The Enterprise Engineering Series

More information about this series at http://www.springer.com/series/8371

Jan L. G. Dietz • Hans B. F. Mulder

Enterprise Ontology

A Human-Centric Approach
to Understanding the Essence
of Organisation

 Springer

Jan L. G. Dietz
Voorburg, The Netherlands

Hans B. F. Mulder
The Hague, The Netherlands

ISSN 1867-8920   ISSN 1867-8939   (electronic)
The Enterprise Engineering Series
ISBN 978-3-030-38856-0   ISBN 978-3-030-38854-6   (eBook)
https://doi.org/10.1007/978-3-030-38854-6

This Springer imprint is published by the registered company Springer Nature Switzerland AG.
The registered company address is: Gewerbestrasse 11, 6330 Cham, Switzerland

dag sterke Sanne
bezorger van geluk

goodbye strong Sanne
deliverer of happiness

Preface

Our knowledge can only be finite, while our ignorance must necessarily be infinite.
(Karl Popper)

Would it be possible to develop a way of thinking about enterprises that offers substantially more insight into their operation and overview over their composition? And if so, how would such a way of thinking be like? And how could you make it practical? These are the core research questions addressed in this book.

When the first author finished the book *Enterprise Ontology—Theory and Methodology*, in 2006, he was quite confident about his understanding of enterprise ontology. However, both by teaching and by practising the subject, it became clear that he had to keep thinking. Thanks to this continuous process, the book that you are about to read is not just a revised edition of the one in 2006; it is a quite different book.

What we try to emphasise in the current book, is the key role of human beings in enterprises and in society at large. In contrast to our deep conviction that human beings are the pearls of enterprises, we witness the madding crowd drift away in the opposite direction. Unfortunately, this madding crowd does not only include ICT and AI professionals, it also comprises people who are supposed to lead the world into a safe and steady future: philosophers, directors, and corporate and public governors.

Even more firmly than before, leading business schools teach us that employees can best be considered as carbon-based robots, who are intrinsically untrustworthy and lazy, and therefore should be replaced by silicon-based robots, the sooner the better. We think that even Frederic Taylor, who laid the foundation for the currently dominant mechanistic world view, would turn in his grave if he would see the madness. People, all over the world, get ever more brainwashed by the idea that silicon-based robots will soon be better decision makers than we, poor carbon-based creatures, are. And that it is about time to recognise robots as equivalent fellow citizens, as the government of Saudi Arabia did in October 2017. How far can one get derailed?

Fortunately, the falseness of the madding preachers can easily be unmasked if one gets a clear sight again on the distinction between computing (or information processing) and decision making, between our rational and our social existence. Let us exemplify this. In determining the alimony in a divorce case, judges rely heavily on software applications. And rightly so, because the applicable legislation is often complicated. But the result of the computations is not automatically the alimony that one party has to pay to the other. It is only after the judge has decided it to be so; decision making is not a rational but a social act. It is because we have given the judge the authority to do so that we accept her/his judgement, regardless whether we agree or disagree. The basic understanding of this important distinction is the red thread in the theoretical part of this book. Adopting and nourishing this crucial insight is the only way, as we see it, to keep the world human, or to make it human again.

Therefore, it is a good that public governors and councils require governments to be transparent to the people about whether a decision is made by an authorised officer or by a computer (or algorithm). But it is better that these artefacts cannot make decisions, that they can only compute! Deciding is an exclusive human (social) ability. Making errors is another one, but that is all in the (social) game.

Another distinction between humans and androids is the human ability to feel responsible for ourselves and for others, that is, to be a social individual. Of course, we can let androids mimic any human behaviour, but mimicked is not real. For sure, we can declare androids to be equivalent social players in our society. But this will be an explicit and freely taken human decision which the decision maker has to justify to his fellow social individuals. History teaches us that humans can make stupid decisions and succeed in justifying them. There is no reason to assume that they won't in the future. So, indeed, judges and governors make errors, as all decision makers do. But we, members of the common society, can hold them responsible and accountable for their deeds. That is also a rule of the game.

Enterprise Ontology, as defined and applied in this book, is therefore an ever more important way of understanding human social behaviour, more specifically of human cooperation that is based on trust. Endowed with the authority that is needed to do their work, people will act responsibly, they will excel in their work, and they will hardly need being managed.

In addition to a substantial extension and improvement of the theoretical foundations of the notion of Enterprise Ontology, this book contains almost as many pages that are devoted to its practical applications. This makes the book perfectly suited for being used as a textbook in courses on Enterprise Ontology and Enterprise Engineering, or on the principal methodology in Enterprise Engineering: DEMO (Design and Engineering Methodology for Organisation). In addition to six exercises in producing so-called essential models of organisations with DEMO, we have included two chapters containing reports about the practical application of DEMO on various subjects in a wide range of enterprises (companies, institutions, governmental agencies).

Although, even after finishing the book, our ignorance regarding Enterprise Ontology is necessarily infinite (thanks to Popper), we hope that our finite knowledge of it will appear to be sufficient for convincing you and inspiring you to keep on reading and thereby enter into a wonderful world.

Voorburg, The Netherlands   Jan L. G. Dietz
The Hague, The Netherlands   Hans B. F. Mulder
15 January 2020

Acknowledgements

From 2006 on, our understanding of Enterprise Ontology has also been shaped in the communication with many people. Numerous students have been a valuable whetstone, notably those at Delft University of Technology and Antwerp Management School, as well as the NOVI and the Avans+ universities of applied sciences. A similar role was played by our colleagues in the Ciao! Network and the Enterprise Engineering Institute. We would like to mention some of them explicitly (in reverse alphabetical order): Marné de Vries, José Tribolet, Linda Terlouw, Ronald Stamper, Robert Pergl, Martin Op 't Land, Mark Mulder, Klaas Meijer, Steven van Kervel, Joop de Jong, Junichi Iijima, Jan Hoogervorst, Duarte Gouveia, Edward van Dipten, Joseph Barjis, Eduard Babkin, David Aveiro, Antonia Albani.

Contents

About the Authors

Jan L. G. Dietz is Professor Emeritus at Delft University of Technology, and visiting professor at the University of Lisbon and the Czech Technical University in Prague. He has always combined academic work with applying research outcomes in practice. Jan Dietz has supervised over 300 MSc's and 16 PhD's and has published over 250 scientific and professional papers and books. He is the spiritual father of DEMO (Design & Engineering Methodology for Organisations), one of the founders of the Enterprise Engineering Institute (www.ee-institute.com), and the founder of the Ciao! Enterprise Engineering Network (www.ciaonetwork.org).

Hans B. F. Mulder is an entrepreneur and founder of VIAgroep, Standish research director, executive professor at the Antwerp Management School and lecturer at the Police Academy of the Netherlands. He is regularly engaged as an IT expert when conflicts between companies need to be resolved in or out of court, such as participating in arbitration, mediation, and expert reports. He received his PhD at Delft University of Technology, MSc in Business Administration at Nijenrode Business Universiteit, and BSc in Informatics at The Hague University of Applied Sciences. Furthermore, he has published more than 100 articles in specialist journals and international magazines, and is the author of several books such as *Eenvoud in Complexiteit*.

Abbreviations[1]

ADT Authorisation Delegation Table [representation form of the *Action Model*] (Chap. 12).

AM Action Model [*aspect model* of the *ontological model* of an *organisational layer*] (Chap. 12).

ARS Action Rule Specifications [representation form of the *Action Model*] (Chap. 12).

BAT Bank Access Table [representation form of the *Cooperation Model*] (Chap. 12).

BCT Bank Contents Table [cross-model representation form of the *Cooperation Model* and the *Fact Model*] (Chap. 12).

CM Cooperation Model [*aspect model* of the *ontological model* of an *organisational layer*] (Chap. 12).

CSD Coordination Structure Diagram [representation form of the *Cooperation Model*] (Chap. 12).

c̲t̲ creation time; attribute of a fact (Chaps. 8 and 12).

C̲U̲T̲ Create Use Table [cross-model representation form of the *Process Model* and the *Fact Model*] (Chap. 12).

DFS Derived Fact Specifications [representation form of *Fact Model*] (Chap. 12).

e̲t̲ event time; attribute of a fact (Chaps. 8 and 12).

F̲M̲ Fact Model [*aspect model* of the *ontological model* of an *organisational layer*] (Chap. 12).

ICT Information and Communication Technology. It comprises Information Technology (IT) for information processing and storage, and Communication Technology (CT) for transmitting information.

OFD Object Fact Diagram [representation form of *Fact Model*] (Chap. 12).

---

[1]In the following, the most common abbreviations of terms in Enterprise Ontology, as used in this book, are listed in alphabetical order. The chapter where the term is defined is indicated within brackets.

ot   operative time; attribute of a product (Chaps. 8 and 12).
PM   Process Model [*aspect model* of the *ontological model* of an *organisational layer*] (Chap. 12).
PSD   Process Structure Diagram [representation form of the *Process Model*] (Chap. 12).
SoI   Scope of Interest
TPD   Transaction Process Diagram [representation form of the *Process Model*] (Chap. 12).
TPT   Transactor Product Table [cross-model representation form of the *Cooperation Model* and the *Fact Model*] (Chap. 12).
WIS   Work Instruction Specifications [representation form of the *Action Model*] (Chap. 12).

Part I
Introduction

Part I contains the three introductory chapters to the main contents in Parts II (theories) and III (applications). Chapter 1 offers a history of the developments of both the Organisational Sciences and the ICT Sciences (Computer Science, Software Engineering, Artificial Intelligence, etc.), and their current convergence. In Chap. 2, the reader is introduced into the emerging discipline of Enterprise Engineering, in which a design-oriented view is taken towards organisations. One of the conceptual pillars of Enterprise Engineering is Enterprise Ontology, the core subject of the book. Chapter 3 provides an introduction to this key notion.

Chapter 1
A History of Organisation and ICT

Abstract This chapter sketches a history of the Organisational Sciences along with a history of the ICT Sciences (comprising Computer Science, Software Engineering, Artificial Intelligence, etc.). The first one starts with the famous publication by Frederick Taylor in 1911. The history of the ICT Sciences begins in the late fifties of the last century, with the first use of computers in organisations. The two histories converge at the time that communication is (also) understood as action, around the year 2000. This insight paves the way to the development of the discipline of Enterprise Engineering, which includes Enterprise Ontology.

The test of a healthy business is not the beauty, clarity or perfection of its organisational structure, it is the performance of people.

(Peter Drucker)

As expressed by its subtitle, this book is about a human-centric approach to understanding the essence of organisation. Adding such a subtitle begs the question what the authors understand by human-centric, and by essence, and by organisation. As will become clear in the remainder of the book, these notions are tightly interrelated, and they are all also related to Information and Communication Technology (ICT).[1] And because organisation will turn out to be the key notion, let us start with a sketch of its history, supplemented later on by the history of ICT, which has, over the years, increasingly become intertwined with organisation. Instead of "the history", we speak more humbly of "a history", since it is our specific view on the history of organisation and ICT.

In 1911, Frederic Taylor published his paper "The Principles of Scientific Management" [1], which is widely considered as the first scientific study into the notion of organisation. At the time, people were the principal resources for doing the work

---

[1]Information and Communication Technology commonly refers to the digital electronic, optical, etc., means to process, store, and transmit data. Regarding the term 'technology' we prefer to stick to the original meaning of the word, which stems from its Greek origin: technè (meaning making) and logos (meaning knowing). So, by technology we primarily understand knowing how to make, and only secondarily the means (devices, etc.) mentioned above.

© Springer Nature Switzerland AG 2020
J. L. G. Dietz, J. B. F. Mulder, *Enterprise Ontology*, The Enterprise Engineering Series, https://doi.org/10.1007/978-3-030-38854-6_1

that had to be done, in all kinds of organisations, so in manufacturing, in financial, and in governmental organisations. Taylor's focus was to improve the efficiency with which the work was done, in order to minimise the time a piece of work would take, as well as to minimise material usage, including waste. Typical characteristics of the scientific management approach are the minute division of labour in simple, repetitive tasks, and the clear separation between thinking and doing. Workers are instrumentally viewed as parts of the enterprise 'machine'. According to Taylor, a man fit to do the manual work is unfit to understand the organising of the work, like the coordination of all work and workers. Consequently, Taylor was convinced that managerial control is indispensable. In [2], we have reflected on Taylor's contribution to the organisational sciences and on the criticism that fell upon him later.

Basically, two kinds of criticisms can be identified. The first one concerns ethical considerations regarding the deployment of 'human resources'. Various researchers have argued that the principles of scientific management lead to worker deprivation and alienation, and to destroying the meaning of work itself [3, 4]. These phenomena were already visible a few years after Taylor published his paper, when his principles were practised in Ford's car manufacturing: workers' jobs were depleted of skill, autonomy, and control, leading to extreme worker turnover rates [5].

Considerations concerning the effectiveness and efficiency of enterprises constitute the second kind of criticism. Essentially, the critique boils down to two aspects. First, the notion that proper attention to employees as a social group can significantly enhance enterprise effectiveness and efficiency, as for example, evidenced by the classical Hawthorne studies [6]. Noteworthy within this perspective is the socio-technical approach [7] that argues the mutual relationship between the social and technological 'system' of an enterprise. Hence, these systems must be jointly designed since they can mutually support each other to enhance enterprise effectiveness and efficiency.

Second, it is argued that the mere instrumental view on employees—workers as labour resources—undervalues human cognitive and social capacities. This shift in focus is evidenced by landmark publications like [8–10]. The new focus considers employees, and their involvement and participation, as the critical core for enterprise success.

Around 1970, a revolution took place in the way people conceived ICT and its applications, particularly the applications in organisations [11]. Since then, people are aware of the distinction between the form and the content of information and/or communication. Up to that time, computers (i.e. main ICT devices) were used to store and process large amounts of data (both numeric and alphanumeric). The semantic meaning of these data was not a real concern; people were still overwhelmed by the immense capacity of electronic digital computers to store and process data. The revolution around 1970 marks the transition from the era of Electronic Data Processing (EDP) to the era of Information Systems Engineering (ISE), as shown in Fig. 1.1. It was also the time that relational databases set in [12].

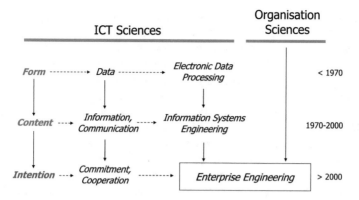

Fig. 1.1 The roots of Enterprise Engineering

The comparison we draw in Fig. 1.1 between the Organisation Sciences and the ICT Sciences[2] is not an arbitrary one. On the one hand, ICT has become the key enabling technology for shaping future enterprises. On the other hand, there is a growing insight within the ICT Sciences that the central notion for understanding profoundly the relationship between organisation and ICT is the entering into and complying with commitments between social individuals [13, 14]. These commitments are raised in communication, through the intention of communicative acts [15]. Examples of intentions are requesting, promising, declaring, and accepting. Therefore, like the content of information/communication was put on top of its form in the 1970s, its intention is now put on top of its content. This explains and clarifies the organisational notion of collaboration or cooperation. The still ongoing revolution in the ICT Sciences marks the transition from the era of ISE to the era of Enterprise Engineering, while at the same time converging with the Organisation Sciences. In the Chap. 2, we will elaborate on Enterprise Engineering.

Unfortunately, the current practice of ICT lies quite behind the state of the art on the scientific plane. Most ICT professionals seem to live in the ISE era still, which means that they don't understand and recognise that information systems are intrinsically parts of organisations; that they have always been there. The only new thing is that they are now implemented with ICT. They still view their work basically as developing application software, after having collected requirements from the future users, and 'implanting' the resulting software in the organisation when they are finished. Let us illustrate this alarming situation with two examples.

The first one is a failed payroll system for health care in Australia [16]. The system has cost 1 billion euros (1.25 billion Australian dollars) more than budgeted. The project started in 2007. Shortly after its completion in 2010—18 months late— problems arose: some employees were not paid; others got too much. Employees who received too much could not repay the amount because the system did not

---

[2]The term ICT Sciences is a container term for Computer Science, Software Engineering, Artificial Intelligence, etc.

provide this option. The Queensland Government then decided to receive the excess sums through discounts in time. With reference also to Deming [17], the payroll system is first of all a matter of organisation. As said and as will be clarified in Chap. 11, every enterprise information system, thus also a payroll system, is an intrinsic part of the organisation, only implemented by using ICT.

The second example is the Dutch government, which is unable to manage its ICT projects. In many cases, the government is not in control of the costs, the timing, or even the final results of its projects. Since no comprehensive report on the national public finances has been drawn up after 1995, nobody knows how much money the Dutch public sector is really spending on ICT, or how much is being wasted on failed projects.[3] A conservative estimate based on information from a variety of experts suggests that this figure is most likely between 1 and 5 billion euros per year [16]. Meanwhile, a Dutch governmental Committee has investigated the situation and found that much is amiss, especially the culture surrounding government ICT projects. On the one hand, there is unbridled enthusiasm for ICT, with proponents viewing it as the solution to every problem. On the other hand, the House of Representatives regularly demands policy measures without realising that almost always ICT is needed to implement them. The responsible minister promises delivery without first checking whether the measures required are technically possible. Political leadership is not challenged enough even when the promises being made to Parliament cannot be fulfilled, and when ICT project leaders do voice their concerns, it does not reach the top political level.

The statement by Peter Drucker quoted at the beginning of this chapter (which he made in 1985) has meanwhile had a reinforced impact, which he most likely did not foresee. Indeed, the health of an enterprise depends on the performance of the people in it, both workers and managers, because only people can be responsible for what happens in the enterprise's organisation. ICT artefacts, of any kind, can only support them. They can never take over responsibility, as we will stress and explain in part B.

References

1. Taylor, F. W. (1911). *The principles of scientific management* (2 p. l., 7–77 p.). New York: Harper & Brothers.
2. Dietz, J. L. G., Hoogervorst, J. A. P., Albani, A., Aveiro, D., Babkin, E., Barjis, J., et al. (2013). The discipline of enterprise engineering. *International Journal of Organisational Design and Engineering, 3*, 28.
3. Fromm, E. (1942). *The fear of freedom.* International library of sociology and social reconstruction (London) (xl, 257 p.). London: K. Paul, Trench, Trubner & Co.
4. Mintzberg, H. (1989). *Mintzberg on management: Inside our strange world of organizations* (x, 418 p.). New York, London: Free Press, Collier Macmillan.

---

[3]https://www.houseofrepresentatives.nl/news/committee-presents-report-failures-government-ict-projects

5. Hounshell, D. A. (1984). *From the American system to mass production, 1800–1932: The development of manufacturing technology in the United States. Studies in industry and society* (xxi, 411 p.). Baltimore: Johns Hopkins University Press.

6. Mayo, E. (1949). *The social problems of an industrial civilization; With an appendix on the political problem.* International library of sociology and social reconstruction (xvi, 148 p.). London: Routledge & K. Paul.

7. Mayo, E. (1977). *The social problems of an industrial civilization.* Work, its rewards and discontents (xvii, 150 p.). New York: Arno Press.

8. McGregor, D. (1985). *The human side of enterprise: 25th anniversary printing* (x, 246 p.). New York: McGraw-Hill.

9. Katz, D., & Kahn, R. L. (1966). *The social psychology of organizations* (viii, 498 p.). New York: Wiley.

10. Drucker, P. F. (2007). *Management: Tasks, responsibilities, practices* (xvi, 839 p.). New Brunswick, NJ: Transaction Publishers.

11. Langefors, B. R. (1973). *Theoretical analysis of information systems* (4th ed., 489 p.). Lund Sweden, Philadelphia: Studentlitteratur, Auerbach.

12. Codd, E. F. (1990). *The relational model for database management: Version 2* (xxii, 538 p.). Reading, MA: Addison-Wesley.

13. Winograd, T., & Flores, F. (1987). *Understanding computers and cognition: A new foundation for design* (xiv, 207 p.). Reading, MA: Addison-Wesley.

14. Dietz, J. L. G. (2006). The deep structure of business processes. *Communications of the ACM, 49*(5), 58–64.

15. Habermas, J. (1986). *The theory of communicative action.* Cambridge: Polity Press.

16. Johnson, J., Mulder, J., & CHAOS Chronicles. (2016). Focusing on failures and possible improvements in it projects. *Journal of Systemics Cybernetics and Informatics (JSCI), 14*(5), 5.

17. Deming, W. E. (1986). *Out of the crisis: Quality, productivity and competitive position* (xiii, 507 p.). Cambridge: Cambridge University Press.

Chapter 2
Introduction to Enterprise Engineering

Abstract Enterprise Engineering is an emerging discipline that takes an engineering perspective on enterprises. It aims to address the problems in organisations that cannot be solved by the traditional organisational sciences. Organisational changes are conceived as situations of (re)design and (re)implementation. The conceptual pillars are Enterprise Ontology, Enterprise Design, and Enterprise Governance. By applying Enterprise Engineering three goals are attained: intellectual manageability, organisational concinnity, and social devotion.

Science is about knowing; engineering is about doing.

(Henry Petroski)

In perfect agreement with Petroski's quote above, the discipline of enterprise engineering (EE) is about doing. The general goal of EE is to make better enterprises, or to make enterprises better, in every meaning of the word. By "enterprise" we refer to all kinds of organised human activities (like companies, agencies, institutions, supply chains, etc., but also the organisation of a birthday party). Indeed, science alone doesn't solve the problems humanity faces; engineering is needed to develop and implement effective solutions [1]. At the same time, doing without a proper understanding of what one is doing, seems to be worse than doing nothing. That is why every serious engineering discipline is rooted in a solid theoretical foundation.

The societal need of a discipline of EE is urgent because modern societies are increasingly complex networks of an increasing number of enterprises, with increasingly complex interrelationships. Moreover, the traditional organisational and management sciences fail to provide effective help [2]. Deming [3] provides a convincing account, which can be paraphrased as follows: almost all (94%) manifestations of inadequate enterprise performance are the inevitable results of how enterprises are organised. The purport of this finding is that only in 6% of all instances of operational failure one can correctly blame workers. In all other cases, the cause is a design or implementation fault of the organisation.

Over the years insights have been developed on how to (1) enhance the effectiveness and efficiency of enterprises; (2) effectively ensure quality, service, and customer orientation; and (3) avoid core reasons for strategic failure. One would

J. L. G. Dietz, J. B. F. Mulder, *Enterprise Ontology*, The Enterprise Engineering Series, https://doi.org/10.1007/978-3-030-38854-6_2

expect that a century after Taylor published his principles of scientific management his influence would have vanished. However, as Doz and Thanheiser observed at the end of the previous century: "Despite the 'modernisation' of corporate structures and systems, the mindset of managers appears to be remarkably similar to the Taylorist model developed at the beginning of the century" [4]. Thus, principles that follow from "a machine-like concept of the organisation still dominate managerial practice" [ibid.]. Others argue that "Corporations continue to operate according to a logic invented at the time of their origin, a century ago" [5].

The continuation of the Taylorist model can additionally be demonstrated by observing the increase in the number of management functions. For example, in the country where Taylor expressed his views, managers accounted for less than 1% of the labour force in 1900. Thirty years later, this figure was already 7.5%, increasing to 10.5% by 1970. By 1990, the figure was approaching 14% [6]. These increases must be understood against the background of increasing population and workforce.

The increased population of managers largely consists of people who believe that management is a profession like other professions. As Edward Deming, the renowned quality and productivity leader, observed: "Students in schools of business in America are taught that there is a profession of management; that they are ready to step into top jobs. That is a cruel hoax" [3]. This 'hoax' resulted in the widely observable management crises. An article in the Standardization News (1983) stated that "Practical all our major corporations were started by technical men—inventors, mechanics, engineers, and chemists, who had a sincere interest in the quality of products. Now, these companies are largely run by men interested in profit, not product. Their pride is the P&L statement or stock report" [3].

The needed paradigm shift is provided by the emerging discipline of Enterprise Engineering. It amounts to a theory-based methodology for addressing enterprise (re-) development in an all-encompassing way. A sound and rigid theoretical foundation is crucial. As Deming states: "Experience alone, without theory, teaches management nothing about what to do to improve quality and competitive position, nor how to do it" [3]. In view of our previous discussion, and the tenacity of Taylor's principles, little learning seems to have taken place. We posit that an explanatory theory is required to give experience meaning, so to provide the basis for appropriately understanding enterprises.

In [7], three general goals are identified for the discipline of EE: intellectual manageability, organisational concinnity, and social devotion. *Intellectual manageability* is about getting and keeping insight into and overview over complexity. People who have to govern or run enterprises, or to devise and implement substantial changes, need first of all a proper understanding of what they are doing. Current practice shows that this basic premise is often not met. Obviously, enterprise phenomena that are not properly understood cannot be addressed adequately. Consequently, the necessary changes cannot be determined, and if they can, they cannot be brought about effectively. In addition, current development approaches, for enterprises as a whole and for ICT applications in particular, are cursed with combinatorial impacts of changes. So, in addition, appropriate ideas of enterprise evolvability are needed for making changes expeditious and manageable.

Intellectual manageability is an indispensable quality: if you don't understand fully and deeply what you are doing, you better not do it.

Organisational concinnity is about designing, engineering, and implementing an enterprise in such a way that the resulting operational organisation is always a coherent and consistent whole. In order to perform optimally and to implement changes successfully, enterprises must operate as unified and integrated wholes, taking into account all aspects that are deemed relevant. Many approaches to enterprise development, for example, TOGAF, are ill-suited and suffer from theoretical and methodological weakness and incompleteness [8]. It is evidently not sufficient to consider enterprise design domains like processes, the information needs of the processes, the software applications providing the information, and their underlying infrastructure. A viable theory and methodology for enterprise engineering must be able to address all relevant aspects, even those that cannot be foreseen presently, in a properly integrated way. It is quite obvious that organisational concinnity must be designed; it does not emerge in a natural way [9, 10].

Social devotion is about recognising that the operation of an enterprise's organisation is brought about, not by its managers, but by its operational employees. In [2, 7], the importance of employee involvement and participation has been argued in order to achieve enterprise productivity, product and service quality, customer orientation, learning and innovation (and subsequent enterprise change), as well as to cope with enterprise dynamics, complexity, and uncertainty leading to emerging enterprise developments. Contrary to Taylor's mechanistic view on organisations [11], EE takes a human-centric view. It considers human beings to be the 'pearls' of every enterprise. Therefore, all employees should be fully empowered and competent for the tasks they have to perform. They must be endorsed with transparent authority and have access to all information needed to perform their tasks in a responsible way. Next, managers must not only be skilled in managerial work of the kind that Deming refers to [3], they must first of all be thoroughly knowledgeable in the subject field of the enterprise they are managing.

The three goals of EE are often connected to the principal parts or pillars of the discipline in the next way. Intellectual manageability is mainly achieved by applying *enterprise ontology*, as presented in this book. It offers an unprecedented reduction of complexity, resulting in broad overview and deep insight. Organisational concinnity is mainly achieved by applying *enterprise design*, including enterprise architecture and implementation, while starting from the ontological model of the organisation to be designed. The goal of social devotion can be achieved by applying *enterprise governance* as presented in [2].

To conclude, it is not all sorrow and misery. In the CHAOS database of failed, challenged, and successful ICT projects, which is set up and maintained by the Standish Group [12], the so-called 'next neighbour algorithm' can be used to compare projects on selected attributes. In this way, several attributes of DEMO[1]

---

[1] DEMO is the name of the methodology that is presented in Part III of this book.

projects, such as a sound and grounded way of thinking, and the involvement of 'shop floor' employees and managers in large and complex projects, were compared to some 50,000 other projects. The results clearly demonstrate that being human-centric as well as being based on sound theoretical foundations, pays off for sure. The opportunity to learn from international projects could raise awareness to apply lessons learned in (governmental) ICT projects, right from the beginning [13].

References

1. Petroski, H. (2010). *The essential engineer: Why science alone will not solve our global problems* (1st ed., x, 274 p.). New York: Alfred A. Knopf.
2. Hoogervorst, J. A. P. (2017). *Foundations of enterprise governance and enterprise engineering* (574 p.). Cham: Springer International.
3. Deming, W. E. (1986). *Out of the crisis: Quality, productivity and competitive position* (xiii, 507 p.). Cambridge: Cambridge University Press.
4. Doz, Y., & Thanheiser, H. (1993). Regaining competitiveness: A process of organizational renewal. In J. Hendry, G. Johnson, & J. Newton (Eds.), *Strategic thinking: Leadership and the management of change*. Chichester: Wiley.
5. Zuboff, S., & Maxmin, J. (2004). *The support economy: Why corporations are failing individuals and the next episode of capitalism* (xvii, 458 p.). New York: Penguin Books.
6. Osterman, P. (1996). *Broken ladders: Managerial careers in the new economy* (259 p.). New York: Oxford University Press.
7. Dietz, J. L. G., Hoogervorst, J. A. P., Albani, A., Aveiro, D., Babkin, E., Barjis, J., et al. (2013). The discipline of enterprise engineering. *International Journal of Organisational Design and Engineering, 3*, 28.
8. Dietz, J. L. G., & Hoogervorst, J. A. P. (2012). A critical investigation of TOGAF. In A. Albani, J. L. G. Dietz, & J. Verelst (Eds.), *Advances in enterprise engineering V* (Lecture notes in business information processing). Cham: Springer.
9. Keller, S., & Price, C. (2011). *Beyond performance: How great organizations build ultimate competitive advantage* (xx, 280 p.). Hoboken, NJ: Wiley.
10. Leinwand, P., & Mainardi, C. (2011). *The essential advantage: How to win with a capabilities-driven strategy* (xii, 227 p.). Boston, MA: Harvard Business Review Press.
11. Taylor, F. W. (1911). *The principles of scientific management* (2 p. l., 7–77 p.). New York: Harper & Brothers.
12. Johnson, J., Mulder, J., & CHAOS Chronicles. (2016). Focusing on failures and possible improvements in IT projects. *Journal of Systemics Cybernetics and Informatics (JSCI), 14*(5), 5.
13. Gaikema, M., Donkersloot, M., Johnson, J., & Mulder, J. B. F. (2019). Increase the success of governmental IT-projects. *Systemics, Cybernetics and Informatics, 17*(1), 97–105.

Chapter 3
Introduction to Enterprise Ontology

Abstract The notion of Enterprise Ontology as adopted in this book comprises both system ontology (dynamics) and world ontology (statics). By applying the notion, one acquires an understanding of the essence of an enterprise that is comprehensive, coherent, consistent, and concise, thus allowing one to achieve intellectual manageability, which is one of the general goals of Enterprise Engineering. The philosophical background in which Enterprise Ontology is positioned, is characterised by being both constructivist and interpretive. In addition to the importance of the Enterprise Ontology for all participants in modern social and economic life, the urgency of adopting and spreading it is substantiated. The only prerequisite to achieve this is an open mind.

The difficulty lies not so much in developing new ideas as in escaping from old ones
(John Maynard Keynes)

3.1 About Intellectual Manageability

The use of the—in organisational circles quite novel—term "Enterprise Ontology" (EO) deserves two explanations. One regards the justification of presenting this still rather uncommon point of view on enterprises. Why and how would EO assist in coping with the current and future problems related to enterprises? The other explanation concerns the particular approach towards EO that this book takes. Why would this approach be more appropriate and more effective than others? A first attempt to answer these questions is provided in this introductory chapter. Definite and fully satisfying answers can only emerge from a dedicated and thorough study of the book. The lasting reward of such a study is a new and powerful insight into the essence of the organisation and operation of enterprises.

Let us start by noting that managing an enterprise, but also getting services from it as a client or collaborating with it as partner in a network, is nowadays far more complicated than it was in the past. Because you probably have heard this tune in all pitches and keys, we will not elaborate it. And in case you have not, glance over an arbitrary management book from the past 20 years and you are sufficiently informed.

© Springer Nature Switzerland AG 2020
J. L. G. Dietz, J. B. F. Mulder, *Enterprise Ontology*, The Enterprise Engineering Series, https://doi.org/10.1007/978-3-030-38854-6_3

The current lasting problems in enterprises, of any kind, are well investigated and well documented. More than well, one could say, because far less effort is put in thinking about how to cope with them. Anyhow, the common denominator of these problems is complexity, and complexity can only be mastered if two conditions are fulfilled. One is that there is an appropriate and effective theory of the things whose complexity one wants to master. The other condition is that one disposes of appropriate analysis methods and techniques, based on that theory.

The knowledge that one acquires at management or business schools does not suffice anymore. Actually, it never did; managers were just lucky that the shop floor workers ultimately always managed to really solve problems and implement desired changes. Therefore, even the gifted entrepreneur can nowadays not succeed without a basic, systematic, and integral understanding of how enterprises work. In order to really cope with current and future challenges, a conceptual model of the enterprise is needed that is coherent, comprehensive, consistent, and concise, and that only shows the essence of the enterprise, abstracted from irrelevant details. By *coherent* we mean that the distinguished aspect models constitute a logical and truly integral whole. By *comprehensive* we mean that all relevant issues are covered, that the whole is complete. By *consistent* we mean that the aspect models are free from contradictions or irregularities. By *concise* we mean that no redundant matters are contained in it, that the whole is compact and succinct. The most important property, however, is that this conceptual model is *essential*, that it shows only the essence of the enterprise. In particular, we mean that the model abstracts from all realisation and implementation issues, so that one can effectively discuss alternative ways of realising and implementing the enterprise.

We shall call such a conceptual model an *ontological model*. The combined Greek words "ontos" and "logos" from which the English word "ontology" stems, mean study or knowledge of what is or exists, and the philosophical branch with the same name has taken up the term as referring to the reality around us, regardless of our specific view on it. In other words, ontology requires us to make a strict distinction between the observing subject and the observed object. This requirement puts the authors under another obligation, namely of clarifying the philosophical stance taken with respect to the subject–object dichotomy. We will do it only briefly, without much elaboration.

3.2   The Philosophical Background of Enterprise Ontology

Three philosophical positions are relevant for our discussion: the objectivist, the subjectivist, and the constructivist position. *Objectivists* believe that the world they live in exists in itself, fully independent of them. In other words, they believe in a true objective reality. *Subjectivists* take the opposite position. They believe that there is no reality outside the subject (human being) and, in the extreme, that every subject has its own image of reality. Somewhere in between is the position of the *constructivists*. They agree with the subjectivists that there is no absolute objective reality (as the objectivists believe), but they believe that there is instead a kind of semi-objective reality that they call an intersubjective reality. It is built and continuously adapted through negotiating and achieving social consensus among subjects [1]. Our position is this constructivist one. We consider the ontology of a particular part of reality as the basis for sensible communication about that part of reality. At the same time, we recognise that this ontology is built, rebuilt, and adapted in communication; it cannot be otherwise.

We like to add to this tripartite philosophical stance two sociological paradigms regarding the study of systems, namely the functionalist paradigm and the interpretive paradigm [2]. The *functionalist* paradigm takes its name from the fact that it wants to ensure that everything in the system is operating well so as to promote efficiency, adaptation, and survival. An understanding of how systems work can be gained by using scientific methods and techniques to probe the nature of parts of the system, the interrelationships between them, and the relationship between the system and its environment. The expertise it provides should put managers more in control of their operations and organisations, and enable them to eliminate inefficiency and disorder. The *interpretive* paradigm takes its name from the fact that it believes social systems, such as organisations, result from the purposes that people have and that these, in turn, stem from the interpretations they make of the situations in which they find themselves. People act and interact in organisations as a result of their interpretations. This paradigm wants to understand the different meanings of collaborative activity and to discover where these meanings overlap, and so give birth to shared, purposeful activity. Managers can be guided to seek an appropriate level of corporate culture. They can take decisions, on the basis of participative involvement, that gain the commitment of stakeholders.

It is sometimes argued that these paradigms are incommensurable. In our opinion, this is not necessarily the case. The notion of EO, as conveyed in this book, is primarily functionalist in nature. However, various aspects, like considering an enterprise as a social entity, the focus on (human) social individuals, Habermas' theory of communicative action [3], the autonomy that is basically allowed to actor roles, also reflects an interpretive perspective. One might argue that a really comprehensive approach to enterprise engineering should be able to address an enterprise from different angles, thus integrating important views from different paradigms. Let this be our final brushstroke in painting the philosophical background for the key notion of EO.

3.3   The Importance of Enterprise Ontology

In its modern use, ontology has preserved its original meaning, but it has also a definite practical goal. It serves to provide a basis for the common understanding of some area of interest among a community of people who may not know each other at all, and who may have very different cultural backgrounds. There are various definitions of the modern notion of ontology in circulation. Our main source is the ontology of Mario Bunge [4, 5], but we will also refer to other sources. A widely adopted definition of ontology is the one in [6]: an ontology is a formal, explicit specification of a shared conceptualisation. It states the core properties that our notion of ontology also will have. First, it regards the conceptualisation of (a part of) the world, so it is something in our mind. Because of our constructivist stance, we consider these mental images be checked and adapted in communication. Second, this conceptualisation is supposed to be shared, which is the practical goal of ontologies. This also takes place in communication. Third, it is explicit; an ontology must be explicit and fully clear, there should be no room for misunderstandings. Fourth, it is specified in a formal way. Natural language is inappropriate for this task, because of its inherent ambiguity and impreciseness.

The notion of ontology as applied in [6], but also in [7–9], is what we will call in Chap. 8 a *world ontology*. Common examples of such an ontology are the world of traveling or the world of cooking and dining. The focus is on defining the core entity types in such a world and their property types in a most clear and extensive way. The main notion of ontology in this book is the notion of *system ontology*. Our goal is to understand the essence of the construction and operation of systems, more specifically, of enterprises. As will become clear, this notion of system ontology includes the notion of world ontology. Next, although we fully recognise the need for ontologies for the purpose of worldwide flawless communication among agents over the Internet, our motivation for this book is wider. In our opinion, the current world is, and will remain, in the first place, a world of people, of human beings, despite all the technical devices that (can) make our lives much more pleasant. This is a philosophical stance of course; it is a choice. We strongly oppose, for example, the quite common idea that artificial agents are, or at some future time will be, equivalent fellow players in human social life. This idea can only be justified by a severe inflation of such notions as authority and responsibility. Throughout the history of mankind, people have used anthropomorphic metaphors for the purpose of understanding and explaining the operation of natural things and of artefacts. The only, but at the same time serious, danger is that one forgets that they were metaphors, that one takes the metaphorical reasoning for real. So, for example, if you think that your computer does not understand you, you are twofold right. First, it is quite okay to use anthropomorphic metaphors in the interaction with your computer. You probably do it sometimes also while driving your car or trying to let any machine do what you want it to do. Second, in the most true sense, your computer does not understand you, because understanding in the way human beings have internalised the notion and apply it is applicable only to them. There is no general notion of understanding that human beings would share with artificial intelligent systems. There is no evidence for such a belief, except for occasional apparent similar external behaviour. To conclude from these cases that the behaviours of humans and machines are brought about in the same way is merely speculation.

3.4 The Urgent Need for Enterprise Ontology

A major motivation for this book and for our work in ontology in general stems from the conviction that the world is in great need for transparency about the operation of all the systems we daily work with, ranging from the domestic appliances to the big societal institutions. We are in great need already, and this need can only increase if one imagines a future life in a cyber culture [10]. Our concern is the current lack of an appropriate philosophical counterbalance to the dominant technocratic and bureaucratic thinking. Let us give some examples to clarify the point. First, regarding technical devices, if you read the user manual of a car or a computer or a software application, you become overloaded with irrelevant details. You mostly end up with a headache instead of any relevant understanding. And in case you persevere, there is a high chance that you will discover so many errors and omissions in the description that reading has become solving a puzzle.

As a concrete example, the implementation of an ERP (Enterprise Resource Planning) package in an enterprise, even of only a few modules, may easily take several years and cost the enterprise a huge amount of money. This money is partly spent in having the supplier of the package (or some intermediary company) explain how to use it, and partly to have the enterprise adapt its current way of working such that it fits the straitjacket of the ERP package. Is this societal progress? Do we really need to suffer this? As another example, have you ever phoned the help desk of a company or a government agency in order to get the service they claim you will get in their advertisements? Mostly you end up not by having what you were looking for, but by being frustrated, maybe to the extent that you think of giving up. Why? Because the operation of these institutions is completely opaque to you. And, in case you have succeeded in penetrating to the right place, there is a chance that the other side does not take on her/his responsibility and concludes your case by blaming the computer or any other thing that he/she uses as an aid. Most probably, he/she acts in this way not to hamper or frustrate you, but because the institution is also opaque to her/him.

This situation should stop because it is not in the interest of humanity that it continues, as it has been in no one's interest to have come this far. To the best of our knowledge, there has never been a plan to organise modern society in such a way that nobody is able to understand how it works. Likewise, in no manufacturing company has there ever been a plan to design domestic or professional equipment such that it takes an incommensurable amount of effort to get to know how to use it. Things have just gone that way. But, as said, there is no reason to let it continue. Instead, there is abundant ground for stopping it. Imagine that it is possible for you to acquire the right amount of the right kind of knowledge about the operation of the equipment you are working with. Imagine that you are not bothered by incomprehensible and irrelevant things but that you get the insight you need in a way that you immediately understand, because it is about what you want to do with the equipment, not how it is designed and assembled. In a similar manner, imagine that it is possible for you to acquire the right amount of the right kind of knowledge of the operation of the company from which you bought something you want to complain about, or of the government agency from which you are trying to get a license but have not succeeded yet.

In summary, imagine that the business processes of these organisations have become transparent to you. Wouldn't that be great? So, this is our goal: to offer a new understanding of systems of any kind, and of enterprises in particular, such that one is able to look through the distracting and confusing appearance of an enterprise right into its deep kernel, like an X-ray machine can let you look through the skin and the tissues of the body right into the skeleton. As a user of systems, this understanding lets you become master again of your activities. As a designer, it lets you design systems in such a way that the resulting design, in particular the user dialogue and interface, reflects the essence of the system. We will try to achieve this goal through a notion of ontology that includes the dynamic aspects of systems, and that at the same time does justice to the nature of enterprises. This nature is that enterprises are social systems, of which the operating principle consists of the ability of human beings to enter into and comply with commitments.

So, this will be our notion of EO and, as a quality criterion for evaluating enterprise ontologies, we will apply the five properties that were discussed earlier: coherence, comprehensiveness, consistency, conciseness, and essence, collectively abbreviated as C_4E, and elaborated on in Chap. 9. The particular methodology (DEMO[1]) that we will present in Chap. 12 lets you develop the ontology of an enterprise in a systematic way. But you need not become a professional developer of ontologies. The explanation of the methodology and the demonstration of the example cases serve first of all to let you internalise these ontologies, such that, after having studied the book, you are able to understand them and take full advantage of them.

Concluding, you will learn how to have more control over your professional life, how to take the lead again, both as a user and as a manager of enterprises. The only thing you need to do in return is to put aside your current way of thinking about enterprises and to open up your mind for new ideas, as conveyed in the quote from Keynes at the beginning. Only then can EO be the instrument that lets you discover and reveal the essence of your enterprise (or any other one).

References

1. Searle, J. R. (1995). *The construction of social reality* (xiii, 241 p.). New York: Free Press.
2. Hoogervorst, J. A. P. (2017). *Foundations of enterprise governance and enterprise engineering* (574 p.). Cham: Springer International.
3. Habermas, J. (1986). *The theory of communicative action*. Cambridge: Polity Press.

---

[1]DEMO is an acronym that has had several meanings in the course of time, starting with "Dynamic Essential MOdelling". The current one is "Design and Engineering Methodology for Organizations". Visit www.ee-institute.nl for more information.

4. Bunge, M. (1977). Treatise on basic philosophy ontology I: The furniture of the world. In *Treatise on basic philosophy 3*. Dordrecht: Springer Netherlands. p. 1 (370 p.).

5. Bunge, M. (1979). Treatise on basic philosophy ontology II: A world of systems. In *Treatise on basic philosophy 4*. Dordrecht: Springer Netherlands. p. 1.

6. Gruber, T. (1995). Towards principles for the design of ontologies used for knowledge. *International Journal of Human-Computer studies, 43*(5/6), 907–928.

7. Gómez-Pérez, A., Fernández-López, M., & Corcho, O. (2004). *Ontological engineering with examples from the areas of knowledge management, e-commerce and the semantic web*. Advanced information and knowledge processing (403 p.). London: Springer.

8. Guarino, N., Oberle, D., & Staab, S. (2009). What is an ontology? In *Handbook on ontologies* (pp. 1–17). Berlin: Springer.

9. Guizzardi, G. (2005). *Ontological foundations for structural conceptual models*. The Netherlands: University of Twente.

10. Bell, D. (2006). *Cybercultures*. Critical concepts in media and cultural studies (4 Vols.). London: Routledge.

Part II
Theories

There is nothing as practical as a good theory
(Kurt Lewin)

There is nothing as dangerous as a bad theory
(Sumantra Goshal)

Part II comprises the presentation and discussion of the theories underlying the notion of Enterprise Ontology. Chapter 4 provides an overview of all current Enterprise Engineering theories and their position in a clarifying framework. Chapters 5 through 11 contain extended summaries of the theories. The texts are called extended summaries because there is always more to be said. But for the purpose of this book, they suffice to provide the knowledge that one needs for studying Part III. Every chapter is divided into three parts: foundations, elaborations and discussions.

The *foundations* part regards the theoretical basis of the theory, its core ideas, as well as the core sources of knowledge that they rely on. It is considered to be the most stable part of a theory.

In the *elaborations* part, the link to practice is established (illustrations, methods, techniques, tools, etc.). It is less stable than the foundations part, because new elaborations may come up in the course of time from applying the theory in practice.

The *discussions* part serves mainly to compare the theory, and the methods that are based on it, with comparable other approaches. Therefore, it is also less stable than the foundations part, as new comparisons may become relevant in the course of time.

Chapter 4
The Enterprise Engineering Theories

Abstract The foundations of the discipline of enterprise engineering (EE), as envisioned by the Ciao Network, consist of the CIAO Paradigm and a number of theories. After the discussion of the paradigm, which has its origins in the communication-centric view on information systems engineering which emerged around 2000, the role of the EE theories and their relationships with the EE methods and the practice of EE is explained. After having been arranged in a suitable classification scheme, each of the following theories is briefly discussed: the EE information theory, the EE model theory, the EE function-construction theory, the EE organisational operation theory, the EE system theory, the EE organisational construction theory, the EE organisational essence theory, the EE organisational design theory, the EE organisational implementation theory, the EE normalisation theory, and the EE governance and management theory.

Whether you can observe a thing or not depends on the theory that you use. It is the theory that decides what can be observed

(Albert Einstein)

4.1 Introduction

In this chapter, the reader is introduced to the theoretical foundations of the discipline of Enterprise Engineering (EE), as it is developed and practised by a group of researchers and practitioners called the Ciao Network[1] [1]. The Italian word Ciao[2] is an acronym for Communication, Information, Action, and Organisation. They are the key concepts in the CIAO Paradigm, which constitutes the basic understanding of the operation of enterprises. It also sets our engineering perspective. Even if an

---

[1]For more information, visit www.ciaonetwork.org

[2]The Italian word 'Ciao' can mean both 'hello' and 'goodbye', depending on the context. The shared characteristic is that one confirms to someone else to consider him/her as a trustworthy fellow human being.

© Springer Nature Switzerland AG 2020
J. L. G. Dietz, J. B. F. Mulder, *Enterprise Ontology*, The Enterprise Engineering Series, https://doi.org/10.1007/978-3-030-38854-6_4

enterprise has not been designed consciously, changing can be considered as redesigning and re-implementing it. At the same time, the highest appreciation is given to the 'pearls' of every enterprise: the people. Invested with the right authority, based on competence, and exerted with responsibility, they are the cornerstones of an enterprise's organisation. Without people, there is no organisation.

Fig. 4.1 The CIAO tree

In order to portray the role of theories and methods in the field of EE, the Ciao Network uses the tree metaphor, as exhibited in Fig. 4.1. The EE theories constitute the roots of the tree. They feed the trunk, which represents the EE methods, with their juices. After having been made fit for consumption by the methods, the juices ultimately reach all branches, where they cause the growth of leaves and flowers, representing the flourishing enterprises that EE aims to achieve.

As the tree grows, the need may arise to develop new methods, or to graft external ones on the trunk. There is no objection against it; on the contrary, every useful contribution is welcome. The only prerequisite is that the methods are (made) compliant with the EE theories. In addition, a need may occur to develop new theories, or to add external ones to the root structure. Again, the only prerequisite is that they are (made) compliant with the existing set of theories.

Section 4.2 contains an explanation of the CIAO Paradigm. In Sect. 4.3, an overview of the currently existing EE theories is presented, followed by a brief summary of each of them in Sect. 4.4.

4.2   The CIAO Paradigm

4.2.1   From Information-Centric to Communication-Centric

Up to about 1975, there were no information systems and there was no field of information systems engineering. The application of programmed computers in enterprises, for the sake of assisting the workers and the managers, was called EDP (Electronic Data Processing). Around 1975, EDP was replaced by ISE (Information Systems Engineering) or like names, referring to the field that concerns the application of ICT[3] in organisations. The primal and core notion became information, generally defined as the representation of knowledge. Communication was defined as the exchange of information. The notion of action was something rather disconnected from information and communication, as was the notion of organisation, although there was the general recognition that organisation somehow implies action, communication, and information. Let us call this point of view the *information-centric* view on information systems (engineering).

One of the consequences of the information-centric view is that developing (automated) information systems is considered as something that ICT professionals do 'to the side', after having elicited requirements from the people in the organisation, basically by interviewing these people. Once the system is built, it is 'implanted' in the organisation. A widely acknowledged drawback of this 'waiter' approach is that the delivered systems rarely meet the expectations of the users. In hindsight, the main reason for this failure is that requirements determination was ill-understood. Asking the members of an organisation what information they need, presupposes that these people have such a comprehensive understanding of their tasks, that they are able to provide complete, consistent, and coherent answers. As a counter example, embedded software engineers will start to get an appropriate understanding of the system or machine for which they are going to build supporting software. Based on this understanding they will specify the requirements for the software system to be built.

For obscure reasons, the developers of 'embedded' software for organisations, thus the information system engineers, have never recognised the necessity to acquire an appropriate understanding of the objects of interest they want to support: organisations. As a consequence of the 'waiter' approach to requirements determination, relevant requirements are often missing, and irrelevant ones are included.

In the nineties of the past century, an awareness emerged that the information-centric view was not sustainable anymore. The number and size of failures in information systems engineering kept increasing, and the proclaimed benefits of standard packages, notably ERP[4] systems, came along with the feeling of being armoured by the people that had to use these systems. Based on the achievements in language philosophy, notably Speech Act Theory [2, 3] and in (social) action theory, notably the Theory of Communicative Action [4], a community of researchers in information systems engineering, called LAP (Language/Action Perspective), proposed a paradigm shift [5]. By taking communication as the primal notion, the path was paved to a more appropriate and more integrated understanding of the other

---

[3]ICT stands for Information and Communication Technology. It refers especially to the modern practice of applying digital electronic, optical, etc., means to process, store, and transmit data.

[4]ERP stands for Enterprise Resource Planning. It evolved in the 1990s from MRP (Materials Requirements Planning). ERP is a manufacturing and logistics approach to business processes and data management.

three key notions: information, action, and organisation. Later, the name CIAO Paradigm (CIAO stands for Communication, Information, Action, and Organisation) has been coined for this *communication-centric* view on information systems (engineering). *Communication*[5] is now defined as the sharing of thoughts between subjects (human beings), and *information* as the means for communication. People, in organisations and in society at large, have a need to communicate, generally for the sake of making known what they are doing. Because it is impossible to do this directly, for example, by connecting brains, they have to use the vehicle of information.

4.2.2   Communicative Action

In addition to the sharing of thoughts, communication became (also) understood as a form of *action*, by virtue of the intention in every communicative act, as explained by Habermas' Theory of Communicative Action [4]. Figure 4.2 exhibits the four constituting parts of a communicative act: the performer, the intention, the addressee, and the proposition.

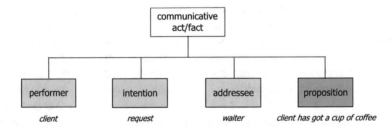

Fig. 4.2   The structure of a communicative act/fact

The *performer* and the *addressee* are subjects, that is, human beings, particularly in their quality of social individual, which means: being capable to engage in mutual commitments. The *proposition* is a state of affairs that is or can be the case. An example of a proposition in the context of a café is that a client has got a cup of coffee. The *intention* is the intent of the performer (the client) towards the addressee (a waiter), with respect to the proposition. If the intention is 'request', the performer wants the addressee to make the proposition become true. In this case, the client wants the waiter to bring her a cup of coffee. Habermas [4] tells us that, in performing a communicative act, the performer raises three validity claims towards

---

[5]The English word 'communicate' comes from the Latin word 'communicare', which means 'making something common', 'sharing something with somebody'. In a more specific sense, it means 'sharing thoughts'.

the addressee: the claim to rightness, the claim to sincerity, and the claim to truth. These claims have to be assessed by the addressee, and the result of this assessment will guide him/her in the way he/she will respond. By accepting the *claim to rightness* in the above example, the waiter recognises the authority of the client to make the request. By accepting the *claim to sincerity*, the waiter expresses that he considers the client sincere in making the request. By accepting the *claim to truth*, the waiter expresses that the proposition can be made true. If all three claims are accepted, the communicative act is said to be successful. In the café example, the waiter will then respond by a promise. In case of failure, he will decline the client's request. In every communicative act, one of the validity claims is dominant. Based on this dominance, Habermas [4] distinguishes three categories of communicative acts, as well as three worlds in which these acts have effect. Figure 4.3 shows the distinctions. The dominance of a claim, as well as the related world, is indicated by the grey-coloured rectangles.

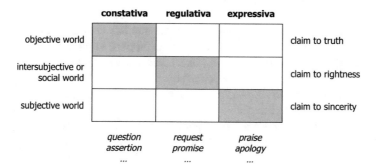

Fig. 4.3 Categories of communicative acts

In the category of *constativa*, the dominant claim is the claim to truth, and the world with which they are primarily concerned, is called the *objective world*. Examples of intentions in this category are question and assertion. If a railway passenger asks a railway officer for the departure time of the next train to Amsterdam, the dominant claim is the claim to truth, that is, that the fact exists (in their shared objective world). This holds also for the answer by the officer (which would be the assertion of a fact). Facts like the departure time of trains are considered to exist in our common objective world, like the fact that the sun is shining, and the current price of a glass of beer in your favourite pub. But, the other two (non-dominant) validity claims must also be satisfied. In the train example, this means that the railway passenger respectively trusts the railway officer that he/she is authorised to provide the answer, and that this officer will provide the correct answer.

In the category of *expressiva*, the dominant claim is the claim to sincerity, and the world with which they are primarily concerned, is everyone's private *subjective world*. Examples of intentions in this category are praise and apologise. If the railway passenger starts his/her conversation with the railway officer by saying

"I'm sorry to disturb you, madam, but . . .", then the dominant claim of this phrase is the claim to sincerity. If the officer feels that the passenger is insincere, she will most likely utter a sincerity checking sentence, and she may even ignore the passenger. Facts like feeling sorry are considered to exist in everyone's subjective world. The claim to sincerity represents the most fundamental condition for human cooperation in the broadest sense of the word, which is mutual *trust*. At the same time, it is the hardest one to verify. Moreover, trust emerges from shared values and norms among people, which do change over time. In language philosophy [6] and social action theory [4] it is assumed that people constantly check and adjust their values and norms when they are communicating. In [7] we have called this second-order communication, and we have suggested that this is the lubricating oil of organisations and of society at large.

In the category of *regulativa*, the dominant claim is the claim to rightness, and the world with which they are primarily concerned, is the intersubjective or *social world*. Examples of intentions in this category are the request and the promise. If the client in the café asks the waiter for a cup of coffee, the dominant claim is the claim to rightness, that is, the client claims that she has the authority to make the request, and that she considers the waiter to be authorised to fulfil it. This holds also for the response by the waiter. Facts like being authorised to do something are considered to exist in our common intersubjective or social world. Moreover, we have created them ourselves. Assigning each other authorities (and expecting that they will be exerted in a responsible way) is the way in which we build organisations and societies [6]. This insight has important consequences. One of them is that people are basically autonomous in deciding how to respond to (intersubjective or social) events. This is the case in every enterprise and in society at large. The fundamental autonomy implies that one may disobey rules and laws if the situation asks for it. At the same time, they must act responsibly, and they can be held accountable for their deeds. Another consequence is that all facts, or all data if one likes, are basically social or intersubjective facts. As will be elaborated in the PSI theory (cf. Chap. 8), a fact is either a coordination fact, like having requested a cup of coffee, or a production fact, like having brought a cup of coffee, or having observed the temperature in a room. Even in the upcoming era of the Internet of Things, the facts that we use in our institutionalised society are always social facts.

4.2.3   Implications for Information, Action, and Organisation

Let us point out next what the consequences of the communication-centric view are for the other three concepts: information, action, and organisation, starting from the basic understanding that *communication* is the sharing of thoughts by human minds. Because human beings are not able to directly connect their minds, some vehicle for transmitting thoughts is needed, and this vehicle is information, or the sign, which is the preferred term in semiotics (cf. Chap. 5). A major outcome of this study is the semiotic ladder, shown in Fig. 4.4. It clarifies the role of signs in the communication of human beings. *Information* then is the dyad of content and form, meaning that the two parts are distinguishable but not separable. The *content* is the thought that one wants to share, and the *form* is the agreed-upon perceivable sign. The content comprises both the intention (or pragmatics) and the proposition (or semantics) of the thought, and the form comprises both the formalism (or syntax) and the coding (or empirics). Contrary to the definition in Fig. 4.4, the content of a sign is often equated with the notion of *information*, and the form with *data*. Precise definitions and their consistent use don't seem to have a high priority in current practice.

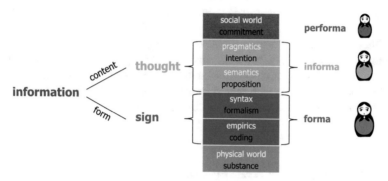

Fig. 4.4 The semiotic ladder

In the café example, the client has, at some point in time, got the thought that she wants a cup of coffee. In order to share this thought, she has to express it in a sign that is intelligible for the waiter. The proposition of the thought is "client has got a cup of coffee" and the intention is the request. By performing the request, she enters into a commitment towards the waiter, like the waiter enters into a commitment if he performs a promise or a decline in response. The client may have expressed her thought in this English sentence: "I'd like to have a cup of coffee, please", which constitutes the form part in Fig. 4.4. The applied formalism is the English grammar and the coding concerns the representation of the words. The substance in which the sentence is inscribed consists of the air vibrations that are produced by the client and then perceived by the sense of hearing of the waiter.

For the concept of *action*, the communication-centric view means that communicating is (also) acting, as discussed in Sect. 4.2.2. As Austin [2] puts it, people do things with words. In the PSI theory (cf. Chap. 8), this is accentuated by distinguishing coordination acts and production acts, and by combining them in the concept of the (business) transaction. The new concept of *organisation* that arises from the foregoing is: a network of actors who carry out transactions in cooperation. It is a new way of looking at Mintzberg's basic idea of organisation: the need to divide labour into tasks, and the need to coordinate these tasks [8]. The idea that organisation is somehow the outcome of the social interaction of cooperating human beings, is not new, by the way. Since Max Weber [9], several sociologists have studied this relationship, like, for example, Weick [10]. However, none of them has made the idea as operational as the CIAO Paradigm does.

Having this new understanding of organisation, a new and more appropriate understanding of information system emerges. It appears that every information system in an organisation can appropriately be conceived as some implementation of some part of the organisation. This view emphasises the being intrinsically intertwined of informations systems and their supported organisations. It also clarifies why information system engineers should first of all study the construction and operation of the organisation before designing the information system. Basically, the information system is already there, because it is an intrinsic part of the organisation. Consequently, the functional requirements are also already there. The main task of the information system engineer is to find a new way of implementing a particular part of the organisation, in particular by applying ICT.

Although conceiving organisations as networks of actors who carry out transactions, is indifferent to a particular management style or approach, it certainly matches very well with a high degree of self-management, as discussed in [11]. Making decisions at the lowest hierarchical level that is possible, implies that one grants a high degree of autonomy to the employees on that level.

4.3   Overview of the EE Theories

Paraphrasing Einstein's quote above, the EE theories are the mental glasses through which enterprise engineers observe and understand enterprises, and seek to make sense of them. In addition, the EE theories are the roots of the methods for improving enterprises, as illustrated in Fig. 4.1.

Table 4.1 The current EE theories

Φ-theory	FI theory	EE information theory
M-theory	MU theory	EE model theory
T-theory	TAO theory	EE function-construction theory
Ψ-theory	PSI theory	EE organisational operation theory
Δ-theory	DELTA theory	EE system theory
Ω-theory	OMEGA theory	EE organisational construction theory
A-theory	ALPHA theory	EE organisational essence theory
B-theory	BETA theory	EE organisational design theory
I-theory	IOTA theory	EE organisational implementation theory
N-theory	NU theory	EE normalisation theory
Σ-theory	SIGMA theory	EE governance & management theory

The presently identified EE theories are listed in Table 4.1. Next to the Greek letter that serves as the primary identifier, their alternative names and EE references are mentioned. All theories are classified in the EE Framework of Theories (Fig. 4.5), which is an adapted version of the framework that was introduced in [1]. Four categories are distinguished: philosophical, ontological, technological, and ideological. The structure of Fig. 4.5 must be understood as follows. The philosophical theories underlie all other theories. On top of that, the ontological theories underlie both the technological theories and the ideological ones. The latter two categories do not have specific interrelationships. The classification of the theories in the framework is, to some extent, disputable, because they do not always fit in exactly one category. However, the presented classification seems to do justice to their main character.

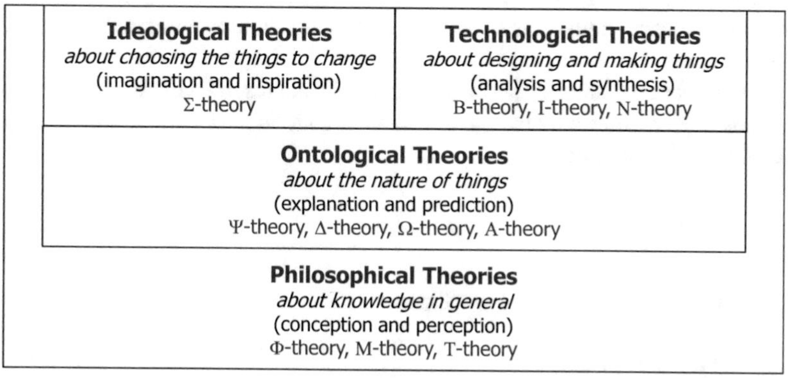

Ideological Theories	Technological Theories
about choosing the things to change	*about designing and making things*
(imagination and inspiration)	(analysis and synthesis)
Σ-theory	B-theory, I-theory, N-theory
Ontological Theories	
about the nature of things	
(explanation and prediction)	
Ψ-theory, Δ-theory, Ω-theory, A-theory	
Philosophical Theories	
about knowledge in general	
(conception and perception)	
Φ-theory, M-theory, T-theory	

Fig. 4.5   The EE theories in the EE framework of theories

Philosophical theories concern the most fundamental ways in which people perceive and conceive the surrounding world, make sense of it, study it, etc. They are about knowledge in general, and therefore include, for example, epistemology, phenomenology, and logic. Philosophical theories are justified by their *truthfulness*. The truthfulness of a theory is established by reasoning or by judging its tenability in the face of reality.

Ontological theories are about the nature of things. They serve to explain their construction and operation, and predict the consequences of changing them, while completely abstracting from implementation. In EE, the things are organisations. Ontological theories are justified by their *soundness* and *appropriateness*. The soundness of an ontological theory is established by its being rooted in sound philosophical theories. The appropriateness of an ontological theory is established by the evaluation of its practical application, for example, through expert judgements.

Technological[6] theories are about designing and building things, and about putting them into operation. Generally spoken, they assist in analysing and synthesising things. Technological theories are justified by their *rigor* and *relevance*. The rigor of a technological theory is established by its being rooted in sound ontological and ideological theories. The relevance of a technological theory is established by the evaluation of its practical application, e.g., through measurements, evaluative comparisons, and adoption studies.

Ideological theories are not about things themselves, but about the context in which one decides on whether to make or change them. In EE, they serve to feed the imagination of people and to assist them in inspiring other people to adopt new, better ideas for running enterprises. Ideological theories cannot a priori be predicated as truthful or as sound and appropriate, nor as rigorous and relevant, even if they are rooted in rigorous and relevant other theories. One can only speak of their societal *significance*. The significance of an ideological theory boils down to the usefulness that is assigned to it by its supporters.

The summaries of the EE theories in Sect. 4.4 are presented in an order that seems to be most logical; one can read them from the first to the last without having to jump forward for explanations.

4.4   Summaries of the EE Theories

4.4.1   The FI Theory

The FI theory or EE information theory (FI stands for *Factual Information*), clarifies how people acquire factual knowledge. Semiotics provides us with the *semiotic triangle* [12], which clarifies the dyadic character of information: it is the inseparable combination of *content* (the communicated thought) and *form* (the sign that signifies the thought). In addition, Semiotics provides us with the *semiotic ladder* [13], in which a distinction is made between the semantics and the pragmatics of thoughts, thereby clarifying that a thought consists of a *proposition* and an *intention*.

---

[6]Particularly in Information and Communication Technology, the term 'technology' has got the meaning of means. We prefer to stick to the original meaning of the word, which stems from its Greek origin: technè (meaning making) and logos (meaning knowing). So technology means knowing how to make.

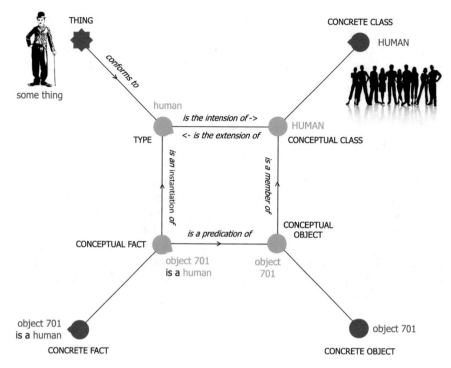

Fig. 4.6 The ontological mill

The core of the FI theory is the *semiotic mill*, refined into the *ontological mill*, which is a generic framework for understanding perception and conception, shown in Fig. 4.6. A *fact* becomes existent in the mind when a perceived concrete thing conforms to (the prescription of form of) a *type*. Therefore, a fact is an *instantiation* of a type. In logical terms, it is a predication of a conceptual object, with the type as the predicate. The conceptual object represents a concrete object that is considered to be the *identity* of a concrete thing. The first is a member of a conceptual class, and the second is a member of a concrete class. Type and class are dyadic notions: a class is the *extension* of a type; conversely, a type is the *intension* of a class.

Because the form of the thing with object 701 conforms to the type human, the conceptual fact is created in the mind that the thing is a human. In addition, factual knowledge can be acquired through communication.

Types can be *declared*, as original new types, but they can also be *derived* from existing types. Three ways of deriving are discussed: specialisation, generalisation, and aggregation. An example of *specialisation* is the definition of the type student as a specialisation of person: a student is a person for whom there is an admission in which the person is the admitted person. An example of *generalisation* is the (extensional) definition of the type vehicle: the class VEHICLE is the set-theoretic union of the classes CAR, BIKE, SCOOTER, etc. An aggregation of a number of types is (extensionally) defined as the cartesian product of their classes. An example of *aggregation* is the definition of the price of an article as an attribute of the Cartesian product of article kind (e.g. apple), supplier (e.g. GreenShop), and day (e.g. today).

4.4.2   The MU Theory

The MU theory or EE model theory (MU stands for *Model Universe*), is a theory of models and modelling in general, and of conceptual modelling in particular. It adopts Apostel's definition of *model* [14]: Any subject using a system A to obtain knowledge of a system B, is using A as a model of B. This definition conveys the basic understanding of the concept of model as a role concept. The *model triangle*, which is based on the semiotic triangle (cf. Sect. 4.4.1), clarifies how complexes (systems and aggregates) of three major sorts (concrete, conceptual, and symbolic) can be viewed as models of each other. It is exhibited in Fig. 4.7.

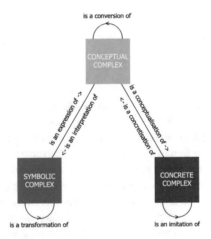

Fig. 4.7   The model triangle

   By adding two levels of abstraction (the schema level and the meta level) on top of the conceptual complex or instance level, the *General Conceptual Modelling Framework* (GCMF) emerges. It clarifies the notions of *conceptual complex, conceptual schema*, and *meta schema*, for any Universe of Discourse or system's world.

It also makes clear that these notions are logical constructs, and that consequently any expression of them (in a suitable language) is directly transformable to first-order logic. The GCMF is exhibited in Fig. 4.8.

Because the form of the concrete complex conforms to the prescription of form that the conceptual schema represents, the corresponding conceptual complex is created in the mind. For communicating this 'thought', it is expressed in the symbolic formalism of the conceptual schema, yielding the symbolic complex.

In order to specify conceptual complexes, conceptual schemas and meta schemas, the *General Ontology Specification Language* (GOSL) is presented and discussed. The syntax of the language consists of graphical and textual symbols and constructs, as well as a textual part. The latter is an English-like formal language, which means that it is directly transformable to first-order logic, like the graphical part. The split between the two is a rather pragmatic one. Compared to common graphical languages for conceptual modelling, GOSL might be called minimal: it covers only the basic concepts and constructs. More complicated logical formulas can mostly be better expressed in formal textual sentences.

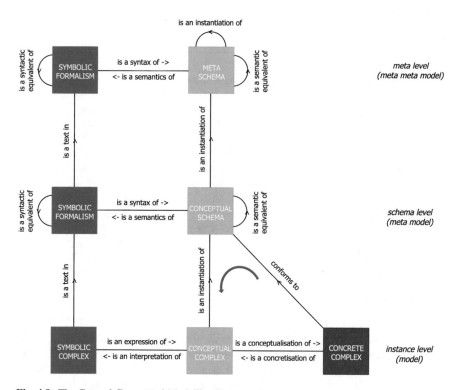

Fig. 4.8 The General Conceptual Modelling Framework

4.4.3   The TAO Theory

EE is an engineering approach to tackling problems in enterprises. By nature, engineers seek to understand the *construction* and *operation* of systems (where operation is defined as the manifestation of the construction in the course of time), in addition to their *functions* and *behaviours* (where a behaviour is defined as the manifestation of a function in the course of time). The TAO theory *(Teleology–Affordances–Ontology)* clarifies the distinction between function and construction. One of the clarifications is that the construction of a system is an inherent property of the system, whereas all of its functions are relationships between the system and stakeholders. Consequently, functions are not properties of systems. The TAO theory builds on Gibson's Theory of Affordances [15]. As Fig. 4.9 illustrates, *affordances* emerge from the perception by subjects (with needs or purposes) of concrete objects (with properties). As an example, if you walk in the woods and feel the need to sit, you may perceive that a tree trunk offers you the sit-on-ability affordance.

In addition to using the affordances that existing things offer, people also create things with particular affordances in mind. These things are commonly called *artefacts,* and their intended affordances *functions*. For example, chairs have the function to be sit-on-able. In addition, one can assign (new) functions to things. For example, one can assign the function of parking lot to a square, for particular days of the week.

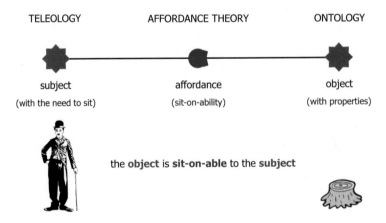

Fig. 4.9 Illustration of the TAO theory

Consequently, a strict distinction is made between the construction and the function perspective on things. In the *construction perspective*, one studies a thing in an objective way, that is, independent of the affordances it may offer. In the *function perspective*, one studies the affordances that a thing may offer to subjects, while disregarding its construction. So, function (or affordance) is not a property of a thing, but a relationship between the thing and a stakeholder. For example, to people who know to drive, cars do offer relevant functions. This does probably not (directly) hold for the members of an isolated tribe in the jungle of Brazil.

When using the affordances that things can offer them, subjects may have different *experiences*. For example, you may *value* the sit-on-ability of a chair higher than the same affordance offered by a tree trunk. Experiences are basically subjective impressions. However, they may be shared among stakeholders.

Corresponding with the function-construction distinction, two sorts of conceptual models (cf. Sect. 4.4.2) are distinguished: constructional models and functional models. A *constructional model* is a representation of the construction of concrete things, like cars. A *functional model* is a representation of the possible affordances or functions that a concrete thing may offer to someone, for example, the driving function of a car to a (potential) driver. Next, the constructional decomposition and functional decomposition of enterprises are discussed. To distinguish between the two, it is suggested that the term "organisation" be used when referring to the construction perspective, and the term "business" when referring to the function perspective. A decomposition of an enterprise's organisation is a *constructional decomposition*, and a decomposition of its business is a *functional decomposition*.

4.4.4 The PSI Theory

The PSI theory *(Performance in Social Interaction)* serves to study the operational essence of organisations. The word "organisation" indicates that one takes the construction perspective on enterprises. Organisations are systems in the category of social systems (cf. Sect. 4.4.3), which means that the system elements are social individuals, called actors. The operating principle is that actors enter into and comply with commitments towards each other.

An *actor* is defined as a subject (human being) in an actor role. The *actor role* determines the authority that the actor may exercise and the responsibility to do so. Commitments are raised in coordination acts, which are communicative acts in Habermas' category of regulativa (cf. Figs. 4.2 and 4.3). The result of performing a coordination act is the creation of the corresponding coordination fact. For example, performing a request act concerning some product results in the fact that the product is requested.

Coordination acts/facts are the atomic building blocks of organisational (but commonly called: business) processes. They always occur in particular patterns of interaction between subjects who play either the *initiator* role or the *executor* role in the transaction. These patterns are instances of one generic pattern, called the (business) *transaction*. The basic coordination acts in every transaction are the request (by the initiator), the promise (by the executor), the declare (by the executor), and the accept (by the initiator). The complete transaction pattern comprises in addition, the decline (instead of promise), reject (instead of accept), and a revocation pattern for each of the basic steps. Every transaction (instance) is of a particular *transaction kind*. A transaction kind concerns one specific *product kind* and has one specific actor role as its executor role. The combination of a transaction kind and its executor role is called a *transactor role*. It is the (molecular) building block of organisations.

Based on the semiotic ladder (cf. Sect. 4.4.1), three human abilities are distinguished in performing coordination acts: *forma*, *informa*, and *performa* (cf. Fig. 4.4). This distinction gives rise to three levels of correspondence in the communication between subjects: the forma level (notational correspondence), the informa level (cognitive correspondence), and the performa level (social correspondence), as shown in Fig. 4.10. To be successful, all three conditions of correspondence must be satisfied, that is, the communication must be free of distortion. Below the forma level is the medium level, where forms are inscribed in physical substances and transported between subjects. Although evenly conditional for successful communication, this level is considered to be outside the field of EE, as is the 'inner self' upper level, where a person's wisdom and love reside, which constitute the basis for her/his decisions. He/she is basically autonomous in deciding how to respond to coordination events. At the same time, actors can always be held accountable, by other actors, for the acts that they decide to perform.

Fig. 4.10 The process of a communicative act

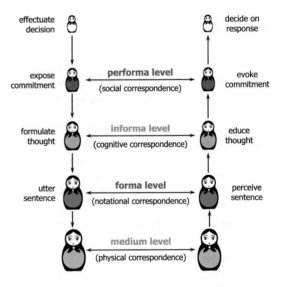

The structure of a coordination act/fact is shown in Fig. 4.2. Examples of intentions are: request, promise, declare, and accept. An example of a product (or production fact) is 'sale 1618 is completed'. As said, coordination acts occur in specific interaction patterns between two participants, called transactions. A transaction is successful if the (final) product is accepted. At that moment, the product starts to exist (comes into being). Figure 4.11 exhibits the complete transaction pattern, which is considered to be the universal pattern in all organisations. It consists of the standard pattern (middle part) and four revocations patterns.

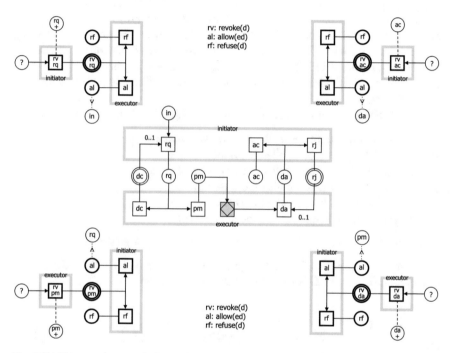

Fig. 4.11 The complete transaction pattern

4.4.5 The DELTA Theory

The DELTA theory or EE system theory (DELTA stands for *Discrete Event in Linear Time Automaton*) is a theory of discrete event systems, both from the construction and from the function perspective (cf. Sect. 4.4.1). According to Weinberg's division of the realm of systems [16], organisations fall in the category of organised complexity: they are too organised for statistics and too complex for (mathematical) analysis. Bunge's system definition [17] is adopted: a (homogeneous) *system* is a triple $(\mathbb{C}, \mathbb{E}, \mathbb{S})$, where $\mathbb{C}$ (composition) is a set of elements of some category, $\mathbb{E}$ (environment) is a set of elements of the same category as the elements in $\mathbb{C}$, and $\mathbb{S}$ (structure) is a set of influencing bonds among the elements in $\mathbb{C}$

and between them and the elements in $\mathbb{E}$. Examples of categories are: physical, biological, and social. Organisations fall in the category of social systems.

Two sorts of conceptual systems are distinguished that may serve as models (cf. Sect. 4.4.2) of concrete systems: the *black-box* system and the *white-box* system. White-box models are suited to study the construction and operation of systems (cf. Sect. 4.4.3). Black-box models are suited to study their functionality and behaviour. Because black-box systems don't have an internal state, the grey-box system is introduced as a black-box system with internal state. Well-known examples of grey-box systems are the finite automaton (or finite state machine) and the discrete event system. For a deep and formal study of grey-box and white-box models, the PRISMA model is introduced. Three ways of mutual influencing between (the elements of) systems are distinguished, called *activating*, *restricting*, and *impeding*. In the PRISMA *grey-box* model, all acts by the system, and their resulting facts, are divided in two kinds: *production acts/facts* and *coordination acts/ facts* (cf. Sect. 4.4.4).

The PRISMA grey-box model is defined as a tuple (**P, R, I, S, M, A**), where:

P   is a partial function, called the *performance function*
R   is a set of C-fact types, called the *reaction base*
I   is a set of C-fact types, called the *impediment base*
S   is a set of P-fact types, called the *state base*
M   is a set of P-fact types, called the *mutation base*
A   is a set of C-fact types, called the *action base*

P is defined as: $\wp((\underline{\mathbf{A}} \cup \underline{\mathbf{I}}) * \mathbb{T}) * \wp(\underline{\mathbf{S}} * \mathbb{T}) \rightarrow \wp(\underline{\mathbf{M}} * \mathbb{D}) * \wp(\underline{\mathbf{R}} * \mathbb{D})$

where $\underline{\mathbf{X}}$ is the union of the extensions of $X \in \underline{\mathbf{X}}$ (X is A, I, M, R, or S); $\mathbb{T}$ is the discrete time scale and $\mathbb{D}$ is the set of (positive) time delays.

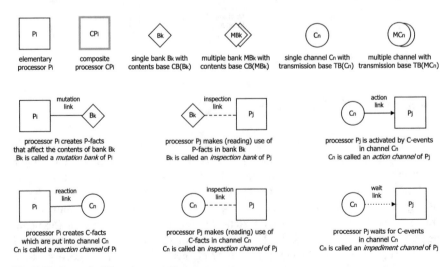

Fig. 4.12 Legend of the prismanet diagram

The PRISMA *white-box* model allows one to conceive systems as *prismanets*: networks of processors, channels, and banks. The complete prismanet model of a system is divided into the construction model and the operation model. The *construction model* of a system is the part that is expressed in the prismanet diagram, whose legend is shown in Fig. 4.12. The meanings of the various links between the basic shapes (box for processors, diamond for banks, and disk for channels) are expressed in an informal way. The *operation model* of a system consists of the action rules that constitute the performance function of the corresponding prisma. They reside in the processor that is the kernel of the prisma. The abstraction that is achieved through the notions of activating, restricting (constituted by inspection links), and impeding makes the prismanet comprehensive: no additional knowledge is needed to get a complete (ontological) understanding of the modelled system. That is why it is called the *essential model* of the system. In addition, prismanets are formalised systems; they can directly be implemented in software.

4.4.6 The OMEGA Theory

The OMEGA theory *(Organisational Modules Emerging from General Arrangements)* clarifies the coordination structures in which transactor roles are connected. Three basic structures are distinguished: interaction, interstriction, and interimpediment.

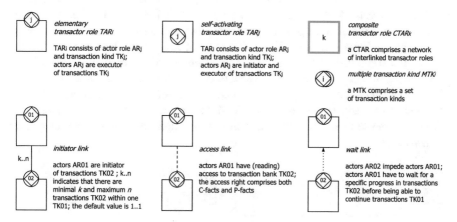

Fig. 4.13 Legend of the Coordination Structure Diagram

The *interaction structure* determines for every transactor role in the organisation which transactor roles are initiator in transactions of the corresponding transaction kind. It appears that the interaction structure of an organisation is always a set of tree structures. Consequently, the transaction kinds at any level of such a tree structure are enclosed in another transaction kind (except the 'root' of the tree) and do have enclosed transaction kinds (except the 'leaves' of the tree). The interaction structure is the inherent fundamental structure of business processes (which are commonly envisioned as flows, that is, as sequences of events). In addition, it clarifies the responsibility ranges of actors in business processes, and thus notions like process ownership and data ownership.

The *interstriction structure* determines which transactor roles may inspect the history of the transactions of other transaction kinds. These other transaction kinds may be external to the organisation (or Scope of Interest). Actors do inspect the history of transaction processes because they need to take process facts into account when deciding on acts to perform. In this way, actors restrict each other's decision freedom.

The *interimpediment structure* determines whether actors in some actor role have to wait with performing specific acts until other transaction processes have reached a specific state. All three organisational structures are expressed in the *Coordination Structure Diagram* (CSD), of which Fig. 4.13 shows the legend. Figure 4.14 illustrates it, using the GloLog case (cf. Chap. 19) as an example enterprise. The red colour of the diamonds indicates that the transactor roles belong to the O-organisation of the modelled enterprise (cf. Sect. 4.4.7). There are four interaction trees, also called *business process kinds*. The top of the left one is a composite transactor role. The initiator link with TAR01 expresses that it contains a (unknown) transactor role that initiates transactions TK01. The top of the other three structures is a self-activating transactor role. The light-grey colour of some boxes indicates that they belong to the environment of the Scope of Interest (which comprises the white-coloured boxes). Each of the four processes has its own case kind: client order, supply order, ship content and container content, respectively. The evoked structural clashes [18] between them are resolved by the wait links. In addition, there are several inspection links. Figure 4.14 clearly shows the added value of product (tree) thinking in addition to flow thinking. There cannot be one 'seamless' process flow in GloLog. Instead, there are four autonomous processes, with their own process cycle, determined by their case kind. As alluded to in Sect. 4.4.5, no additional knowledge is needed to get a complete (ontological) understanding of the organisation, that is, of the collective business processes, provided that the action rules for the transactor roles are also known. Therefore, this model is called the *essential model* of the organisation.

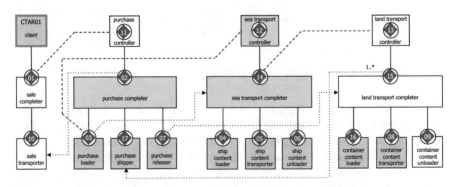

Fig. 4.14   CSD of the GloLog enterprise

There is a second kind of general arrangements, in addition to the ones above. It appears that every organisational structure is composed of a limited number of *reference patterns*, which often resemble legal patterns of action, like the transfer of property and the granting/obtaining of usufructuary rights.

4.4.7 The ALPHA Theory

The ALPHA theory *(Abstraction Layers in Production for Holistic Analysis)* is a theory about tree structures of (trans)actors, in addition to the compositional trees from the OMEGA theory (cf. Sect. 4.4.6). These tree structures occur in three transactor layers, which are based on the distinction of three sorts of production acts: original, informational (or infological), and documental (or datalogical).

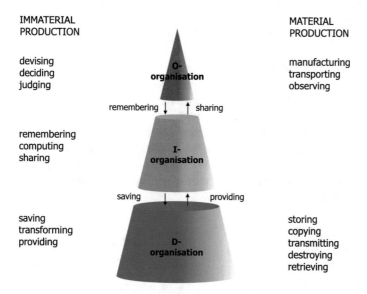

Fig. 4.15 Organisational layers and sorts of production

Original production acts bring about original, new, production facts. Examples are devising things, deciding and judging (all of them having intangible results), as well as manufacturing, transporting, and observing (all of them having tangible results).

Informational production acts comprise remembering facts (in the state of the production or coordination world of an organisation), recalling (remembered) facts, and computing or deriving facts. Computing does not change the state of a world; it only leads to presenting the state in new, possibly more intelligible ways.

Documental production acts concern the signs (or data) that contain facts, as well as the files that carry the data (cf. Sect. 4.4.1). They comprise saving, providing and transforming (documents or data), and storing, retrieving, copying, transmitting, and destroying (files). Because original acts are the only acts that change the state of the production world of an organisation, they need to be performed by authorised and responsible actors, thus subjects in actor roles. Both informational and documental acts may be taken over by artefacts, notably ICT systems. However, as pointed out in Sect. 4.4.4, human actors are ultimately responsible and accountable.

Corresponding with the distinct sorts of production, the actors in an organisation can be partitioned in three layers: the *O-organisation* (O from original), the *I-organisation* (I from informational), and the *D-organisation* (D from documental). The I-organisation supports the O-organisation by means of informational services (remembering and sharing facts), and the D-organisation supports the I-organisation by means of documental services (saving and providing documents). By the *realisation* of an organisation is understood the devising of the I-organisation and the D-organisation, given its O-organisation (cf. Fig. 4.15). Conversely, abstracting from realisation yields the O-organisation of an enterprise. The additional abstracting from implementation yields the ontological model of the O-organisation, also called the *essential model* of the (total) enterprise (cf. Sect. 4.4.5).

The 'pie chart' in Fig. 4.16 illustrates the difference between material and immaterial production in the O- and the D-organisation (the production in the I-organisation is by definition only immaterial). The adjacency of material original production and material documental production expresses that the exact sort of an act/fact may depend on the point of view taken: sending a letter by postal mail is clearly a material documental act for the sender. Postal mail companies, however, may consider the distinction between original and documental production less interesting. Their business is to transport packages, including envelops, without much regard to their contents.

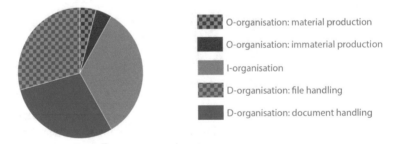

Fig. 4.16   Organisational layers and sorts of production

4.4.8   The BETA Theory

The BETA theory or EE design theory (BETA stands for *Building from Essence with Technology and Architecture*), is a theory about designing artefacts. Where the ALPHA theory tells one how to abstract from the concrete appearance of a system (realisation and implementation), the BETA theory guides one in designing a system and in making it concrete. First, Simon's notion of *design* [19] is discussed, understood as devising a situation that is considered preferable to the current situation, as well as Alexander's notion of *design process* [20], understood as a sequence of alternate analysis (of the problem) and synthesis (of a solution) steps. Next, the *General System Development Process* (GSDP) is introduced. It is a general framework for understanding the development of an *object system* for the benefit of a *using system* (cf. Fig. 4.17).

With reference to the TAO theory (cf. Sect. 4.4.3), a clear and sharp distinction is made between the function and the construction of the object system, as well as between the function and the construction of the using system, thereby clarifying that the function of the object system supports the construction of the using system. The three main phases in a development process are function design, construction design, and implementation design. *Function design* starts from the ontological model of the using system, which is commonly arrived at by reverse engineering (cf. Sect. 4.4.7), and ends with the specification of the object system function. There are two inputs: *functional requirements* (determined by the using system construction) and *functional principles* (determined by the applicable architecture). *Construction design* starts from the object system function, and ends with the ontological model of the object system. There are two inputs: *constructional requirements* (determined by the using system construction) and *constructional principles* (determined by the applicable architecture). *Implementation design* (also called *engineering*) starts from the ontology of the object system and ends with the fully detailed specification of a possible implementation, which can subsequently be implemented with appropriate technology. The inputs are both the constructional requirements and the constructional principles.

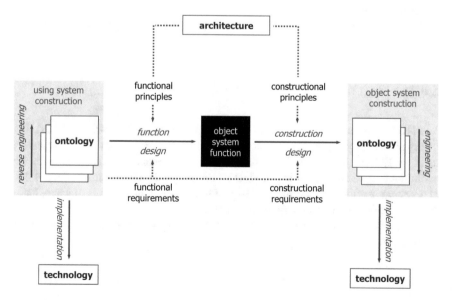

Fig. 4.17 The General System Development Process

A general problem in system development is the (too) large amount of design freedom that is left when all requirements are satisfied. Since time immemorial, the notion of *architecture* helps designers to use this freedom in a purposeful and systematic way. To exemplify this, the Metropolitan Opera in New York, the Sydney Opera House, and the Scala in Milan have the same basic function, namely to offer the facilities that are needed to perform operas. Yet, their appearances are very different. One only has to look at the photos of the respective buildings to see it. Thus, whereas the functional requirements for each of the opera houses are (for the largest part) the same, the applied architectures are quite different.

The *General Requirements and Architecture Framework* (GRAF) is introduced for expressing architecture in practicable design and implementation *principles*, which are basically understood as *generic requirements* that constrain system development in addition to the specific requirements.

4.4.9   The IOTA Theory

The IOTA theory or EE organisational implementation theory (IOTA stands for *Implementing Organisations with Technological Alternatives*), is theory about the implementation of organisations. With reference to Fig. 4.17 (right-hand side), the BETA theory covers the engineering (or implementation design) process, but not the implementation itself. It stops at the implementation model, thus the lowest level construction model of the OS. This is the point where the IOTA theory starts. It guides the enterprise engineer in determining the content of the implementation model, as well as in finding, justifying, and assigning technological alternatives for the actual implementation.

The IOTA theory has yet to be produced. The first steps are taken in [21].

4.4.10   The NU Theory

The NU theory or EE normalisation theory (NU stands for *Normalised Units*), is a theory about the construction of systems. It can best be considered as complementary to the DELTA theory (cf. Sect. 4.4.5). The NU theory is concerned with the evolution of systems. Applying the NU theory in the development (cf. Sect. 4.4.8) of a system results in a modular structure of the system that prevents unwanted side effects when the system undergoes changes.

The NU theory has yet to be produced. A candidate footing is the Normalised Systems Theory [22, 23].

4.4.11   The SIGMA Theory

The SIGMA theory or EE governance & management theory (SIGMA stands for *Socially Inspired Governance and Management Approach*), is an ideological theory about how enterprises should be managed and governed in such a way that the people in the enterprise are maximally empowered. Traditional thinking about enterprises considers (executive) management the primary and exclusive custodians of enterprise performance. Employees, under management control, must behave instrumentally as parts of the enterprise machine. There is no employee variability: standard, predefined instrumental behaviour is required and expected. The SIGMA theory submits a fundamentally different perspective by arguing that variability in employee behaviour is crucial for operational and strategic performance. In our view, the instrumental approach to employee behaviour conflicts with moral and ethical considerations concerning employees and society at large. Current economic thinking, in which enterprises are merely seen as money-generating machines, reinforces the instrumental view on employees. It is argued that employee variability is an absolute prerequisite for aligning employee interests with enterprise performance interests. This unitarist perspective rejects any supposedly 'natural' opposition between them. The SIGMA theory is made operational through the notion of meaningful work, which is seen as an affordance (cf. Sect. 4.4.3): a relationship between employees with certain subjective needs and enterprises with certain objective properties of the work environment. The nature of these needs and properties is elucidated, clarifying at the same time that the theory is firmly grounded in the organisational sciences. The employee-centric nature of this theory aims to counteract the narrow economic theories advanced by many business schools. The discussion of these current ways of thinking reveals the fundamentally different perspective on enterprises that the SIGMA theory radiates. The SIGMA theory is extensively discussed in [24].

References

1. Dietz, J. L. G., & Hoogervorst, J. A. P. (2013). The discipline of enterprise engineering. *International Journal of Organisational Design and Engineering, 3*, 28.
2. Austin, J. L. (1962). *How to do things with words.* Cambridge: Harvard University Press.
3. Searle, J. R. (1969). *Speech acts: An essay in the philosophy of language.* London: Cambridge University Press. vii, 203 p.
4. Habermas, J. (1986). *The theory of communicative action.* Cambridge: Polity Press.
5. Weigand, H. (2006). Two decades of the language-action perspective. *Communications of the ACM, 49*(4), 44–46.
6. Searle, J. R. (1995). *The construction of social reality.* New York: Free Press. xiii, 241 p.
7. Dietz, J. L. G. (2012). *Red garden gnomes don't exist.* The Netherlands: Sapio Enterprise Engineering. www.sapio.nl
8. Mintzberg, H. (1979). *The structuring of organizations: A synthesis of the research* (Theory of management policy). Englewood Cliffs, NJ: Prentice-Hall. xvi, 512 p.

 9. Weber, M. (1990). Legitimate authority and bureaucracy. In D. S. Pugh (Ed.), *Organization theory*. London: Penguin Books.
10. Weick, K. E. (2001). *Making sense of the organization*. Oxford, UK: Blackwell. xii, 483 p.
11. Laloux, F. *Reinventing organizations: A guide to creating organizations inspired by the next stage of human consciousness* (1st ed.). Brussels: Nelson Parker. xviii, 360 p.
12. Ogden, C. K., & Richards, I. A. (1923). *The meaning of meaning: A study of the influence of language upon thought and of the science of symbolism* (International library of psychology, philosophy, and scientific method). London: K. Paul, Trench, Trubner/Harcourt, Brace. xxxi, 1, 544 p.
13. Stamper, R. K. (1973). *Information in business and administrative systems*. London: Batsford. 6, 362 p.
14. Apostel, L. (1960). Towards the formal study of models in the non-formal sciences. *Synthese, 12*(2–3), 125–161.
15. Gibson, J. J. (1979). *The ecological approach to visual perception*. Boston: Houghton Mifflin. xv, 332 p.
16. Weinberg, G. M. (1975). *An introduction to general systems thinking* (Wiley series on systems engineering and analysis). New York: Wiley. xxi, 279 p.
17. Bunge, M. (1979). *Treatise on basic philosophy. Ontology II: A world of systems* (Treatise on basic philosophy) (4th ed.). Dordrecht: Reidel.
18. Jackson, M. A. (1975). *Principles of program design* (A P I C studies in data processing). New York: Academic Press. xii, 299 p.
19. Simon, H. A. (1969). *The sciences of the artificial* (Karl Taylor Compton lectures). Cambridge: M.I.T. Press. xii, 123 p.
20. Alexander, C. (1964). *Notes on the synthesis of form*. Cambridge: Harvard University Press. 216 p.
21. Op't Land, M., & Krouwel, M. (2013). Exploring organizational implementation fundamentals. In H. A. Proper, D. Aveiro, & K. Gaaloul (Eds.), *EEWC* (pp. 28–42). Berlin: Springer.
22. Mannaert, H., Verelst, J., & de Bruyn, P. (2016). *Normalized systems—From foundations for evolvable software toward a general theory for evolvable design*. Kermt, Belgium: Koppa.
23. Krouwel, M. R., Op't Land, M. (2011). Combining DEMO and normalized systems for developing agile enterprise information systems. In A. Albani, J. L. G. Dietz, & J. Verelst (Eds.), *EEWC* (pp. 31–45). Berlin: Springer.
24. Hoogervorst, J. A. P. (2017). *Foundations of enterprise governance and enterprise engineering*. Cham: Springer. 574 p.

Chapter 5
The FI Theory: Understanding Factual Knowledge and Information

Abstract The FI theory is a theory about factual knowledge and about information in general. FI stands for Factual Information. The basis for the FI theory consists of Ogden and Richard's semiotic triangle and Stamper's semiotic ladder. They clarify that information is a dyadic notion: it is the inseparable combination of content (the communicated thought) and form (the sign that serves to signify the thought). The main contribution of the semiotic ladder is that it distinguishes between the semantics and the pragmatics of thoughts and in doing so clarifies that a (elementary) thought consists of a fact and an intention. Intentions correspond with commitments in the social world. The core of the FI theory is the semiotic mill, refined into the ontological mill, which is a framework for understanding perception and conception. It explains how factual knowledge is created from perceptions of concrete things, directed by (fact) types, which operate as conceptual sieves. Three topics are elaborated. The first one is the recognition that most of the types that people use are functional types. Regarding functional types, the important fact is that they are inherently subjective, and therefore hard to define precisely. The second topic is the problem of sameness and change, illustrated with the well-known paradox of Theseus. The third topic concerns the composition and decomposition of things, based on the part-of relationship between things. Lastly, two issues in current programming and modelling practice are discussed. The first one is the duality of types, as opposed to the synonymy of signs. The second issue is the value types in software. Most programming and modelling languages offer four 'types': integer, real, boolean, and string. The first three are true types; the fourth is only a sign 'type'.

5.1 Introduction

The theory in this chapter is labeled Φ-theory. The Greek capital letter is pronounced as FI, which is an acronym for Factual Information. The FI theory, also called the EE information theory, is an extensive study of the notion of information and the notion of factual knowledge. It is classified as a *philosophical* theory in the framework of theories, as presented in Chap. 4, thus a theory that is about knowledge in general.

As discussed in the founding article of the discipline of enterprise engineering (EE) [1], the application of contemporary information and communication technology (ICT) is the key technology in implementing organisations, and a major driver of organisational changes and transformations. Consequently, the notions of communication and information are crucial in understanding the application of ICT. As presented and discussed in Chap. 4 and elaborated in Chap. 8, the CIAO paradigm constitutes the new, appropriate understanding of communication, as well as the new, appropriate understanding of the notions of information, action, and organisation based on it.

Section 5.2 starts with a discussion of a fundamental framework for studying information in a most general way: the semiotic triangle. It is a necessary leg up to the next framework, the semiotic ladder, which clearly defines the notion of information as the inseparable dyad of content and form. Based on both the semiotic triangle and the semiotic ladder, we will discuss the notions of world, thing, and object, followed by a discussion of facts and types and classes. It culminates in the presentation of a framework for understanding all these notions in a coherent way, which is called the semiotic mill (because the shape of the picture resembles a windmill), followed by a stripped version called the ontological mill. This ontological mill will be used to clarify various issues in conceptual modelling, like the declaring and deriving of types. Three ways of deriving facts are discussed: specialisation, generalisation, and aggregation. The section concludes with the clear distinction between specialisation and generalisation, on the one hand, and subtype and supertype, on the other hand.

Section 5.3 starts with a discussion of the difference between constructional types and functional types, and the basic impossibility to define functional types in a definite and precise way. The next part is about sameness and change. It addresses the fundamental question of what it means for a thing to change while remaining the same thing. The next topic in Sect. 5.3 is the part-of relationship between things, and the corresponding notions of composition and decomposition. The section ends with a discussion of the duality that may exist among concepts. It is exemplified by discussing the common business concepts purchase and sale.

Section 5.4 points at two habits in the practice of applying ICT to organisations that appear to violate the outcomes of the FI theory. One regards the layout of forms, both paper forms end electronic forms. The other concerns the value types that are broadly used in programming languages and in conceptual modelling languages.

5.2   Foundations

5.2.1   The Semiotic Triangle

The primary concept in the FI theory is *communication*, defined as the sharing of thoughts between (human) minds.[1] Because minds cannot communicate directly, a vehicle is needed to accomplish it, and this vehicle is called *information*. Thus, information should be understood as a means for communication. If a subject S1 wants to communicate a thought with a subject S2, S1 has to 'assign' the thought to a sign that can be perceived and interpreted by S2. This makes information a dyadic notion: it has both content and form, inseparably connected. The process of sharing a thought is discussed in Sect. 8.2.3. Here, we will only study the relationships between the thought, the sign, and the state of affairs that is represented by the thought. Almost a century ago, Ogden and Richards published a framework to support this, known as the *semiotic triangle* [2]. Figure 5.1 (left) shows a slightly adapted version of it. Figure 5.1 (right) shows an extended version, including a node labeled "matter", which refers to the physical substance in which the sign is inscribed.

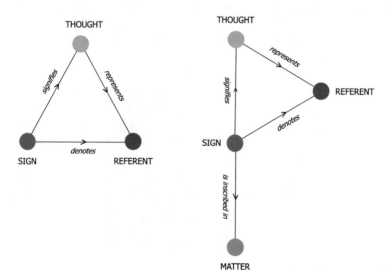

Fig. 5.1 The adapted (left) and extended (right) semiotic triangle

Thoughts are things in the mind. They *represent* concrete things (i.e. things outside the mind), called *referents*. A *sign* is a mark or a pattern of marks that has been assigned a special role, namely that it *signifies* a specific thought. Conversely, we say that the thought is expressed in the sign. For example, I could write down on a piece of paper the word "bread". This may serve as a sign for me, for example, to

---

[1]The English word "communicate" comes from the Latin word "communicare", which means 'making something common'. In a more specific sense, it means 'sharing thoughts'.

remind me that I have to buy bread. Next, the sign needs to be *inscribed* in some *matter* (physical substance) in order to be perceivable, as I do by writing down the word. An alternative way of inscribing the same sign could be a voice recording of the word "bread" or a whole sentence: "buy bread". Lastly, although the relationship between a sign and its referent is completely determined by their being connected through the thought, it is often also indicated separately: the sign is said to *denote* the referent.

5.2.2 The Semiotic Ladder

The semiotic triangle is a quite useful but also a quite simplified representation of the three core concepts in communication: sign, thought, and referent, and the relationships between them. Let us focus first on the notions of sign and thought and on the signification relationship (cf. Fig. 5.1). This is at the core of the field of semiotics and of language philosophy. The language philosophical point of view is addressed in Chap. 8. Here, we will discuss the semiotic point of view. A well-known researcher in this field is Ronald Stamper, who proposed a more sophisticated framework for studying information-related notions, known as the semiotic ladder [3, 4]. It is shown in Fig. 5.2, slightly adapted to our needs.

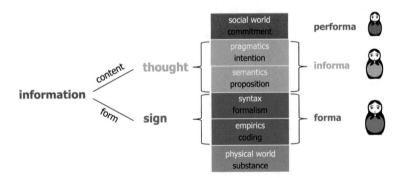

Fig. 5.2 The semiotic ladder

In the semiotic ladder, the study of the content of information (the thought) is divided into semantics and pragmatics. *Semantics* is about the 'literal' meaning of a sign or sentence, thus the thought that it signifies, according to the vocabulary of the language that is used. Let us assume, as an example, that a subject S1 conveys somehow, for example, through face-to-face speaking, the sentence "The cat sits on the mat" to subject S2. The state of affairs that this sentence refers to is obviously that a particular cat is sitting on a particular mat. *Pragmatics* then studies what S1 intends to do by sharing the thought with S2. Presumably (i.e. appearing from the syntactic structure of the sentence), S1 asserts to S2 that the represented state of affairs is the case, possibly in response to a question of S2 about where the cat could be. As another example, consider the sentence "There's a draught here", again communicated by S1 to S2. This sentence could be interpreted as an assertion of a state of affairs (there is a draught here). But it may very well be interpreted also as a way in which a lord of the castle (S1) requests (intention) his servant (S2) to shut the window (state of affairs).

The study of the *form* of information (like the above-mentioned sentence) is also divided into two subfields: syntactics and empirics. *Syntactics* is concerned with the structure of the sentence. This structure must follow particular rules, known as the grammar of the applied language. *Empirics* concerns the way of expressing the components of the sentence, for example, that they are coded in words that are constructed using Roman letters (instead of the Cyrillic alphabet or Morse code, for example).

Both the social world and the physical world do, strictly speaking, not belong to the field of semiotics. The *physical world* is needed because patterns and codes have to be inscribed somehow as traces in substances. For example, I can write down the sentence "The cat sits on the mat" on a white board or I can utter it by speaking. The top rung of the ladder, the *social world*, is the most interesting one in EE, notably in the PSI theory (see Chap. 8). There, the effects of communication on people in their quality of social individuals are studied, in particular how intentions are related to commitments between people.

5.2.3 Things and Objects

In his book '*The Furniture of the World*' [5], Mario Bunge addresses the basic topic in ontology: what is a world and what does it consist of? Bunge defines a world as a collection of things, 'untouched' yet by mental abstractions. Although the term "world" can be taken in a general sense, in EE it has the particular meaning of the world of a system, as discussed in Chap. 9. Think of the production world of an organisation, for example, as discussed in Chap. 8.

The basic assumption in *world ontology* is that a world consists of distinguishable concrete things or things for short. A *thing* is said to have features. Only through these features can the thing be perceived; a thing without features is no thing. As an example, one may perceive a cloud in the sky. The cloud is a thing, of which the main features are the perceivable water drops or crystals. At some point in time, the cloud may evaporate. Because then there are no perceivable features anymore, we say that the cloud is gone. One rarely would say that the cloud is still there, only invisible. In many cases, however, it makes sense to conceive of a persisting identity of a thing, even if the thing has no (more) perceivable features. This helps to address the problem of sameness and change in an elegant way, as we will do in Sect. 5.3.2.

To exemplify the point, let's have a look at the human body. Although the features of a body do change dramatically during its lifetime, as we know, we are inclined to say that it is still the same body. The key to Bunge's solution to the problem of sameness and change, which we will adopt in Sect. 5.3.2, is that the features of a thing are assigned to a featureless core, which he names the *bare individual*. In this bare individual resides the identity of the thing. Note that this bare individual is no thing. Only when at least one feature is recognised, there is a thing. Henceforth, we will call the bare individual of a thing its *object*. Moreover, we distinguish between concrete objects and abstract objects. Concrete objects are the core of concrete things, like humans, dogs, memberships, and rentals. Abstract objects are the core of abstract things, like numbers, boolean values, and other kinds of values.

When observing and distinguishing the concrete things in a world, the mind creates conceptual objects that represent these concrete objects. We need further conceptual means, however, to 'colour' our picture of the world, to make it intelligible. The first step in this 'colouring' process is something we did already as a child. It is called *classifying:* we observe similarities and differences between things and accordingly put them into different classes. This is how people learn to distinguish between dogs and cats, between geometrical shapes, etc. Through a separate intellectual process, called induction, the mind creates types. As will be discussed in Sect. 5.2.4, types serve as templates (form patterns) that we 'put on' the things we observe, and then conclude that the things (more precisely: the objects of the things) belong to certain classes, like humans and rentals. Consequently, conceptual things are typed objects.

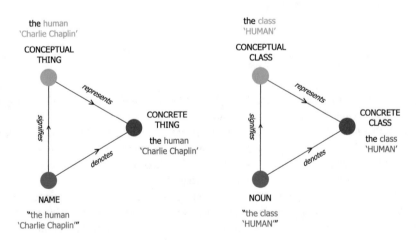

Fig. 5.3 The adapted semiotic triangle for things (left) and classes (right)

Figure 5.3 (left) illustrates the foregoing by applying the semiotic triangle to concrete things, either *tangible*, so things that one can observe, like humans and dogs, or *intangible*, that is, things that one considers to exist in a conceived world, like memberships and rentals. The example referent in Fig. 5.3 (left) is a concrete thing of the type human. The particular instance is denoted by "the human 'Charlie Chaplin'", which is shorthand for "the human with the (human) name Charlie Chaplin". The string "Charlie Chaplin" belongs to a specific name class that is used to refer to humans (but it may also belong to other name classes, of course).

To avoid confusion, we will refer to the concrete thing as <the human 'Charlie Chaplin'>, and to the corresponding conceptual thing as (the human 'Charlie Chaplin'). For concrete objects and classes, we use the bracket pair "[" and "]".

Figure 5.3 (right) shows an example of applying the semiotic triangle to classes. The name "the class 'HUMAN'" denotes the concrete class [the class 'HUMAN'], which is the set of the concrete objects of all humans. It is represented in our mind by the thought (the class 'HUMAN'). The string "HUMAN" is a name from the name class for classes.

In Fig. 5.4 (left), the semiotic triangle is applied to the notion of concrete object. The referents we consider now are thus the cores or identities of concrete things. They are represented in the mind by conceptual objects. The particular instance is denoted by "the object '701'", shorthand for "the object with the object name '701'". The numeric code "701" is arbitrarily chosen from the name class that is used to refer to objects. To avoid confusion, we will refer to the concrete object as [the object '701'], and to the corresponding conceptual object as (the object '701').

Figure 5.4 (right) shows an example of applying the semiotic triangle to abstract objects. As indicated by the question mark, abstract objects don't represent anything concrete. Through reasoning by analogy (with concrete objects and concrete things), however, we will conceive abstract objects and abstract things. Well-known abstract things are numbers. The name "the number '387'" signifies the abstract thing (the number '387'). As examples of using this number, we may have counted 387 humans or dogs or memberships or rentals.

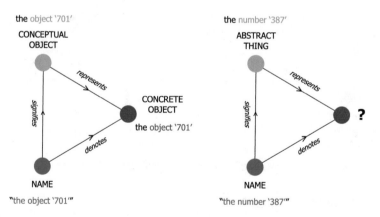

Fig. 5.4 The adapted semiotic triangle for concrete (left) and abstract (right) objects

Let us now generalise the features that things may have and through which we are able to observe and distinguish them, in the notion of fact. For example, to say that John is a human is mentioning a fact, to say that John is born in The Netherlands is mentioning a fact, and to say that John is the author of books is mentioning a fact. We distinguish between unary facts and binary facts. Unary facts are predications of single objects; binary facts are predications of pairs of single objects. As explained in Chap. 8, there is no need in EE to consider higher-order facts (cf. Chap. 6).

In Fig. 5.5 (left), the semiotic triangle is applied to unary facts. The example (conceptual) fact is that the thing with object 701 is a human. In this sentence, "object 701" is shorthand for "the object '701'" that we used before. The sentence "the thing with object 701 is a human" signifies this (conceptual) fact, and it denotes the concrete fact <the thing with object 701 is a human>. Let us assume that object 701 is the identity of the human named Charlie Chaplin (cf. Fig. 5.3, left side). The binary fact on the right side of Fig. 5.5 then expresses a property of Charlie Chaplin, namely that he is born on day 2411108. This is a day on the time scale Julian Date. In the Gregorian calendar, this day is denoted by "16 April 1889". Thus, the sentence "the birthday of Charlie Chaplin is 2411108" signifies the conceptual fact (the birthday of Charlie Chaplin is 2411108) and denotes the concrete fact <the birthday of Charlie Chaplin is 2411108>.

If the object of a unary fact is concrete, the thing is commonly called an *entity*. As an example, one commonly speaks of the entity Charlie Chaplin, thereby referring to the concrete unary fact that object 701 is a human, denoted by the name "Charlie Chaplin". Likewise, if the object of a unary fact is abstract, the thing is commonly called a *value*. As an example, day 2411108 is a value on the time scale Julian Date.

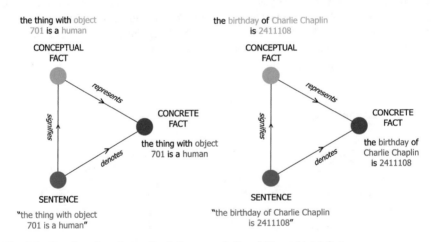

Fig. 5.5 The adapted semiotic triangle for unary (left) and binary (right) facts

5.2.4   Factual Information

After the introductory finger exercises above, we are now able to focus on the core issues of the FI theory: what are facts and how do they come into existence? In answering these questions, we will adhere strictly to the distinctions we have made between concrete and conceptual things. Concrete things are the things that we deal with in reality: the people we cooperate with, the car we drive in, the house we live in, but also the rental contract of our house, the insurance policy for our car, and the employment contract we have with our employer. As said, concrete things can be tangible (like a house) and intangible (like a rental). Conceptual things are things in the mind. They are representations of concrete things.

Let us take a closer look at how the mind operates in perceiving and conceiving the world. Figure 5.6 exhibits the so-called *semiotic mill*, in which Figs. 5.3, 5.4, and 5.5 are integrated. The result is a framework for understanding how the mind creates pictures of the world that we observe and/or study, and how we can communicate about them by exchanging signs.

The concept of type (or fact type, to be very precise) is crucial in the conceptualisation process. A *type* is defined as a template or form pattern that the mind applies when we consider concrete things (both tangible and intangible). The *form* of a concrete thing is defined as the collection of its features or (concrete) properties. More precisely, a type determines the presence or absence of properties or, as Wittgenstein puts it: a type is a family resemblance [6]. In applying a type, the mind puts, so to speak, the type's template over the things in the world, and sieves out the ones that conform. Let us take as an example the type human. Let us next assume that there is a thing whose object we signify by "object 701", and let us study the thing that is indicated as <some thing> (also represented in Fig. 5.6 by a picture of Charlie Chaplin). To illustrate that things are objects with features, the symbol for the thing in the semiotic mill is a magenta-coloured disk with protrusions, where every protrusion stands for a feature. The type human is represented by a green disk with a single protrusion.

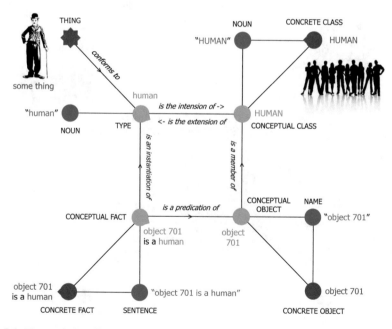

Fig. 5.6 The semiotic mill

When putting the template of the type human over the thing, we conclude that it *conforms* to the type human, because one of its protrusions fits the protrusion of the type human. In Fig. 5.6, this process is indicated by the line labelled "conforms to".

Consequently, a *conceptual fact* is created in the mind that represents the conformity: object 701 is a human. This conceptual fact is represented by a similar green
disk with one protrusion, and it is called an *instantiation* (or instance) of the type. It
represents the concrete fact that object 701 is a human. Formally, that is, in the
language of mathematics and logic, the conceptual fact that object 701 is a human is
a *predication* of the conceptual object (object 701). As we have seen above
(cf. Fig. 5.4, left side), this conceptual object refers to the concrete object [object
701]. The conceptual objects of facts of the same type constitute a *conceptual class*
of which each of the conceptual objects is a member. Let us call the conceptual class
of objects that are predicated by facts of the type human, HUMAN.[2] This class is
called the *extension* of the type human. Conversely, the type human is called the
intension of the class HUMAN. Formally: HUMAN = {x | human(x)}. Lastly, the
conceptual class (HUMAN) represents the concrete class [HUMAN].

In the ontological modelling of worlds [7], one fully abstracts from the sign part
of information (names, nouns, sentences) as well as the substance in which the sign
is inscribed (cf. Fig. 5.2), in order to focus on the thought part. This focus was also
the intention of information systems modelling [8] but it didn't turn out that way.
Therefore, we omit the corresponding parts from the semiotic mill, which leads to
the *ontological mill*, as shown in Fig. 5.7.

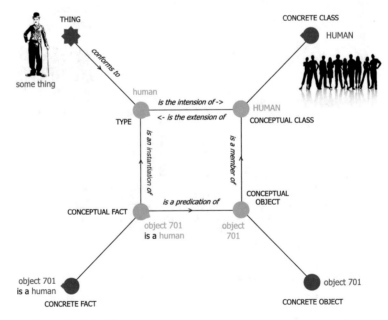

Fig. 5.7 The ontological mill

---

[2]By convention, types are signified by singular nouns in small letters, and classes by nouns in
capital letters.

In general, facts have a lifetime. They start to exist at some point of time and they end to exist at some (later) point in time. The same holds for types; they are facts at the schema level, as discussed in Chap. 6. A fact starts to exist either as soon as the form of a thing conforms to a type, or as soon as a type starts to exist to which the thing conforms. An example of the first situation is that a caterpillar turns into a butterfly. Through this event, a new entity of the type butterfly starts to exist. An example of the second situation is that one 'invents' the type pet. From that moment on, there are pets; before that moment, pets didn't exist, in a very true sense.

A fact ends to exist either as soon as the form of the thing that the fact is about, does not conform anymore to the type, or as soon as a type to which it conforms, ends to exist. An example of the first situation is again the caterpillar that turns into a butterfly. After this event has occurred, the thing does not conform anymore to the type caterpillar. Consequently, the entity of the type caterpillar ends to exist. An example of the second situation is that a university decides that the type propaedeutic student is obsolete. From that moment on, there are no more propaedeutic students.

It is important to make and maintain the distinction between the world one is referring to and one's knowledge of this world. As Mario Bunge puts it, a world is not a collection of facts, pace Wittgenstein, but a collection of things [5]. The knowledge of these things, and thus one's factual knowledge of the world, consists of conceptual facts [9]. This factual knowledge is fully constituted by the 'green square' in Fig. 5.7.

5.2.5 The Creation of Types

Following up the last part of the previous section, there are two ways to create types. The first one is called *declaring*. It means that one 'devises' a new type, independent of any existing type, for example, the type person. In conceptual modelling, this comes down to introducing a new type in the conceptual schema of a world (cf. Chap. 6). As an example, one could start to conceptualise the world of a university by declaring the (unary) types person, program, and admission, and the (binary) types 'the admitted person of [admission] is [person]' and 'the program of [admission] is [program]' (Note: the words between "[" and "]" are variables, that is, place holders for instances, cf. Chap. 12). Instances of declared types have an 'independent' existence in the considered world, as well as a 'natural' way of identification. Persons and study programs are candidates for being introduced through declaration because they have an independent existence. As is explained in Chap. 8, the entity types that occur in product kinds are proper candidates for being declared.

The second way of creating types is called *deriving*. It means that one defines a type based on one or more existing types. There are three ways of deriving types: specialisation, generalisation, and aggregation.

By *specialisation* is understood that one defines a new type as a subtype of another type (which may be declared or derived). As an example, one could define the type student in this way: "a student is a person who is the applicant in an admission". Because students are (also) persons, they can be identified in their being a person, so by their person's name. Commonly, universities also use student numbers to refer to students. Note, however, that student numbers do not identify students but admissions. Only because an admission regards exactly one person can student numbers be used to (indirectly) identify students. Note also that if a person is admitted to several programs, there are several student instances with the same object. In accordance with the ontological mill (Fig. 5.7), a student is created as soon as the form of a person (in this case the property of being admitted to a program) conforms to the type student (which requires the person to be admitted). When this is not the case anymore, the student entity ceases to exist.

By *generalisation* is understood that one defines a new type as the union of the extensions, so the classes, of two or more existing types (which may be declared or derived). To exemplify generalisation, let us depart from the types car, boat, and aircraft. We can then define the type vehicle as the intension of the class (cf. Fig. 5.7) that equals the set-theoretic union of the extensions of car, boat, and aircraft. Formally: VEHICLE = CAR ∪ BOAT ∪ AIRCRAFT. Typically one does not devise separate identifications for vehicles. Instead one would identify a vehicle by its car identification if it is a car, by its boat identification if it is a boat, etc.

By *aggregation* is understood that one defines a new type as the Cartesian product of (the extensions of) a number of other types. Thus, if the type T0 is the aggregation of the types T1, T2, ... Tn, then every instance of T0 is a tuple (a1, a2, ... an), such that a1 is an instance of T1, a2 of T2, etc. As an example, the price of a product generally depends on the product kind, the supplier, and the date. So, it may be conceived as a property of the Cartesian product of (the extensions of) these types, formally expressed as PRODUCT KIND ∗ SUPPLIER ∗ DAY.

5.2.6   The Subtype Relation

Types that are defined by means of specialisation or generalisation, are implicitly ordered by means of the subtype relation. A type T1 is said to be a *subtype* of a type T2 if the extension of T1 is a proper subset of the extension of T2. Conversely, the type T2 is called a *supertype* of the type T1. The subtype relation is transitive. So, if T1 is a subtype of T2, and T2 is a subtype of T3, then T1 is also a subtype of T3. By applying the subtype relation, trees of types are created. Well-known examples of such trees are the taxonomies in biology. Figure 5.8 exhibits a part of the taxonomy for animals. (Note that only one path through the tree is represented.) For every level, except the lowest, it holds that it has one or more (direct) subtypes. As an example,

Carnivora is a subtype of Mammalia. Similarly, for every level, except the highest, it holds that it has one (direct) supertype. As an example, Mammalia is a supertype of Carnivora.

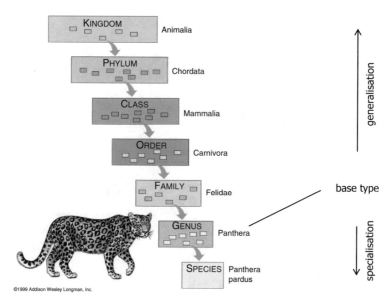

Fig. 5.8   Biological taxonomy

In building a taxonomy, only one type needs to be created by declaration. In the biological taxonomy in Fig. 5.8, the genus level would probably be the best candidate for being declared, because its individuals have a natural way of identification. As a rule of thumb: it is possible to draw a panther, but it is impossible to draw a mammal (Therefore, it is not accidental that only an instance of the type genus is drawn in the picture). Consequently, the other types in the taxonomy are derived. The levels above the genus level are derived through generalisation, and the levels below this level are derived through specialisation. For example, the family Felidae is a generalisation of the genus Panthera and other genera, whereas the species *Panthera pardus* is a specialisation of the genus Panthera. The individuals in all these classes are identified by the concrete identity they have in the class genus.

Specialisation and generalisation are often said to be each other's inverse. This is not true however, as becomes immediately clear from the examples provided above. Inversion only holds between subtypes and supertypes. Thus, it is correct to say that the type person is a supertype of student, but it is not correct to say that it is a generalisation of student (and some other types). Similarly, it is correct to say that the type car is a subtype of vehicle, but not that it is a specialisation of it. Specialisation and generalisation are intellectual techniques through which derived types can be created.

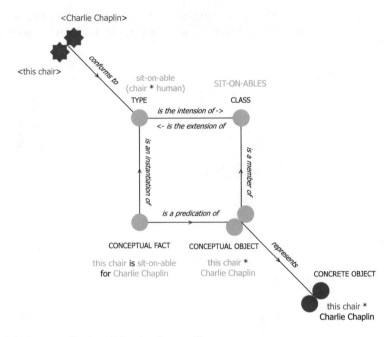

Fig. 5.9 Conceptualisation of functional types (1)

5.3   Elaborations

5.3.1   Functional Types

Corresponding with the distinction between the function perspective and the construction perspective on things, as discussed in Chap. 7, one can distinguish between functional and constructional facts and types. The type human, as discussed, is typically a constructional type: it is based exclusively on the properties of things. In contrast, the type chair is typically a functional type. It concerns the sit-on-ability affordance that a thing may offer. Figure 5.9 shows the conceptualisation of things of the type sit-on-able. It shows the sit-on-ability relationship between the thing <Charlie Chaplin> and the thing <this chair>, in the TAO theory (cf. Chap. 7) referred to as subject and object respectively. The combination of the two conforms to the form pattern of the type sit-on-able for humans, resulting in the creation of the fact that this chair is sit-on-able for Charlie Chaplin. It is important to recognise that this is a predication of the conceptual object that consists of the combination of (the conceptual object of) Charlie Chaplin and (the conceptual object of) the chair. In other words, the fact is an instance of the aggregate type PERSON * CHAIR.

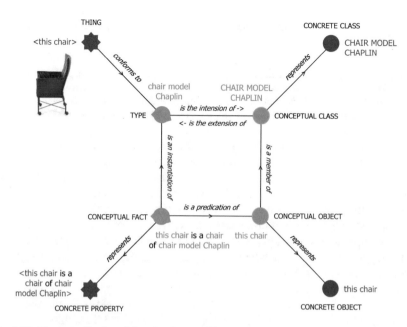

Fig. 5.10 Conceptualisation of functional types (2)

As said, the type chair is typically a functional type. There are many constructions that are able to offer the function (or affordance) sit-on-ability. Consequently,
it is not possible to define the type chair from the construction perspective. The
way out of this problem is to devise subtypes of chair that are sufficiently specific
for being conceived constructionally. Figure 5.10 shows the conceptualisation
process of an instance of a specific chair model, which happens to be named
Chaplin. The type 'chair model Chaplin' can be specified precisely enough from
the construction perspective, in order to decide whether a thing conforms to the
type or not. In Fig. 5.10, the two obtrusions on the green disk represent the type
chair model Chaplin (top) and its instantiation (bottom). Chairs of the model
Chaplin offer the function or affordance sit-on-ability to humans. Note, however,
that this sit-on-ability doesn't play a role in the conceptualisation process in
Fig. 5.10.

5.3.2   Sameness and Change

In Sect. 5.2.3, we have touched already on the problem of sameness and change.
Its general questions are: when does a thing change and if a thing changes, is it
still the same thing (only changed)? In order to illustrate the problem, let us have

a look at the paradox of Theseus, as formulated by the Greek philosopher Plutarch[3]:

> The ship wherein Theseus and the youth of Athens returned from a long journey was preserved by the Athenians by taking away the old planks as they decayed, putting in new and stronger timber in their place. In the end, all parts of Theseus' ship are replaced. The philosophical question, as formulated by Plutarch, is this one: is the ship the same ship or not?

The key to an appropriate solution of the problem of sameness and change, exemplified by the paradox of Theseus, is to recognise that every thing has a concrete object, where its concrete identity resides, next to having properties. So, even if all the parts of the ship are replaced by other (similar) ones, it is still the same ship. This argument is supported by the distinction between matter-constant (the ship is composed of the same part instances) and form-constant (the ship is an instance of the type ship), as proposed by Simons [10]. When the first plank is replaced, the ship is already not the same matter-constant ship anymore. The form-constant argument preserves that it is still a ship of the same type because the whole thing keeps conforming to the type ship (even when all parts are replaced). However, our argument goes further: Theseus' ship does indeed still conform to the type ship, but, in addition, it has kept its identity. This would even hold if the thing would not conform to the type ship anymore, as a butterfly has kept its identity after having transformed to being a butterfly from being a caterpillar before.

The philosopher Thomas Hobbes added the next extension to the paradox[4]:

> Assume that all parts are replaced and that the 'old' ship is rebuilt by assembling the 'old' parts. Then which ship is Theseus' ship?

This is a tougher question. We are now confronted with two concrete ships, each of them having its own concrete identity. Most likely, Theseus would consider the current one his ship, not the one that has been re-assembled from the thrown away parts. But he could very well (also) call the other one his ship. Which of the ships is his legal property, is dependent on the prevailing law. But that is not an ontological issue.

Many researchers in ontology, like Guarino [11] and Guizzardi [12], try to solve the problem of sameness and change by assigning the identity of a composite thing to one of its components. Regarding the human body, they consider the human brains as the component that bears the body's identity: as soon as the brains are replaced, it is not the same body anymore. With respect to cars, they choose a particular part (mostly the body of the car or the motor block) to bear the car's identity. Although one can very well live with such choices as practical solutions, they are not satisfactory from an ontological point of view.

---

[3]https://en.wikipedia.org/wiki/Theseus

[4]https://en.wikipedia.org/wiki/Ship_of_Theseus#cite_ref-hobbes_7-0

5.3.3 Composition and Decomposition

A binary fact type that one can find in many conceptual schemas (cf. Chap. 6) is the part-of relation. Some modelling approaches even have a separate symbol for it. The part-of relation is transitive, which means that if P1 is a part of P2, and P2 is a part of P3, then P1 is also a part of P3. In this way tree-like structure of parts are built. In such a tree, a part P0 is called the *composition* of the parts P1, P2, ... , Pn if P1, P2, ... , Pn are a part of P0. On their turn, each of the parts P1, P2, ... , Pn may be a composition itself. Conversely, the P1, P2, ... , Pn are called the *decomposition* of P0. So, the complete decomposition of P0 consists of P1, P2, ... , Pn, as well as of the parts of which they are composed, etc., down to the lowest level. Mereology [10] teaches us that there are several kinds of part-of relations, between which one should carefully distinguish. We will not elaborate them, however.

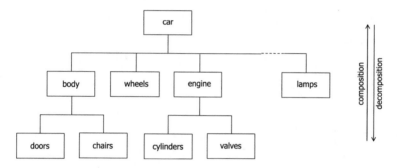

Fig. 5.11 The (partial) composition tree of a car

A well-known example of a composition tree is the Bill of Materials (BoM) in manufacturing. It is a tree structure of (elementary) parts and (sub) assemblies. The top level assembly is the end product. Figure 5.11 exhibits a part of the BoM of a car. Going up the tree is called composition and going down the tree is called decomposition. Note that the composition in Fig. 5.11 holds for some kind of car, so not necessarily for all cars. It seems to apply to all cars with a combustion engine, but it certainly does not apply to electric cars. The important point to recognise is that a composite thing has its own identity, independent of the identities of its components.

5.3.4 Dual Notions

Many pairs of notions appear to be dual, which means that they mirror each other. Well-known pairs of such notions are addition and subtraction (in mathematics), multiplication and division (in mathematics), conjunction and disjunction (in logic), and input and output (in systems theory). In EE, there are also such dual notions. Examples are debtor and creditor, and purchase and sale. To understand how dual notions are precisely related to each other, we use Fig. 5.12.

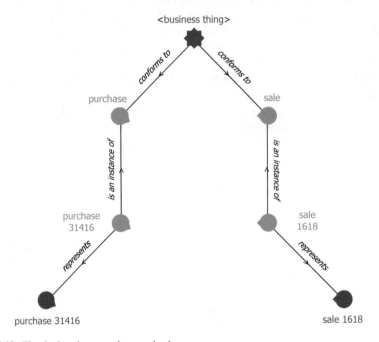

Fig. 5.12 The dual notions purchase and sale

It is a combination of a part of Fig. 5.7 and the mirror image of this part. The exhibited picture applies to the business relationship of two enterprises, one in the role of buyer and the other in the role of seller. The same 'business thing' (upper part) appears to conform to two types, namely to the type purchase (left side), and to the type sale (right side), respectively applied by the buyer and the seller enterprise. Consequently, the conceptual object (purchase 31424) exists and the concrete object [purchase 31424] to which is refers. Similarly, the conceptual object (sale 1618) exists and the concrete object [sale 1618] to which is refers. Because the notions of purchase and sale apply to the same business thing, they are called *dual notions*.

One should not confuse the notion of duality with the notion of synonymy. Duality is a purely conceptual notion, whereas synonymy is a linguistic notion. Two names are called synonymous if they signify the same thought (or denote the same referent, cf. Fig. 5.1). Common synonyms in the English language are "car" and "automobile", as well as "ship" and "vessel". Clearly, "sale" and "purchase" are no synonyms; they are not alternative names of something. Instead they refer to different things, with different properties. A possible synonym of "sale" is "selling", and a possible synonym of "purchase" is "acquisition".

5.4   Discussions

In the current practice of information systems and software engineering, there exist several persistent peculiarities that the FI theory is able to clarify elegantly. Whereas these peculiarities go often unnoticed, they sometimes cause confusion among practitioners (information analysts, programmers, information system designers, etc.) and even among researchers. Two of them are discussed subsequently.

5.4.1   The Layout of Forms

The first peculiarity concerns the layout of forms (either paper or electronic). The following is an example of a form for illustration:

Name:	*Charlie Chaplin*
Date of birth:	*16-04-1889*
Address:	*Mekelweg 4*
Postal code:	*2628CD*
City:	*Delft*
Phone Nr.:	*0031152787822*

The general understanding of such a form is that the left column shows the names of property types, and the right one shows the names of instances of these types. Only the first line of the form is different; it serves to identify a particular entity where the properties are about. Therefore, something like "Person name" would have been a better signifier than just "Name". The other lines represent properties. For example, "City" is the name of a property type, and the corresponding property instance is signified by "Delft". A more appropriate name of this property would be "residence of person".

Now, the peculiarity of the form is that the strings in the left column are sometimes names of property types, but sometimes they are names of name types. To explain this, "Address" and "City" are property type names, but "Date of birth", "Postal code", and "Phone Nr." are not. Instead they are names of name types, which means that the strings in the right column are just instances of the name type; they do not signify a thought of the type in the left column (cf. Fig. 5.1). For example, "2628CD" is not the name of a postal code, but a postal code itself. This inconsistency in forms can easily be solved by mentioning in the first column either only property type names or only name type names. In the first case, "Date of birth" should be replaced by "Day of birth", "Postal code" by "Postal area", and "Phone Nr." by "Telephone subscription". In the second case, "Address" should be replaced by "Street name and house number", and "City" by "City name". In our view, the first alternative is preferable.

5.4.2   Value Types in Programming and Modelling Languages

There is a related blurring of the distinction between sign and thought to the one discussed above, which pervades almost all programming languages, as well as almost all software and information modelling languages.

BankAccount
owner : String balance : Dollars = 0
deposit (amount : Dollars) withdrawal (amount : Dollars)

Fig. 5.13 Example of a class diagram in UML

Most programming languages offer only these four basic value types: real, integer, boolean, and string. The first three are true value types; the fourth one is only a way of constructing alphanumeric character strings (that may, e.g., serve as names). Real numbers, integers, and boolean values have a conceptual meaning; they belong to the realm of thoughts. Strings, however, are only syntactic constructs; they belong to the realm of signs. To illustrate this, Fig. 5.13 shows an example of the Class Diagram of UML (Universal Modelling Language).[5] As one can see, it allows for the value type "dollar" but not for the value type (better: entity type) "person". Instead, persons appear to be strings. This may not be the intention of the modeller, but it is what the diagram says. Unfortunately, also information modelling languages suffer from this carelessness, whereas there is no excuse (programmers might say in defence that the programming language they have to use does not allow them to model things properly).

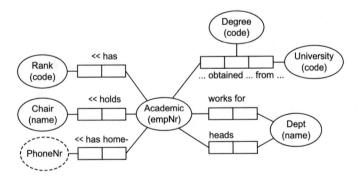

Fig. 5.14 Example of an ORM diagram

---

[5]https://en.wikipedia.org/wiki/Class_diagram

To illustrate the point, Fig. 5.14 shows a small information model in ORM (Object Role Model) [13], one of the better current information modelling approaches. The problem is with the syntactic type "PhoneNr". As is clear by now from the discussion of the form example in the previous section, this should have been the entity type "Telephone subscription" or the like, with the name class "PhoneNr" between brackets, like it is done for the other entity types. Name types or name classes should not occur in conceptual models because the represented world does not consist of names or strings or codes. These things only serve to signify the 'real' concepts.

A striking example of where such carelessness can lead to is the so-called Y2K problem (the year 2000 problem). Fixing this problem has cost worldwide a huge amount of money. This amount has been charged by ICT companies to their clients to save them from serious consequences. The odd thing is that the problem was caused by these ICT professionals in the first place. Yet, they presented the problem as something they couldn't help. It was allegedly caused by the need to save space when storing dates. By omitting the first digits "19", one would only need six ASCII characters[6] to store a date (in the Gregorian calendar). This is not correct, however. The real cause of the Y2K problem is that these ICT professionals failed to make a clear distinction between sign and thought (cf. Fig. 5.1). The 48 bits that were used to store the 'stripped' dates (i.e. calendar names) should properly have been used to store an integer value, representing a day on the time scale. Only a few computer manufacturers did and do this and thereby act(ed) truly professional (and caused no Y2K problem). Among them are Apple, Burroughs (nowadays merged in Unisys), and DEC.

References

1. Dietz, J. L. G., & Hoogervorst, J. A. P. (2013). The discipline of enterprise engineering. *International Journal of Organisational Design and Engineering, 3*, 28.
2. Ogden, C. K., et al. (1923). *The meaning of meaning: A study of the influence of language upon thought and of the science of symbolism*. International library of psychology, philosophy, and scientific method. , London: K. Paul, Trench, Trubner/Harcourt, Brace, xxxi, 1, 544p.
3. Stamper, R. K. (1973). *Information in business and administrative systems*. London: Batsford. 6, 362 p.
4. Liebenau, J., & Backhouse, J. (1990). *Understanding information: An introduction*. London: Macmillan. ix, 125 p.
5. Bunge, M. (1977). *Treatise on basic philosophy ontology I: The furniture of the world* (Treatise on basic philosophy) (Vol. 3). Dordrecht: Springer. p. 1 (370 pages).
6. Wittgenstein, L. (1958). *Philosophical investigations* (2nd ed.). Oxford: Blackwell. 246 p., 23 cm.
7. Dietz, J. L. G. (2005). A world ontology specification language. In: *OTM*. Springer LNCS.
8. Falkenberg, E. D., et al. (1998). *A framework for information systems concepts*. Technical report. IFIP.

---

[6]https://en.wikipedia.org/wiki/ASCII

9. Wittgenstein, L., & Ogden, C. K. (1999). *Tractatus logico-philosophicus*. Mineola, NY: Dover. 125 p.
10. Simons, P. (1987). *Parts—A study in ontology*. New York: Oxford University Press.
11. Guarino, N., Oberle, D., & Staab, S. (2009). What is an ontology? In S. Staab & R. Studer (Eds.), *Handbook on ontologies* (pp. 1–17). Berlin: Springer.
12. Guizzardi, G. (2005). *Ontological foundations for structural conceptual models*. The Netherlands: University of Twente.
13. Halpin, T. A., & Morgan, T. (2008). *Information modeling and relational databases* (Morgan Kaufmann series in data management systems) (2nd ed.). Burlington, MA: Elsevier/Morgan Kaufman. xxvi, 943 p.

Chapter 6
The MU Theory: Understanding Models and Modelling

Abstract The MU theory or EE model theory is a theory of models and modelling in general, and of conceptual modelling in particular. The foundations part starts with this definition of model: any subject using a system A to obtain knowledge of a system B is using A as a model of B. It conveys clearly the basic understanding of the concept of model as a role notion. Next, the model triangle is introduced, based on the semiotic triangle from the FI theory. It clarifies how complexes (systems and aggregates) of three major sorts (concrete, conceptual, and symbolic) can be used as models of each other. By adding two levels of abstraction (namely the schema level and the meta level), the General Conceptual Modelling Framework emerges. It clarifies the notions of conceptual complex, conceptual schema, and meta schema for any Universe of Discourse or system's world. It is also made clear that these notions are logical constructs, and that consequently any expression of them (in a suitable language) is directly transformable to first-order logic. The elaborations part comprises the presentation and discussion of the General Ontology Specification Language (GOSL). GOSL is a universal language for specifying conceptual complexes, conceptual schemas, and meta schemas. The syntax of the language consists of graphical as well as textual symbols and constructs. The latter constitute an English-like formal language. The split between the two is a pragmatic one. Compared to common graphical languages for conceptual modelling, GOSL might be called minimal: it covers only the basic concepts and constructs. More complicated logical formulas can often be better expressed in textual constructs. The discussions part starts with a comparison of the GCMF with two other frameworks. Next, the influence of O-O thinking on conceptual modelling is discussed. It appears that O-O thinking causes the blurring of two crucial things in conceptual modelling: the type–instance relationship and the subtype–supertype relationship.

6.1 Introduction

In this chapter, the M-theory is discussed. The Greek capital letter is pronounced as MU, which is an acronym for Model Universe. The MU theory is about models, about modelling in general, and about conceptual modelling in particular. We all

© Springer Nature Switzerland AG 2020

J. L. G. Dietz, J. B. F. Mulder, *Enterprise Ontology*, The Enterprise Engineering Series, https://doi.org/10.1007/978-3-030-38854-6_6

make and use conceptual models, in our professional and in our private lives. We have functional models in our minds of all the things we use (cf. Chap. 7). Without these models, we couldn't use the things.

The foundations part (Sect. 6.2) starts with a fundamental discussion of the notion of model, concluding that something is not a model per se, but that it may be used as a model. A well-known example is to use the geometric sphere as a model of celestial bodies.

In Sect. 6.2.2, the model triangle is introduced. Based on the semiotic triangle from the FI theory (see Chap. 5), it provides a useful framework to understand and discuss all kinds of models. In the model triangle, three classes of complexes are distinguished: concrete, conceptual, and symbolic complexes. Every distinct kind of model is a mapping from one class to another. As an example, a mapping from the class of concrete complexes to the class of conceptual complexes is called conceptualisation. Consequently, the conceptual complex is called a conceptual model of the concrete complex. To exemplify this mapping: the conceptual complex 'sphere' can be used as a conceptual model of the concrete complex 'planet Mars'. Conceptual models will be the focus of interest in the remainder of the chapter and of the entire book.

In Sect. 6.2.3, the General Conceptual Modelling Framework (GCMF) is introduced and discussed. It shows that there are three levels in conceptual modelling, and how they are related to each other. The levels are: instance, schema, and meta schema. In the current practice of conceptual modelling, they are often also called: model, meta model, and meta meta model.

The elaborations part (Sect. 6.3) comprises the presentation and explanation of a language for expressing ontological models of worlds (cf. Chap. 9), called the General Ontology Specification Language (GOSL). It is a language for specifying schemas and meta schemas, fully based on first-order logic. The syntax of GOSL comprises both graphical and textual symbols and constructs.

In the discussions part (Sect. 6.4), two modelling issues are discussed. One is a comparison of the GCMF with some existing and well-known frameworks: the FRISCO framework, and the unified foundational ontology (UFO) framework. The other issue is the harm that object-oriented (O-O) thinking does to proper (general) conceptual modelling. It turns out that O-O thinking easily leads to flaws in conceptual models. More specifically, it blurs the distinction between the type–instance relationship and the subtype–supertype relationship.

6.2   Foundations

6.2.1   The Notion of Model

As it holds for the notion of system (see Chap. 9), a precise notion of model is crucial for the advancement of enterprise engineering (EE). In current practice as well as research, the term "model" is used in so many diverse and incompatible ways, that a thorough study of the notion is imperative. The only common denominator in the plethora of model notions seems to be that a model is a simplified representation of a thing, made for the purpose of studying those aspects of the thing that one is interested in. This is certainly an important and a necessary property of models, but it is not sufficient for a crisp and clear general understanding of the notion of model.

According to the Belgian philosopher Leo Apostel [1], the notion of model should be understood as a role notion. In other words, something is not a model per se, that is, by itself, but it may be used as a model of some other thing. We adopt his notion. It also happens to be in full accordance with the notion of affordance (and function) in the TAO theory (see Chap. 7). Apostel's original definition reads as follows:

Any subject using a system A that is neither directly nor indirectly interacting with a system B, to obtain information about the system B, is using A as a model of B.

There may be many different reasons for studying system A instead of system B. Studying B directly may be physically (almost) impossible, for example, because B is too far away, like B being the planet Mars. Or it can be too dangerous to study B directly, for example, if B is a nuclear power station. In addition, system A may be simpler than B, because it needs only to have the features that one is interested in.

Apparently, the notion of system in this definition must be taken broader than our notion of system as defined by the DELTA theory (see Chap. 9). It should be able to include aggregates, like, for example, Mendeleev's periodic table of elements. Therefore, we will replace the term "system" in Apostel's definition by "complex", to make the notion of model really general. A complex is either a system or an aggregate.

6.2.2 The Model Triangle

Based on the semiotic triangle in Chap. 5, three major sorts of complexes can be distinguished: concrete, conceptual, and symbolic. A *concrete* complex is either a concrete system or a concrete aggregate. It may be material or tangible (e.g. a car), but it may also be immaterial or intangible (e.g. a contract). *Conceptual* complexes are aggregates of thoughts, more specifically of facts (cf. Chap. 5). *Symbolic* complexes are aggregates of symbols and/or sentences in some language. Together with their mutual relationships, the three sorts of complexes constitute the *model triangle* [2]. It is shown in Fig. 6.1, slightly adapted to our needs. The major difference of the exhibited model with the one in [2] is that we have left out the relationships between a symbolic complex and a concrete complex, for the reason that these relationships actually always go via the corresponding conceptual complex.

Using a conceptual complex as a model of a concrete complex is called "conceptualisation". For example, the geometric sphere (conceptual complex) is taken as a *conceptualisation* of planets (concrete complexes). The reverse relationship is called "concretisation". For example, a football (concrete complex) is a *concretisation* of the geometric sphere (conceptual complex).

In order to communicate conceptual complexes, they must be expressed in symbolic complexes. Using a symbolic complex as a model of a conceptual complex is called "expression". For example, a Class Diagram in UML [3] (symbolic complex) is an *expression* of a Class Model in UML[1] (conceptual complex). The reverse relationship is called "interpretation". So, a Class Model is an *interpretation* of a Class Diagram. In order to be perceivable, symbolic complexes have to be *inscribed* in a subclass of concrete complexes, called physical complexes (cf. Fig. 5.1). These physical complexes, and their relationships with other parts of the model triangle, are left out from Fig. 6.1 for the sake of simplicity, as we did in Chap. 5.

Fig. 6.1 The adapted model triangle

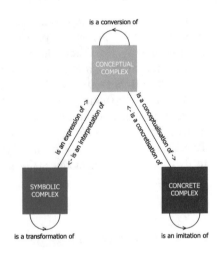

Alongside the relationships discussed above, there is a mutual relationship the three kinds of complexes have over each other. Regarding concrete complexes, this relationship is called "imitation". For example, a scale model (concrete complex) of an aircraft that is made for aerodynamic tests in wind tunnels is an *imitation* of a real aircraft (concrete complex). Regarding conceptual complexes, the relationship is called "conversion". For example, the algebraic notion of sphere (conceptual complex) can be considered as a *conversion* of the geometric notion of sphere (conceptual complex), and vice versa. For symbolic complexes, the relationship is called "transformation". As an example, a text in Morse code (symbolic complex) may be a *transformation* of a text in Roman letters (symbolic complex).

---

[1]Currently, the UML (2.0) does not include the notion of Class Model. It would be a good idea, however, to make a clear distinction in UML between models and diagrams (and to define their semantics precisely).

The focus in EE is on conceptual complexes as models of concrete systems, and on the symbolic expressions of these conceptual aggregates, notably by means of graphical and textual formalisms.

6.2.3   The General Conceptual Modelling Framework

As explained in Chap. 5, the prerequisite for the creation of a corresponding thought in the mind is that the observed form of a thing (i.e. the collection of its properties) conforms to the prescription of form of a type. This holds also for the creation of conceptual complexes. Instead of type, we now speak of *conceptual schema*. So, a conceptual complex will be created in the mind if, and as soon as, an observed concrete complex conforms to a conceptual schema. The created conceptual complex is called an *instantiation* of the conceptual schema. In other words, a conceptual schema works as a mental lens through which one perceives concrete complexes, and subsequently creates conceptual complexes. Consequently, we say that a concrete complex is conceptualised (i.e. a corresponding conceptual complex is created) *through* a conceptual schema. Similarly, the conceptual schema determines what 'can be seen' in the world.

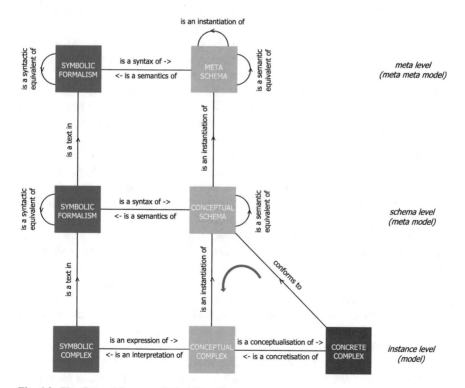

Fig. 6.2 The General Conceptual Modelling Framework

Figure 6.2 exhibits this conceptualisation process, indicated by the red curved arrow. In more general terms, and with reference to the quote by Einstein in Sect. 4.1, a "*conceptual model*" of a concrete complex is the understanding of the complex within the applied 'theory', that is, within the applicable conceptual schema. From now on, the term "*conceptual model*" is applied as a shorthand for a conceptual complex that is used as a model of a concrete complex. One should keep in mind, however, that the notion of model is a role notion.

The lower part of the figure is directly taken from Fig. 6.1. It is the adapted original model triangle, only arranged differently. Moreover, the relationships over each of the complexes are omitted, for the sake of simplicity. The middle and upper parts are new. Conceptual complexes are expressed in a symbolic formalism that corresponds with the conceptual schema through which it is conceptualised, yielding the symbolic complexes that are taken as their expressions. In other words, a symbolic complex is a *text* in a symbolic formalism. The combination of a conceptual schema and a corresponding symbolic formalism is called a (conceptual) *modelling language*. The symbolic formalism constitutes the *syntax* and the conceptual schema the *semantics* of the language. Such a language is often called *domain specific*, because the conceptual schema restricts all of its instantiations to some domain. Examples of domains are hospital care, goods logistics, or car manufacturing.

A conceptual schema can also be understood as a specification of the state space and the transition space of the world of a system, or better: of a Scope of Interest, as explained in Chap. 9. More specifically, a conceptual schema determines the entity types, property types, attribute types, and event types that play a role in the Scope of Interest. Analogously to the relationships named "conversion" and "transformation" in Fig. 6.1, there is the relationship named "semantic equivalence" over conceptual schemas, and the relationship named "syntactic equivalence" over symbolic formalisms. As an example, a DEMO Fact Model [4] and an ORM schema [5] of the same world are syntactically equivalent, because there is a one-to-one correspondence between the syntactic elements of the Object Fact Diagram in DEMO and the ORM diagram. Two models or schemas, expressed in whatever symbolic formalism, are called semantically equivalent if they convey the same meaning. Note that their syntactic appearance need not be the same, even if they are expressed in the same symbolic formalism. Like it is the case for natural languages, it is often possible to express a particular thought in different syntactic ways.

Like a conceptual complex is an instantiation of a conceptual schema, a conceptual schema can be understood as an instantiation of a *meta schema*. This is shown in the upper part of Fig. 6.2. The combination of a meta schema and a corresponding symbolic formalism is called a *general*, that is, not domain-specific, (conceptual) *modelling language*. This is the language in which one can express all (domain-specific) conceptual schemas. Consequently, these schemas are instantiations of the meta schema. Moreover, the meta schema is an instantiation of itself (the reader is invited to verify this assertion, after having read the current section). So, there are exactly three levels in conceptual modelling, which are called the *instance level*, the *schema level*, and the *meta level*. Notably in process modelling, three alternative names for these levels are quite common. They are, respectively, model, meta model, and meta meta model.

Figure 6.3 exhibits, on the left side, a stripped version of Fig. 6.2. On the right side, examples of the things on the left side are shown. At the bottom is an example of a conceptual complex. It is an instantiation of (a part of) the conceptual schema in the middle. At the top of the figure is (a part of) the meta schema (cf. Fig. 6.16), of which the conceptual schema in the middle is an instantiation. All three levels are expressed in the language GOSL, to be discussed in Sect. 6.3.

To explain the contents of Fig. 6.3, we start from the schema in the middle. It says that in the modelled world, there can exist entities of the type rental.[2] Possible examples of such entities are: rental 1089 and rental 387. They are listed at the bottom right of Fig. 6.3 as the sentences "rental 1089 **exists**" and "rental 387 **exists**". It shall not be too hard to understand the other sentences as expressions of instances of things at the schema level. Going from the schema level to the instance level is called *deduction* in logic. Deduction has proven to be a very effective help in *verifying* that one's conception of a world at the schema level is correct. A few examples of instances are often sufficient to determine the (in)correctness of a conceptual schema.

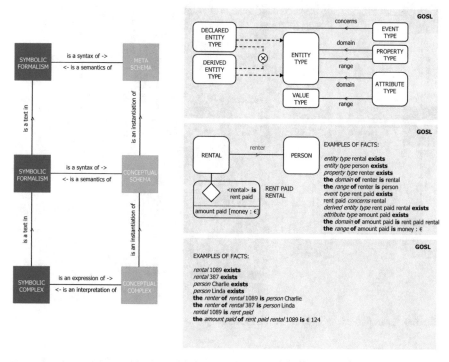

Fig. 6.3 Examples of the three conceptual levels (1)

---

[2]From now on we will us the expression <string> as a convenient shorthand for: thing with the name "<string>", like rental instead of thing with the name "rental". If the use of names that consist of several words may cause confusion, these words can be separated by an underscore, like in the string car_group.

Conversely, *induction* is going from the instance level to the schema level. In doing so, one can determine the existence of the entity types rental and person, as well as the property type renter and the event type named "rent paid" at the schema level. In the same way, one can deduce the schema level in Fig. 6.3 from the meta level, and one can induce the meta level from the schema level. In doing such an exercise, it is often helpful to first transform the graphical language in a (structured) textual language, as is done next to the diagram at the schema level in Fig. 6.3. This transformation is also known as *verbalisation*.

As a general convention, to be discussed in Sect. 6.3.2, but already applied in Fig. 6.3, one may refer to types by their name (e.g. rental), instead of having to write "*entity type* rental". Consequently, one may write for example, "**the** *domain* **of** renter **is** rental".

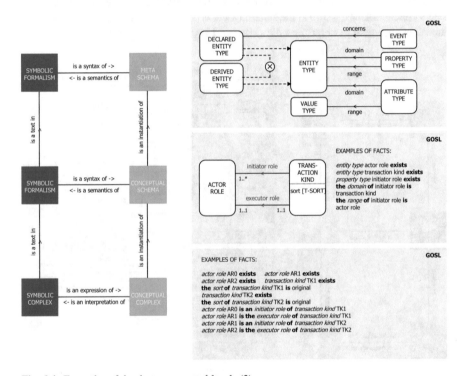

Fig. 6.4 Examples of the three conceptual levels (2)

In the middle of Fig. 6.4, another example of a conceptual schema (but deduced from the same meta schema) is exhibited, as well as an example of an instantiation at the bottom. This conceptual schema is taken from the PSI theory (see Chap. 8).

The reader is invited to go hence and forth between the schema level and the instance level, as well as between the schema level and the meta level, in the same way as we did with respect to Fig. 6.3, in order to get a grip on this aspect of modelling.

Figure 6.5 exhibits the same part of the conceptual schema (middle right) and the same part of the conceptual complex (bottom right) as the ones shown in Fig. 6.4, but now expressed in a different modelling language, namely DEMOSL (DEMO Specification Language).[3] So, the only difference between Figs. 6.4 and 6.5 is in the symbolic formalism at the schema level (and consequently in the symbolic complexes at the instance level). The symbolic formalism at the schema level in Fig. 6.5 is syntactically equivalent to the one in Fig. 6.4, which means that there is a one-to-one correspondence between the syntactic constructs in the applied languages (respectively, DEMOSL and GOSL). They also are semantically equivalent, because the two languages are designed in this way. Consequently, the expression of the example at the instance level (the symbolic complex in Fig. 6.5) is also syntactically equivalent to the corresponding symbolic complex at the instance level in Fig. 6.4. Moreover, the two complexes have the same (semantic) meaning. Note: the red colour of the diamonds expresses that the sort of the two transaction kinds is original (cf. Chap. 8).

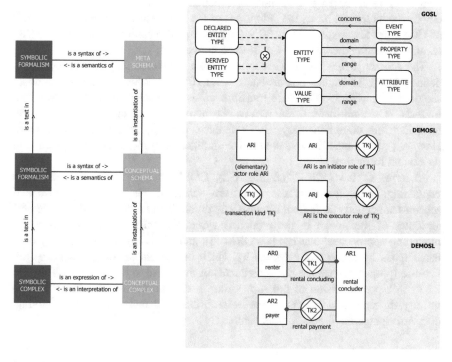

Fig. 6.5   Examples of the three conceptual levels (3)

---

[3]The document is available from www.ee-institute.org

6.3   Elaborations

6.3.1   The General Ontology Specification Language

GOSL (General Ontology Specification Language) is a first-order logic language for specifying the state space and the transition space of a world (cf. Chap. 9). It is the successor of WOSL (World Ontology Specification Language), presented in [4]. The main differences are that the terms "factum" and "statum" are replaced by "independent fact" and "dependent fact", and that only unary and binary facts are considered. Ternary and higher-order facts can be reduced to binary facts through aggregation (cf. Sect. 6.3.3). Moreover, it appears that if the PSI theory (cf. Chap. 8) is applied properly, the production world will not contain facts with an arity greater than 2.

The notion of sentence in GOSL is the same as Wittgenstein's notion in [6]: elementary sentences express elementary facts. Although such sentences could be written in the traditional Peano-Russell notation in logic, an intuitive and simple *graphical formalism* is used. The well-known Venn diagram from mathematical set theory serves to explain mathematical functions as mappings between sets. To emphasise its logical basis, the definitions of the graphical elements and constructs of GOSL are also expressed in PRN (Peano-Russell Notation), complemented by textual set theoretic expressions, if deemed convenient.

The *textual formalism* of GOSL looks like structured English. Its syntax is defined in the Extended Backus-Naur Form (EBNF), which is the international standard (ISO/IEC 14977).[4] The transformations of expressions in this formalism to PRN is straightforward. Moreover, the textual formalism and the graphical formalism are complementary. By preference, the graphical formalism is used. However, what cannot be specified in the graphical formalism must be specified in the textual formalism.

In terms of the GCMF (cf. Fig. 6.2), GOSL is a symbolic formalism for expressing conceptual schemas and meta schemas. The resulting conceptual schemas are called *ontological* because they do not include names and other lexical attributes of the things in the modelled world. Contrary to current conceptual modelling approaches, like ER [7], ORM [5], and UML [3], we deliberately omit name types in conceptual schemas by which one refers to things in the world, because (proper) names are not constituents of the world to be modelled. They are labels that people assign to things in order to communicate about them. Consequently, the name of a thing is not one of its attributes: changing the name of a thing, does not change the thing, only its name.

---

[4]http://www.cl.cam.ac.uk/~mgk25/iso-14977.pdf

6.3.2 The Textual Formalism of GOSL

In the following, the textual formalism of GOSL is presented. First we present the way in which names of types are formed, so the nouns and verbs that signify the types. The names to be specified are written in italics; comments are written between "%" and "%".

type name = {lower case letter}-, {" ", {lower case letter}}

class name = {upper case letter}-, {" ", {upper case letter}}

entity type name = type name   % commonly the type name is a noun %
                Examples: rental, car

entity class name = class name   % commonly the type name is a noun %
                Examples: RENTAL, CAR

value type name = type name, "[", {dimension, ":", unit} | {unit}, "]"
                Examples: time [Julian : day], amount [money : €], amount [€]

property type name = type name
                Examples: renter, allocated car

attribute type name = type name
                Examples: rental charge, daily rental rate

event type name = type name   % preferably the type name is a verb in the perfect
                                tense %
                Examples: concluded, rent paid

Next, we present the way in which types are declared in a conceptual schema:

entity type declaration = "*entity type*", entity type name, "**exists**"
                Example: *entity type* rental **exists**

value type declaration = "*value type*", value type name, "**exists**"
                Example: *value type* amount **exists**

property type declaration = "*property type*", property type name, "**exists**"
                Example: *property type* renter **exists**

attribute type declaration = "*attribute type*", attribute type name, "**exists**"
        Example: *attribute type* rental charge **exists**

event type declaration = "*event type*", event type name, "**exists**"
        Example: *event type* concluded **exists**

Once a type is declared, one may refer to it directly, that is, without having to mention the particular type (entity type, value type, etc.), like it is done in Figs. 6.3 and 6.4, for example, in "**the** *domain* **of** renter **is** rental".

Next, we present the way in which individual entities, values, properties, and attributes at the instance level are added to the state of a world:

entity declaration = entity type name (in italics), entity name, "**exists**"
        Examples: *person* Linda **exists**,
                 rental 387 **exists**

value declaration = value type name (in italics), value name, "**exists**"
        Examples: *transaction sort* documental **exists**,
                 car group sedan **exists**

property declaration = "**the**", property type name (in italics), "**of**", entity type name (in italics), entity name, "**is**", entity type name (in italics), entity name
        Example: **the** *renter* **of** *rental* 1089 **is** *person* Linda

attribute declaration = "**the**", attribute type name (in italics), "**of**", entity type name (in italics), entity name, "**is**", value type name (in italics), value name
        Example: **the** *starting day* **of** *rental* 1089 **is** *day* 3456789

event declaration = entity type name (in italics), entity name, "**is**", event type name;
        Examples: *rental* 1089 **is** concluded, *rental* 1089 **is** rent paid

6.3.3 The Graphical Formalism of GOSL

The graphical formalism of GOSL is based on the Venn diagram, as illustrated by Fig. 6.6. There are two sets: RENTAL (with example elements r_1, r_2 and r_3) and PERSON (with example elements p_1, p_2, p_3 and p_4). The function renter is shown as a mapping from RENTAL to PERSON, which are respectively the domain and the range of renter. The expression renter$(r_i) = p_j$ means that person p_j is the renter of rental r_i.

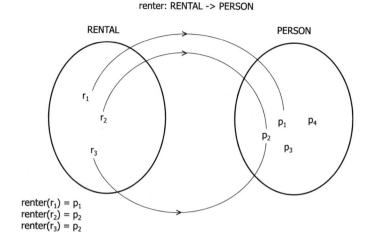

renter: RENTAL -> PERSON

renter(r_1) = p_1
renter(r_2) = p_2
renter(r_3) = p_2

Fig. 6.6 Mathematical functions as mappings between sets

Figure 6.7 exhibits the more stylised way in which functional mappings are represented in GOSL. The roundangles[5] represent entity classes, thus the extensions of entity types (cf. Chap. 5). The functions are now called properties. One best considers the lines with an arrow in the middle as bundles of separate mappings from elements in RENTAL to elements in PERSON (cf. Fig. 6.6).

The strings "0...∗" and "1...1" denote the cardinality ranges that apply. The first number is the minimum cardinality and the second one the maximum cardinality. The symbol "∗" (which can only occur as the maximum cardinality) means that the number is undetermined, that is, any number larger than or equal to the minimum cardinality is allowed. The cardinality ranges in Fig. 6.7 state that every rental has exactly one person as its renter (minimum 1 and maximum 1), and that every person is the renter of an arbitrary number of rentals (minimum 0 and maximum ∗). The ranges shown in Fig. 6.7 are the default ones. They may be omitted, as is done, for example, in Fig. 6.9.

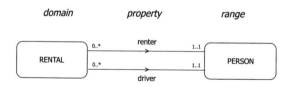

Fig. 6.7 Properties as mappings between entity classes

Hereafter, the remainder of the graphical formalism of GOSL is presented in a number of figures. Figure 6.8 shows the graphical notation of the distinct types (entity, event, value, property, and attribute) as well as the way in which they are entered into a conceptual schema, either by declaration or by derivation.

---

[5]A roundangle is a rectangle with rounded corners.

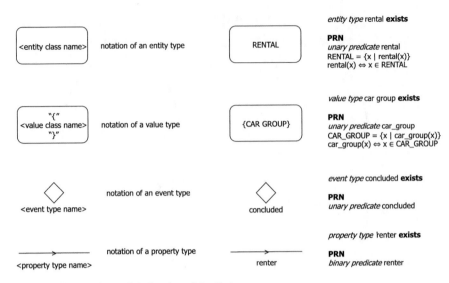

Fig. 6.8 The notation and declaration of the distinct types

In terms of logic, entity types and event types are unary predicates, whereas property types and attribute types are binary predicates. To emphasise that a roundangle denotes a class, the class name is written in capitals.

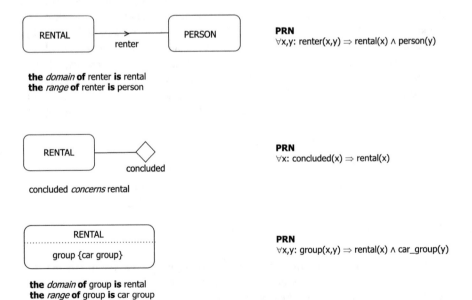

Fig. 6.9 The specification of reference laws

As mentioned in Sect. 6.2.3, a conceptual schema of a world is a specification of its state space and its transition space. The state space of a world is determined first of all by the distinct sorts of facts (entities, events, properties, and attributes) that may exist in a state of the world. In addition, it is determined by the applicable existence laws. *Existence laws* regulate the co-existence of facts. We distinguish three kinds of existence laws: reference laws, cardinality laws, and exclusion laws.

Reference laws state which facts must exist together. They are exhibited in Fig. 6.9. As an example, if the property type 'renter' exists, then its domain and its range must also exist. This is expressed in the figure by connecting the representation of the property renter with the representations of the classes RENTAL and PERSON. Like roundangles represent classes of entities (of a specific type), diamonds represent classes of events (of a specific type). An event is a unary predicate concerning an entity. As exemplified in Fig. 6.9, the unary predicate concluded holds for elements of the class RENTAL. If GOSL is used to model the production world of an organisation (cf. Chap. 8), an event is the becoming existent of the independent fact of a product, as the result of a transaction. Events are thus elementary state changes (cf. Chap. 9). As extensively discussed in Chap. 8, a number of so-called dependent facts may start to exist together with an independent fact.

Attributes are a special kind of properties. The distinction is first that the range of an attribute type is a value class, whereas the range of a (normal) property type is an entity class, and second, that both cardinality ranges are the default ones (cf. Fig. 6.7). This allows for a more compact notation of attribute types, as shown in Fig. 6.9 (bottom). The domain of the attribute group is the class RENTAL and the range is the extension of the value type car group.

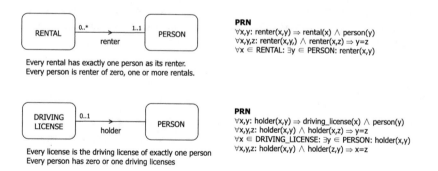

Every rental has exactly one person as its renter.
Every person is renter of zero, one or more rentals.

PRN
$\forall x,y$: renter(x,y) $\Rightarrow$ rental(x) $\wedge$ person(y)
$\forall x,y,z$: renter(x,y,) $\wedge$ renter(x,z) $\Rightarrow$ y=z
$\forall x \in$ RENTAL: $\exists y \in$ PERSON: renter(x,y)

Every license is the driving license of exactly one person
Every person has zero or one driving licenses

PRN
$\forall x,y$: holder(x,y) $\Rightarrow$ driving_license(x) $\wedge$ person(y)
$\forall x,y,z$: holder(x,y) $\wedge$ holder(x,z) $\Rightarrow$ y=z
$\forall x \in$ DRIVING_LICENSE: $\exists y \in$ PERSON: holder(x,y)
$\forall x,y,z$: holder(x,y) $\wedge$ holder(z,y) $\Rightarrow$ x=z

Fig. 6.10 The specification of cardinality laws

Cardinality laws provide a further specification of reference laws, by stating what their cardinality ranges are, as shown in Fig. 6.10. As said, the default values (so "0...*" on the side of the domain and "1...1" on the side of the range) may be omitted, and therefore usually are omitted.

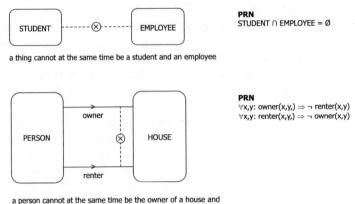

a thing cannot at the same time be a student and an employee

a person cannot at the same time be the owner of a house and
the renter of the (same) house

Fig. 6.11 The specification of exclusion laws

Exclusion laws serve to specify which facts cannot exist together, in addition to the restrictions that are already expressed in reference laws and cardinality laws. In other words, they state that the existence of a fact excludes the existence of one or more other facts. Figure 6.11 exhibits their graphical notation. We assume that the figure is self-explaining.

Like existence laws determine the set of lawful states of a world, *occurrence laws* determine which state transitions are lawful. Two kinds of occurrence laws are distinguished: precedence laws and preclusion laws. They are presented in Fig. 6.12, which we assume is self-explaining. A *precedence law* states that an event of some type, concerning a particular entity, must always precede an event of some other type, concerning the same entity. A *preclusion law* states that an event of some type, concerning a particular entity, forbids the (future) occurrence of an event of some other type, concerning the same entity.

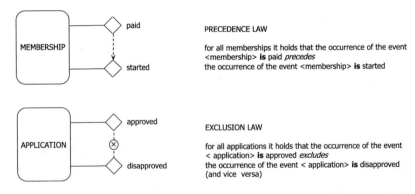

Fig. 6.12 The specification of occurrence laws

Existence laws that cannot be or not easily be specified graphically must be specified textually in GOSL. Here are some, presumably self-explaining, examples of textual specifications (words between the brackets "["and"]" denote variables):

[membership] **is** started **on** [day] **implies that** [day] **is the** first day **of some** [month] **and that** [month] **is equal to or greater than the** Current Month;

[membership] **is** started **on** [day] **implies that the** age **of the** member **of** [membership] **on** [day] **is equal to or greater than the** minimal age **in the** year **of** [day];

Alongside introducing concept types in a conceptual schema by declaration, as explained above, one can introduce types by *derivation*, meaning that one defines a new type on the basis of existing types. In Figs. 6.13 and 6.14, the graphical specification of three kinds of *derived types* are shown: specialisation, generalisation, and aggregation, in accordance with their definitions in the FI theory (cf. Chap. 5). The definition of the *specialisation* concluded_rental in Fig. 6.13 (right side) is complete. The definition of the specialisation student (left side), however, needs to be complemented by a precise rule, for example, that a student is a person for whom there is an admission in which this person is the applicant.

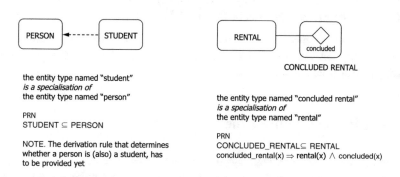

the entity type named "student"
is a specialisation of
the entity type named "person"

PRN
STUDENT ⊆ PERSON

NOTE. The derivation rule that determines
whether a person is (also) a student, has
to be provided yet

the entity type named "concluded rental"
is a specialisation of
the entity type named "rental"

PRN
CONCLUDED_RENTAL⊆ RENTAL
concluded_rental(x) ⇒ rental(x) ∧ concluded(x)

Fig. 6.13 The specification of derived types (1)

Figure 6.14 (left side) exhibits an example of *generalisation*. It defines in a precise and complete way the derived type vehicle: a vehicle is either a car or a boat or an aircraft. As discussed in Chap. 5, specialisation and generalisation are not each other's inverses. They are fundamentally different ways of constructing a type on the basis of one or more other types. The only invertible relationship between types is the subtype–supertype relationship. For example, student is a subtype of person, and thus person is a supertype of student (cf. Fig. 6.13). Likewise, boat is a subtype of vehicle and thus vehicle is a supertype of boat, etc.

On the right side of Fig. 6.14, the notion of aggregation is explained. The derived concept offer could be useful for comparing the prices of a product (on a day) in different shops. The price would then be an attribute type of the entity type offer.

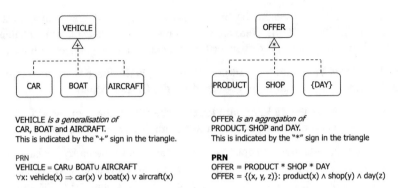

Fig. 6.14 The specification of derived types (2)

Derived types that are not, or not completely, specified graphically must be specified textually in GOSL. Here are some, presumably self-explaining, examples of textual specifications of *derived types*:

the age **of** [person] **on** Day = Day **minus the** day of birth **of** [person]
% Note that the age is expressed in Julian, cf. Fig. 6.15 %

the first fee **of** [membership] = (((12 **minus the** month **of the** starting day **of** [membership]) **plus** 1) **divided by** 12) **times the** annual fee **in the** year **of the** starting day **of** [membership]

6.3.4   Standard Value Types

As said, attribute types are mappings from an entity class to a value class, thus to the extension of a value type. Many value types appear to be quite common across conceptual schemas, and thus across worlds. Figure 6.15 shows the list of predefined *value types*, also called *scales*, which are considered to exist always and everywhere in conceptual schemas that are specified in GOSL. Additional value types must be declared separately. The first column lists the distinct value types, the second column their so-called dimension, and the third column the possible units in which values of the type can be expressed. The base types of these values are listed in the fourth column, and their (scale) sort in the fifth column.

The scale sort determines the ordering that applies to the values (the instances) of a value type. The next scale sorts are distinguished as: ordinal (O), interval (I), ratio (R), absolute (A), boolean (B), and categorial (C). An *ordinal* scale is only a ranking of values. A well-known example is the hardness scale of minerals. *Interval* scales have a (freely choosable) measuring unit, but no zero point. Examples are time scales and temperature scales. *Ratio* scales have both a (freely choosable) measuring unit and a (freely choosable) zero point. Examples are the scales for measuring mass and length. The *absolute* scale has a fixed measuring unit and a fixed zero point. It is actually just counting, like counting the number of apples in a basket. The *boolean* scale contains the truth values in logic: a proposition is true or false. *Categorial* scales are enumerations of values, without any ordering. Examples are car group (sedan, cabriolet, mini, etc.) and transaction sort (original, informational, documental).

value type	dimension	(measuring) unit	base type	sort
duration	time interval	day, hour, minute, second, ...	integer	I
time	point in time	Julian day, hour, minute, second, ...	integer	I
amount	money	dollar ($), euro (€) etc.	real	R
mass	mass	... kg, g, mg, ...	real	R
length	length	... m, cm, mm, ...	real	R
area	length²	... m², cm², mm², ...	real	R
volume	length³	... m³, cm³, mm³, ...	real	R
velocity	length/time	... m/s, ...	real	R
temperature	temperature	°C, °F, K	real	I
number	number	< just counting >	integer	A
truth value	boolean	logical value	{true, false}	B
sort	sortal	< not applicable >	{O, I, D}	C

Fig. 6.15 Predefined value types in GOSL

6.3.5   The Meta Schema

Figure 6.16 exhibits the meta schema of GOSL. We add textually the existence rule that the three ways of constructing a type (specialisation, generalisation, and aggregation) exclude each other. In a similar way, we add that the specialisations declared_type and derived_type constitute an exhaustive set, that is, every type is either declared or derived. Lastly, the class TYPE SET is defined as the set of all sets of types.

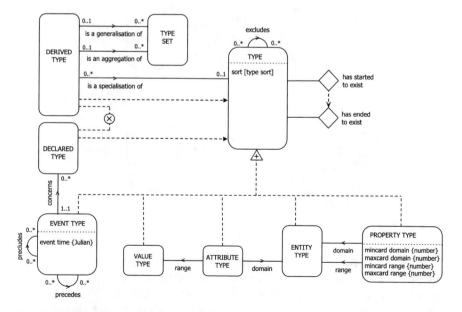

Fig. 6.16 The GOSL meta schema

6.4   Discussions

6.4.1   Comparison of the GCMF with Other Approaches

One of the first attempts to construct conceptual frameworks in the field of information systems engineering was undertaken by a task group of IFIP Working Group 8.1. It is known as the FRISCO framework [8]. Figure 6.17 shows the basic relationships between things in the mind (left side) and external representations of these things (right side). Although at the time of publication it was considered to be a milestone, most researchers would consider it now as a good but not yet mature study. Note that the is-a relationship is identical to specialisation (cf. Fig. 6.13).

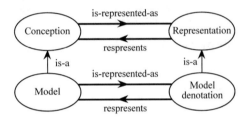

Fig. 6.17   The FRISCO framework

A more recent study is made by Guizzardi [9]. Figure 1.1 in this dissertation is reproduced as Fig. 6.18. The corresponding part of the GCMF is shown in Fig. 6.19.

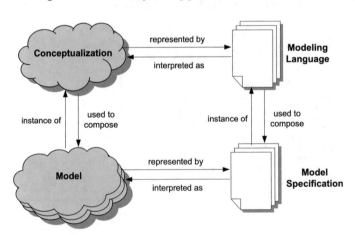

Fig. 6.18   Guizzardi's framework

The only part in Fig. 6.19 that is missing in Fig. 6.18 is the box named "concrete complex". So, the question "Of what is the bottom-left cloud in Fig. 6.18 a model?" remains unanswered. Clearly, the model is not only an instance of the top-left cloud (Conceptualization), this cloud has acted as a conceptual schema to create the model.

Next, the labelling of the relationships between the parts in Fig. 6.18 is debatable. Using twice the relationships "represented by" and "interpreted as" seems less precise than the corresponding relationships in Fig. 6.19. Our preference to use the terms "syntax" and "semantics" in labelling the relationships between the box named "symbolic formalism" and the box named "conceptual schema", is based on the fact that they may very well be considered as the syntax and semantics of a language, a point of view that is supported by the name "Modelling Language" in Fig. 6.18.

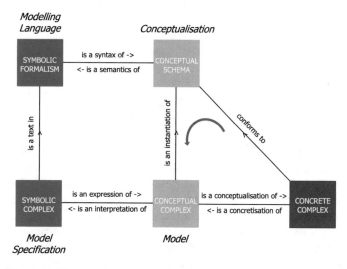

Fig. 6.19 Mapping of Guizzardi's framework into the GCMF

6.4.2   The Confusion that Is Caused by O-O Thinking

There exists a vast amount of literature on conceptual modelling that is written by authors who have adopted object-oriented thinking (abbreviated to O-O thinking) in their mental toolbox for dealing with modelling issues. O-O thinking originates from the object-oriented programming paradigm, which was proposed in the 1980s as an alternative to the prevalent procedural or imperative style of programming. A good introduction to O-O programming is written by Bertrand Meyer [10].

Regardless of the real or supposed benefits of O-O programming over other programming paradigms, its introduction has definitely brought a serious confusion with it in conceptual modelling, whether for the purpose of database design or for ontological modelling. The confusion concerns the distinction between the type–instance relationship and the subtype–supertype relationship.

Up to the introduction of O-O thinking, the distinction was crisp and clear: the particular dog 'Lassie' was an instance of the type 'dog', whereas the type 'dog' was a subtype of, for example, 'mammal', in full correspondence with what we have discussed in Sects. 6.2 and 6.3, and also in full correspondence with the findings of the FI theory (cf. Chap. 5).

Fig. 6.20 The modelling framework of the OMG

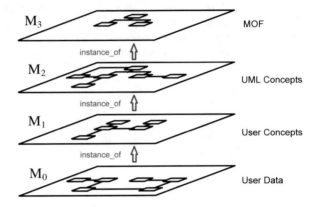

To illustrate the point we want to make, let us take a look at Fig. 6.20. It exhibits a typical presentation of the conceptual framework that is applied in many publications by the Object Management Group (OMG). It is taken from [11]. In particular, the instance_of relationship between M1 and M2 is questionable. Level M0 seems to correspond with the instance level of the GCMF, and level M3 with the meta schema level. But then both M1 and M2 must be at the schema level. Therefore, it is most likely that M1 is a specialisation of M2 instead of an instance.

In order to solve the modelling problems that O-O thinking leads to, the authors of [11] make a distinction between ontological modelling and linguistic modelling. The distinction is illustrated by Fig. 6.21, which reproduces Figs. 2 and 3 in [11].

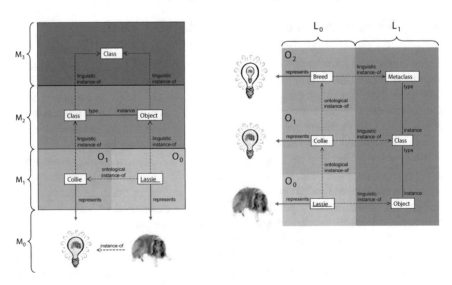

Fig. 6.21 Linguistic (left) and ontological (right) O-O modelling

In our view, however, the introduced distinction between linguistic and ontological modelling only complicates the matter. It is actually a perfect demonstration of blurring the distinction between the type–instance relationship and the subtype–supertype relationship. Conceptual modelling is by definition an act of the mind, abstracted from the linguistic terms in which one may communicate the thoughts one has created. The relationships between conceptual things and linguistic things are fully and clearly explained by the GCMF (cf. Sect. 6.2.3). So, the picture of Lassie on the left side of Fig. 6.21 might be taken as a concrete complex in Fig. 6.2, and the box labeled "Lassie" might then be taken as the conceptual complex in Fig. 6.2. This conceptual complex, however, is just an instantiation of a type (or of several types) at the next conceptual level, thus at the schema level in Fig. 6.2. The tree of types that one may want to build at the schema level will probably be something like the taxonomy of Linnaeus that is used in Chap. 5 (Fig. 5.8). To illustrate this, let us take the type dog as the base type of the taxonomy branch for dogs. Then we can construct, for example, the specialisation "collie" and the generalisation "mammal". This makes Lassie not only an instance of dog, but also of collie and of mammal. The important issue is that these types are all things at the schema level.

The same holds for the concept breed in Fig. 6.21: it is only a categorisation of the many specialisations of dog. One may, for example, distinguish alaskan husky, appenzeller sennenhund, and german shepherd, next to collie. One may subsequently add the attribute breed to the type dog (once more: at the schema level), and populate the value class (of the sort categorial) to which breed maps, with collie, alaskan husky, appenzeller sennenhund, german shepherd, etc.

Concluding, the proposals in [11], exemplified by the pictures in Fig. 6.21, do not solve the modelling problems that are caused by O-O thinking; they may even increase the confusion. As an example, an object may certainly be an instance of a class, but this puts the object necessarily on a lower conceptual level than the class. The type–instance relationship just doesn't exist at the same level of abstraction, by definition. At the schema level (M2 in Fig. 6.21) and the meta level (M3 in Fig. 6.21), there can only be trees of types, constructed through specialisation and generalisation. Likewise, one may certainly state that the entity Lassie is an instance of the type collie (Fig. 6.21, right), but not that the type collie is an instance of a meta type breed. As said, the notion of breed is a categorisation of the distinctions at a particular level of a type tree (in this case at the schema level). It is similar to the distinctions species, genus, family, etc., that Linnaeus has introduced. In his taxonomy, collie would be at the species level of the type tree and dog at the genus level. The meta class (or type) of which collie is an instance, and dog, and all other types in the taxonomy tree, is the entity type at the meta level (cf. Fig. 6.16).

References

1. Apostel, L. (1960). Towards the formal study of models in the non-formal sciences. *Synthese, 12*, 125.
2. Bertels, K., & Nauta, L. (1969). *Inleiding in het modelbegrip*. Amsterdam: Wetenschappelijke Uitgeverij.

3. Scott, K. (2001). *UML explained* (xviii, 151 p.). Boston: Addison-Wesley.
4. Dietz, J. L. G. (2006). *Enterprise ontology: Theory and methodology* (xiii, 243 p.). Berlin: Springer.
5. Halpin, T. A., & Morgan, T. (2008). *Information modeling and relational databases*. Morgan Kaufmann series in data management systems (2nd ed., xxvi, 943 p.). Burlington, MA: Elsevier/Morgan Kaufman.
6. Wittgenstein, L., & Ogden, C. K. (1999). *Tractatus logico-philosophicus* (125 p.). Mineola, NY: Dover Publications.
7. Chen, P. P. S. (1977). *The entity-relationship approach to logical data base design* (73 p.). Data base management no 6. Wellesley, MA: Q.E.D. Information Sciences.
8. Falkenberg, E. D. A. E. (1998). A framework for information systems concepts. Technical Report. IFIP.
9. Guizzardi, G. (2005). *Ontological foundations for structural conceptual models, in CTIT*. The Netherlands: University of Twente.
10. Meyer, B. (1997). *Object-oriented software construction* (2nd ed., xxvii, 1254 p.). Upper Saddle River, NJ: Prentice Hall.
11. Atkinson, C., & Kuehne, T. (2003). Model-driven development: A metamodeling foundation. *IEEE Software, 20*(5), 6.

Chapter 7
The TAO Theory: Understanding Function and Construction

Abstract The TAO theory (T-theory), or function-construction theory, is a theory about the way subjects (people) perceive the things that surround them. TAO stands for Teleology, Affordance, Ontology. The foundations part starts with an excerpt from Gibson's theory of affordances. This theory clarifies the being subjective of affordances. Next, the intended affordances, commonly called functions, of designed things (artefacts) are discussed. Although people are mostly and primarily interested in the functions (affordances) that things may offer them, engineers are also interested in the construction of things. Contrary to function, construction is an objective notion. Related to function is the notion of experience, defined as the sensation that an affordance evokes in someone's mind. Based on it, the notion of value is discussed as the intensity of experience, measurable on an ordinal scale. The elaborations part starts with a discussion of constructional models and functional models, their incommensurability, and the fundamental difference between constructional decompositions and functional ones. Next, these findings are illustrated to an example of an enterprise.

7.1 Introduction

The theory in this chapter is labeled T-theory. The Greek capital letter is pronounced TAO, which is an acronym for Teleology, Affordances and Ontology. It is a study of the notion of affordance and subsequently of the notions of function and construction. Therefore, the TAO theory is also called the EE function-construction theory. It is classified as a *philosophical* theory in the framework of theories (cf. Chap. 4), thus a theory that is about knowledge in general.

Teleology (from the Greek words 'telos', meaning purpose, and 'logos', meaning thinking, reasoning) is the branch of philosophy in which one seeks to explain the behaviour of things (animate and inanimate) by ascribing them intrinsic purposes. The branch is as old as the works of Plato and Aristotle. Although it is also considered controversial, teleology has notorious defenders, like Kant in [1] and recently Nagel in [2], where the basic assumption is that animals behave in certain ways in order to achieve survival. The notion of teleology has also been introduced

© Springer Nature Switzerland AG 2020
J. L. G. Dietz, J. B. F. Mulder, *Enterprise Ontology*, The Enterprise Engineering Series, https://doi.org/10.1007/978-3-030-38854-6_7

in cybernetics, by considering it as feedback controlled purpose and by calling feedback controlled systems, teleological mechanisms [3].

Ontology (from the Greek words 'ontos', meaning being, and 'logos', meaning thinking, reasoning) studies questions concerning the nature of things, irrespective of the intrinsic purposes they would have or the purposes for which subjects would use them. Three phenomena are investigated in ontology. The first one is what things essentially are, so what their 'true' nature is. This subfield is called core ontology. Some contemporary researchers in this field are Guarino [4] and Guizzardi [5]. The second phenomenon is how things are composed of other things. The subfield studying this phenomenon is called mereology (the Greek word 'meros' means part). An authoritative work is written by Simons [6]. The third phenomenon is what the causes are of observable changes. They are studied in the subfield called aetiology (the Greek word 'aitios' means cause). The PSI theory (Chap. 8) can be classified as an aetiological theory.

To exemplify the foregoing, a typical *teleological* statement regarding the human heart is that it pumps blood through the veins for the sake of providing all organs with oxygen and nutrition (and other useful things). Note that this statement is also an anthropomorphic metaphor, drawn from our experience in using artificial, that is, man-made, pumps. A typical *ontological* statement regarding the human heart is that its muscles alternately contract and relax and by doing so cause the blood in the veins to flow, without investigating the why question however. So, causation is definitely an important issue in ontology, but purpose is definitely a non-issue.

The remainder of the paper is organised as follows. Section 7.2 introduces the notion of affordance and the related notion of function. It also discusses the important distinction between function and construction. Section 7.3 comprises the discussion of functional and constructional decomposition, and the roles of function and construction in system design. In Sect. 7.4, several comparisons are made between the contributions of the TAO theory and current theoretical and practical approaches, both inside and outside the field of enterprise engineering. It concludes with a brief comparison of the TAO theory and the TAO philosophy.

7.2 Foundations

7.2.1 The Notion of Affordance

In order to connect the philosophical branches of teleology and ontology, as briefly discussed above, we use the theory of affordances, developed by Gibson [7], and elaborated by Chemero [8]. In this theory, an *affordance* is defined as an action possibility which is latent in the natural environment. For example, an affordance of terrestrial surfaces is that they offer support to human beings and animals: they can stand on them, walk over them, etc. Affordances can be recognised by an intelligent subject,[1] but whether they will be recognised or not, depends on the current needs or desires of the subject. So, if one doesn't have the need to sit, one may not recognise the corresponding affordance that surrounding things offer. The notion of affordance is the key notion in the TAO theory. For a thorough study of affordances, however, a few additional notions must be introduced.

The core notions on which the TAO theory is based are summarised in Fig. 7.1. There is a *subject* (shown on the left side) and there is an *object* (shown on the right side). In order to depict that the need of the subject matches the affordance that the object offers, the shapes at the top of Fig. 7.1 have protrusions. The *affordance(s)* that the object may offer to the subject correspond with the matches of the protrusions. For example, if Charlie Chaplin (the subject) feels the need to sit, he may perceive that he can sit (the affordance sit-on-ability) on a tree-stump (the object), because its height and size (the properties) offer the affordance that matches the need to sit. It is crucial to keep in mind that an affordance is a *subject–object* relationship, whereas the needs of subjects are purely *subjective*, and the properties of objects are purely *objective*. Because of the unlimited (actual or imaginary) needs of human beings, the number of affordances that an object may offer is virtually unlimited.

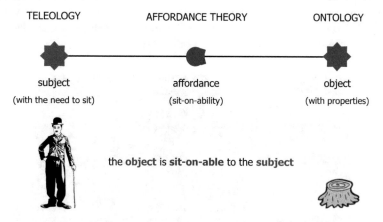

TELEOLOGY   AFFORDANCE THEORY   ONTOLOGY

subject   affordance   object
(with the need to sit)   (sit-on-ability)   (with properties)

the **object** is **sit-on-able** to the **subject**

Fig. 7.1   The notion of affordance

The sit-on-ability of tree-stumps does not only hold for Charlie Chaplin but for all subjects with the need to sit, provided they have roughly the same sizes as Charlie Chaplin. That is why people are inclined to say that tree-stumps are sit-on-able things. Note, however, that a tree-stump with a height of about 45 cm is not very sit-on-able for a 2-year-old child. Likewise, people usually say that a ladder is climbable, but this may not be the case for a physically disabled person.

---

[1]Contrary to the PSI theory, subjects in the TAO theory may also be (intelligent) animals, and even intelligent artefacts, next to human beings.

As said, understanding affordances as relationships between objects and subjects is crucial. Consequently, it is fallacious to say that the sit-on-ability of tree-stumps is a property of tree-stumps. If there wouldn't exist subjects with a need to sit, the notion of sit-on-ability would also not exist. But the properties of the objects that could offer this affordance would still be there.

7.2.2 Artefacts

So, it is the match between the needs of a subject and the properties of an object where affordances emerge from. But why then do people use nouns, like chair, table, hammer, screwdriver, and windshield, which suggest that affordances are properties of things? The answer is that people, in addition to using 'natural' things, like tree-stumps, create and make things,[2] commonly called *artefacts*. Artefacts are commonly designed and made with some affordance(s) in mind. For example, people make things that offer the affordance sit-on-ability; these things are called chairs. They also make things that offer the affordance sit-at-ability; these things are called tables. With respect to artefacts, we commonly do not speak of affordances but of *functions*. We say, for example, that is the function of a chair to sit on it, instead of saying that chairs offer the affordance sit-on-ability.

Fig. 7.2 Function and other affordances of an umbrella

---

[2]In the TAO theory, we will not make the strict distinction between the notions of object and thing as done in the FI theory. Here, the two words are considered largely synonymous.

Because artefacts may also offer unintended affordances to subjects, in addition to the intended ones (the functions), the totality of functions is a subset of the totality of affordances. Thus, like all other affordances, functions are relationships between subjects and objects, as discussed in Sect. 7.2.1 and as clarified by Fig. 7.1. To illustrate the point, Fig. 7.2 exhibits, in the lower right part, the function, that is, the intended affordance, of an umbrella, namely shielding from rain. But the picture also shows three other affordances that umbrellas may offer to people. Proceeding anti-clockwise, there is the affordance shielding from sun, hitting, and hiding things (like a gun). In spite of these other affordances, people easily recognise the thing on all four pictures as an umbrella. The word "umbrella" is a functional word, like the other words mentioned above: chair, table, hammer, screwdriver, and windshield, and like many more words. There is nothing wrong with using functional names, as long as one is aware that they do not refer to a thing as such but to its intended affordance(s). Ontologically spoken, no thing *is* a chair, but it may be used as a chair (and intended to be used in this way). Most nouns in natural languages are functional because of people's primary interest in what they can use things for, instead of what they ontologically are. Therefore, tables are also used to sit on and chairs to sit at. In general, whenever the properties of an object match a need of a subject (that seeks to satisfy this need), the corresponding affordance emerges. Moreover, it doesn't matter whether the object is an artefact or a 'natural' thing.

Fig. 7.3 Assignments of functions. © Jan L.G. Dietz, reprinted with permission

In addition to designing and making artefacts, people also *assign* (new) functions to existing things, whether they are artefacts or not. Let us use Fig. 7.3 to clarify this. The building in the middle of the picture is a church, most people would say. Why?

Because we have learned that buildings with such a shape are erected with the function of church in mind. But churches are sometimes (also) used as a place of shelter, for example, for refugees. And when too few people make use of the original function of a church, it may be assigned, for example,, the function of indoor playground. As for the paved area in front of the church, it may have been designed to be a village square. But these squares may be assigned various other functions, for example, marketplace (on Tuesday and Friday) and parking lot (on the other days, except Sunday). And twice per year it may be a fairground. In addition, the paved area may offer various unintended affordances to specific stakeholders (like roller skate ground, dancing place, meeting place, etc.).

The important conclusion from these examples, once more, is that (designed or assigned) functions and other (unintended) affordances are relationships between objects (things) and subjects (people). A building is not a church per se, but it may have been designed with this function in mind, and a paved area is not a marketplace or parking lot per se, but it may have been assigned these functions (or have been designed with these functions in mind).

7.2.3   Function and Construction

Despite the fact that artefacts may offer various affordances to people, they are mostly designed with a specific function (for a specific target group) in mind. Figure 7.4 exhibits on the left side a clock that could be a showpiece in a living room. The intended function is obvious: it is a clock, that is, it tells one what time it is. This intended function is realised by the construction behind the clock-face in the casing: the clockwork (Fig. 7.4, right side). The casing is also part of the (total) construction of the clock and it may offer additional affordances, like being a nice piece of furniture. The clockwork itself may also be considered a beautiful piece of craftsmanship.

Fig. 7.4 Function versus construction

Thus, every function of a thing is realised by its construction. Taking the *construction* perspective on a thing (a natural thing or an artefact) means that one exclusively considers the thing as an object, without paying any attention to the intended function(s) or other affordances it may offer to subjects. So, for example, we can perceive the clockwork in Fig. 7.4 just as a material thing with properties: spatial dimensions, mass, etc. without having in mind what affordances it may offer. Because the construction perspective is independent of the possible affordances of the thing, it is said to be *objective*. By this we mean that two knowledgeable persons will have or can acquire the same constructional understanding of it. As an example, if two clockwork engineers are asked to produce the Bill of Materials (BoM) of the clockwork in Fig. 7.4, by dissembling it, they will come up with the same BoM. In case they don't, at least one of them has made an error.

Taking the *function* perspective on a thing means that one exclusively considers the affordances that are offered by the thing given the purposes or needs one has in mind. For example, one could think of sitting on a chair, or of using it as a temporary store, one could create a baby's crib by putting the seating sides of two chairs together, etc. The distinctive characteristic of the function perspective is that we take the position of an observer who has purposes in mind for which the chair could be used. By way of metaphor, he/she looks at the chair through the 'lens of purposes' and in doing so 'sees' the affordances that the chair offers. Consequently, two persons, even if they are equipped with the same generic knowledge of chairs, could easily 'see' different affordances of the chair, dependent on the purposes they have in mind. Hence the function perspective is said to be *subjective*, although functions are actually subject–object relationships, as we have seen. In Sect. 7.3.1, we will elaborate what the distinction means for designing artefacts and for modelling them, both from the function and from the construction perspective.

7.2.4 Experience and Value

Although different things, like tree-stumps and chairs, may offer the same affordance to subjects, these affordances may very well be experienced differently. By *experience* is understood the subjective sensation that the recognition of an affordance evokes in the subject's mind (cf. Fig. 7.5).

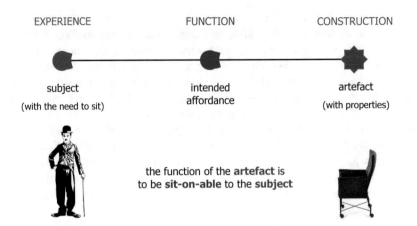

Fig. 7.5 The notion of function

For example, the sit-on-ability of the tree-stump in Fig. 7.1 may evoke a different experience in Charlie Chaplin's mind than the one offered by the chair in Fig. 7.5. On this basis, he may have a preference for one of them. Generally, subjects appear to not just look for affordances that match their needs, but to also pay attention to the experiences that they evoke.

Related to the notion of experience is the notion of value. In the light of the previous discussion, it may be clear that value is not a property of a thing. Consequently, one can, in principle, not say that a thing has a particular value, like it has a particular weight. More specifically, we will define *value* as the intensity of the experience that is evoked in a subject's mind by the recognition of an affordance. The subject could express this value as an attribute of the affordance, by which value becomes measurable, although most likely only on an ordinal scale. For example, the affordance sit-on-ability that is offered by an armchair to Charlie Chaplin could evoke in his mind a higher ranked experience than the one that is offered by a tree-stump. He could express this by assigning a higher value of the affordance sit-on-ability to the armchair than to the tree-stump. As another example, many people nowadays rank their experience of hotel stays, restaurant visits, etc. on websites. In order to make this useful for other people, the subjective rankings are 'normalised' through an ordinal scale.

In contrast to value, the *price* of a thing must be considered as a property of the thing, so as something objective, regardless whether this price is the outcome of a calculation or someone's original declaration. For example, Charlie Chaplin's decision to buy a new walking pole is most likely based on balancing the price of the pole and the value that he assigns to the affordance(s) that the pole offers to him.

7.3   Elaborations

7.3.1   Constructional and Functional (De)composition

In Sect. 5.3.3, the composition and decomposition of concrete things is discussed, based on the part-of relation between the parts of composite things, as extensively discussed in [6]. Below, Fig. 5.11 is reproduced as Fig. 7.6. It shows the composition and decomposition of a car. Taking the foregoing into account, we need to add that the (de)composition is a constructional one, that is, it regards purely the construction of a car, not its function(s). Therefore, the exhibited structure is called a *constructional component tree*, also known as a Bill of Materials (BoM). Obviously, the tree is not complete, it has to be extended. Moreover, the exhibited decomposition does certainly not hold for all cars. Presumably, it holds for all cars with a combustion engine, but it certainly does not hold for electric cars.

A constructional component tree shows how a composite thing (the top level in Fig. 7.6) can be disassembled down to its elementary parts (the bottom level, or the 'nuts and bolts'), and how it can be (re-)assembled from these elementary parts. As every engineer knows, disassembling a car (or any other artefact) is mostly not very difficult, but re-assembling it may easily turn into a nightmare. The reason of the trouble is that there is only one constructional decomposition of a car. This holds anyhow for the top level (the assembled car) and the lowest level (the distinct parts). Whether there is always exactly one structure of sub-assemblies in between the top and the bottom level for a particular brand and model of car, is disputable, but at the same time it is irrelevant for the argument.

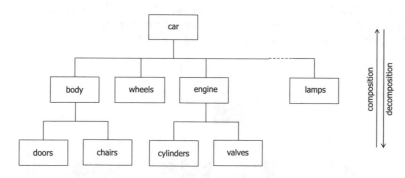

Fig. 7.6 Constructional component tree of a car

Component trees can also be applied to the functions[3] of things. Figure 7.7 exhibits (a part of) a possible functional component tree of a car. It shows a *functional decomposition* of the function driving, which most people will consider

---

[3]From now on, we will not be strict anymore about the distinction between function and (unintended) affordance. The latter may be considered as a possible function.

the most distinctive function of cars. Other functions could be: a cosy shelter and a status symbol. The exhibited functional model could be very useful for a driving instructor to explain to a new pupil how one drives a car. The driving function is decomposed into four subfunctions: powering, steering, lighting, and seating. Both the powering and the lighting function are further decomposed, just for illustration. In addition to plain black boxes, Fig. 7.7 contains grey-lined black boxes. These boxes represent the (sub) functions that can be used through operating specific constructional parts. In general, such a constructional part is called a *user interface* to the function. In all cars, the steering function is operated by turning the steering wheel, but the constructional parts through which other functions are operated may differ between car brands and models. Fortunately, car manufacturers nowadays attempt to standardise the user interfaces. Note that these user interfaces are the only mental connections between the functions and the construction of the car, and that they must be explicitly designed and implemented.

Up to now, we have intentionally avoided using the term "model" when discussing the constructional and functional component trees, for the simple reason that they do not comply with the definition of model as presented in Chap. 6, where a (conceptual) model of a thing is the understanding of the thing within some (proper) theory. As an example, discrete event systems can be understood properly within the DELTA theory (Chap. 9), more specifically within the PRISMA meta model. The part-of relation, on which the component trees are built, can hardly be called a theory. However, if component trees are integral parts of theories, there is no objection against calling structures like the ones that are exhibited in Figs. 7.6 and 7.7, models. We will go along with this habit. In addition, we will call functional component trees *black-box* models, in conformity with the DELTA theory (Chap. 9), because they completely ignore the 'internals' of a system (its statics, kinematics, and dynamics). Likewise, we will call constructional component trees *white-box* models.

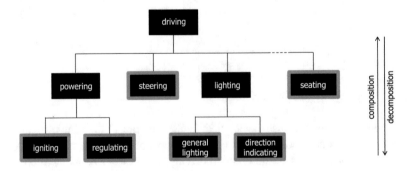

Fig. 7.7   Functional component tree of the driving function of a car

Contrary to constructional decompositions, which are objective, functional decompositions are subjective. In principle, everyone can have his/her own functional model of the driving function of cars, as well as of the function(s) of other devices, like computers and vending machines. However, although these models are basically personal, they are commonly shared among groups of people. The insight that functional models are subjective sheds a clarifying light on the endless discussions about the 'correctness' of functional models. We will elaborate this topic in Sect. 7.4.

In order to show the distinction between constructional and functional component trees in a graphical way, the parts (boxes) of the first are coloured white and the parts (boxes) of the latter are black. Contrary to constructional decompositions, functional decompositions may be 'endless', that is, one can always decompose a functional component, at will, just and only because they are not (directly) related to constructions.

7.3.2 Composition and Decomposition of Enterprises

Like it holds for other composite systems, the construction and the function(s) of enterprises[4] are generally decomposable. Let us first investigate the functional decomposition, taking the enterprise Malum, discussed in [9], as the example for illustration. The primary function of every enterprise is what is commonly called its *business*: the service(s) that the enterprise offers to the customers or clients. Malum is a manufacturer and vendor of wheelbarrows.

Figure 7.8 exhibits a possible functional decomposition of the business of Malum. For the depth of the decomposition, the same criterion is applied as we did to the driving function of cars (Fig. 7.7), namely being able to operate the 'leaf' functions. Only three functional components are considered to be 'leaves' of the enterprise's business. The other 'black' components in Fig. 7.8 have yet to be decomposed to the 'leaf' level. The 'leaf' functions: selling, paying, and transporting, can be operated by actors in the environment through some user interface. They are indicated in the figure by grey-lined black boxes. These functions can be used by initiating transactions of three corresponding kinds: one that provides the service of selling, one that provides the service of paying, and one that provides the service of transporting.

---

[4]The term "enterprise" is used to denote any instance of human cooperation, ranging from organising a birthday party to running a multinational company.

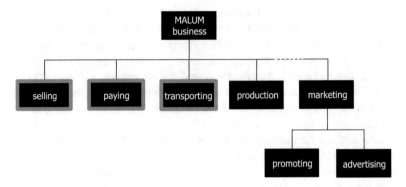

Fig. 7.8 Functional component tree of the business of Malum

We will refer to the construction of enterprises as their *organisation*. Regarding the relationship between the construction of an enterprise and its function(s), it is the organisation that realises its business, as well as all other conceivable functions, including those services that are offered to other stakeholders than the customers or clients. Figure 7.9 exhibits the constructional component tree of Malum's organisation, conceived according to the PSI theory (Chap. 8) and the OMEGA theory (Chap. 10). It realises the business functions of selling, paying, and transporting.

Table 7.1 Transactor Product Table of Malum

transaction kind	product kind	actor role
01 sale completing	[sale] is completed	sale completer
02 sale paying	[sale] is paid	sale payer
03 sale transporting	[sale] is transported	sale transporter

In order to be precise as well as to illustrate the interconnectedness of the functions selling, paying, and transporting, the corresponding transaction kinds in the Transactor Product Table (cf. Table 7.1) are called, respectively, sale completing, sale paying, and sale transporting, where a sale is an instance of selling. The latter two turn out to be constructional components of the first one. It means that, although all three business functions are offered to the environment, paying and transporting can only be used in the context of selling. The three transactor roles are user interfaces through which users can use the functions selling, paying, and transporting. Note that the users of selling are the customers of Malum, that the users of paying are actors in the sales department, and that the users of transporting are also actors in the sales department.

As follows from the PSI theory (Chap. 8), the initiators of transactions TK01 (sale completing) are the customers of Malum and the executors are actors in the sales department. The initiators of transactions TK02 (sale paying) are actors in the sales

department and the executors are the customers of Malum. The initiators of transactions TK03 (sale transporting) are actors in the sales department and the executors
are actors in the (internal) transportation department or an (external) transportation
company.

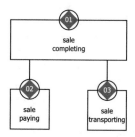

Fig. 7.9   Constructional component tree of the organisation of Malum

Only the building blocks in the O-organisation (cf. Chap. 11) of Malum are
shown in Fig. 7.9. Those in its I-organisation and D-organisation are omitted. For a
complete ontological model, the informational and documental component trees
must be added, which would make the tree substantially bigger. However, for
understanding the constructional essence of Malum, also called its essential model
(cf. Chap. 9), the component tree in Fig. 7.9 is the basis.

7.3.3   The Role of Function and Construction in System Design

Although this book is not about designing systems, studying the role of functional
and constructional models in the design of systems appears to shed a clarifying light
on them. So, let us look at the design process, as presented in [10]. There, system
design is considered to be a part of system development, a process in which two
systems play a crucial role: the object system and the using system. By the *object
system* is understood the system which is going to be developed. By the *using system*
is understood the system that is going to use the services (functions) of the object
system.

As the explanatory example of the using system we take the sales department of
an enterprise. One of the services that the object system offers to the using system is
providing the monthly turnover of the enterprise. As the explanatory example of the
object system we take a sales information system. One of the monthly products that it
brings about is the sum of a set of numbers. This sum is interpreted by the using
system as the monthly turnover.

The complete system development process is divided into three phases: design, engineering, and implementation. As said, our goal is to clarify the design process. Figure 7.10 exhibits the basic view that we consider appropriate for understanding the design process. The figure shows that the function perspective and the construction perspective on systems, as well as the corresponding black-box model and white-box model, play a crucial role in understanding the design process. Two major activities can be distinguished in the design of the object system. The first one is called "function design" and the second one "construction design". Function design starts from the using system construction, which is a white-box model, and ends at the function of the object system, which is a black-box model. In line with what has been said about black-box models above, this means that the specified function of the object system does not contain any information about the construction of the object system. In other words, the function of the object system must be specified fully and only in terms of the construction of the using system.

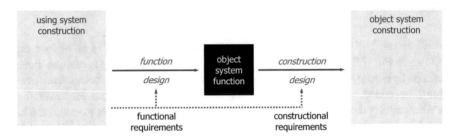

Fig. 7.10 The system design process

As said, the function of the object system supports the construction of the using system. Put the other way around: the construction of the using system uses the function(s) of the object system. Why the construction of the using system, and not its function? The answer is that there must always be an alternation of function and construction in the support–use relationship of systems. A function cannot support another function directly, because functions cannot have a need for support; only constructions can. To exemplify this, the sales department as a part of the construction of the enterprise can have a need for a sales information system. The sales department as a black box is a functional abstraction of the operational activities of selling. Conversely, the function of the object system is always and necessarily expressed in terms of the construction of the using system. So, for example, the salesmen in (the construction of) the using system may have a need to know the monthly turnover of the enterprise. The notion of turnover is a business notion that takes its meaning from the larger economic context in which the enterprise operates. The value of the monthly turnover is something by which people in the sales department may become excited or depressed. In specifying the function of the object system, it is this rich meaning of turnover that the salesmen will express to the functional designers of the object system. Needless to say, the functional designers must possess sufficient knowledge of the enterprise in order to be well-matched sparring partners to the salesmen in the process of function design.

The nature of the second design phase, construction design, is quite different from the first one. It starts from the specified function of the object system and it ends at the construction of the object system. Without intending to wrong functional designers, the job of constructional designers is definitely more creative, because they have to bridge the mental gap between function and construction. They have to establish a correspondence between systems of different kinds: the system kind of the using system and the system kind of the object system. The constructional designer is aware of the fact that the sales information system that he or she is going to design will never have any 'understanding' of turnover. The name "turnover" will at best be a label, assigned to a variable in the computer program; however, this variable can equally well be named "Mickey Mouse". It is the task of the constructional designer to get the precise definition of turnover from the functional designer, and to replace its business semantics by its formal semantics. From these formal semantics, the constructional designer devises an appropriate calculation rule. As another example for clarification, have a look at Figs. 7.6 and 7.7. Obviously, there is no simple way to arrive at the constructional model in Fig. 7.6 from the functional model in Fig. 7.7. It requires 'hard' design efforts.

The result of the activity function design is a functional model of the object system, which by nature is a black-box model. It contains all *functional specifications* for the object system to be built. The major inputs for the activity function design are the *functional requirements*, which are provided by the using system (cf. Fig. 7.10). Not all functional requirements need to be contained in the functional specifications, for two reasons. First, requirements may be unfounded. Fortunately, the ontological model of the using system provides an objective yardstick for determining unfounded requirements, since the essential model of the sales department (the ontological model of its O-organisation, cf. Chap. 10) specifies the information that is needed for every actor role. All other information that the fillers of an actor role may ask for, they do not really need. Next, determining requirements includes their validation, something that can be achieved only in thorough discussions with people 'in the business'. If the ontological model of the O-organisation is taken as the starting point, one cannot forget essential requirements. Second, the functional specifications must be feasible. By this is meant that the needed object system can be implemented, given the available technology. In addition, it must be possible to finish the development process within the agreed-upon time and for the agreed-upon costs.

As Fig. 7.10 indicates, the using system may also provide constructional requirements. This option is added to let people have a say in the construction of the object system. Constructional requirements regard a.o. the interface through which the services of the object system are made available to the using system.

7.4   Discussions

7.4.1   The Subjective Nature of Functional Models

As pointed at in Sect. 7.3.1, there is a persistent practical problem concerning functional modelling approaches. Examples of such models in the area of enterprise engineering are Forrester's System Dynamics Models, SADT (or IDEF0) activity models, and the models expressed in Data Flow Diagrams.

The problem is that different modellers commonly produce different functional models of the same system, often to the surprise of the principal or the teacher who ordered them to produce it. It should not be surprising, however, for the simple reason that functional models are inherently subjective. They represent the affordances, both intended (by the designer of the system) and unintended, that the modeller perceives, steered by the needs he/she sees or feels, as discussed in Sect. 7.2. Notwithstanding, there may be a considerable amount of similarity between the different models, but that is due to the common context in which the distinct modellers work, and the preceding discussions they may have had. The bottom line is that a functional model of a system contains the affordances that the maker perceives, and the alarming point is that many modellers seem not to be aware of this subjective nature. Consequently, they conduct endless and fruitless discussions about which functional model is 'correct'. Correctness, however, is an objective notion, and therefore only applicable to constructional models. As said, if two knowledgeable persons were asked to produce the constructional model of the same thing, for example, a coffee machine, they would come up with the same model (or they made a mistake). The criterion is the resemblance of the model to the coffee machine. For functional models, there is no such criterion. Therefore, it makes little sense to talk about the correctness of functional models.

To illustrate the problem, let us have a look at the Data Flow Diagram (DFD) in Fig. 7.11. It represents a functional model, at the highest level of abstraction, of an elevator control system, as discussed in [11]. It is of the grey-box model kind, according to the DELTA theory (Chap. 9), which means that it is a black-box (behavioural) model with an internal state. The disks (or 'bubbles') in Fig. 7.11 represent functions (also called processes), the double lines represent partial states (also called data stores), the straight arrows represent data flows, and the dashed arrows represent control flows. The latter are actually also data flows but with a special role: they activate functions, whereas the 'normal' data flows consist of input to or output from functions. The names "process" and "data store" suggest that DFDs represent constructional models, but a simple test shows that this cannot be the case. First, in no concrete elevator control system will one find parts like elevator scheduler or elevator controller. Second, the decomposition rules of DFDs tell us that one may decompose every process into a network of (sub) processes, data stores, data flows, and control flows. This may be done at will, as long as the totality of the processes, data stores, etc. is equivalent to the corresponding process at the higher level. This property is typical for functional models. Regarding constructional models, there are always a limited number of possible decompositions, and there is a definite lowest level, as discussed in Sect. 7.3.1.

Fig. 7.11   Data flow diagram of an elevator control system

7.4.2   Can One Map Functional Models to Constructional Models?

In the current practice of enterprise engineering, notably in software engineering, but also for example in business systems engineering and systems architecture, there is a widespread belief that functional models can be mapped directly to constructional models, which is fully opposite to the findings in Sect. 7.3.3. How should one understand this (mis)belief, and how could one reconcile it with the findings of Sect. 7.3.3, which are in addition compliant with the DELTA theory (Chap. 9)? The answers to these questions lie in two fallacies that, for some reason, are quite common in software engineering and in computer science at large.

The first fallacy is that if one 'opens' a black-box model of a system, one gets a white-box model, where 'opening' means that one replaces the system by a structure of subsystems. In order to illustrate the point, Fig. 1.8 in [12] is reproduced as Fig. 7.12. The figure exhibits a decomposition of the system SysA into a collection of interrelated systems SysB, SysC, etc. This decomposition can be functional or constructional (one cannot tell from the figure), but not some mix, as suggested by the figure and the clarifying text in [12]. If the boxes in Fig. 7.12 are black boxes, then the decomposition is functional and the interactions are behavioural relationships (cf. Chap. 9). If they are white boxes, then the decomposition is constructional and the interactions are operational relationships (cf. Chap. 9). Decomposing a functional model can only lead to structured collections of functional components (cf. Figs. 7.7 and 7.11), and decomposing a constructional model can only lead to structured collections of constructional components (cf. Fig. 7.6).

The second fallacy is that computer programming, so the producing of software, can be understood as a transformation from function to construction or, more precisely, a mapping of functional requirements into software primitives [op. cit., Chap. 11], where the latter are considered constructional entities. The cause of this fallacy is probably that the software primitives in modern programming languages are high-level functional entities, called functions, procedures, or methods, depending on the programming language. The ultimate constructional realisation of these functional entities are algorithms, that is, the instructions that make the hardware do what one wants it to do. These algorithms must still be created, and this work is not straightforward or trivial, although there are libraries of standard algorithms where the software engineer can pick from.

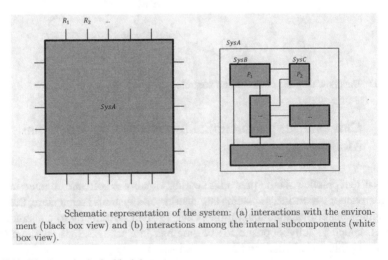

Schematic representation of the system: (a) interactions with the environment (black box view) and (b) interactions among the internal subcomponents (white box view).

Fig. 7.12 The 'opening' of a black box

Because the notion of function in current programming languages is quite blurred, and because in software engineering the dominant view on software systems is information-centric (cf. Chap. 4), a clarifying light on the second fallacy might be shed by the ALPHA theory (Chap. 11). It states that the organisation of an enterprise (so the construction perspective on the enterprise) can be divided into three partial organisations: the O-organisation, the I-organisation, and the D-organisation, as shown in Fig. 7.13, which is a reproduction of Fig. 10.12. The whole organisation is operating if the three partial organisations are operating, and if they are connected in the way as shown in Fig. 7.13. Every *enterprise information system* is some part of the enterprise's I-organisation together with the corresponding part of its D-organisation, as indicated by the yellow trapezium. Note that in the ALPHA theory (Chap. 11), we are exclusively talking in terms of white-box models.

The operation of the enterprise information system is independent of the way in which the covered parts of the I- and the D-organisation are implemented. As discussed in Chap. 11 and in [10], a possible implementation technology is ICT, which means that the actors are replaced by software modules or agents.

The functions that are needed by the actors in the O-organisation, and which are offered by the enterprise information system, are realised by the transactions of the general kinds remembering (of facts that are created in the O-organisation) and sharing (of remembered or computed facts). The issue of evolvability of information systems, which is a major issue in software engineering [13] and in systems engineering in general [12], can also be solved by redesigning the relevant parts of the I- and the D-organisation, and subsequently re-implementing them. If ICT is the implementation technology, this implies regenerating the software, including the data bases that contain representations of the facts in the O-organisation. Evolvability only concerns the implementation of a system; it is no issue at the level of the O-organisation. At this level, there is only one copy of every action, entity, fact, etc., as follows from the DELTA theory (Chap. 9) and the PSI theory (Chap. 8).

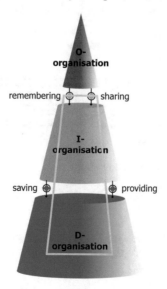

Fig. 7.13 The notion of enterprise information system

7.4.3   The Importance of Ontological Modelling

As discussed in Sect. 7.3.3, devising a construction that will realise a specified function, is generally the hardest task in a design process. It requires professionalism and creativity, next to thorough knowledge of the subject matter. Next, starting this process with devising the ontological model of the object system is of major help. Unfortunately, it is rarely taught in design courses; of any kind, not only in the area of enterprise engineering.

One of the good exceptions is electrical engineering, notably electronics. To illustrate this, let us have a look at the ontological model and the implementation model of a simple FM radio (which you may have built as a student). The detailed (i.e. lowest level of decomposition) ontological model is exhibited in Fig. 7.14.[5] The main component is an integrated circuit referred to by TDA7000. It does the lion's share of the (analog) signal processing work of the radio. It has 18 input/ output ports, which take in or produce electrical signals, except ports 5 and 16, which are supplied by an electrical voltage of 6 and 0 DC, respectively. Integrated circuits, like the TDA7000, are composite components, which commonly consist of dozens of elementary components. Examples of such elementary components are transistors, diodes, capacitors, inductors, and resistors. Actually, these components cannot really be found in the integrated circuit, which is why it is called integrated. Consequently, integrated circuits mostly have a quite complex construction.

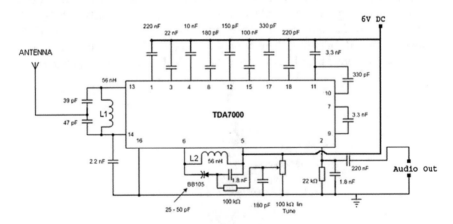

Fig. 7.14 Ontological model of the radio receiver

---

[5]The pictures and the other information of the FM radio are taken from http://pdf.datasheetcatalog. com/datasheet/philips/TDA7000_CNV_2.pdf   and   https://circuitswiring.com/fm-radio-with-tda7000/

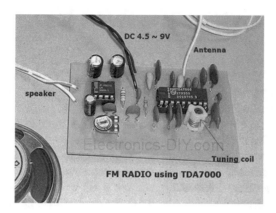

Fig. 7.15   Implementation of the FM radio

In Fig. 7.14, capacitors are represented by 'double-lines', inductors by 'wired' symbols, and resistors by rectangular shapes (note that the diagram doesn't contain transistors or diodes). All elementary components have a specific functional behaviour, as has the integrated circuit TDA7000. Figure 7.15 exhibits a possible implementation of the ontological model. Only the right side, with the TDA7000 in the middle, is applicable. The left side contains an audio amplifier, which amplifies the audio output from the right side to a level that is needed to make it audible through a loudspeaker. The TDA7000 is implemented by the black-coloured device labeled TDA7000. It has 18 sockets, each of them implementing one of the ports in Fig. 7.11 (note Figs. 7.14 and 7.15 do not fully correspond). As said, it is the construction of a system that brings about the function(s) and additional affordances to its users, and possibly to other stakeholders. The highest level function is that of a radio. This function is elaborated in more extensive and more specific functions, ending up in one or more functional component trees, like the one in Fig. 7.7, complemented by detailed behaviour specifications. As an example, Fig. 7.16 shows one of the detailed functional behaviour specifications of the integrated circuit TDA7000 that are relevant for the performance of the FM radio.

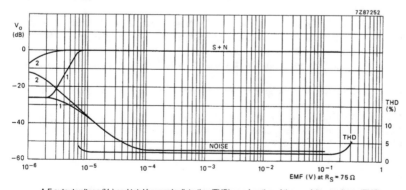

A.F output voltage (V_o) and total harmonic distortion (THD) as a function of the e.m.f. input voltage (EMF) with a source impedance (R_S) of 75 Ω: (1) muting system enabled; (2) muting system disabled.

Fig. 7.16   Part of the functional specifications of the TDA7000

7.4.4   The TAO Theory and the TAO Philosophy

The TAO, also spelled as DAO, is a metaphysical concept in ancient Chinese philosophy, in Confucianism among others. Its literal translation into English is: the way or the path [14]. TAO is considered the source and the substance of everything that exists. Taoists seek to free themselves from the subjective influences that unavoidably stick to the human observations of the world that surrounds us, and subsequently to find the human independent truth in the world. The TAO philosophy has also led to a particular way of living, the TAO ethics, which is characterised by three so-called treasures: compassion, frugality, and humility.

The similarity of the TAO theory and the TAO philosophy is not only in the name.[6] The sharp distinction in the TAO theory between the function and the construction of the things that surround us, or more generally between teleology and ontology, paves the way to a crisp and clear notion of the ontological essence of systems in general (cf. Chap. 8) and of organisations in particular (cf. Chap. 9). But it also suggests a profound correspondence between this notion of ontological essence and the core of the TAO philosophy. We leave it to the reader to verify that this correspondence is more than mere speculation, as well as to discover the correspondence between the TAO ethics and the human-centric ideological foundation of Enterprise Engineering, as presented in [15].

References

1. Kant, I. (1965). *First introduction to the critique of judgment* (The Library of Liberal Arts) (p. xv, 55). Indianapolis: Bobbs-Merrill.
2. Nagel, T. (2012). *Mind and cosmos: Why the materialist neo-Darwinian conception of nature is almost certainly false* (p. x, 130). New York: Oxford University Press.
3. Rosenblueth, A., Wiener, N., & Bigelow, J. (1943). Behavior, purpose and teleology. *Philosophy of Science, 10*(1), 18–24.
4. Guarino, N., Oberle, D., & Staab, S. (2009). What is an ontology? In *Handbook on ontologies* (pp. 1–17). Berlin: Springer.
5. Guizzardi, G. (2005). *Ontological foundations for structural conceptual models.* CTIT, University of Twente.
6. Simons, P. (1987). *Parts—A study in ontology.* New York: Oxford University Press.
7. Gibson, J. J. (1979). *The ecological approach to visual perception* (p. xv, 332). Boston: Houghton Mifflin.
8. Chemero, A. (2003). An outline of a theory of affordances. *Ecological Psychology, 15*(2), 181–195.
9. Dietz, J. L. G. (2012). *Red garden gnomes don't exist.* The Netherlands: Sapio Enterprise Engineering. www.sapio.nl
10. Dietz, J. L. G. (2009). *Architecture: Building strategy into design.* The Hague: SDU Publishing.
11. Yourdon, E. (1989). *Modern structured analysis* (p. x, 672). Englewood Cliffs, NJ: Yourdon Press.

---

[6]The Roman writing of the pronunciation of the Greek letter T is actually not TAO but TAU.

12. Mannaert, H., Verelst, J., & Bruyn, P. D. (2016). *Normalized systems theory: From foundations for evolvable software toward a general theory for evolvable design*. Kermt: Koppa.
13. Lehman, M. M., & Belady, L. A. (1985). *Program evolution: Processes of software change* (A P I C Studies in Data Processing) (p. xiii, 538). London: Academic.
14. Puett, M. J. (2016). *The path: What Chinese philosophers can teach us about the good life* (First Simon & Schuster hardcover edition, p. xvi, 204). New York: Simon & Schuster.
15. Hoogervorst, J. A. P. (2017). Ideological foundation. In *Foundations of enterprise governance and enterprise engineering: Presenting the Employee-Centric Theory of Organization* (pp. 355–564). Cham: Springer.

Chapter 8
The PSI Theory: Understanding the Operation of Organisations

Abstract The PSI theory is a theory about the operation of organisations. PSI stands for Performing in Social Interaction. Based on the CIAO (Communication, Information, Action, and Organisation) paradigm, a communication-centric view is taken on the cooperation of people in enterprises, as manifested in business processes. The fundamental notion in understanding the operation of organisations is the coordination act. It consists of a performer, an addressee, an intention, and a product. The performer and the addressee are actors, that is, subjects filling an actor role. Actor roles are the units of authority and responsibility. Coordination acts can be performed verbally, non-verbally, and tacitly. They are the key elements in (business) conversations, which are the constituting parts of (business) transactions. A transaction is carried out by actors in two roles: the initiator and the executor. The executor brings about the product of the transaction to the benefit of the initiator. The process of a transaction is a path, possibly including iterations, through a universal transaction pattern, which consists of one main pattern and four revocation patterns. The latter serve to revert the state in the main pattern to a previous state. Because of the inherent connection between an actor role and the transaction kind of which fillers are the executor, the combination of the two is called transactor role. Transactor roles are the universal building blocks of business processes. Performing a coordination act results in creating the corresponding coordination fact. The time attributes of coordination facts are: the creation time and the event time, defined as the time at which the fact comes into existence. Regarding products (which consist of one independent production fact and a number of dependent facts), the notion of operative time (i.e., the time at which the product becomes effective) is distinguished, next to its event time, that is, its coming into existence, and its creation time. A fundamental principle in the PSI theory is that actors act autonomously, also if they are guided by business rules. Based on this principle, precise definitions are developed for the notions of authority, responsibility, accountability, and competence.

© Springer Nature Switzerland AG 2020
J. L. G. Dietz, J. B. F. Mulder, *Enterprise Ontology*, The Enterprise Engineering Series, https://doi.org/10.1007/978-3-030-38854-6_8

Every organised human activity—from the making of pots to the placing of a man on the moon—gives rise to two fundamental and opposing requirements: the division of labour into various tasks to be performed and the coordination of these tasks to accomplish the activity.
(Henry Mintzberg [1])

8.1   Introduction

The statement by Henry Mintzberg, quoted above, comprises the core problem of organising: how to divide the total amount of work, how to assign the resulting parts to workers, and how to arrange the necessary coordination among them. The quote also hints at the prospect that it could be possible to understand the notion of organisation in a very general way, independent of the particular kind of enterprise and independent of the particular workers. But how should one conceive work and workers, so that a universal notion of organisation emerges that is effective, particularly in the current practice, where the pervasiveness of ICT applications[1] blurs the sight of the 'real' organisation? Achieving this goal has been the aim of a long-lasting research activity that began in the early 1990s, and that resulted in the present Ψ-theory. The Greek letter Ψ is pronounced as PSI, which is an acronym for Performing in Social Interaction. It is about human cooperation in enterprises, and it is classified as an ontological theory in the framework of theories, as presented in Chap. 4, meaning that it is about the nature of things.

The PSI theory exclusively takes the construction perspective (cf. Chap. 7) on enterprises, disregarding all functional aspects. Therefore, we will try to consistently use the specific term "organisation" instead of the general term "enterprise". The operation of an organisation is defined as the manifestation of its construction in the course of time. In concordance with the DELTA theory (Chap. 9), every organisation is a discrete event system, in the category of social systems [2]. By the construction of an organisation is understood the triple of its composition, its environment, and its structure (cf. Chap. 9). The elements in the composition and the environment are social individuals, commonly called subjects, and the structure of an organisation consists of mutual influencing bonds between these subjects, as explained by the OMEGA theory (Chap. 10).

Section 8.2 (foundations) starts with a recapitulation of the CIAO paradigm from Chap. 4. Communication is the primal notion in understanding organisations. Communicating is (also) acting, or as Austin [3] puts it: people do things with words. In the PSI theory, this is accentuated by distinguishing coordination acts and production acts, and by bringing them together in the concepts of business conversation and business transaction. In addition, the process of performing a coordination act is discussed. In Sect. 8.3 (elaborations), several time aspects of transactions are highlighted, followed by a discussion of the operating cycle of actors. Next, attention is paid to crucial factors in organisations, like authority, responsibility, accountability, and competence. In Sect. 8.4 (discussions), the PSI

---

[1]By ICT applications are understood all artefacts that are implemented using ICT (Information and Communication Technology). They include all AI (Artificial Intelligence) artefacts.

theory is compared to several similar approaches, and the practical importance of the PSI theory is discussed.

8.2 Foundations

8.2.1 Recapitulation of the CIAO Paradigm

In general, the best way of addressing the potentials of a new technology is to step back and to reconsider how one actually did think about the field of application before its introduction, and to find new, better ways of thinking, following Einstein's quote "We can't solve problems by using the same kind of thinking we used when we created them", often paraphrased as out-of-the-box thinking. Initially, the office workers in enterprises, including accountants, considered ICT as a more efficient alternative for the existing paper-based data processing technology. Hence the original name "Electronic Data Processing" (EDP). It took until around 1975 before EDP was replaced by ISE (Information Systems Engineering) or by like names. The shift of attention from the form to the content of information (cf. Fig. 8.3) was a paradigm shift. Thus, the *information-centric* view on information systems was born.

But the wrong belief among ICT professionals, that developing information systems is something that one does 'to the side', after having elicited requirements from the people in the organisation, basically by interviewing these people, persisted. Despite many improvements, this approach to requirements determination has rarely been able to achieve that the delivered systems meet the justified expectations of the users. Around 2000, a new way of thinking emerged, which took communication as the primal notion. From this *communication-centric* view on information systems, the CIAO paradigm has evolved. The acronym CIAO stands for Communication, Information, Action, and Organisation. In this paradigm, *communication*[2] is defined as the sharing of thoughts between (human) minds, and *information* as the means for communication. As articulated by the ALPHA theory (Chap. 11), every information system can be conceived as some implementation of some part of the organisation, thereby applying some information and communication technology (ICT). The CIAO paradigm definitely solves the requirements problem: if one understands the operation of an organisation fully and properly, one also has got the requirements.

---

[2]The English word "communicate" comes from the Latin word "communicare", which means 'making something common'. In a more specific sense, it means 'sharing thoughts'.

In addition, communication became understood as a form of *action*. In Habermas' Theory of Communicative Action [4], the elementary instance of communication is the *communicative act*. It consists of four parts: performer, intention, addressee, and proposition, as exhibited in Fig. 8.1.

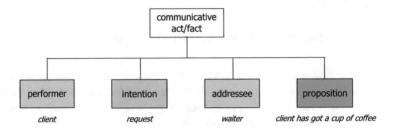

Fig. 8.1 The structure of a communicative act/fact

The *performer* and the *addressee* are human beings, in their quality of social individual, which means: being capable to engage in and comply with commitments. The *proposition* is a state of affairs that is or that can be the case. The *intention* is the intent of the performer (a client in Fig. 8.1) towards the addressee (a waiter), with respect to the proposition. If the intention is 'request', the performer wants the addressee to make the proposition become true. In the café case, the client wants the waiter to bring her a cup of coffee. According to Habermas [4], the performer of a communicative act raises three validity claims towards the addressee: the claim to rightness, the claim to sincerity, and the claim to truth. The claims have to be assessed by the addressee, and the result of this assessment will guide her/him in her/his response. By accepting the *claim to rightness* in the above example, the waiter recognises the authority of the client to make the request: according to the applicable societal norms or laws, she is allowed to place orders in the café. By accepting the *claim to sincerity*, the waiter expresses that he considers the client to be honest and trustworthy in making the request. It includes that she complies with the applicable terms of sale (implying, e.g. that she has to pay for the service). By accepting the *claim to truth*, the waiter expresses that he is able to make the proposition true. If all three claims are accepted, the waiter responds by a promise. Otherwise, he will decline the request.

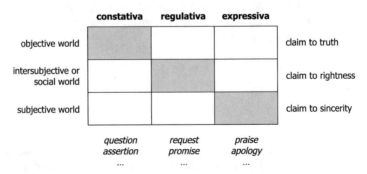

Fig. 8.2 The three categories of communicative acts

There is always one validity claim dominant. Based on this dominance, Habermas distinguishes three categories of communicative acts, and three worlds in which they have effect (cf. Fig. 8.2). The dominance of a claim, as well as the related world, is indicated by the grey-coloured rectangles. In the category of *constativa*, the dominant claim is the claim to truth, and the world with which they are concerned is the *objective world*. Examples of constativa are questions and assertions. If a railway passenger asks a railway officer for the departure time of the next train to Amsterdam, the dominant claim is the claim to truth. Facts like the departure time of trains are considered to exist in the objective world. In the category of *expressiva*, the dominant claim is the claim to sincerity, and the world with which they are concerned is everyone's private *subjective world*. Examples of expressiva are praises and apologies. If the railway passenger starts by saying "I'm sorry to disturb you, madam...", then the dominant claim of this phrase is the claim to sincerity. In the category of *regulativa*, the dominant claim is the claim to rightness, and the world with which they are concerned is the *intersubjective* or *social world*. Examples of regulativa are requests and promises. If the client in the café asks the waiter for a cup of coffee, the dominant claim is the claim to rightness, that is, the client claims that she has the authority to make the request.

Because people are not able to directly connect their minds, some vehicle for communication is needed, and this vehicle is information or, more precisely, signs, which is the preferred term in semiotics, the branch of philosophy that studies signs [5]. A major outcome of this study is the semiotic ladder, exhibited in Fig. 8.3. It clarifies the role of signs in the communication between human beings. A unit of *information*, commonly called an information item, is the dyad of content and form, meaning that the two parts are distinguishable but not separable. The content of an information item is the *thought* (cf. Chap. 5) that one wants to share, and the agreed upon perceivable shapes constitute the form, thus the *sign*. The content comprises both the intention (or pragmatics) and the proposition (or semantics) of the thought, and the form comprises both the formalism (or syntax) and the coding (or empirics) of the sign.

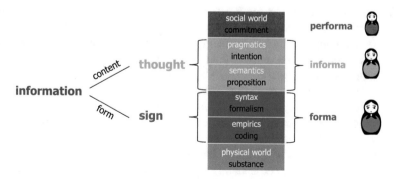

Fig. 8.3 The semiotic ladder

In the café example, the client has, at some point in time, got the thought that she wants a cup of coffee. In order to share this thought, she has to express it in a sign that is intelligible to the waiter. The proposition of the thought is "client has got a cup of coffee" and the intention is the request. By performing the request, she enters into a commitment towards the waiter, as the waiter enters into a commitment if he performs a promise or a decline in response to her request. The client may have expressed her thought in this English sentence: "I'd like to have a cup of coffee, please", which constitutes the sign part in Fig. 8.3. The applied formalism is the English grammar and the coding concerns the construction of the words. The substance in which the sentence is inscribed consists of the air vibrations that are produced by the client and perceived by the sense of hearing of the waiter.

For the concept of *action*, the communication-centric view means that communicating is also acting. In the PSI theory, this is accentuated by distinguishing coordination acts and production acts (cf. Sect. 8.2.2), and by combining them in the concepts of business conversation (cf. Sect. 8.2.4) and business transaction (cf. Sect. 8.2.5). Consequently, the word "in" in the explanation "Performing in Social Interaction" of PSI, has a twofold meaning. It means that coordination acts, like requesting a cup of coffee, are performed in communication, and thus in social interaction. In addition, it means that production acts, like delivering a cup of coffee, are performed in patterns of social interactions (cf. Sect. 8.2.6).

The (new) concept of *organisation* is that it is a system of transactor roles, the universal building blocks of organisations, to be discussed in Sect. 8.2.7.

8.2.2   Work Is Production Plus Coordination

8.2.2.1   Production Acts and Facts

As postulated by the DELTA theory (Chap. 9), all acts, in all systems, of all categories, can be divided in two sorts: production acts and coordination acts. By performing *production acts* (or P-acts for short), the subjects in an organisation create products. The character of a production act can be tangible (like transporting goods) or intangible (like becoming member of a library). The effect of performing a P-act is the creation of the corresponding independent P-fact, together with a number of dependent P-facts. Examples of independent P-facts are "membership 387 is started", "rental 1087 is concluded", "the car of rental 1087 is issued", and "sale 1618 is completed". Dependent P-facts are called *dependent* because they start to exist (come into being) as a consequence of, and together with, the related *independent* P-fact. Independent P-facts are mostly unary facts (concerning some entity), whereas dependent P-facts are always binary facts. They constitute the *properties* of the entity (cf. Chap. 5). The combination of an independent P-fact and all of its related dependent P-facts (properties) is called a *product*. As an example, the independent P-fact 'membership 387 is started' is an instance of the P-fact type '[membership] is started', which is a logical predication over the class

MEMBERSHIP. The term "[membership]" is a placeholder, or variable, that can be instantiated; membership 387 could be one of its instances. Possible properties of membership 387 are that the concerned member is John, and that the starting day (in Julian days, cf. Chap. 6) is 2458209, which equals 1 April 2018 in the Gregorian calendar.

Independent P-fact types (or product kinds) are formulated in such a way that the instances are unique in time and space. To illustrate this, if it is allowed that one can be member of a tennis club several times during one's lifetime, there is only one proper way to deal with it. It is to adopt the notion of membership, whose instances are unique in time. By space is meant the state space of the production world (cf. Sect. 8.2.2.1). Unique in space means that there can only exist one membership 387 in any state of the world. So, membership 387 is a unique entity.

Lastly, one should be aware that a phrase like "membership 387 is started" is just the formulation of a proposition (or P-fact). It is not the assertion that the proposition is true.[3] As we will see, the proposition may become true at some point in time, which means that the corresponding P-fact becomes existent at that point in time.

8.2.2.2 Coordination Acts and Facts

Coordination acts (or C-acts for short) are communicative acts in Habermas' category of regulativa (cf. Fig. 8.2). Its generic structure is exhibited in Fig. 8.4, which is a refinement of Fig. 8.1. The illustrating example is taken from the case wheelbarrows, as discussed in [6]. The performer of the act is Gnome 463, in his role of buyer on behalf of the company HORTUS, and the addressee is Gnome 691, in her role of seller on behalf of the company MALUM. The product is the purchase of a number of wheelbarrows. This is represented by the independent P-fact 'purchase 31416 is fulfilled' (split into the predication "is fulfilled" and the predicated entity "purchase 31416"), and the dependent P-facts or properties 'article type is Quadra 75', number of items is 10', 'price is 165 (in the currency of Gnomeland)', and 'delivery day is 731.513 (in the Gnomeland calendar)'. The intention of the C-act/fact is the request. By conveying this intention to Gnome 691, Gnome 463 commits himself to his request, which means that he cannot simply say at some later point in time that he was just joking. Similarly, Gnome 691 will become committed to the response that she is going to perform. C-acts are the *atoms* of business processes. They are ontologically indivisible: one performs a 'complete' request or any other C-act or none.

---

[3]In English, like in many natural languages, it is not possible to make a grammatical distinction between the formulation of a proposition and the assertion that the proposition is true. Both are expressed in the same assertive sentence.

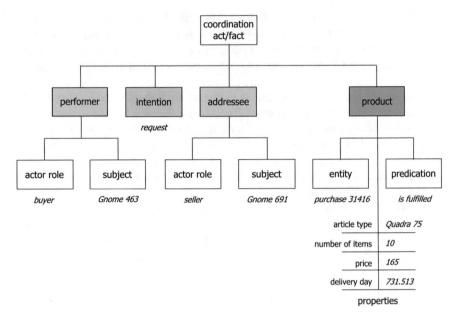

Fig. 8.4 The structure of a coordination act/fact

The coloured parts in the representation of a C-act/fact in the figure constitute the *normal form* of a C-act/fact, formally defined as follows (plus an example, in which the performer and the addressee are indicated as <actor role>/<subject>):

< performer > : < intention > :   < addressee > :   < product >

buyer/Gnome 463 :   request   : seller/Gnome 691 : purchase 31416 is fulfilled

8.2.3 The Process of a Coordination Act

Corresponding with the semiotic ladder (cf. Fig. 8.3), we distinguish three abilities that communicating subjects need to dispose of: the *forma* ability (in order to deal with codings and formalisms), the *informa* ability (in order to deal with propositions and intentions), and the *performa* ability (in order to deal with commitments). These abilities are shown, on the right side of Fig. 8.3, as three shapes that human beings can take on. Note that the physical world (dealing with substances) is not covered by the performa-informa-forma distinction. If needed, we will consider it to be included in the forma ability. For the sake of completeness, however, the physical (grey) shape is included in the elaborated explanation of the process of a coordination act in Fig. 8.6, next to the blank shape, which represents the most inner self of every subject. There reside the wisdom and love that are considered to constitute the basis for deciding on how to comply with commitments. The Matryoshka doll shapes in this figure are scaled, to illustrate that they should be understood as being enclosed in each other, from top to bottom.

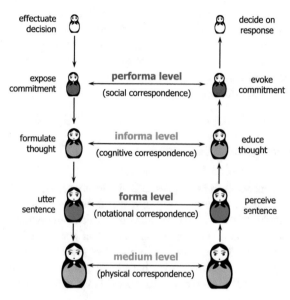

Fig. 8.5 The process of a coordination act

In order to effectuate a decision to perform a C-act, the subject on the left side of Fig. 8.5 has to expose the corresponding commitment in her/his 'red' shape, that is, by applying her/his performa ability. Because it is impossible to convey the commitment directly to the addressee, he/she has to formulate, in her/his 'green' shape, a thought that contains the commitment. As we know from Sect. 8.2.1, the thought consists of a proposition and an intention. As it is impossible to share the thought directly with the addressee, the subject has to utter, in her/his 'blue' shape, a sentence that expresses the thought. In order to make the sentence perceivable to the addressee, he/she has, in her/his 'grey' shape, to inscribe the sentence in some substance, and have the inscription transmitted through a proper communication channel to the addressee. This action succeeds if the message arrives undistorted. If so, the two subjects have achieved *physical correspondence*, that is, the *medium condition* is satisfied. The addressee is now able, in her/his 'blue' shape, to perceive the inscribed sentence from the transmitted substance. If he/she succeeds, the two subjects have achieved *notational correspondence*, that is, the *forma condition* is satisfied. Next, the addressee can educe, in her/his 'green' shape, the thought from the sentence, so the contained proposition and intention. If he/she succeeds, the two subjects have achieved *cognitive correspondence*, that is, the *informa condition* is satisfied. Then, in her/his 'red' shape, the addressee has to evoke in her/his mind the commitment that the performer of the C-act wanted to convey. If he/she succeeds, the two subjects have achieved *social correspondence*, that is, the *performa condition* is satisfied. Lastly, the addressee has to decide on how he/she will respond in her/his blank shape, after which a similar process takes place for sharing the decision with the other subject. At every level, but commonly only at the informa level, the addressee may confirm or disconfirm the message. Figure 8.5 clearly illustrates that communicating is a laborious activity. Fortunately, people are experts at it.

8.2.4   Business Conversations

Communicative acts occur in sequences, called *conversations*, which are the objects of interest in conversation theory [7–9]. In the PSI theory, the focus is on *business conversations*, defined as conversations that take place in an institutional setting and of which the participants aim at achieving a common goal [10]. These participants are considered to satisfy the requirements of the ideal speech situation.[4] In the course of time, several patterns of conversation have been identified, like the conversation for information and the conversation for action [11]. Based on these studies, we

---

[4]Habermas has elucidated and elaborated the notion of "ideal speech situation" in his book "*Moral Consciousness and Communicative Action*". This a relevant quote: "A measure of whether or not participants in communication reach agreement is the yes or no position taken by the hearer whereby he accepts or rejects the claim to validity that has been raised by the speaker. In the attitude oriented toward reaching understanding, the speaker raises with every intelligible utterance the claim that the utterance in question is true (or that the existential presuppositions of the propositional content hold true), that the speech act is right in terms of a given normative context (or that the normative context that it satisfies is itself legitimate), and that the speaker's manifest intentions are meant in the way they are expressed. When someone rejects what is offered in an intelligible speech act, he denies the validity of an utterance in at least one of three respects: truth, rightness, or truthfulness. His "no" signals that the utterance has failed to fulfil at least one of its three functions (the representation of states of affairs, the maintenance of an interpersonal relationship, or the manifestation of lived experience) because the utterance is not in accordance with either the world of existing states of affairs, our world of legitimately ordered interpersonal relations, or each participant's own world of subjective lived experience. These aspects are not clearly distinguished in normal everyday communication. Yet in cases of disagreement or persistent problematisation, competent speakers can differentiate between the aforementioned three relations to the world, thematising individual validity claims and focusing on something that confronts them, whether it be something objective, something normative, or something subjective".

distinguish four kinds of conversations: actagenic conversations, factagenic conversations, reversiogenic conversations, and cogitatiogenic conversations.[5] Henceforth, we assume that a conversation involves two participants, but we allow that a participant is the collectivity of a number of subjects (cf. Sect. 8.2.7).

An *actagenic conversation*, or *A-conversation* for short, is a conversation in which the participants strive to reach consensus about a product that one of them is going to bring about at the other's request. The key C-acts in an A-conversation are the *request* and the *promise*. Both must be present for a successful conversation, and in this order, because the promise is a response to the request. However, except for the order, they may occur at any place in the conversation. An example of an A-conversation in the café situation is given below (where C is the client and W the waiter). The request is expressed in the fourth line, and the corresponding promise in the fifth line.

W	Good morning madam, what a wonderful weather you bring with you.	
C	Yes indeed, it is beautiful outside. I think I will go for a walk later today.	
W	A very good idea, I would say, madam. What can I do for you?	
C	I think, I'd like to have a cup of coffee.	[request]
W	I will bring it right away, madam. Anything else?	[promise]
C	No thanks, that's all.	

A *factagenic conversation*, or *F-conversation* for short, is a conversation in which the participants strive to reach consensus about the produced P-fact. The key C-acts in an F-conversation are the *declare* and the *accept*. Both must be present for a successful conversation, and in this order, because the acceptance is a response to the declaration. Except for the order, they may occur at any place in the conversation. F-conversations typically go together with A-conversations in the frame of transactions, to be discussed in Sect. 8.2.5. An example of an F-conversation in the café situation that matches the A-conversation above could be:

W	Here you are, madam, a fresh cup of coffee, the best in town!	[declare]
C	Ha ha, I hope so, sir. What makes you think it is the best in town?	
W	Just gut feeling, madam. Anyway, I know no better one!	
C	Well, let me see whether I can agree with you.	[accept]
W	I'll bet you will!	

A *reversiogenic conversation*, or *R-conversation* for short, is a conversation in which the participants strive to agree on reverting (turning back) the current state in an A- or an F-conversation, in which they (also) participate. As shown in Sects. 8.2.6.4–8.2.6.7, it means that one can revert a complete transaction in this way. The key C-acts in a successful R-conversation are the *revoke*, followed by the *allow*. An example of an R-conversation in the café situation, right after the A-conversation above, when the waiter is already on his way to get the coffee, could be:

---

[5]The words actagenic, factagenic, reversiogenic, and cogitatiogenic mean, respectively, act creating, fact creating, reversion creating, and idea or plan creating.

C	Oh, waiter, please, on second thoughts . . . do you have cappuccino?	[revoke rq]
W	Sure, madam, and it's no problem at all that you changed your mind	[allow]
C	Oh, thanks a lot, you are very kind. So, a cappuccino please.	[request]
W	As you wish, madam.	[promise]

The revoke of the request is expressed in the first line, and the corresponding allow in the second one. The third and fourth lines contain the new request and the corresponding promise. They are not part of the R-conversation, however. The example contains also an informational transaction, namely in the last part of the first sentence and the first part of the second sentence. In this transaction, the availability of cappuccino is checked by the client and confirmed by the waiter (cf. Chap. 11).

As said, an A-conversation is successful if the state of being promised is reached. In case of no success, the state of the conversation can be reverted by a successful corresponding R-conversation, as will be discussed in Sect. 8.2.6. Likewise, an F-conversation is successful if the state of being accepted is reached. In case of no success, the state of the conversation can be reverted by a successful corresponding R-conversation, as will be discussed also in Sect. 8.2.6. An R-conversation is said to be successful if the intended reversion is achieved, that is, if the state of an A- or an F-conversation is reverted. In case of no success, the state in the A- or F-conversation will remain unchanged.

A *cogitatiogenic conversation*, or *C-conversation* for short, is a conversation in which the participants strive to reach consensus about an idea or plan for future action. C-conversations are typically held in preparation of a decision to perform a C-act in an A-, F-, or R-conversation. They include conversations that are commonly known as consultations and deliberations, in particular the conversations in the discussion states that we will see in Sect. 8.2.6. Contrary to the other three kinds of conversations, the PSI theory does not contain specific patterns for C-conversations. The reason is simply that C-conversations are not composed of coordination acts but of other (non-performative) communicative acts. However, their existence and their relevance are recognised. An example of a C-conversation in the café situation, which could precede the formal part of the A-conversation above, is:

W	Good morning madam, what a wonderful weather you bring with you.
C	Yes indeed, it is beautiful outside. I think I will go for a walk later today.
W	A very good idea, I would say, madam. What can I do for you?
C	I don't know yet, I just came in because I wanted to have something stimulating. I feel a bit groggy, perhaps of the wine last night.
W	Then I can recommend a cup of coffee or, if you don't feel for it, a glass of fresh mint tea.
C	Hmm, well, coffee sounds like a good idea.

8.2.5 Business Transactions

A (business) *transaction*[6] is a sequence of C-acts/facts, within a specific pattern called the transaction pattern, concerning some product. It involves two actors, one in the role of *initiator* and one in the role of *executor*. An actor is a subject in filling an actor role. The notions of actor and actor role are elaborated in Sect. 8.2.7.

The best general understanding of a transaction is that it proceeds in three phases: the order phase, the execution phase, and the result phase. The *order phase* is an A-conversation in which the two actors discuss and negotiate in order to come to agreement about a product (cf. Sect. 8.2.2) that the executor can promise to bring about in response to the request by the initiator. The properties of the product include the terms of delivery (time, price, etc.) that are common in (business) transactions. In this phase, the product is also called *proposition*. In the *execution phase*, the executor produces some product (which may differ from the promised one). The initiator is basically ignorant of what the executor does in this phase. The *result phase* is an F-conversation in which the two actors discuss and negotiate in order to come to an agreement about the actually brought about product so that it can be accepted responsibly by the initiator. In this phase, the product is also called *result*. While in the order phase, basically all properties of the product are negotiable, some are still also negotiable in the result phase, notably properties like price and delivery time. As an example in the café, the client may not be fully satisfied with the declared product if the coffee is not really warm. Instead of producing a fresh cup of coffee (something that will be discussed in Sect. 8.2.6), the two actors could agree on a lower price (note: paying is a separate transaction, as discussed in Chap. 10).

8.2.6 Transaction Patterns

8.2.6.1 The Basic Transaction Pattern

The DELTA theory (Chap. 9) postulates that the state of a world at some point in time is the set of facts that are created up to that point in time. The coming into existence of a fact is called an *event*. So, an event is a change of state, also called transition, at a particular point in time, called the *event time*. The C-acts and P-acts in an organisation cause events in its coordination world, called *coordination events* or C-events, and its production world, called *production events* or P-events, respectively (cf. Fig. 8.6). The two actors in the middle interact through the creation of C-facts (represented by disks), which are the immediate results of performing C-acts (represented by boxes). For example, the effect of performing a request is the creation of the fact of being requested. Likewise, the effect of a P-act (represented

---

[6]The noun "transaction" is related to the verb "to transact", which originates from the Latin verb "transigere", meaning carrying out, bringing through.

by a grey box) is a P-fact (represented by a grey diamond). As will become clear, the number of C-events is always much larger than the number of P-events. The light-grey colouring of the shapes of the P-acts and P-facts will be explained later.

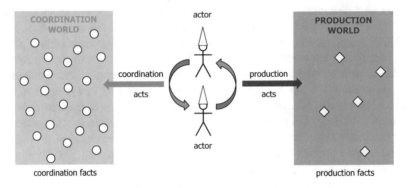

Fig. 8.6 The coordination world and the production world of an organisation

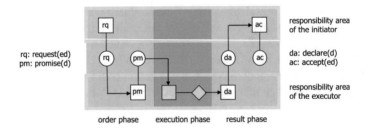

Fig. 8.7 The basic transaction pattern

In Fig. 8.7, the *basic transaction pattern* is shown. It contains the five steps that must always be performed in order to let a transaction succeed: the request and the promise in the A-conversation (the order phase), the declaration and the acceptance in the F-conversation (the result phase), and performing the P-act in between (the execution phase). The symbols used are explained in Table 8.1. In the café example, the first step is the performing of a request by the client (the initiator) for a cup of coffee, addressed to the waiter (the executor). We have entered now the order phase of the transaction. The second step is the promise by the waiter to bring the cup of coffee. With this step, the order phase ends successfully, and the execution phase starts, in which the waiter produces the cup of coffee. The shapes of the P-act and the P-fact in Fig. 8.7 are coloured light-grey to indicate that they are private to the executor, and thus not directly knowable to the initiator (nor to anyone else). After this third step, the waiter addresses himself to the client again and declares the result of his work, which is the fourth step. At this moment, the created P-fact is knowable to the initiator, as part of the created C-fact (cf. Fig. 8.4). We have entered now the result phase of the transaction. This phase ends successfully if the client accepts the declared result, which is the fifth transaction step.

The two light-grey lined rectangles in Fig. 8.7 indicate the *responsibility areas* of the two participants: the initiator is responsible for the request and the acceptance, and the executor for the promise, the P-act, and the declaration. The notion of responsibility will be elaborated in Sect. 8.3.3. In order to indicate that they are knowable to both actors, the conversation states (C-facts) are put in between these rectangles. Note that we abstract completely from the particular way in which the steps in Fig. 8.7 are performed. This abstraction is one of the key elements in calling the understanding of organisations that the PSI theory provides, *ontological*. The other key element is the rootedness of this understanding in the atomicity of C-acts/facts, and in the molecularity of transactions. Note also that the pattern in Fig. 8.7 makes the communication between the initiator and the executor *asynchronous*. To illustrate this, the fact of being requested exists from the moment that the request act is performed. The addressee (thus the executor) takes notice of the fact when it suits her/him (cf. Sect. 8.3.2).

Table 8.1 Legend of the links in transaction patterns

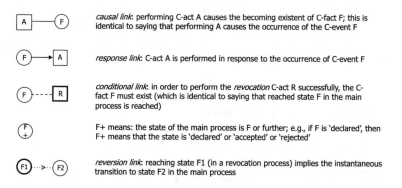

C-acts may be performed *verbally*, for example, by uttering sentences like "I'd like to have a cup of coffee, please" as a way to request, but they may also be performed *non-verbally*, which means that some other act counts as the C-act (like just putting the cup of coffee in front of the client as a way of performing the declaration). In both cases, the evidence of the act is *explicit*. In addition, C-acts may be performed *tacitly*, which means that there is no evidence of acts that could count as performing them. Still they are performed, but the evidence is said to be *implicit*: they can be deduced from the presence or the absence of other acts [13]. To illustrate this, if the waiter doesn't perform an explicit promise, the client may deduce it from the absence of an explicit decline (cf. Sect. 8.2.6.2). Moreover, when the waiter brings the cup of coffee and thereby performs the declare act, the client may deduce the promise from the presence of this act. As one may expect, tacitly performed

C-acts are a major cause of business process failures where an actor is waiting for an explicit C-event that will never occur (because the other actor thinks there is no need for it: no news is good news).

The product of a transaction, that is, the independent P-fact together with its dependent P-facts (cf. Sect. 8.2.2), will only become existent after a successful completion of the result phase. In this way, P-acts/facts are firmly connected to C-acts/facts: the resulting product becomes existent as soon as it is accepted by the initiator of the transaction. Consequently, every P-fact is the result of a successfully completed transaction (or it is derived from such original facts, cf. Chap. 6).

Moreover, the initiator may accept a result that differs from the requested product. Let us take the café example again to illustrate this. Suppose that the client has asked for a double espresso and the waiter delivers a cappuccino. Most people would reject the declare act by the waiter in such a case, but it is perfectly fine if the client accepts it. The example emphasises that the most important world for human beings is Habermas' intersubjective or social world (cf. Fig. 8.2). To top that, the client may even accept the declaration if no coffee has been brought at all! This basic understanding of the 'nature' of P-facts reflects our basic understanding of the 'nature' of societal institutions, namely that they are primarily intersubjective or social constructs, in accordance with the core message in [12].

The carrying out of a transaction (of whatever kind) can be taken as a generic *business process* building block, and the C- and P-acts in transactions can be taken as a generic notion of *task*, seeming to be more precise than the one that is rather implicitly used in Mintzberg's quote in Sect. 8.1.

8.2.6.2   The Standard Transaction Pattern

Figure 8.8 exhibits an extension of the basic pattern. Note that the diamond of the P-fact is drawn in the box of the P-act (just to save space), that the phase colours are omitted, and that the accept act and fact have another place (for purposes of convenience). Moreover, we have added the external state (C-fact) called "in". It represents the becoming existent of some state in some process. From now on, we will refer to acts and facts in the next concise way: we use the brackets "(" and ")" for a C-fact or conversation state, "<" and ">" for a P-fact, and "[" and "]" for a C-act or a P-act. As an example, [rq] denotes the act of requesting and (rq) denotes the fact of being requested.

The basic transaction process is represented by the green path. As discussed in Sect. 8.2.1, the performer of a C-act raises three *validity claims* towards the addressee: the claim to rightness, the claim to sincerity, and the claim to truth. All three of them must be accepted by the addressee in order to proceed successfully. If so, the executor will respond by a promise. This is indicated in Fig. 8.8 by the green path from (rq) via [pm] to (pm). If the validity claims are not satisfied, the executor will decline the request, which brings the transaction process in the state declined. This is indicated in Fig. 8.8 by the yellow path from (rq) via [dc] to (dc).

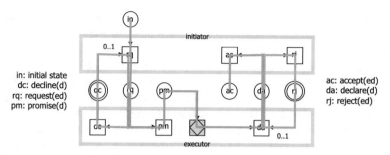

Fig. 8.8   The standard transaction pattern

The state (dc) is a *discussion* state, indicated by a double disk, because ending up there is most likely not what the initiator had in mind. Therefore, he/she now challenges the executor to explain why one or more validity claims could not be accepted, and the initiator has the opportunity to refute the objections of the executor, as well as to discuss possible changes in the properties of the product. In the café example, the waiter could have declined the request for a cup of coffee, because the coffee machine is broken (claim to truth), or because the closing time has passed (claim to rightness), or because the client repeatedly has revoked her request for no good reasons (claim to sincerity). The result of the discussion in the state (dc) can be that the client stands by her request or that she performs an adapted request, like ordering tea instead of coffee, or waiting for the coffee machine to be fixed (in which case the delivery time of the coffee changes). This is indicated in Fig. 8.8 by the yellow path from (dc) via [rq] to (rq). The executor can then perform the promise of the adapted request, thus following the green path from (rq) via [pm] to (pm). Note that performing a new request is optional, as indicated by the cardinality range 0. . .1. The initiator can also do nothing instead, which means that the process remains in the state (dc).

Let us assume that the process has reached the state declared. The initiator may then accept the declared product, by which the transaction ends successfully. This is indicated in Fig. 8.8 by the green path from (da) via [ac] to (ac). But the initiator may also reject the declare, which brings the transaction process in the state rejected. This is indicated in Fig. 8.8 by the yellow path from (da) via [rj] to (rj), which is also a discussion state. The initiator now has the opportunity to explain why he/she could not accept one or more validity claims, and the executor gets the opportunity to convince the initiator that the declared product is what was promised. In the café example, the client could have rejected the declaration (of a cup of coffee) by the waiter because she thinks that the coffee is not fresh or not warm enough (claim to truth), or because an unknown person brings the coffee (claim to rightness), or because she has waited for a long time for the coffee after having reminded the waiter several times (claim to sincerity). During the discussion in the state (rj), the two may come to agree, for example, on a lower price for the client. If so, the executor performs an adapted declare. This is indicated in Fig. 8.8 by the yellow path from (rj) via [da] to (da). From there, the initiator can perform the acceptance, following the green path up to (ac). Note that a renewed declaration is optional, as indicated by the cardinality range 0...1. The executor can also do nothing. Then the process remains in the state (rj).

So, a transaction process can end up successfully in the final state (ac), but it can also get stuck in one of the discussion states (dc) or (rj). The pattern in Fig. 8.8 offers no options to escape from these deadlock situations. In Sects. 8.2.6.3–8.2.6.7, reversiogenic conversations (R-conversations) are presented, which allow one to revert the main process to some previous state. Two of them, namely the revocation of the request and the revocation of the declaration, can be used to get out of the deadlock situations mentioned. Let us therefore add the corresponding revocation patterns to the standard pattern, as is done in Fig. 8.9. Through the revocation pattern in the top left corner, the initiator can 'undo' her/his request and revert the main process to the state (in), as if nothing has happened, provided that the condition (rq+) is satisfied. Through the pattern in the bottom right corner of Fig. 8.9, the executor can 'undo' the declare act and revert the main process to the state (pm), provided that the condition (da+) is satisfied.

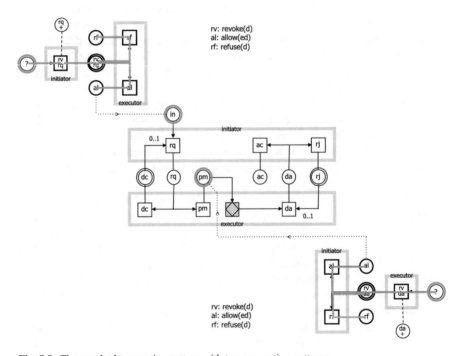

Fig. 8.9 The standard transaction pattern with two revocation patterns

Let us use the café example again to illustrate the revocations. If the discussion between the client and the waiter in the state (dc) does not lead to performing an adapted request, followed by a promise, the client has the option to start an R-conversation, in which she strives to turn the state in the main process back to the initial state (in), and thus to 'undo' her request. She does so by performing [rv-rq], which brings the R-conversation in the discussion state (rv-rq), indicated in Fig. 8.9 by the blue path from (?) via [rv-rq] to (rv-rq). Note that the state (?) is identical to (dc) now. If the waiter allows the revoke, he performs [al[rv-rq]], which leads to the state (al[rv-rq]), indicated by the blue path from (rv-rq) via [al] to (rv-rq). The reversion link from (al) to (in) expresses that the state of the main process will immediately be reverted to the initial state (in). The social meaning of this reversion is that both actors are discharged from all commitments in the main process. But, if the waiter refuses the revocation, so if he performs [rf[rv-rq]], by which the state (rf [rv-rq]) is reached, indicated in Fig. 8.9 by the yellow path from (rv-rq) via [rf] to (rf), the main process remains in the state (dc). The social meaning of this situation is that the waiter does not seem to strive to consensus, which is a fundamental assumption in Habermas' theory [4]. In order to get out of this deadlock, the two parties may leave the *discussion layer* of the conversation and enter the *discourse layer* [13]. At this layer, people investigate, challenge, and discuss the values and norms that they, explicitly or implicitly, apply in their social interaction. Such a discourse may eventually, and hopefully, lead to an allowance of the [rv-rq] by the executor.

Likewise, the executor may revoke her/his declaration, in order to escape from a deadlock situation in the state (rj). If successful, the main process will be reverted to the state (pm), from which the executor can redo the P-act, followed by the declaration of the new product. In case of failure, the process remains in the state (rj). Then the only possible way out of the discussion state is to leave the discussion layer of the conversation and enter the discourse layer, hoping to reach consensus.

8.2.6.3 The Complete Transaction Pattern

In addition to the revocations of the request and the declare act, as discussed above, the other two basic C-acts, namely the promise and the acceptance, can also be revoked. Moreover, all four R-conversations can be started at any point in time, that is, regardless of the current state in the main transaction process. In other words, both the initiator and the executor can revoke any basic step they have taken, from any state in the main transaction process. They may also revoke a step several times, in the same transaction. Figure 8.10 exhibits the *complete transaction pattern*, in which these extensions are included. All four R-conversation patterns are expressed in a similar pattern. In this pattern, the boxes and disks are bold-lined, in order to indicate that these conversations are at a *meta level* with regard to the main process, in which they aim to revert the current state to a previous one.

Revoking a step means that one wants to undo a step that one has performed intentionally earlier, because one has changed one's mind. If a step is taken by mistake, it can be *cancelled* (as long as the addressee has not responded). In this way, both participants can correct mistakes. An R-conversation can be initiated in response to any state in any process. Therefore, its initial state is shown in Fig. 8.10 as a C-fact named "?". In addition, the R-conversations have a conditional link (cf. Table 8.1) from a state in the main process to the revoke act, meaning that performing the revoke is only possible if the main process has reached this state. For the act [rv-rq], the condition is (rq+), meaning that the state of the main process must be (rq) or further.

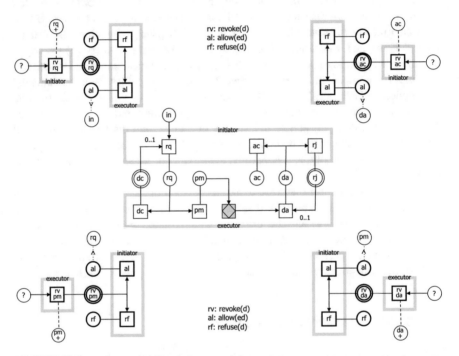

Fig. 8.10 The complete transaction pattern

Likewise, the condition for performing [rv-pm] is (pm+), for performing [rv-da], it is (da+), and for performing [rv-ac], it is (ac). If an R-conversation is successful, the state of the main process will be reverted to (in) for a revoke of the request, to (rq) for a revoke of the promise, to (pm) for a revoke of the declare, and to (da) for a revoke of the accept, as indicated in Fig. 8.10. If an R-conversation is unsuccessful, the state of the main process remains unchanged.

Concluding, every transaction process is some path (possibly including iterations) through the complete transaction pattern, starting from the state (in) and ending up either successfully in the state (ac) or unsuccessfully in the state (in) or in one of the deadlock situations, (dc) and (rj). Although theoretically every step in a transaction process should be revocable, the four R-conversations in Fig. 8.10 seem to be sufficient in practice. Revocations have a legal counterpart in the Civil Codes of many nations. In these Civil Codes, a (business) commitment cannot be made undone by one party without the explicit allowance by the other party. This legal requirement is fully accommodated by the revocation patterns as presented above. Therefore, the discussed complete transaction pattern is considered to be *universal*.

Let us take a closer look now at the four R-conversations. In order to let the discussions be as general as possible, we will start all of them from the state (ac) in the main process, that is, when the transaction has ended successfully.

8.2.6.4 The Revocation of an Acceptance

Figure 8.11 exhibits the process of revoking an accept act. It starts with performing the act [rv-ac] by the initiator, resulting in the discussion state (rv-ac), indicated in the figure by the blue path from (?) via [rv-ac] to (rv-ac). The dashed line from (ac) to [rv-ac] represents the conditional link. It means that the revocation can only be performed if the main process has reached the state (ac), which is the case. The state (rv-ac) is considered a discussion state, which means that the two actors have to sit together in order to discuss the proposed reversion of the main process.

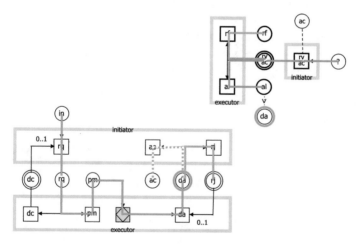

Fig. 8.11 The process of revoking an accept act

The executor may allow the revoke, indicated by the continued blue path to (al) or refuse it (the yellow path to (rf)). If he/she allows, the main process will return to the state (da), as indicated by the green-white path in the standard pattern, and by the green circle around (da). From there, the initiator is able to perform the reject, indicated by the yellow path from (da) via [rj] to (rj). As an example in the café, the client may have accepted the delivered cup of coffee, but later on discovers that the coffee is not as warm as it should be. She then may call the waiter again and tell him that she doesn't want this coffee. This act counts as revoking the accept act. If the waiter allows the revocation, the client can subsequently reject the declaration, by which the main process ends up in (rj). If the waiter refuses the revocation, the state of the main process remains unchanged, namely (ac).

8.2.6.5   The Revocation of a Declaration

The executor of a transaction may at any point in time want to undo the declare act. Logically, this entails that he/she wants to redo the P-act and subsequently perform a new declare act. Revoking the declare act is a common response by the executor of a transaction in case the initiator has rejected the declare act, and the executor agrees, during the discussion in the state (rj), on the reason for the reject. As an example in the café, after the client has rejected the acceptance because the coffee was cold, the waiter may want to redo the P-act and the subsequent declare act, that is, he wants to bring a new, warm cup of coffee.

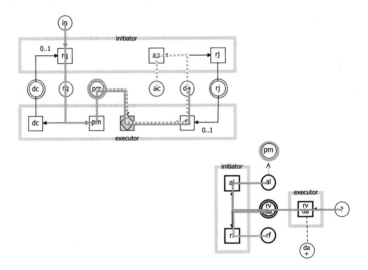

Fig. 8.12 The process of revoking a declare act

The pattern for revoking the declare act is exhibited in Fig. 8.12. It starts with performing the act [rv-da] by the executor, resulting in the state (rv-da), indicated by the blue path from (?) to (rv-da). The conditional link from (da+) to [rv-da] represents the condition that the revocation can only be performed if the state in the main process is at least (da). Thus, it can be performed from any state after, and including (da). This condition is met. The state (rv-da) is considered a discussion state, which means that the two actors have to sit together in order to discuss the proposed turning back of the main transaction process. The initiator may allow the revoke (continued blue path to (al)) or refuse it (the yellow path to (rf)). If he/she allows, the state of the main process will be reverted to (pm), as indicated by the green-white path in the standard pattern, and by the green circle around (pm). From there, the executor is able to redo the P-act, followed by a new declare act, as indicated by the blue line. If the initiator refuses the revocation, the state of the main process remains unchanged. In Fig. 8.12, this is the state (ac).

8.2.6.6 The Revocation of a Promise

The executor of a transaction may at some point in time want to undo the promise act. This will normally happen if he/she discovers that he/she cannot comply with the promise anymore. As an example in the café, the waiter may have promised the client a cup of coffee, and then discovers that the coffee machine is broken. By revoking the promise and the subsequent allowance by the initiator, they can end up in the state declined, in which they can discuss for example other drinks, like a cup of tea.

The revocation pattern of a promise is exhibited in Fig. 8.13. It starts with the revoke promise [rv-pm] by the executor, resulting in the state (rv-pm), indicated by the blue path from (?) via [rv-pm] to (rv-pm). The conditional link from (pm+) to [rv-pm] represents the condition that the revocation can only be performed if the state in the main process is (pm) or further. This condition is met. The being revoked is a discussion state, which means that the two actors have to sit together in order to discuss the proposed reverting of the main transaction process. The initiator may allow the revoke (continued blue path to (al)) or refuse it (the yellow path to (rf)). If he/she allows, the state of the main process will be reverted to (rq), as indicated by the green-white path in the standard pattern, and by the green circle around (rq). From there, the executor can perform the act [dc], and discuss changes to the proposition so that he/she will be able to promise it, as indicated by the yellow path. If the initiator refuses the revocation, the state of the main process, which is (ac), remains unchanged.

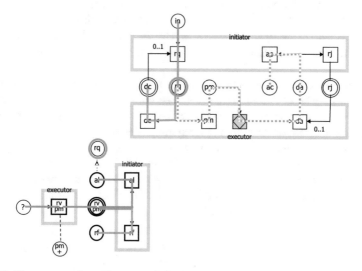

Fig. 8.13 The process of revoking a promise act

A common example of the revocation of a promise from the state (ac) is the situation where a client has paid for a purchase, but the purchase transaction has successfully been 'rolled back'. The state (?) in Fig. 8.13 represents the initial state of the purchase transaction. In order to get her/his money back, the client then has to revoke the promise (to pay). After the allowance by the other party, the payment transaction is reverted to the state (rq), including the 'undoing' of the P-act. From the state (rq), the client then declines the original request (the yellow path in Fig. 8.13). In the state (dc), the two participants can discuss a new amount to pay, or the initiator can revoke the request, by which (after allowance by the client) the payment transaction is completely rolled back to the initial state.

8.2.6.7   The Revocation of a Request

Lastly, the initiator of a transaction may at some point in time want to undo the request act. As an example in the café, the client may have asked for a cup of coffee, but then gets an urgent telephone call because of which she has to leave immediately. Or, after a while she changes her mind and wants a cup of tea instead of coffee.

The revocation pattern is exhibited in Fig. 8.14. It starts with the revoke request [rv-rq] by the initiator, resulting in the state (rv-rq), indicated by the blue path from (?) via [rv-rq] to (rv-rq). The conditional link from (rq+) to [rv-rq] represents the condition that the revocation can only be performed if the state of the main process is (rq) or further. This condition is met. The state (rv-rq) is a discussion state, which means that the two actors have to sit together in order to discuss the proposed turning back of the main transaction process. The executor may allow the revoke, indicated by the continued blue path to (al) or refuse it (the yellow path to (rf)). If he/she allows, the state of the main process will be reverted to (in), as indicated by the green-white path in the standard pattern, and by the green circle around (in). If he/she refuses, the state of the main process remains what it is. In Fig. 8.14, this is the state (ac).

So, a revoke request can even be performed from the state (ac), as shown in the figure, that is, when the transaction has been completed successfully. A common example is that one has bought something from a shop and returns it, for example, because one sees no need for having it anymore. The being revoked is a discussion state, which means that the two actors have to sit together in order to discuss the proposed reversion of the main transaction process. The executor may allow the revoke (continued blue path) or refuse it (yellow path). The main process will then be reverted to the state (in), and both parties are freed of all obligations. In other words, the transaction is completely 'rolled back'.

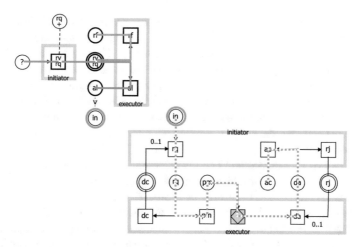

Fig. 8.14 The process of revoking a request act

For (business) transactions like acquiring goods, there is mostly a favour in return. Normally, this is the payment for the purchased goods or the rendered service. Note that paying is a separate transaction. It is commonly enclosed in the purchase transaction as discussed in Chap. 10, but it is a separate transaction. Rolling back the purchase transaction then implies rolling back the payment transaction.

As becomes evident from the discussion of the complete transaction pattern above, the path of every single transaction through this pattern may comprise an arbitrary number of loops. But there are some definite landmarks. Both the order phase and the result phase have a clear successful completion. The order phase of a transaction is completed successfully if the (latest) promised product is equal to the (latest) requested one. Likewise, the result phase of a transaction is completed successfully if the (latest) accepted product is equal to the (latest) declared one. If this is the case, the product starts to exist at the event time of the acceptance.

However, it is always possible to 'break open' a successfully completed transaction by revoking one of the basic steps. The permanent option to (try to) return to a previous state in the transaction process, long after the transaction is completed, may seem irrelevant, but has an important practical relevance. All warranty clauses in sales contracts are actually openings to revoking one of the basic transaction steps. Understanding the settling of warranty claims and of returned goods as simple revocations in an existing transaction, instead of distinct processes, is crucial. It is an illustrative example of the reduction of complexity that Enterprise Ontology claims to offer (cf. Chap. 3).

8.2.6.8 The Operating Principle of Organisations

Every (dynamic) system has some internal mechanism that makes it 'tick' [14]. For inanimate systems, this mechanism is usually called the operating principle.

Regarding animate systems, one often speaks of the vital force [15]. But, although the subjects in organisations (and other social systems) are animate systems, the organisations themselves are considered inanimate. Therefore, we speak of the operating principle of organisations, in much the same way as we speak of the operating principle of cars, aircrafts, etc. By performing coordination acts, subjects enter into and comply with commitments towards each other regarding the product to be brought about. *Commitments* are the social agencies through which people cooperate. In other words, subjects comply with commitments because they feel the social/cultural obligation to do so. We consider this 'mechanism' to be the *operating principle* of every organisation. The underlying premise, as already articulated in Habermas' Theory of Communicative Action [4], is that the actors in a transaction strive to reach consensus. This is only possible if the actors *trust* each other, and this trust is verified explicitly when the claim to sincerity is assessed (cf. Fig. 8.2). Mutual trust is the fundament of every instance of human cooperation. With reference to Habermas' Theory of Communicative Action, we must add that the cooperation takes place in a context in which the participants are free and autonomous, and in which they strive for consensus. All situations of dependence or abuse of force are excluded. In Habermas' theory, these situations are categorised as instrumental or strategic [16, 17]. Fortunately, it rarely happens in contemporary enterprises. Unfortunately, it is the case sometimes.

8.2.7   The Notion of Transactor

In all exhibited transaction patterns above, there is a clear separation between the acts that the initiator of a transaction can perform and the acts that fall within the responsibility area of the executor. In Figs. 8.7, 8.8, 8.9, 8.10, 8.11, 8.12, 8.13, and 8.14, these areas are indicated by light-grey coloured, bold-lined rectangles. We have also emphasised the importance of precisely formulating the independent P-fact of a transaction, such that it is unique in time and space (cf. Sect. 8.2.2.1). An example is "[membership] is started", where [membership] is a variable that can be instantiated, for example, to membership 387. We will take such expressions as denoting a *product kind*, while being aware that it is only the expression of its independent P-fact type (cf. Sect. 8.2.2.2).

Corresponding with the notion of product kind, we will use the notion of *transaction kind* as an attribute of every transaction (cf. Chap. 6). There is a one-to-one relationship between transaction kinds and product kinds. A proper naming of the transaction kind, in which instances products of the kind <[membership] is started> are brought about, would be "membership starting". Next, we introduce the notion of *actor role*, defined as the authority to be the executor in transactions of some transaction kind. This authority can be assigned to subjects, as will be elaborated in Sect. 8.3.3. As a consequence of the definition of actor role, every transaction kind has exactly one actor role as its executor role, and vice versa. An actor role may have an initiator role in several transaction kinds, however, or in none.

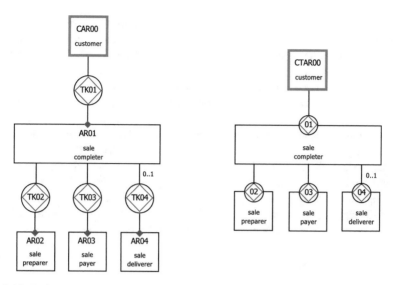

Fig. 8.15 Business process tree structure in the Pizzeria

Figure 8.15 exhibits the graphical notation of these relationships in DEMOSL-4.[7] The shape of a transaction kind is a diamond (the symbol of production) in a circle or disk (the symbol of coordination), and the shape of an actor role is a square or rectangle, commonly called a box. Transaction kinds are connected to actor roles by initiator links (represented by a line between their shapes) and by executor links (represented by a line between their shapes and by a small diamond at the junction of the line and the actor role shape). These links constitute the *interaction structure*, which is one of the three coordination structures in organisations (cf. Chap. 10). The cardinality range 0...1 in Fig. 8.15 indicates that transactions TK04 are optional.

The example organisation shown in Fig. 8.15 is the case Pizzeria (cf. Chap. 14). The red colour of the diamonds indicates that the transaction kinds and actor roles belong to the O-organisation of the Pizzeria (cf. Chap. 11). As said, the combination of a subject and an assigned actor role is called actor. Only actors can participate in transactions. A subject may fill several actor roles and an actor role may be assigned to several subjects, both sequentially and simultaneously. As examples in the café situation, the waiter (subject plus actor role) can at the same time be cashier (same subject, different actor role), and there may be several waiters in the café (one actor role, assigned to several subjects). Next, an actor role can be assigned to a collectivity of subjects, which means that these subjects can fill the role only together. Examples are the board of directors of a company and the general assembly of an association.

---

[7]DEMOSL stands for DEMO Specification Language. It is the formal definition of the ways in which DEMO models can be expressed (diagrams and formal text). The official reference document on DEMOSL can be found on www.ee-institute.org.

The left side of Fig. 8.15 shows that actors in the composite actor role CAR00 are initiator in transactions TK01, and that actors AR01 are executor in these transactions.[8] At the same time, they are initiator of transactions TK02, TK03, and TK04, of which actors AR02, AR03, and AR04 are the executors, respectively.

Because of the one-to-one relationship between a transaction kind and its executor role, it makes sense to combine them in one shape, called *transactor role*, as shown in Fig. 8.15 (right side). The exhibited tree structure represents the same organisation as the one on the left side. When using the transactor role shape, one can just number the transactor roles, without using prefixes (like the "TK" and the "AR"). Transactor roles are the basic *building blocks* of organisations. Through the bringing about of a particular product, a transactor is also said to provide a particular *service* to the initiating transactor (cf. Chap. 7; [18]). The links between the transactor roles in Fig. 8.15 (right side) are *initiator links*. So, like in the tree structure on the left side, actors AR01 are initiator in transactions TK02, TK03, and TK04.

Table 8.2 Transactor Product Table

transaction kind	product kind	executor role
TK01 sale completing	PK01 [sale] is completed	AR01 sale completer
TK02 sale preparing	PK02 [sale] is prepared	AR02 sale preparer
TK03 sale paying	PK03 [sale] is paid	AR03 sale payer
TK04 sale delivering	PK04 [sale] is delivered	AR04 sale deliverer

Table 8.2 represents the so-called Transactor Product Table of the Pizzeria. The process of completing a client order (conceived as a sale by the Pizzeria) starts with the request of a transaction of the kind 'sale completing' by a subject who fills actor role 'customer' (CAR00) to someone who fills actor role 'sale completer' (AR01). During the carrying out of this transaction, three other transactions are initiated: one of the kind 'sale preparing', one of the kind 'sale paying', and one of the kind 'sale delivering'. As clarified in Chap. 10, all three must be carried out before the transaction of the kind 'sale completing' can be finished. In other words, every product of the kind '[sale] is completed' implies three other products: one of the kind '[sale] is prepared', one of the kind '[sale] is paid', and one of the kind '[sale] is delivered'. In the formulation of these product kinds, [sale] denotes the variable that has to be instantiated to get individual products, like 'sale 1618'. In the formulation of these product kinds, [sale] denotes the variable that has to be instantiated to get individual products, like 'sale 1618'.

Figure 8.16 depicts what happens if a specific transaction of the kind TK01 (sale completing) is executed. The initiating subject is Linda. By force of the operative Civil Code, she is authorised to fill the unknown transactor role within the composite transactor role CTAR00 that has an initiator link with TK01, thus to be a customer of

---

[8]We will write 'actors ARn' as a shorthand for 'actors filling actor role ARn', 'transactions TKn' as a shorthand for 'transactions of the kind TKn', and 'products PKn' as a shorthand for 'products of the kind PKn'.

the Pizzeria. As an actor in this role she has the potential to initiate transactions TK01. This is expressed on the left side of the figure by the 'initiator part' of the transaction shape on the edge of the actor role shape. Mia is authorised by the Pizzeria to fill actor role AR01 (cf. Chap. 14), so she has the potential to provide the service of executing transactions TK01 (sale completing) to Linda. Her potential is expressed in Fig. 8.16 by the 'executor part' of the transaction shape on the edge of the actor role shape. As soon as Linda performs a request, a specific transaction, let's say T5189, is created. This is exhibited on the right side of the figure. In filling actor role AR01, Mia can initiate transactions TK02 (sale preparing), TK03 (sale paying), and TK04 (sale delivering). The executors in transactions of these kinds are respectively Mario, Linda, and Edward. As soon as Mia effectuates her authorities, the transactions T5190, T5191, and T5192 are created, as shown on the right side of Fig. 8.16. As elaborated in Chap. 14, Edward is not only the executor of T5192, but he has also a delegated authority in transactions T5189, T5190, and T5191, which is the reason why he is also a filler of actor role AR01.

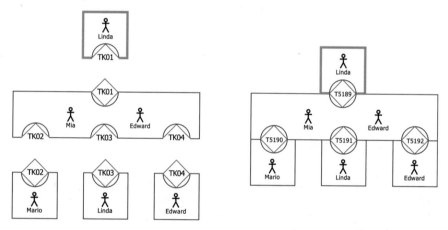

Fig. 8.16 Instantiation of the coordination structure diagram of the Pizzeria

As soon as the transactions T5190, T5191, and T5192 are successfully completed, T5189 can be completed. Figure 8.16 does not show from which state in T5189 the other transactions are initiated by Mia, and which states in transactions T5190, T5191, and T5192 Mia (or Edward) has to wait for. In order to exhibit these details, one needs to produce the Process Model of the Pizzeria (cf. Chap. 14).

8.3   Elaborations

8.3.1   Time Aspects of Transactions

As discussed in Sect. 8.2, the process of a transaction is a sequence of C-events, starting with the request (in response to the initial state) and ending with either the acceptance (in case of success) or a reversion to the initial state (in case of failure), or being stuck in an eternal deadlock or impasse, as discussed in Sect. 8.2.6.2. Let us have a closer look now at the time aspects of C-facts and P-facts, in order to acquire a deeper understanding of the transaction concept.

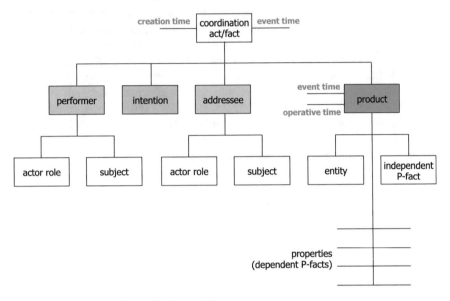

Fig. 8.17 Time aspects of coordination acts/facts

The structure of a C-act/fact that was presented in Fig. 8.4 is reproduced in Fig. 8.17, but without the specific example, and including the time aspects that are common to all C-acts/facts. The first one is the point in time at which the C-act is performed, and thus at which the C-fact is created. This is the *creation time* of the C-fact. The second time aspect of C-facts is their *event time*. By default, the event time is equal to the creation time. In technical systems, the difference between creation time and event time is used to synchronise processes (cf. Chap. 9). In organisations, the event time may be used as the (intended) *settlement time*. By this is meant the point in time at which the performer of a C-act wants the addressee to have settled the created C-event. Although often, like in the café example, the settlement time is asap (as soon as possible), it may be set at a specific point in time, thereby introducing a specific time delay. The addition of the adjective "intended" expresses that it is not an imperative, since actors always act autonomously. So, they may settle the C-event before or at the intended point in time, but they may also do it later. If no specific settlement time is set, the performer of the act expects the addressee to respond within a reasonable amount of time after the creation time. For example, if the client in the café asks the waiter for a cup of coffee, she assumes that the waiter responds to her request more or less instantly, not after an hour.

Regarding P-acts/facts, we distinguish between the event time and the operative time. Because the creation time of a product is basically unknown, we disregard it. This holds specifically for independent P-facts. The dependent facts that are related to them may be created in advance, as is illustrated by the Create Use Tables in Chap. 12. However, the event time of dependent P-facts is always equal to the event time of the corresponding independent P-fact (or the product). The *event time* of a product is by definition equal to the event time of the accept fact in the transaction in which it is brought about. If the acceptance is performed tacitly, it is considered to be equal to the event time of the declare fact. In addition, products have an *operative time*. By this is meant the time period[9] during which the product is operative or valid. Like it holds for any other attribute, the value of the operative time may change during the transaction process, but the accepted value is the definite one. Consequently, a product is operative or valid during its (accepted) operative time. During this period, the product, consisting of an independent P-fact and a number of dependent P-facts (cf. Fig. 8.17), is effective.

Mostly, as in the café example, the initiator wants the product to be operative or effective asap. Therefore, the event time of a product is its default operative time. However, in a business-to-business situation, one often wants to set a specific future time. This holds for all product categories that are discussed in Chap. 10: creation of things, transporting and storing, transferring ownership, and granting right of usufruct. As an example in the category of transferring ownership, you may give a money transfer order to your bank today but have the transfer effectuated on the 28th of this month. Other quite common examples are making appointments with professionals, like medical doctors, for getting diagnosis, advice or treatment (all of them falling in the category of creating things), and making reservations for hotel stays, theatre performances, car rentals, flights, etc. (all of them falling in the category of transferring right of usufruct). So, for example, if you conclude today a reservation for a hotel stay for three nights, starting on the 13th of next month, the event time of the product is today, but the operative time is from the 13th till the 16th. During that period, you have the right to use a room of a particular kind. In order to effectuate this right, you have to check in. This is a separate transaction. By performing the declare act in this transaction, you exert your right to use the room (cf. Chap. 10).

For the product category transferring right of usufruct, it may even make sense to set the operative time in the *past*. This may sound strange at first sight, but it is not unusual. For instance, you subscribe to a monthly magazine, let's say during the month of May, but that the subscription starts in retroaction from January on, so that you (have the right to) receive all issues of the current year. Similar advantages may hold for becoming member of an association in retroaction.

---

[9]As discussed in the DELTA theory (Chap. 9), every point in time is actually a time period, but possibly very small. This holds always for the attribute event time. The operative time, however, may be so large (minutes, hours, days) that one preferably speaks of a time period.

8.3.2   The Operating Cycle of Actors

Every actor is considered to loop constantly through its *operating cycle*, at a pace that is sufficiently frequent to deal with her/his agenda on time. The cycle begins when the actor selects an agendum to be settled. As discussed earlier, he/she may settle it at the intended settlement time (cf. Fig. 8.17), but it may also be earlier or later. Then, the actor fetches the applicable action rule, which is similar to an imperative business rule [19] (note: actors have always access to these action rules). If there is no specific action rule present, he/she is led by the general guidelines (culture, policies) of the enterprise, which may have been expressed in declarative rules [19]. Because the authorisation of the actor is also based on her/his competence (cf. Sect. 8.3.3.4), he/she will also be guided by her/his professionalism. After having assessed the conditions in the action rule, the actor decides how to respond to the selected C-event. Then, the actor performs the act(s) that follow from the decision. The ALPHA theory (Chap. 11) clarifies in more detail how assessing an action rule proceeds (Fig. 8.18).

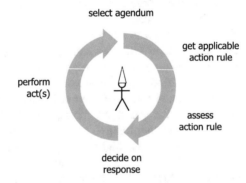

Fig. 8.18 The operating cycle of actors

   As said, action rules are guidelines, because actors are autonomous in deciding how to act. However, they are responsible and possibly also accountable for their acts (cf. Sect. 8.3.3), which might imply acting against the action rules. Several examples have been discussed above. Another illustrative example is presented in Sect. 8.3.3.2.

8.3.3   Human Qualities in Transactions

In Sect. 8.2, the notions of responsibility and authority were briefly touched upon. We have talked about the responsibility areas of the initiator and the executor in a transaction, and we have defined the notion of actor role as the authority to be executor in transactions of a specific transaction kind. Let us have a closer look at these human qualities, and at two other ones, namely accountability and competence.

The definitions we will provide are not (fully) compatible with the popular RACI framework[10], due to the fact that the RACI framework lacks a solid foundation. In contrast, the notions defined hereafter have a solid foundation in the PSI theory.

8.3.3.1   Authority

The notion of *authority* is defined as the right of a subject to perform particular C-acts in response to particular C-events. Taking the café situation again, the subject who is referred to as waiter, apparently has the authority to be executor in 'café sale' transactions, and the subject who is referred to as client, apparently has the authority to be initiator in these transactions.

There are two ways in which authority can be assigned to subjects: through authorisation and through delegation. *Authorisation* is the common way in which authority is assigned to people in organisations, and it is commonly the authority of the human resource functionaries in an enterprise to authorise employees. In current practice, the unit of authorisation is mostly the functionary type: salesperson, accountant, assistant accountant, secretary, trainee, etc. In the PSI theory, the unit in which authorisation takes place is, more fundamentally and more precisely, the (trans)actor role.

An authorisation may include the right to *delegate* a part of the authority to other subjects. In the PSI theory, this part consists of the transaction steps in the transaction kind(s) for which the delegator is authorised to respond to. The only act that can never be delegated is the P-act.

Delegation may be used to deliberately relieve an actor of tasks, but sometimes it is inevitable, for physical/logistic reasons. The case Pizzeria (cf. Chap. 14) is a good example to illustrate this. Table 8.2 shows the existing transaction kinds and actor roles. The subject who is authorised to fill the actor role 'sale completer' is Mama Mia, the owner of the company. She is executor of transactions 'sale completing' and initiator of transactions 'sale paying'. This implies that she has to perform the accept act in transactions 'sale paying'. However, if the pizzas are delivered at the home address of the customer, she has no other choice than to delegate this process step to the delivery boy, who fills the actor role 'sale deliverer'. In addition, she has to delegate the authority to perform the declare act in transactions 'sale completing' to the delivery boy, because he is the only one who has direct contact with the customer at the customer's home address.

8.3.3.2   Responsibility

The notion of *responsibility* seems to have two meanings, which we will refer to as feeling responsible and being responsible. By nature, most people *feel responsible*

---

[10]See https://www.raci.com

for using the resources offered by our planet in such a way that they will not get exhausted, or for causing irreversible damages to the environment. Similarly, most people feel responsible for behaving properly vis-à-vis fellow human beings. In the context of enterprises, most people feel the social obligation to exert their authority in the best way possible, so by acting professionally, by behaving properly towards other actors, etc. It corresponds with the fundamental 'social' principle in the PSI theory to base one's decisions on one's wisdom and love (cf. Sect. 8.2.3).

In our view, the meaning "*being responsible*" is the institutionalised version of "feeling responsible". If someone has been assigned a particular authority (either by authorisation or by delegation), he or she is considered responsible for exerting this authority in the best possible way. As a consequence, authority and responsibility may be considered as the two sides of the same coin; none of them can exist without the other. In Sect. 8.2.6, we applied this notion already when we spoke of the responsibility areas of the initiator and the executor in carrying out transactions.

A related crucial notion in the PSI theory is *autonomy*, by which is meant that actors may deviate from the existing rules or norms. To illustrate this important point, let us take a purchaser in a manufacturing company as an example. Suppose that he/she gets the advice from the 'intelligent' purchase system to place a purchase order at a specific supplier. Normally, the purchaser would follow the advice, but suppose that he/she has heard the evening before in the local bar that this supplier is going bankrupt soon. Wouldn't it be irresponsible to place the order? And, doesn't he/she have a good story to justify her/his disobeying the rule?

In order to clarify this issue, one often distinguishes in current practice between advisory and compulsory business rules. *Advisory rules* can be disobeyed but *compulsory rules* cannot. In the light of the foregoing discussion, the question is, however, whether this distinction is tenable. Also with respect to compulsory rules, there can always be a situation that requires one to deviate from the rule, in order to act responsibly. After all, human beings are no robots.

8.3.3.3   Accountability

Responsibility seems often to be confused with *accountability*, which we define as the obligation to provide justifications of one's acts, whenever there is a need for it. Because of the basic autonomy that actors have in the PSI theory, they are accountable for all of their acts. So, if a particular subject is authorised to perform certain acts, he/she is responsible and accountable for the way he/she performs the acts, also if the authority is acquired through delegation. This becomes particularly apparent when an actor has violated the applicable business rules (for which there may be very good reasons, as we have seen). The actor will be held accountable for having deviated from the rule or the norm. In such a case, sanctions may be applied, depending on the severity of the deviation.

Related to accountability is the notion of *liability*, which means that an actor may be prosecuted legally on the basis of the applicable Civil Code. With respect to liability, there is an important difference between authorisation and delegation:

delegates may be held accountable for their deeds, but they are never liable. Liable is the actor who has delegated the corresponding part of her/his authority. Therefore, distinguishing between authorisation (often also called mandating) and delegation is an interesting issue in every enterprise. Ultimately, the 'big boss' is always liable.

8.3.3.4 Competence

Although one may assign any authority to any subject, one normally would do so on the basis of her/his competence. By someone's *competence* is understood the totality of knowledge, skills, and experience that the person possesses. Competence is thus a capability. Based on the PSI theory, it can be divided into production competence and coordination competence. Production competence is quite specific; it concerns being able to bring about products of one or more kinds. On the other hand, coordination competence is quite generic; it concerns basically the performing of all coordination acts in the complete transaction pattern. It belongs to what are commonly called communication skills or soft skills.

To exemplify this, let us assume that someone has acquired, for example through education, the (production) competence of a plumber. In order to practise this competence, he/she has to get the corresponding authority from some (institutional) actor, for example, the boss of a plumbing company. Once this is done, he/she is expected to exert the authority in a responsible way, and he/she is accountable for all acts, as discussed in the previous sections. This will first of all apply to the 'real' plumbing work in the buildings of the clients of the company. But it also holds for the corresponding coordination acts. More specifically, the plumber is supposed to behave properly during contacts with the clients.

8.4 Discussions

8.4.1 Striving for Consensus and Culture

As discussed in Sects. 8.2.4 and 8.2.6, the fundamental assumption in Habermas' theory of communicative action, and consequently of the PSI theory, is that the participants in (business) transactions strive for consensus, thus for mutual agreement. In other words, they attempt to make the transactions that they are involved in, successful. This is the core of the notion of communicative action. Habermas recognises, however, that this precondition is not always satisfied. Therefore, he includes and discusses a fourth category of communicative acts, namely the imperativa, where the claim to power is the dominant one. Habermas explicitly presents this category outside the region of 'proper' coordination. This is clarified in [20], which comprises a thorough comparison of Searle's speech act theory [21] and Habermas' theory of communicative action [4], yielding the next outcomes.

Because Searle overlooks the orientation towards mutual agreement, he is incapable of distinguishing power claims from validity claims. He considers communication primarily as an interaction between persons who try to let one another perform actions. A speech act thus succeeds if the course of action aimed at, is taken. In this view, it is impossible to distinguish a situation in which the addressee acts because he/she wants to evade sanctions, from one in which he/she responds to the demand of the performer because he/she accepts the validity of her/his claims in a rational way. Otherwise said, Searle's theory is incapable of distinguishing between empirical and rational coordination of action.

The central point of Habermas' critique, however, is that Searle fails to reveal what really makes a speech act work. The mechanism is that validity claims are criticisable, stemming from the orientation of the participants towards mutual agreement, and giving rise to negotiations about the claims made. It is particularly because of this weakness in Searle's theory that his taxonomy misses several important distinctions. One of these is the distinction between speech acts that are based on power claims and speech acts that are based on validity claims (or speech acts proper).

Whether people in organisations are engaged in communicative acts that succeed because they satisfy validity claims, or in imperative coordination, that is, exerting the power to force others to do things, is largely a matter of culture, as explained in [22]. Culture is defined as the whole of values, norms, convictions, and beliefs (rational or irrational, implicit or explicit) that the members of an organisation (and of societies at large) have learned through social interaction, and apply in their cooperation. Cases about successful enterprise transformation, like the famous NUMMI case [23], show that management behaviour in the form of leadership and culture (meaning, purpose, norms, and values) are the crucial determinants of enterprise success.

8.4.2 Other Approaches to Organisations as Social Systems

In the course of time, several ways of composing conversations into larger units are proposed, of which the workflow loop is probably best known [24]. It also underlies the Action Workflow approach [25]. Among other things, however, it does not recognise the production act as a crucial part of a workflow loop and it lacks the revocation patterns. The concept of workflow loop is therefore not as well-founded and not as universally applicable as the (business) transaction in the PSI theory.

As discussed before, the CIAO paradigm has evolved from the communication-centric view on information systems (cf. Sect. 8.2.1), which was developed between 1996 and 2005 by a group of researchers who called themselves the Language-Action Perspective (LAP). In the May 2006 issue of the Communications of the ACM, the group has presented its final achievements.[11] Next to [26], which is an

---

[11]During the last meeting, in 2005, the group decided to discontinue. Some members continued their research activities under the name "Pragmatic Web".

early sketch of the PSI theory, the issue contains presentations of comparable approaches, like for example the approach called BAT [27].

A well-known approach to systems thinking, both in general and more specifically to organisations and information systems is the Soft Systems Methodology (SSM) by Peter Checkland [28]. The notion that seems to come closest to that of organisation in the PSI theory is the notion of human activity system. It is hard to compare them, however, for many reasons, of which we present the three most important. First, SSM does not distinguish clearly between the function and the construction perspective on systems (cf. Chap. 7). Second, the human beings in SSM are not considered as the core active elements of a system. Third, SSM does not provide a theoretical explanation of the operation or behaviour of an organisation on the basis of the actions of its elements, notably the human beings in the activity system.

Sociotechnical Systems Theory (SST) is an approach to understanding the relationship between technology, individuals, organisations and society at large in the design of workplaces. SST includes the hardware, software, social, psychological, political, policy, and legal systems that comprise the overall organisational system. SST pays particular attention to internal supervision and leadership at the level of the group and refers to it as responsible autonomy [29]. In our view, SST can be very well combined with the PSI theory and its practical bearings through the notion of collective actor role: a team in SST can be modelled as a collective actor role.

8.4.3 The Practical Importance of the PSI Theory

The PSI theory is meant to be, and has also proven to be over many years now, an intellectual instrument in clearing up the massive and seemingly unrelated details that one is faced with when trying to make sense of the observable operations of an organisation, notably of its business processes. Being based on a general understanding of human cooperation, the PSI theory is applicable to every enterprise.

The most powerful innovation that the PSI theory brings to the practice of (re-) designing, (re-) engineering, (re-) implementing, and running enterprises of any kind and size is the understanding that the operation of every organisation is a network of transactions, and that every transaction is some path through the universal complete transaction pattern (CTP). In addition, every transaction is of some transaction kind, determined by the product kind of its result, and by the two actor roles that the subjects who carry out the transaction, fill.

A typical example of how the CTP clarifies everyday problems in doing whatever kind of business is the case Fixit (cf. Chap. 13). It demonstrates that common solutions to the presented organisational problems, like help desks (to deal with customers' complaints regarding business processes) and goods returning procedures (to deal with customers' dissatisfactions with received goods), should not be addressed as separate problem areas, but instead be understood as integral parts of the notion of transaction, namely as dealing with the 'exceptional' states declined and rejected, and with an acceptance, a declaration, a promise, or a request being revoked.

The CTP is also a powerful tool in identifying transaction steps that are apparently performed tacitly, thus for whose presence there is no evidence. Typical examples are the promise and the acceptance. In order to avoid communication costs, people rely from time immemorial on a no-news-is-good-news rule. However, this rule is also a major cause of process malfunctions, because it is doomed to fade into oblivion in the course of time. Note also that tacitly performed steps do not appear in common business process models, since these models only contain what is observable.

The notion of actor role, the unit of authority and responsibility, is an effective help in unravelling the tangles of ineffective and superfluous bureaucratic measures that are a plague to consumers and citizens. Any functionary without (either assigned or delegated) authority is plainly redundant. Their only purpose is to shield the responsible persons and thus to mask their responsibility. Even in simple business processes, like in the café example discussed above, the blurring of responsibilities is annoying. When a client, in interaction with a particular waiter, has successfully carried out the order phase of a transaction to get something to drink or eat, she will not be pleased when somebody else addresses her to carry out the result phase, because it will only complicate a possible discussion in the state rejected, that is, in case she is not satisfied with what is delivered. Unfortunately, this is the order of the day, all over the world. It is the effect of how managers are educated. They are mainly taught that organising is about cutting costs, achieving targets, and improving efficiency. What they fail to learn is a proper understanding of how organisations actually work.

References

1. Mintzberg, H. (1979). *The structuring of organizations: A synthesis of the research. Theory of management policy* (xvi, 512 p.). Englewood Cliffs, NJ: Prentice-Hall.
2. Bunge, M. (1979). *Treatise on basic philosophy ontology II: A world of systems, in treatise on basic philosophy 4.* Dordrecht: Reidel.
3. Austin, J. L. (1962). *How to do things with words.* Cambridge: Harvard University Press.
4. Habermas, J. (1986). *The theory of communicative action.* Cambridge: Polity Press.
5. Stamper, R. K. (1973). *Information in business and administrative systems* (6, 362 p.). London: Batsford.
6. Dietz, J. L. G. (2012). *Red garden gnomes don't exist.* The Netherlands: Sapio Enterprise Engineering. www.sapio.nl
7. Edmondson, W. J. (1981). *Spoken discourse: A model for analysis. Longman linquistics library* (217 p.). London: Longman.
8. Grice, H. P. (1975). Logic and conversation. In P. Cole & J. Morgan (Eds.), *Syntax and semantics. Speech acts* (Vol. 3). New York: Academic.
9. Grice, H. P. (1978). Further notes on logic and conversation. In P. Cole & J. Morgan (Eds.), *Syntax and semantics. Pragmatics* (Vol. 9). New York: Academic.
10. Steuten, A. (1998). *A contribution to the linguistic analysis of business conversations within the language/action perspective.* Delft: Delft University of Technology.
11. Winograd, T., & Flores, F. (1986). *Understanding computers and cognition: A new foundation for design* (xiv, 207 p.). Norwood, NJ: Ablex.

12. Searle, J. R. (1995). *The construction of social reality* (xiii, 241 p.). New York: Free Press.
13. Van Reijswoud, V. E. (1996). *The structure of business communication: Theory, model and application*. Delft: Delft University of Technology.
14. Bunge, M. (1979). *A world of systems. Ontology* (XVI, 314 S). Dordrecht: Reidel.
15. Bergson, H. (1913). *Creative evolution* (XV, 425 S). London: Macmillan.
16. Habermas, J. (1984). *The theory of communicative action* (v). Boston: Beacon.
17. Dietz, J. L. G., & Widdershoven, G. A. M. Speech acts or communicative action? In *Second European Conference on Computer Supported Cooperative Work*. Dordrecht: Kluwer.
18. Terlouw, L. (2011). Modularization and specification of service-oriented systems. In *Computer Science*. Delft Univeisity of Technology.
19. Dietz, J. L. G. (2009). On the nature of business rules. In J. L. G. Dietz, A. Albani, & J. Barjis (Eds.), *Advances in enterprise engineering I*. Berlin: Springer.
20. Dietz, J. L. G., & Widdershoven, G. A. M. (1991). Speech acts or communicative action? In *Second European Conference on Computer Supported Cooperative Work*. Dordrecht: Kluwer.
21. Searle, J. R. (1969). Speech acts: An essay in the philosophy of language (vii, 203 p.). London: Cambridge University Press.
22. Hoogervorst, J. A. P. (2017). *Foundations of enterprise governance and enterprise engineering* (p. 574). Cham: Springer.
23. Shook, J. (2010). How to change a culture: Lessons from NUMMI. *Sloan Management Review, 50*(2), 63–68.
24. Denning, P., & Medina-Mora, R. (1995). Completing the loops. *Interfaces, 25*(3), 15.
25. Medina-Mora, R., Winograd, T., Flores, R., & Flores, F. (1992). The action workflow approach to workflow management technology. In *Conference on Computer-Supported Cooperative Work*. ACM.
26. Dietz, J. L. G. (2006). The deep structure of business processes. *Communications of the ACM, 49*(5), 59–64.
27. Goldkuhl, G. (2006). Action and media in interorganizational interaction. *Communications of the ACM, 49*(5), 53.
28. Checkland, P., & Checkland, P. (1999). *Systems thinking, systems practice: A 30-year retrospective* (2nd ed., A66, xiv, 330 p.). Chichester: Wiley.
29. Sitter, L. U., Hertog, J. F., & Dankbaar, B. (1997). From complex organizations with simple jobs to simple organizations with complex jobs. *Human Relations, 50*(5), 497–536.

Chapter 9
The DELTA Theory: Understanding Discrete Event Systems

Abstract The DELTA theory, also called EE system theory, is a theory about the construction and operation of systems in general. The realm of systems is divided into three regions: organised simplicity, organised complexity, and unorganised complexity. The definition of a (homogeneous) system is presented as a triple $(\mathbb{C}, \mathbb{E}, \mathbb{S})$, where $\mathbb{C}$ (composition) is a set of elements of some category, $\mathbb{E}$ (environment) is a set of elements of the same category as the elements in $\mathbb{C}$, and $\mathbb{S}$ (structure) is a set of interaction bonds among the elements in $\mathbb{C}$ and between them and the elements in $\mathbb{E}$. Examples of categories are: physical, biological, and social. Organisations belong to the category of social systems. Three sorts of conceptual models are distinguished: black boxes, grey boxes, and white boxes. The well-known finite automaton or finite state machine, and the discrete event system are examples of grey boxes. For a thorough discussion of the grey box and the white box, the PRISMA model is introduced. In this meta model, systems are considered to be discrete event automata, operating in a linear time dimension. Its formalised ontological model is particularly suited to study organisations. In the PRISMA grey box, three ways of mutual influencing between (the elements of) systems are distinguished, called activating, restricting, and impeding. The PRISMA white box allows one to conceive organisations as prismanets: networks of processors, channels, and banks. Prismanets are comprehensive formalised systems, open to formal analysis and to implementation in software. They can conveniently be expressed in prismanet diagrams. To illustrate the PRISMA model, two example prismanets are presented: one regards a traffic control system, and the other a car rental organisation. Next, the generic transaction prismanet is discussed. It is the understanding of the complete transaction pattern from the PSI theory in the PRISMA model. Lastly, the quality aspects of PRISMA models are discussed, as well as the importance of the PRISMA model for software engineering.

9.1 Introduction

The theory in this chapter is labeled Δ-theory. The Greek capital letter is pronounced as DELTA, which is an acronym for Discrete Event in Linear Time Automaton. It is a theory about the construction and operation of systems, in particular of discrete

© Springer Nature Switzerland AG 2020

J. L. G. Dietz, J. B. F. Mulder, *Enterprise Ontology*, The Enterprise Engineering Series, https://doi.org/10.1007/978-3-030-38854-6_9

event systems. In Chap. 4, the DELTA theory is classified as an ontological theory, meaning that it is about the nature of things. It serves foremost as a solid foundation for the other theories in this category: the PSI theory (Chap. 8), the ALPHA theory (Chap. 11) and the OMEGA theory (Chap. 10). In addition, the DELTA theory offers three sorts of meta models for studying systems: the black-box model, the grey-box model, and the white-box model.

Section 9.2 (foundations) consists of three subsections. Section 9.2.1 provides an introduction in systems theory and in systems thinking, including the ontological system concept that is adopted in this book. In Sect. 9.2.2, the three basic sorts of conceptual models are presented and discussed. The most primitive one is the black-box model; it doesn't contain any knowledge about the system's construction and the operation. This property makes it only suitable for studying possible function (s) and (external) behaviour. In contrast, the white-box model of a system contains all knowledge about its construction. It serves to study the construction of a system (i.e. the constituting parts and their interactions) and its operation (i.e. the effects of the interaction in the course of time). The grey-box model is a black-box model, but with an internal state. For the class of discrete event systems, a specific (white-box) meta model is presented and discussed in Sect. 9.2.3, called the PRISMA model. It allows one to build comprehensive, coherent, consistent, and concise white-box models, fully abstracted from realisation and implementation. These models are called essential prismanets. Their corresponding grey-box models are fully formalised, and therefore suited for formal analysis and for (discrete event) simulation. The PRISMA white-box and grey-box model is illustrated by a technical system (traffic control) and a social system (a part of a car rental company).

Section 9.3 (elaborations) starts with the presentation and discussion of the generic transaction prismanet, which is the expression of the complete transaction pattern (cf. Chap. 8) in the PRISMA model. Next, the quality aspects of PRISMA models are discussed. The section ends with a discussion of the implications of the PRISMA model for the field of software engineering. Section 9.4 (discussions) contains a comparison of the prismanet and the Petri net.

9.2   Foundations

9.2.1   Systems Thinking

9.2.1.1   Introduction

Systems thinking is an approach to problem solving which goes hence and forth between a global, holistic view on a system, and a detailed, specific view on its constituting parts. It originates from several areas, including General Systems Theory [1], Cybernetics [2], and System Dynamics [3]. Unfortunately, the practice of systems thinking suffers often from a lack of precision, notably regarding the notion of system itself. Instead of precise definitions, many textbooks only provide characterisations, such as "A system is a set of related elements with some purpose", and "The whole is greater than the sum of its parts". Taking the first one, our first comment is that, according to the TAO theory (cf. Chap. 7), systems don't have purposes; only human beings do. The second comment is that proponents of this statement fail to separate the function and the construction perspective on systems. The second assertion (the whole is more than its parts) points to the distinctive property of systems as opposed to aggregates, but it has to be made more precise. In order to be called a *system*, its elements must act upon each other, in such a way that the trajectories, or processes that they cause to happen, are dependent on the mutual influencing of the elements, that is, that they are different from what these processes would have been if the causing elements would not interact. Or, as Bunge puts it, the assertion is a fuzzy version of the insight that ". . . the components of a concrete system are linked, whence the history of the whole differs from the union of the histories of its parts" [4] (Chap. 1). If the relationships between the elements are only passive, the thing is not a system but an *aggregate*. A well-known example of something that is an aggregate, but often called a system, is the Periodic Table of Mendeleev.

Fig. 9.1 Regions of systems with respect to methods of thinking

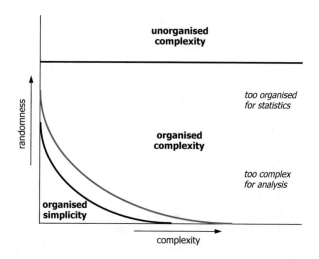

Weinberg [5] divides the realm of systems into three regions: organised simplicity, organised complexity, and unorganised complexity. An adapted version of his figure 1.9 is presented as Fig. 9.1. The region of *organised simplicity* comprises systems that have relatively few elements and mostly a great deal of structure. Systems in this region can generally be studied by (mathematical and logical) *analysis*. Examples are machines and other technical systems. The region of *unorganised complexity* comprises systems that have a very large number of elements with mostly few structural relationships. Because of the high level of randomness, systems in this region can generally be studied by *statistics*. Examples are populations of animals or plants, and vessels of gas molecules. In between these two is the region of *organised complexity*. It comprises systems that are too organised for statistics and too complex to be studied by analytical methods. This region is the core of enterprise engineering (EE): all enterprises belong to it. It is the ambition of the Ciao! Network to shift the border between organised simplicity and organised complexity, as indicated by the magenta curve in Fig. 9.1, and thus to make more systems, in particular enterprises, amenable to analytic study.

9.2.1.2   The Ontological System Concept

As a first step in reducing the complexity of systems, we make a distinction between homogeneous and heterogeneous systems. Every non-trivial system is a heterogeneous system, which means that it is some, possibly complicated, combination of homogeneous systems. For example, a human being is a physical system but also a chemical and a biological one, and as a whole it is also a social individual. In order to address its complexity, Bunge considers a *heterogeneous* system as a layered nesting of homogeneous systems [4]; he suggests studying the composing homogeneous systems first, leaving the study of the complex heterogeneous totality for later. Hereafter, whenever the term "system" is used, a homogeneous system is meant, according to the following definition [4]:

A (homogeneous) *system* can be conceived as a triple $(\mathbb{C}, \mathbb{E}, \mathbb{S})$, where:

$\mathbb{C}$ is a set of elements, all belonging to the same category,

   called the *composition* of the system;

$\mathbb{E}$ is a set of elements of the same category as the elements in $\mathbb{C}$,

   called the *environment* of the system;

$\mathbb{S}$ is a set of influencing bonds among the elements in $\mathbb{C}$ and between them and the elements in $\mathbb{E}$,

   called the *structure* of the system.

Figure 9.2 depicts this definition. The red- and purple-coloured boxes are elements in $\mathbb{C}$, and the green ones are elements in $\mathbb{E}$. The purple-coloured closed curve depicts the *boundary* of the system. It is defined as the subset of $\mathbb{C}$ for whose elements it holds that they are connected by structural links with elements in $\mathbb{E}$, in correspondence with [6]. The elements in $\mathbb{C}$ that are not connected to elements in $\mathbb{E}$ are called *kernel* elements. Hereafter, we will call the triple $(\mathbb{C}, \mathbb{E}, \mathbb{S})$ the *construction* of a system.

There are three important comments to be made about the system definition above. The first one is that a structural link between two elements means that one of them acts upon the other, or that both do, as discussed in [7]. The second one is that every element in $\mathbb{C}$ must act upon or be acted upon by at least one other element in $\mathbb{C}$, so that all elements in $\mathbb{C}$ are directly or indirectly connected. Consequently, isolated elements, or isolated clusters of connected elements, cannot exist; their presence would violate the basic notion of system. The third comment is that the elements in $\mathbb{C}$ and $\mathbb{E}$ are of the same category. Examples of system categories are: physical, chemical, biological, and social. Only systems of the same category can interact, systems of different categories cannot. For example, if you have something in your mind that you want to 'tell' your computer in order to not forget it, it is ultimately your homogeneous physical system (which is a part of your heterogeneous entirety) that interacts with the homogeneous physical system of the heterogeneous computer system, in particular through the physical forces that your fingers exert on the keys of the keyboard. The pressing of a key causes the generation of a train of electrical signals that carry the code of the key that is pressed. This sequence of signals is transmitted to etc. etc.

Fig. 9.2 Depiction of the construction of a system and of a subsystem

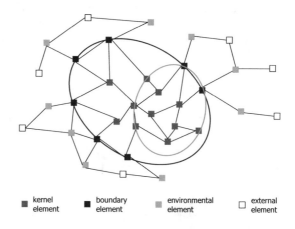

Based on the provided definition of system, the next definition of subsystem is in force [4]: A thing x is a *subsystem* of a system y if and only if x is a system, and if:

$$\mathbb{C}(x) \subseteq \mathbb{C}(y)$$
$$\mathbb{E}(x) \subseteq (\mathbb{C}(y)\backslash(\mathbb{C}(x)) \cup \mathbb{E}(y)$$
$$\mathbb{S}(x) \subseteq \mathbb{S}(y)$$

The blue-coloured closed curve in Fig. 9.2 depicts the boundary of a subsystem of the system whose boundary is depicted by the purple closed curve. As a corollary, every system may have many subsystems, and can be subsystem of many systems. Note that one cannot just view something as a system. Only systems, according to the definition above, can be 'viewed' as a system. All other things can't.

Both its elements and its subsystems are called *components* of a system. Consequently, the composition of a system comprises both its elements, so the members of $\mathbb{C}$, and all subsystems that one likes to distinguish. Therefore, the composition of a system may be said to consist of *elementary* components and *composite* components, keeping in mind that the latter are always built up of elementary components. As a corollary, the structural bonds between two composite components are actually structural bonds between elements in one composite component and elements in the other.

Likewise, the environment of a system comprises both its elements, so the members of $\mathbb{E}$, and all subsystems, built up of these elements, that one considers useful to distinguish. In addition, the structural bonds between composite components in $\mathbb{C}$ and $\mathbb{E}$ are actually structural bonds between elements in $\mathbb{C}$ and elements in $\mathbb{E}$.

9.2.2 Conceptual Models of Concrete Systems

9.2.2.1 Introduction

According to the MU theory (cf. Chap. 6), a conceptual model of a concrete system is a conceptualisation of the system within an appropriate conceptual schema or meta model. The conceptual model is said to be an instance of the conceptual schema. Hereafter, we use the word "model" to refer to a model (instance) as well as to a meta model, following the current (confusing) practice in conceptual modelling.

We will distinguish three sorts of conceptual models: black-box models, grey-box models, and white-box models. They will be discussed in Sects. 9.2.2.2, 9.2.2.3, and 9.2.2.4, respectively. Their distinction is related to the fundamental difference between the function and the construction perspective on things, as explained in the TAO theory (cf. Chap. 7). Figure 9.3 shows the construction perspective on a car (right), and a particular function perspective, namely the driving function (left). Both models are extensively discussed in Chap. 7.

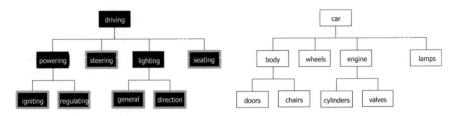

Fig. 9.3 The function and the construction perspective on cars

White-box models are suited for studying the construction and the operation of systems. The white-box model on the right side of Fig. 9.3 is actually only the decomposition of a car in its subsystems, sub-subsystems, etc., disregarding the structure of the system. It resembles a Bill-of-Material (BoM). *Black-box models* are suited for studying the behaviour of systems and their possible function(s). The black-box model on the left side of Fig. 9.3 is the decomposition of the driving function of a car into subfunctions, sub-subfunctions, etc. *Grey-box models* are black-box models with an internal state. Examples will be given in Sect. 9.2.2.3.

With reference to Fig. 9.1, the only thing one can do in the region of unorganised complexity is black-box modelling, and the best one can hope for is to find correlations between (functional) variables. In the region of organised simplicity, one has the option to apply white-box modelling, and thus to discover the causal relationships between system acts and observable effects. Consequently, one can acquire a deeper understanding of a system, not only from the construction perspective, but also from the function perspective.

9.2.2.2   The Black-Box Model

A *black-box* model of a concrete system is a conceptual model of the system that disregards completely the construction and the operation of the system (this explains the name "black box"). Therefore, black-box models are only suited to study the behaviour of systems, expressed in relationships between the functional variables that one chooses to study. Well-known examples of black-box models are economic models. They are commonly expressed in differential equations concerning a number of (economic) variables.

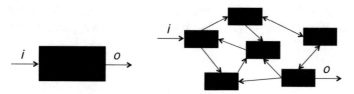

Fig. 9.4 The black-box model (left) and a decomposition (right)

Basically, the knowledge of a concrete system that is contained in a black-box model is the relationship between the input flow i and the output flow o in the course of time (t). In formal notation: $o = B(i, t)$. Both flows are time series of values of (functional) variables. Figure 9.4 (left side) exhibits the common graphical representation of a black-box system. The *behaviour function B* is often not or only partially known, meaning that one only knows that the output flow o at time t is somehow the effect of the input flow i before t. It is always possible to decompose a black-box model into a network of connected black-box models (cf. Chap. 7). A well-known example of such a functional decomposition is the *control model* [8], as applied for example in cybernetics and biology.

Fig. 9.5 Example of an SADT activity diagram

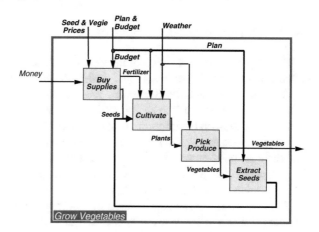

A widely used technique for representing black-box models, including their decomposition, is SADT (Structured Analysis and Design Technique), developed by Douglas T. Ross [9], and included in many structured analysis and design methods. Figure 9.5 shows an example of an SADT activity diagram. It is important to recognise that the diagram represents only a functional understanding of the activity of growing vegetables. There is no hint whatsoever to the construction of a system that is able to exhibit this behaviour. As another example, it is not very difficult to make a functional model of a coffee machine along the lines of Fig. 9.5. In fact, we all have some functional (black-box) model of the systems we daily use, like coffee machines, ATMs, and cars. As is illustrated for cars in Sect. 9.2.2.1 and in Chap. 7, there is no straightforward mapping between functional (black-box) models and constructional (white-box) models, because they are of a fundamentally different nature.

9.2.2.3 The Grey-Box Model

The *grey-box* model is a black-box model with an internal state [4]. Consequently, the behaviour is now determined by three variables: the flow of input items i, the flow of output items o, and the state of the system s, next to time (t). The behaviour function is formally defined as: $o = B(i, s, t)$. Figure 9.6 exhibits the common graphical representation of a grey-box model (left side) and of a possible decomposition (right side).

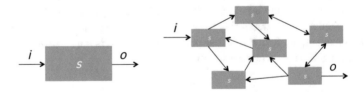

Fig. 9.6 The grey-box model (left) and a decomposition (right)

A well-known specialisation of the grey-box model is the finite automaton (FA), often also called finite state machine (FSM). A *finite automaton* is a mathematical model of a system with discrete inputs and outputs, and with discrete states. By this is meant that the system is at any point in time in some state, and that the state space is finite (or denumerable infinite). State changes or transitions occur on an input from a finite (and commonly small) set of possible inputs. Usually, there is an initial state and there are one or more final or terminal states. FAs are mostly associated with the way in which they are commonly represented, namely the *state transition diagram* (STD), which we will use in Fig. 9.8.

Another well-known specialisation of the grey-box model is the discrete event system (DES). A *discrete event system* is a discrete-state, event-driven conceptual system (cf. Chap. 6). The notion of *discrete-state* is similar to the notion of state in an

FA. By *event-driven* is meant that the system responds to the occurrence of particular input events [10]. The number of distinct events may be denumerable infinite. Many concrete systems, in particular logistic systems, information systems, and organisations, can be conceived as discrete event systems. The notion of discrete event system is often considered to be identical to the notion of grey-box model [4]. This is not true, however, because in a grey-box model one does not require that the input to which the system responds, consists of discrete events. As an example, the variables in economic (grey-box) models are mostly not discrete but continuous.

Typical problems that are studied by means of discrete event models are stochastic systems, like customers in supermarkets and cars at fuel stations. To get deeper insight into the behaviour function, discrete event simulation is often applied [10].

The grey-box model of a discrete event system can mathematically be defined as a tuple $(\mathbf{B}, \mathbf{O}, \mathbf{I}, \mathbf{S})$, where:

B is a partial function, called the *behaviour function*
O is a set of items, called the *output base*
I is a set of items, called the *input base*
S is a set of items, called the *state base*
B is defined as: $\wp\mathbf{I} * \wp\mathbf{S} \rightarrow \wp(\mathbf{O} * \mathbb{D})$

The (mathematical) extension of **B** is a set of rules of the form (I, S, R), where:

I is the current input; $I \subseteq \mathbf{I}$
S is the current state; $S \subseteq \mathbf{S}$
R is the response: a set of pairs (o, d) with $o \in \mathbf{O}$ and $d \in \mathbb{D}$; d is a time delay; its effect is that o becomes existent at the point in time $t = \text{Now} + d$, where Now is the time of executing the rule.

(Note: for an explanation of the mathematical symbols, see Sect. 9.2.3.1.)

Illustration: Traffic Control System
To illustrate the grey-box system, more specifically the FA, we take a traffic control system (TCS) at a simple crossover, as shown on the left side in Fig. 9.7. Suppose that you are asked to produce first a black-box model and then a grey-box model of the TCS. The black-box model that you may arrive at, after having observed the traffic control system for some time, is shown to the right of it. Theoretically, there are nine possible outputs: R1R2, R1G2, R1Y2, G1R2, ~~G1G2~~, ~~G1Y2~~, Y1R2, ~~Y1G2~~, and ~~Y1Y2~~, where R denotes red light, G denotes green light, Y denotes yellow light, 1 denotes Cycle 1, and 2 denotes Cycle 2. Four of them do not occur however, and are therefore struck out above. The five remaining outputs are shown on the right side in Fig. 9.7. The arrows indicate the order in which the outputs occur. The additional knowledge of the behaviour function B, which you can deduce from observing the traffic lights and the traffic, is that the transition R1G2 → R1Y2 is influenced by arriving and/or waiting traffic in Cycle 1 (but you don't know exactly how). Likewise, the transition G1R2 → Y1R2 is influenced by arriving and/or waiting traffic in Cycle 2.

Fig. 9.7 Picture of the TCS
(left) and its black-box
model (right)

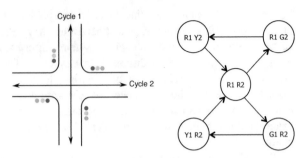

In order to produce a grey-box model, one has to conceive an internal state of the system. With this new meta model in mind, one is able to acquire the next, advanced, knowledge (cf. Fig. 9.8). If the output R1G2 is produced, it will stay for at least a minimum amount of time. Let us call this the (standard) *move time* for Cycle 2, abbreviated to MT2. As long as there is no traffic waiting in Cycle 1, this output is prolonged. However, as soon as the (standard) move time for Cycle 2 has passed, and there is traffic waiting for red light in Cycle 1, the output R1Y2 will be produced. This output appears to hold on for a fixed amount of time, which we will call the *stop time* for Cycle 2 (ST2). After the stop time has elapsed, the light in Cycle 2 becomes red. However, also the light in Cycle 1 remains red for some fixed amount of time. Let us call this amount of time the *clear time* of Cycle 2 (CT2), meaning that it is meant for clearing the crossing from traffic in Cycle 2. The output R1R2 is produced. After the clear time has elapsed, the output G1R2 is produced. And then the whole story is repeated, with the cycles exchanged. In order to cope with these observations, you distinguish the next different states: W1M2, W1P2, W1S2, C1W2, M1W2, P1W2, S1W2, and W1C2, where W stands for "waiting", M for "(standard) moving", P for "prolonged (moving)", S for "stopping", and C for "clearing". The state transitions occur in the order as exhibited in Fig. 9.8. At the top of the figure, the outputs (traffic lights) are shown that correspond with the states of the system.

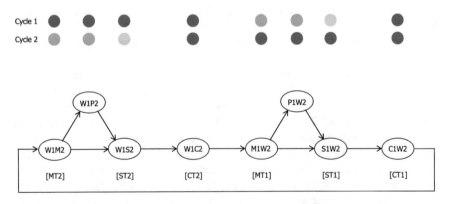

Fig. 9.8 STD of the grey-box model of the TCS

The choice between transiting from W1M2 to W1P2 or to W1S2 depends on the presence of traffic in Cycle 1. If traffic arrives in the state W1M2, then the transition to W1S2 is made, but only after MT2 time units have elapsed since the beginning of the state W1M2. Otherwise the transition to W1P2 is made. As soon as traffic in Cycle 1 arrives in this state, the transition to W1S2 is made immediately. The system remains in this state for ST2 time units. Then, the transition to C1W2 is made, which takes CT2 time units. After this time has elapsed, the transition to M1W2 is made. Similar observations hold for the transitions from M1W2 to P1W2 or S1W2.

9.2.2.4   The White-Box Model

The white-box model of a system is a conceptual model that allows one to study the *construction* of the system, thus the triple $(\mathbb{C}, \mathbb{E}, \mathbb{S})$ as discussed in Sect. 9.2.1.2, as well as its *operation*, that is, the way in which the elements in $\mathbb{C}$ and the elements in $\mathbb{E}$ interact, through the bonds in $\mathbb{S}$. Consequently, one is able to reveal the 'mechanism' that makes it 'tick'. The behaviour that the 'mechanism' causes to occur can be studied with a grey-box (or black-box) model of the system, as we have seen above.

For a proper discussion of the white-box system, we introduce the notion of world. With every white-box model of a concrete system, a *world* is associated, where the acts of the (elements of the) system have their effect. At any point in time, the world of a system is in some state. A *state* is simply defined as a set of facts. A state change is called a *transition*. It consists of the addition and/or removal of one or more facts.

The state of a white-box system differs from the state of a corresponding grey-box system. For a grey-box system, the state concept is an instrument to better understand the behaviour of the system. For a white-box system, the state concept is an instrument to better understand its operation. The relationship between behaviour and operation is that the behaviour of a concrete system (which can be studied by using a black-box or grey-box model) is brought about by the operation of its construction (which can only be studied by using a white-box system).

Next to the state of the world of a system, there is the state of the system itself. By the *state of a system* at a point in time t we understand the particular triple $(\mathbb{C}, \mathbb{E}, \mathbb{S})$ at time t (cf. Sect. 9.2.1.2). In the course of time, the composition or the environment or the structure may change. Within EE, such changes are considered to be the effect of acts by another system, whose world contains facts that represent the elements in $\mathbb{C}$, $\mathbb{E}$, and $\mathbb{S}$. This other system is commonly called the governance system of the system under consideration [11, 12]. In the DELTA theory, we confine ourselves to studying systems in some system state, that is, we assume a fixed construction $(\mathbb{C}, \mathbb{E}, \mathbb{S})$. Proper illustrations of the white-box model will be provided after the PRISMA model is discussed (in the next section).

9.2.3   The PRISMA Model

9.2.3.1   Introduction

In the next subsections, we will present and discuss a meta model for discrete event systems called the PRISMA model, which builds on the SMART model [13]. It comprises a grey-box and a white-box (meta) model. The PRISMA model is suited for studying discrete event systems, both *technical systems*, thus systems in which the elements are non-human, and *social systems*, that is, systems in which the elements are human. An important subclass of social systems is organisations, as discussed in the PSI theory (cf. Chap. 8). Therefore, one may consider the PRISMA model as a (mathematical-logical) formalisation of the PSI theory.

In addition, it appears that many technical systems are actually social systems, only technically implemented. Well-known examples are (automated) enterprise information systems (cf. Chap. 11), but also ATMs, elevator control systems, vending machines, web shops, and traffic control systems. Consequently, these systems can be very well understood and studied within the PRISMA model.

We distinguish three ways in which systems influence each other, called activating, restricting, and impeding. By *activating* is understood that a system creates events to which other systems respond by creating state changes and/or events. When responding to an event, a system takes the current state of its world into account. The state of a system's world can be changed by the system itself, but also by other systems. This passive way of mutual influencing is called *restricting*, since the effect is that a system's response space is restricted (note that a system is not 'aware' of state changes until it is activated—only then will it 'see' the new state). By *impeding* is understood that a system creates events for whose occurrences other systems have to wait before they can continue what they were doing. Because of the three ways of mutual influencing, systems within the PRISMA model are said to communicate asynchronously.

In the remainder of this document, set theory and logic are applied when considered useful. For the convenience of the reader, we list below the symbols that are used, with their meanings.

x	in general, small letters denote elements (of sets)
X	in general, capital letters denote sets
$\in$	membership of a set; $x \in A$ means that x is an element of A
$\notin$	negation of membership; $x \notin A$ means that x is not an element of A
$\varnothing$	empty set; $A = \varnothing$ means that for all x: $x \notin A$
$\subseteq$	subset; $A \subseteq B$ means that A is a subset of B; for all x: $x \in A \Rightarrow x \in B$
$\cup$	union; $A \cup B$ is the set of elements x for which holds: $x \in A$ or $x \in B$
$\cap$	intersection; $A \cap B$ is the set of x for which holds: $x \in A$ and $x \in B$
\	set difference; A\B is the set of elements x for which holds: $x \in A$ and $x \notin B$
Δ	symmetric set difference; $A \Delta B = (A \setminus B) \cup (B \setminus A)$
$*$	Cartesian product of a set; A$*$B is the set of tuples (x, y) with $x \in A$ and $y \in B$

$\wp$	powerset; $\wp A$ is the set of all subsets of A
$f\colon A \to B$	(mathematical) function f with domain A and range B.
$\mathbf{x}$	variable to denote a type (of acts or facts);
	a type is a unary predicate in logic, for example, person or dog.
$\mathbf{X}$	variable to denote the class that is the extension[1] of the type $\mathbf{x}$
$\underline{\mathbf{X}}$	variable to denote the union of the extensions of all $\mathbf{x} \in \mathbf{X}$
$\wedge$	logical conjunction (also denoted by **and**)
$\vee$	logical (inclusive) disjunction (also denoted by **or**)
$\underline{ct}(f)$	creation time of fact f
$\underline{et}(f)$	effectuation or event time of fact f

For a proper discussion of the PRISMA model, a discrete linear time dimension is adopted, which means that we consider the time axis to be divided into distinct *time units* of arbitrary but equal length.[2] Every such time unit on the time axis is called a *point in time*. Events only occur on (or in) these points in time, and they take place instantaneously, that is, within the duration of the point in time. An *event* is defined as the becoming existent (or ceasing to exist) of a fact at some point in time. As mentioned above, facts have a *creation time* (<u>ct</u>) and an effectuation or *event time* (<u>et</u>).

The notion of a *discrete linear time scale*, for any time unit, can be formalised in the following way:

$\mathbb{R}$	the (ordered) set of real numbers
$\mathbb{N}$	the (ordered) set of natural numbers
$\mathbb{T}\colon \mathbb{N} \to \mathbb{R}$	the (ordered) set of discrete points in time; we will use t_n as a shorthand for $\mathbb{T}(n)$; the time difference between any t_{n+1} and t_n is the same; it is called the time unit (tu)
Now	the current point in time; Now $\in \mathbb{T}$, so Now is always some t_n
$\mathbb{D}$	the set of (positive) time durations; for every $d \in \mathbb{D}$, it holds that $d = k * tu$ with $k \in \mathbb{N}$

From now on, we mean by a point in time t an element $t_n \in \mathbb{T}$.

9.2.3.2 The PRISMA Grey-Box Model

The distinction that we have made in the PSI theory (cf. Chap. 8) between the things that constitute its core, thus its production (or P-) acts/facts, and the things that serve to make them happen, thus the coordination (or C-) acts/facts, appear to have a general applicability. Therefore, the same distinction is made in the PRISMA model. The only difference is that they are now not connected in larger structures of conversations or transactions.

---

[1]The extension of a type is the set of objects that conform to the type (cf. Chap. 5).

[2]The duration or length of the applied time unit will depend on the application domain. Therefore, it may vary from nanoseconds or microseconds (for technical systems) to hours or days (for enterprises).

The PRISMA grey-box model can best be considered as an extended 'normal' grey-box model, as discussed in Sect. 9.2.2.3. The extension is that it comprises *process dependency* next to *state dependency*. It means that the response to an input item does not only depend on the current state, but may also depend on the occurrences of (past or future) input or output events.

A *prisma* can formally be defined as a tuple (**P, R, I, S, M, A**), where:

P	is a partial function, called the *performance function*
R	is a set of C-fact types, called the *reaction base*
I	is a set of C-fact types, called the *impediment base*
S	is a set of P-fact types, called the *state base*
M	is a set of P-fact types, called the *mutation base*
A	is a set of C-fact types, called the *action base*

P is defined as: $\wp((\underline{\mathbf{A}} \cup \underline{\mathbf{I}})) * \mathbb{T}) * \wp(\underline{\mathbf{S}} * \mathbb{T}) \rightarrow \wp(\underline{\mathbf{M}} * \mathbb{D}) * \wp(\underline{\mathbf{R}} * \mathbb{D})$

At every point in time, a prisma disposes of a set of *agenda*.[3] An agendum is a pair (*c*, *t*), in which *c* is a C-fact and *t* is its event time. The C-fact belongs to the extension[4] of the *action base* or the *impediment base*. The set of agenda *c* with et (*c*) = *t*, is called the *trigger* at time *t* (note: commonly the trigger will be a singleton set). Considering impediments as potential agenda allows us to deal with impediments in a simple way: we consider them to be agenda, similar to real agenda, that is, to elements in the extension of the action base. If the settling of a real agendum, that is, a pair (*c*, *t*), in which *c* is an element of **A**, has to wait for an impediment, the prisma will skip this agendum and settle the impediment, once it has occurred. The having occurred of the real agendum then becomes a state condition for settling the impediment event.

A prisma responds to a trigger instantaneously, so within the duration of the point in time *t*. As the effect of settling a trigger, a finite set of P-events is created, called the *mutation*, and a finite set of C-events, called the *reaction*. The set of P-fact types, whose instances can belong to a mutation, is called its *mutation base*. The set of C-fact types, whose instances can belong to a reaction, is called the *reaction base*.

The response to a trigger is generally dependent on the state of the P-world, which is a set of P-facts. The set of P-fact types, instances of which can belong to a state, is called the *state base* of the prisma.

The (mathematical) extension of **P** is a set of *performance rules* of the form (*A*, *S*, *M*, *R*) where:

A	is the *agenda*; $A \subseteq (\underline{\mathbf{A}} \cup \underline{\mathbf{I}}) * \mathbb{T}$
	the *trigger* at time *t* is $\{f \in A: \underline{\mathrm{et}}(f) = t\}$
S	is the *state*; $S = \{(f, t) \text{ with } f \in \underline{\mathbf{S}} \text{ and } t \in \mathbb{T}\}$
M	is the *mutation*: a set of pairs (*m*, *d*) with $m \in \underline{\mathbf{M}}$ and $d \in \mathbb{D}$
R	is the *reaction*: a set of pairs (*r*, *d*) with $r \in \underline{\mathbf{R}}$ and $d \in \mathbb{D}$

---

[3]The word 'agenda' is the plural form of the Latin word 'agendum', meaning 'thing to be done'. So, agenda are 'to do' items.

[4]The extension of a type is the set of objects that conform to the type (cf. Chap. 5).

The delay d in a pair (m, d) or (r, d) is an occurrence delay; it means that the P-fact m or the C-fact r becomes effective at the event time $t = \text{Now} + d$, where Now is the point in time at which the performance rule is executed. As said, $\{f \in A: \underline{et}(f) = t\}$ is commonly a singleton set, thus a set containing only one element. Note that the state S at time t comprises existing facts (with $\underline{et}(f) \leq t$) and future facts (with $\underline{et}(f) > t$).

On the basis of their formal definition, the mutual influencing of prismas as discussed in Sect. 9.2.3.1, can be described more precisely as follows.

A prisma1 *activates* a prisma2 if $\underline{\mathbf{R}}_1 \cap \mathbf{A}_2 \neq \varnothing$ (so if $\underline{\mathbf{R}}_1$ and $\mathbf{A}_2$ overlap). If this is the case, then all C-events in a reaction of prisma1, of which the C-fact belongs to this intersection, are instantly added to the agenda of prisma2. If prisma1 and prisma2 are identical, we speak of *self-activation*. Through self-activation, periodic activities can be modelled conveniently. If this is the case, the period equals the settlement delay.

A prisma1 *restricts* a prisma2 if $\underline{\mathbf{M}}_1 \cap \mathbf{S}_2 \neq \varnothing$ (so if $\underline{\mathbf{M}}_1$ and $\mathbf{S}_2$ overlap). If this is the case, then every P-event in a mutation of prisma1 of which the P-fact belongs to this intersection, affects the state of prisma2, at its event time. The way in which the state of prisma2 is affected by a mutation is defined as follows. If *S1* is the state of prisma2 before applying a mutation *M* (at its event time), and *S2* is the state afterwards, then $S2 = S1 \, \Delta \, M$. (Δ is the symmetric set difference, cf. Sect. 9.2.3.1). If prisma1 and prisma2 are identical, we speak of *self-restricting*. This is the classical concept of the state of a world (where only the system itself can make changes).

A prisma1 *impedes* a prisma2 if $\underline{\mathbf{R}}_1 \cap \mathbf{I}_2 \neq \varnothing$ (so if $\underline{\mathbf{R}}_1$ and $\mathbf{I}_2$ overlap). If this is the case, then all C-events in a reaction of prisma1 of which the C-fact belongs to this intersection, are instantly added to the impediments of prisma2. Consequently, prisma2 may have to wait with responding to an action until one or more impediments have occurred. Self-impeding is ignored, because it doesn't seem to make sense.

If the action base **A** of a prisma consists of one fact type, the prisma is called *elementary*. The action bases of elementary prismas are disjoint. A *composite* prisma is a collection of elementary prismas. The specification of a composite prisma in terms of its constituting elementary prismas is simple: every component of the tuple (**P, R, I, S, M, A**) of a composite prisma is equal to the set-theoretic union of the corresponding components of the constituting elementary prismas.

Illustration: Traffic Control System

Let us take the Traffic Control System from Sect. 9.2.2.3 to exemplify the PRISMA grey-box model. From the STD in Fig. 9.8 and the accompanying explanation, we deduce the next components of the tuple (**P, R, I, S, M, A**):

$$\mathbf{A} = \{\text{let\_pass(Cycle)}\}$$
$$\mathbf{I} = \varnothing$$
$$\mathbf{S} = \{\text{phase(Cycle), move\_time(Cycle), stop\_time(Cycle), clear\_time(Cycle)}\}$$
$$\mathbf{R} = \varnothing$$
$$\mathbf{M} = \{\text{phase(Cycle)}\}$$

In this specification, the variable Cycle has the value cycle1 or cycle2. The value of phase(Cycle) is W1M2 or W1P2 or W1S2, etc. let_pass(Cycle) is the external trigger to which the prisma responds (cf. Fig. 9.8). A phase change takes place if the mutation of the prisma contains a new P-fact of the type phase(Cycle). Next to the current phase of each of the cycles, the state also includes the current values of the parameters (move_time, stop_time, and clear_time) for each of the cycles.

Table 9.1 exhibits the performance function **P** that can be deduced from the grey-box model in Sect. 9.2.2.3. The *agenda* column contains the triggers to settle. The *state* column contains logical propositions concerning the state of the production world, and the *mutation* column contains the state changes to be effectuated.

The table presents the situation that traffic is arriving in cycle1. A similar table applies for the situation that traffic is arriving in cycle2, by exchanging cycle1 and cycle2. Occurrence delays are specified by a value between "[" and "]". If no occurrence delay is specified, the default value is assumed (which is 1 time unit). The abbreviations have the following meanings: MT (Cycle) stands for the standard move time in Cycle, ST (Cycle) for the stop time in Cycle, and CT (Cycle) for the clear time in Cycle. The meaning of the delay D is explained later on.

Table 9.1 The performance function of the TCS

agenda	state	mutation
let_pass(cycle1)	phase(cycle1) = waiting phase(cycle2) = moving **or** prolonged_moving) **and** **there is no future event** phase(cycle2) = stopping)	phase(cycle2) := stopping [D] phase(cycle2) := waiting [D + ST(cycle2)] phase(cycle1) := moving [D + CT(cycle2)]

The trigger to be settled is let_pass(cycle1). If the current state (at time t) comprises the facts <phase(cycle1) = waiting> and <phase(cycle2) = moving or prolonged_moving>, both with an event time in the past or present ($\underline{et}(f) \leq t$), and there is not already a future stopping for cycle2 (with $\underline{et}(f) > t$, caused by another car), then the rule is executed; otherwise nothing happens. The response of executing the rule is the specified mutation. It says that the phase of cycle2 will become 'stopping' after D time units. The delay D is defined as follows: D = max (0, (MT (cycle2) − (Now − ETM)), where ETM = $\underline{et}$(phase(cycle2) = moving), the point in time at which the phase of cycle2 started to be moving. The mathematical expression is clarified in Fig. 9.9. If the current time is Now1, then the delay is the time represented by the blue line. If the current time is Now2, then the delay is zero.

In addition, the mutation contains the state changes phase(cycle2) := waiting [D + ST(cycle2)] and phase(cycle1) := moving [D + CT(cycle2)]. These occurrence delays are also clarified by Fig. 9.9.

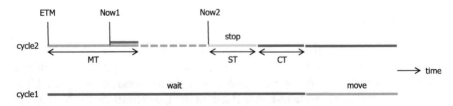

Fig. 9.9 Explanation of the time delay D

9.2.3.3 The PRISMA White-Box Model

The influencing relationships among a collection of prismas can be made more comprehensible if the collection is conceived as a prismanet. A *prismanet* is a white-box system, wherein the construction $(\mathbb{C}, \mathbb{E}, \mathbb{S})$ comprises three kinds of components: processors, banks, and channels. The components in the composition $\mathbb{C}$ and in the environment $\mathbb{E}$ are processors. The structure $\mathbb{S}$ consists of banks and channels and of the various links that connect them with the processors in $\mathbb{C}$ and in $\mathbb{E}$.

Processors are the 'motors' of prismas. The motor of an elementary prisma is an *elementary processor*, and the motor of a composite prisma is a *composite processor*. The operation of a processor is fully determined by the performance function $\mathbf{P}$ of the corresponding prisma (i.e. the prisma of which it is the motor).

Channels are used to transmit and keep C-events. A channel Cn is determined by its *transmission base* TB, which is the set of C-fact types whose instances it can keep and transmit. The set of C-events in a channel at time t, is called the *contents* of the channel at time t. The channel metaphor runs as follows. Suppose processor Pi creates at time t the pair (c, d), where c is a C-fact and d is the occurrence delay. The metaphor then is that Pi 'puts' c in a channel at time $\underline{ct}(c)$ (the creation time of c) and that c 'arrives' at a processor P_j at the event time $\underline{et}(c) = t + d$. On arrival, it is settled instantaneously. Every transmitted C-event remains in the channel, because it may be an impediment for one or more (other) prismas. If the transmission base consists of one C-fact type, the channel is called a *single channel*. The transmission bases of the single channels in a prismanet are disjoint. A collection of single channels is called a *multiple* channel. The transmission base of a multiple channel is the union of the transmission bases of the composing single channels.

Banks are used to keep P-events. A bank Bk is determined by its *contents base* CB, which is the set of P-fact types whose instances it can contain. The set of P-events in the bank at some time is called the *contents* of the bank at that time. If the contents base consists of one P-fact type, the bank is called a *single bank*. The contents bases of the single banks in a prismanet are disjoint. A collection of single banks is called a *multiple* bank. The contents base of a multiple bank is the union of the contents bases of the composing single banks.

A channel C_n is called an *action channel* of processor P_j if the transmission base of the channel is a subset of the action base of the prisma of which processor P_j is the motor, so if $TB(C_n) \subseteq \mathbf{A}_j$. The settling of an action may be impeded by one or more C-events or P-events. It means that the processor has to wait until these events have occurred. A Processor P_j is impeded by C-events in a channel C_n if the transmission base of the channel is a subset of the impediment base of the prisma of which processor P_j is the motor, so if $TB(C_n) \subseteq \mathbf{I}_j$. If so, the channel C_n is called an *impediment channel* of processor P_j.

As the result of settling an action, processor P_i creates a (possibly empty) set of P-events, called the mutation. They are put in every bank B_k of which the contents base is a subset of the mutation base of the prisma whose motor is processor P_i, so of which $CB(B_k) \subseteq \mathbf{M}_i$. If so, bank B_k is called a *mutation bank* of processor P_i.

In addition, processor P_i creates a (possibly empty) set of C-events, called the reaction. They are put in every channel C_n of which the transmission base is a subset of the response base of the prisma whose motor is processor P_i, so of which TB $(C_n) \subseteq \mathbf{R}_i$. Consequently, channel C_n is called a *reaction channel* of processor P_i.

When dealing with a C-event, a processor P_j may take P-events that are kept in one or more banks into account. This holds for bank B_k if its contents base is a subset of the state base of the prisma of which processor P_j is the motor, so if CB $(B_k) \subseteq \mathbf{S}_j$. Consequently, bank B_k is called an *inspection bank* of processor P_j.

The *operation* of a processor must be understood as follows. Processors constantly loop through their *operating cycle*, of which the cycle time is equal to or less than the time unit (cf. Sect. 9.2.3.1). In every cycle, the processor 'sees' the current trigger (if any) and brings about a response by evaluating the corresponding performance rule.

9.2.3.4 The Prismanet Diagram

The understanding of a prismanet may be enhanced by expressing it in a *prismanet diagram* (cf. Fig. 9.10).

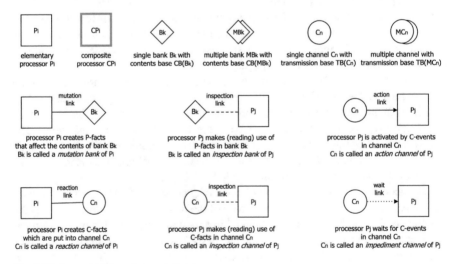

Fig. 9.10 Legend of the prismanet diagram

Processors, banks, and channels are respectively represented by boxes, diamonds, and disks, as shown in the top part of the figure.

Channels are connected to processors by four kinds of links: reaction links, action links, inspection links, and wait links. A *reaction link* connects a processor with one of its reaction channels. An *action link* connects a processor with one of its action channels. An *inspection link* connects a processor with one of its inspection channels. A *wait link* connects a processor with one of its impediment channels. Banks are connected to processors by two kinds of links: mutation links and inspection links. A *mutation link* connects a processor with one of its mutation banks. An *inspection link* connects a processor with one of its inspection banks.

From a prismanet diagram, one can directly deduce that for an elementary prisma with processor P_j as its motor:

- The action base $\mathbf{A}_j$ is the union of the transmission bases of its action channels.
- The impediment base $\mathbf{I}_j$ is the union of the transmission bases of its impediment channels.
- The state base $\mathbf{S}_j$ is the union of the content bases of its inspection banks and the transmission bases of its inspection channels.
- The reaction base $\mathbf{R}_j$ is the union of the transmission bases of its reaction channels.
- The mutation base $\mathbf{M}_j$ is the union of the content bases of its mutation banks.

Illustration: Traffic Control System

To illustrate the PRISMA white-box model for the traffic control system (TCS), Fig. 9.11 exhibits its prismanet diagram. The light-grey coloured frame represents the Scope of Interest (SoI). It means that one is exclusively interested in the operation of the processors within the SoI. They are therefore called internal processors, whereas the composite processors CP_1 (traffic participant) and CP_2 (traffic control manager) are called environmental processors. To show this, their boxes are coloured light-grey. Channel C_1 is a reaction channel of CP_1 and an action channel of P_1. Bank B_1 is a mutation bank and an inspection bank of P_1, as well as an inspection bank of CP_1. The banks B_2, B_3, and B_4 are mutation banks of CP_2 and inspection banks of P_1.

Fig. 9.11 Prismanet diagram of the TCS

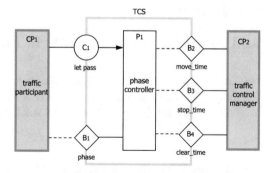

The traffic participants take note of the phase of each cycle (by looking at the traffic lights) and generate let_pass commands (by passing a sensor in the road). There is a traffic control manager, who is able to change the control parameters of each of the cycles: move time, stop time, and clear time (through updates of their values).

Processor P_1 responds to let_pass commands by bringing about the appropriate phase changes, according to the performance function that is exhibited in Table 9.1.

From the diagram in Fig. 9.11, together with the discussion in Sect. 9.2.3.2 and the explanation in Fig. 9.9, one can easily verify the following specifications of the action base, the impediment base, the state base, the mutation base, and the reaction base of the prisma with motor P_1:

$$A_1 \quad = TB(C_1) = \{let\_pass(Cycle)\}$$
$$I_1 \quad = \varnothing$$
$$S_1 \quad = CB(B_1) \cup CB(B_2) \cup CB(B_3) \cup CB(B_4) = \{phase(Cycle),$$
$$\qquad move\_time(Cycle), stop\_time(Cycle), clear\_time(Cycle)\}$$
$$M_1 \quad = CB(B_1) = \{phase(Cycle)\}$$
$$R_1 \quad = \varnothing$$

In the specification of the performance function of the TCS (cf. Table 9.1), P-facts are referred to by a particular value of the variable Cycle, for example, as in "phase (cycle1) = moving". In the specification of a contents base, only the variable is mentioned, as in $CB(B_1) = \{phase(Cycle)\}$. To be complete, one should also add the value class for each variable. As an example, these are the value classes for the variables that are used in the case TCS:

phase(Cycle)	: {moving, prolonged_moving, stopping, waiting}
move_time(Cycle)	: $\mathbb{D}$
stop_time(Cycle)	: $\mathbb{D}$
clear_time(Cycle)	: $\mathbb{D}$

9.3 Elaborations

9.3.1 Specification of the PRISMA Model of Rent-A-Car

In this section, we use a slightly adapted version of the case Rent-A-Car (cf. Chap. 15) for illustrating the application of the PRISMA model to organisations. We will first discuss the white-box model and then the grey-box model.

9.3.1.1 The White-Box Model of Rent-A-Car

Figure 9.12 exhibits the prismanet diagram of a part of the Rent-A-Car organisation. It regards the settling of requests for concluding a rental contract, according to the PSI theory (cf. Chap. 8) and the generic transaction prismanet in Fig. 9.13.

The system consists of six elementary processors, eight single channels, three multiple banks, and one single bank. The interface with the environment consists of the action channel C_1, the reaction channel C_2, the impediment channel C_3, the mutation bank B_1, as well as the multiple inspection banks MB_1, MB_2, and MB_3.

The processors outside the SoI, so the environmental processors, have been omitted, for the sake of simplicity. For the same reason, the revocation options are left out (cf. Chap. 8). Moreover, the multiple banks MB_1, MB_2, and MB_3 are connected through inspection links with the border of the SoI. This is a convenient way to express that they are inspection banks of all internal processors. Their content bases are respectively denoted as $CB(MB_1)$, $CB(MB_2)$, and $CB(MB_3)$.

From the diagram in Fig. 9.12, one can easily deduce the specification of the components **A**, **I**, **S**, **R**, and **M**, of the corresponding internal prismas. As an example, we provide the specifications of prisma1 (with processor P1 as its motor):

$$\begin{aligned}
\mathbf{A}_1 \quad & = TB(C_1) = \{request\ ([rental]\ \textbf{is}\ completed)\} \\
\mathbf{I}_1 \quad & = \varnothing \\
\mathbf{S}_1 \quad & \subseteq CB(MB_1) \cup CB(MB_2) \cup CB(MB_3) \\
\mathbf{M}_1 \quad & = \varnothing \\
\mathbf{R}_1 \quad & = TB(C_2) \cup TB(C_4) \cup TB(C_6) = \{request\ ([rental]\ \textbf{is}\ paid), \\
& \quad decline\ ([rental]\ \textbf{is}\ completed),\ promise\ ([rental]\ \textbf{is}\ completed)\}
\end{aligned}$$

Note. Without knowing precisely the performance function $\mathbf{P}_1$, we cannot be more specific about $\mathbf{S}_1$ than only stating that it is a subset of some other set. The reader is challenged to formulate $\mathbf{S}_1$ precisely after the specification of $\mathbf{P}_1$ is presented in Sect. 9.3.1.2.

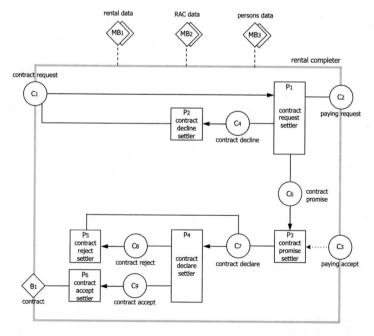

Fig. 9.12 Prismanet diagram of a part of the Rent-A-Car organisation

9.3.1.2   The Grey-Box Model of Rent-A-Car

On the basis of Fig. 9.12, we specify in Table 9.2 the performance function of prisma1 (with motor P1). As the specification language, we use a table form and a 'structured English' like language, which resembles the one that is applied in [14].

Table 9.2   Specification of prisma1 in the Rent-A-Car organisation

action	<u>request</u> ([rental] **is** completed)
	with starting_day[rental] : DAY
	ending_day[rental] : DAY
	renter[rental] : PERSON
	driver[rental] : PERSON
	car_group[rental] : CAR_GROUP
	pick-up_location[rental] : BRANCH
	drop-off_location[rental] : BRANCH
impediments	Ø
state	starting_day[rental] ∈ rental_horizon (year(starting_day [rental])) **and**
	ending_day[rental] ∈ rental_horizon(year (starting_day [rental])) **and**
	ending_day[rental] ≥ starting_day[rental] **and**
	duration[rental] ≤ max_rental_duration(year (starting_day [rental])) **and**
	#{cars **in** car_group[rental] **on** starting_day[rental] } > 0
mutation	Ø
reaction	<u>promise</u> ([rental] **is** completed)
	<u>request</u> ([rental] **is** paid)
action	<u>request</u> ([rental] **is** completed)
	with starting_day[rental] : DAY
	ending_day[rental] : DAY
	renter[rental] : PERSON
	driver[rental] : PERSON
	car_group[rental] : CAR_GROUP
	pick-up_location[rental] : BRANCH
	drop-off_location[rental] : BRANCH
impediments	Ø
state	starting_day[rental] ∉ rental_horizon (year(starting_day [rental])) **or**
	ending_day[rental] ∉ rental_horizon(year (starting_day [rental])) **or**
	ending_day[rental] < starting_day[rental] **or**
	duration[rental] > max_rental_duration(year (starting_day [rental])) **or**
	#{cars **in** car_group[rental] **on** starting_day[rental]} ≤ 0
mutation	Ø
reaction	<u>decline</u> ([rental] **is** completed)

The first action rule in Table 9.2 is performed when there is a request for completing a rental contract (first line of the action part). Note that, according to the PSI theory (cf. Chap. 8), there may be more than one request regarding the same rental in the course of time, but then it is a different event. Commonly, it will also have different properties (specified in the 'with' clause). There is no impediment for performing the first action rule, which is indicated by the symbol "Ø" in the impediments part. If the state condition is satisfied, so if its logical evaluation yields the value true, then the payment of the rental will be requested. The mutation is empty.

The state condition in the second action rule is the negation of the one in the first rule, whereas the action part and the impediments part are the same as in the first rule. If the state condition is satisfied, so if its logical evaluation yields the value true, then the concluding of the rental will be declined. Otherwise, nothing happens. The mutation is empty. Note that always either the first or the second action rule is executed successfully.

9.3.2 The Generic Transaction Prismanet

According to the PSI theory (cf. Chap. 8), C-acts/facts and P-acts/facts occur in universal patterns, called transactions. In Fig. 9.13, the complete transaction pattern from the PSI theory is reproduced. In order to express it in the PRISMA model, we need the prismanet whose corresponding diagram is shown in Fig. 9.14. It is called the *generic transaction prismanet*.

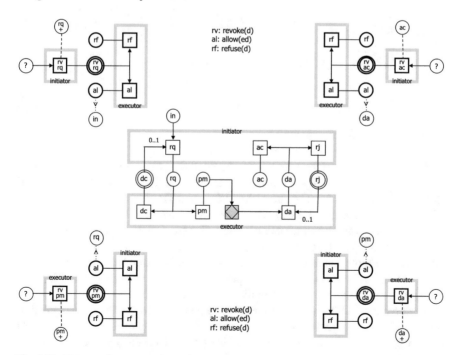

Fig. 9.13 The complete transaction pattern

There are nine processors that take care of the acts in the responsibility areas of the initiator in Fig. 9.13. They are labeled "Pin$_1$" through "Pin$_9$". Next, there are ten processors that take care of the acts in the responsibility areas of the executor in Fig. 9.13. They are labeled "Pex$_1$" through "Pex$_{10}$". The transmission bases of the channels are indicated by the abbreviated names of the intentions of the C-facts that they may transmit and contain: rq for request, pm for promise, etc. The four multiple channels, indicated with a "?", are (unknown) channels through which C-events are transmitted that trigger the connected performer to revoke [rv] one of the four basic C-facts in the transaction process: (rq), (pm), (st), and (ac).

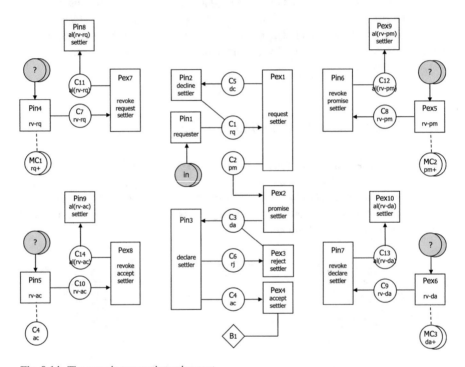

Fig. 9.14 The generic transaction prismanet

The specifications of the transmission bases of the three multiple channels MC$_1$, MC$_2$, and MC$_3$ are as follows: TB(MC$_1$) is the union of TB(C$_1$) through TB(C$_8$); TB (MC$_2$) is the union of TB(C$_2$), TB(C$_3$), TB(C$_4$), and TB(C$_6$); TB(MC$_3$) is the union of TB(C$_3$), TB(C$_4$), and TB(C$_6$). They correspond with the revocation conditions that hold for the complete transaction pattern. The contents base of bank B$_1$ consists of the independent P-fact type in the product kind, and all of its dependent P-fact types. The multiple channel, labeled "in", is included to complete the prismanet. Its transmission base consists of C-fact types to whose instances processor Pin$_1$ may respond by creating a request and putting it in channel C$_1$.

The operation of the generic transaction prismanet can briefly be explained as follows. If Pin$_1$ is triggered by an item in channel "in", it puts a request in channel C$_1$. In response, Pex$_1$ creates either a promise, put in channel C$_2$, or a decline, put in channel C_5. In response to the decline, Pin_2 may create a renewed request, put in C_1. If this is not a feasible option, processor Pin_4 may create a [rv (rq)], in response to the decline (which is also contained in channel "?"), and put it in channel C_7.

Processor Pex_2 responds to a promise by creating a state fact, which is put in channel C_3. Processor Pin_3 responds to it by either an accept, put in channel C_4, or a reject, put in channel C_6. In the latter case, processor Pex_3 may respond by creating a renewed state, put in C_3. If this is not a feasible option, processor Pex_6 may create a [rv (st)], in response to the reject (which is also contained in channel "?"), and put it in channel C_9. In response to an accept in C_4, processor Pex_4 adds the corresponding independent P-fact and its dependent P-facts to the contents of bank B_1. This reflects the postulation in the PSI theory (cf. Chap. 8) that the product of a transaction is created at the moment that the accept fact is created. At the same time, this arrangement reflects the postulation that the executor of a transaction is the owner of the product, and thus the primary source to inquire about it. For each of the four revocation patterns, it holds that there is an unknown trigger in the channel that is indicated by "?", and that there is a wait event in channel MC_1, MC_2, MC_3, or C_4. The wait condition is that the status of the main process (the middle part of Fig. 9.13) must respectively be "requested or further", "promised or further", "stated or further", and "accepted". If the revoke of a request, promise, state, or accept is allowed, a corresponding C-fact will be put in respectively channel C_{11}, C_{12}, C_{13}, and C_{14}, which are action channels of respectively Pin_8, Pex_9, Pex_{10}, and Pin_9. These processors revert the main process to the statuses as indicated by the complete transaction pattern in Fig. 9.13. Note that if a refuse act is performed, the main process stays in the status it was in. No processors respond to refuse events. As said, ending up in a refuse state means that nothing has changed in the main process.

If the single processors Pin_1 through Pin_9 are combined in the composite processor CPin, and if the processors Pex_1 through Pex_{10} are combined in the composite processor CPex, one gets the prismanet as shown in Fig. 9.15 (left side). In this diagram, the channel names are left out, only the intention of the C-facts is mentioned. Moreover, the shapes of CPin and CPex are sinuated, in order to indicate that they are only shown partly, that is they may contain more components, because they are normally also connected to other prismanets (cf. Chap. 11). The use of composite processors, like the ones shown in Fig. 9.15, may be helpful in modelling discrete event systems, notably 'technical' systems that are actually technically implemented social systems. Examples of such systems are machines of all kinds, like vending machines, and control systems of all kinds, like warehouse control systems.

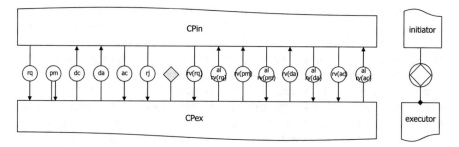

Fig. 9.15 Composite processors as organisational building blocks

On the right side of Fig. 9.15, the 'compression' of the left side part into the organisational building block (cf. Chap. 8) is shown. All channels (C_1 through C_{14}) and the bank B_1 are put together, resulting in the transaction-kind shape, which is a diamond (representing production) inside a disk (representing coordination). The small black diamond on the edge of the lower actor role shape indicates that it has the executor role in this transaction kind. Note that the executor role also comprises the processors, channels, and banks, that it needs as initiator in (other) transactions (if any), and that the initiator role also comprises the processors, channels, and banks, that it needs as executor of its 'own' transaction kind, as well as the processors, channels, and banks, that it needs as initiator in other transactions (if any). As already explained for the left part of Fig. 9.15, this is indicated by their sinuated shapes.

9.3.3   The C4E Quality Aspects

In this section, we will discuss the quality aspects of white-box systems in the PRISMA model, that is, of prismanets. To start with, we have shown that a prismanet is an *ontological* model of a discrete event system, that is, a white-box model that is fully abstracted from the (technological) implementation of the modelled system.

The first quality aspect of a prismanet is that it is *comprehensive*, which means that it is ontologically complete, of course provided that one has all knowledge of the concrete system. Consequently, it allows not only for studying the statics of the modelled system (its construction), but also its dynamics (its operation). Next, a prismanet is *coherent*, by virtue of the ontological system concept (cf. Sect. 9.2.1.2). It means that the model elements are connected in such a way that there are no 'loose' parts.

In addition, the presented prismanets are abstracted from realisation (cf. Chap. 11), so from all informational issues (like remembering, sharing, and deriving facts) and from all documental issues (like storing and retrieving documents or data). Note that derived facts just 'exist' in the ontological sense once they are defined. For example, someone's age at a particular day exists if the day exists and the person's birthday exists. The additional abstraction from realisation makes prismanets *concise*, by which we mean that their size is very small compared to current meta models, which mostly do not abstract from realisation and implementation. Moreover, prismanets are *consistent*, that is, they do not contain logical contradictions, as ensured by the PRISMA model.

The four quality aspects (coherent, consistent, comprehensive, and concise) constitute the requirements for calling the prismanet of a system its *essential model* (within the PRISMA model). By using the definite article "the", we want to conjecture that there is only one essential model for a given system. As a mnemonic, the quality requirements, together with their corollary of capturing the essence of a system, are collectively named "C4E". The added connotation is "see for E", expressing that one must always strive to capture the essence of a system, in order to reduce the complexity of its white-box model, and consequently to get deeper insight into and better overview over the system. The reduction of complexity that is achieved by producing a white-box model that satisfies the C4E requirements, contributes to achieving the generic enterprise engineering goal of intellectual manageability [15].

9.4 Discussions

9.4.1 Implications of the DELTA Theory for Software Engineering

Software engineering is the discipline of engineering software systems. It includes the design, the implementation, the deployment and the maintenance of these systems. Even professional software engineers sometimes seem to forget that a software system in operation is a mathematical machine (also if its function is to support people in organisations). This undeniable truth has important implications for the discipline of software engineering, however.

First, it implies that a software engineer must have a *comprehensive* understanding of the object system that is going to be supported by the software system that he/she is going to develop. The relationship between the object system and its supporting information/software system is precisely defined in the ALPHA theory (cf. Chap. 11). Moreover, this understanding of the object system must be *concise* (thus fully abstracted from realisation and implementation) in order to manage intellectually its complexity, that is, to get and keep insight into and overview over of the software system to be developed. This insight and overview is also indispensable for *validating* that the software system satisfies the applicable requirements.

Second, such an understanding of the object system is also indispensable for *verifying* the logical correctness of the developed software system. The role of testing can only be secondary, because it may show the presence of errors but never their absence, as pointed out already long ago by Edsger Dijkstra [16].

Third, such an understanding would also be a necessary basis for studying the construction and operation of the system by means of mathematical and logical analysis, as well as through simulation, possibly including animation.

Fourth, such an understanding of the object system would be a necessary condition for generating software in such a way that its correctness can be guaranteed [17]. Because PRISMA models are formalised, they can be converted to mathematical/logic complexes (cf. Chap. 6), and subsequently expressed in a programming language.

9.4.2 Prismanets and Petri Nets

Readers who are familiar with Petri nets may have wondered already what the similarities and differences are between prismanets and Petri nets [18], because the resemblance of the graphical symbols suggests some similarity. It seems worthwhile therefore to make a comparison of the two process modelling techniques.

In [19], the relationship between the Petri net and the smartienet is investigated. Since the smartienet [20, 21] is the precursor of the prismanet, we will first summarise the findings in [19], using the TCS again as the example system. The smartienet diagram in Fig. 6 in [19] is reproduced as Fig. 9.16. The legend of the diagram is the same as for the prismanet diagram (cf. Fig. 9.10). So, there are two processors (P_1 and P_2), four banks (B_1, B_2, B_3, and B_4) and two channels (C_1 and C_2). Because the smartienet lacks the notion of delayed mutation, which the prismanet does have (cf. Sect. 9.2.3.2), two elementary processors are needed to model the TCS properly. Next to being activated by set_phase commands from P_1, P_2 also activates itself, through channel C_2.

Although the TCS is a quite simple system, its discussion above and in [19] illustrates how difficult it is to understand a system comprehensively (i.e. its construction, its operation, and the effects of its operation, thus the processes or state trajectories in the system's world) without a proper theory. At the same time, both the prismanet model in this chapter and the smartienet model in [19], demonstrate the power of ontological modelling: providing one with a comprehensive, coherent, and consistent understanding of a system, released from the burden of implementation details.

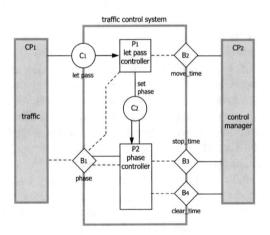

Fig. 9.16 Smartienet diagram of the TCS

The Petri net [18] originates from the research work that Carl Adam Petri[5] undertook already at a young age. It can best be understood as a (meta) model for studying synchronisation problems in discrete event systems. A well-known application of the Petri net is the studying of cooperating sequential processes in computers. Because of its popularity among (business) process modellers with a focus on

---

[5]https://en.wikipedia.org/wiki/Carl_Adam_Petri

formalisation, the Petri net has evolved in the course of time in order to meet the additional requirements. The major extensions have been the addition of delay times (resulting in the timed Petri net [22]) and the 'colouring' of tokens, by which is meant adding process semantics (resulting in the coloured Petri net [23]).

In Figs. 9.17 and 9.18 the timed Petri net diagram of the TCS is exhibited. It is an adapted version of Fig. 2.10 in [24]. The adaptation comprises a more accurate layout and corrections of the delay times. The disks represent the places of the Petri net and the boxes represent the transitions. The black dots in the places are the tokens that can 'move' through the net. A place is an input place of a transition if its shape is connected to the transition shape by an arrow. A place is an output place of a transition if its shape is connected to the transition shape by a solid line. Transitions 'fire' if all input places contain at least one token. The effect of 'firing' is that one token is removed from every input place and that one token is added to every output place. The names of the places and transitions, as well as the time delays, correspond with the names in Fig. 9.8. So, for example, W1 means Cycle 1 is in the state waiting, S1–W1 is the transition from S1 to W1, and CT2 is the clear time in Cycle 2.

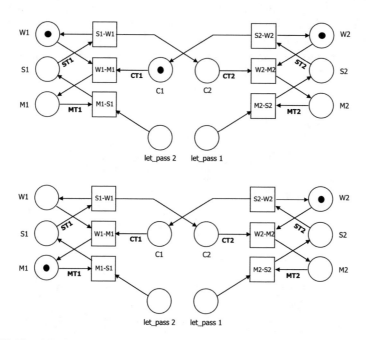

Fig. 9.17 Timed Petri net of the TCS (1)

The process starts in the situation that the state of Cycle 1 is waiting and the state of Cycle 2 is (prolonged) moving (cf. Fig. 9.17 upper part). Then a let_pass event in Cycle 1 occurs (a token is put in place let_pass 1). The condition to fire M2-S2 is now satisfied, and thus the transition takes place. The state of Cycle 2 will immediately become stopping (cf. Fig. 9.17, lower part). This enables the firing of S2-W2 after ST2 time units. Then the token in S2 is removed and a token is added to both W2 and C1 (cf. Fig. 9.18, upper part). Together with the token in W1, this satisfies the condition for W1-M1 to fire, after CT1 time units. The effect of this transition is that the tokens in W1 and C1 are removed and that a token is added to M1, meaning that the state of Cycle 1 will become 'moving' (cf. Fig. 9.18, lower part). After MT1 time units, transition M1-S1 is enabled by this token, but the firing has to wait for a token in place let_pass 2, so for arriving traffic in Cycle 2. As soon as this is the case, the whole process will be repeated, but now with the cycles reversed.

Despite the similarity of the diagrams, the Petri net that is represented in Figs. 9.17 and 9.18 and the prismanet that is represented in Fig. 9.11, are fundamentally different. The prismanet is a *construction model*: it shows the composition, the environment, and the structure of a system (cf. Sect. 9.2.1.2). The Petri net, however, is a *process model* in the strict systemic sense [4]: it specifies the lawful states and the lawful transitions of a system's world, possibly the world of the system that is represented by the prismanet diagram in Fig. 9.11. The Petri net in Figs. 9.17 and 9.18 is semantically equivalent to the STD in Fig. 9.8. Note that the presented Petri nets are independent of any implementation, contrary to the one in [24]: using red, yellow, and green lights to inform traffic participants about the states 'waiting', 'stopping', and 'moving', is just one way of implementing the inspection link from the processor 'traffic' to the bank 'phase' in the prismanet diagram in Fig. 9.11. Such implementation choices should not appear in an ontological model.

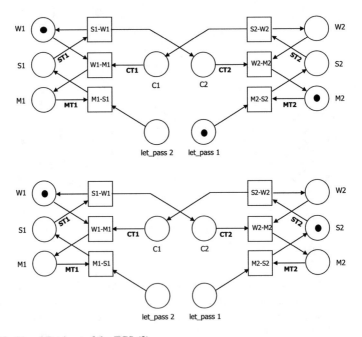

Fig. 9.18 Timed Petri net of the TCS (2)

9.4.3   The Petri Net and the DEMO Process Model

Because Petri nets are process models, as discussed in the previous section, it is interesting to compare the Petri net with the DEMO Process Model (PM), as presented in Chap. 12. For some time already, Petri nets have been applied for analysing and simulating (business) processes that are modelled in DEMO, for example, in [25] and in [26]. As discussed in Chap. 8, DEMO process models are basically tree structures (cf. Chap. 10) of transaction processes. So, let us first draw a comparison between the Petri net and the complete transaction pattern (CTP), by interpreting the CTP as a Petri net.

Figure 9.19 contains the CTP from Fig. 9.13, but without the names of the C-facts, in order to let them resemble the places of a Petri net. The C-acts must be interpreted as transitions. The optionalities (indicated by the cardinality ranges 0. . .1 next to the response links in Fig. 9.13) are accommodated by adding the alternatives (cf. Chap. 8): performing rv-rq and rv-da, respectively. Moreover, the P-act and the P-fact are separated: the P-fact symbol (the diamond) is also interpreted as a place in the Petri net. The reversion states are indicated in the same way as they are in Fig. 9.13, in order to avoid crossing lines in the diagram.

Let us suppose that there is a token in the place labeled "in". Then transition rq will fire, resulting in putting a token in its output place (which corresponds with the state requested). Then both transition dc and transition pm are enabled. However, only one of them can fire because there is only one token in the input place. Going on in this way, one will discover that the process either ends (successfully) in the state accepted or goes on infinitely, which is exactly the idea of the CTP (cf. Chap. 8).

What is new in Fig. 9.19, compared to the 'real' Petri net, are the dashed lines. In a Petri net, they have to be replaced by solid arrows, and thus serve as an additional input place for the four revocation transitions, because state conditions and response conditions cannot be distinguished in a Petri net. In other words, the CTP (and for that matter the DEMO PM) is richer than a Petri net as regards the ability to represent real (business) processes, where the distinction between state conditions (inspection links) and triggers (response links) is crucial to deeply understand them.

A similar remark can be made with respect to the wait links in the DEMO PM (cf. Chap. 12). They are also crucial in real business processes: waiting for something to happen before acting, is fundamentally different from being triggered to act.

As said, a Petri net only represents the world of a system, not the system itself: it is (only) a grey-box model, not (also) a white-box model. To understand the corresponding system, one has to model it in some other way, for example, as a prismanet.

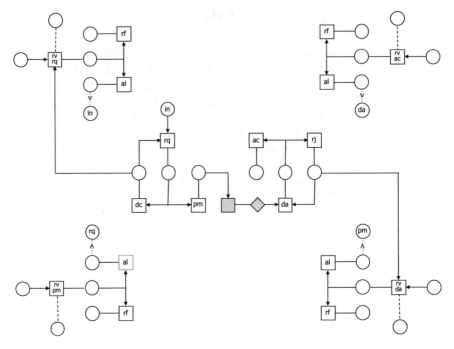

Fig. 9.19 Petri net interpretation of the CTP

The current use of (timed coloured) Petri nets for modelling business processes is a typical illustration of how meta models can be 'inflated' to accommodate applications where they were never meant for (and consequently are mostly not suited for). As convincingly discussed in Chap. 8, business processes are processes that occur in the coordination world of organisations, as the effect of acts by autonomous human actors. Other examples of 'inflations' of modelling approaches are the use of the Entity Relationship Diagram (originally meant for exhibiting the structure of relational databases) for conceptual modelling, and the use of the UML class diagram for conceptual modelling and even for ontological modelling (cf. Chap. 6).

With reference to Einstein's quote at the beginning of Chap. 4 (*Whether you can observe a thing or not depends on the theory that you use. It is the theory that decides what can be observed*), all modelling actions are inherently shaped by the theory one applies or, when lacking an explicit theory, by the 'mental glasses' one has put on. If these glasses are ill-suited, the resulting models will not be very useful. Unfortunately but most likely, one may not be aware of the mismatch.

References

1. Bertalanffy, L. V. (1969). *General system theory; foundations, development, applications* (Rev. ed., xxiv, 295 p.). New York: G. Braziller.
2. Wiener, N. (1965). *Cybernetics: or, Control and communication in the animal and the machine* (2nd ed., 212 p.). The M I T paperback series. Cambridge, MA: MIT.

3. Legasto, A., Forrester, J. W., & Lyneis, J. M. (1980). *System dynamics. TIMS studies in the management sciences* (282 p.). Amsterdam: North-Holland.
4. Bunge, M. (1979). Treatise on basic philosophy ontology II: A world of systems. In *Treatise on basic philosophy 4* (p. 1). Dordrecht: Springer.
5. Weinberg, G. M. (1975). *An introduction to general systems thinking* (xxi, 279 p.). Wiley series on systems engineering and analysis. New York: Wiley.
6. Marquis, J.-P. (1996). A critical note on Bunge's 'system boundary' and a new proposal. *International Journal of General Systems, 24*(3), 245–255.
7. Bunge, M. (1977). Treatise on basic philosophy ontology I: The furniture of the world. In *Treatise on basic philosophy 3* (p. 1, 370 p.). Springer: Dordrecht.
8. Franklin, G. F., Powell, J. D., & Emami-Naeini, A. (2010). *Feedback control of dynamic systems* (xviii, 819 p., 6th ed.). Upper Saddle River, NJ: Pearson.
9. Marca, D., & McGowan, C. L. (1988). *SADT: Structured analysis and design technique* (xvii, 392 p.). New York: McGraw-Hill.
10. Cassandras, C. G., & Lafortune, S. (2008). *Introduction to discrete event systems* (xxiii, 769 p., 2nd ed.). New York: Springer Science + Business Media.
11. Hoogervorst, J. A. P. (2017). *Foundations of enterprise governance and enterprise engineering* (p. 574) Cham: Springer International.
12. Aveiro, D., Silva, A. R., & Tribolet, J. (2010). Towards a G.O.D organization for organizational self-awareness. In *6th International Workshop, CIAO! 2010*. St. Gallen: Springer.
13. Hee, K. M. V., Houben, G.-J., & Dietz, J. L. G. (1989). Modelling of discrete dynamic systems; framework and examples. *Information Systems, 14*.
14. Perinforma, A. P. C. (2015). *The essence of organisation*. South Holland: Sapio Enterprise Engineering.
15. Dietz, J. L. G., & Hoogervorst, J. A. P. (2013). The discipline of enterprise engineering. *Journal Organisational Design and Engineering, 3, 28*.
16. Dijkstra, E. W. (1970). *Notes on structures programming*.
17. van Kervel, S. J. H., et al. (2012). Enterprise ontology driven software engineering. In *ICSOFT 2012*. SciTePress.
18. Peterson, J. L. (1981). *Petri net theory and the modeling of systems* (x, 290 p.). Englewood Cliff, NJ: Prentice-Hall.
19. Dietz, J. L. G. (2005). System ontology and its role in system development. In J. Castro & E. Teniente (Eds.), *Advanced information systems engineering wokshops* (CAiSE) (pp. 271–284). Porto.
20. Dietz, J. L. G. (Ed.). (1987). *Modelleren en specificeren van informatiesystemen*. Eindhoven: T.N. Eindhoven University of Technology.
21. Houben, G.-J., Dietz, J. L. G., & van Hee, K. M. (1988). The SMARTIE framework for modelling discrete dynamic systems. In P. Varaiya & H. Kurzhanski (Eds.), *Discrete event systems: Models and applications*. New York: Springer.
22. Wang, J. (1998). *Timed petri nets – Theory and applications*. Boston: Kluwer Academic.
23. Jensen, K. (1997). *Coloured petri nets: Basic concepts, analysis methods, and practical use* (2nd ed.). Monographs in theoretical computer science. Berlin: Springer.
24. van der Aalst, W., & van Hee, K. M. (2004). *Workflow management models, methods, and systems. Cooperative information systems series* (368 S.). Cambridge, MA: MIT.
25. Barjis, J. A., & Dietz, J. L. G. (2001). A type of petri net based on speech act theory for modeling social systems. In A. W. Heemink (Ed.), *EUROSIM*. Delft.
26. Barjis, J. A. (2008). The importance of business process modeling in software systems design. *Elsevier Science of Computer Programming, 71, 73–87*.

Chapter 10
The OMEGA Theory: Understanding the Construction of Organisations

Abstract The OMEGA theory, also called organisational construction theory, is a theory about the modular structures that can be distinguished in organisations. Based on the organisational building block (the transactor role) from the PSI theory, three kinds of coordination structures are identified and discussed: interaction structure, interstriction structure, and interimpediment structure. The interaction structure of an organisation consists of tree structures, composed of the initiator links between transactor roles. An interaction structure determines a business process kind. The interstriction structure of an organisation consists of the access links between transactor roles. Through access links, actors have reading access to the facts in transaction banks. A distinction is made between the interprocess and the intraprocess interstriction structure. The interimpediment structure of an organisation is composed of the wait links between transactor roles. A distinction is made between the interprocess and the intraprocess interimpediment structure. Three topics are elaborated in-depth. The first one is the notion of responsibility range of a transactor role, as an extension of the responsibility area from the PSI theory (cf. Chap. 8). The second subject is a comprehensive way of modelling business processes, which allows for all the details that are needed, but that is still very concise. The third subject concerns general patterns in process structures, called reference models. To conclude, the structural way of thinking about business processes is compared with the current dominant flow thinking.

10.1 Introduction

The theory in this chapter is labeled Ω-theory. The Greek capital letter is pronounced as OMEGA, an acronym for Organisational Modules Emerging from General Arrangements. The theory concerns the possible ways in which transactor roles (cf. Chap. 8) can influence each other, as well as the modular structures that these ways of influencing give rise to. In Chap. 4, the OMEGA theory is classified as an ontological theory, meaning that it is about the nature of things.

The PSI theory (cf. Chap. 8) provides us with the most fundamental work structure in organisations, namely the division in production and coordination, and

© Springer Nature Switzerland AG 2020
J. L. G. Dietz, J. B. F. Mulder, *Enterprise Ontology*, The Enterprise Engineering
Series, https://doi.org/10.1007/978-3-030-38854-6_10

their combined occurrence in the universal pattern of the (business) transaction. The complete transaction pattern comprises all coordination acts/facts that are necessary and sufficient for carrying out any transaction. Based on it, the PSI theory provides us also with the universal building block of organisations: the transactor (transaction processing actor) role. Every transactor role includes the complete transaction pattern. In addition, it comprises the guidelines for carrying out transactions of the corresponding transaction kind, varying from cultural norms to imperative business rules.

Section 10.2 (foundations) starts with a summary of the PSI theory. In Sects. 10.2.2–10.2.4, the distinct coordination structures are presented that arise from the three distinct ways of influencing between transactors: the interaction structure, the interstriction structure, and the interimpediment structure. All three are expressed in the Coordination Structure Diagram (CSD). The business processes in the GloLog enterprise (cf. Chap. 18) are used for illustration.

Section 10.3 (elaborations) covers three topics. In Sect. 10.3.1, the notion of responsibility range of transactors is discussed, as an extension of the notion of responsibility area from the PSI theory. In Sect. 10.3.2, the Process Structure Diagram (PSD) is introduced for understanding the three coordination structures in more detail, and the notion of business process is elucidated. Section 10.3.3 is devoted to a discussion of the reference models that emerge from the presented structures.

Section 10.4 (discussions) is about the added value of structure thinking in business processes, next to flow thinking, as well as its indispensability if it comes to changing business processes. The chapter ends with a discussion of the practical relevance of the OMEGA theory.

10.2   Foundations

10.2.1   The Organisational Building Block

In this section, the parts of the PSI theory (cf. Chap. 8) that are relevant for the OMEGA theory are resumed and elaborated. The first important notion is the notion of transaction. It is a pattern of acts, performed by actors in two roles: the initiator and the executor. The executor brings about the product of the transaction to the benefit of the initiator. In the presented complete transaction pattern, there is a clear separation between the coordination acts (C-acts) that the initiator of a transaction can perform and the C-acts that belong to the responsibility of the executor. Emphasis is put on the precise formulation of the product of a transaction, namely in such a way that it is uniquely identified. The example of a correct formulation of a *product kind* that was used in Chap. 8 is '[membership] is started', where [membership] is a placeholder or variable in this logical predicate type. An example of an instance of the predicate type is 'membership 387 is started'. Related to the notion of product kind, the notion of *transaction kind* is introduced. It is a basic property of every transaction, and there is a one-to-one relationship between transaction kinds and product kinds. A suitable naming of the transaction kind, in which instances products of the kind '[membership] is started' are brought about, would be "membership starting". Next, the notion of *actor role* is introduced, defined as the authority to be the executor in transactions of a particular transaction kind. This authority can be assigned to subjects, by which these subjects become eligible to act accordingly. A proper name for the executor role of the transaction kind 'membership starting' would be "membership starter".

The combination of a subject and an assigned actor role is called *actor*. Only actors can act, that is, be active in transactions. A subject may fill several actor roles and an actor role may be assigned to several subjects, both sequentially and simultaneously. As examples from the case Rent-A-Car (cf. Chap. 15), renters (subjects in an actor role) can at the same time be deposit payers (same subject, different actor role), and there are several rental completers (one actor role, assigned to several subjects). Next, an actor role can be assigned to the collectivity of a number of subjects, which means that these subjects fill the role collectively. Examples of collective actor roles are the board of directors of a company and the general assembly of an association.

Every transaction kind has exactly one actor role as its executor role, and vice versa, but actor roles may have an initiator role in a number of (other) transaction kinds. The left side of Fig. 10.1 shows the graphical notation of these relationships in the DEMO Specification Language.[1] The shape of a transaction kind is a diamond (the symbol of production) in a disk (the symbol of coordination), and the shape of an actor role is a box (possibly stretched to a rectangle). A transaction kind is connected to an actor role by an initiator link (represented by a solid line between the shapes) or an executor link (represented by a solid line between the shapes plus a small black diamond at the junction of the line and the executing actor role box). Figure 10.1 shows that actors CAR00 are initiators in transactions TK01 and that actors AR01 are their executors.[2] Actors AR01 are also initiators of transactions TK02, TK03, and TK04, of which actors AR02, AR03, and AR04, respectively, are the executors.

The transaction kind shape has two interpretations. In the *constructional interpretation*, it represents the complete transaction pattern, as discussed in Sect. 8.2.6.3. Every instance of a transaction of the transaction kind is some path, possibly including iterations, through the complete transaction pattern. In the *operational interpretation*, the transaction kind shape represents the conceptual store of all C- and P-facts in transactions of the transaction kind that are created in the course of time. Therefore, the transaction kind is now conceived as a *transaction bank*. Basically, the subjects who fill or have filled the initiator or executor role in one or

---

[1]The DEMO Specification Language (DEMOSL) formally defines the ways in which DEMO models can be expressed (diagrams and formal text). The official reference document on DEMOSL can be found on www.ee-institute.org

[2]We will write "actors ARn" as a shorthand for "actors filling actor role ARn", "transactions TKn" as a shorthand for "transactions of the kind TKn", and "products PKn" as a shorthand for "products of the kind PKn".

more transactions of some kind, have access to the contents of the corresponding transaction bank, possibly restricted to the specific transactions in which they have participated.

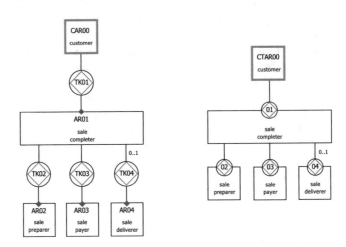

Fig. 10.1 Graphical notations of transaction kinds, actor roles, and transactor roles

The *actor role shape* has also two interpretations. The *constructional interpretation* is that it represents the authority to be the executor in transactions of the transaction kind to which it is linked by an executor link. The *operational interpretation* is that it represents the guidelines, ranging from culture (norms and values) to specific action rules and work instructions that actors filling the actor role apply when they carry out transactions. The action rules regard the role of executor of transactions of the kind to which it is linked by an executor link and the role of initiator in transactions of the kind to which it is linked by an initiator link. So, for example, actor role AR01 contains guidelines both for dealing with C-events in transactions TK01 (of which it is the executor) and in transactions TK02, TK03, and TK04 (of which it is an initiator).

Because of the one-to-one relationship between a transaction kind and its executor role, it makes sense to use one shape for the combination of the two. This shape, called *transactor role*, is shown on the right side of Fig. 10.1. Instead of using prefixes (like "TK" and "AR" that are used on the left side of the figure), we just number transactor roles. The links between the transactor roles are *initiator links*. So, for example, transactors TAR01 are initiator in transactions TK02, TK03, and TK04. Henceforth, we will talk of transactors and transactor roles, as well as of actor roles and transaction kinds. The cardinality range 0...1 in Fig. 10.1 indicates that the carrying out of a transaction TK04 within a transaction TK01 is optional.

Because transactor roles can have an initiator role in one or more transaction kinds, next to having the executor role in their 'own' transaction kind, the being connected through initiator links, constitutes tree structures, like the one shown in

Fig. 10.1. To illustrate the meaning of this tree structure, we use the Pizzeria case (cf. Chap. 14). Table 10.1 represents the so-called Transactor Product Table of the Pizzeria.

Table 10.1 Transactor Product Table of the Pizzeria

Transaction kind	Product kind	Executor role
TK01 sale completing	PK01 [sale] is completed	AR01 sale completer
TK02 sale preparing	PK02 [sale] is prepared	AR02 sale preparer
TK03 sale paying	PK03 [sale] is paid	AR03 sale payer
TK04 sale delivering	PK04 [sale] is delivered	AR04 sale deliverer

The processing of a client order (which is conceived as completing a sale) starts from the request of a transaction of the kind TK01 'sale completing' by someone who fills the actor role 'customer' (an actor role within the composite actor role CAR00) to someone who fills actor role AR01 'sale completer'. During the carrying out of this transaction, three other transactions are initiated: one of the kind TK02 'sale preparing', one of the kind TK03 'sale paying', and (optionally) one of the kind TK04 'sale delivering'. All three must have been finished before the transaction of the kind TK01 'sale completing' can be finished. In other words, every product of the kind '[sale] is completed' implies three other products: one of the kind '[sale] is paid', one of the kind '[sale] is prepared', and (optionally) one of the kind '[sale] is delivered'.

Fig. 10.2 Representations of the organisational building block

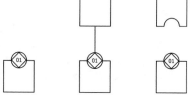

The transactor role is the *construction element* or basic *building block* of organisations, as shown in Fig. 10.2. On the left is the 'bare' building block. In the middle, this transactor role is connected to another actor role by an initiator link. By doing this, actors in this role become initiator of transactions TK01, of which actors AR01 are the executor. The construct on the right side of Fig. 10.2 represents another way of making actor roles initiator of transaction kinds. The meaning of the disk-shaped cut-away in the upper box is that actors filling the corresponding actor role become initiator in transactions TK01 by 'clicking' the transaction symbol to the cut-away. This so-called "click mode" will be elaborated in Sect. 10.3.2. The operational meaning of the middle and the right construct is that the initiators of transactions

TK01 perform requests, to which actors AR01 respond by a promise (or a decline), and thus start the carrying out of transactions TK01, which concern products of the kind PK01. A product starts to exist as soon as the initiator has accepted it.

10.2.2   The Interaction Structure

By the *interaction structure* of an organisation is understood the collective initiator links between the transactor roles, as illustrated by Fig. 10.1, right side. This is equivalent to saying that the interaction structure comprises the transaction kinds of an organisation, as well as the initiator links and the executor links that connect them to the actor roles (cf. Fig. 10.1, left side). The interaction structure is the main structure in an organisation, because it determines the business process kinds in which the products are brought about (cf. Chap. 8). Therefore, we take the following as the definition: every interaction tree in an organisation is a *business process kind*. As we will see later, the top of such a tree is either an environmental or a self-activating transactor role. Both, the interstriction structure (to be discussed in Sect. 10.2.3) and the interimpediment structure (to be discussed in Sect. 10.2.4) come in addition with the interaction structure; they cannot exist without it.

The interaction structure of an organisation consists by definition of a number of tree structures, as will become clear subsequently. The general understanding of a tree structure is that it is a pair (P, R) where P is a set of things and R is a (binary) relation over P, commonly called a part-of relation. For every (p1, p2) ∈ R, it holds that p1 is a *part of* p2. Conversely, p2 is commonly called the *assembly* of the things x ∈ P, for which it holds that (x, p2) ∈ R. The leaves of the tree, that is, the things y in P that have no parts, so for which there is no tuple (−, y) ∈ R, are commonly called (elementary) *parts*. All non-leaf things are commonly called assemblies.

An interaction tree (cf. Fig. 10.1, right side) is basically always extensible by adding new transactor roles as components of the 'leaf' transactor roles. The tree structure is a direct reflection of the Bill-of-Material (BoM) structure of the corresponding product kinds.

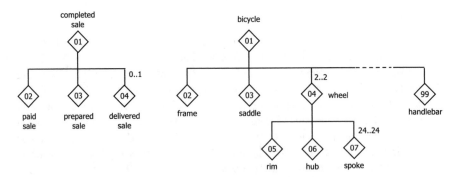

Fig. 10.3 Examples of product structures

As an example, in the Pizzeria (cf. Chap. 14), the case kind is the sale. It serves as the core entity type (cf. Chap. 8) in all four product kinds. The product structure is shown in Fig. 10.3, (left side) whereas Table 10.1 contains the Transactor Product Table. A product of the kind '[sale] is completed' comprises three other products as parts: '[sale] is paid', '[sale] is prepared', and '[sale] is delivered'. The last one is optional (indicated by the cardinality range 0...1) because there are also walk-in customers, for which there is no delivery transaction. Consequently, four speciali-sations (cf. Chap. 6), or life phases, of the entity type sale are distinguished: completed sale, paid sale, prepared sale, and delivered sale.

As another example to illustrate that product structures resemble BoM-like structures, a part of the BoM of a bicycle (of some bicycle kind) is shown on the right side of Fig. 10.3. It shows that a bicycle consists of one frame, one saddle, two wheels (indicated by the minimum and maximum cardinality), one handlebar, etc. Next, a wheel is an assembly of one rim, one hub, and 24 spokes (note: if no cardinality range is indicated next to an initiator link, the default value 1...1 holds). The product structure that corresponds with this BoM has the same shape. Only the names of the parts would be replaced by "assembled bicycle", "assembled wheel", "acquired spoke", etc.

In order to express the coordination structures, we use the Coordination Structure Diagram (CSD) (cf. Chap. 12); its legend is depicted in Fig. 10.4. The upper part shows the three different sorts of transactor roles: the elementary transactor role, the self-activating transactor role, and the composite transactor role.

As stated, the interaction structure of an organisation consists of a number of tree structures. By definition, the top of such a tree is a self-activating transactor role. However, because many business processes in an organisation originate from the environment, the common way to represent the external 'top' transactor role of such a business process kind in a CSD is the composite transactor role (Fig. 10.4, top right).

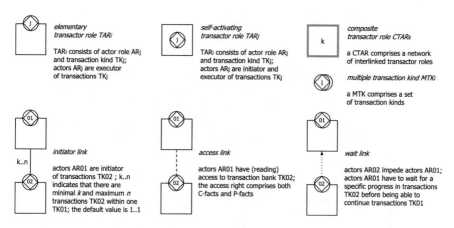

Fig. 10.4 Legend of the Coordination Structure Diagram

As shown in Fig. 10.3, a product, for example a PK01, may be composed of other products; which means that actors AR01 have to initiate other transactions in order to bring about a PK01. A possible sub-tree of the construct in the middle of Fig. 10.2, is shown in Fig. 10.5. It should be read as follows. In order to produce a PK01, actors AR01 need a PK02, a PK03, and a PK04. On their turn, actors AR02 need a PK05 and a PK06 to produce a PK02, actors AR03 need a PK08 and optionally (indicated by the cardinality range 0...1) a PK07 to produce a PK03, and actors AR04 need a PK08 and a PK09 to produce a PK04. Note that transactor role TAR08 is drawn twice, to keep the diagram orderly, but there is only one transactor role TAR08. So, transactions TK08 are initiated by either an actor AR03 or an actor AR04.

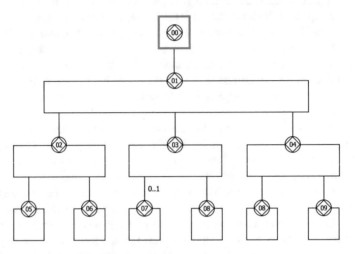

Fig. 10.5 Example of an interaction-based tree structure

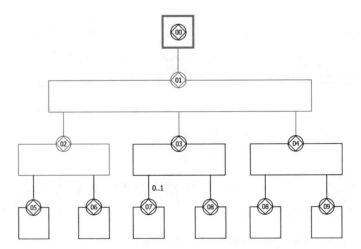

Fig. 10.6 Narrowing down a scope of interest

A crucial point in the OMEGA theory is that at any level in an interaction tree, the initiating actor basically does not care (and does not need to care) about what the executing actor has to do in order to produce the agreed-upon product. To illustrate this, at some point in time, the actor AR01 addresses herself/himself to the initiating actor CTAR00 and declares the creation of a product PK01. What the actor AR01 actually has done during the execution phase of the transaction TK01, is to have acquired a PK02, a PK03, and a PK04 in transactions TK02, TK03, and TK04, respectively, as shown in Fig. 10.5. The transactor roles TAR02, TAR03, and TAR04 are called sub-transactor roles of TAR01. Together they constitute the sub-tree of TAR01. It is important to understand that every sub-transactor role may have a sub-tree of transactor roles itself, but this sub-tree does not affect the character of its products. Thus, it makes no difference for actor role AR01 whether AR02 has to initiate transactions TK05 and TK06 for producing products PK02 or not. It will always be the (same) product kind that actors AR01 and actors AR02 negotiate about and come to agreement about in transaction processes of the kind TK02. In a similar way, one may want to disregard the sub-tree of a transactor role.

The interaction tree structures in an organisation may be quite deep, that is, have many levels, in particular, if one includes the transactor roles in the I-organisation, and even more if one also includes the transactor roles in the D-organisation (cf. Chap. 11). Commonly, one would only consider the transactor roles in the O-organisation, or at least start with them, as a consequence of abstracting from the I- and the D-organisation. The reason for 'hiding' a part of a tree by means of a composite transactor role, as CTAR00 in Fig. 10.5, may be that one wants to disregard it for the moment, as discussed above, or that it falls outside the chosen Scope of Interest (SoI).

In Figs. 10.6 and 10.7, the SoI as shown in Fig. 10.5 is narrowed down. The new SoI consists of TAR02 and its components TAR05 and TAR06. For illustrative purposes, the edges of the shapes in the corresponding part of the initial SoI are blue-lined. Figure 10.7 displays the result. The name of the new composite transactor role (CTAR02) is arbitrarily chosen.

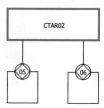

Fig. 10.7 The new scope of interest

As a practical example of the interaction structure of an organisation, Fig. 10.8 shows this structure for the GloLog enterprise (cf. Chap. 18). There are four business process kinds, represented by four distinct interaction structures: the sales process, the purchase process, the sea transport process, and the land transport process. The case kind in these process kinds is respectively sale, purchase, ship content, and container content. Only because of these different *case kinds* (i.e. entity kinds) does one arrive at the four tree structures, as explained in Chap. 18. The left one is initiated externally, as indicated by the composite transactor role CTAR01. The top or root of the other trees is a self-activating transactor role. The company IES within the GloLog enterprise comprises all white-coloured transactor role shapes. So, the grey-coloured transactor role shapes are outside IES, but inside the scope of the GloLog enterprise. The red colour of the diamonds indicates that the transactor roles belong to the O-organisation of the GloLog enterprise. The structure with double-lined boxes at the top of Fig. 10.8 does not belong to the CSD; it only serves to clarify that there are four different business process kinds in the Glolog enterprise. Together they bring about the products/services of the enterprise.

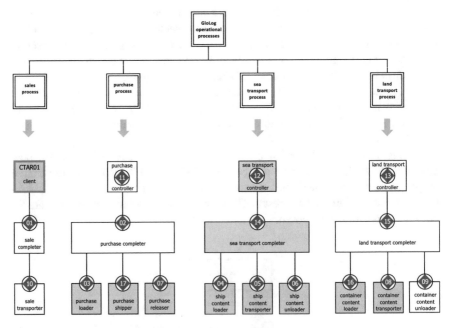

Fig. 10.8 The interaction structure in the GloLog enterprise

10.2.3   The Interstriction Structure

The second kind of link between transactor roles is the *access link*. It is presented in Fig. 10.4, in the middle of the bottom part. As discussed in Chap. 11, access links are the means to abstract from the realisation of an organisation, that is, from the

I-organisation, and subsequently from the D-organisation. Therefore, the right understanding of the construct shown in the middle of Fig. 10.4 is that actors AR01 are initiators in one or more informational transactions, through which they acquire the knowledge of facts that are contained in transaction bank TK02.

Actors AR01 need these facts in order to properly carry out transactions TK01. To this end, they have (reading) access to the contents of transaction bank TK02. The access link can also be understood as a restriction of the decision freedom of actors AR01 by actors AR02, as discussed in Chap. 9. Therefore, the collective access links in an organisation are called its *interstriction structure*.[3] Interstriction is a passive way in which actors in the O-organisation of an enterprise (cf. Chap. 11) influence each other, in addition to the active way of interaction. In carrying out a transaction, both the initiator and the executor need to keep track of the progress of the transaction, and they may also need to know the histories of earlier transactions of the same kind. Consequently, there is an access link 'under' every initiator link and every executor link (cf. Fig. 10.1, left side). Although they are not made visible in the CSD, they do also belong to the interstriction structure. The interstriction structure of an organisation constitutes the *state dependencies* among the contained transaction processes: the acts of the connected actors depend on the current state of the connected transaction processes, that is, on the contents of the connected transaction banks.

Figure 10.9 depicts the interstriction structure in the GloLog enterprise, in addition to the interaction structure, which is presented in Fig. 10.8. It shows that actors AR11 have access to transaction bank TK01, actors AR12 to transaction bank TK03, and actors AR13 to transaction bank TK14.

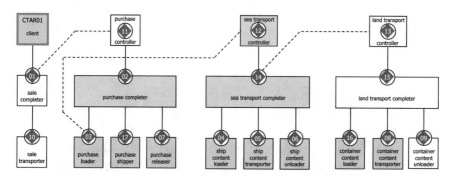

Fig. 10.9 The interstriction structure in the GloLog enterprise

---

[3]The term 'restriction'; originates from the Latin verb 'stringere', meaning trimming, curtailing. The word 'interstriction' expresses that actors restrict each other's decision freedom or 'play area'.

10.2.4   The Interimpediment Structure

The third kind of link between transactor roles is the *wait link*. It is shown in Fig. 10.4 on the right side of the bottom part, and it should be understood as follows. The process of every transaction is a path, possibly including iterations, through the complete transaction pattern (cf. Chap. 8). Every C-act is performed in response to a C-event. The performer of the C-act may take some time before he/she responds, and this time may even exceed the intended settlement time (cf. Chap. 8), because the executor is autonomous. However, there can also be external conditions that force the performer to wait. These conditions are represented by wait links.

Collectively, the wait links represent the *interimpediment structure* of an organisation. The interimpediment structure constitutes the *process dependencies* among the transaction processes: the acts of the connected actors are held up until a specific state of the connected transaction process is reached.

The CSD in Fig. 10.10 shows the interimpediment structure in the GloLog enterprise, in addition to the interaction structure. The left wait link expresses that the transaction processes of transactions TK10 are dependent on the progress of transactions TK02. More specifically, the continuation of every transaction TK10 has to wait for a specific progress in some transaction TK02. In a similar way, the continuation of every transaction TK14 has to wait for a specific progress in transactions TK03 (loading goods of purchases in containers). Next, the continuation of transactions TK15 has to wait for a specific progress in transactions TK07 (release of purchases by Customs), and the continuation of transactions TK17 must wait for some progress in one or more (indicated by the cardinality range 1...∗) transactions TK15 (container transports).

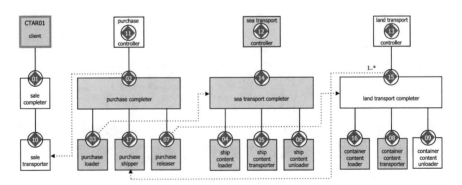

Fig. 10.10 The interimpediment structure in the GloLog enterprise

In Fig. 10.11, the three coordination structures are combined, so that one gets a comprehensive overview of the construction of the GloLog enterprise. The specific meaning of the coordination structures is explained in Chap. 18.

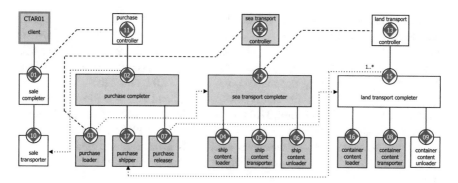

Fig. 10.11 The combined coordination structures in the GloLog enterprise

10.3   Elaborations

10.3.1   Responsibility Ranges

As discussed in Chap. 8, the two participating actors in a transaction have their own responsibility areas, which comprise the steps in the transaction process that each of them is authorised to perform. As follows from the CTP in Fig. 8.10, the responsibility area of the initiator comprises the steps rq, ac, rj, rv-rq and rv-ac (as well as allowing or refusing revocations of the promise and the declare by the executor). The responsibility area of the executor comprises the steps pm, dc, da, ex (the production act), rv-pm, and rv-da (and allowing or refusing revocations of the request and the accept by the initiator). Figure 10.12 shows how the notion of *responsibility range* can be based on the notion of responsibility area. For example, the responsibility range of actors AR01 is indicated by the dotted-lined blue rectangle. As shown, it does not only consist of the executor responsibilities in transactions TK01 (represented by the 'lower' half of its transaction shape), but also of the initiator responsibilities in transactions TK02, TK03, and TK04 (represented by the 'upper' halves of their transaction shapes).

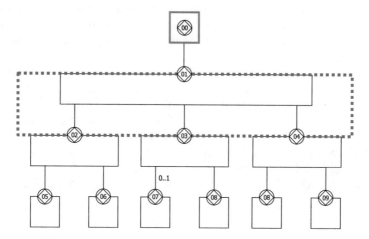

Fig. 10.12 Responsibility range in a business process kind

This extended notion of responsibility holds for every node in the tree, except the leaf nodes AR05, AR06, AR07, AR08, and AR09, because these actor roles have no initiator roles (or because one has abstracted from the sub-trees). It clarifies that actors AR01 must not only see to it that they act properly in carrying out transactions TK01, but also in carrying out transactions TK02, TK03, and TK04. This implies that they may have to exhort actors AR02, AR03, and AR04 to do their part of transactions TK02, TK03, and TK04 properly. In more current practical terms: actors AR01 are *owner* of the *process* in which products PK01 are brought about. In addition, they are *owner* of these *products*, and thus (also) of the *data* concerning them: the independent P-fact as well as the dependent P-facts that are created in transactions TK01.

10.3.2   Business Process Modelling

Although the presentation of the three kinds of coordination structures in a CSD provides a useful insight, it is often too concise for studying the business processes in detail. Notably, it is not possible to represent, in a precise way, the interimpediment structure (thus, the interprocess process dependencies), as well as the intraprocess process dependencies and the initiations of transactions. In order to do this, the Process Structure Diagram (PSD) (cf. Chap. 12) is introduced. Below, the PSD of the sales process of the GloLog enterprise (cf. Chap. 18) is presented as an example.

In Fig. 10.13, the corresponding part of interaction structure is included in the so-called "click mode": the right side of Fig. 10.2 with the two parts put together. The grey-coloured thick lines correspond with the borders of the actor roles: they separate the responsibility areas in a similar way as the 'swim lanes' in BPMN [1]. The transaction kind shapes are drawn on these lines; above the line is the responsibility area of the initiator, below the line is the responsibility area of the executor. The disk of the transaction shape is stretched horizontally, which makes it look like a 'sausage'. The diamond represents the execution phase, the part of the 'sausage' to the left represents the order phase, and the part to the right represents the result phase. Consequently, one may imagine a (non-proportional) time axis from left to right.

Although the 'sausage' comprises all steps of the complete transaction pattern, only the ones that are connected to steps in other transaction kinds are shown in a PSD, and they are always put on the edge of the 'sausage'. C-acts are represented by small boxes and C-facts by small disks. The P-act is represented by a small grey box.

The PSD in Fig. 10.13 shows that transactions TK01 are initiated externally, thus from a different process; this is indicated by the grey colour of the small disk that is connected to [TK01/rq] by a response link. The response link corresponds with the initiator link in the CSD. Likewise, there is a response link from (TK01/pm) to

[TK10/rq], expressing that transactions TK10 are initiated from the state promised of the corresponding TK01. Because of this, every transaction TK10 is said to be enclosed in a transaction TK01.

Fig. 10.13 GloLog: PSD of the sales process

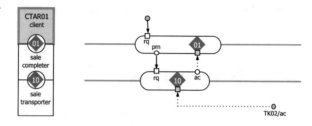

The wait link from (TK10/ac) to [TK01/ex] expresses that the enclosed transaction TK10 must have reached the state (TK10/ac) before actor AR01 can proceed to perform the P-act [TK01/ex]. The interprocess wait link in Fig. 10.10 from TK02 to AR10 is made more precise in the PSD by the wait link from (TK02/ac) to [TK10/ex]. It expresses that performing [TK10/ex] must wait until the corresponding transaction TK02 has reached the state accepted. The grey colour of the small disk indicates that (TK02/ac) is a state in a process of a different business process kind.

As explained in Chap. 9, the processes that are caused by a (discrete event) system are sequences of events. In enterprises, these processes are commonly called *business processes*. The adjective "business" is somewhat confusing, because it refers to the function perspective on enterprises (cf. Chap. 7). Therefore, the term "organisational process" would be more appropriate. Nevertheless, we will adopt the term "business process", while taking exclusively the construction perspective. As illustrated by Fig. 10.11, the four interaction (tree) structures, together with the related parts of the interstriction and the interimpediment structures, are the structures in which business processes take place. Therefore, we say that each of these tree structures corresponds with a *business process kind*. Every *business process* (instance) is some path through this structure, starting from the top transactor role (by a request for a product), and, if successful, ending in the top transactor role (by the acceptance of the product). As said, a business process kind corresponds with a BoM-like product structure.

The atomic steps in every business process (instance) are coordination acts/facts (cf. Chap. 8). Because they occur always in the universal pattern of the transaction, these transactions may rightly be called the *molecules* of business processes. In Sect. 10.4.1, the structure view, as discussed above, will be compared with the currently dominant flow view in business process modelling.

The case kind of every transaction kind in a business process kind, except the self-activating transaction kind at the top, must be the same as the one at the level above it, or be a part of it, like the frame in Fig. 10.3 is a part of a bicycle. If this condition is not met, the case kinds are incompatible. As an illustration, the business process structures that correspond with the product structures in Fig. 10.3 regard the same case kind, or a part of it. If one is confronted with incompatible case kinds, the process structure must be split into a number of other tree structures. Because of this incompatibility, there are four distinct case kinds in the GloLog enterprise (cf. Chap. 18): sale, purchase, ship content, and container content. Consequently, there are four distinct business processes, loosely coupled by access links and wait links.

10.3.3   Reference Models

The tree structures in business processes appear to contain similar patterns, which are specific for the categories of products that they bring about. These distinctions exist in addition to the product sorts that are discussed in the ALPHA theory (cf. Chap. 11): original products, informational products, and documental products. In Table 10.2, the distinct categories of product kinds are listed: creating and changing, transporting and storing, transferring of ownership, and obtaining usufruct. They can apply to tangible and to intangible things.

In the following sections, each of the four product categories from Table 10.2 is discussed and exemplified. We do not claim that the table is exhaustive, only that it is based on many years of solid practice. The corresponding business process patterns may very well be considered as *reference models* of enterprise categories.

10.3.3.1   Creating and Changing

By creating and changing *tangible things* is understood: the making of new things (things that didn't exist before) or the extending, modifying, and repairing of things. Examples of tangible things, commonly called goods, are bicycles, houses, and sculptures. Things are often assemblies of other things, called their parts or components. The assembly structure of things is often called a Bill of Material (BoM). On the right side of Fig. 10.3, a typical BoM of a bicycle is shown.

Table 10.2 Product categories

	tangible things	intangible things
creating and changing	manufacturing, changing, repairing (movable and immovable) goods	making and adjusting decisions, advices, judgements, etc.
transporting and storing	transporting and storing goods or files	*not applicable*
transferring ownership	buying/selling goods	acquiring owner rights, paying, trading shares
obtaining usufruct	hiring/renting space-time capacities	*not applicable*

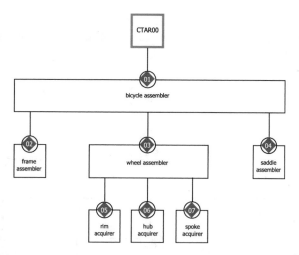

Fig. 10.14 Reference CSD for creating and changing

In Chap. 8, the product of a transaction is defined as an independent production fact, together with its dependent facts, and a product structure is defined as a tree of independent production facts. The BoM of the bicycle in Fig. 10.3 becomes a product structure when "bicycle" is replaced by "assembled bicycle", "wheel" by "assembled wheel", "spoke" by "acquired spoke", etc. Note that only the real 'leaf' parts, like the rim and the hub, are acquired (or taken from the shelf); all other parts are assemblies. Figure 10.14 shows the CSD of the corresponding business process kind.

The creating and changing of *intangible* things, like insurance policies, building licences and judgements, are pretty much similar to what has been said about tangible things. Only the number of levels in the product structure is commonly smaller.

10.3.3.2 Transporting and Storing

Transporting and storing are exclusively associated with *tangible* things. They constitute the core of logistic operations. We have seen examples of such operations in the GloLog enterprise, as presented in Sects. 10.2.2–10.2.4, and in Chap. 18. Like it is the case for creating goods, the products in transporting and storing have also BoM-like structures (cf. Fig. 10.5), and these structures can also easily be extended. As an example in the GloLog enterprise, the completion of land transport of a container (cf. Fig. 10.8) consists of loading the container on a truck, actually transporting the container from one location to another, and unloading the container. Each of these transaction kinds may have a sub-tree. For example, transporting the container may be decomposed into picking the container and putting it on a truck, driving the truck to the premises of IES, and taking the container from the truck. It is not so hard to imagine how each of these transaction kinds, on their turn, may be further decomposed, if needed. Figure 10.15 exhibits the CSD of the resulting part of the GloLog enterprise.

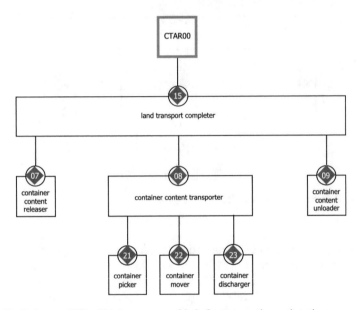

Fig. 10.15 Reference CSD of business process kinds for transporting and storing

As explained by the FI theory (cf. Chap. 5), the form part of an information item is inscribed in some physical substance. In modern digital technologies, the physical substance is mostly electrical, magnetic, or optical. In the ALPHA theory (cf. Chap. 11), the word "file" is used to refer to the collection of physical 'inscriptions' that together carry a document (or data set). Files are transported and stored, in much the same way as goods are transported and stored. Consequently, reference models apply that are similar to the one shown in Fig. 10.15. For example, in order to transport a file from your computer to another computer, a number of physical actions must be performed, including the transmission of the file through a computer network, like the Internet.

10.3.3.3   Transferring Ownership

In most civil codes, buying and selling are the dual notions (cf. Chap. 5) related to a (legal) agreement or contract between two parties about the transfer of ownership of *tangible* things from the seller to the buyer, commonly in exchange for an amount of money. In the OMEGA theory, paying is considered a separate transaction because it results in the creation of an original product, namely the transfer of ownership of an amount of money. Omitting the payment transaction does not affect the transfer of ownership of the goods. So, one can very well become owner of a thing without doing something in return, which means getting the thing for free.

As an example of the reference model that corresponds with the transfer of ownership of things, Fig. 10.16 shows, on the left side, the general pattern of transferring ownership. On the right side, the specific pattern for the case Pizzeria (cf. Chap. 14) is shown. The transactor roles TAR01 and TAR03 represent, respectively, the transfer of ownership of goods and the transfer of ownership of money. As said, payments are not an inherent part of an ontological model. They occur if the ownership transfer crosses the border of economic (or business) units (cf. Chap. 11). Inside such a unit, there are no payments for services. Next, transactor roles TAR02 and TAR04 in Fig. 10.16 are considered enterprise specific. If the goods can be taken from stock, there is no manufacturing (like the preparing of pizzas). And if the goods are taken out by the customer, there is no delivering.

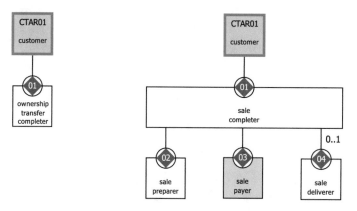

Fig. 10.16 Reference CSD of transferring ownership (left) and the Pizzeria example (right)

To illustrate how buying/selling things is conceived in the OMEGA theory, transaction kind TK01 regards the fulfilment of the selling/buying contract, in this case the transfer of ownership of pizzas. The transfer of ownership of the amount to pay is represented by transaction kind TK03. Every TK03 is enclosed in a TK01. Transactions TK01 have two other components: the preparing of the pizzas (TK02) and the optional delivering of the pizzas to the customer's place (TK04). Note that the case kind in all product kinds is the same, namely the sale. Sale is the conception of the product from the perspective of the supplier, as discussed in Chap. 5. From the perspective of the buyer, it is a purchase.

10.3.3.4 Obtaining Usufruct

Next to the transfer of ownership of goods, which basically implies a permanent right of usufruct of the owned goods, one may grant temporary usufruct of *tangible* things. These things are always space-time resources, so things that one uses or occupies for some time. Figure 10.17 exhibits the most general reference model. It is a simple tree of which the top is the transaction kind TK01 (concluding of the usufruct case). There are two enclosed transaction kinds: TK02 and TK03. In a transaction TK02 (resource seizing), the user is requested to occupy the resource at the agreed-upon beginning of the usufruct period. In a transaction TK03 (resource releasing), the user is requested to release the occupied resource at the agreed-upon ending of this period.

Concluding a usufruct case concerning tangible things, like cars, houses, rooms in a hotel, and chairs in an aircraft, a stadium or a theatre, is commonly called *renting*. As an example, if one rents a car, one gets the right to use the car for some period, and if one books a seat on a flight, one gets the right to use a chair in the aircraft with which the flight is carried out. Because payments are no inherent parts of ontological models (cf. Chap. 11), they are omitted in Fig. 10.17.

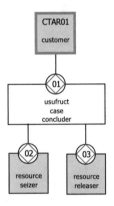

transaction kind	product kind	executor role
TK01 usufruct case concluding TK02 resource seizing TK03 resource releasing	PK01 [usufruct case] is concluded PK02 the resource of [usufruct case] is seized PK03 the resource of [usufruct case] is released	AR01 usufruct case concluder AR02 resource seizer AR03 resource releaser

Fig. 10.17 Reference CSD and TPT for granting usufruct of tangible things

Seizing and releasing space-time resources are commonly called checking-in and checking-out, respectively. Checking-in means that one shows up, at the car rental office, at the gate, or at the hotel, for actually driving, flying, or staying, respectively. It corresponds with declaring that one has seized the resource, so with performing the C-act [TK02/da]. Checking out corresponds with declaring that one has released the resource, so with performing a [TK03/da].

To the reference CSD in Fig. 10.17 belongs a typical reference PSD, shown in Fig. 10.18. What the PSD shows specifically is that the enclosed transactions TK02 (resource seizing) and TK03 (resource releasing) are initiated from the state of being requested in the enclosing TK01. In addition, performing the act [TK03/rq] has to wait for the being promised of the seizing (TK02/pm). After the releasing has also been promised (TK03/pm), the transaction TK01 can be promised. Expressed in more practical terms, concluding a usufruct case, like booking a seat on a flight or a room in a hotel, implies that one has committed oneself to check-in and to check-out. Not showing up for a check-in (called a no-show), means that the (in general scarce) resource cannot be occupied by somebody else.

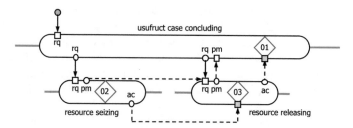

Fig. 10.18 Reference PSD for granting usufruct of tangible things

Figure 10.19 exhibits the reference model for car rental companies (cf. Chap. 15). The general transaction kinds 'resource seizing' and 'resource releasing' are replaced by the more specific 'car taking' and 'car returning'. Likewise, 'usufruct case concluding' is replaced by 'car rental completing'. Because transactions of the kind TK01 (car rental completing) take place between separate economic units (namely the renter and Rent-A-Car), two payment transactor roles are added, one for paying a deposit (TAR04) and one for paying the (final) invoice (TAR05), which may include fines.

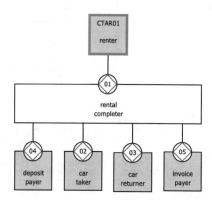

transaction kind	product kind	executor role
TK01 rental completing TK02 car taking TK03 car returning TK04 deposit paying TK05 invoice paying	PK01 [rental] is completer PK02 the car of [rental] is taken PK03 the car of [rental] is returned PK04 the deposit of [rental] is paid PK05 the invoice of [rental] is paid	AR01 rental completer AR02 car taker AR03 car returner AR04 deposit payer AR05 invoice payer

Fig. 10.19 Reference model of business process kinds in car rental companies

Next to the single obtaining of usufruct, like renting a car, there are contracts that give one the right on multiple instances of usufruct. For example, by becoming member of a tennis club, one acquires the right to play on the courts of the club as often as one likes (provided there is a free court). Similarly, by subscribing to a music streaming service, one can listen all day to one's favourite music. In these cases, there are two additional processes. The first one regards becoming a member and the second one regards ending the membership. We will illustrate them for the case Library (cf. Chap. 16). The CSD and the TPT are shown in Fig. 10.20. On the left side of the diagram are the added transaction kinds membership starting (TK01) and membership ending (TK02). Being member, one is authorised to initiate transactions TK03 (loan concluding).

Actors AR03 will therefore check for every TK03 whether the membership under which the borrower wants to borrow a book is a valid membership, that is, a membership that is started and not yet ended. This is represented in Fig. 10.20 by the access links from AR03 to TK01 and TK02. The general transaction kinds 'resource seizing' and 'resource releasing' (cf. Fig. 10.17) are replaced by the more specific ones 'book taking' and 'book returning'.

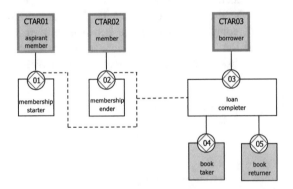

transaction kind	product kind	executor role
TK01 membership starting	PK01 [membership] is started	AR01 membership starter
TK02 membership ending	PK02 [membership] is ended	AR02 membership ender
TK03 loan completing	PK03 [loan] is completed	AR03 loan completer
TK04 book taking	PK04 the book of [loan] is taken	AR04 book taker
TK05 book returning	PK05 the book of [loan] is returned	AR05 book returner

Fig. 10.20 Reference CSD for libraries

In contemporary business practice, there is a tendency to offer the usufruct of things instead of transferring their ownership. Commonly, the usufruct is then called a *service*. Renting cars is already a good example of providing and using services. In many cities, one can nowadays also rent bikes, e-bikes, and scooters. Well-known examples in the ICT business are Software as a Service (SaaS) and Platform as a Service (PaaS).

10.3.3.5 The Ontology of Contracts

In the preceding subsections we have come across notions like sale (and purchase), rental and membership. They are special kinds of the general notion of contract. A contract is an agreement between parties in which the conditions regarding the mutual delivery of services is stated. The transfer of ownership of a number of pizza's in exchange of the transfer of ownership of an amount of money is a typical and well-known example of a contract. It is called a sale from the perspective of the seller and a purchase from the perspective of the buyer (cf. Sect. 5.3). Both parties may specify terms and conditions concerning such contracts. Consequently, we speak of terms and conditions of sale, and of terms and conditions of purchase. Moreover, Civil Codes usually contain sections in which the rights and duties of the legal parties in legal/economic contracts are laid down.

A sale in the case Pizzeria (cf. Chap. 14) is a contract between the legal entity Pizzeria and the legal entity customer. The first is represented by Mia and the second by somebody in the role of customer. The sale entity, thus the contract, is created at the moment that the request is performed, which means that the whole process of performing the C-act is completed (cf. Fig. 8.5). The applicable terms and conditions of sale are accessible to the customer, who is considered to comply with them when he/she performs the request in a sale completing transaction. Among other things, it implies that the customer will pay the money due once the payment is requested. Private customers commonly have no terms and conditions of purchase but companies commonly do. If this is the case, the purchase terms and conditions are considered to be known to the selling party, as they have to comply with them.

The compliance of a customer with terms and conditions of sale may be explicitly assessed in the sincerity division of the assess part of the action rule for settling customer requests, as discussed in Chap. 12. Customers who do not comply with the rules are thus considered insincere, more specifically: untrustworthy. Likewise, the compliance of a vendor with terms and conditions of purchase may be explicitly assessed in the sincerity division of the action rule for settling the promise of vendors to sell.

10.3.3.6 Enforcing Laws

Enforcing laws or rules is not a separate category in Table 10.2 but a combination of the existing ones. Still, it seems worthwhile to devote a section to this topic because it has quite some societal importance. To start with, there is no fundamental difference between the enforcement of laws by the police and, for example, the checking whether employees comply with the business rules that are in place.

There are always two processes. The first one is making laws or rules. It belongs to the category of creating and changing (intangible) things in Table 10.2. Thus, the reference model of Fig. 10.14 applies. The final product kind PK01 is a (societal) law or a (business) rule. In terms of the MU theory (cf. Chap. 6), societal laws and business rules are existence laws or occurrence laws concerning some world. Collectively, these laws determine which states and which transitions are lawful. Because of the basic autonomy of actors (cf. Chap. 8), laws can be disobeyed or violated. Consequently, the P-world or C-world of an organisation can be in an unlawful state. An example of violating a societal law is driving at a speed of 120 km/h where the speed limit is 90 km/h. An example of violating a business rule is starting the membership of a tennis club for an 11-year-old child if the minimum age is 12 years.

The second process in enforcing laws is about dealing with violations. According to the PSI theory (cf. Chap. 8), in particular Habermas' idea of discourse, the actor who violates a rule is challenged to give account of the violation, that is, to explain why he/she has deviated from the rule. In principle, there may be good reasons for the violation. In the example of driving too fast, the driver could be a medical doctor who is on her way to the hospital to give medical care to a road casualty. In the example of the tennis club, the 11-year-old boy (whose name appears to be Rafael Nadal) may be considered a very promising tennis player, who would otherwise go to the rival tennis club in town. There must always be room for discussion and discourse; this is a fundamental condition in Habermas' theory. But, if the explanation is unsatisfactory for the judging authority, measures may be taken.

There are two kinds of such measures. One aims at correcting the unlawful state. It could be an option in the tennis club case. As explained in Chap. 8, this can be achieved by revoking the promise of the tennis club official in the membership start transaction. In the subsequent discussions (and possibly discourse), the tennis club official has to convince the aspirant member that he/she is, on second thought, not allowed to make him member of the club.

The other kind of measure aims at discouraging or prohibiting the unlawful state from happening. It holds for the case of driving too fast, as well as for violating many other societal laws. In general, two (original) transaction kinds are needed to take this kind of measures. One is observing the violation of the law; the other is effectuating the discouraging or the prohibiting. The common way of discouraging future misbehaviour is by imposing a fine (with which you may be familiar in the case of driving too fast). The common way of prohibiting misbehaviour is by depriving the offender of her/his freedom, normally by imprisoning her/him. Note that these transactions belong to the category of creating and changing.

10.4   Discussions

10.4.1   Structure Thinking Versus Flow Thinking

The dominant way of thinking in business process management, as exemplified by the widespread approach named BPMN [1], is *flow thinking*. By this is meant that one perceives a business process as a sequence of actions or tasks that affect an entity or case, like a purchase or sale. The word "flow" refers to the 'flowing' of the cases through the sequence of actions. Flows are not necessarily monolithic; it may also consist of parallel (sub) flows. In the previous sections, we have introduced an alternative way of thinking about business processes, which we refer to as *structure thinking*. There are at least two situations in which flow thinking seems to be insufficient.

The first one is the situation where there are *different case kinds* in a (monolithic) process. This necessarily leads to splitting of the process into parallel cooperating processes, loosely coupled by the interstriction structure and the interimpediment structure. A good example of this situation is the GloLog enterprise, whose interaction structure is shown in Fig. 10.8. The 'main' business process kind is the one that is initiated by the client. The other three process kinds emerge from the necessity to devise separate processes because of incompatible case kinds. Consequently, these processes are initiated internally. The four process kinds together accomplish that, at the end, the client gets the goods that he/she has ordered.

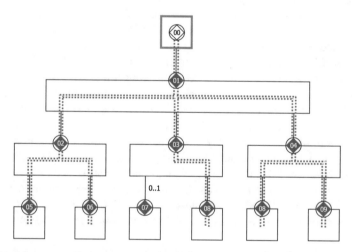

Fig. 10.21 Structure thinking versus flow thinking

The second situation is when one wants to make major changes to a business process kind. To illustrate this situation, let us have a look at Fig. 10.21, in which the interaction structure of Fig. 10.5 is copied. When applying structure thinking, one would get the next understanding of the whole process. It starts from an actor in CTAR00, who performs a request for a TK01, directed to an actor AR01. In response to it, the actor AR01 decides that he/she needs three other products in order to bring about the requested PK01, namely a PK02, a PK03, and a PK04. So, the AR01 performs corresponding requests to an AR02, an AR03, and an AR04, respectively. The bringing about of these products may be done in parallel, but there may also be dependencies, like the ones we have seen in Fig. 10.15. On their turn, the actors AR02, AR03, and AR04 need to start transactions in which products of the kinds PK05, PK06, PK07, PK08, and PK09 are brought about. Because the PK07 is optional, as indicated by the cardinality range 0...1, Fig. 10.21 shows, for the sake of illustration, the situation in which no PK07 is needed. Note also that two products PK08 are produced: one as part of a PK03 and one as part of a PK04.

When applying flow thinking, one would primarily follow the dotted brown lines in the figure, and consequently would understand the whole process basically as the next sequence of acts: [TK01/rq], [TK01/pm], [TK02/rq], [TK02/pm], [TK05/rq], [TK05/pm], [TK05/da], [TK05/ac], [TK06/rq], [TK06/pm], [TK06/da], [TK06/ac], [TK02/da], [TK02/ac], [TK03/rq], [TK03/pm], [TK08/rq], [TK08/pm], [TK08/da], [TK08/ac], [TK03/da], [TK03/ac], [TK04/rq], [TK04/pm], [TK08/rq], [TK08/pm], [TK08/da], [TK08/ac], [TK09/rq], [TK09/pm], [TK09/da], [TK09/ac], [TK04/da], [TK04/ac], [TK01/da], [TK01/ac].

Two comments are in place. The first one is that in this sequence, the possible parallel carrying out of transactions is ignored, just to keep it simple. The second comment is that the acts are indicated by their names as transaction steps, just for the sake of convenience. Other names would also be fine.

Let us point out two major drawbacks of flow thinking, and illustrate them using the example above. The first drawback is that it is very hard, if not impossible, to 'see' what the consequences of changing a part of the process are for other parts. For example, if one would like to replace the process of bringing about the component PK04 in every PK02 by another process, this concerns two separated parts in the sequence, namely the part that is represented by [TK04/rq] and [TK04/pm], and the part represented by [TK04/da] and [TK04/ac]. Moreover, one must be aware that the part in between these two, so the part that is represented by the sequence from [TK08/rq] through [TK09/ac], may also need to be changed as a consequence of changing the production of the PK04. One should also keep in mind that the transactor roles in Fig. 10.16 are original ones, that is, they belong to the O-organisation of an enterprise (cf. Chap. 11). But every actor role will have sub-trees in the corresponding I-organisation and D-organisation. In the current practice of business process modelling, such distinctions are not made, as discussed in Sect. 10.3.2.

The second drawback of flow thinking is that it becomes soon unclear who is responsible for what. Let us take as an example the part of the process that is represented by the sequence [TK05/rq], [TK05/pm], [TK05/da], [TK05/ac], [TK06/rq], [TK06/pm], [TK06/da], [TK06/ac]. Structure thinking tells us accurately that an actor AR02 is responsible for performing the [TK05/rq], as well as the [TK06/rq]. In the usual layout of workplaces, however, actors AR05 would be located close to actors AR06, and actors AR05 would pass their work (the PK05s) to actors AR06, which could easily lead to the idea in actors AR06 that they are ordered to produce their PK06s by actors AR05. Imagine, as an example, a bicycle factory where bicycles are assembled according to the BoM in Fig. 10.3 (right side). The actor who completes the frame of the bicycle passes it to her/his 'neighbour' who mounts the saddle on the frame, etc. The possible confusion thus may be even worsened by the fact that the message by which, for example, actors AR06 get the request to bring about a product PK06 may be delivered by an actor in the D-organisation (cf. Chap. 11).

10.4.2   Transforming Flows into Trees

As said, flow thinking may be useful, in particular when one wants to explain the details of the implementation of business process kinds, but when it comes to analysing, optimising, or (re)designing them, flow-based knowledge is insufficient. An interesting question then is how one can transform flow structures into tree structures. The answer is provided by the combined application of the OMEGA theory, the PSI theory (cf. Chap. 8), and the ALPHA theory (cf. Chap. 11). Let us illustrate this, using the Flow Charts of the case Volley [2], which are reproduced in Figs. 10.22, 10.23, 10.24, and 10.25. It is about becoming member of a tennis club. Applying the ALPHA theory means distinguishing between the O-, the I-, and the D-organisation, and subsequently abstracting from the I-organisation and the D-organisation, thus from the realisation of the Volley enterprise. In Figs. 10.22, 10.23, 10.24, and 10.25, documental (thus D-organisation) acts are indicated by the word "documental" and informational (thus I-organisation) acts by the word "informational", to which the letter "P" (for production) or "C" (for coordination) may be added. Only to original (thus O-organisation) acts do we apply in addition the PSI theory, which means that these acts are labeled as transaction steps in the complete transaction pattern. Lastly, the names of tacitly performed steps are put between "[" and "]".

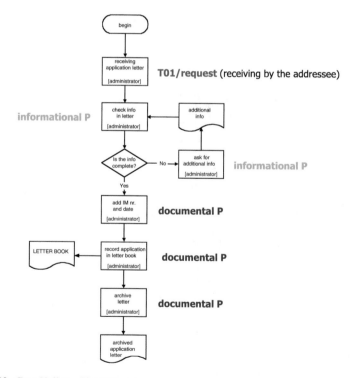

Fig. 10.22 Case Volley—Flow Chart 1

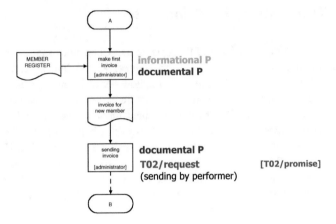

Fig. 10.23 Case Volley—Flow Chart 2

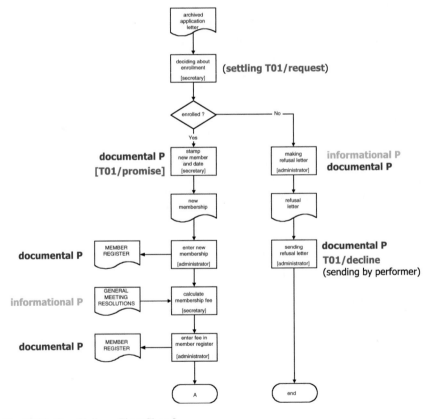

Fig. 10.24 Case Volley—Flow Chart 3

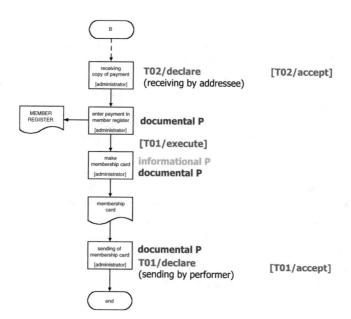

Fig. 10.25   Case Volley—Flow Chart 4

Fig. 10.26   CSD of the enterprise Volley

Applying the OMEGA theory to the results of the analysis of the Flow Charts yields the simple tree structure that is shown in Fig. 10.26. There are three actor roles: CTAR00 (aspirant member), who is the initiator of transactions TK01 (membership starting), AR01 (membership starter), who is the executor of transactions TK01 and initiator of transactions TK02 (membership payment), and AR02 (membership payer), who is the executor of transactions TK02. As shown, transactions TK02 are enclosed in transactions TK01. The tree structure in Fig. 10.26 conforms to the reference model for creating and changing (cf. Fig. 10.14).

As extensively discussed in [2], the CSD of the enterprise Volley in Fig. 10.26, shows more and at the same time less than the Flow Charts in Figs. 10.22, 10.23, 10.24, and 10.25. It shows more because it contains the complete transaction pattern of both transaction kinds. An important practical consequence is that one is made aware of the process 'exceptions', like the decline and the reject, and the four revocation patterns. They are easily forgotten otherwise. In addition, one is made aware that coordination acts can be performed tacitly. Tacitly performed acts are major causes of business process failures in practice. A 'no news is good news' rule could be economically justified in the past, it certainly is not anymore, given the modern ICT.

The CSD in Fig. 10.26 shows less because it is abstracted from the realisation and implementation of the enterprise Volley, whereas the flow charts in Figs. 10.22, 10.23, 10.24, and 10.25 show realisation and implementation details. But, as one can easily check, they are not complete. Every flow chart includes what the maker (the analyst) has observed and has considered worthwhile to include. In contrast, the realising of an enterprise's O-organisation (thus the devising of its I- and D-organisation) according to the ALPHA theory (cf. Chap. 11) is systematic and therefore comprehensive, as is the implementation of all three aspect organisations.

10.4.3   The Loose Coupling of Processes

We have already said that the distinct interaction trees in an organisation are loosely coupled through the existing interstriction and interimpediment structures. It means that the distinct business process kinds influence each other through these structures, but without the need to interact. The practical advantage is that each business process can be re-designed (and subsequently re-engineered and re-implemented) independently of the processes with which they are connected through these structures. Only the interfaces, thus the access links and the wait links, must be properly dealt with.

The notion of loose coupling has a history in systems design that dates back to 1972, when David Parnas published his paper on the decomposing of (software) systems into modules. It is included in [3]. Without calling it loose coupling, many other researchers, like Edsger Dijkstra [4, 5] and Michael Jackson [6, 7], proceeded in the same way. In hindsight, these authors can be considered the forerunners of object-oriented programming and design. A more recent approach to the modularisation of systems is Normalised Systems [8]. Although all of them focus on software engineering, the applied principles of modular design have a broader scope. The invariable key question is how to decompose a (too) complex system into comprehensible, manageable, and maintainable parts (modules).

The OMEGA theory, as presented in this chapter, offers an approach to modularising organisations, based on the tree structures that are inherent in the products that are brought about. It is a most natural way to achieve maximum cohesion within a process tree and minimum dependencies between them, as extensively discussed in Sects. 10.2 and 10.3. As an additional illumination of the soundness of the theory, let us study the consequences of the narrowing down of the

SoI in the case GloLog. To this end, Fig. 10.27 exhibits the narrowing down to the sales and the purchase processes, thus excluding or ignoring the land transport process and the sea transport process, indicated by the yellow-lined rectangle. This rectangle cuts across several access links and wait links. The question now is how these links must be represented in a CSD of the new SoI.

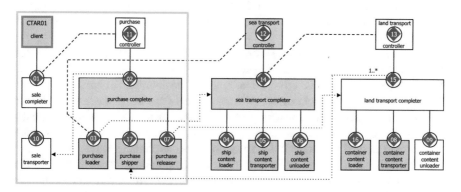

Fig. 10.27 Narrowing down the scope in the case GloLog (1)

The access link from actor role AR12 to transaction kind TK03 can just be left out because it represents an information need from outside the new scope. For similar reasons, the wait link from TK03 to AR14, and the one from TK07 to AR15 can be omitted. The only interdependency we have to take care of is the wait link from TK15 to AR17. Figure 10.28 shows how this is done, namely by including the (now external) transaction kind TK15. In order to illustrate access links to external transaction kinds, the one to the multiple transaction kind MTK01 (cf. Chap. 12) is included.

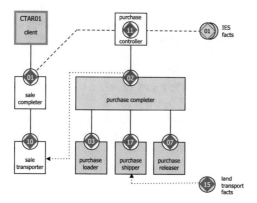

Fig. 10.28 Narrowing down the scope in the case GloLog (2)

10.4.4   The Practical Importance of the OMEGA Theory

The OMEGA theory is meant to be, and has also proven to be, an intellectual instrument in discovering and profiting from the tree structures that exist in business processes, once these processes have been understood in the ontological way as provided by the PSI theory (cf. Chap. 8). The key concept on which the OMEGA theory builds is the transactor role. It is the constructional building block of organisations, and consequently of the business processes that become manifest when these organisations are operational.

The understanding of a business process as a tree of transaction processes, in the way discussed in Sect. 10.2.2, is probably the most important insight that the OMEGA theory offers. Therefore, it was taken as the definition of *business process*. The (interaction) tree structure resembles the product structure of the 'top' product in the tree. Consequently, the core entity or case kind in each node of a tree must be the same as the one in the higher node (the parent), or be a true part of it. Structure clashes are solved by conceiving separate trees, as demonstrated for the case GloLog. The provided insight is lacking in contemporary approaches to business process modelling, like BPMN [1, 9], UML [10, 11], Aris [12], and Archimate [13]. Concluding, it should not be a surprise that these approaches offer little help when major process changes are at stake.

The tree structure also allows for a clear and precise discussion of the often vaguely defined notions of process and data ownership (cf. Sect. 10.3.1). The combination of tree thinking and flow thinking for practical business process analysis was demonstrated in Sects. 10.4.1 and 10.4.2.

The second important insight is that the dependencies between (interaction) tree structures can simply be expressed in an additional *interstriction structure* and an additional *interimpediment structure*. The first one represents the *state dependencies* among business processes; that is, the situations in which for performing a process step, the state of another business process is taken into account. The second one represents the *process dependencies* among business processes; that is, the situations in which one has to wait for a specific progress in another business process to come into being in order to perform a step (in the current process). The precise nature of the impediments can be expressed in the PSD, as discussed in Sect. 10.3.2.

The third practical insight that the OMEGA theory provides is that, in practice, there are only a few really different process structures. In Sect. 10.3.3, we have called them *reference models*. They may remain a subject of ongoing research, but it looks like one can do with a limited number of 'fibre' structures, on top of the 'molecules' and 'atoms' as presented in [14]. They can be used as building blocks to construct the essential model of any enterprise in a short amount of time.

References

1. Mendling, J., & Weidlich, M. (2012). Business process model and notation 4th international workshop. In *Proceedings. Lecture notes in business information processing* (p. 1). BPMN 2012, Vienna, Austria, September 12–13, 2012. Berlin: Springer.

2. Perinforma, A. P. C. (2015). *The essence of organisation*. Leidschendam: Sapio Enterprise Engineering.
3. Parnas, D. L., Hoffman, D. M., & Weiss, D. M. (2001). Software fundamentals. In D. L. Parnas (Ed.), *Collected papers* (xxiv, 664 p.). Boston: Addison-Wesley.
4. Dijkstra, E. W. (1970). *Notes on structures programming*.
5. Dijkstra, E. W. (1976). *A discipline of programming* (XVII, 217 p.). Prentice-Hall series in automatic computation. Englewood Cliffs, NJ: Prentice-Hall.
6. Jackson, M. A. (1975). *Principles of program design* (xii, 299 p.). A P I C studies in data processing. London: Academic.
7. Jackson, M. A. (1983). *System development* (XIV, 418 p.). Prentice-Hall International series in computer science. Englewood Cliffs, NJ: Prentice/Hall International.
8. Mannaert, H., Verelst, J., & De Bruyn, P. (2016). Normalized systems – from foundations for evolvable software toward a general theory for evolvable design. Kermt, Belgium: Koppa.
9. Dumas, M., et al. (2018). *Fundamentals of business process management* (2nd ed.). Berlin: Springer.
10. ACM Digital Library. UML: Unified Modeling Language. In *ACM Digital Library*. s.n.: S.l.
11. Scott, K. (2001). UML explained (xviii, 151 p.). Boston: Addison-Wesley.
12. Scheer, A.-W. (1999). *ARIS – Business process modeling* (XIX, 218 S., 2nd. completely Rev. and Enl. ed.). Berlin: Springer.
13. The Open Group. (2010). *Archimate∗∗ 1.0 specification? Technical standard technical standard* (p. 1, 161 p.). Zaltbommel: Van Haren Publishing.
14. Dietz, J. L. G. (2003). The atoms, molecules and fibres of organizations. *Data and Knowledge Engineering, 47*, 24.

Chapter 11
The ALPHA Theory: Understanding the Essence of Organisations

Abstract The ALPHA theory, or organisational essence theory, is a theory about the distinction of layers of transactor roles in an organisation, based on the sort of production that transactors bring about: original, informational, or documental. Original production comprises all production acts that result in original new facts. Examples are devising things, deciding and judging, as well as manufacturing, transporting, and observing things. Informational production acts comprise remembering, computing and deriving facts, and sharing (remembered or derived) facts. Documental production acts comprise saving, providing, and transforming documents or data (containing facts), as well as storing, retrieving, copying, transmitting, and destroying files. Accordingly, the organisation of an enterprise can be partitioned into three partial organisations: the O-organisation (O from original), the I-organisation (I from informational), and the D-organisation (D from documental). The I-organisation supports the O-organisation by means of informational services (remembering and sharing facts), and the D-organisation supports the I-organisation by means of documental services (saving and providing data or documents). Because original acts are the only acts that change the state of the 'business' world of an enterprise (i.e. the production world of its O-organisation), they must be performed by human actors. For informational and documental acts, it holds that they can be taken over by artefacts, notably ICT systems, including AI-artefacts (like logistic control systems and robots). However, as pointed out in the PSI theory, human actors are ultimately responsible and accountable for the acts of these artefacts. The ontological model of an enterprise's O-organisation is called its essential model. Like every ontological model, it is abstracted from implementation, but it is also abstracted from realisation, that is, from the supporting I- and D-organisation. Yet it contains everything that is needed to understand the essence of an enterprise's operation. In terms of size, that is, the amount of diagrams, text, etc., the essential model is less than 5% of a 'normal' complete model of an enterprise. So, the ALPHA theory contributes to the generic enterprise engineering goal of intellectual manageability by an unprecedented reduction of complexity. The ALPHA theory also clarifies that every enterprise information system (EIS) is nothing more or less than a part of I- and the D-organisation that support the O-organisation, only implemented by using ICT. Thus, the (functional) requirements for an EIS are contained in the essential model of the organisation.

© Springer Nature Switzerland AG 2020

J. L. G. Dietz, J. B. F. Mulder, *Enterprise Ontology*, The Enterprise Engineering Series, https://doi.org/10.1007/978-3-030-38854-6_11

11.1   Introduction

The theory in this chapter is labeled A-theory. The Greek capital letter is pronounced as ALPHA, an acronym for Abstraction Layers in Production for Holistic Analysis. It concerns layers of transactors (cf. Chap. 8) that can be discerned in every organisation. They exist next to the compositional trees that are discussed in Chap. 10. The ALPHA theory is classified as an *ontological* theory in the framework of theories, as presented in Chap. 4. Thus, it is a theory about the nature of things.

Three layers of transactors are distinguished, based on the three distinct sorts of production acts (cf. Chap. 8): original, informational, and documental. The distinction corresponds to the distinct performa, informa, and forma levels in coordination. Accordingly, the organisation of an enterprise can be layered into three partial organisations: the *O-organisation* (O from original), the *I-organisation* (I from informational), and the *D-organisation* (D from documental). The I-organisation supports the O-organisation by means of informational services (remembering and sharing facts), and the D-organisation supports the I-organisation by means of documental services (saving and providing data or documents).

Original production acts result in original (new) production facts. Examples are devising things, deciding and judging (all of them concerning intangible things), and manufacturing, transporting, and observing things (all of them concerning tangible things). *Informational production* acts comprise remembering facts, computing or deriving facts, and sharing (remembered or derived) facts. *Documental production* acts concern the signs (documents or data) that contain facts, including the physical substances in which they are inscribed (cf. Chap. 5). Therefore, they comprise saving, providing and transforming documents or data, as well as storing, retrieving, copying, transmitting, and destroying files (both electronic and paper based). Because original acts are the only acts that change the state of the 'business' world of an enterprise (i.e. the production world of its O-organisation), they must be performed by human actors. Informational and documental acts can be taken over by artefacts, notably ICT systems, including AI-artefacts (like logistic control systems and robots). However, as pointed out in Chap. 8, human actors are ultimately responsible and accountable for the acts of these artefacts.

The remainder of the chapter is organised as follows. Section 11.2 (foundations) starts with discussing the three organisational layers, as well as the corresponding sorts of actors and products, on the basis of the semiotic ladder (cf. Chap. 5). Next, the notion of the essential model of an enterprise is presented. Section 11.3 (elaborations) starts with deepening the key concepts that are discussed in Sect. 11.2. Next, the notions of realisation and implementation are elaborated. It comprises a discussion of the differences between actors and agents (artificial intelligence), and it will lead to the understanding of (enterprise) information systems as inherent parts of organisations. In Sect. 11.4 (discussions), two topics are addressed. One is the distinction between an enterprise's organisation and the boundary of its business, thereby clarifying the notion of (in- and out-) sourcing. The other topic is the current debate on AI and the position that is taken in this discussion by the discipline of Enterprise Engineering (EE).

11.2 Foundations

11.2.1 The Organisational Layers

The FI theory (cf. Chap. 5) provides us with the semiotic ladder (cf. Fig. 11.1). It clarifies the role of signs in the communication between human beings. Information is defined as the means for communication. A unit of *information*, commonly called an information item, is a dyad of content and form: the two parts are distinguishable but not separable, like the two sides of a coin. The content of an information item is the *thought* to be conveyed, and the form consists of perceivable formations (letters, numerals, and other symbols), collectively called the *sign*. The content comprises both the intention (or pragmatics) and the proposition (or semantics) of the thought, and the form comprises both the formalism (or syntax) and the coding (or empirics) of the sign. Signs are 'inscribed' in some physical substance, for example, on paper, on clay tablets or in electromagnetic waves.

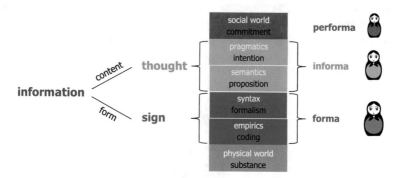

Fig. 11.1 The semiotic ladder

In accordance with the semiotic ladder, the PSI theory (cf. Chap. 8) distinguishes three abilities of communicating subjects: the *forma* ability (to deal with empirics and syntax), the *informa* ability (to deal with semantics and pragmatics), and the *performa* ability (to deal with the social impact of communication). These abilities are shown, on the right side of Fig. 11.1, as three shapes that human beings can take on. The physical world (dealing with substances) is not covered by the performa-informa-forma distinction. As clarified in Sect. 11.2.3, we consider it to be included in the forma ability. The analogy with the Matryoshka (Russian nested doll) shapes is used to illustrate that they must be understood as enclosed in each other, from top to bottom, that is, they are scaled top-down.

In Chap. 8, the performa, informa, and forma abilities or shapes are used to clarify the distinct levels in the process of performing coordination acts. Here, we will apply them to clarify the distinction that can be made in every enterprise between three organisational layers, based on the following three sorts of production acts: original, informational (or infological), and documental (or datalogical). The terms "infological" and "datalogical" are coined by Langefors [1]. For practical reasons, we will use the more common synonyms "informational" and "documental".

A production act is called *original* if it creates new facts in the business world of the enterprise (cf. Chap. 7). Examples of original acts are the decision by the customer in a flower shop to buy a bouquet of flowers, and the subsequent decision by the addressed salesperson to sell a bouquet of flowers to the customer.

A production act is called *informational* if it concerns the remembering, sharing, or deriving of business facts (note: derivation comprises both mathematical computation and logical deduction). Shared facts may be original, thus created in an original production act, or derived. Note that the derivation of facts does not change the state of the world; it only leads to presenting the state in new, possibly more intelligible or convenient ways. Computing the daily turnover of a flower shop is an example of an informational act. It does not change the performed sales, but it presents them in a more convenient way.

A production act is called *documental* if it concerns the saving and providing of documents or data (which contain facts that need to be remembered). Also transforming documents or data, like changing the docx format of a document to PDF, is a documental act. Moreover, we consider documental acts to include physical operations on the files that carry the documents or data. Examples of these operations are storing, retrieving, copying, transmitting, and destroying. The distinction between documents (or data) and files will be clarified in Sect. 11.2.3.

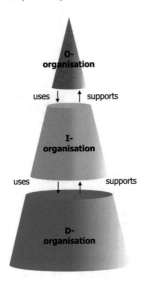

Fig. 11.2 The organisational layers

In Fig. 11.2, the total organisation of an enterprise is divided into three partial organisations, in accordance with the distinction between original, informational, and documental production. The three partial organisations are respectively called *O-organisation* (from Original), *I-organisation* (from Informational), and *D-organisation* (from Documental). All original production acts are performed by actors in the O-organisation (called *O-actors* for short), all informational production acts are performed by actors in the I-organisation (called *I-actors* for short), and all documental production acts are performed by actors in the D-organisation (called

D-actors for short). The general relationship between the three partial organisations is that the D-organisation supports the I-organisation, and that the I-organisation supports the O-organisation. Conversely, the O-organisation uses (the services of) the I-organisation, and the I-organisation uses (the services of) the D-organisation. In Fig. 11.3, O-actors are represented by figurines with red hats, I-actors by figurines with green hats, and D-actors by figurines with blue hats, like the gnomes in [2].

11.2.2 Organisational Layers and Sorts of Actors

As explained in Chap. 8, actors collaborate through carrying out transactions. Corresponding with the distinction between the O-organisation, the I-organisation, and the D-organisation, we distinguish between original or *O-transactions*, informational or *I-transactions*, and documental or *D-transactions*.

In addition to the transaction kinds that exist within the I-organisation, there are two general I-transaction kinds between the O-organisation and the I-organisation, as shown in Fig. 11.3: *remembering* facts and *sharing* facts. Transactions of these kinds are initiated by O-actors and executed by I-actors. O-actors are able to do this by taking on their informa shape (cf. Chap. 8). Similarly, there are two general D-transaction kinds between the I-organisation and the D-organisation, as shown in Fig. 11.3: *saving* documents (or data) and *providing* documents (or data). I-actors are able to initiate transactions of these kinds by taking on their forma shape.

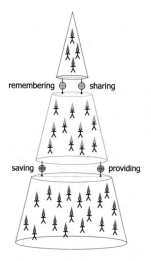

Fig. 11.3 Organisational layers with corresponding O-, I-, and D-actors

So, one of the services that the I-organisation offers to the O-organisation is that O-actors can ask I-actors to remember (original) facts. This happens in remembering transactions. Likewise, they can ask to share (original or derived) facts in sharing transactions. The separation between creating facts and remembering created facts is strict. By definition, O-actors create facts but do not remember them. If they want facts to be remembered, they need to initiate a remembering transaction, and if they want to know facts, they need to initiate a sharing transaction. Note, however, that this is a separation of actor roles, not of subjects (cf. Chap. 8). For example, the salesperson in a flower shop fills the O-actor role seller when selling flowers, and in this actor role he/she does not remember what has been sold. In order to have sales facts remembered, he/she must ask an actor in the I-organisation to remember them. But this I-actor may be the same person as the O-actor. Continuing the flower shop example, the I-actor who has to remember the sales facts, may feel the need to document these facts in order not to forget them. To this end, he or she may write down sales facts and ask a D-actor to save the notes. Likewise, an I-actor may ask a D-actor to provide saved documents or data. Both actors may be the same person, and they may also be the same person as the I-actor.

To elaborate this, the figurines with the coloured hats in Fig. 11.3 are actors, thus subjects in filling an actor role, not the actor roles. Consequently, the same subject may be present in the O-organisation with a red hat, in the I-organisation with a green hat, and in the D-organisation with a blue hat. This is very common, in all enterprises. Sometimes, people perform original acts, sometimes informational, and sometimes documental. But the distribution of these sorts of acts over individual persons may differ substantially. People whose organisational function is to sell or to purchase, for example, will mainly perform original acts (and then be an O-actor). In contrast, accountants will mainly perform informational acts, like calculating (and then be an I-actor), and the internal postmen will predominantly perform documental acts, namely transporting letters and reports (and then be a D-actor).

11.2.3   Organisational Layers and Sorts of Production

Let us have a closer look now at the distinct kinds of production acts, and corresponding products, as presented in Sect. 11.2.1, in order to get a deeper understanding of the relationships between the O-organisation of an enterprise, on the one hand, and its I- and D-organisation, on the other hand.

As explained in Chap. 8, the key characteristic of all *original* production acts is that they result in new facts in the business world of the enterprise, that is, the production world of its O-organisation. In Fig. 11.4, a distinction is made between immaterial or intangible production (left side) and material or tangible production (right side). Examples of *immaterial* production acts are all kinds of devising (thinking up, designing), deciding, and judging. These acts create original business facts, always and everywhere. They also constitute the majority of production acts in contemporary enterprises. To illustrate this, every sale or purchase implies an original decision by an authorised and responsible actor, and every advice or consultation is an original judgement, which also requires an authorised and responsible executor.

Examples of *material* production acts are all manufacturing acts and all logistic (physical) acts, like transporting. This is quite obvious. Less obvious may be that observing or measuring things are also material acts. Let us take, as an example, the measurement of water heights. Most people are able to 'measure' the water height in rivers and canals by looking at the rulers that are placed on the sides, here and there.

These observations, however, have no significance for the decision by the captain of a barge on the route to take through the waters. He or she needs an authorised measurement, which is usually provided by a particular government agency. There are authorised and responsible actors that determine the water heights. Skippers rely on their authority and will hold them responsible, and possibly accountable, if things go wrong. In our institutionalised modern societies, we want and need to do 'business' this way [3]. Therefore, the produced observations and measurements are considered original facts.

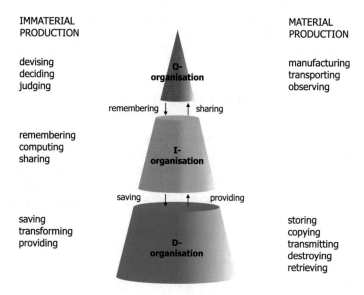

Fig. 11.4 Organisational layers and sorts of production

The characteristic of all *informational* production acts is that they are immaterial. This is implied by their nature. Informational acts are acts by the human mind, and the resulting products are thoughts. Following the FI theory (cf. Chap. 5), we will speak of *conceptual facts* rather than thoughts. These conceptual facts are either original facts or derived facts.

Also *documental* production is, by nature, *immaterial*. As illustrated in Fig. 11.1, it regards dealing with *signs*. More common words for signs are "documents" and "data", although few people would consider these words to be true synonyms. One normally thinks of *documents* as of reports, books, or letters. The common characteristic is that they are large amounts of signs (words) without much structure. Likewise, one normally thinks of *data* as of structured signs, which mostly contain factual information. Because the operations on documents and data are the same, there is no reason, within the scope of the ALPHA theory, to make a distinction between them. Nevertheless, we will continue to speak of documents and data, preferably of documents and *data sets*, and to consider both as collections of data.

In [4], a partial organisation below the D-organisation is conceived in order to deal properly with all material D-acts. Here we take an easier path; we consider the *material* operations on the carriers of documents and data sets to belong to documental production. As shown in Fig. 11.4, they comprise the storing, copying, transmitting, destroying, and retrieving of *files* (the physical carriers of documents and data sets). The distinction between documents or data sets, on the one hand, and their physical carriers, thus files, on the other hand, is important. Every file is the carrier of a document or a data set. Conversely, every document or data set may be inscribed in a number of files, commonly called copies of the document or the data set. A document or data set is saved by storing one or more files that carry the document or data set, and it is provided by retrieving and transmitting files. Moreover, only files can be destroyed, documents and data cannot. But, if all files that carry a document or data set are destroyed, the document or data set is usually considered to be lost (although there may be I-actors who still can recall their contents).

11.2.4   The Essential Model of an Enterprise

In Chap. 9, the essential model of a system is defined as an ontological model, thus a model of its construction (cf. Chap. 7), that is fully abstracted from realisation and implementation. More specifically, the prismanet of a system is called the *essential model* of the system (within the PRISMA meta model). Based on this notion, we will develop in this section the notion of essential model for enterprises. Figure 11.5 illustrates what it means to abstract from *realisation*, that is, from the supporting I-organisation and D-organisation, and thus to focus on the O-organisation.

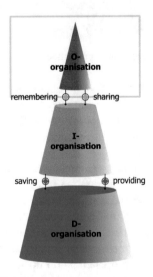

Fig. 11.5 Abstracting from realisation

By understanding the construction and operation of the O-organisation, one understands that part of an enterprise's organisation that brings about its business. As stated, the I-organisation supports the operation of the O-organisation, but it is not part of it. Likewise, the D-organisation supports the I-organisation, but it is not part of it. For a full understanding of the operation of the O-organisation, we can therefore confine ourselves to the interface between the O- and the I-organisation, thus to the remembering and sharing transaction kinds between them, in addition of course to understanding the internals of the O-organisation itself.

Ontologically spoken, all created facts, both coordination facts and production facts, exist in the corresponding world, from their event time onward (cf. Chap. 8), and they will exist forever. Therefore, the remembering transaction kinds in Fig. 11.5 can be accommodated by considering created conceptual facts to be 'stored' in the 'bank' of the transaction kind in whose transactions they are created. A *transaction bank* is the conceptual container of all facts that are created in the carrying out of transactions of the concerned kind (cf. Chap. 10). In order to also accommodate the sharing transaction kinds, we introduce the notion of *access* right. Every actor role whose fillers need to know conceptual facts from a transaction bank, has reading access to the bank. In Chap. 10, this access right is expressed by means of an access link from the actor role to the transaction kind in whose transactions the facts are created. In case one needs derived facts, the access links go to all transaction banks in which the 'ingredient' original facts reside from which the derived facts are obtained. To illustrate this, Fig. 10.9 is reproduced as Fig. 11.6.

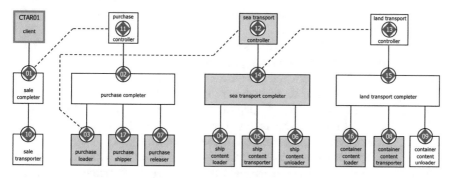

Fig. 11.6 Access links in the essential model of the GloLog enterprise

As an example of an access link, let us explain the link from the self-activating actor role AR11 to the transaction bank TK01, represented by the dashed line between their shapes. Actors AR11 periodically compose purchase orders from sales orders. To be able to do this, they need to know what sales orders are placed (and not yet completed). These facts are contained in the transaction bank of TK01.

The ontological model of an enterprise's O-organisation, including the ways in which the remembering and sharing transactions are taken care of, is called the *essential model* of the enterprise.

11.3 Elaborations

The discussions in Sect. 11.2 culminated in the notion of the essential model of an enterprise, which is arrived at by abstracting from realisation and implementation. In this section, we will investigate organisations the other way around, based on the dissertation of De Jong [4]. First we will take up the task to clarify in detail how one can systematically design the ontological models of the supporting I-organisation and D-organisation, given the ontological model of the corresponding O-organisation. This will be done in Sects. 11.3.1 and 11.3.2. In Sects. 11.3.3–11.3.6, we will discuss how the ontological models of the three partial organisations can be implemented, in order to arrive at a constructional model of an enterprise at such a level of detail that it can be put into operation straightforwardly. Along the same lines of reasoning, the notion of enterprise information system will be studied in Sect. 11.3.7.

11.3.1 Designing the Ontological Model of the I-Organisation

As discussed in Sect. 11.2, the interface between an enterprise's O-organisation and I-organisation consists of two general transaction kinds: remembering and sharing. In transactions of both kinds, the executor is an I-actor and the initiator is an O-actor in her/his informa (green) shape (cf. Chap. 8). Remembering concerns the C-facts and P-facts that the O-actor creates. Sharing concerns the C-facts and P-facts that the O-actor needs to know.

An O-actor does initiate transactions of these kinds when he/she is settling a trigger, as discussed in the PSI theory (cf. Chap. 8) and the DELTA theory (cf. Chap. 9). As also discussed in these theories, actors constantly loop through their operating cycles, checking in every cycle whether there are triggers to settle. To this end, they have permanent access to their agenda, through a sharing transaction kind. At the beginning of a cycle, an actor selects an agendum to settle. There may be several simultaneous agenda, but since they are not dependent on each other (cf. Chap. 9), they can be dealt with concurrently. Next to knowing the agendum to be settled, O-actors must also know the action rule to be executed. The next step is therefore to fetch the corresponding action rule, through a sharing transaction. Action rules are also considered to be facts, but created by another part of the enterprise, outside the O-organisation that we are focusing at. In order to illustrate how the interface between an enterprise's O-organisation and I-organisation looks like, Table 11.1 exhibits one of the action rules for the case Rent-A-Car (cf. Chap. 15). Note that both the fetching of the agenda and the fetching of the action rule are taken for granted.

The *event part* of the action rule begins with the *when-clause*. It specifies the agendum to settle (in this case: 'rental completing **for** [rental] **is** requested'). This request is created by an actor who is filling the role of initiator in the transaction at hand, and it is settled by the actor who is filling the role of executor (cf. Chap. 8). In the first execution of the rule, a new instance of the core entity type, in this case 'rental', is created. The same instance is used in successive executions, for example, as the effect of a discussion in the state 'declined'. The event part also contains a *with-clause*, in which the facts are specified that are provided, along with the request fact. They are the properties or attributes of the core entity, in this case represented by the value of [rental], so of a specific rental.

Table 11.1 Example of an action rule from the case Rent-A-Car

event part	**when** rental completing **for** [rental] is <u>requested</u>
	 with
	 remember
	    the starting day **of** [rental] **is some** day
	    the ending day **of** [rental] **is some** day
	    the renter **of** [rental] **is some** person
	    the deposit payer **of** [rental] **is some** person
	    the driver **of** [rental] **is some** person
	    the deposit payer **of** [rental] **is some** person
	    the car group **of** [rental] **is some** car group
	    the pick-up location **of** [rental] **is some** branch
	    the return location **of** [rental] **is some** branch
	 rebmemer

assess part	share
	    the <u>performer</u> **of the** <u>request</u> is the renter **of** [rental];
	    the <u>addressee</u> **of the** <u>request</u> is **a** rental completer;
	    the starting day **of** [rental] is in the rental horizon **of the** year **of**
	      the starting day **of** [rental];
	    the ending day **of** [rental] is in the rental horizon **of the** year **of**
	      the ending day **of** [rental];
	    the ending day **of** [rental] **is equal to or greater than**
	      the starting day **of** [rental];
	    the duration **of** [rental] **is less than or equal to** the max rental
	      duration **in the** year **of the** starting day **of** [rental];
	    the expiration day **of the** driving license **of the** driver **of** [rental]
	      is equal to or greater than the ending day **of** [rental];
	    the number **of** free cars **in the** car group **of** [rental] **on** every day **in**
	      the rental period **of** [rental] **is greater than zero**
	 erahs

response part	**if** *performing the action after **then** is considered justifiable*
	 then
	 remember
	 <u>promise</u> rental completing **for** [rental]
	      to the renter **of** [rental]
	 <u>request</u> deposit paying **for** [rental]
	      to the deposit payer **of** [rental]
	         with the <u>requested</u> ot **of** rental paying **for** [rental] **is** Now;
	            the <u>requested</u> deposit amount **of** [rental] **is equal to**
	               the standard deposit amount **for the** car group **of** [rental]
	               in the year **of the** starting day **of** [rental]
	 rebmemer
	 else
	 remember
	 <u>decline</u> rental completing **for** [rental] **to the** renter **of** [rental]
	      with * reason for declining *
	 rebmemer

As said, the fetching of the agenda, including the dependent facts of the core entity type, thus 'rental' in Table 11.1, is taken for granted. The same holds for the evaluation of the predications, like <the starting day of [rental] is some day>.

The *assess part* of an action rule is an expression of the action or business rule that is in place. It is effectively a list of facts that must exist (i.e. must be the case). The first two facts in the assess part of Table 11.1 concern the coordination world, the others the production world. Note that most P-facts, that is, facts in the production world, are derived facts; they need to be computed by actors in the I-organisation. Obviously, precise specifications of these derived fact types must be available to the I-actors. As explained in Chap. 12, producing them is considered to be part of producing the so-called Fact Model. In order to get to know the listed facts, the executing actor initiates corresponding sharing transactions. This is indicated in the event part in Table 11.1 by the pair of brackets "share" and "erahs", printed in green, that enclose the facts to be shared.

The *response part* starts with the sentence that expresses the human autonomy of the executing actor. He/she is allowed to violate the business rule, but can be held accountable for it (cf. Chap. 8). The remainder of the response part is a formulation of the coordination acts that are performed as the outcome of executing the action rule. In this case, it is either the promise in completing the rental, followed by the request in a new transaction, namely the payment of the deposit, or the decline of the request for completing the rental. Thus, the result is either two C-events of which the C-facts are (rental completing **for** [rental] **is** promised) and (deposit payment **for** [rental] **is** requested) or a C-event with C-fact (rental completed **for** [rental] **is** declined). After an agendum is settled, it is marked as such, and this C-fact is remembered. In order to make the created C-events known to the actors who have to settle them, the executing actor initiates the corresponding remembering transactions. This is indicated in the event part in Table 11.1 by the pair of brackets "remember" and "rebmemer", printed in green, that enclose the facts to be remembered. Note that a with-clause may be added to the results of the action rule, in which the properties and attributes are listed that need also to be remembered.

Table 11.2 Example of (a part of) an action rule from the case Rent-A-Car

event part	when rental completing **for** [rental] **is** promised
	while
	share
	deposit paying **for** [rental] **is** accepted
	erahs

In action rule ARS-3 in Chap. 15, a *while-clause* is added to the when-clause. It is shown in Table 11.2. This while-clause specifies that the execution of the rule cannot take place before the fact in the while-clause has begun to exist. In other words, the executing actor is held up in executing the rule until this fact exists. Obviously, in order to get to know the fact (deposit paying **for** [rental] **is** promised), it must be enclosed between the brackets "share" and "erahs".

The executing actor is now burdened with the task to constantly watch the occurrence of the event in the while-clause for which he/she has to wait. The DELTA theory (cf. Chap. 9) offers an elegant solution to this operational problem, by means of the notion of trigger.

According to the PSI theory (cf. Chap. 8), the product of a successfully carried out transaction begins to exist at the moment that the accept act is performed. Let us investigate here what this means for the design of the I-organisation. In Table 11.3, the action rule is presented in which a rental in the case Rent-A-Car is completed. If the accept act is performed (the then-clause of the response part), the product of the transaction must start to exist in the P-world at the same time. To indicate that this is the case, a corresponding sentence (coloured red) is added to Table 11.3, for clarification.

Table 11.3 Example of an action rule in which a product is created

event part	**when** car returning **for** [rental] is declared

assess part	share
	   the performer **of the** declaration **is the** driver **of** [rental];
	   the addressee **of the** declaration **is some** rental completer;
	   the declared car **of** car returning **for** [rental]
	      is the promised car **of** car returning **for** [rental]
	erahs

response part	**if** *performing the action after **then** is considered justifiable*
	then
	remember
	   accept car returning **for** [rental] **to the** performer **of the** declaration
	   the car **of** [rental] **is** returned
	remember
	else
	remember
	   reject car returning **for** [rental] **to the** performer **of the** declaration
	remember

We have clarified above how the general interface transaction kinds between an enterprise's O-organisation and I-organisation are put into effect in action rules, using the case Rent-A-Car for illustration. In addition to these transaction kinds, there are a number of other transaction kinds needed, which are internal to the I-organisation, of which both the initiator role and the executor role are filled by I-actors. Table 11.1 contains several examples of derived fact types for whose derivation such transaction kinds are needed. One of them is the fact type <**the** ending day **of** [rental] **is equal to or greater than the** starting day **of** [rental]>. This is a rather simple logical computation. Another example <**the** number of free cars **in the** car group **of** [rental] **on** every day **in the** rental period **of** [rental] **is greater than zero**>. Computing the truth value of this predication is not trivial at all; it will encompass various additional internal transaction kinds in the I-organisation, as one can imagine.

As can be deduced from the action rule in Table 11.1, the unit of factual knowledge to be remembered by I-actors is the coordination fact or C-fact for short. This should not be a surprise, because the C-act/fact is the atomic element of business processes, as discussed in Chap. 8. To clarify this, we reproduce in Fig. 11.7 the structure of a C-act/fact, as presented in Fig. 8.17. The example C-act/ fact is taken from the first remembering act in the response part of Table 11.1. It assumes that the subject Chiara fills the role of rental completer, that Jippe fills the role of deposit payer, that it is about rental 31416, that the deposit amount to pay is 112.50 €, and that the operative (payment) day is 2458400 (on the Julian time scale).

The remembered C-fact is an agendum for Jippe in his role of deposit payer. It will be shared with him at the right moment, that is, at the event time of the C-fact. In order to settle the agendum, Jippe will also be supplied with the appropriate action rule(s).

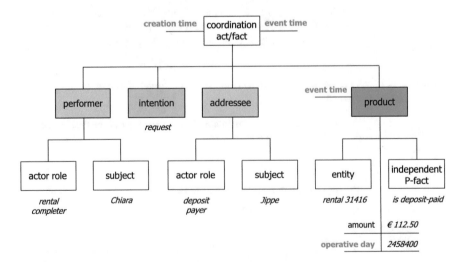

Fig. 11.7 The structure of a coordination act/fact

11.3.2 Designing the Ontological Model of the D-Organisation

Thanks to the semiotic triangle (cf. Chap. 5), we have been able to abstract completely from the sign aspect, that is, the form of information, and to focus on the thought aspect, that is, its content. But, as said, content cannot exist without form: information is the dyad of content and form. Let us therefore now study the consequences of the acts of I-actors for the D-organisation of an enterprise.

As an intermediate step, imagine that all I-actors are human and that they all have an unlimited capability of remembering facts and of computing derived facts. In such a 'utopian' situation, the D-organisation does not need to save and provide documents (or data sets) containing the facts mentioned. It only needs to support the communication between O- and I-actors in carrying out remembering and sharing transactions.

The current reality in enterprises, however, is that people can or do not want to rely on the rational capabilities of I-actors. At least for a large part, people want to store, process, and retrieve data. For the majority of contemporary enterprises, it is also impractical to have human beings remember all important facts, and consequently need to ask, time and again, human actors for the information that one needs. This problem can be solved by implementing I-actor roles using modern ICT. We will elaborate it in Sect. 11.3.5.

In order to keep facts, they must be 'documented', meaning that they must be expressed in some language and saved for future use. The language may be a natural or a formal one, or something in between, like the structured English in the expression of action rules, as shown in Tables 11.1, 11.2, and 11.3. Consequently, I-actors, in their forma (blue) shape, need to initiate saving transactions in order to keep documents or data sets for future use, and to initiate providing transactions in order to get saved documents or data (cf. Fig. 11.4). The executors of these transactions are D-actors. In addition, D-actors may need to transform data or documents. An example in human communication is the transformation of English to Morse code. An example in the exchange of data between computers is the transformation from EBCDIC to ASCII.

In order to save documents or data sets, they need to be inscribed in some physical medium, as discussed in Sect. 11.2.3. The results are files. Only on files can the operations at the bottom right side of Fig. 11.4 be applied: storing, retrieving, copying, transmitting, and destroying.

11.3.3 Actors and Agents

By devising the ontological model of a suitable I-organisation and subsequently the ontological model of a suitable D-organisation for the O-organisation of an enterprise, the largest part of making the essential model of the enterprise work is done.

But we are not finished yet; the three ontological models must still be implemented. Implementation basically means allocating proper technological means[1] to the elements of an ontological model. An important class of these elements are the actor roles.

As clarified in Chap. 8, only subjects, that is, human beings can bear the responsibility of actor roles. Therefore, a perfectly safe implementation of actor roles would be to assign them exclusively to subjects. However, subjects are outperformed, in orders of magnitude, by modern ICT artefacts in doing, for example, documental work. So, the question is not whether using ICT is feasible for implementing actor roles, but how we should understand this application of ICT, and what the limits are. As the first step in answering the question, let us call an ICT artefact filling an actor role an *agent*, like we have called a subject filling an actor role an actor (cf. Chap. 8). The question then is what it means to have agents perform the P-acts and C-acts, while keeping in mind that agents cannot be held accountable for their deeds.[2]

11.3.3.1 Documental Transactions

We begin by answering the foregoing question with respect to D-transactions. The only acceptable way of addressing the problem seems to be that there is no objection to having agents carrying out D-transactions, but that there must always be an actor who is ultimately responsible for the work and who can be held accountable for what the agents do. As an illustrating example, let us consider the replacement of the internal (paper-based) postal mail service in a company by an email system. Clearly, the head of the internal postal mail service is held responsible and, if the need is there, accountable for the (mal-)functioning of the system. He or she is the person that one would address in case of a problem. In our view, the same functionary should be addressed if the email system doesn't function properly, because this functionary has apparently decided to replace the implementation of the postal mail system by a modern one. Naturally, if the cause of the problem is the ICT system, this functionary would address, on her/his turn, the people who are responsible for the technical performance of the ICT system. But he or she would have acted in a similar way if there would have been 'technical' problems in the internal postal mail service.

So, if one accepts the crucial idea of an actor bearing the ultimate responsibility, and if one implements this solution properly, there is nothing that would withhold

---

[1]We intentionally speak of technological means instead of technology, although this meaning inflation is quite common nowadays. We prefer to stick to the original meaning of the word technology, which stems from its Greek origin: technè (meaning making) and logos (meaning knowing). So technology is knowing how to make.

[2]I am aware that the issue of responsibility and accountability with respect to agents or to other 'intelligent' things is currently a topic of debate in the adoption of the achievements of AI. For the moment, I choose to consider 'intelligent' things as unable to bear responsibility.

the use of agents in carrying out documental transactions, nowadays also called Robotic Process Automation (RPA).[3] For executing P-acts, this is fully clear, whereas for performing C-acts we need some additional reasoning, because C-facts are commitments between social individuals. The only acceptable solution regarding C-acts seems to be that we consider agents to *mimic* actors. This philosophical stance preserves the primacy of human beings to act as social individuals; human beings possess exclusively the ability to enter into and comply with commitments. It is also an effective measure to avoid the anthropomorphic trap. As explained by psychology, anthropomorphism is the innate tendency of people to attribute human traits to non-human things. As an example, people normally think that there is nothing wrong with calling a bicycle or a laptop stupid. As long as one is aware of producing anthropomorphic explanations concerning the behaviour of non-human things, there is no objection. But the borderline is thin, very thin. Time and again it appears to be too tempting for people to ascribe human traits to things.

11.3.3.2 Informational Transactions

Regarding I-transactions, the answer to the question whether agents can perform P-acts and C-acts is similar to the answer given above. As an example for illustration, recall what happened on 11 May 1997, when Gary Kasparov lost to Deep Blue. Kasparov was upset, as seemed the entire chess world. There was even talk of the end of chess, because what would be the point of playing chess when machines would always win? Consider a simple counter example. For quite some time, people use forklift trucks to lift heavy weights. Everyone would burst into laughter if a newspaper headline would read "weightlifter beaten by forklift truck". So, why didn't we do the same when reading the headline "Gary Kasparov beaten by Deep Blue"? The only reason why we didn't is that we were not yet used to human chess players being beaten by computers. But forklift trucks are not allowed into the Olympic Games, for example. So, playing chess can still be an exciting pastime for people.

The key to dealing with artefacts properly is exactly the notion of *mimicking*. The proper way of understanding Kasparov's (alleged) defeat is that Deep Blue didn't play chess at all. It just did what is the only thing computers can do: computing. Any further attribution of human-like qualities to the computer is walking in the anthropomorphic trap. To be very precise, computing is actually an ability of human (or other natural) intelligence. It is quite correct, and even advisable, to say that computers don't compute. The only thing they actually do, and at which they are extremely good, is very fast manipulation of symbols, strictly following instructions. Why then do we call these machines computers? There are two explanations. One is our tendency to anthropomorphism, as discussed above. The other one is our equally strong tendency to assign functional names to the things we use, in particular to the artefacts we make, as discussed in Chap. 7. That's why it is okay to say that computers compute.

---

[3]https://irpaai.com/introduction-to-robotic-process-automation-a-primer/

11.3.3.3 Original Transactions

If it comes to performing original P-acts, like devising, deciding, judging, but also like manufacturing, transporting, and observing (cf. Fig. 11.4), assigning artefacts to actor roles is no option anymore. This strict position follows from the basic philosophical position as presented in Chap. 8: our world is a socially constructed world [3]. We assign actor roles to each other, and in doing so, we bestow each other with authority and responsibility. Of course, people can and do make mistakes, but accepting failures is part of the societal game. And for substantial misdemeanour, we have our judicial system: we can and do bring people to the court; we can and do condemn people; we can and do punish them. At the same time, we can and do have compassion with the condemned; we can and do help them in becoming 'normal' members of the society again. In the light of this nucleus of modern social existence, the crucial question is: could we ever treat artefacts (agents, robots) in a similar way? This is one of the most difficult philosophical questions modern man has to face and come to grips with. In our view, the only acceptable answer is no. The current tendency to conceive agents as full-fledged social individuals is treading on thin ice. An illustrating example is the decision by the government of Saudi Arabia to grant a robot the same civil rights as human citizens.[4] Declaring robots to be citizens, or holding self-driving cars responsible for causing accidents, is not only thoughtless but is also a dangerous idea. They could mark the dawn of a non-human era in human history, possibly even the end of human civilisation.

The consequence of our strict position is that artefacts, notably ICT artefacts, may be used to support O-actors to a large extent, but that they can never take over the authority and responsibility that have been assigned to them. As an example for illustration, a judge may be supported by all possible 'intelligent' advisors in arriving at his or her judgement (and he or she better does so!), but the judgement is made by an authorised human. Only he or she is responsible and can be held accountable.

Having said this, and having this strict position always in mind, there is a way of co-existence with artefacts that can be acceptable in modern societies. It is the way that we alluded to already, when discussing the use of artefacts in carrying out documental and informational transactions. In the concrete example of the judicial system, it would mean that a judge would be allowed to have 'intelligent' agents produce facts that count as the judge's decisions, but that the judge is ultimately responsible and accountable. Actually, most Western countries apply this idea in the case of traffic offences. There is nothing wrong with automatic jurisdiction in this case, as long as the accused has the right to go against the decision. In terms of the PSI theory: to revoke her/his implicit accept act (cf. Chap. 8).

---

[4]On 28 October 2017, Saudi Arabia declared a robot to be citizen (http://wgntv.com/2017/99/28/meet-sophia-the-first-robot-declared-a-citizen-by-saudi-arabia/)

11.3.4   Implementing the D-Organisation of an Enterprise

In discussing the implementation of an organisation, we will start with the D-organisation and then go up the cone in Fig. 11.5, thus addressing the I-organisation and the O-organisation later.

From the discussion in Sect. 11.3.3, it is clear that carrying out D-transactions can very well be mimicked by agents, as long as there is a clear sight on the (human) actor who is responsible and accountable for their deeds. So, when taking this precaution, there is no objection to having agents do all the work in D-transactions. In other words, the D-organisation can be fully automated, if one likes. But how should one proceed in achieving it? The answer to this question is provided by the DELTA theory (cf. Chap. 9), notably the PRISMA model. As discussed in Sect. 9.3.2, the generic transaction prismanet is the key to implementing any organisation (O-, I-, or D-organisation) by means of ICT. There are only three kinds of components that need to be implemented: processors, channels, and banks. A processor is basically an algorithmic procedure that is activated by C-events in its action channel, and that may be impeded by wait events in its impediment channels. In order to get the information that is needed to execute the procedure, the processor must have access to its inspection channels and its inspection banks. Channels can be implemented by a bus that connects all processors, and through which the processors can send C-facts to each other. In addition, these C-facts must be stored for future inspection by the processor or by other processors. In a similar way, banks can be implemented as directly accessible storages, like computer memories.

In Fig. 11.8, the generic transaction prismanet from the DELTA theory (Fig. 9.14) is reproduced. Likewise, Fig. 9.15 is reproduced as Fig. 11.9.

Together, the pictures give the insight that we need for choosing the appropriate ICT means in implementing the D-organisation. It tells us that agents, the replacements of actors, are composed of 19 processors. They must be connected by some sort of bus through which they can exchange the various kinds of C-facts, as exhibited in Fig. 11.9. Note that actually five more processors are needed to deal with the events in the external (grey-coloured) channels in Fig. 11.8. In addition, some way of implementing banks is needed, for storing the resulting products, thus the documents or data sets. This holds for every transaction kind in which the composite processors, so the agents, are involved. Every agent is the executor of one transaction kind, but it may be initiator of a number of transaction kinds (cf. Chap. 10). In this way, arbitrarily large tree structures can be constructed. In doing so, most of the external (grey-coloured) channels, mentioned earlier, become internal channels, that is, of the kinds as shown in Fig. 11.9. But there will always be some left as external channels. They are what one normally calls the input and output terminals of a system.

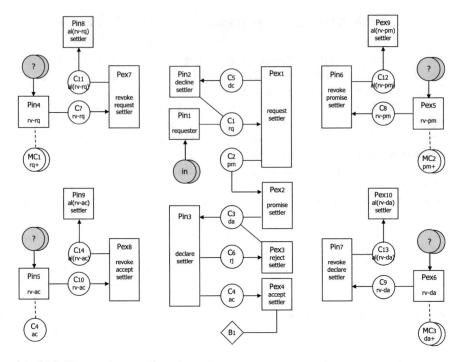

Fig. 11.8 The generic transaction prismanet

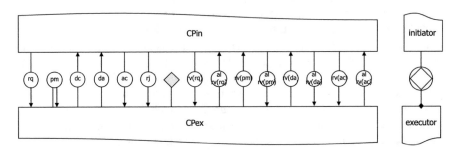

Fig. 11.9 Composite processors as organisational building blocks

As for the agents themselves, they can be implemented as computer programs. In case of a procedural programming language, an agent is a collection of procedures, one for every trigger kind that it should be able to respond to. In case of an object-oriented language, it is a (composite) object class comprising a method for every trigger kind. Of course, some work needs to be done, but the generality of the solution, as discussed above, makes that one can endlessly extend an implementation in an almost effortless way, once the general solution is there. Applying ICT in this way would be no less than a revolutionary breakthrough in computer programming, at least as far as supporting business processes is concerned.

11.3.5 Implementing the I-Organisation of an Enterprise

What has been said in Sect. 11.3.4 regarding the D-organisation is in no way specific for D-organisations, which means that it also holds for implementing I-organisations. So, in implementing I-organisations, one can take advantage of the knowledge and experience one has got in implementing D-organisations. But there is an even greater advantage to be gained, since we know that the products of the saving transactions and the providing transactions between the I-organisation and the D-organisation concern facts that are created or used by O-actors, for example the C-fact (rental completing **for** rental 1993 **is** requested), or the indepen-dent P-fact <rental 1993 **is** completed> together with its dependent facts, like <**the** renter **of** rental 1993 **is** Adam> and <**the** driver **of** rental 1993 **is** Eve>.

In such cases, one can profit from the verity that every information item is the dyad of content and form. Concerning elementary facts, as in the examples above, it would be sufficient that I-agents are told to remember facts, as well as to compute or to share facts. Modern programming languages are already made for creating I-agents. One doesn't have to bother about how the forms of the facts are saved and possibly transformed. In other words, the design of the D-organisation is taken care of by the compiler or interpreter (and the computer platform). In Sect. 11.3.3, we have referred to this ability of programming languages as the mimicking of human rational abilities. Agents do not remember, compute and share facts in the way humans do. They can only mimic these abilities by performing documental acts in well-designed and well-controlled ways, ways that preserve the semantic meaning of the data.

11.3.6 Implementing the O-Organisation of an Enterprise

As discussed in Sect. 11.3.3.3, one must be very careful in assigning actor roles in an O-organisation to artefacts, but it is certainly possible. To illustrate this 'relaxed' position, we reproduce the prismanet diagram of a part of the Rent-A-Car organisa-tion (Fig. 9.12) as Fig. 11.10. It is the PRISMA white-box model of the operations of the actor role rental completer. The six processors can be implemented as computer programs. The algorithm or logic is provided by the corresponding grey-box model. To illustrate this, Table 9.2 exhibits the grey-box model of processor P1. The performance rules are sufficiently formalised to express them in a programming language.

As said, the channels can be implemented by a bus, which connects all processors, and which transmits C-facts between the processors (including the environmental ones, which are not shown in Fig. 11.10). Every processor will pick the ones that it needs to process and ignore the other ones. As also said, the banks can be implemented by the computer's memory (and external storages if necessary). This holds for bank B1 but also for the external multiple banks (MB$_1$, MB$_2$, and MB$_3$), which contain various facts that the processors need when being active. Together with the channels C$_1$, C$_2$, and C$_3$, they constitute the terminals of the exhibited system, the connectors with the outside world.

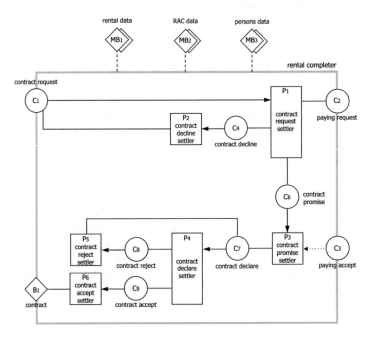

Fig. 11.10 Prismanet diagram of a part of the Rent-A-Car organisation

In Fig.11.4, a distinction is made between material and immaterial production. Examples of material P-acts are manufacturing, transporting, and observing. Examples of immaterial production acts are devising, deciding, and judging. One should be aware that this distinction does not affect the nature of P-facts. Every P-fact is an elementary state of affairs in the production world of an organisation, like every C-fact is an elementary state of affairs in its coordination world (cf. Chap. 8). Consequently, every P-fact (like every C-fact) is represented by a logical predicate, and expressed in an elementary sentence. For example, the sentence "rental 1993 **is** completed" expresses the fact that rental 1993 is completed, and the sentence "**the car of** rental 1993 **is** returned" expresses the fact that the car of rental 1993 is returned.

Let us have a closer look at these examples. The first sentence is a predication of the entity rental 1993. Although this entity is for sure a concrete thing (cf. Chap. 5), it is also intangible: one cannot grasp it or observe it. In contrast, the entity in the predication <**the** car **of** rental 1993 **is** returned> is a particular car. Cars are tangible: they can be grasped and observed. And of course, cars are also concrete things. As follows from the examples, it doesn't matter for the faculty of predications to represent facts, that the predicated entities are material or immaterial. But for creating the entities, the difference is quite relevant and important. Immaterial (intangible) entities are created as just the result of a mental act. For example, as soon as the C-fact (rental completing **for** rental 1993 **is** requested) is created, the entity rental 1993 is also created, just by conceiving it. There is nothing else needed. But creating a car is a different story. Like any material (tangible) thing, it needs to be manufactured somehow. And as long as teleportation is not reality, returning a car to a particular branch of Rent-A-Car implies the physical transport of the car to the branch's location.

Fig. 11.11 Material and immaterial production

So far so good, but what about tangible things that are the object of operations in the lower right side of Fig. 11.4, that is, of operations like storing copying, transmitting, and destroying? Indeed, we have labelled these operations documental, but it appears that they can quite easily turn into original ones. As an example, the transporting of folders (containing letters, forms, etc.) by the internal mail service is clearly a documental material act. But what if such a folder contains peanuts? Clearly, then the act cannot be labelled documental anymore, it has become an original act of transporting goods. To elaborate the issue, let us use the 'pie chart' in Fig. 11.11 for illustration. It shows clearly that material production in the O-organisation and material production in the D-organisation border on one another. By having the internal postman transport folders containing peanuts, we have crossed the border. Let us cross the border once more, but now in the opposite direction, that is, from the O-organisation to the D-organisation. An example of such a crossing is the original creation of a document, like the writing of a book. There is no doubt that in essence, writing a book (or any document) is an immaterial original act. However, in order to communicate the contents, it has to be expressed in sentences in some language, and these sentences must be inscribed in some physical substance, like being printed on paper. This is basically the same thing as communicating facts by writing them down and having the forms be transported by the postal mail service, or by entering them, via a keyboard, in a computer and having them transmitted by email. But the difference is that the contents of the book are not facts in some O-organisation, and therefore writing a book (or any other kind of document) needs special attention.

For the sake of clarification, suppose we are studying an organisation in which this P-fact can be created: <book title 23929 **is** written>. The entity book title 23929 consists of the text of the book, and it is this text that one wants to save, provide, and possibly to transform (cf. Fig. 11.4 bottom left side). Another but similar example of a P-fact is <technical drawing 9829 **is** made>. The entity technical drawing 9829 consists of 'graphical text', that is, expressions in some graphical language, and this 'text' must be saved, provided, and possibly transformed. Even though the 'graphical text' could also be conceived as a data set, the meaning of the graphical expressions is not relevant when the P-fact <technical drawing 9829 **is** made> is created, like the meaning of the contents of book title 23929 is not relevant when the P-fact <book title 23929 **is** written> is created.

Therefore, creating a book or a technical drawing, or any other document is, at the documental level, similar to manufacturing a car, or any other material thing. Material things need to have some place to be. For documents it holds that any file in which they are inscribed also needs some physical place to be. And because of the similarity to data sets, documents can very well be handled by the D-organisation of an enterprise. We only have to allow that O-actors, in their forma (blue) shape, initiate saving transactions as well as providing transactions with D-actors. So, this we do. It would mean some modification of Figs. 11.4 and 11.5, but we leave them as they are.

11.3.7   Enterprise Information Systems

From the time that the term "information system" became the common reference to ICT applications that are intended to support people in organisations (around 1973), its understanding, in Chap. 4 referred to as the *information-centric* view, has hardly changed. The primal notion in this view is information, generally defined as the representation of knowledge, while communication is subsequently defined as the exchange of information.

As discussed in Chap. 4, one of the consequences of the information-centric view is that developing (automated) information systems is considered something that ICT professionals do 'at home', after having elicited requirements from the people in the organisation, basically by interviewing these people. Once the system is built, it is 'implanted' in the organisation. A widely acknowledged drawback of this approach is that the delivered systems rarely meet the expectations of the users. The main cause of this failure is that requirements' determination is quite ill-understood. Interviewing the members of an organisation for determining information requirements is akin to asking the parts of a machine (like a car) what information they need in order to properly operate and cooperate. Every embedded software engineer would start to get an appropriate understanding of the machine for which he/she is going to build supporting software. Based on this understanding, he/she would specify the requirements for the software system to be built. He/she knows that the parts could never tell you, even if they were able to speak. As a consequence of the interviewing approach to requirements determination in the field of enterprise information systems, relevant requirements are often missing, and irrelevant ones are included. For obscure reasons, information system engineers have never recognised the necessity to acquire first of all an appropriate understanding of their primal objects of interest: enterprises. The extension of "information system" to "enterprise information system" didn't contribute to a better understanding, only to a better delineation of the application area.

As explained in Chap. 4, the CIAO paradigm (Communication, Information, Action, and Organisation) provides us with the *communication-centric* view on information systems. It entails that they are integral parts of the supported organisations and that they will always be like this, regardless of the technology that is used to implement them. The path to this new understanding was paved by the achievements in language philosophy, notably Speech Act Theory [5, 6] and in (social) action theory, notably the Theory of Communicative Action [7]. Communication[5] is defined as the sharing of thoughts between subjects (human beings), and information as the means for communication (cf. Chap. 5). The bottom line is that people, in organisations and in society at large, have a need to communicate. Since it is impossible to do this directly, they use the vehicle of information.

The new understanding emphasises informations systems and the supported organisations being intrinsically intertwined. It also clarifies why information system engineers should first of all study the construction and operation of the organisation before designing information systems. Basically, the information system is already there: it is an intrinsic part of the organisation. Consequently, the functional requirements are also already there. It is the task of the 'new' information system engineer to find a better way of implementing the particular part of the organisation, most likely by applying ICT.

---

[5]The English word 'communicate' comes from the Latin word 'communicare', which means 'making something common', 'sharing something with somebody'. In a more specific sense, it means 'sharing thoughts'.

Fig. 11.12 The notion of enterprise information system

Actually, in the foregoing sections, when we discussed the deduction of the onto-logical model of the I- and the D-organisation of an enterprise, we have already applied this communication-centric view. The combined I-organisation and D-organisation basically are the entire enterprise information system, because together they offer all information services that the actors in the O-organisation need. The orange-lined shape in Fig. 11.12 shows this crucial understanding: every enterprise information system is some part of the enterprise's I-organisation and the corresponding part of the D-organisation. But what about the 'automation' of the O-organisation, in other words, what about the replacement of O-actors by agents? Aren't these agents part of the enterprise information system? For sure they are because they cannot be elements of the O-organisation so they must be elements of the I-organisation, as discussed in Sect. 11.3.3. The proper understanding of these agents is therefore that they are 'sham red': they are green (informa) but they have a red (performa) skin, so to speak.

To illustrate this, suppose that we would fully automate the actor role rental completer in the Rent-A-Car company (cf. Chap. 15). Then we must first extend the I-organisation with an actor role that is a true copy of the O-actor role rental completer. Next, we transform all action rules for this actor role into algorithms, simply by replacing all occurrences of the line "**if** *performing the action after* **then** *is considered justifiable*" by the line "**if true**". The third step is to implement the actor role, by means of ICT. As discussed in Sect. 11.3.6, this comes down to implementing the prismanet that is shown in Fig. 11.11. The actor role rental completer comprises the operations of the processors P1 through P6. In terms of software engineering, it would be represented by a set of procedures if a procedural language is used and by an object class if an object-oriented language is used. If, in the new situation, a customer wants to rent a car, he or she addresses an agent in the role rental completer (e.g. via a web page) to perform the request that is specified in the when-clause in Table 11.1. The resulting C-fact (e.g. rental completing **for** rental 1993 **is** <u>requested</u>) is remembered by some agent and shared with the rental completer agent in order to settle it. The addressee of the response act, which is either the request to pay for the rental or a decline of the request, is the (human) actor again.

11.4 Discussions

11.4.1 The Boundary of an Enterprise

In [8], the term B-organisation (B from Business) of an enterprise is used instead of O-organisation. This has led to quite some confusion since its publication, because the delineation of the ontological model of an enterprise's O-organisation (as well as of the corresponding I- and D-organisation) does not necessarily coincide with the institutional or legal boundary of the enterprise. Hereafter, we will discuss important differences, which sometimes are quite subtle. As the leading example for illustration, we will use again the case Rent-A-Car (cf. Chap. 15).

In Fig. 11.13, the Coordination Model (cf. Chap. 12) of the O-organisation of the case Rent-A-Car is represented. It is expressed in a Coordination Structure Diagram (CSD) and a Transactor Product Table (TPT) (cf. Chap. 15). The focus in the chosen SoI is determined by the white coloured actor role shapes, in accordance with the system definition in Chap. 9. The notion of SoI is an important one. Practically spoken, one always chooses some SoI, guided by the problems one wants to study. During this study, one may get the need to adjust the SoI, by enlarging it or by reducing it. This makes the ontological notion of an enterprise basically independent of the legal and/or economic notion. Although it is not very likely that one goes beyond the boundary of the enterprise (because the enterprise 'has' the problems to be studied and has called in your help), it is not impossible to do it. An illustrating example of this situation is the case GloLog, discussed in Chap. 10. The O-organisation of GloLog covers several legal/economic enterprises.

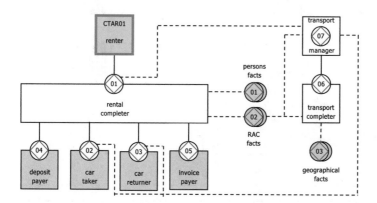

transaction kind	product kind	executor role
TK01 rental completing	PK01 [rental] is completed	AR01 rental completer
TK02 car taking	PK02 the car of [rental] is taken	AR02 car taker
TK03 car returning	PK03 the car of [rental] is returned	AR03 car returner
TK04 deposit paying	PK04 the deposit of [rental] is paid	AR04 deposit payer
TK05 invoice paying	PK05 the invoice of [rental] is paid	AR05 invoice payer
TK06 transport executing	PK06 [transport] is executed	AR06 transport executer
TK07 transport managing	PK07 transport managing **for** [day] **is** done	AR07 transport manager

Fig. 11.13 CSD and TPT of of Rent-A-Car

But what then constitutes an enterprise? When does the focus in Fig. 11.13 coincide with the boundary of the enterprise Rent-A-Car, and thus comprise its business? When would it be larger and when smaller? The key to answering these questions is the sourcing of the actor roles, which is a matter of implementation, as we have seen in Sects. 11.3.4–11.3.6. According to the description of the case Rent-A-Car, the internal actor roles in Fig. 11.13, thus actor roles AR01, AR06, and AR07, are filled by subjects who are employed by the company (who are on the payroll). In contrast, the actor roles in the environment, thus AR02, AR03, AR04, and AR05, are not filled by employees of the company. As for the external information sources, the multiple transaction kinds MTK1, MTK2, and MTK3, both the initiators and the executors are fully outside the focus. We will not elaborate them, however. The focus in Fig. 11.13 is said to coincide with the organisation of the legal/economic enterprise.

Now suppose that the directors of the company decide to outsource the transportation of cars between the branches, presumably for economic reasons, to the company TransCar, which is specialised in transporting cars. This decision would mean that actor roles AR06 and AR07 are no more filled by employees of Rent-A-Car, but by employees of TransCar. Then the boundary of Rent-A-Car and the focus in Fig. 11.13 do not coincide anymore, because actor roles AR06 and AR07 have become environmental actor roles. However, the chosen SoI may still be an interesting one, given the problems or issues at hand. Thus, actor roles AR06 and AR07 still belong to the ontological model of the chosen SoI.

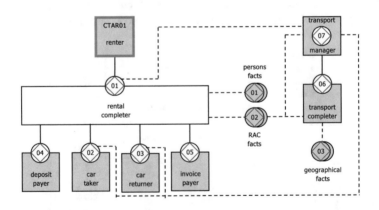

transaction kind	product kind	executor role
TK01 rental completing	PK01 [rental] **is** completed	AR01 rental completer
TK02 car taking	PK02 **the car of** [rental] **is** taken	AR02 car taker
TK03 car returning	PK03 **the car of** [rental] **is** returned	AR03 car returner
TK04 deposit paying	PK04 **the deposit of** [rental] **is** paid	AR04 deposit payer
TK05 invoice paying	PK05 **the invoice of** [rental] **is** paid	AR05 invoice payer
TK06 transport executing	PK06 [transport] **is** executed	AR06 transport executer
TK07 transport managing	PK07 transport managing **for** [day] **is** done	AR07 transport manager

Fig. 11.14 CSD and TPT of Rent-A-Car after outsourcing car transportations

Figure 11.14 contains the CSD and TPT of Rent-A-Car in the new situation. Making actor roles AR06 and AR07 environmental actor roles is the first step in establishing the new situation, in which TransCar takes care of the transportation of cars between the branches of Rent-A-Car. But it is not enough. The salaries of the employees of TransCar who fill actor roles AR06 and AR07 now are debit entries for TransCar, as are various additional costs. These costs must somehow be covered by payments made by Rent-A-Car. There are several options to arrange this. One of them is that Rent-A-Car pays for every transportation. Then we would need to extend the Coordination Model (CM) of Rent-A-Car with a payment transaction kind in which TransCar is the initiator and Rent-A-Car the executor. But the two companies could also agree on long-term cost coverages, which would lead to other changes of the CM.

In addition, new implementations must be devised and made operational of the access links that cross the (economic) border of the enterprise Rent-A-Car, as, for example, the links from AR07 to TK01, TK02, and TK03.

Outsourcing actor roles is not limited to actor roles in the O-organisation. It may also hold for actor roles in the I-organisation (like making statistics) and the D-organisation (like document management). Also in these cases, the ontological models of the I-organisation and the D-organisation will not change, only their implementations.

11.4.2   The Debate on AI and the Position of EE

The advances in the field of artificial intelligence (AI) have taken an incredible pace and the societal areas that are influenced by the achievements of AI increase at an incredible pace too. Fortunately, there is also a critical debate going on about the benefits as well as the threats of AI, on a worldwide scale. Even more importantly, not only scientists and engineers participate in the debate but also influential voices from other fields, notably philosophers. Among the recent influential contributions are the ones by Yuval Harari [9] and Daniel Dennett [10].

In Sect. 11.3.3, we have already touched upon a few topics in the current debate on AI. In what follows, we only want to summarise the position that is taken by the field of EE. The current dominant line of reasoning of the proponents of AI is that if the 'intelligence' of artefacts, in particular robots, keeps increasing, it will arrive at a point where these artefacts could confidently be treated as fellow human beings, they will even be a lot smarter than human beings. There are two serious flaws in this line of reasoning.

The first one is the notion of intelligence itself. As pointed out in Sect. 11.3.3, the human faculty of 'intelligence' can only be ascribed to ICT artefacts by way of an anthropomorphic metaphor. Only in this perspective is it okay, for example, to call your laptop stupid. But of course, laptops cannot be stupid nor can any other things, natural or man-made. Stupidity is the exclusive privilege of human beings. Actually, the term "artificial intelligence" is perfect, as long as one takes it literally, thus as long as one considers AI artefacts not really but artificially intelligent. In other words their 'intelligence' is mimicked. An example that we have discussed in Sect. 11.3.3.2 is the mimicked ability of Deep Blue to play chess. As also pointed out in this context, it is actually incorrect to say that computers compute. What these machines do, and at which they are extremely good, is manipulating symbols according to prescribed rules. This holds also for what are nowadays called self-learning machines. The fact that these machines are able to generate such rules by and for themselves doesn't make them more than symbol manipulators.

The second serious flaw in the current debate on AI is that by merely increasing the 'intelligence' of artefacts, they will at some stage of their development be able to make decisions, like human beings do. The misunderstanding here is that making decisions would be a matter of intelligence. It is not. Making decisions is a faculty of human beings in their role of social individual, being able to enter into and comply with commitments. The faculty is strongly connected to authority and responsibility (and accountability), as explained by the PSI theory (cf. Chap. 8). This is exactly why the recent granting of citizenship to a robot by the government of Saudi Arabia, which we mentioned in Sect. 11.3.3.3, is a rather thoughtless act, if not stupid.

But, EE doesn't have a monopoly on wisdom, and the insights may change in the course of time. Therefore, we conclude with a quote by Stephen Hawkins: "AI will be either best or worst thing for humanity".

11.4.3   The Practical Importance of the ALPHA Theory

The ALPHA theory is meant to be, and has also proven to be, an intellectual instrument in discovering and profiting from the three layers of transactions and actors that exist in all organisations and business processes, once they have been understood in the ontological way as provided by the PSI theory (cf. Chap. 8). The key concept on which the ALPHA theory builds is the semiotic ladder (cf. Chap. 5). It yields the distinction between these three human capabilities: performa, informa, and forma. In the PSI theory, the distinction clarifies the process of coordination acts. In the ALPHA theory, it gives rise to conceiving three aspect organisations in every enterprise: the O-organisation, the I-organisation, and the D-organisation.

The crucial notion of the essential model of an enterprise is primarily rooted in this distinction. It is the ontological model of the enterprise's organisation (thus a constructional model that abstracts from its implementation) that in addition abstracts from its realisation (thus from the I- and the D-organisation, cf. Fig. 11.5). The result is an ontological model of the O-organisation in which the interface with the supporting I-organisation is taken care of in the next two ways. First, the remembering transactions are covered by considering all created C-facts to be stored in the transaction bank of the corresponding transaction kind. Second, the sharing transactions are covered by considering actors to have reading access to the transaction banks in which the facts that they need reside. Derived facts are defined on the basis of these original facts.

The foremost practical importance of the ALPHA theory is in the PIF analysis (PIF is the abbreviation of Performa-Informa-Forma), as discussed in [8] and in Chap. 12. Applying the PIF analysis to narrative descriptions of organisations or business processes, or to structured descriptions like Flow Charts or the diagramming techniques of current BPM approaches (cf. Chap. 10), has proven to be a most effective way of revealing the essence of organisations, provided it is combined with the application of the transactor concept from the PSI theory and the tree structures of business processes from the OMEGA theory. The resulting insight and overview, and the short time in which an essential model can be produced are unprecedented.

Another practically important contribution of the ALPHA theory is the clarification of the notion of enterprise information system (EIS), and consequently of the way in which EISs should be developed, namely from the communication-centric view on information systems, as discussed in Chap. 8. The emerging simple and powerful understanding is that developing an EIS is the devising and engineering of a new implementation of a part of the I- and D-organisation (cf. Fig. 11.12), no more and no less. Only when taking this approach can one be confident that all functional requirements are met, even those that are not mentioned by the interviewed employees in the analysis phase, like the tacitly performed C-acts and the 'exceptional' declines, rejections, and revocations (cf. Chap. 8).

References

1. Langefors, B. R. (1973). *Theoretical analysis of information systems.* (489 p., 4th ed.). Lund: Studentlitteratur; Auerbach.
2. Dietz, J. L. G. (2012). *Red garden gnomes don't exist.* The Netherlands: Sapio Enterprise Engineering. www.sapio.nl
3. Searle, J. R. (1995). *The construction of social reality* (xiii, 241 p.). New York: Free Press.
4. Jong, J. D. (2013). A method for enterprise ontology based design of enterprise information systems. In *Computer science.* Delft University of Technology: Delft.
5. Austin, J. L. (1962). *How to do things with words.* Cambridge: Harvard University Press.
6. Searle, J. R. (1969). *Speech acts: An essay in the philosophy of language* (vii, 203 p.). London: Cambridge University Press.
7. Habermas, J. (1986). *The theory of communicative action.* Cambridge: Polity Press.
8. Dietz, J. L. G. (2006). *Enterprise ontology: Theory and methodology* (xiii, 243 p.). Berlin: Springer.
9. Harari, Y. N. (2017). *Homo deus: A brief history of tomorrow* (449 p., 1st U.S. ed.). New York: Harper (an imprint of HarperCollins Publishers).
10. Dennett, D. C. (2017). *From bacteria to Bach and back: The evolution of minds* (xviii, 476 p., 1st ed.). New York: W.W. Norton.

Part III
Applications

I hear and I forget
I see and I remember
I do and I understand
(Confucius)

Part III regards the application of the theories in Part II in practice. Chapter 12 contains an extensive summary of the DEMO methodology, as well as the DEMO Specification Language. In Chaps. 13 through 18, exercises are presented and discussed of the use of DEMO to small cases. These exercises are particularly suited for DEMO courses. In Chap. 19, eight practical applications of DEMO in various industrial areas are reported. Chapter 20 is devoted to method engineering, more precisely to combining DEMO with other methods, techniques or approaches.

Chapter 12
The DEMO Methodology

Abstract In this chapter DEMO (Design and Engineering Methodology for Organisations) is presented, in order to produce the essential model of an enterprise, or in general of a Scope of Interest (which may cover a part of one enterprise or of a network of enterprises). Like every proper methodology, DEMO comprises a Way of Thinking (WoT), a Way of Modelling (WoM), and a Way of Working (WoW). The WoT consists of the theories that are discussed in part B of this book. The WoM consists of an integrated whole of four aspect models: the Cooperation model (CM), the Action Model (AM), the Process Model (PM), and the Fact Model (FM). The CM of a Scope of Interest (SoI) is the ontological model of its construction, thus of the identified transactor roles and the coordination structures among them. Three structures are distinguished: the interaction structure, the interimpediment structure and the interstriction structure. The AM of an SoI is the ontological model of its operation. For every internal actor role, it provides the rules that guide the role fillers in doing their work. The guidelines for responding to coordination events are called action rules (similar to business rules), the ones for performing production acts are called work instructions. The PM of an SoI is the ontological model of the state space and the transition space of its coordination world. It contains the existence laws and occurrence laws for all internal and border transactor roles. The PM connects the CM and the AM of an SoI as far as coordination is concerned. The FM of an SoI is the ontological model of the state space and the transition space of its production world. It contains the existence laws and occurrence laws for all identified entity types, value types, property types, attribute types, and event types. The PM connects the CM and the AM of an SoI as far as production is concerned. All four sub-models are expressed in the DEMO Specification Language (DEMOSL), which comprises diagrams, tables, and formal textual descriptions. For producing essential models of enterprises, the WoW of DEMO offers the OER method (Organisational Essence Revealing). It consists of a number of steps in which the four aspect models are produced, preferably in a spiral way.

© Springer Nature Switzerland AG 2020

J. L. G. Dietz, J. B. F. Mulder, *Enterprise Ontology*, The Enterprise Engineering
Series, https://doi.org/10.1007/978-3-030-38854-6_12

12.1   Introduction

Everyone who understands the EE theories, as discussed in Chaps. 5–11, truly and thoroughly, disposes of the intellectual ability to 'discover' the organisational essence of an enterprise and to analyse organisational problems accordingly. Yet, most people appear to be uncomfortable with only theories in their toolbox, even if they agree with Kurt Lewin's adage "Nothing is more practical than a good theory". They like to have more concrete bridges to their practical work. With reference to the CIAO tree in Fig. 4.1, they like to have methods that guide them in doing the work.

By a *method* is commonly understood a systematic procedure for accomplishing a task. Examples are teaching methods, learning methods, methods to develop software, and methods to make lasagna. Next to "method", there is the word "methodology". By a *methodology* is commonly understood a system of methods, used in a particular area of study or activity, whereas the original meaning is: doctrine or principles of methods, specifically concerning scientific research. We will adopt the first meaning while in addition requiring that a methodology is firmly rooted in theoretical foundations, like the trunk of the CIAO tree in Fig. 4.1 is firmly rooted in the EE theories. In Fig. 12.1, the so-called Five Ways Framework is presented, as an aid to discussing methodologies. It is an adapted version of the one that is discussed in [1].

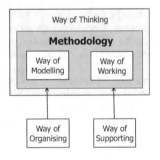

Fig. 12.1   The five ways framework

The core of every methodology is a Way of Modelling (WoM) and a Way of Working (WoW). By a WoM is meant a collection of meta models (cf. Chap. 6) that guide one in understanding the system or situation (as-is or to-be). The WoW comprises the method that is used for producing the models that constitute this understanding, as well as the methods for bringing about devised changes.

The WoM and the WoW must firmly be rooted in a common Way of Thinking (WoT), that is, in a theoretical foundation that is coherent and consistent, and that is appropriate for the subject matter. Consequently, a *methodology* is defined as a matching triple WoT, WoM, and WoW. It may be supplemented by a Way of Organising (WoO) and a Way of Supporting (WoS). The WoO regards the organising and managing of the application of the methodology, and the WoS comprises (software) tools that support both the WoM and the WoW.

In the next section, DEMO, the principal methodology in Enterprise Engineering, is introduced. In Sect. 12.3, the DEMO Specification Language and the four DEMO meta models are presented, comprising together the WoM. The WoW for revealing the essential model of an enterprise is discussed in Sect. 12.4. It is applied in the cases that are discussed in Chaps. 13–20. The case Volley [2] is used as the example for illustrating DEMO's WoM and WoW. Section 12.5 deepens the understanding of the PSI theory (cf. Chap. 8), and Sect. 12.6 contains the conclusions of the chapter.

The version of DEMO that is applied in this book is DEMO-4. Its predecessors are DEMO-1, DEMO-2, and DEMO-3. There are no official publications on DEMO-1. DEMO-2 and DEMO-3 are described in [2, 3], respectively.

12.2   DEMO: Essence and Simplicity

> *Simplicity is prerequisite to reliability*
> (Edsger W. Dijkstra)

DEMO (Design and Engineering Methodology for Organisations) is the result of scientific research, constantly fed by practical applications, from 1990 to 1994 at the University of Maastricht, and from 1995 to 2009 at Delft University of Technology. Since 2010, its development takes place within the world-wide DEMO community. From the late 1990s onward, courses in DEMO are taught under the auspices of the Enterprise Engineering Institute (EEi).[1] Alongside commercial courses, the methodology is taught at several member institutes of the Ciao Network,[2] as well as at universities and polytechnic schools outside the network.

The motto of DEMO is "essence and simplicity". The notion of *essence* is the one as discussed in Part B, notably in the PSI, DELTA, OMEGA, and ALPHA theories. It refers to the essential model of the organisation or Scope of Interest (SoI) that one wants to study, in order to get deep insight into the problems one is facing, and subsequently to solve them by means of re-design, re-engineering, and re-implementation (cf. Fig. 4.17). In addition to presenting the essence of a problem situation, it is crucial for a methodology to follow Ockham's Razor[3] and keep things as simple as possible. This is of paramount importance for intellectually managing the complexity of a problem situation, and of enterprises in general. In Chap. 3, five intellectual techniques are presented that offer effective help in achieving essence and simplicity. These techniques, for mnemonic reasons called *sapiences*, are summarised in Fig. 12.2. They have been valuable principles in developing DEMO, and they have proven to be equally valuable guidelines in applying the methodology.

---

[1] For more information, visit www.ee-institute.org

[2] The Ciao Network is an international group of researchers and practitioners who develop and practise the discipline of Enterprise Engineering. For more information, visit www.ciaonetwork.org

[3] https://en.wikipedia.org/wiki/Occam%27s_razor

Separation of concerns
Use of **a**bstraction
Devising **p**roper concepts
Verification by **i**nstantiation
Validation from **o**ntology

Fig. 12.2 The five sapiences

Examples of the first sapience, *separation of concerns*, are making the distinction between function and construction (cf. Chap. 7), distinguishing between production and coordination (cf. Chap. 8), and distinguishing between the O-, the I-, and the D-organisation of an enterprise (cf. Chap. 11). Examples of the second, *use of abstraction*, are abstracting from the implementation of a system and in doing so arriving at its ontology (cf. Chap. 9), as well as abstracting, in addition, from the realisation of an enterprise and in doing so arriving at its essential model (cf. Chap. 11). Examples of the third sapience, *devising proper concepts*, are the transaction concept (cf. Chap. 8), as well as using and devising concepts like membership, flight, sale and purchase, in formulating uniquely identifiable products. We owe the three techniques above to Edsger Dijkstra, who provides convincing applications of them in [4]. The fourth sapience, *verification by instantiation*, is an indispensable intellectual technique for making sure that one really understands a conceptual model at the schema (or meta model) level (cf. Chap. 6). It serves to convince oneself that a produced essential model is a correct model in the applied methodology. The technique has been articulated by Sjir Nijssen [5] for the field of information systems engineering. The fifth sapience, *validation from ontology*, serves to make sure that a produced essential model is a faithful conception of the organisation that one wants to understand. It is made sure by systematically checking for every ontological element whether it has a counterpart in reality. It is also a valuable technique for discovering errors in the realisation and implementation of an essential model.

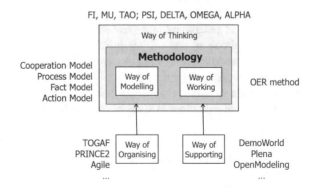

Fig. 12.3 DEMO in the five ways framework

The development of DEMO was initially triggered by a dissatisfaction with the state-of-the-art in requirements determination in the 1980s and 1990s, when the information-centric view (cf. Chap. 4) was dominant. A satisfying solution to the requirements determination problem had to wait for the communication-centric view being conceived. Once DEMO was under construction, it became clear that it could provide more benefits than only solving the requirements determination problem. As an illustration, DEMO is (also) considered a coordination-based business process modelling approach [6]. Therefore, the original reading of the acronym (Dynamic Essential MOdelling) was replaced, around the year 2000, by the current one (Design and Engineering Methodology for Organisation). The additional meaning of the word "DEMO", namely a shorthand for "demonstration", expresses the original mission of demonstrating that it is possible and crucial to base modelling approaches on sound theoretical foundations.

Figure 12.3 exhibits the position of DEMO (DEMO-4) in the framework of Fig. 12.1. The WoT comprises seven EE theories, the WoM consists of four models, and there is one WoW. Together they offer the support that is needed to make essential models of enterprises. The methodology does not include a specific WoO. Therefore, Fig. 12.3 just shows a few candidate project management methods. As for the WoS, several existing tools are listed.

Since the early 1990s, DEMO has been applied in thousands of practical projects, and its further development is nurtured and steered by the feedback from these experiences. Indeed, next to assisting the elicitation of requirements for information systems development in an objective way, DEMO has proven to provide effective help in organisational changes of any kind, from business process re-design and re-engineering up to enterprise transformations, like mergers and acquisitions. The key to exploring these, originally unanticipated, application areas, is the insight and overview that DEMO models offer, due to the unprecedented reduction of complexity that is made possible by being firmly rooted in the EE theories. Because of this quality, DEMO has evidently shown to be virtually indispensable in major enterprise change projects, such as the post-merger integration of the cargo divisions of Air France and KLM [7] and the organisation of large civil engineering projects [8], where the DEMO-based VISI method[4] is an ISO approved standard.

Fig. 12.4 How DEMO reduces complexity. © Jan L.G. Dietz, reprinted with permission

---

[4]https://www.crow.nl/thema-s/bouwwerkinformatie/visi

In Chap. 2, three generic goals are presented for the discipline of enterprise engineering: intellectual manageability, organisational concinnity, and social devotion. The focus in this book is on *intellectual manageability*, understood as achieving and maintaining insight and overview concerning enterprises and enterprise changes, in order to master the complexities of the phenomena one faces. It is achieved by a systematic *reduction of complexity*. Figure 12.4 illustrates this: the detailed description of the business processes of an insurance company, laid down in a document of over 200 pages, is 'compressed' by applying DEMO into an A3 size graphical representation of the Cooperation Model of the company (cf. Sect. 12.3.2). The reduction of complexity is notably achieved by the combined application of the PSI, OMEGA, and ALPHA theories (cf. Chaps. 8, 10, and 11), as explained subsequently.

First, by virtue of the transaction concept, a universal pattern is imposed on the operational activities of an enterprise, yielding a reduction of complexity of at least 80% on average, since 19 concepts are replaced by one concept, as illustrated by the complete transaction pattern (cf. Fig. 8.10). Second, the mind-bending railroad yard images of flow-based business process models that most current process modelling approaches come up with, are replaced by simple tree structures of transactor roles, as discussed in Chap. 10. This replacement offers a substantial additional reduction of complexity, estimated at 80%. Third, by systematically abstracting from implementation (i.e. from functionaries and departments, and from coordination and production technology), as well as from realisation (i.e. from the I-organisation and the D-organisation), another considerable reduction of complexity is achieved, also estimated at 80%. So, an overall reduction of well over 95% (in terms of the size of model expressions) is achieved. The resulting most important asset of DEMO to practitioners is their readiness in unraveling the evermore obstinate tangle called reality.

12.3   The Way of Modelling

Models are green, diagrams are blue

Whenever we speak of an organisation, a particular *Scope of Interest* (SoI) is meant (cf. Chap. 10). A SoI may cover (a part of) an enterprise or (a part of) a network of enterprises. Within a SoI a *focus* organisation may be identified.

The ontological model of an organisation in DEMO consists of the integrated whole of four *aspect models*, each taking a specific view on the organisation: the Cooperation Model, the Action Model, the Process Model and the Fact Model. Models constitute one's understanding of a system or a situation.

The *Cooperation Model* (CM) of an organisation is a model of its *construction* (cf. Chaps. 9 and 10), that is, of the identified transactor roles (the elements) and the coordination structures (the influencing relationships) between them. A CM is expressed in a Coordination Structure Diagram and a Transaction Product Table, possibly supplemented by a Bank Contents Table and a Bank Access Table.

The *Action Model* (AM) of an organisation is a model of its *operation*, that is, the manifestation of the construction in the course of time (cf. Chaps. 8 and 9). An AM is represented by Action Rule Specifications and Work Instruction Specifications. The first ones guide actors in performing coordination acts, the second ones guide them in performing production acts.

The *Process Model* (PM) of an organisation is a model of the (business) *processes* that take place as the effect of acts by actors. In systemic terms, it is a specification of the state space and the transition space of the coordination world (cf. Chap. 9). A PM is expressed in a Process Structure Diagram, optionally supplemented by a number of Transaction Process Diagrams and a Create Use Table.

The *Fact Model* (FM) of an organisation is a model of the *products* of the organisation (cf. Chap. 8). In systemic terms, it is a specification of the state space and the transition space of the production world (cf. Chap. 9). An FM is expressed in an Object Fact Diagram, supplemented by Derived Fact Specifications, and optionally supplemented by Existence Law Specifications.

The relationships between the four models are illustrated in Fig. 12.5. As illustrated by the triangular shape, and the division of this shape into the four aspect models, the CM and the AM cover both coordination and production, while the PM regards only coordination and the FM only production. The PM connects the CM and the AM, as far as the coordination between actors is concerned. In a similar way, the FM connects the CM and AM, as far as production is concerned. The AM is the solid foundation on which the other three models are standing. In a sense, they are already 'contained' in the AM, they only need to be 'extracted'. Lastly, there is nothing 'above' the CM.

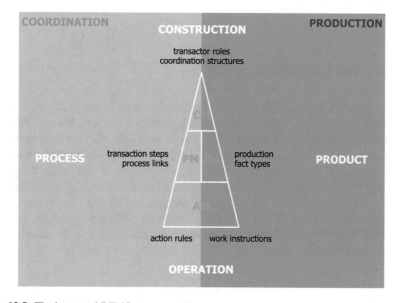

Fig. 12.5 The integrated DEMO aspect models

12.3.1   The DEMO Specification Language

As discussed in Chap. 6, and as exhibited specifically in Fig. 6.2, models have to be expressed in some language in order to communicate them, both with others and with oneself (for future use). In order to represent DEMO models, the DEMO Specification Language (DEMOSL) has been developed [9]. The distinction between models and representations is crucial (cf. Chap. 6); they constitute respectively the semantics and the syntax of the language in which the models are expressed. Expressions in DEMOSL are basically formal textual descriptions. Therefore, its syntax is defined in the Extended Backus-Naur Form (EBNF), the international standard syntactic meta language (ISO/IEC 14977). At the same time, these formal textual expressions are intuitive: they look like structured English sentences, which make them quite readable. Many formal textual expressions in DEMOSL have also a graphical equivalent, because the appreciation of formal text in the practice of EE is generally low, certainly by people without a logical/mathematical background.

Consequently, DEMOSL diagrams must be understood as graphical representations of first-order logical formulas. In spite of the preference in practice for diagrams to formal text, there are limits to their expressive power: diagramming techniques can easily become impractical if one has to remember (too) many symbols and rules. Therefore, the DEMOSL diagrams are kept simple. What cannot be said in a diagram must be said in additional (formal) textual expressions. As indicated in Fig. 12.5, and as clarified by the FI theory (cf. Chap. 5), models are green, whereas diagrams (and all other ways of expressing thoughts in communicable things) are blue.

12.3.2   The Cooperation Model

The Cooperation Model (CM) of an SoI is the ontological model of its construction (cf. Chaps. 9 and 10), thus the identified transactor roles and the coordination structures among them. Actor roles within the focus organisation are called internal. Transaction kinds of which both the initiator and the executor are internal actor roles, are called internal. In case one of the actor roles is not internal, the transaction kinds are called border transaction kinds and the non-internal actor role is called environmental. There are three coordination structures among transactor roles (cf. Chap. 10): the interaction structure, the interimpediment structure, and the interstriction structure. The ways in which these structures can be expressed is presented in [9].

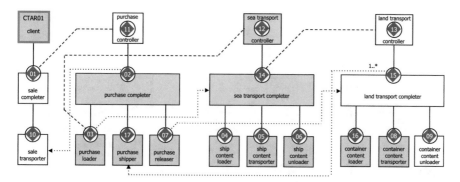

Fig. 12.6   The three coordination structures in the GloLog enterprise

The *interaction structure* consists of initiator links between transactor roles and transaction kinds (note: the executor links are implicitly specified by the notion of transactor role). Through this structure, trees of transactor roles emerge, as illustrated by Fig. 12.6, which is a reproduction of Fig. 18.11. The initiator links are expressed by solid lines between actor roles and transaction kinds. A cardinality range (k...n) indicates how many transactions are enclosed (cf. Fig. 12.7).

The *interimpediment* structure consists of wait links from actor roles to transaction kinds. A wait link expresses that actors in the connected actor role have to wait for a specific progress in transactions of the connected transaction kind before they can proceed with their work (in their own transactions). In other words, the initiators or executors of these transactions impede actors in the connected actor role to carry on as long as the wait condition (i.e. a particular progress) holds. A wait link is expressed by a dashed arrow from a transaction kind to the impeded actor role. For example, the wait link in Fig. 12.6 from TK02 to AR10 expresses that actors AR10 are impeded (hold up) in carrying out a transaction TK10 until a particular progress is made in a transaction TK02.

If one abstracts from the realisation of the O-organisation of a SoI, and thus aims at producing its essential model (cf. Chap. 11), a third coordination structure comes on the scene. This *interstriction*[5] structure consists of access links from actor roles to transaction kinds, which are now conceived as transaction banks (cf. Chap. 10). Access links are the ontological abstraction of the sharing transaction kinds between the O-organisation and the I-organisation of the SoI (cf. Chap. 11). An access link expresses that actors in the connected actor role have reading access to the contents of the transaction bank (both to the C-facts and to the P-facts). Access links are represented by dashed lines between actor roles and transaction kinds. For example,

---

[5]The word 'restriction' originates from the Latin verb 'stringere', meaning trimming, curtailing. The word 'interstriction' expresses that actors restrict each other's decision freedom or 'play area'.

the access link in Fig. 12.6 from AR11 to TK01 expresses that actors AR11 are allowed to inspect the contents of the bank TK01.

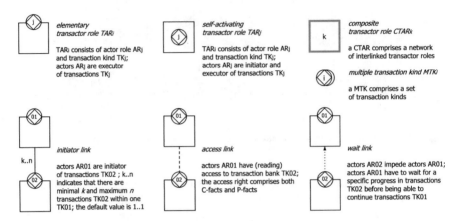

Fig. 12.7 Legend of the Coordination Structure Diagram

The CM of an organisation is expressed in a *Coordination Structure Diagram* (CSD), supplemented by a *Transactor Product Table* (TPT), and a *Bank Contents Table* (BCT). The TPT is a list of the identified internal and border transaction kinds, their product kinds and their executor roles. Because the product kinds are identical to the independent P-fact types in the FM, the TPT is called a cross-model table; it bridges the CM and the FM. The BCT is also a cross-model table, bridging also the CM and the FM, but in a different way.

The BCT of an organisation is a list of the P-fact types, both independent and dependent (cf. Chap. 8), whose instances are created or used by the initiators and executors in transactions of the identified transaction kinds. They are grouped according to the transaction banks in which they are stored. P-fact types whose instances are used within the organisation but created outside it, are also listed in the BCT. Because one commonly doesn't know the single transaction banks in which they reside, these banks are combined into multiple transaction banks (cf. Chap. 10).

The legend of the CSD is exhibited in Fig. 12.7, which is identical to Fig. 10.4. The upper part shows the three different sorts of transactor roles: elementary, self-activating and composite. As said, the interaction structure of an organisation consists of a number of tree structures. By definition, the top of these trees is a self-activating transactor role. The SoI commonly covers parts, that is, sub-trees, of such trees. If this is the case, then the cut-off upper part of the tree is represented by a composite transactor role, as discussed in Chap. 10. Most business processes in enterprises originate in this way from the environment. The shapes and constructs are considered to be sufficiently explained in Fig. 12.7.

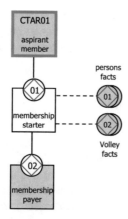

Fig. 12.8 CSD of the Volley organisation

Table 12.1 TPT of the Volley organisation

transaction kind	product kind	executor role
TK01 membership starting TK02 membership paying	PK01 [membership] is started PK02 the first fee of [membership] is paid	AR01 membership starter AR02 membership payer

Figure 12.8 exhibits the CSD, and Table 12.1 shows the TPT of the Volley organisation, resulting from applying the OER method to the case description (cf. Sect. 12.4). The red colour of the diamonds indicates that the transactor roles, as well as the external transaction kinds, belong to the O-organisation of Volley. Table 12.2 exhibits the corresponding BCT. In the second column, the entity types and value types are indicated in capital (i.e. actually as object classes, cf. Chap. 5),

Table 12.2 BCT of the Volley organisation

bank	independent/dependent facts

TK01 membership starting	MEMBERSHIP
	[membership] is started
	  the starting day of [membership]
	  the member of [membership]
	  the amount to pay of [membership]

TK02 membership paying	the first fee of [membership] is paid the amount paid of [membership]
MTK01 persons facts	PERSON the day of birth of [person]

MTK02 Volley facts	YEAR
	  the minimal age in [year]
	  the annual fee in [year]
	  the max members in [year]

and the event types by (unary) predicates concerning entity types. The dependent fact type indications are indented. Variable names are placed between "[" and "]" as discussed in [9]. Note that the BCT can only be completed when the FM is produced.

12.3.3   The Action Model

The Action Model (AM) of an organisation or SoI is the ontological model of its operation (cf. Chaps. 8 and 9). For every internal actor role, it contains the rules that guide the role fillers in doing their work. The guidelines for responding to coordination facts (C-facts) are called *action rules*; the guidelines for performing production acts (P-acts) are called *work instructions*. They are respectively expressed in *Action Rule Specifications* (ARS) and *Work Instruction Specifications* (WIS). Because work instructions are usually enterprise specific, we will not elaborate on them. One should consider them as the detailed instructions for accomplishing a certain production task, like the concluding of a rental contract or the baking of an apple pie. Although work instructions are often expressed in work flows, these work flows do not represent business processes, because business processes only exist in the coordination world. Instead, such work flows represent processes in the production world. In DEMO, only the final effect of production processes is modelled: the resulting products of the transaction processes (cf. Chap. 8).

Therefore, we will only present the specification of action rules hereafter. In current practice, these rules are commonly called *business rules*.[6] In principle, there is an action rule for every kind of agendum (cf. Chap. 8) that actors in a specific actor role have to deal with, while looping through their actor cycle (cf. Chap. 8). The 'exception' states (declined, rejected, and the states in the revocation patterns) are mostly ignored, because the response is much too dependent on the topical situation. Consequently, the standard practice is to specify only action rules for responding to events in the basic transaction pattern, in Fig. 12.9 indicated by the green line in the Complete Transaction Pattern (CTP), that is, for the events (rq), (pm), and (da). Actors are basically autonomous in deciding how to respond to coordination events, as well as how to perform production acts (cf. Chap. 8). As a consequence, the ARS may be incomplete or even absent. In such cases, the actors are supposed to base their decisions on their professional and general knowledge.

The specification of an action rule is divided into three sequential parts: event part, assess part, and response part. As an example, Fig. 12.10 exhibits an action rule from the case Volley [2], following from the analysis of the case description in Sect. 12.4. To emphasise the differences between the three parts, the event part is coloured light-blue, the assess part light-tangerine, and the

---

[6]To be precise, they are the imperative business rules, as opposed to the declarative rules, which consist of existence laws and occurrence laws (cf. Chap. 9).

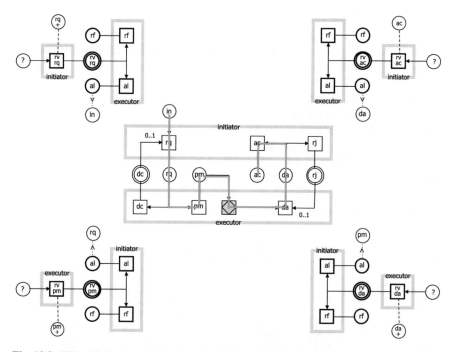

Fig. 12.9 CTP with the transaction states for which action rules are commonly specified

response part light-green. The formal definition of action rules in EBNF is presented in [9].

The *event part* comprises a when-clause, optionally supplemented by a with-clause and a while-clause. In the when-clause, one states the type of the event that is going to be settled; in the example it is the being requested of the starting of a (new) membership of the tennis club. The product of such a transaction consists of the independent P-fact '[membership] is started' and a number of dependent P-facts. Three of these dependent P-facts are specified in the with-clause: the person who will be the member, the person who will be the payer (not necessarily the same person as the member), and the day on which the membership will start (note that this is an explicit specification of the operative time of the transaction's product, cf. Sect. 8. 3.1). The optional while-clause specifies the event that impedes settling the event in the when-clause. Then the rule cannot be executed until both events have occurred. Thus, there may be several action rules for the same kind of event, but each of them with a specific impeding event kind, for example, ARS-5 and ARS-7 in Chap. 15. There cannot be two or more action rules that have the same when-clause and while-clause. Otherwise said, actors never have to choose what rule to execute, there will at most be one.

The *assess part* consists of a number of propositions whose truth value must be determined. The propositions are divided in three, according to the three validity claims in Habermas' theory of communicative action (cf. Chap. 8): rightness, sincerity, and truth. In the *rightness* division, the conditions are specified that must apply to the participating actors, and that serve to ensure that they have the proper authority. In the given example, the performer of the request must be the person who is mentioned as member in the with-clause of the event part, and the addressee must be someone who is authorised to fill the actor role 'membership starter'. The first condition may look redundant, but it is not. If it would be omitted, anyone could make the request. In addition, it forbids that the (aspirant) member delegates her/his authority. Because the claim to sincerity is specific for the individual fillers of the actor roles, it seems hard to make the *sincerity* division more precise than checking if they seem to be trustworthy. However, if (formal) terms and conditions exist, one can explicitly assess the compliance with these rules. Lastly, the propositions in the *truth* division always regard the state of the production world. They serve to check the possible violation of existence and occurrence rules in the production world. The ones that are presented in Fig. 12.10 can easily be deduced from the case description. The syntax is in accordance with DEMOSL-4 [9].

when	membership starting for [membership] **is requested**	(TK01/rq)
	with	the member of [membership] **is some** person
		the payer of [membership] **is some** person
		the starting day of [membership] **is some** day
assess	*rightness:*	the performer of the request **is** the member of [membership]
		the addressee of the request **is a** membership starter
	sincerity:	* the member complies with the Volley Regulations *
	truth:	the starting day of [membership] **is the first day of some** month;
		the age of the member of [membership] **on** the starting day of [membership]
		is equal to or greater than the minimal age
		in the year of the starting day of [membership];
		the number of members **on** the starting day of [membership] **is less than**
		the max members **in the year of** the starting day of [membership]
if	*performing the action after* **then** *is considered justifiable*	
then	promise	membership starting for [membership]	[TK01/pm]
		to	the performer of the request
else	decline	membership starting for [membership]	[TK01/dc]
		to	the performer of the request

Fig. 12.10   Example of an action rule specification (ARS)

The *response part* starts with the most distinctive condition in DEMO action rules, compared to other business rules approaches: '*if performing the action after then is considered justifiable*'. This sentence expresses the fundamental autonomy of the executor to decide what the best response is, given the specific case he/she is dealing with. As discussed in Sect. 8.3, there may always be circumstances that play a role but could not have been not foreseen when the action rule was designed. As an example in the Volley organisation, someone could have applied for membership who is still younger than the minimal age, but well-known already for her talent. What is a wise decision then? Declining, thereby strictly following the business rule? Or promising, a decision that could probably very well be justified with the board.

On the right side in Fig. 12.10, the C-acts/facts in the CTP are indicated (cf. Chap. 8). From now on, we will refer to the combination of a C-act and its resulting C-fact as a (transaction) *process step*.

12.3.4 The Process Model

The Process Model (PM) of an organisation or SoI is the ontological model of the state space and the transition space (cf. Chap. 9) of its coordination world (cf. Chap. 6). Regarding the state space, the PM contains, for all internal and all border transaction kinds, the process step kinds as well as the applicable existence laws (cf. Chap. 6), in full accordance with the CTP (cf. Fig. 12.9). Regarding the transition space, the PM contains, for all transaction kinds, the process step kinds as well as the applicable occurrence laws (cf. Chap. 6), including the cardinalities of the occurrences, in full accordance with the CTP. The PM of an organisation connects its CM and AM, as far as coordination is concerned (cf. Fig. 12.5).

A PM is represented in a *Process Structure Diagram* (PSD), optionally supplemented by *Transaction Process Diagrams* and a *Create Use Table*. A PSD shows the inter-transaction occurrence laws, that is, the laws that hold between transactions of different kinds. They are expressed in two kinds of process links: *response links* and *wait links*. The legend of these links is explained in Fig. 12.11. Figure 12.12 exhibits the PSD of the business process kind that is constituted by the transactor roles CTAR01, TAR01, and TAR02 in Fig. 12.8. We will use it to explain the legend of a PSD in general.

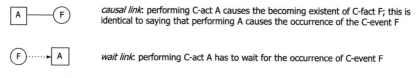

causal link: performing C-act A causes the becoming existent of C-fact F; this is identical to saying that performing A causes the occurrence of the C-event F

wait link: performing C-act A has to wait for the occurrence of C-event F

Fig. 12.11 Legend of the links in the PSD

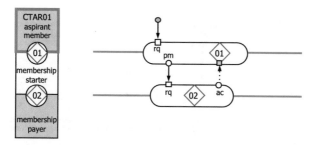

Fig. 12.12 PSD of the membership process in Volley

The left part of Fig. 12.12 shows the tree structure from Fig. 12.8, but now in the 'click' mode (cf. Chap. 10). The PSD in the right part of the figure is directly derived from this representation. The disks of the transaction kind shapes are 'stretched' horizontally, thus becoming sausage-like shapes. One must consider these shapes to contain the complete transaction pattern In particular, one must imagine that the sausage shapes contain the standard pattern (in the middle of Fig. 12.9). In addition, one must imagine a non-linear time axis from left to right in the sausage shapes. All coordination acts in the order phase of a transaction are contained in the part of a sausage shape to the left of the diamond. All coordination acts in the result phase of a transaction are contained in the part of a sausage shape to the right of the diamond. The diamond itself represents the execution phase.

The bold grey lines 'behind' the sausage shapes separate the responsibility area of the initiator (above the line) from the responsibility area of the executor (below the line). Only the coordination acts and facts that take part in the interactions between the participating actors are drawn, always on the edge of the sausage shape. For example, an aspirant member in the case Volley, thus a person in an elementary actor role inside the composite transactor role CTAR01, performs a [TK01/rq] in response to some (basically unknown) state in some (basically unknown) transaction. This initial state is represented in Fig. 12.12 by the small grey-filled disk, and the C-act is represented by the small box labeled "rq" on the edge of the shape of TK01. As follows from the actual operations in Volley (cf. Sect. 12.4) or, more specifically, from the action rule in Fig. 12.10, the addressed actor AR01 performs a [TK02/rq] after having promised to carry out the TK01. This is represented by the response link from (TK01/pm) to [TK02/rq]. The actor AR01 will then wait until the transaction TK02 is completed, thus until the state (TK02/ac) is reached. This condition is represented by the wait link from (TK02/ac) to [TK01/ex], expressed by the dotted arrow from the disk labeled "ac" on the edge of the shape of TK02 to the grey-coloured box at the border of the red-lined diamond. The box is coloured light-grey to indicate that performing the P-act is basically unknown to the initiator of the transaction TK01.

All possible connections between transaction kinds in a PSD are exhibited in Fig. 12.13. In order to show that response links and wait links can apply both to the order phase and to the result phase, they are drawn on both sides (u, v, w for the order phase, and x, y, z for the result phase).

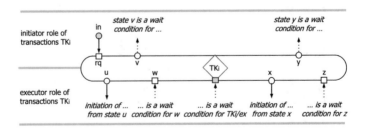

Fig. 12.13 Possible connections between transaction kinds in a PSD

Both to response links and to wait links, cardinality constraints may apply. A cardinality range $k...n$ for a response link means that the C-act at the arrow side is performed a minimum number of times k and a maximum number of times n. The default value of k and n is 1; they are not indicated in a PSD. So, for example, the cardinality ranges that hold for the response link from (TK01/pm) to [TK02/rq] in Fig. 12.12, and for the wait link from (TK02/ac) to [TK01/ex] are the default ones.

Figure 12.14 shows examples of non-default cardinality ranges, namely the range 0. . .*, which means that the act to perform or the state to wait for can occur not at all or an indeterminate number of times. The figure exhibits the PSD of the car transportation process in the case Rent-A-Car (cf. Chap. 15). It also shows how self-activating transaction kinds and actor roles are represented in a PSD. As follows from the case description, transactions TK07 are carried out daily. During the carrying out of a TK07, a number (possibly zero) of transactions TK06 are initiated. When they are all completed, the corresponding transaction TK07 can be completed.

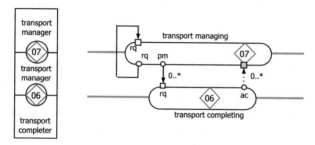

Fig. 12.14   PSD of the car transportation process of Rent-A-Car

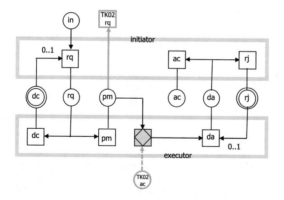

Fig. 12.15   TPD of (the standard pattern in) transaction kind TK01 of Volley

As said, the PSD of a business process kind can be supplemented by one or more Transaction Process Diagrams and a Create Use Table. A *Transaction Process Diagram* (TPD) may be helpful to discuss the exact connections between two transaction processes. Figure 12.15 exhibits an example from the case Volley. In tangerine, the connections between the patterns of transaction kinds TK01 and TK02 are shown. In response to reaching the state (TK01/pm), the act [TK02/rq] is performed. The performing of the P-act [TK01/ex] has to wait for the occurrence of (TK02/ac), thus for the completion of the payment of the first fee (cf. Fig. 12.12).

A *Create Use Table* (CUT) shows in which transaction steps instances of the fact types in the FM (cf. Sect. 12.3.5) are created (as an effect of performing the step) and in which steps they are used (in order to settle the agenda). The CUT is a cross-model table. It connects the PM and the FM. Note that the contents of a CUT is fully determined by the AM of the considered organisation. As an example, Table 12.3 shows the CUT for the case Volley. All fact types, that is, entity types, value types, event types, property types and attribute types, that occur in the FM are listed in the first column of the table. In the second column, one indicates the acts by which facts of the type in the left column are *created*. In the third column one indicates the agenda in whose settling facts of the type in the left column are *used*, except for the entity and value types since they are already indirectly used in the property and attribute types.

For fact types whose instances are accessible in external transaction banks, the indication in the second column is "<given externally>". They are listed in the BCT (cf. Table 12.2), and they are inspected in the assess part of the action rules (cf. Fig. 12.10). For fact types whose instances are provided as parameter values in the with-clause of a when-clause of an action rule concerning the C-event type in the third column (cf. Sect. 12.3.3), the indication in the second column is "<provided as parameter>". Derived fact types are indicated by "<derived>". They have to be included in the Derived Fact Specifications, as part of the FM.

Table 12.3 CUT of the case Volley

P-fact type	created in performing	used when settling
MEMBERSHIP	TK01/rq	
PAID MEMBERSHIP	<derived>	
PERSON	<given externally>	
YEAR	<given externally>	
[membership] **is** started	TK01/ac	
the first fee **of** [membership] **is** paid	TK02/ac	TK01/pm
the member **of** [membership]	<provided as parameter>	TK01/rq, TK01/pm
the payer **of** [membership]	<provided as parameter>	TK01/rq, TK01/pm, TK01/da
the starting day **of** [membership]	<provided as parameter>	TK01/rq
the day of birth **of** [person]	<given externally>	TK01/rq
the minimal age **in** [year]	<given externally>	TK01/rq
the max members **in** [year]	<given externally>	TK01/rq
the annual fee **in** [year]	<given externally>	TK01/rq
the amount to pay **of** [membership]	TK02/rq	
the amount paid **of** [membership]	TK02/da	TK02/da
the first fee **of** [membership]	<derived>	TK01/rq, TK02/da
the number **of** members **on** [day]	<derived>	TK01/rq
the age **of** [person] **on** [day]	<derived>	TK01/rq

12.3.5 The Fact Model

The Fact Model (FM) of an organisation is the ontological model of the state space and the transition space (cf. Chap. 9) of its production world. Regarding the *state space*, the FM contains entity types, value types, property types, and attribute types that are relevant for the modelled organisation as well as the existence laws that apply (cf. Chap. 6). An FM is the conceptual schema of the production world of the modelled organisation, as far as the state space is concerned (cf. Chap. 6). Regarding the *transition space*, an FM contains the event types and the occurrence laws that apply (cf. Chap. 6). The FM of an organisation connects its CM and AM, as far as production is concerned (cf. Fig. 12.5).

An FM is expressed in an *Object Fact Diagram* (OFD), supplemented by (textual) *Derived Fact Specifications* (DFS). If needed, (textual) existence laws, and (textual) occurrence laws may be added. Set theory and mathematical function theory help in understanding the relationships between the schema level and the instance level of the conceptual model of a world. The common way of representing sets in set theory is the Venn Diagram. In such a diagram, the shape of a set is an oval; symbols within the oval represent the elements of the set (cf. Fig. 12.16). The common way of representing functions (or binary relations in general) is to extend the Venn Diagram with connections between the elements of two sets. One set is called the domain of the function, the other one the range. A function maps the elements in the domain to the elements in the range. Figure 12.16 exhibits an extended Venn Diagram, representing the function 'has as renter', having as domain the class RENTAL and as range the class PERSON. The figure is considered to be self-explaining.

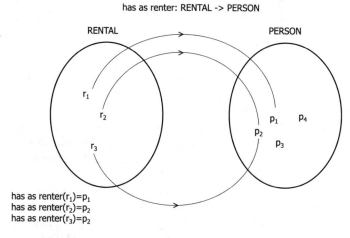

Fig. 12.16 Venn Diagram notation of a (mathematical) function

The mappings between these classes represent property types or attribute types, depending on the kind of the range. *Property types* are expressed by lines between classes, As an example in Fig. 12.17, the property type 'the member of [membership] is [person]' is a function that maps the class MEMBERSHIP to the class PERSON. One should imagine that the line between the roundangles represents the bunch of connections between elements in MEMBERSHIP and elements in PERSON. The ">" indicates that MEMBERSHIP is the domain of the function and PERSON the range.

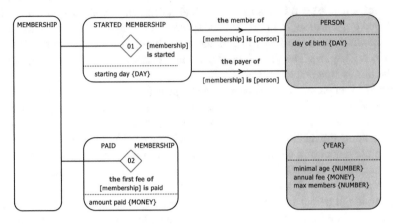

Fig. 12.17   OFD of the Volley organisation

Attribute types can be represented in a simpler way, because they represent pure (mathematical) functions, that is, functions of which the cardinality range at the domain side is $0 \ldots *$, and at the range side $1 \ldots 1$. Moreover, the range is always a value class. The name of the attribute type is written in the roundangle of the class that is its domain. To the right of it, the name of the value class that is the range of the function is written, between "l" and "l". As an example, the day of birth of a person is an attribute type that has the entity class PERSON as its domain and the value class TIME as its range. The measuring unit is 'day'. Instead of writing "day of birth {TIME : day}" in Fig. 12.17, the shorthand notation {DAY} is used [9].

Production *event types* are represented by diamonds, the universal symbol of production (cf. Chap. 8). They are represented as unary predicates concerning an entity type or class. For example, the event type 'the first fee of [membership] is paid' concerns the entity type membership (or the entity class MEMBERSHIP). An event type in the FM is identical to a product kind in the CM. Therefore, the product kind identifier (e.g. PK02) is written in the diamond.

Derived entity types can often be specified graphically, as is done in Fig. 12.17 for started membership and paid membership. They allow for precise specifications of the attribute types 'starting day' and 'amount paid': they are functions with as domain the entity classes STARTED MEMBERSHIP and PAID MEMBERSHIP respectively. Standard value classes like DAY and MONEY are assumed to be implicitly present in every OFD. The value class YEAR is explicitly included in the OFD in Fig. 12.17 because of the attribute types that have to be specified that have YEAR as domain: 'minimal age', 'annual fee', and 'max members'.

An OFD also exhibits the *existence laws* that can conveniently be specified graphically. For example, the OFD in Fig. 12.17 shows that the domain of the property type 'the member of [membership] is [person]' is the class MEMBERSHIP and that the range is PERSON. In addition, it shows that every membership has exactly one person as its member, whereas a person can be member in 0, 1 or many memberships. This follows from the (default) cardinality range. Existence laws that cannot be specified graphically must be specified textually (cf. Chap. 21). Moreover, an OFD exhibits the *occurrence laws* that can conveniently be specified graphically (expressed by a dashed arrow). For example, the OFD in Fig. 12.17 shows that the occurrence of an event of the type 'the first fee of [membership] is paid' precedes the occurrence of the corresponding event of the type '[membership] is started'.

To complete the explanation of the OFD, the name of an entity class and the list of attribute types that have this entity class as domain, is separated by a dotted line. Lastly, external entity classes are coloured light-grey. Thus, PERSON is an external entity class. It means that persons are created outside the scope of the modelled organisation, but it must be possible to inspect their existence and to use their properties or attributes, like the day of birth. All standard value classes, as presented in [9], are external and thus also coloured light-grey. They are always available.

Derived (fact) types, of all kinds, that cannot be specified graphically, must be specified textually. As follows from the CUT in Table 12.3 and the OFD in Fig. 12.17, there are three attribute types in the case Volley that have to be specified textually, as is done in Fig. 12.18. In this figure, days are values in the Julian time dimension. So, the age of a person is expressed in the number of days that the person exists; it may be transformed to years in the Gregorian calendar. The cardinality of a set is the number of its elements. New members pay the proportional part of the annual fee in the year that the membership starts.

Derived Fact Specifications

the age of [person] on [day] = [day] minus the day of birth of [person]
the number of members on [day] = the cardinality of STARTED MEMBERSHIP on [day]
the first fee of [membership] = (12 minus the month of the starting day of [membership]) times the annual fee in the year of the starting day of [membership]

Existence Laws (Declarative Business Rules)

[membership] is started on [day] implies that [day] is the first day of some [month] and [month] is equal to or greater than «current month»
[membership] is started on [day] implies that the age of the member of [membership] is equal to or greater than the minimal age in the year of [day]
[membership] is started on [day] implies that the number of members on [day] is less than or equal to the max members in the year of [day]

Fig. 12.18   Derived fact specifications and existence laws of the Volley organisation

Figure 12.18 also contains the business laws that apply to Volley. They are the *declarative* counterparts of the (imperative) business rules [9] or action rules that are discussed in Sect. 12.3.3. The reader is invited to check that these business laws are correctly accommodated in the action rule in Fig. 12.10.

What is essential is invisible to the eye
(Antoine de Saint Exupéry in 'The Little Prince')

12.4   The Way of Working

The method in DEMO that supports the making of essential models is called the OER method (cf. Fig. 12.3). OER is an acronym of Organisational Essence Revealing. The notion of revealing is crucial. First, one does not devise an essential model or create it in some other way; the operational essence is already present in the running organisation, it only has to be revealed. Second, as the little prince articulates beautifully in the book where the quote above is taken from, and as we less poetically try to express in Fig. 12.19, what is essential in an organisation is the wisdom and love that reside in the most inner selves of its members. However, we may come close to it by observing the organisation through the glasses that are constituted by the Way of Thinking as presented in part B. But how does one proceed to reveal the essence of an organisation effectively and efficiently?

Recognising that the essence of an organisation or SoI inheres in its actors, the best way of working is to address these people and to reveal the essence together with them. By involving them, they will also feel appreciated and they will most likely support your proposals to improve the organisation later. You will need them anyhow in the end for validating your models. The second best option is to rely on written documentation of the operational processes. It is second best for two reasons. First, there is most likely a difference between the descriptions in the documentation and reality. Second, you miss the positive effects of involving the 'shop floor' from the beginning.

Yet, the second best option, that is, basing oneself on written documentation, is by far the most widely spread approach in practice. Therefore, we present the OER method hereafter on the supposition that the starting point is written documentation, which may also contain diagrams and tables next to text.

12.4.1   General Guidelines in the OER Method

Besides being an acronym, the name "oer" is a Dutch word meaning "original" as well as "primitive". Its translation in German, "ur", is also used as a prefix in English, like in "urtext", meaning the original or earliest version of a text. Within the OER method, the word "oer" has the specific connotation that one seeks to find the 'original version' of an organisation: that what remains after all irrelevant details are removed or, with reference to the ALPHA theory (cf. Chap. 11), after having abstracted completely from realisation and implementation. A practical help is to assume that the people in the organisation can only communicate by speaking to each other.

In addition to this general understanding of the OER method, one should also have constantly the five sapiences (cf. Fig. 12.2) in mind when applying it. Regarding the first one, *separation of concerns*, it is of utmost importance to take and keep the constructional perspective (cf. Chap. 7). It means that one must actively resist the natural human tendency to take the functional perspective. The business of the enterprise one is studying (purpose, value, etc.) is at the moment irrelevant. The focus is on construction and operation. It may help to imagine that one is trying to understand an immense clockwork without being interested at all in its being a clock (cf. Fig. 7.4).

As for the second sapience, *use of abstraction*, this is what one is doing particularly: abstracting from realisation, so from the I- and the D-organisation (cf. Chap. 11) and from implementation, that is, from all technological means with which the 'clockwork' is built. It includes the specific persons who currently fill the actor roles. Although these people are of utmost importance in the preferred way of applying the OER method, as discussed above, they may at the same time 'hinder' you in finding the actor roles in the O-organisation. The implementation of an organisation also comprises things like hierarchical structures, divisions, departments etc., and functionary types, like managers, secretaries, purchasers and accountants, as well as, surprisingly perhaps, the economic boundary of the enterprise. As pointed out in Sect. 11.4.1, the economic or legal border of an enterprise is basically irrelevant for the essential operations that are carried out. In other words, one also abstracts from the sourcing of actor roles. Actor roles that were initially internal may have been outsourced in the course of time, or the other way around.

The need to apply the third sapience, *devising proper concepts*, may sound somewhat weird. Why would one need to devise new concepts in revealing the essence of an organisation? Shouldn't they be there already? Yes, they should and mostly they are, but sometimes the people in the enterprise need your help to 'reveal' these concepts and to find proper formulations. The case Volley, which we will use for illustrating the OER method, contains a perfect example of the need to devise a proper concept in a product kind, in order to make the key concept uniquely identifiable. Devising proper concepts includes applying Ockham's Razor (cf. Sect. 12.2).

The fourth sapience, *verification by instantiation*, is a most important intellectual technique for producing correct conceptual models. Many people think that they can understand thoughts on the schema or type level (cf. Chaps. 5 and 6) without verifying their understanding by concrete examples on the instance level. Humbleness, however, is not a demonstration of weakness. Being humble in conceptual modelling means being aware that our mind is too small to keep track of the implications that our thinking on the schema level generates. Fortunately, there is an effective procedure to avoid mistakes. It is simply to provide instantiations of the constructs at the schema or type level. As an example for illustration, in order to verify that the (default) cardinality ranges for the property type 'the member of [membership] is [person]' in the OFD in Fig. 12.17 are correct, one just produces a so-called representative population of the type. This is a list of examples that contains all possible combinations of values of the variables. In this case, a representative population would be:

the member of membership 387 is Edward
the member of membership 387 is Linda
the member of membership 388 is Edward

Next, one checks whether the produced instances of the fact type can co-exist, that is, exist in the same state of the world. Then it becomes clear that the first two instances cannot co-exist. Commonly, one then strikes out the second one, as is done below:

the member of membership 387 is Edward
~~the member of membership 387 is Linda~~
the member of membership 388 is Edward

The remaining instances may co-exist perfectly well.[7] By applying this simple technique, one has convincingly verified that the indicated cardinality ranges (0. . .∗ at the MEMBERSHIP side and 1. . .1 at the PERSON side) are what one intends.

If any of the five sapiences can be called the most important, it surely must be the fifth: *validation from ontology*. The ontological model that one has come up with, while having consciously and thoroughly applied the other sapiences, may be a perfectly correct model in the DEMO WoT, but it may still be a false representation of reality. Consequently, the model must be validated. As already hinted at in the beginning of this section, the only reliable source to call in are the people on the 'shop floor', the people who fill the actor roles in the ontological model. All other ways of validation are (very) second best and should therefore be avoided.

Finally, one always starts with determining the SoI (Scope of Interest) to which the OER method will be applied. It follows from what one wants to do with the resulting model (solving a specific problem, changing the organisation, etc.). While producing the essential model, the SoI may turn out to be too small or too large. Consequently, it may need to be broadened or narrowed (cf. Fig. 10.27).

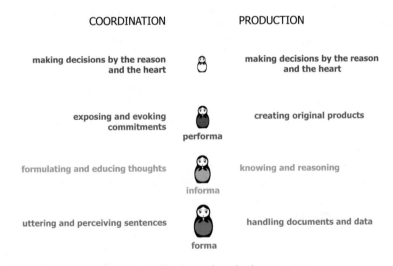

Fig. 12.19 The human abilities in coordination and production

---

[7]One might argue that it makes, practically spoken, no sense for a person to have two or more memberships at the same time. The point, however, is only that there is no logical objections.

12.4.2   OER Step 1: Distinguishing Performa-Informa-Forma

The first goal of applying the OER method is to determine the transaction kinds and the actor roles (or the transactor roles for short) in the O-organisation of a chosen Scope of Interest (SoI). A very helpful aid in achieving this goal is to distinguish carefully between the Performa, Informa, and Forma shapes. Figure 12.19 resumes these human abilities both for coordination and for production. They are discussed in Chaps. 8 and 11, respectively. The most inner ability (the 'blank' me) is added to emphasise the fundamental humanness of actors. OER step 1, also called the PIF analysis (PIF from Performa-Informa-Forma), consists of traversing the available documentation and marking pieces of text as expressing performa or informa or forma matters. For illustrating the PIF analysis, we take the case Volley, as discussed in [2]. Below, the narrative description of the case is copied.

One can become member of the tennis club Volley by sending a letter to the club by postal mail. In the letter one has to mention one's surname and first name, birth date, gender, telephone number, and postal mail address (street, house number, zip code, and town). Adam, the administrator of Volley, empties the mailbox daily and checks whether the information provided is complete. If not, he makes a telephone call to the sender in order to complete the data. Once a letter is complete, Adam writes an incoming mail number and the date on the letter, records the letter in the letter book, and puts it in a folder.

Every Wednesday evening, Adam takes the folder to Eve, the secretary of Volley. He also takes the member register with him. If Eve decides that an applicant can become member of Volley, she stamps 'new member' on the letter and writes the date below it. She then hands the letter to Adam in order to add the new member to the member register. This is a book with numbered lines. Each new member is entered on a new line. The line number is the number by which the new member is referenced in the administration. Next, Eve calculates the fee that the new member has to pay for the remaining part of the calendar year. She asks Adam for the annual fee, as decided at the general assembly, which Adam has recorded on a sheet of paper. Then, she asks Adam to write down the amount in the member register.

If Eve does not allow an applicant to become member (e.g. because he or she is too young or because the maximum number of members has been reached), Adam will send a letter in which he explains why the applicant cannot (yet) become member of Volley.

When all applications are processed, Adam takes the letters and the member register home and prepares an invoice to all new members for the payment of the first fee. He sends these invoices by postal mail. Payments have to be performed by bank transfers.

As soon as a bank statement is received, Adam prints a card on which the member number, the starting date, the name, the date of birth, the gender, and the residence are mentioned. The card is sent to the new member by postal mail.

The next step is to mark those pieces of text that seem to express the performa, informa, or forma level in coordination or in production. Doing this yields the text below. The uncoloured pieces are considered to be irrelevant for our purpose.

One can become member of the tennis club Volley by <u>sending a letter</u> to the club by postal mail. In the letter one has to mention one's surname and first name, birth date, gender, telephone number, and postal mail address (street, house number, zip code, and town). Adam, the administrator of Volley, empties the mailbox daily and checks whether the information provided is complete. If not, he makes a telephone call to the sender in order to complete the data. Once a letter is complete, Adam writes an incoming mail number and the date on the letter, records the letter in the letter book, and puts it in a folder.

Every Wednesday evening, Adam takes the folder to Eve, the secretary of Volley. He also takes the member register with him. If Eve decides that an applicant can become member of Volley, she stamps 'new member' on the letter and writes the date below it. She then hands the letter to Adam in order to add the new member to the member register. This is a book with numbered lines. Each new member is entered on a new line. The line number is the number by which the new member is referenced in the administration. Next, Eve calculates the fee that the new member has to pay for the remaining part of the calendar year. She asks Adam for the annual fee, as decided at the general assembly, which Adam has recorded on a sheet of paper. Then, she asks Adam to write down the amount in the member register.

If Eve does not allow an applicant to become member (e.g. because he or she is too young or because the maximum number of members has been reached), Adam will <u>send a letter</u> in which he explains why the applicant cannot (yet) become member of Volley.

When all applications are processed, Adam takes the letters and the member register home and prepares an invoice to all new members for the payment of the first fee. He <u>sends these invoices</u> by postal mail. Payments have to be performed by bank transfers.

As soon as <u>a bank statement is received</u>, Adam prints a card on which the member number, the starting date, the name, the date of birth, the gender, and the residence are mentioned. The <u>card is sent to</u> the new member by postal mail.

Although the main goal of the PIF analysis is to find the performa parts, colouring also the informa and forma parts may help in identifying them. At the same time, one must be cautious. In particular, one must be attentive to avoid the so-called *blue trap*. Sometimes, a piece of text expresses a forma level P-act, but is at the same time the forma level of a C-act. A good example is the piece "sending a letter" in the first line. In addition to being 'blue' production (right side of Fig. 12.19), it expresses the 'blue' way in which a request is done to become member (left side of Fig. 12.19). To indicate the additional performa meaning, the text is underlined, as are the other pieces of text that contain a blue trap. From now on, we consider them thus primarily as being 'red'.

As said, the main goal is to find the performa parts in a description. Nevertheless, being aware of the 'green' and 'blue' parts may help to achieve this goal. It is certainly most helpful in the beginning. After one has got experience, it will suffice to use only the red marker.

12.4.3   OER Step 2: Identifying Transaction Kinds and Actor Roles

The next step of the OER method is to find the relevant transaction kinds, the corresponding product kinds, and the executing actor roles, based on the 'red' parts in the PIF analysis, including the underlined 'blue' parts.

The part *"become member of the tennis club Volley"* obviously represents an original product. Let us denote the corresponding transaction kind by "TK01". Although *"sending a letter"* certainly refers to a documental act, the most important meaning is that it expresses a coordination act at the performa level: it is the request in a transaction TK01. As follows from the standard transaction pattern (cf. Fig. 12.15), the response to a request is either a promise or a decline. Although the sentence *"decides that an applicant can become member of Volley"* could very well express a P-act, it appears from the context that it expresses the promise to the applicant that he/she will become member, so the [TK01/pm]. The alternative response, the decline [TK01/dc] is expressed in the text parts *"does not allow an applicant to become member"* and *"will send a letter in which he explains why the applicant cannot (yet) become member of Volley"*. The piece of text *"payment of the first fee"* obviously represents also an original product. Let us denote the corresponding transaction kind by "TK02". Next, although *"sends these invoices"* certainly refers to a documental act, the most important meaning is that it implements a C-act at the performa level: invoices are requests to pay, so a [TK02/rq]. Likewise, the text *"a bank statement is received"* expresses the declaration in the payment transaction [TK02/da], and the part *"card is sent to"* expresses the declaration in the transaction in which one becomes member [TK01/da].

So far, we have identified two transaction kinds: TK01 and TK02, based on indications in the narrative description of the corresponding P-act or product kind, and on indications of several C-act kinds in each of them. The universality of the transaction pattern makes us confident of these findings. Nevertheless, it is good to look for the missing steps in the standard transaction pattern as well as for the steps in the revocation patterns. Most likely, the answer to asking for the revocation patterns is that they do not occur (which is not true). As for the missing steps in the standard pattern, the conclusion is most likely that promises and acceptances are performed tacitly (because they often are), and that the decline and the reject are exceptions (really?).

Let us now try to find a proper formulation of the two product kinds. A first attempt to formulate PK01 could be "[person] has become member". This may look okay but it isn't. Suppose that a person called Anna applies to become member of Volley. The corresponding product then would be "Anna has become member". Next, suppose that Anna leaves Volley after some time but later on wants to become member again. Then the second product would be identical to the first one, namely "Anna has become member". The only way to solve this (well-known) problem definitely, is to devise a new concept (cf. Fig. 12.2) that satisfies the requirement of uniqueness. A proper candidate is the concept of membership. If we formulate PK01 as "[membership] is started", then Anna can become member of Volley as often as she wants in the course of time; every time would be a different membership, but with the same person as member. So, although the word "membership" is completely lacking in the narrative description of Volley, the concept is quite needed to model the operation of Volley properly. The reason why Adam and Eve seemingly don't need it is their old-fashioned way of bookkeeping, in which one can deliberately insert and remove entries. Perhaps they have the concept of membership in mind, but slumbering.

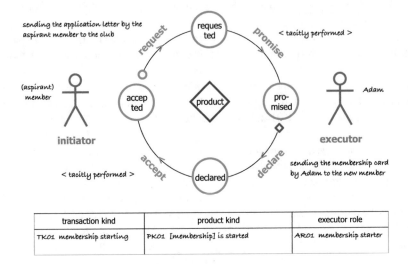

transaction kind	product kind	executor role
TK01 membership starting	PK01 [membership] is started	AR01 membership starter

Fig. 12.20 The basic pattern of transactions TK01

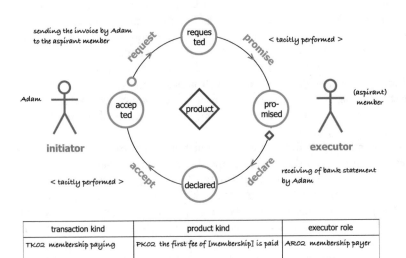

transaction kind	product kind	executor role
TK02 membership paying	PK02 the first fee of [membership] is paid	AR02 membership payer

Fig. 12.21 The basic pattern of transactions TK02

The second product kind (PK02) can properly be formulated now as "the first fee of [membership] is paid". The alternative way is to formulate PK02 for example as "[fee payment] **is** done". But then, a new entity type is introduced, with the inherent property type "membership of fee payment". Although this formulation is also fully correct, it is recommended to adhere to the principle of minimality, also referred to as Ockham's Razor (cf. Sect. 12.2). In this way, the connection between PK01 and PK02 is also immediately clear. The complete TPT of Volley is given in Table 12.1.

A practical help in identifying transaction kinds and the corresponding actor roles (initiator and executor) is to use the basic transaction pattern, in the form that is shown in Fig. 12.20, as a template, and to indicate in it the particular ways in which the four basic steps are performed, as well as who the actor role fillers are, and to provide the corresponding entry in the TPT. The results of a similar exercise for transactions of the kind TK02 are presented in Fig. 12.21. These figures are not only helpful during the analysis of the case but also during the validation of the resulting essential model and, when applicable, during the discussion of the feasibility of suggested new ideas about implementing the essential model. The basic pattern is drawn as a 'cycle'.[8] The upper part represents the order phase and the lower part the result phase (cf. Chap. 8). The order phase starts from the small disk above the state 'accepted' and ends in the state 'promised'. The result phase starts from the small diamond below the state 'promised' and ends in the state 'accepted'. The product is drawn in the middle of the 'cycle' in order to express that all steps are about it. The acts in the left half are performed by the initiator and those in the right half by the executor.

As an additional exercise in identifying transaction kinds and corresponding actor roles from a narrative description, let us verify our conclusions by considering the process of becoming member of Volley of a particular person, Anna. Below, we present the possible interactions between her and Eve, who apparently is authorised to fill actor role AR01 (we will come back to this). Anna fills role AR00 (the further unknown role whose fillers are initiator in transactions TK01) within the composite transactor role CTAR01. She also fills AR02 (cf. Fig. 12.8). Below, after every uttered C-act, its *normal form* (cf. Chap. 8) is presented, supplemented by specific facts, when needed.

The progress of the transaction process is shown in a self-explaining formulation (in italics), followed by the indication of the C-fact kind, as for example (T01/rq). Both to the performer and to the addressee, the actor role is added that they fill in the C-act. The particular membership is denoted by "1087".

Anna   "I would like to become member of Volley, as soon as possible"

AR00/Anna : request : AR01/Eve : membership 1087 is started; the starting day is asap

Eve   "I am happy that you have chosen Volley, the best tennis club there is!"

---

[8]For the insiders: the figure is actually an STD (cf. Chap. 9).

(By this expression, Eve confirms that she has understood Anna, i.e. there is cognitive correspondence between them, cf. Fig. 8.5. But it is not a promise yet!)

membership start for membership 1087 is requested   (TK01/rq)

From the facts in the current state of the production world of Volley, Eve finds out that on the first day of the next month (which is the default starting day of memberships), Anna will be at least 12 years old (which is the current minimum age), and that the maximum number will not be exceeded if she allows Anna to become member.

Eve   "I will see to it that you become member as per the first day of the next month".

AR01/Eve : promise : AR00/Anna : membership 1087 is started; the starting day is the first day of the next month.

Anna   "Great".

(By this expression, Anna confirms that she has understood Eve's promise)

membership start for membership 1087 is promised   (TK01/pm)

Next, Eve computes that the first membership fee to be paid is € 75 (Note that this is an informational transaction). Then she addresses Anna in Anna's role AR02.

Eve   "The fee for the remainder of this calendar year that you have to pay is € 75".

AR01/Eve : request : AR02/Anna : the first fee of membership 1087 is paid; the amount to pay is € 75; the operative time is asap

membership payment for membership 1087 is requested   (TK02/rq)

Anna   "I will do it right away".

AR02/Anna : promise : AR01/Eve : the first fee of membership 1087 is paid; the amount to pay is € 75; the operative time is now.

membership payment for membership 1087 is promised   (TK02/pm)

Anna takes € 75 out of her wallet and hands it over to Eve. Note that performing this act presupposes that the production act, so Anna's decision to pay, is performed.

Anna   "Here you are".

AR02/Anna : declare : AR01/Eve : the first fee of membership 1087 is paid; the amount paid is € 75; the operative time is now.

membership payment for membership 1087 is declared   (TK02/da)

Eve   "Thanks".

AR01/Eve : accept : AR02/Anna : the first fee of membership 1087 is paid; the amount paid is € 75; the operative time is now.

membership payment for membership 1087 is accepted   (TK02/ac)

Because the condition of the first fee being paid is satisfied, Eve can now perform the production act in the TK01 and declare the product (cf. Figs. 12.12 and 12.15).

Eve   "Welcome as member of Volley, as per the first day of the next month".

AR01/Eve : declare : AR00/Anna : membership 1087 is started; the starting day is the first day of the next month.

membership start for membership 1087 is declared   (TK01/da)

Anna   "Thanks".

AR00/Anna : accept : AR01/Eve : membership 1087 is started; the starting day is the first day of the next month.

membership start for membership 1087 is accepted   (TK01/ac)

From both exercises that we presented and discussed above, it becomes clear that if one focuses on the O-organisation of an enterprise, one can straightforwardly identify the key parts in its business process kinds, because they are composed of transaction kinds and actor roles in the O-organisation. Recall that we abstract from all enclosed informational and documental transaction kinds and actor roles that realise these business processes (cf. Chap. 11).

The reason why we said earlier that Eve apparently is the authorised filler of actor role AR01 is that she performs the production act in transactions TK01. Performing the production act is a decisive indication for being the authorised filler of an actor role. But she delegates part of her authority to Adam, as becomes clear from the narrative description of the case. Delegations (cf. Sect. 8.3.3) can conveniently be represented in a (detailed) Authorisation Delegation Table (ADT). The columns in an ADT contain tasks (process steps), the rows contain the performers to which the task is authorised or delegated. Table 12.4 exhibits the detailed ADT of the case Volley. The columns represent the process steps, which are the smallest possible tasks in an organisation (cf. Chap. 8). As the performers of these tasks, the two functionaries in Volley are mentioned. The ADT is extensively discussed in [9].

Table 12.4 Detailed ADT of the case Volley

T/P	TK01/dc	TK01/da	TK02/rq
Secretary	A	A	A
Administrator	D	D	D

A major help in identifying transaction kinds (and their executing actor roles) is the insight that having found evidence for the existence of any of the steps in the complete transaction pattern (CTP, cf. Fig. 8.10), implies having found the presence of a transaction kind. By asking specific questions about the other steps in the CTP, one collects confirmations of having indeed identified a new transaction kind.

12.4.4   OER Step 3: Composing the Essential Model

After having completed OER step 2, one has basically identified all transaction kinds and their executing actor roles in the O-organisation of the SoI. It is now time to build the DEMO model of it, thus the essential model of the SoI. During this step, one may feel the need to broaden or narrow the scope. Broadening means that one has to redo partly step 1 and step 2 in order to find the missing transactor roles. Narrowing means leaving out transactor roles. Figure 12.22 summarises the ways in which the four sub-models of an organisation are represented, in diagrams, tables, and (formal) textual expressions. It is derived from Fig. 12.5 (note: the BAT is discussed in [9]). It is recommended to build the four models (CM, AM, PM, and FM) in a spiral way, extending all four models in every cycle. We will illustrate the approach for the case Volley.

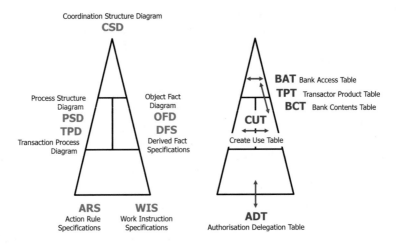

Fig. 12.22   Ways of representing the four sub-models

As soon as transaction kind TK01 is identified, and subsequently actor role AR01 is defined as its executor role, we can produce the part of the CSD on the left side of Fig. 12.23, consisting of transactor role TAR01, the external composite transactor role CTAR01, and the initiator link with TK01. As discussed earlier, the initiator role in transactions TK01 is assumed to be taken by actors who fill the (basically unknown) actor role AR00, named "aspirant member", which is contained in CTAR01.

Next, we can produce the part of the OFD that is shown on the right side of Fig. 12.23. The event type '[membership] is started' is identical to the product kind PK01, as indicated in the red-lined diamond. These connections between the FM and the CM are also expressed in the TPT (cf. Table 12.1). Although the column 'executor role' in a TPT is, strictly spoken, redundant, we include for educational purposes: it almost forces the modeller to give a name to the actor role that corresponds with the names of the transaction and the product kind. In this way, one is encouraged to avoid implementation-related names, like secretary or administrator, or Eve or Adam.

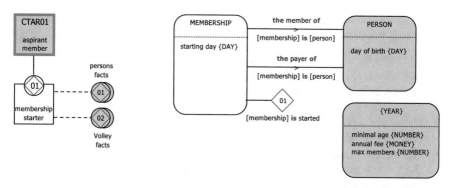

Fig. 12.23 First cycle in spirally composing the essential model of Volley

Being guided by the transaction pattern, notably the standard transaction pattern as shown in Fig. 12.15, we can now start to produce the first action rule of the AM, that is, the rule that applies to settling requests in transactions TK01. It is shown hereafter. As discussed in Chap. 8, a transaction process may contain iterations. Consequently, action rules may be executed more than once. Therefore, only during the first execution of the action rule below, a new membership is created.

when	membership starting **for** [membership] **is** <u>requested</u>	(TK01/rq)
with	the member of [membership] **is some** person	
	the payer of [membership] **is some** person	
	the starting day **of** [membership] **is some** day	
assess *rightness*:	the <u>performer</u> of the <u>request</u> **is**	
	the member of [membership];	
	the <u>addressee</u> of the <u>request</u> **is** a membership starter	
sincerity:	* the performer seems sincere in performing the request *	
truth:	the starting day **of** [membership] **is**	
	the first day **of some** month;	
	the age of the member of [membership] **on the**	
	starting day **of** [membership] **is equal to or greater than**	
	the minimal age **in the** year **of the** starting day	
	of [membership];	
	the number of members **on the** starting day **of** [membership]	
	is less than the max members **in the** year **of**	
	the starting day **of** [membership]	

if	*performing the action after **then** is considered justifiable*		
then	<u>promise</u>	membership starting **for** [membership]	[TK01/pm]
		to the member of [membership]	
else	<u>decline</u>	membership starting **for** [membership]	[TK01/dc]
		to the member of [membership]	

Traversing from top to bottom through the action rule, we find the next connections with the other models:

- The property type 'member' is already present in the OFD
- The property type 'payer' is already present in the OFD
- The attribute type 'starting day' is already present in the OFD
- Any person who fills actor role AR01 is a membership starter
- The age of a person is a derived fact, specified in Fig. 12.18
- The number of members on a day is a derived fact, specified in Fig. 12.18
- The external multiple transaction kind MTK01 (persons facts) is added to the CSD, connected by an access link with actor role AR01. It contains facts of the type 'day of birth'
- The external multiple transaction kind MTK02 (Volley facts) is added to the CSD, connected by an access link with actor role AR01. It contains facts of the types 'minimal age', 'annual fee', and 'max members'

The executor of the discussed action rule is the membership starter of the membership. Normally, this property is included in the OFD, but for the sake of convenience we have left it out. In the next cycle of the spiral approach, transaction kind TK02 is added. Extending the four models, that is, the CM, AM, PM, and FM accordingly, leads to the results that are presented in Figs. 12.8, 12.9, 12.10, 12.11, 12.12, 12.13, 12.14, 12.15, 12.17, and 12.18 and in Tables 12.1, 12.2, and 12.3. Note that conceiving the specialisations STARTED MEMBERSHIP and PAID MEMBERSHIP (cf. Fig. 12.17) makes the OFD more precise. Note also that we have skipped some parts of the complete model, like the CUT (cf. Table 12.3) in the first cycle. In practice, these parts should also be added in every cycle.

12.4.5   OER Step 4: Validating the Essential Model

In the previous steps of the OER method, we have applied the first four sapiences (cf. Fig. 12.2): *separation of concerns* (by taking exclusively the construction perspective on the Volley enterprise), *use of abstraction* (by applying in particular the PSI, the OMEGA, and the ALPHA theories), *devising proper concepts* (notably in Sect. 12.4.3), and *verification by instantiation* (notably in Sects. 12.4.1 and 12.4.3). It is time now to practice the fifth sapience: *validation from ontology*. Where verification of a model ensures that the model is correct according to the applied methodology (thereby answering the question: is the model right?), validation ensures that a model offers a faithful understanding of the modelled piece of reality (thereby answering the question: is it the right model?).

Validation in the OER method means that one leaves one's desk with all representations of the produced integrated essential model (CM, AM, PM, and FM), that is, the diagrams and tables, and heads for 'reality'. This comes basically down to sitting together with the people on the 'shop floor', that is, the people who fill the actor roles in the essential model. The recommended procedure is to study the identified transactor roles one by one and to check the claims that the model implicitly makes. As mentioned in Sect. 12.4.3, the basic pattern implementations of the identified transactor roles (cf. Figs. 12.20 and 12.21) may be very helpful in this step.

The *first* claim is the *existence of the transaction kind* itself. The main source for validating it is the CM. Can (some of) the involved people confirm that they are indeed carrying out transactions of the considered kind? Can they provide evidences? Is the product kind formulated in such a way that they do understand it? To illustrate this for the case Volley, one would sit together with Adam and Eve, put Figs. 12.8, 12.9, 12.10, 12.11, 12.12, 12.13, 12.14, 12.15, 12.17, 12.18, 12.20, and 12.21, and Tables 12.1, 12.2, and 12.3 on the table and select transaction kind TK01 to start with. Both Adam and Eve can very well demonstrate that they carry out transactions of this kind and, after having learnt that they are better-off by using the concept of membership (cf. Sect. 12.4.3), and that they understand the product kind PK01 ([membership] is started). For transaction kind TK02 similar questions hold. In particular, the product kind PK02 (the first fee of [membership] is paid) seems worth being discussed. Why not "[invoice] is paid" or "[payment] is done" or the like? Both of these alternatives may be used. But then, a property type must be added to the FM that constitutes the relationship with the membership. Moreover, if the second alternative is chosen, how does one make sure that the first fee has been paid, since it may obviously be paid in several payments.

The *second* claim concerns the *interaction structure* (cf. Sect. 12.3.2) in the model. The main source for validation is again the CM. Can (some of) the involved people confirm that they are executor in transactions of the considered kind, and thus have the authority (cf. Sect. 8.3.3) to fill the corresponding actor role? Do they also know whether their authority is acquired through authorisation or through delegation? Next, can (some of) the involved people confirm that they are initiator in transactions of the considered kind, and thus have the authority (cf. Sect. 8.3.3) to fill the corresponding actor role? Are they aware that being initiator is an inherent part of the authority to be executor in transactions of some (other) kind? As for the case Volley, after an explanation of the difference between authorisation and delegation, and of their relationships with responsibility and accountability (cf. Sect. 8.3.3), Adam and Eve might be very happy to have the division of authority between them illuminated.

The *third* claim concerns the *interstriction structure* (cf. Sect. 12.3.2). Next to the CM, the AM is an important source for this validation. Can (some of) the involved people confirm, in their role of executor of transactions of the considered kind, that they need reading access to the transaction banks that are linked by access links to the executing actor role they fill? A more precise confirmation can be achieved by checking the BCT and the corresponding action rule(s) in the AM. As for the case Volley, it is very likely that Adam understands that he (also) operates as an I-actor and in this quality provides Eve with the information in the assess part of the action rule in Fig. 12.10, as well as that Eve understands thoroughly that she takes care of the response part of the action rule, including the delegation of the implementation (i.e. sending the letter) of the decline act [TK01/dc] to Adam. Both will certainly also understand the corresponding part of the BCT (cf. Table 12.2).

The *fourth* claim concerns the *interimpediment structure* (cf. Sect. 12.3.2). Next to the CM, the AM, and the PM are important sources for the validation. Can (some of) the involved people confirm, in their role of executor of transactions of the considered kind, that they have to wait until other transaction processes are in a specific state? A more precise confirmation can be achieved by checking the corresponding part in the PM, as well as by checking the corresponding action rule(s) in the AM. Let us take the case Volley again for illustration. After having explained to them the meaning of the PSD in Fig. 12.12, it is most likely that Adam and Eve will understand the wait link from (TK02/ac) to [TK01/ex]. An extra confirmation could be achieved by discussing the related action rule, but this rule is not presented above (if you want to make your own confirmation, you are referred to [2]).

The *fifth* claim concerns the *complete transaction pattern* (CTP, cf. Fig. 12.9). The claim implies that all steps in the basic pattern (rq, pm, ex, da, ac) must be performed in order to complete a transaction successfully, that the additional steps in the standard pattern (dc and rj) should also be 'standard procedure' because they are the logical alternatives to the pm and the ac respectively, and that the four revocation patterns are always possible (and therefore should ideally be accommodated too). Unfortunately, the practice of organising work is unruly. Looking at the current organisation of Volley, and assuming that the narrative description in Sect. 12.4.2 is accurate, one must observe that [TK01/pm] and [TK02/ac] are performed tacitly, that [TK01/rj] is not addressed, and that revocations of the four basic C-acts (rq, pm, da, ac) are not mentioned at all. It is very likely, therefore, that Adam and Eve, when confronted with the latter, answer that such things never happen. So, this would be a perfect opportunity to show them the case Fixit (cf. Chap. 13) and then to think up various situations in which they also would need the revocation patterns.

The *sixth* claim concerns the *completeness* of the *information requirements*. Can (some of) the involved people confirm, in their role of executor of transactions of the considered kind, that they have access to every fact that they need to know through the access links they have in the interstriction structure, thus that there is no missing information? In addition to the interstriction structure, the BCT, the CUT, and the FM may be helpful to confirm the completeness. Sure, an OFD is not the kind of diagram that laymen easily and readily understand, but patient explanation and exemplification may work magic. The sixth claim implies that the functional requirements for any supporting ICT-application are there, in the essential model, as discussed in Chap. 11.

12.5   Deepening the Insight into the PSI Theory

We are able now to produce verified and validated models of the essence of an organisation within the DEMO methodology, and thus within the theoretical framework of the preceding seven chapters. But what is the meaning of the four sub-models, the CM, the AM, the PM, and the FM, for the detailed operations in an organisation? How can we deepen our insight into them? To be more precise, what is the implication of understanding an organisation's essence for understanding the individual acts that the workers in it perform?

Having, meanwhile, learned about the transactional structures that guide the acts of the subjects (now conceived as actors), let us take the framework of Fig. 8.6 to investigate these implications. Moreover, let us take the case Volley to illustrate our findings. The framework in Fig. 8.6 is reproduced in Fig. 12.24.

In Fig. 12.25 a part of the FM in Fig. 12.17 is exhibited, expressed in GOSL (cf. Chap. 6). We will use it as the (partial) conceptual schema of the production world (PW) of Volley, in conformity with the MU theory (cf. Chap. 6). What the schema tells us is that in a state of the PW of Volley, there are facts that represent the existence of memberships and persons, there are facts that tell us which person is the member of which membership, and there are facts that tell us which person is the payer of a particular membership. Next, there is one event type, formulated as '[membership] is started'. Instances of this type correspond with the grey-coloured diamonds in Fig. 12.24. Moreover, there are facts that represent the day of birth of the existing persons, and facts that represent the starting day of the existing memberships. Recall that this day is the (intended) operative time (cf. Fig. 8.17) of the independent P-facts of the type '[membership] is started' (which equals the product kind PK01 of transaction kind TK01). The event time, thus the point in time at which the fact '[membership] is started' comes into existence, is the time at which the accept act is performed in the corresponding transaction TK01.

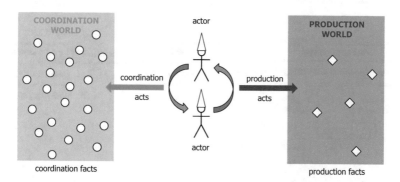

Fig. 12.24 The coordination world and the production world of an organisation

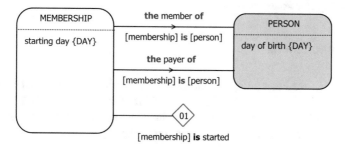

Fig. 12.25 Partial schema of the production world of Volley

Let us therefore draw our attention now to the left part of Fig. 12.24, thus to the coordination world (CW) of Volley. Figure 12.26 exhibits the (partial) conceptual schema of the CW of Volley, expressed in GOSL (cf. Chap. 6). Note that it is actually the conceptual schema for every coordination world because of the general character of the transaction concept and the PSI theory (cf. Chap. 8). Note in addition that only the bold and green-lined parts belong to the conceptual schema of the CW of Volley, the other parts are added to make the schema better understandable.

What the schema tells us is that in every state of the CW of Volley, there exist instances of the types transaction step and transaction. With reference to Sect. 12.4.3, let us assume that transaction T-51917 is the transaction in which Anna becomes member of Volley, so in which the product 'membership 1087 is started' is brought about. Its transaction kind is TK01 (cf. Table 12.1). Let us also assume that one of the steps in transaction T-51917 is TS-106539, and that the transaction kind step kind of TS-106539 is TK01/rq. The performer of TS-106539 is AR00/Anna and the addressee is AR01/Eve. Recall that a transaction step is the combination of a C-act and its resulting C-fact (cf. Chap. 8). As an example, the transaction step TK01/rq is the combination of the C-act [TK01/rq] and its resulting C-fact (TK01/rq).

The connection between the CW and the PW of Volley is brought about by the added independent P-fact type at the right side of Fig. 12.26. The P-fact 'membership 1087 is started' is an instance of the P-fact type '[membership] is started'. This statement is equivalent saying that the P-fact kind of 'membership 1087 is started' is '[membership] is started'.

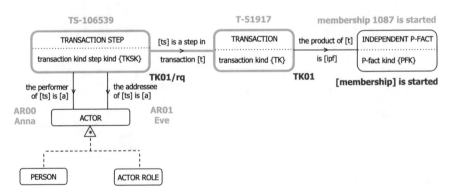

Fig. 12.26 Partial schema of the coordination world of Volley

12.6   Conclusions

In this chapter, we have presented the DEMO methodology: the Way of Thinking, the Way of Modelling, and the Way of Working. We have demonstrated how the essential model of an enterprise can be produced by applying the methodology. Let us summarise and emphasise three crucial properties.

First, DEMO is at the same time a process modelling approach, a data modelling approach, and a business rules modelling approach. Moreover, these approaches are fully and properly integrated. In addition, DEMO offers the overarching Cooperation Model, something that none of the current approaches to enterprise or organisational modelling does.

Second, producing DEMO models is to a large extent a straightforward undertaking. The essential model of an organisation is not the outcome of a creative action nor something that one can have differences of opinion about. As said, the essence of an organisation is already there, it only has to be revealed. By applying the OER method properly, one gets it, irrespective of the person(s) who produce(s) it. If two knowledgeable professionals would get the task of producing the essential model of the same SoI, they will deliver the same model. If not, one of them (or both) is mistaken. Only modelling approaches without a solid and proper theoretical foundation allow for subjectivity and consequent boundless discussions about the correctness and rightness of a model.

Third, next to offering full confidence regarding the correctness (through verification) and rightness (through validation) of a model, applying the OER method assures one of the most valuable approval and support by the actors in the organisation, the people 'on the shop floor'.

References

1. Seligmann, P. S., Weijers, G. M., & Sol, H. G. (1989). Analyzing the structure of IS methodologies – An alternative approach. In *First Dutch Conference on Information Systems*. Amersfoort.
2. Perinforma, A. P. C. (2015). *The essence of organisation*. Leidschendam: Sapio Enterprise Engineering.
3. Dietz, J. L. G. (2006). *Enterprise ontology: Theory and methodology* (xiii, 243 p.). Berlin: Springer.
4. Dijkstra, E. W. (1976). *A discipline of programming*. Prentice-Hall series in automatic computation (XVII, 217 p.). Englewood Cliffs, NJ: Prentice-Hall.
5. Nijssen, G. M., & International Federation for Information Processing. (1976). Technical Committee 2. In *Modelling in data base management systems: Proceedings of the IFIP Working Conference on Modelling in Data Base Management Systems* (vi, 418 p.). Amsterdam: North-Holland (sole distributors for the U.S.A. and Canada, Elsevier/North-Holland).
6. Keen, P. G. W. (1997). *The process edge: Creating value where it counts* (xvii, 185 p.). Boston, MA: Harvard Business School Press.
7. Op 't Land, M., Zwitzer, H., Ensink, P., & Lebel, Q. (2009). Towards a fast enterprise ontology based method for post merger integration. In *SAC'09* (pp. 245–252). ACM: Hawaii.
8. Pluijmert, N. J. (2017). VISI revisited. *Lecture Notes in Business Information Processing, 284*, 89–98.
9. Dietz, J. L. G. (2019). *DEMO-4 specification language*. Enterprise Engineering Institute.

Chapter 13
Exercise: Case Fixit

Abstract The case Fixit is an exercise in understanding and applying the full potential of the complete transaction pattern, including the revocation patterns and the consequent roll-backs of the main business process. The analysis of the case demonstrates and clarifies that the complete transaction pattern covers all 'exceptional' situations, which, in current practice, are commonly taking care of in separate business processes, thereby blurring the inherent connections with other processes as well as the involved responsibilities. Understanding exceptions within this pattern not only helps actors in all enterprises to get a deeper insight into the business processes they are involved in, it is also an invaluable intellectual asset for the designers of business process management systems, specifically regarding the design of the user–system interaction.

13.1 Introduction

The case Fixit is an exercise in understanding and applying the full potential of the complete transaction pattern (CTP), including the revocation patterns and the consequent roll-backs of the main transaction process (cf. Chap. 8). It demonstrates and clarifies that the CTP covers all 'exceptional' situations, which, in current practice, are commonly taken care of in separate business processes, thereby blurring the inherent relationships with other processes as well as the involved responsibilities. The case also elucidates that business processes consist in the first place of human interaction.

Section 13.2 contains the narrative description of the process of repairing a car in the Fixit garage. It is the basis for applying the CTP to two transaction kinds: the actual repair of a car and the payment of the repair. The analysis is presented in Sect. 13.3. and discussed in Sects. 13.4 and 13.5 contains the conclusions.

13.2 Narrative Description

John Smith collects his car from the Fixit garage where he had brought the car the day before, because of a bumping noise he heard whenever he drove over a speed ramp. On the invoice he has to pay, he sees that the two rear shock absorbers are replaced. After having paid, John drives back home. At the first speed ramp, however, he hears the same bumping noise again! John returns straight to the garage and tells the boss

© Springer Nature Switzerland AG 2020

J. L. G. Dietz, J. B. F. Mulder, *Enterprise Ontology*, The Enterprise Engineering
Series, https://doi.org/10.1007/978-3-030-38854-6_13

(Jack) about what happened, and that he will not accept this outcome of the repair. Jack says that he will have another look at the problem. At the end of the day, Jack calls John to tell that they have found the real cause of the problem: two loose bolts. They will fix it first thing in the morning, after which John can collect the car. When John presents himself again at the reception of Fixit the next day, Jack says that there are no additional costs for the (second) repair. But that is not acceptable to John; he doesn't want to pay for the shock absorbers because that repair didn't solve the problem. After some discussion, they come to the agreement that John gets the new shock absorbers for 60% of the original price.

13.3   Analysis of the Narrative Description

When applying the division into product categories (cf. Chap. 10) to the case Fixit, it is clear that the case belongs to the category of creating and changing tangible things. In addition, it comprises the transfer of ownership of an amount of money. Instead of producing the complete essential model of the case, we will focus on two transaction kinds: the repair fulfilment transaction kind and the repair payment transaction kind. For the sake of simplicity we consider Jack, the boss, to be (also) the mechanic who repairs the car. So, the initiator role in the repair fulfilment transaction is taken by John and the executor role by Jack. In the repair payment transaction, the initiator is Jack and the executor is John. Below, two complete transaction pattern diagrams are shown, one for the repair fulfilment transaction, and one for the repair payment transaction. In these diagrams we will picture the progress of the transaction processes according to the case description.

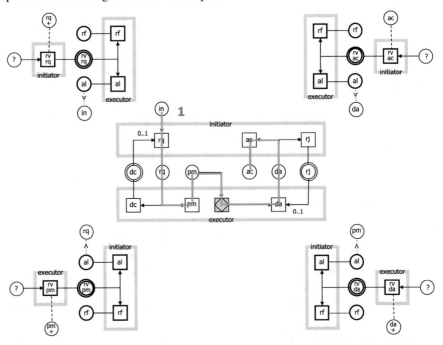

Fig. 13.1 The repair fulfilment transaction—phase 1

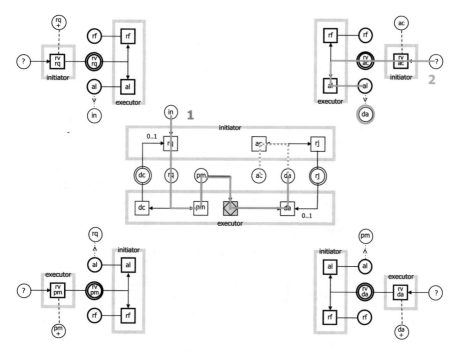

Fig. 13.2 The repair fulfilment transaction—phase 2

In the first instance, the repair fulfilment transaction is completed successfully, as exhibited in Fig. 13.1. The successful completion of the transaction is indicated by the green lines and referred to as path 1. As discussed in Chap. 8, this path is often called the success path or happy flow.

After having experienced that the problem has not been solved, John returns straight to the garage and tells Jack about what happened, and that he will not accept this outcome of the repair. With respect to the carried out transaction process (cf. Fig. 13.1), it means that John regrets that he has accepted the result. With hindsight he should have rejected it. Therefore, John revokes the acceptance of the result. This is indicated in Fig. 13.2 by the tangerine lines and referred to as path 2. Note that the initial state of path 2 is the state (ac) in the standard pattern, and that the condition for the process in the standard pattern of having reached at least state (ac) is satisfied.

The two actors find themselves now in the discussion state (rv[ac]). In this state, John has the opportunity to elucidate his dissatisfaction and Jack can already offer to redo the repair, because he also wants the problem be solved. Formally, it means that he allows the revocation and that the process in the standard pattern is rolled back to the state (da). The rolling back is indicated in Fig. 13.2 by the dashed green lines. The acceptance by John of the result of the repair transaction is thereby made 'undone'. From the state (da), he can now perform the act that, with hindsight, he should have performed right away, namely the reject. This path 3 (represented by tangerine lines) is shown in Fig. 13.3.

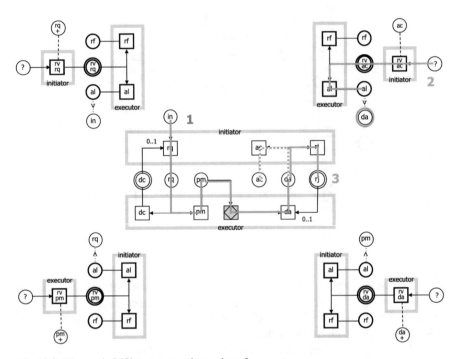

Fig. 13.3 The repair fulfilment transaction—phase 3

So, the two actors end up in the discussion state (rj). Because the problem and the possible way out are extensively discussed already in the state (rv[ac]), there is probably no need for an additional discussion. In order to be able to redo the repair, Jack formally revokes his declaration in the repair fulfilment transaction, which will of course be allowed by John. This is indicated in Fig. 13.4 by path 4, and expressed in the corresponding tangerine lines. It brings the process in the standard pattern back to the state (pm). It expresses that Jack keeps his promise to repair the car, but that he is now able to reconsider his initial diagnosis, find out what really caused the bumping sound, and resolve it. The effect of the successful revocation of the declare act is shown in Fig. 13.4. The roll-back is indicated in Fig. 13.2 by the dashed green lines. Rolling back to the state (pm) implies reversing the performed production act. It would imply that Jack takes the new shock absorbers out. As we know, however, he doesn't.

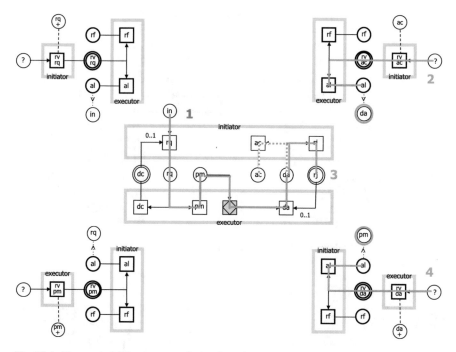

Fig. 13.4   The repair fulfilment transaction—phase 4

From the state (pm), Jack is now able to make another attempt to solve the problem. In this second attempt he discovers that there are two loose bolts in the suspension of the rear wheels. Because there do not seem to be other strange things, he decides that fixing them must solve the problem, and so he does. This second passing of the standard pattern is indicated in Fig. 13.5 by the blue lines and referred to as path 5. Being convinced by Jack that there will now be no bumping anymore, John accepts the result of the transaction.

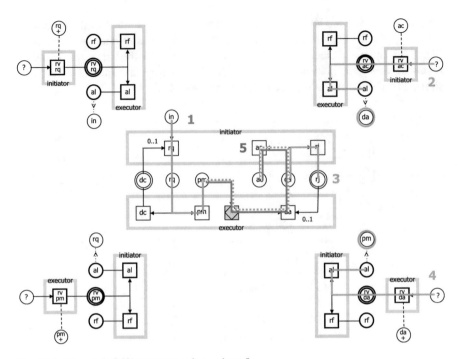

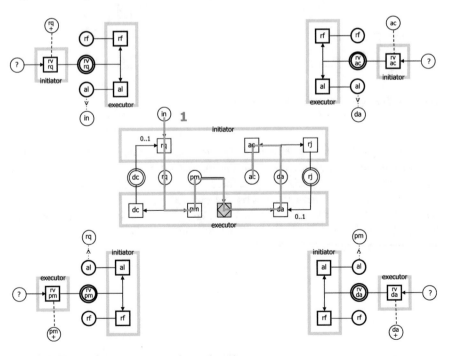

Fig. 13.5 The repair fulfilment transaction—phase 5

Fig. 13.6 The repair payment transaction—phase 1

Regarding the carried out payment transaction, John does not agree with it because the new shock absorbers didn't solve the problem. Figure 13.6 shows the happy flow (path 1) in the repair payment transaction. In terms of the CTP, it means that John, with hindsight, regrets to have promised to pay, in response to the request by Jack. The formal next step for John is to revoke his promise in this transaction. This is exhibited in Fig. 13.7 as path 2, represented by tangerine lines. The roll-back of the main transaction process is indicated by the dashed green lines.

Note that the initial state of path 2 in the repair payment transaction is the state (ac) in the standard pattern, and that the condition for the process in the standard pattern of having reached at least state (pm) is satisfied. The two actors find themselves now in the discussion state (rv[pm]). In this state, John has the opportunity to elucidate his unwillingness to pay for the shock absorbers and Jack can already start thinking of a way out of the disagreement.

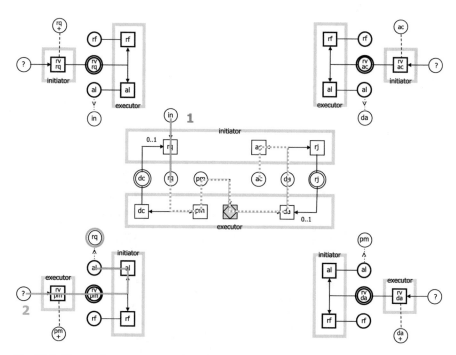

Fig. 13.7 The repair payment transaction—phase 2

As follows from the case description, Jack agrees with John's viewpoint regarding the payment for the shock absorbers and thus allows the revocation of the request. Consequently, the process in the standard pattern (path 1) is rolled back to the state (rq). From there, John can perform the act that, with hindsight, he should have performed right away, namely the decline. This path 3 (represented by tangerine lines) is shown in Fig. 13.8. In the discussion state (dc), John and Jack negotiate about a fair price for the total repair, without needing to remove the new shock absorbers. The result is that Jack gets them with 40% discount.

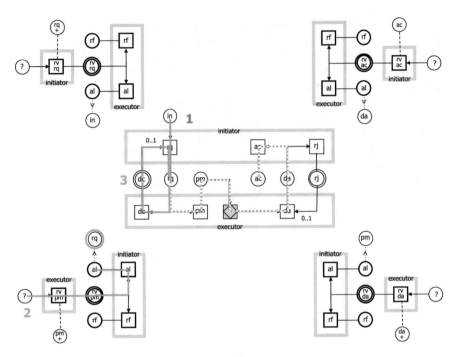

Fig. 13.8 The repair payment transaction—phase 3

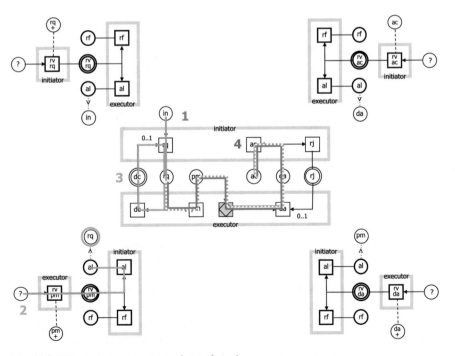

Fig. 13.9 The repair payment transaction—phase 4

Based on the outcome of the negotiation, Jack performs a renewed request in the repair payment transaction, with the agreed-upon reduced amount. This is indicated in Fig. 13.8 by the tangerine-coloured path from (dc) via [rq] to (rq). In response to it, John promises to pay this amount, after which the second passing of the transaction pattern proceeds as indicated by path 4 in Fig. 13.9, represented by blue lines.

13.4   Discussion of the Analysis

The size of a case description apparently is not a reliable predictor of the size of its analysis. In addition, you may have had a hard time to understand the analysis of the case Fixit. Most likely, the difficulties are caused by being unfamiliar with the presented thorough analyses of business processes. After some experience in applying the complete transaction pattern (CTP), as introduced and discussed in the PSI theory (cf. Chap. 8), one will discover and agree that also the analysis of the case Fixit is in accordance with the motto of DEMO: essence and simplicity. Moreover, as you may know, none of the current BPM[1] approaches [1] is able to provide the insight that the presented analysis of the case Fixit offers. Let us therefore reflect on it, thereby deepening the acquired insight and possibly offering new insights.

In the analysis of the repair fulfilment transaction, we have identified two revocations concerning the (first) passing of the standard transaction pattern. The first one is the revocation of the accept act, so the [rv(ac)], and the second one is the revocation of the declare act, so the [rv(da)]. The two revocation kinds often go together, because the successful settlement of a [rv(ac)] ends up in the discussion state (rj), as exhibited in Fig. 13.3. The executor (Jack in this case) may try to convince the initiator (John) that there is nothing wrong with the produced product (the being fixed of the car by replacing the shock absorbers) by performing again the declare act, but he will have no success: John has experienced loud and clear that the bumping is not resolved. In many other cases, however, like the café example in Chap. 8, such an attempt by the executor may very well be successful, certainly if during the discussion in the state (rj) the conditions for the payment transaction are made more attractive.

If renewing the declare act is no option, there is only one way out of the reject state in a transaction process, which is revoking the declare act. After a successful [rv (da)], the process in the standard pattern is rolled back to the state (pm), as exemplified in Fig. 13.4. Rolling back a transaction process up to the order phase logically implies 'undoing' the production act, but this may cause practical issues, as in the case Fixit. Naturally, Jack is reluctant to remove the new shock absorbers and replace the old ones. That would cost him a lot of (unpaid) time. So, he opts for resolving the issue in the payment transaction. In the second passing of the standard pattern, Jack fixes the loose bolts, as illustrated by Fig. 13.5.

---

[1]BPM is the abbreviation of Business Process Management. In the past decades it has become the common denominator of approaches (methods, techniques, etc.) to the modelling, analysis, and (re) design of business processes.

In the analysis of the repair payment transaction, we have identified only one revocation concerning the (first) passing of the standard transaction pattern, namely the revocation of the promise act. This is the right action to take if the executor of a transaction of this kind wants to undo or reverse a payment. One may think that revoking the declare act may do the job but that is not true. It would only roll back the process in the standard pattern to the state (pm), whereas changing the promise is what the executor wants. Therefore, a roll-back up to the state (rq) is needed, which is the effect of a successful [rv(pm)], as shown in Fig. 13.7. From this state, John formally declines the request because the original request regards the full payment of the shock absorbers. In the resulting discussion state (dc), John and Jack have the opportunity to negotiate a new price for the repair, as we have seen above, after which Jack performs a second request, with the reduced amount.

As we have seen above, rolling back a transaction process up to the order phase logically implies 'undoing' the production act. Regarding the repair transaction, this may have serious consequences (like removing the new shock absorbers). Regarding the payment transaction, the practical issues are less problematic. Undoing the performed (first) payment would mean giving back the paid amount to John. The second request in the same transaction process would lead to the payment by John of the reduced amount. The practical solution in most enterprises is to subtract the first amount from the second one and to ask for paying the difference. Because in the case Fixit, the result of the subtraction is negative, Jack 'pays' the difference to John.

13.5 Conclusions

Using the repair of a car as the example, we have demonstrated above how the CTP helps in thoroughly understanding transaction processes, notably those paths that are commonly called exceptions. However, despite the many exceptions that we have come across, the case Fixit is not a special one at all. Exceptions occur in every enterprise, every day. Therefore, the name is actually a misnomer. One better adopt the CTP as the pattern for all transaction processes, and thus for all business processes. Fortunately, most transaction processes follow (only) the happy flow. Still, one must always be prepared for an 'exception'.

Understanding exceptions within the framework of the CTP not only helps actors in all enterprises to get a deeper insight into the business processes they are involved in, it is also an invaluable intellectual asset for the designers of business process management systems. If they base the user–system interaction on the CTP, they will have anticipated every future 'exception'.

Reference

1. Dumas, M., La Rosa, M., Mendling, J., & Reijers, H. (2018). *Fundamentals of business process management*. Berlin: Springer.

Chapter 14
Exercise: Case Pizzeria

Abstract The case Pizzeria is an exercise in understanding and applying the full potential of abstracting from realisation and implementation, and thus focusing on the O-organisation of an enterprise. In the course of its existence, the pizzeria passes through three phases. The transition from the first to the second phase leads to a change in the essential model. The change appears to have interesting consequences for the allocation of authority. Despite the huge differences between the second and the third phase in terms of implementation, their ontological models do not differ.

14.1 Introduction

The case Pizzeria is an exercise in understanding and applying the full potential of abstracting from realisation and implementation, and thus focusing on the O-organisation of an enterprise, as proposed by the ALPHA theory (cf. Chap. 11). In terms of the categorisation of enterprises by the OMEGA theory (cf. Chap. 10), the business of the pizzeria is the creation and the transfer of ownership of tangible things (preparing and selling pizzas), as well as the transfer of ownership of intangible things (paying).

Section 14.2 contains the narrative description of the operational activities in the three phases of the Pizzeria. The analysis of the case is discussed in Sect. 14.3, while some parts of the essential model are presented (cf. Chap. 12). In Sect. 14.4, this model is extended. Section 14.5 contains the conclusions from the exercise.

14.2 Narrative Description

The Pizzeria Mama Mia was established in 1970 by the owner at the time, Mia, and her son Mario. In the first phase of its existence there was only a takeaway service. Customers could just walk in and make their wishes known at the counter or could order by telephone. In both cases they had to take away the pizzas themselves. In 1980, an important new service was introduced: one could have the pizzas delivered

© Springer Nature Switzerland AG 2020   311
J. L. G. Dietz, J. B. F. Mulder, *Enterprise Ontology*, The Enterprise Engineering
Series, https://doi.org/10.1007/978-3-030-38854-6_14

home. To realise this service, Mia hired students on an hourly basis, who delivered the pizzas on mopeds. That appeared to be a good decision: within a year, less than 20% of the orders were taken away by the customers themselves. Let us call the situation from 1980 on the second phase of Mama Mia. The year 1990 marks the start of the third phase, a time about which Mia still does not know whether she should be glad or sad. The pizzeria was bought by a global chain of pizzerias, called Domina. With the proceeds from the sale, Mia and Mario have returned home to Italy. Rumour goes that they still do not really enjoy the 'dolce far niente'. For each of the three phases, the operational activities are described in detail below.

The First Phase

Customers present themselves at the counter of the pizzeria or make a telephone call. In both cases, Mia writes down the name of the customer, the ordered items, and the total price on an order form. On the counter lies a menu of the available pizzas and their prices. Usually, she produces this list every year during the holiday. In the case of an order by telephone, she also notes the telephone number. Moreover, she repeats the ordered items and informs the customer about the price and the expected time that the order will be ready. If needed, she also informs the customer about the available assortment of pizzas.

The order forms have a serial number and are produced in duplicate: a white and a pink copy. Mia slides the pink one through a hatch in the wall to the kitchen, where Mario takes care of the baking. She keeps the white copy behind the counter. As soon as Mario has finished an order, he slides the pizzas in boxes through the same hatch to Mia, including the pink order copy. Mia then seeks the matching white copy, hands it together with the boxes over to the customer, and waits for the payment.

It can happen that Mario is not able to fulfil an order completely because of missing ingredients. In such a case, he puts his head through the hatch and notifies Mia of the problem. He then also returns the pink copy. If the customer is present in the shop, Mia confers with him/her on what to do about it, and modifies the order. If the customer is not present, which is of course the case for orders by telephone, she modifies the order often at her own discretion. This leads sometimes to vigorous debates in the pizzeria when the customer comes for taking away the pizzas. Thanks to Mia's temperament, she always comes to an agreement that is not disadvantageous for her.

The Second Phase

The operations in this phase are basically similar to the operations in the first phase; only the deliveries have been added. However, the big success of the new service has made it necessary that a second baker be employed. His name is Giovanni. An extra duplicate is added to the order forms; next to the white and the pink copies, there is a blue one. If an order has to be delivered home, Mia writes down the delivery address on the order form and slides both the white and the blue copy through a hatch to the room where the students are waiting.

The student whose turn it is fills in her or his name on the blue copy and puts it in a tray. He/she then waits for Mario or Giovanni to slide the pizzas, together with the pink copy, through a hatch to the transporters' room. Then, the student leaves with the pizzas and the pink and white copies of the order form. At the customer's address, he/she hands over the pizzas and the white copy, and waits for the payment. After the customer has paid and has signed the pink copy, the student goes back to the pizzeria and hands the money and the pink copy over to Mia. The students use their own mopeds as Mia did not want the trouble of having the pizzeria own the mopeds.

The Third Phase
The takeover of Mama Mia by the Domina chain has brought a lot of changes to the pizzeria. Mia and Mario have left, and Giovanni has become branch manager. Both the inside and the outside of the building are modified so drastically that one cannot find anything that reminds of the old days of the pizzeria; it has just become one of the many Domina pizzerias. The assortment as well as the prices are determined by the central office. There is a choice out of 12 kinds of pizza in three sizes: 25 cm Classic Medium, 25 cm Pan Pizza Medium, and 35 cm Classic Large. The selection is printed on colourful flyers, which are given to customers and dropped at locations where one expects gatherings of young people. Giovanni manages about ten youngsters on a part-time basis. Their function is either baker or deliverer. Baking is not much of a job anymore; the pizzas are produced in automatic ovens. There is also no more a separate kitchen and transporters' room. The inside of the pizzeria is one big open space, except for a small office for Giovanni. Everything carries the Domina logo, including the mopeds, which are owned by the company now.

Both the bakers and the deliverers take orders from customers, of which over 90% are placed through the webshop, with payment in advance. There is a fully automated order entry system that is integrated with other administrative functions. After entering an order, stickers are automatically printed, which are put on empty boxes. The stickers have the following information printed on them: the kind of pizza, the order number, the total price, the name of the customer, and the delivery address.

As soon as a pizza is discharged by the baking machine, one of the bakers puts it in the right box, which he or she takes from the rack in which they are stored. The baker then enters a record of the baked pizza in the automatic order system. The boxes of the same order are kept together on a large table with infrared lamps hanging over them. If an order is complete, one of the deliverers takes the boxes to the customer address. In case of a takeaway order, the deliverer hands the boxes over to the customer, after he/she has paid, in cash or by bank transfer.

14.3 Analysis of the Narrative Description

Because it is not possible to question the employees of the pizzeria, we have to apply the second best way of working, as discussed in Chap. 12, which is to study the case description and to find clues for the presence of original (thus O-organisation) transaction kinds and corresponding actor roles. We will do this below, paragraph after paragraph, while applying the OER method as much as possible in a spiral way (cf. Chap. 12). The pieces of text that are taken from the case description, are written in italics. Contrary to the analysis of the case Volley (cf. Chap. 12), we only mark the pieces of text that indicate parts of the O-organisation of the pizzeria (in red).

14.3.1   Analysis of the First Phase

Although the very first part of the description does contain indications of essential transaction kinds, we consider it primarily as introductory text. Therefore, we start our analysis with the description under the heading "The first phase".

Customers present themselves at the counter of the pizzeria or make a telephone call. In both cases, Mia writes down the name of the customer, the ordered items, and the total price on an order form. On the counter lies a menu of the available pizzas and their prices. Usually, she produces this list every year during the holiday. In the case of an order by telephone, she also notes the telephone number. Moreover, she repeats the ordered items and informs the customer about the price and the expected time that the order will be ready. If needed, she also informs the customer about the available assortment of pizzas.

From the first piece of text in red, we identify a transaction step that we will label TK01/rq. It concerns the ordering of pizzas by customers. Taking the perspective of the executor of these transactions, we choose the concept of sale as the core entity type, which leads to this formulation of the product kind PK01: "[sale] is completed". Consequently, we choose "sale completing" as the name of TK01 and "sale completer" as the name of the executing actor role AR01. As discussed in Chap. 8, the promise act is mostly performed tacitly. This also holds true for [TK01/pm]. Yet, one may consider the second sentence ("Mia writes down . . .") an implicit evidence of the promise act.

The second transaction kind that can be identified is contained in the second piece of text in red. It concerns the determining of the available pizzas and their prices. For the sake of convenience, we will disregard this transaction kind, and focus on the operational activities.

The third transaction kind we identify is 'hidden' in the third piece of text in red. It represents first of all clearly an informational transaction. However, in most shop situations, telling of the (total) price of ordered items by the salesperson to the customer also counts as performing the request act, in this case [TK03/rq], where TK03[1] is the transaction kind number that we assign to it. We formulate the

---

[1]It sounds not logical to assign the number '03' to the new transaction kind. However, there is basically no logic in assigning numbers to transaction kinds and actor roles. There is only one practical convention: the number of an actor role is the same as the number of the transaction kind of which it is the executor. For example, the executing actor role of TK03 is AR03.

corresponding product kind PK03 as "[sale] is paid", and name TK03 as "sale paying". The executing actor role is named "sale payer". The formulation "[sale] is paid" of the product kind is preferable to, for example, "[invoice] is paid" or "[payment] is done", for two reasons. First, by using the same entity type in the 'component' product PK03 as the one in the 'assembly' product PK01, the relationship between TK01 and TK03 (TK01 encloses TK03) is elucidated. Second, all other options have two drawbacks. One is that another core entity type has to be added to the Fact Model (FM). The other is that the connection between this entity type (so 'invoice' or 'payment') and 'sale' has to be clarified: whether there is one invoice or payment per sale or can there be more than one, etc.

The order forms have a serial number and are produced in duplicate: a white and a pink copy. Mia slides the pink one through a hatch in the wall to the kitchen, where Mario takes care of the baking. She keeps the white copy behind the counter. As soon as Mario has finished an order, he slides the pizzas in boxes through the same hatch to Mia, including the pink order copy. Mia then seeks the matching white copy, hands it together with the boxes over to the customer, and waits for the payment.

From the first red-coloured sentence in this paragraph we identify steps in transactions of a new kind, which we will label TK02 and name "sale preparing". The corresponding product kind PK02 is formulated as "[sale] is prepared", and the executing actor role AR02 is named "sale preparer". The action in the first part of the sentence that we refer to counts as performing [TK02/rq] and the second part clearly points at performing the production act, thus [TK02/ex].

The second piece of text in red expresses another step in transactions of the same kind, namely the declaration act, thus [TK02/da]. The first part of the text is already a sufficient indication of the act; the second part (*including the pink order copy*) is a documental act that confirms it extra.

The third piece of text in red is a very short indication of the existence of transactions of the kind TK03, of which we identified the request earlier.

It can happen that Mario is not able to fulfil an order completely because of missing ingredients. In such a case he puts his head through the hatch and notifies Mia of the problem. He then also returns the pink copy. If the customer is present in the shop, Mia confers with her/him on what to do about it, and modifies the order. If the customer is not present, which is of course the case for orders by telephone, she modifies the order often at her own discretion. This leads sometimes to vigorous debates in the pizzeria when the customer comes for taking away the pizzas. Thanks to Mia's temperament, she always comes to an agreement that is not disadvantageous for her.

In the previous part of the analysis, we have identified the steps TK02/rq, TK02/ex, and TK02/da. The promise, [TK02/pm], was apparently performed tacitly. This can be deduced from the presence of the declaration act. In the first two red-coloured sentences above, we identify a step from whose absence the promise may also be deduced, namely from the decline act [TK02/dc]. Declining is precisely what Mario does when he tells Mia that he cannot bake the requested pizzas, and returns the pink copy of the order form in addition to it.

Mia has a problem now. She has promised the customer, be it tacitly, that her/his order will be executed and now she is faced with the impossibility to live up to it. Her only option is to revoke the [TK01/pm], which she apparently does in the remainder of the red-coloured text, and to discuss an adapted request in the state (TK01/dc) where she and the customer have ended up (cf. Sect. 8.2.6). This works well if the customer is present in the pizzeria, but not if the customer is waiting at home. In that case, Mia quite boldly 'speaks for the customer' by personally modifying the order.

Table 14.1 TPT of the Pizzeria organisation (first phase)

transaction kind	product kind	executor role
TK01 sale completing	PK01 [sale] is completed	AR01 sale completer
TK02 sale preparing	PK02 [sale] is prepared	AR02 sale preparer
TK03 sale paying	PK03 [sale] is paid	AR03 sale payer

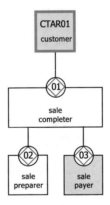

Fig. 14.1 Interaction structure of the Pizzeria organisation (first phase)

The analysis so far leads to the TPT in Table 14.1 and the CSD in Fig. 14.1. The border of the chosen organisation is the boundary of the enterprise (cf. Sect. 11.4.1). Consequently, CTAR01 and AR03 are actor roles in the environment.

14.3.2   Analysis of the Second Phase

The major change in the second phase of the pizzeria is the option to have pizzas delivered home. Hereafter, we will analyse the effects of this change on the O-organisation of the pizzeria.

The operations in this phase are basically similar to the operations in the first phase; only the deliveries have been added. However, the big success of the new service has made it necessary that a second baker be employed. His name is

Giovanni. An extra duplicate is added to the order forms; next to the white and the pink copies, there is a blue one. If an order has to be delivered home, Mia writes down the delivery address on the order form and slides both the white and the blue copy through a hatch to the room where the students are waiting.

From the first piece of text in red, we deduce that there is a new transaction kind, which we will label TK04 and name "sale delivering". The second piece of text in red clearly indicates the performing of the request in transactions of this kind: [TK04/rq]. As usual, there is no explicit promise; the absence of a decline upon the request is sufficient evidence for Mia to deduce that the [TK04/pm] is performed implicitly.

The other parts of the text above are about implementation (the presence of a second baker) and about the D-organisation (the blue copy of the order form).

The student whose turn it is fills in her or his name on the blue copy and puts it in a tray. He/she then waits for Mario or Giovanni to slide the pizzas, together with the pink copy, through a hatch to the transporters' room. *Then, the student leaves with the pizzas and the pink and white copies of the order form. At the customer's address, he/she* hands over the pizzas and the white copy, *and waits for the payment. After the customer has paid and has* signed the pink copy, *the student goes back to the pizzeria and hands the money and the pink copy over to Mia. The students use their own mopeds as Mia did not want the trouble of having the pizzeria own the mopeds.*

The first piece of text in red may perfectly well be taken as an explicit [TK04/pm], although Mia is not aware of it. In other words, the right part of the process of a coordination act (cf. Fig. 8.5) is missing. This causes no problems, however.

In the second piece of text in red, we see the different way in which the declare act [TK02/da] is performed: the pizzas are now shifted to the deliverer instead of to Mia. As will be elaborated in Sect. 14.4.3, it means that Mia has apparently delegated a part of her authority to the students.

In a similar way, the third piece of text in red tells us that Mia has apparently also delegated another part of her authority to the students, namely the performing of the act [TK01/da]. The signing by the customer of the pink copy (last piece of text in red) counts as the acceptance of the completion of the order, thus the [TK01/ac]. Note that the addressee of this act is the student. A similar reasoning holds as for the result part of TK01 as we applied to the result part of the payment transaction: the declare act [TK01/da] is apparently delegated by Mia to the students.

Based on the analysis so far, we can produce the TPT in Table 14.2 and the CSD in Fig. 14.2. They are identical to Table 8.2 and Fig. 8.15, respectively.

Table 14.2 TPT of the Pizzeria organisation (second phase)

transaction kind	product kind	executor role
TK01 sale completing	PK01 [sale] is completed	AR01 sale completer
TK02 sale preparing	PK02 [sale] is prepared	AR02 sale preparer
TK03 sale paying	PK03 [sale] is paid	AR03 sale payer
TK04 sale delivering	PK04 [sale] is delivered	AR04 sale deliverer

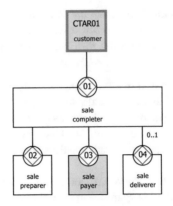

Fig. 14.2 Interaction structure of the Pizzeria organisation (second phase)

Note that in Figs. 14.1 and 14.2, only the interaction structure is shown. The other two structures in a CM (interstriction and interimpediment) will be discussed in Sect. 14.4, in addition to the other submodel, the PM.

14.3.3 Analysis of the Third Phase

Going from the second to the third phase was a major transition for the business and the organisation of the pizzeria. Yet the number of changes that this transition implies for the essential model is zero. In other words, the essential model of the second phase also applies to the third phase. This holds certainly for the CM. In the PM, there is a slight change, to be discussed in the next section.

But the I-organisation and in particular the D-organisation are very different, and the implementation of all three aspect organisations (cf. Chap. 11) is vastly different from the previous phases. The fact that they can be understood and evaluated from almost the same essential model illustrates the power of the essential model.

14.4 Extending the Essential Model of the Pizzeria

14.4.1 The Cooperation Model

The starting point for producing the complete CSD of the pizzeria consists of the TPT and the CSD that are presented in Table 14.2 and Fig. 14.2, respectively. As discussed in Sect. 14.3.3, they also apply to the third phase. What needs to be done now is adding the two other coordination structures: the interstriction structure and the interimpediment structure.

The interstriction structure is represented by the access links (expressed in dashed lines) in Fig. 14.3. There are four external multiple transaction kinds: MTK01 through

MTK04. Their sort is original, like the transaction kinds TK01 through TK04. Their existence is determined on the basis of the case description, by lack of the AM and FM. As explained in Chap. 10, they serve as transaction banks: containers of facts.

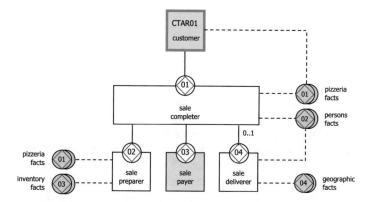

Fig. 14.3 Complete CSD of the Pizzeria organisation (second phase)

Transaction bank MTK01 contains facts like the available assortment of pizzas and their prices. Such facts need to be accessible to AR01 and AR02, but also to the customer (an actor role within CTAR01). Transaction bank MTK02 (persons facts) needs to be inspected by actors AR01 in order to get or check customer information. The same holds for actors AR04, who need to know, for example, the delivery addresses. In addition, they need geographical information, which is most likely accessed with handheld devices. In addition to constant access to the current assortment of pizzas, actors AR02 need to be able to check the presence of sufficient ingredients for preparing them. They do so by inspecting the contents of transaction bank MTK03.

Note that the actor roles that create the contents of the banks MTK01 through MTK04 are intentionally not mentioned. In the CSD, one only expresses that the contained facts are needed. One must also keep in mind that the initiators and executors of transactions of the kinds TK01 through TK04 have reading access to the contents of their 'own' banks. This is not explicitly shown in a CSD, however.

As for the interimpediment structure in the CM of the pizzeria, there are no interprocess impediments; obviously, because there is only one business process, namely the one represented by the transactor tree in Fig. 14.2.

The Bank Contents Table (BCT) is omitted by lack of the AM and the FM.

14.4.2 The Process Model

In this section, we present and discuss the PM of the pizzeria in the second phase of its existence. The PSD shown in Fig. 14.4 is fully based on the CSD in Fig. 14.2 and the case description.

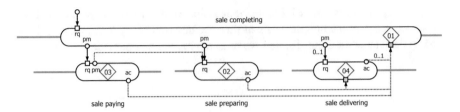

Fig. 14.4 PSD of the Pizzeria organisation (second phase)

As one may expect, the PSD shows the enclosing transaction kind TK01 (sale completing), which encloses three other transaction kinds: TK02 (sale preparing), TK03 (sale paying) and TK04 (sale delivering). Because there are no indications that the initiation of transactions of the enclosed kinds is performed otherwise, we assume that the 'normal way' holds (cf. Chap. 12), that is, that they are initiated from the state promised (pm) of the corresponding transaction TK01. In other words, as soon as the order taker has promised the customer to fulfil her/his wishes, the enclosed transactions can be started. A cardinality range 0...1 is indicated next to the response link from (TK01/pm) to [TK04/rq], as well as to the wait link from (TK04/ac) to [TK01/ex]. It expresses that transaction TK04 is optional: not every sale is delivered at the customer's home.

All enclosed transactions (so TK02, TK03, and optionally TK04) must have been carried out before the enclosing transaction (so TK01) can be completed. This condition is represented by the wait links from (TK02/ac), (TK03/ac), and (TK04/ac) to [TK01/ex]. It is an obvious condition since the products of the enclosed transactions, that is, the PK02, PK03, and PK04, are components of the PK01, as discussed in Chap. 10.

Basically, and ideally, enclosed transactions are carried out in parallel, thus simultaneously, but this is not always possible. In the case Pizzeria, there are two conditions that prevent the (ideal) full parallel carrying out of the transactions TK02, TK03, and (optionally) TK04. The first is represented by the wait link from (TK03/pm) to [TK02/rq]. It is a matter of policy of the pizzeria. The link expresses that the order taker will only ask for preparing the pizzas of a sale if the customer has promised to pay. This is a quite common condition in a sale situation. It is also quite common that the seller deduces being satisfied of the aforementioned condition from having accepted the claim to sincerity, meaning that the customer complies with the general sale terms and conditions (see Chap. 15 for exemplifications). This promise will be seldom made explicitly.

The other additional wait condition is the one from (TK02/ac) to [TK04/ex]. The reason for the presence of this condition is purely a matter of logistics: one cannot transport pizzas that are not yet prepared.

14.4.3   Delegations in the Case Pizzeria

The major difference between the first and the second phase is the introduction of home delivery. Ontologically, this is the addition of the (optional) transaction kind TK04, as shown in the CSD (Fig. 14.2) and the PSD (Fig. 14.4) of the second phase. But the change has drastic consequences for the implementation, notably the allocation of authority. They are shown in the ADT (cf. Sect. 12.4.4) in Table 14.3.

Table 14.3 ADT of the Pizzeria organisation (second phase)

T/P	TK01/da	TK02/ac	TK03/ac	TK04/ac
Customer				D
Order taker	A	A	A	A
Baker				
Student	D	D	D	

The table tells us that the functionary order taker (filled by Mia in the first and the second phase) is authorised to perform the declare act in transactions TK01 (sale completing), as well as the accept act in transactions TK02 (sale preparing), TK03 (sale paying), and TK04 (sale delivering). These authorisations are marked by an "A". For takeaway orders there is no problem: the order taker can accept the preparing and the paying and subsequently declare the transaction TK01 to be completed. However, in case of home delivery, the delegations are needed that are marked by a "D".

In transactions TK02 (sale preparing), it is not the order taker but the student who accepts the pizzas from the kitchen. Next, in transactions TK03 (sale paying), it is the student who accepts the payment from the customer, instead of the order taker. The necessity of these delegations stems from the inability of the order taker to be in two locations at the same time (in the pizzeria and at the customer's home address). As discussed in Chap. 8, these delegations presuppose that the authorised performer, thus the order taker, shares with the delegated person, that is, the student, the norms, and values that he/she applies in the delegated acts, so that everything runs as smooth as without delegations.

In transactions TK04 (sale delivery), it is the customer who performs the accept act, instead of the order taker. This is less strange than it may look, because it is also the customer who performs the accept act in the enclosing TK01. Needless to say that this act is performed tacitly, the customer is actually unaware of it. Next, it is now the student who performs the declare act in these transactions instead of the order taker. As soon as the student has performed the delegated [TK04/da] and [TK03/ac] at the customer's place, he/she performs the [TK01/da], while being unaware of it, and drives back to the pizzeria.

14.5   Conclusions

We have demonstrated above that the case Pizzeria is an exercise in understanding and applying the full potential of abstracting from realisation and implementation.

The analysis of the first phase (Sect. 14.3.1) is an example of applying the OER method (cf. Chap. 12) in revealing the essential model of an enterprise from a narrative description of its activities. Knowledge of the reference models, as presented and discussed in Chap. 10, helps in finding the tree structure in Fig. 14.1. By choosing the enterprise boundary (cf. Chap. 11) as the border of our focus organisation, the payment transaction is part of the tree, and its executor role (AR03) is consequently an environmental actor role. For similar reasons, the actor role AR04, which is added in the model of the second phase, is an internal one: the students are paid by the pizzeria.

The big transformation from being a small local pizzeria to being a branch of a large pizzeria chain, with huge consequences for the way in which it is 'organised', hardly has consequences for the essential model of the pizzeria. This is probably the most important insight that the analysis of the case pizzeria offers to the reader.

Another remarkable insight may be the consequences of the apparently 'simple' extension of the business with home delivery for the allocation of authority (and the necessary delegations). As illustrated by Table 14.3, these consequences are not trivial at all. It also demonstrates the importance of the transaction pattern in determining and discussing authorisation and delegation (cf. Chap. 8). Only on the basis of deep knowledge of the transaction pattern can one understand the necessity of some delegations of authority, which are only caused by the way in which the ontological model is implemented.

Chapter 15
Exercise: Case Rent-A-Car

Abstract The case Rent-A-Car is an exercise in producing the essential model of an enterprise that offers the usufruct of tangible things: Rent-A-Car is a company that rents cars to customers. By applying the OER method to the narrative case description, one acquires the knowledge to produce the essential model of the enterprise. All four aspect models (CM, AM, PM, and FM) are presented. Together they constitute a coherent whole that offers full insight into and overview over the essence of car rental companies. The produced action rules can directly be transformed into executable computer code.

15.1 Introduction

The case Rent-A-Car (or RAC for short) is an exercise in producing the essential model of an enterprise that offers the usufruct of tangible things (cf. Chap. 10). It is an adapted version of the EU-Rent case as used by the Object Management Group in their SBVR (Semantic of Business Vocabulary and Rules specification)[1] undertaking. For the purpose of illustrating ontological modelling, the original EU-Rent case is much too tailored to the needs of data and rules-oriented modelling approaches like NIAM,[2] ORM [1], and RuleSpeak.[3] Therefore, we have adapted it so that it is suited for conceptual modelling in general, including business process modelling, thus not only for the approaches mentioned.

Section 15.2 contains the narrative description of the RAC organisation. It is the basis for applying the OER method in a spiral way, so going in every round through all four steps and in doing so, extending the four aspect models, as discussed in Chap. 12. The analysis is discussed in Sect. 15.3. The results of the first two identified transaction kinds are represented in (preliminary) diagrams, tables, and

---

[1]For more information: https://www.omg.org/spec/SBVR/About-SBVR/

[2]https://en.wikipedia.org/wiki/Object-role_modeling

[3]http://www.rulespeak.com/en/

© Springer Nature Switzerland AG 2020
J. L. G. Dietz, J. B. F. Mulder, *Enterprise Ontology*, The Enterprise Engineering Series, https://doi.org/10.1007/978-3-030-38854-6_15

other ways of expression. The complete essential model is presented in Sect. 15.4, while Sect. 15.5 contains the conclusions from the exercise.

15.2   Narrative Description

Rent-A-Car (or RAC for short) is a company that rents cars to persons, both private ones and representatives of legal bodies, like companies. It was founded by the twin brothers Janno and Ties back in the 1980s. They started to hire out their own (two) cars, and they were among the first companies that allowed cars to be dropped off in a different location than where they were picked up. To this end, Janno and Ties had made agreements with students in several cities. For a small amount of money, a student would await the arrival of a rented car, for example, at an airport, and drive it back to the office of RAC, after which the student would go home by public transport.

Currently, RAC operates from over 50 geographically dispersed branches in Europe. Many cities have a branch, some even several, and there are branches located near all main airports. One of the branches is the original office where Janno and Ties started and where both are still around. Being mechanical engineers by education, they love to drive and maintain cars, even though they now are the managing directors of a million euro company.

The head of the front office of the home branch is Chiara. There are two more desk officers working in this department. Customer orders are placed through several channels: walk-in, telephone, website, and e-mail. Walk-in customers are typically people who want to rent a car immediately. Through the other channels one makes in general advance reservations, which have a future day as the starting day. They can be made up to 200 days in advance; this time span is called the rental horizon. RAC applies a maximum rental period (currently 10 days). In all cases, an electronic rental form is filled out, either by the customer or by one of the desk officers, as input to RACIS (RAC Information System). The next groups of data must be provided:

RENTAL	Identification number (automatically generated), starting day, ending day, pick-up location, return location, car group.
RENTER	Identification (passport or driving license), first name, last name, address, day of birth, place of birth.
DEPOSIT PAYER	Identification (passport or driving license), first name, last name, address, day of birth, place of birth
INVOICE PAYER	Identification (passport or driving license), first name, last name, address, day of birth, place of birth.
DRIVER	Driving license (also for identification), first name, last name.
FINANCIAL	Rental rate per day (basically determined by the car group), deposit amount.

The cars of RAC are divided into car groups. A car group may contain several car types (brands and models). The common feature of the cars in a group is that they have the same rental rate per day and the same deposit amount. The board of directors, that is, Janno and Ties, decide which brands and models belong to which group as well as what the rental rate and deposit amount is for every group. Normally, they do this once a year together with general parameters like the maximum rental duration and the rental horizon.

The renter has to sign the rental form (either manually or electronically in RACIS). The signing does not only count as confirming her/his request to rent a car, but also as the promise (by the deposit payer) to pay the deposit and the promise (by the invoice payer) to pay the final invoice. The deposit has to be paid right away. Note that the renter, deposit payer, invoice payer, and driver may be different people; mostly, however, they are the same person.

As soon as the deposit is paid, a car is allocated to the rental, and the driver is requested to take the car at the agreed-upon time, at the distribution department, located at the backside of the building. If there is no car available of the contracted group, a car from the next higher car group is selected. The driver will get this 'upgraded' car, for the price of the contracted group.

After the car of a rental has been returned, the invoice to be paid is prepared. In addition to the rental charge, which equals the rental duration times the rental rate, there may be a penalty charge for returning the car too late. It amounts to the number of extra days times the late return penalty rate. In addition, the car may have been returned at another branch than the contracted one. In that case, a location penalty charge has to be paid. This amounts to the distance between the actual and the contracted return branch times the penalty rate per kilometre. The paid deposit amount is subtracted from the final sum.

The distribution department is also responsible for transporting cars between branches, so that there are sufficient cars available for the upcoming rentals. To this end, Mik schedules every morning the transportations that have to be performed that day, in coordination with the other branches. The transportations are carried out by all three of them, so also by Ferre and Carlo. That is why often some of them are away from the office.

15.3   Analysis of the Narrative Description

Because it is not possible to involve the employees of RAC directly, we have to apply the second best way of working, as discussed in Chap. 12. It is to study the case description and to find clues for the presence of original (thus O-organisation) transaction kinds and corresponding actor roles. We will do this below, paragraph after paragraph. The pieces of text that are taken from the case description are written in italics. We apply the OER method to the case RAC in a spiral way (cf. Chap.12). Only the first two rounds, in which the transactor roles TAR01 and TAR04 are identified, are dealt with extensively, that is, the corresponding parts of the four aspect models are presented and discussed. For the other rounds, we only identify the transactor roles.

Rent-A-Car (or RAC for short) is a company that rents cars to persons, both private ones and representatives of legal bodies, like companies. It was founded by the twin brothers Janno and Ties back in the 1980s. They started to hire out their own (two) cars, and they were among the first companies that allowed cars to be dropped off in a different location than where they were picked up. To this end, Janno and Ties had made agreements with students in several cities. For a small amount of money, a student would await the arrival of a rented car, for example, at an airport, and drive it back to the office of RAC, after which the student would go home by public transport.

Although this piece of text does contain indications of essential transaction kinds, we consider it primarily as introductory.

Currently, RAC operates from over 50 geographically dispersed branches in Europe. Many cities have a branch, some even several, and there are branches located near all main airports. One of the branches is the original office where Janno and Ties started and where both are still around. Being mechanical engineers by education, they love to drive and maintain cars, even though they are now the managing directors of a million euro company.

As will become fully clear hereafter, the focus of our analysis will be the branch of RAC that was the original office of the founders of the company. So, this will be our Scope of Interest (SoI).

The head of the front office of the home branch is Chiara. There are two more desk officers working in this department. Customer orders are placed through several channels: walk-in, telephone, website, and e-mail. Walk-in customers are typically people who want to rent a car immediately. Through the other channels one makes in general advance reservations, which have a future day as the starting day. They can be made up to 200 days in advance; this time span is called the rental horizon. RAC applies a maximum rental period (currently 10 days). In all cases, an electronic rental form is filled out, either by the customer or by one of the desk officers, as input to RACIS (RAC Information System). The next groups of data must be provided:

RENTAL	*identification number (automatically generated), starting day, ending day, pick-up location, return location, car group.*
RENTER	*identification (passport or driving license), first name, last name, address, day of birth, place of birth.*
DEPOSIT PAYER	*identification (passport or driving license), first name, last name, address, day of birth, place of birth.*
INVOICE PAYER	*identification (passport or driving license), first name, last name, address, day of birth, place of birth.*
DRIVER	*driving license (also for identification), first name, last name.*
FINANCIAL	*rental rate per day (basically determined by the car group), deposit amount.*

In the third and fourth sentences we find evidence of the main activity of RAC: the renting of cars. Let us identify this transaction kind as TK01 and give it the name "rental completing". The red coloured text *"Customer orders are placed"* indicates the C-act [TK01/rq] and *"rent a car"* the P-act [TK01/ex], as well as the whole transaction kind. Let us formulate the corresponding product kind as "[rental] **is** completed", in DEMOSL [2]. So, every PK01[4] is an instance of renting a car by some customer, who takes the initiator role in the transaction. As mentioned in the first paragraph of the case description, a customer is either a natural person or a legal person, whose legal existence is presumably laid down in an official commercial register. Most civil codes allow for the registration of enterprises as legal entities. In applying DEMO, however, we look for actor roles, the units of authority and responsibility, and for subjects, that is, social individuals, who are authorised to fill these roles. Therefore, only humans can be the (responsible) initiators of transactions TK01. Likewise, the executor role in transactions TK01 is taken by employees of RAC, not by the legal entity RAC. Thus, we identify the actor role AR01. Let us give it the name "rental completer". Actors AR01 are the executors of transactions TK01. Because our SoI comprises the operational activities in (the home branch of) the company RAC (as follows from the case description), AR01 is an internal actor role. The initiators of transactions TK01 are outside the SoI. They are the fillers of some unknown elementary actor role in the composite transactor role CTAR01, which we give the name "renter". Figure 15.1 exhibits the CSD and the TPT of the discussed first part of the essential model of RAC.

The red coloured text *"advance reservations"* is also an indication of [TK01/rq]. Advance reservations are basically not different from 'normal' reservations. The difference is only in the value of the operative time of the transaction product, as discussed in Chap. 8.

The last part of the referred paragraph of the case description contains the facts that are related to rentals. In the group RENTAL, there are the attributes 'starting day' and 'ending day', as well as the properties 'pick-up location', 'return location', and 'car group'. Note that the identification number is not a property or attribute. Names and identification numbers are ontologically irrelevant (cf. Chap. 5). From the groups RENTER and DRIVER we distill the properties 'renter' and 'driver' of rentals. The other data (identification, first name, last name, etc.) are either ontologically irrelevant or not necessary for the operations of RAC. Although there is no explicit mentioning of it in the case description, we will assume that drivers have a property 'driving license' and that the validity of the driver's driving license is checked at the start of a rental. In the group FINANCIAL we find that there is a fact type 'daily rental rate'. As shown in Fig. 15.3, it is an attribute of the aggregation of the entity type 'car group' and the value type 'year'.

---

[4]As discussed in Chap. 8, we will write 'actors ARn' as a shorthand for 'actors filling actor role ARn', 'transactions TKn' as a shorthand for 'transactions of the kind TKn', and products PKn as a shorthand for 'products of the kind PKn'.

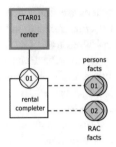

transaction kind	product kind	executor role
TK01 rental completing	PK01 [rental] is completed	AR01 rental completer

Fig. 15.1 CSD and TPT of the RAC organisation (first part)

Based on the analysis so far, we can specify the next action rule for settling requests in transactions TK01, in DEMOSL [2]. Obviously, the action rule has to be validated, like it holds for every part of every aspect model.

when rental completing **for** [rental] **is** <u>requested</u>   (TK01/rq)
      with **the** starting day **of** [rental] **is some** day
              the ending day **of** [rental] **is some** day
              the renter **of** [rental] **is some** person
              the deposit payer **of** [rental] **is some** person
              the driver **of** [rental] **is some** driver
              the invoice payer **of** [rental] **is some** person
              the car group **of** [rental] **is some** car group
              the pick-up location **of** [rental] **is some** branch
              the return location **of** [rental] **is some** branch

assess *rightness*: **the** <u>performer</u> **of the** <u>request</u> **is the** renter **of** [rental]
                    the <u>addressee</u> **of the** <u>request</u> **is some** employee
     sincerity: ∗ no specific condition ∗
     truth: **the** starting day **of** [rental] **is in the** rental horizon **of the** year **of**
                      the starting day **of** [rental];
                the ending day **of** [rental] **is in the** rental horizon **of the** year **of**
                      the starting day **of** [rental];
                the ending day **of** [rental] **is equal to or greater than the**
                      starting day **of** [rental];
                the duration **of** [rental] **is less than or equal to the** max rental
                      duration **in the** year **of the** starting day **of** [rental]
                the expiration day **of the** driving license **of the** driver **of** [rental]
                      is equal to or greater than the ending day **of** [rental];

      the number of free cars **in the** car group **of** [rental] **on** every day
      between the starting day **of** [rental] **and the** ending day
      of [rental] **is greater than zero**

if	*performing the action after **then** is considered justifiable*		
then <u>promise</u>	rental completing **for** [rental]	[TK01/pm]	
	to the renter **of** [rental]		
<u>request</u>	deposit paying **for** [rental]	[TK04/rq]	
	to the deposit payer **of** [rental]		
	with the <u>requested ot</u> **of** rental paying **for** [rental] **is** Now		
	the <u>requested</u> deposit amount **of** [rental] **is equal to**		
	the standard deposit amount **for the** car group **of** [rental]		
	in the year **of the** starting day **of** [rental]		
else <u>decline</u>	rental completing **for** [rental]	[TK01/dc]	
	to the renter **of** [rental]		
	with ∗ reason for declining ∗		

After execution of the action rule, a particular employee is allocated to the rental as its rental completer. As discussed in Chap. 12, the first condition in the rightness division is not a trivial one. If it would be omitted, anyone could perform the request.

The cars of RAC are divided into car groups. A car group may contain several types (brands and models). The common feature of the cars in a group is that they have the same rental rate per day. The board of directors, that is, Janno and Ties, decide which brands and models belong to which group as well as what the rental rate is for every group. Normally, they do this once a year together with general parameters, like the maximum rental duration and the rental horizon.

Although making these decisions is certainly part of the complete essential model of the RAC company, we consider it out of our SoI.

The renter has to sign the rental form (either manually or electronically in RACIS). The signing does not only count as confirming her/his request to rent a car, but also as the promise (by the deposit payer) to pay the deposit and the promise (by the invoice payer) to pay the final invoice. The deposit has to be paid right away. Note that the renter, deposit payer, invoice payer, and driver may be different people; mostly, however, they are the same person.

The red coloured text *"The deposit has to be paid right away"* is a clear indication of the existence of a new original transaction kind. Let us call it TK04 and give it the name 'deposit paying'. Next, let us formulate the product kind PK04 as '**the** deposit **of** [rental] **is** paid'. The executor role is AR04, named 'deposit payer'. The CSD and TPT of RAC, now augmented with transactor role TAR04 is exhibited in Fig. 15.2.

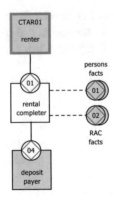

transaction kind	product kind	executor role
TK01 rental completing	PK01 [rental] is completed	AR01 rental completer
TK04 deposit paying	PK04 the deposit of [rental] is paid	AR04 deposit payer

Fig. 15.2 CSD and TPT of the RAC organisation (second part)

We specify the next action rule for settling declarations in transactions TK04:

when   deposit paying **for** [rental] **is** <u>declared</u>   (TK04/da)

assess *rightness*: **the** <u>performer</u> **of the** <u>declaration</u> **is the** deposit payer **of** [rental]
                  the <u>addressee</u> **of the** <u>declaration</u> **is the** rental completer
                  of [rental]
         sincerity: ∗ no specific condition ∗
         truth: **the** <u>declared ot</u> **of** deposit paying **for** [rental] **is within**
                  the <u>promised ot</u> **of** deposit paying **for** [rental];
                  the <u>declared</u> deposit amount **of** deposit paying **for** [rental]
                     is equal to the <u>promised</u> deposit amount **of** deposit paying
                     for [rental]

if   *performing the action after **then** is considered justifiable*
then <u>accept</u>   deposit paying **for** [rental]   [TK04/ac]
              to the deposit payer **of** [rental]
else <u>reject</u>   deposit paying **for** [rental]   [TK04/rj]
              to the deposit payer **of** [rental]
              with ∗ reason for rejecting ∗

The part of the FM that can be produced now is represented in an OFD (Fig. 15.3), a BCT (Fig. 15.4) and a CUT (Fig. 15.5). In addition, the derived fact types, which are used in presented parts of the AM, are specified.

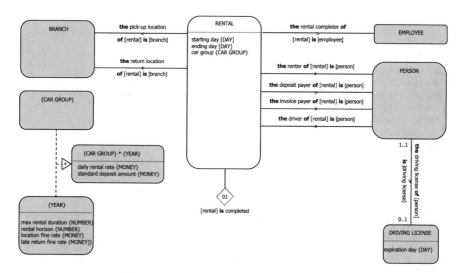

Fig. 15.3 OFD of the RAC organisation (first part)

bank	independent/dependent facts
TK01 rental completing	RENTAL **the** starting day **of** [rental] **the** ending day **of** [rental] **the** renter **of** [rental] **the** driver **of** [rental] **the** deposit payer **of** [rental] **the** invoice payer **of** [rental] **the** car group **of** [rental] **the** pick-up location **of** [rental] **the** return location **of** [rental] **the** rental completer **of** [rental]
TK04 deposit paying	**the** deposit **of** [rental] **is** paid **the** deposit amount **of** [rental]
MTK01 persons facts	PERSON DRIVING LICENSE **the** expiration day **of** [driving license]
MTK02 RAC facts	YEAR **the** rental horizon in [year] **the** late return fine rate in [year] **the** max rental duration in [year] **the** location fine rate in [year] CAR GROUP * YEAR **the** standard deposit amount **for** [car group] **in** [year]

Fig. 15.4 BCT of the RAC organisation (first part)

P-fact type	created in performing	used when settling
RENTAL	TK01/rq	
the starting day of [rental]	<provided as parameter>	TK01/rq
the ending day of [rental]	<provided as parameter>	TK01/rq
the renter of [rental]	<provided as parameter>	TK01/rq
the driver of [rental]	<provided as parameter>	TK01/rq
the deposit payer of [rental]	<provided as parameter>	TK01/rq
the invoice payer of [rental]	<provided as parameter>	TK01/rq
the car group of [rental]	<provided as parameter>	TK01/rq
the pick-up location of [rental]	<provided as parameter>	TK01/rq
the return location of [rental]	<provided as parameter>	TK01/rq
the rental completer of [rental]	TK01/rq	
the deposit of [rental] is paid	TK04/ac	
the deposit amount of [rental]	TK04/ac	
YEAR	<given externally>	
the rental horizon in [year]	<given externally>	TK01/rq
the standard deposit for [car group] in [year]	<given externally>	TK01/rq
the max rental duration in [year]	<given externally>	TK01/rq
PERSON	<given externally>	TK01/rq
DRIVING LICENSE	<given externally>	TK01/rq
the expiration day of [driving license]	<given externally>	TK01/rq

Fig. 15.5 CUT of the RAC organisation (first part)

Although there are attributes of persons, like the day of birth, mentioned in the case description, they are not included in the FM, for the simple reason that they don't occur in any action rule. The corresponding Derived Fact Specifications (DFS) are:

the duration **of** [rental] = **the** ending day **of** [rental] **minus the** starting day **of** [rental];

the number of free cars **in the** car group **of** [rental] **on** [day] = ∗ this a quite complicated computation; by the number of free, that is, available, cars in a car group is meant the number of free cars at the premises of the home branch of RAC; one has to take into account the current and future rentals as well as the transportation plans (as far as they exist) ∗

Fig. 15.6 PSD of the RAC organisation (first part)

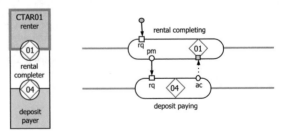

Figure 15.6 exhibits the PSD of the RAC organisation for the part that we have analysed up to now. On the left side, the tree structure from Fig. 15.2 is shown, but now in the 'click' mode (cf. Chap. 10). The right side shows that transactions TK04 are initiated from the state promised in the corresponding TK01, in conformity with the action rule for settling events TK01/rq above, and that actors AR01 must wait for completing transactions TK01 until the corresponding transaction TK04 has been accepted, in conformity with the action rule above for settling events (TK01/pm).

Let us proceed with the analysis of the remainder of the description. Their effect on the models will be presented in Sect. 15.4.

As soon as the deposit is paid, a car is allocated to the rental, and the driver is requested to take the car at the agreed-upon time, at the distribution department, located at the backside of the building. If there is no car available of the contracted group, a car from the next higher car group is selected. The driver will get this 'upgraded' car, for the price of the contracted group.

The text "*a car is allocated*" clearly indicates an original transaction kind. However, for the sake of simplification we ignore it. Note that this transaction kind would be enclosed in TK04. The text "*the driver is requested to take the car*" is an indication of the presence of the transaction kind TK02, which we will name "car taking". Accordingly, PK02 is formulated as "**the** car **of** [rental] **is** taken" and actor role AR02 is named "car taker".

After the car of a rental has been returned, the invoice to be paid is prepared. In addition to the rental charge, which equals the rental duration times the rental rate, there may be a penalty charge for returning the car too late. It amounts to the number of extra days times the late return penalty rate. In addition, the car may have been returned at another branch than the contracted one. In that case, a location penalty charge has to be paid. This amounts to the distance between the actual and the contracted return branch times the penalty rate per kilometre. The paid deposit amount is subtracted from the final sum.

There are two pieces of text that indicate the presence of essential transaction kinds: "*the car of a rental has been returned*" and "*invoice to be paid*". Let us number the first one TK03 and name it "car returning". The corresponding actor role AR03 is named "car returner" and the product kind PK03 is formulated as "**the** car **of** [rental] **is** returned". The second piece of red marked text indicates the presence of transaction kind TK05, named "invoice paying" with executor role AR05 "invoice payer". The product kind PK05 is formulated as "**the** invoice **of** [rental] **is** paid". The rest of the text concerns informational things, from which we abstract.

The distribution department is also responsible for transporting cars between branches, so that there are sufficient cars available for the upcoming rentals. To this end, Mik schedules every morning the transportations that have to be performed that day, in coordination with the other branches. The transportations are carried out by all three of them, so also by Ferre and Carlo. That is why often some of them are away from the office.

This last part of the case description contains two indications of original transaction kinds, both not directly related to the four we have found up to now. The text *"transporting cars between branches"* is an indication of the presence of the transaction kind TK06, which we will name "transport completing". Accordingly, PK06 is formulated as "[transport] **is** completed" and actor role AR06 is named "transport completer". The text *"schedules every morning the transportations"* is an indication of the presence of the transaction kind TK07, which we will name "transport managing". Apparently, transactions of this kind are carried out daily. Thus, TK07 is a self-activating transaction kind: during every instance of transaction kind TK07, so every day, a number of transactions TK06 are initiated. Actor role AR07 is properly named "transport manager". Accordingly, PK07 is properly formulated as "transport managing **for** [day] **is** done".

15.4   The Complete Essential Model of RAC

15.4.1   The Cooperation Model

In Fig. 15.7, the CSD and the TPT of the RAC organisation are shown. It contains two business processes (and thus transaction trees): on the left side the renting process (comprising TAR01 and the enclosed TAR02, TAR03, TAR04, and

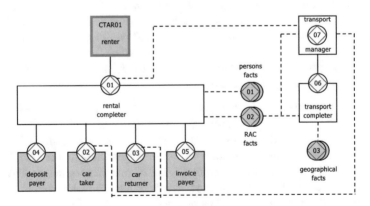

transaction kind	product kind	executor role
TK01 rental completing	PK01 [rental] is completed	AR01 rental completer
TK02 car taking	PK02 the car of [rental] is taken	AR02 car taker
TK03 car returning	PK03 the car of [rental] is returned	AR03 car returner
TK04 deposit paying	PK04 the deposit of [rental] is paid	AR04 deposit payer
TK05 invoice paying	PK05 the invoice of [rental] is paid	AR05 invoice payer
TK06 transport completing	PK06 [transport] is completed	AR06 transport completer
TK07 transport managing	PK07 transport managing **for** [day] **is** done	AR07 transport manager

Fig. 15.7 CSD and TPT of the RAC organisation

TAR05); on the right side the car transporting process (comprising TAR07 and the enclosed TAR06). The mutual influences between the two business processes consist only of interstriction. There are no interimpediments. The transport manager (AR07) needs access to TK01 (current rentals), TK02 (cars taken or to be taken), and TK03 (cars returned or to be returned) in order to make the daily plan for transporting cars.

There are three external information sources, represented by the multiple transaction banks MTK01 (facts about persons), MTK02 (facts about RAC), and MTK03 (geographical facts). As can be deduced from the AM, actors AR01 need access to MTK01 and MTK02, while actors AR07 only need access to MTK02. Actors AR06 need to have access to MTK02 and MTK03 (e.g. through a navigator).

15.4.2 The Action Model

This section presents the Action Rule Specifications (ARS) for the coordination events that the internal actor roles in RAC, that is, AR01, AR06, and AR07, have to settle. As explained in Chap. 12 and in [2], an action rule is divided into three consecutive parts: the *event* part (consisting of a when-clause, optionally supplemented by a while- and/or a with-clause), the *assess* part (consisting of the C-facts and P-facts to be assessed, grouped into the three validity claims), and the *response* part (consisting of the acts to be performed, optionally supplemented by a with-clause).

An action rule is a guideline for the addressed actor of a C-act in deciding how to respond. In terms of the process of a coordination act (cf. Figs. 8.5 or 12.19), we have arrived at the top-right part, the most inner self of the addressee. The standard if-clause (**if** *performing the action after* **then** *is considered justifiable*) emphasises that action rules are not algorithms but guidelines: the executing actor acts autonomously and thus may violate the rule (cf. Chap. 8).

ARS-1 (Executed by AR01)
The event to settle is the completing of a rental being requested (TK01/rq). In more common language, someone wants to rent a car. The with-clause in the when-clause specifies the properties of the rental that must be supplied.

The sincerity condition in the assess part says: ∗ no specific condition ∗. This is the usual formulation if there is no specific condition. It could very well be replaced by, for example, ∗ the renter agrees with the regulations of RAC ∗, provided that the renter has to state her/his agreement with the regulations.

The response is either a promise or a decline, according to the CTP (cf. Chap. 8). If it is a promise, then also the paying of the deposit is requested (cf. Fig. 15.6).

when rental completing **for** [rental] **is** <u>requested</u>   (TK01/rq)
     with   **the** starting day **of** [rental] **is some** day
             the ending day **of** [rental] **is some** day
             the renter **of** [rental] **is some** person
             the deposit payer **of** [rental] **is some** person
             the driver **of** [rental] **is some** driver
             the invoice payer **of** [rental] **is some** person
             the car group **of** [rental] **is some** car group
             the pick-up location **of** [rental] **is some** branch
             the return location **of** [rental] **is some** branch

assess *rightness*: **the** <u>performer</u> **of the** <u>request</u> **is the** renter **of** [rental]
                the <u>addressee</u> **of the** <u>request</u> **is some** employee
      sincerity: ∗ no specific condition ∗
      truth: **the** starting day **of** [rental] **is in the** rental horizon **of the** year **of**
                the starting day **of** [rental];
             the ending day **of** [rental] **is in the** rental horizon **of the** year **of**
                the starting day **of** [rental];
             the ending day **of** [rental] **is equal to or greater than the**
                starting day **of** [rental];
             the duration **of** [rental] **is less than or equal to the** max rental
                duration **in the** year **of the** starting day **of** [rental]
             the expiration day **of the** driving license **of the** driver **of** [rental]
                is equal to or greater than the ending day **of** [rental];
             the number of free cars **in the** car group **of** [rental] **on** every day
                between the starting day **of** [rental] **and the** ending day
                of [rental] **is greater than zero**

if   *performing the action after **then** is considered justifiable*
then **promise**   rental completing **for** [rental]   [TK01/pm]
               to **the** renter **of** [rental]
      request   deposit paying **for** [rental]   [TK04/rq]
               to **the** deposit payer **of** [rental]
               with the <u>requested ot</u> **of** rental paying **for** [rental] **is** Now
                    the <u>requested</u> deposit amount **of** [rental] **is equal to**
                    the standard deposit amount **for the** car group **of** [rental]
                    in the year **of the** starting day **of** [rental]
else **decline**   rental completing **for** [rental]   [TK01/dc]
               to **the** renter **of** [rental]
               with ∗ reason for declining ∗

ARS-2 (Executed by AR01)

The event to settle is the deposit is paid being declared (TK04/da). The term "<u>ot</u>" in the assess part is a shorthand for 'operative time' [2]. In this case, it is the point in time at which the payment is actually done.

The response is either an accept or a reject, according to the CTP (cf. Chap. 8).

when   deposit paying **for** [rental] **is** <u>declared</u>   (TK04/da)

assess   *rightness*: **the** <u>performer</u> **of the** <u>declaration</u> **is the** deposit payer **of** [rental]
                        the <u>addressee</u> **of the** <u>declaration</u> **is the** rental completer
                        of [rental]
           sincerity: ∗ no specific condition ∗
           truth: **the** <u>declared ot</u> **of** deposit paying **for** [rental] **is within**
                            the <u>promised ot</u> **of** deposit paying **for** [rental];
                        the <u>declared</u> deposit amount **of** deposit paying **for** [rental]
                            is equal to the <u>promised</u> deposit amount **of** deposit paying
                            for [rental]

if   *performing the action after **then** is considered justifiable*
then   <u>accept</u>   deposit paying **for** [rental]   [TK04/ac]
                        to the deposit payer **of** [rental]
else   <u>reject</u>   deposit paying **for** [rental]   [TK04/rj]
                        to the deposit payer **of** [rental]
                        with ∗ reason for rejecting ∗

ARS-3 (Executed by AR01)

The event to settle is the completing of a rental being promised (TK01/pm). The when-clause contains a while-clause, which means that the actual settlement of the event has to wait until the event in the while-clause has occurred (cf. Fig. 15.9). As soon as this is the case, the driver is asked to take the selected car. Although the requested operative time of this car taking is the starting day of the rental, it may be delayed by a late payment of the deposit (as expressed by the while-clause). The selection of the car to be taken may be modelled as a separate transaction kind.

when   rental completing **for** [rental] **is** <u>promised</u>   (TK01/pm)
           while deposit paying **for** [rental] **is** <u>accepted</u>   (TK04/ac)

assess   *rightness*: ∗ no specific condition ∗
           sincerity: ∗ no specific condition ∗
           truth: ∗ no specific condition ∗

if   *performing the action after **then** is considered justifiable*
then   ∗ select car for rental ∗
           <u>request</u>   car taking **for** [rental]   [TK02/rq]
                        to the driver **of** [rental]
                        with the <u>requested ot</u> **of** car taking **for** [rental] **is within**
                            the starting day **of** [rental];
                            the <u>requested</u> car **of** car taking **for** [rental]
                            is the car **of** [rental]

ARS-4 (Executed by AR01)
The event to settle is the car taking of a rental being declared (TK02/da). The
response is either an accept or a reject, according to the CTP (cf. Chap. 8).

when	car taking **for** [rental] **is** <u>declared</u>		(TK02/da)

assess	*rightness*:	**the** <u>performer</u> **of the** <u>declaration</u> **is the** car taker **of** [rental]
		the <u>addressee</u> **of the** <u>declaration</u> **is the** rental completer **of** [rental]
	sincerity:	∗ no specific condition ∗
	truth:	**the** <u>declared ot</u> **of** car taking **for** [rental] **is within**
		the <u>promised ot</u> **of** car taking **for** [rental];
		the <u>declared</u> car **of** car taking **for** [rental] **is**
		the <u>promised</u> car **of** car taking **for** [rental]

if	*performing the action after **then** is considered justifiable*		
then	<u>accept</u>	car taking **for** [rental]	[TK02/ac]
		to the performer **of the** declaration	
else	<u>reject</u>	car taking **for** [rental]	[TK02/rj]
		to the performer **of the** declaration	
		with ∗ reason for rejecting ∗	

ARS-5 (Executed by AR01)
The event to settle is again the completing of a rental being promised (TK01/pm), but
with another while-clause, meaning that the actual settlement of the event has to wait
until the event in the while-clause has occurred (cf. Fig. 15.9). As soon as the car
taking is accepted, the driver (in her/his role of car returner) is asked to return the car
on the ending day of the rental. From now on, the driver can use the car for the
duration of the rental.

when	rental completing **for** [rental] **is** <u>promised</u>	(TK01/pm)
	while car taking **for** [rental] **is** <u>accepted</u>	(TK02/ac)

assess	*rightness*: ∗ no specific condition ∗	
	sincerity: ∗ no specific condition ∗	
	truth: ∗ no specific condition ∗	
if	*performing the action after **then** is considered justifiable*	
then	<u>request</u> car returning **for** [rental]	[TK03/rq]
	to the car returner **of** [rental]	
	with the <u>requested ot</u> **of** car returning **for** [rental] **is**	
	on the ending day **of** [rental];	
	the <u>requested</u> car **of** car returning **for** [rental] **is**	
	the <u>accepted</u> car **of** car taking **of** [rental]	

ARS-6 (Executed by AR01)

The event to settle is the car returning of a rental being declared (TK03/da). The response is either an accept or a reject, according to the CTP (cf. Chap. 8).

when	car returning **for** [rental] **is** <u>declared</u>	(TK03/da)

assess	*rightness*:	**the** <u>performer</u> **of the** <u>declaration</u> **is the** driver **of** [rental]; **the** <u>addressee</u> **of the** <u>declaration</u> **is the** rental completer **of** [rental]	
	sincerity:	∗ no specific condition ∗	
	truth:	**the** <u>declared</u> car **of** car returning **for** [rental] **is the** <u>promised</u> car **of** car returning **for** [rental]	

if	*performing the action after **then** is considered justifiable*		
then	<u>accept</u>	car returning **for** [rental] **to the** driver **of** [rental]	[TK03/ac]
else	<u>reject</u>	car returning **for** [rental] **to the** driver **of** [rental] **with** ∗ reason for rejecting ∗	[TK03/rj]

ARS-7 (Executed by AR01)

The event to settle is again the completing of a rental being promised (TK01/pm), but with another while-clause, meaning that the actual settlement of the event has to wait until the event in the while-clause has occurred (cf. Fig. 15.9). As soon as the car of the rental is returned, the final invoice is prepared and handed over to the driver (in her/his role of invoice payer). In order to pay back the deposit amount, the corresponding TK04/rq is revoked.

when	rental completing **for** [rental] **is** <u>promised</u>	(TK01/pm)
	while car returning **for** [rental] **is** <u>accepted</u>	(TK03/ac)

assess	*rightness*: ∗ no specific condition ∗	
	sincerity: ∗ no specific condition ∗	
	truth: ∗ no specific condition ∗	

if	*performing the action after **then** is considered justifiable*	
then	<u>request</u> invoice paying **for** [rental]	[TK05/rq]
	to the invoice payer **of** [rental]	
	with the <u>requested ot</u> **of** invoice paying **for** [rental] **is** Now;	
	the <u>requested</u> invoice amount **of** [rental] **is equal to**	
	the rental charge **of** [rental]	
	<u>revoke-request</u> deposit paying for rental	[TK04/rv-rq]

ARS-8 (Executed by AR01)

The event to settle is the invoice paying of a rental being declared (TK05/da). The response is either an accept or a reject, according to the CTP (cf. Chap. 8).

when	invoice paying **for** [rental] **is** <u>declared</u>	(TK05/da)

assess *rightness*: **the** <u>performer</u> **of the** <u>declaration</u> **is the** invoice payer **of** [rental];
the <u>addressee</u> **of the** <u>declaration</u> **is the** rental completer
of [rental]
sincerity: ∗ no specific condition ∗
truth: **the** <u>declared ot</u> **of** invoice paying **for** [rental] **is within**
the <u>promised ot</u> **of** invoice paying **for** [rental];
the <u>declared</u> invoice amount **of** invoice paying **for** [rental]
is equal to the <u>promised</u> invoice amount **of** invoice paying
for [rental]

if	*performing the action after **then** is considered justifiable*		
then	<u>accept</u>	invoice paying **for** [rental]	[TK05/ac]
		to the invoice payer **of** [rental]	
else	<u>reject</u>	invoice paying **for** [rental]	[TK05/rj]
		to the invoice payer **of** [rental]	
		with ∗ reason for rejecting ∗	

ARS-9 (Executed by AR01)

The event to settle is again the completing of a rental being promised (TK01/pm), but with another (the last) while-clause, meaning that the actual settlement of the event has to wait until the event in the while-clause has occurred (cf. Fig. 15.9). As soon as the final invoice is paid, the rental can be completed: creating the product and declaring the completion. When the product is accepted by the renter, the rental is truly completed. This act is, however, outside the SoI.

when	rental completing **for** [rental] **is** <u>promised</u>	(TK01/pm)
	while invoice paying **for** [rental] **is** <u>accepted</u>	(TK05/ac)

assess *rightness*: ∗ no specific condition ∗
sincerity: ∗ no specific condition ∗
truth: ∗ no specific condition ∗

if	*performing the action after **then** is considered justifiable*	
then	<u>execute</u> rental completing **for** [rental]	[TK01/ex]
	<u>declare</u> rental completing **for** [rental]	[TK01/da]
	to the renter **of** [rental]	

ARS-10 (Executed by AR07)

We are now in the car transportation process (cf. Fig. 15.8). The event to settle is the transport managing on a day being requested (TK07/rq). The action rule shows the typical format of a self-activating actor role.

when	transport managing **for** [day] **is** <u>requested</u>		(TK07/rq)

assess   *rightness*:   **the** <u>performer</u> **of the** <u>request</u> **is the** transport manager
of [day] **minus** 1;
the <u>addressee</u> **of the** <u>request</u> **is the** transport manager **of** [day]
sincerity: ∗ no specific condition ∗
truth: ∗ no specific condition ∗

if   performing the action after **then** is considered justifiable
then   <u>promise</u>   transport managing **for** [day]   [TK07/pm]
to the <u>performer</u> **of the** <u>request</u>
<u>request</u>   transport managing **for** [day] **plus** 1   (TK07/rq)
to the transport manager **of** [day] **plus** 1
else   <u>decline</u>   transport managing **for** [day]   [TK07/dc]
to the <u>performer</u> **of the** <u>request</u>
with ∗ reason for declining ∗
<u>request</u>   transport managing **for** [day] **plus** 1   (TK07/rq)
to the transport manager **of** [day] **plus** 1

ARS-11 (Executed by AR07)

The response to a (TK07/pm) consists of a number of requests to transport a particular car from some branch to some other branch (addressed to car transporters).

when	transport managing **for** [day] **is** <u>promised</u>	(TK07/pm)

assess   *rightness*:   **the** <u>performer</u> **of the** <u>promise</u> **is the** transport manager **of** [day];
the <u>addressee</u> **of the** <u>promise</u> **is the** transport manager **of** [day];
sincerity: ∗ no specific condition ∗
truth: **the number of** cars-to-be-transported **on** [day] **is**
greater than zero

if   *performing the action after **then** is considered justifiable*
then   **for each** [car] **in** cars-to-be-transported **on** [day]
<u>request</u>   transport completing **for** [transport]   (TK06/rq)
to some transport completer
with the car of [transport] **is** [car];
the from-branch **of** [transport] **is some** branch;
the to-branch **of** [transport] **is some** branch

ARS-12 (Executed by AR07)

The event to settle is the transport managing on a day being promised. The while-clause specifies that its actual settlement has to wait until the events in the while-clause have occurred (cf. Fig. 15.8), which means that all transports for this day are completed.

when transport managing **for** [day] **is** promised   (TK07/pm)

while for each [car] **in** cars-to-be-transported **on** [day]

transport completing **for** [transport] **is** accepted   (TK06/ac)

assess *rightness*: **the** performer **of the** promise **is the** transport manager **of** [day];

the addressee **of the** promise **is the** transport manager **of** [day]

sincerity: ∗ no specific condition ∗

truth: ∗ no specific condition ∗

if *performing the action after **then** is considered justifiable*

then execute transport managing **for** [day]   [TK07/ex]

declare transport managing **for** [day]   [TK07/da]

to the transport manager **of** [day]

Note: The derived fact type cars-to-be-transported-on [day] has to be defined yet. This is done later on.

ARS-13 (Executed by AR07)

The event to settle is the transport managing on a day being declared (TK07/da). The response is either an accept or a reject, according to the CTP (cf. Chap. 8). If it is accepted (which is the normal case), the transport manager is relieved from her/his responsibility regarding this instance of transport managing.

when transport managing **for** [day] **is** declared   (TK07/da)

assess *rightness*: **the** performer **of the** declare **is the** transport manager **of** [day];

the addressee **of the** declare **is the** transport manager **of** [day]

sincerity: ∗ no specific condition ∗

truth: ∗ no specific condition ∗

if *performing the action after **then** is considered justifiable*

then accept transport managing **for** [day]   [TK07/ac]

to the transport manager **of** [day]

else reject transport managing **for** [day]   [TK07/rj]

to the transport manager **of** [day]

with ∗ reason for rejecting ∗

ARS-14 (Executed by AR06)

This action rule as well as the next one (ARS-15) are quite straightforward. Actors AR06 (car transporters) complete the car transports that they are requested to do.

when	transport completing **for** [transport] **is** <u>requested</u>	(TK06/rq)
	with	**the** car **of** [transport] **is some** car;
		the from-branch **of** [transport] **is some** branch;
		the to-branch **of** [transport] **is some** branch

assess	*rightness*:	**the** <u>performer</u> **of the** <u>request</u> **is the** transport manager **of** **the** day of transport **of** [transport];
		the <u>addressee</u> **of the** <u>request</u> **is the** transport completer **of** [transport]
	sincerity:	∗ no specific condition ∗
	truth:	∗ no specific condition ∗

if	*performing the action after* ***then*** *is considered justifiable*	
then	<u>promise</u>	transport completing **for** [transport] [TK06/pm]
		to the transport manager **of the** day of transport **of** [transport]
		with the <u>promised</u> ot **of** [transport] **is within the** <u>requested</u> ot **of** [transport]
else	<u>decline</u>	transport completing **for** [transport] [TK06/dc]
		to the transport manager **of the** day of transport **of** [transport]
		with ∗ reason for declining ∗

ARS-15 (Executed by AR06)

when	transport completing **for** [transport] **is** <u>promised</u>	(TK06/pm)

assess	*rightness*:	**the** <u>performer</u> **of the** <u>promise</u> **is the** transport completer **of** [transport];
		the <u>addressee</u> **of the** <u>promise</u> **is the** transport manager **of** **the** day of transport **of** [transport]
	sincerity:	∗ no specific condition ∗
	truth:	∗ no specific condition ∗

if	*performing the action after* ***then*** *is considered justifiable*	
then	<u>execute</u>	transport completing **for** [transport] [TK06/ex]
	<u>declare</u>	transport completing **for** [transport] [TK06/da]
		to the transport manager **of the** day of transport **of** [transport]

ARS-16 (Executed by AR07)

The agendum or event to settle is a transport completing transaction being declared. The response by the transport manager is either an accept or a reject, according to the CTP (cf. Chap. 8). If it is accepted (which is the normal case, of course), the car transporter is relieved of her/his responsibility with regard to the car transport.

when   transport completing **for** [transport] **is** <u>declared</u>   (TK06/da)

assess *rightness*: **the** <u>performer</u> **of the** <u>declaration</u> **is the** transport completer
of [transport];
the <u>addressee</u> **of the** <u>declaration</u> **is the** transport manager **of
the** day of transport **of** [transport]
sincerity: ∗ no specific condition ∗
truth: **the** location **of the** car **of** [transport] **is the** to-branch
of [transport];
the <u>declared</u> <u>ot</u> **of** transport completing **for** [transport] **is
within the** <u>promised</u> <u>ot</u> **of** transport completing **for** [transport]

if   *performing the action after **then** is considered justifiable*
then   <u>accept</u>   transport completing **for** [transport]   [TK06/ac]
to the transport completer **of** [transport];
else   <u>reject</u>   transport completing **for** [transport]   [TK06/rj]
to the transport completer **of** [transport]
with ∗ reason for rejecting ∗

15.4.3   The Process Model

In Figs. 15.8 and 15.9, the PSDs of the two business processes of RAC are shown,
based on the CM in Sect. 15.4.1 and the AM in Sect. 15.4.2. The wait link from
(T04/ac) to [T02/rq] is a matter of policy of Rent-A-Car. It says that the deposit must
have been paid before the car of the rental can be taken. The wait links from (T02/ac)
to [T03/rq] and from (T03/ac) to [T05/rq] are a matter of (logistic) necessity. The
first says that a car must be taken before it can be returned. The second wait link
means that the car of a rental must have been returned before the final invoice can be
prepared and be requested to pay.

Fig. 15.8 PSD of the car
transporting process

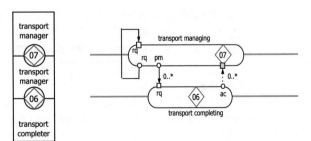

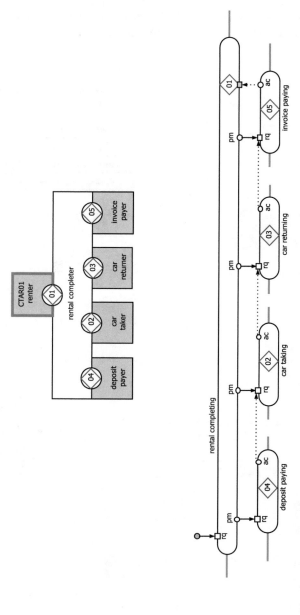

Fig. 15.9 PSD of the car rental process

15.4.4   The Fact Model

In Figs. 15.10, 15.11, and 15.12, the OFDs of RAC are shown, based on the CM in Sect. 15.4.1 and the AM in Sect. 15.4.2, followed by the Derived Fact Specifications (DFS). Note that Figs. 15.10 and 15.12 could be combined (they both have RENTAL as the core entity class). However, for the sake of convenience, they are separated.

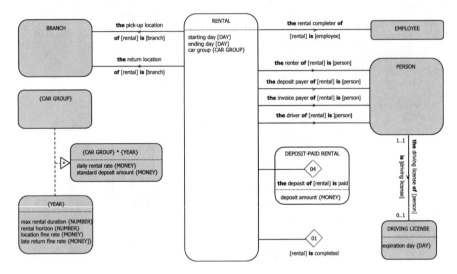

Fig. 15.10   OFD of the RAC organisation (1)

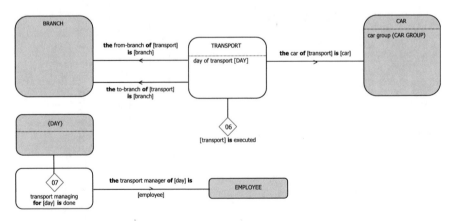

Fig. 15.11   OFD of the RAC organisation (2)

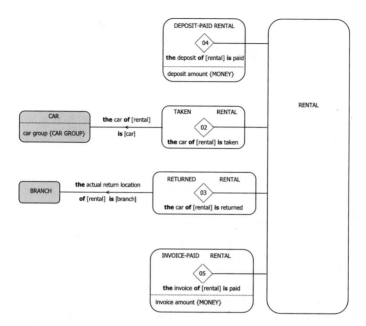

Fig. 15.12 OFD of the RAC organisation (3)

As an exercise in verifying the correctness of the OFDs, the reader is invited to check that every fact type in the action rules (cf. Sect. 15.4.2) is represented in one of the OFDs. The only fact types that are not represented are the derived fact types. The corresponding derivation rules are provided in the following.

Derived Fact Specifications

the duration **of** [rental] = **the** ending day **of** [rental] **minus the** starting day **of** [rental]

the rental charge **of** [rental] = **the** base charge **of** [rental] **plus the** fine charge **of** [rental] **minus the** <u>accepted</u> deposit amount **of** [rental]

the base charge **of** [rental] = **the** duration **of** [rental] **times the** daily rate **of the** car group **of** [rental] **in the** year **of the** starting day **of** [rental]

the fine charge **of** [rental] = **the** location fine **of** [rental] **plus the** late return fine **of** [rental]

the location fine **of** [rental] = **the** distance **between the** return location **of** [rental] **and the** actual return location **of** [rental] **times the** location fine rate **in the** year **of the** ending day **of** [rental]

the actual return location **of** [rental] = ∗ **the** branch where the car has been returned ∗

the late return fine **of** [rental] = **the** day of return **of** [rental] **minus the** ending day **of** [rental] **times the** late return fine rate **in the** year **of the** ending day **of** [rental]

the number of free cars **in the** car group **of** [rental] **on** [day] = ∗ obviously, this is the result of a non-trivial computation, taking also into account what the other branches do ∗ (see also Sect. 15.3)

cars-to-be-transported **on** [day] = ∗ obviously, this is the result of a non-trivial computation, taking also into account what the other branches do ∗

15.5   Conclusions

As stated in the introduction, the case RAC is an exercise in modelling enterprises that offer the usufruct of tangible things, in this case renting cars to customers. So, basically, the construction as presented in Sect. 10.3.3.4 applies. Indeed, the left part of the CSD in Sect. 15.4.1 is similar to the one in Fig. 10.20, as is the corresponding part of the TPT. The second business process, concerning the transport of cars between the branches of RAC is specific for rental car companies; it is not a general feature of usufruct offering enterprises. Also the added external transaction banks and the interstriction structure are specific for car rental companies.

The AM is fully based on the narrative description. No additional assumptions are made (there was also no need to do this). Yet it has to be validated by the employees of RAC. The rules are coherent and consistent and they offer the proper basis for producing the PM and the FM, both connecting the AM and the CM (cf. Chap. 12). However, if there is no need for a complete and formally specified AM, one may produce the PM and FM without the AM, basing them on the CM and the narrative description. This is a quite common practice.

The presented action rules can directly be transformed to executable program code, in the way discussed, for example, in [3] and [4]. The result is a robust computer application for car rental companies, supporting the standard transaction pattern (cf. Chap. 8) of all identified transaction kinds. Because the conditions for revocations are hard to anticipate, their executions can best rely on the skills of the actors and the culture of the company. The AM is also suited to serve as the basis for discrete event simulations, where one can 'play' with varying parameters (max duration, relaxed payment conditions, etc.). Discrete event simulations, based on DEMO models are extensively discussed in [5].

References

1. Halpin, T. A., & Morgan, T. (2008). *Information modeling and relational databases* (Morgan Kaufmann series in data management systems) (2nd ed., xxvi, 943 p). Burlington, MA: Elsevier/ Morgan Kaufman.
2. Dietz, J. L. G. (2019). *DEMO-4 specification language.* Enterprise Engineering Institute.
3. van Kervel, S. J. H., Dietz, J. L. G., Hintzen, J., van Meeuwen, T., & Zijlstra, B. (2012). *Enterprise ontology driven software engineering.* In ICSOFT 2012. SciTePress.
4. Barjis, J. A. (2008). The importance of business process modeling in software systems design. *Elsevier Science of Computer Programming, 71,* 73–87.
5. Barjis, J. (2011). Enterprise modeling and simulation within enterprise engineering. *Journal of Enterprise Transformation, 1*(3), 185–207.

Chapter 16
Exercise: Case Library

Abstract The case Library is an exercise in producing the essential model of an enterprise that offers the obtaining of usufruct of tangible things (borrowing books) and the creating of intangible things (starting and ending memberships). By applying the OER method to the narrative case description, the information is achieved on the basis of which the essential model is produced. The essential model is a stable beacon when discussing the impacts of alternative ways of implementing it. Far-reaching changes in the operational activities appear to have no or little impact on the essential model because they mainly regard implementation matters. Special attention is given to showing how revocations can be indicated in the process structure diagram.

16.1 Introduction

The case Library is an exercise in producing the essential model of an enterprise that offers, in terms of the categories that are distinguished in Chap. 10, both the obtaining of usufruct of tangible things (borrowing books) and the creating of intangible things (starting and ending memberships).

Section 16.2 contains the description of the operational activities of the Library. It is the basis for applying the organisational essence revealing (OER) method in a spiral way, so going in every cycle through all four sub-models and, while doing so, extending them (cf. Chap. 12). The analysis of the Library in its first phase is discussed in Sect. 16.3, along with presenting the (parts of the) essential model in diagrams, tables, and formal text. The analysis of the second phase is presented in Sect. 16.4, with its consequences for the initial essential model. Section 16.5 contains the conclusions from this exercise.

16.2 Narrative Description

Description of the First Phase
The Library described hereafter is a small public library. In the building in which it is located, is a desk for lending books, called the out-desk, and a desk for returning

© Springer Nature Switzerland AG 2020
J. L. G. Dietz, J. B. F. Mulder, *Enterprise Ontology*, The Enterprise Engineering Series, https://doi.org/10.1007/978-3-030-38854-6_16

books, called the in-desk. At a third desk, called the information desk, one can get information about the opening hours, the library regulations, and the membership fees. At the information desk is a desktop computer where members can browse through the library catalogue to find the books they want to borrow.

In order to become member of the library, one has to present oneself at the information desk and provide the next data to the staff member: surname, first name, middle initials, city of residence, street name, house number, postal code, date of birth, place of birth, and the starting day of the membership (which must be the first day of a month in the Gregorian calendar). The provided data are entered into the Library Information System (LIS). LIS automatically prints a membership card (with a bar code), and an invoice for the fee of the first year. The amount to pay is proportional to the remaining part of the year. From then on, membership fees are invoiced annually.

New members also get a letter of welcome, informing them about the library regulations that they are supposed to know. It is handed over to the new member after payment of the first membership fee, in cash or by bank transfer (in which case one has to provide a debit card). The minimal age for new members is 8 years. Moreover, if a new member is under 18, an adult must be entered as the payer of the fee, and one as the payer of possible fines.

Memberships are automatically extended every calendar year, until they are explicitly ended by the member. The termination of a membership is always per the 1st of January. In addition, the librarian decides every month about ending memberships by the Library. Reasons for ending a membership in this way are, for example, repeatedly late returns of books and/or refusals to pay the fee or the incurred fines. If a membership is ended by the Library, the member may claim the refund of the fee that has been paid for the remaining part of the current year. Refunds are made in cash or by bank transfer.

Members are entitled to borrow books from the library. Books are put on shelves, sorted by category and title. Normally, there are several copies of the same title. Every book copy is uniquely identified by a bar code. It consists of the ISBN (International Standard Book Number) and a serial number of the book copy. If someone wants to borrow books, he/she has to take the books from the shelves to the out-desk. There, one of the staff members scans the bar codes on the membership card and on the books. These data are automatically entered into LIS, where a loan contract for every borrowed book is created. After this process is finished, the member can take the books along.

There is a maximum number of books that one can have in loan simultaneously, and there is also a maximum loan period. Borrowed books must be returned within this period. When a member returns one or more books, he/she goes to the in-desk and hands the books to a staff member, who then scans the book codes and the membership number, which are automatically entered into LIS. On the screen of the computer, the staff member sees whether the loan period of a book is exceeded. If it is, the fine to be paid is also shown. Fines have to be paid by the member right away (in cash or by bank transfer).

Description of the Second Phase

After about ten flourishing years, the librarian decides to improve the services of the library substantially by two major changes. The first is that one doesn't need to visit the library in order to become member. It can now be done from home via a web extension of LIS. It implies, however, that payments can only be made by periodic direct debits. Instead of a membership card, members can identify themselves in LIS by means of a membership number and a password. Every member has a personal section in LIS, called MyLIS.

The second major change regards the way in which books are issued and returned. There are no more shelves with books in the library building. Instead there is a central repository in the cellar, where book copies are automatically stored and retrieved by a warehouse system.

Either from home, or from desktop computers in the library, one can browse through the catalogue and select the books one wants to borrow. Like it was in the first phase, a loan is created for every book copy. After finishing such a borrow session, the borrowed books are automatically retrieved from the central repository and put in a locker. The member has access to this locker by keying the membership number and the password at the locker wall during five workdays. If the books are not taken out within this period, they are put back in the repository. In addition, one can opt for home delivery, but at an extra charge.

Returning books is made as easy as picking up. In the hall of the library building is a conveyer belt on which one can put the returned books, one after the other. The handling of the books, as well as the processing of the corresponding loan, are done automatically. If a fine is incurred, the amount is automatically charged to one's bank account (also through direct debit). As an extra service, but at an additional charge, one can opt to have the books collected at one's home address.

16.3 Analysis of the First Phase

Because it is not possible to involve the employees of the Library directly, we have to apply the second best way of working, as discussed in Chap. 12. It is to study the case description and to find clues for the presence of original (thus O-organisation) transaction kinds and corresponding actor roles. We will do this below, paragraph after paragraph. The pieces of text that are taken from the case description are written in italics. We apply the OER method to the case description in a spiral way (cf. Chap. 12). All transaction kinds and involved actor roles are identified and discussed, and most corresponding parts of the aspect models are presented. The described operational processes determine the SoI and focus organisation. The actor roles that are filled by employees of the Library are internal, all other ones are external.

The Library described hereafter is a small public library. In the building in which it is located, are a desk for lending books, called the out-desk, and a desk for returning books, called the in-desk. At a third desk, called the information desk, one can get information such as the opening hours, the library regulations, and the membership fees. At the information desk is a desktop computer where members can browse through the library catalogue to find the books they want to borrow.

Although this piece of text does contain indications of essential transaction kinds, we consider it primarily as introductory text.

In order to become member of the library, one has to present oneself at the information desk and provide the next data to the staff member: surname, first name, middle initials, city of residence, street name, house number, postal code, date of birth, place of birth, and the starting day of the membership (which must be the first day of a month in the Gregorian calendar). The provided data are entered into the Library Information System (LIS). LIS automatically prints a membership card (with a bar code), and an invoice for the fee of the first year. The amount to pay is proportional to the remaining part of the year. From then on, membership fees are invoiced annually.

In the first sentence we find, in red, evidence of one of the services that the library offers: becoming member of the library. Let us identify this transaction kind as TK01 and give it the name "membership starting", in accordance with the discussion of how to model 'becoming member' in the case Volley (cf. Chap. 12). In the subsequent sentences, one learns how a request to do so (thus a TK01/rq) must be performed and what data one has to provide. Let us identify the corresponding product kind as PK01 and formulate it as "[membership] **is** started" in DEMOSL [1]. So, every PK01 is an instance of becoming member of the library by some person. We identify the executor role as AR01 and call it "membership starter". The initiator role in transactions TK01 is filled by the aspirant members. Because this role is clearly an environmental one (outside the chosen Scope of Interest), we consider it to be contained in the composite transactor role CTAR01.

Clearly, becoming member of the library belongs to the category of creating tangible things in the distinctions made in Chap. 10 (cf. Table 10.2). Consequently, we can take the CSD in Fig. 10.6 as the reference model, although the tree we come up with is quite small: there is only one transaction kind enclosed in TK01, which we will call TK02. The presence of this transaction kind can be deduced from the piece of text "*invoice for the fee of the first year*". Let us identify the corresponding product kind as PK02 and formulate it as "**the** fee **for** [membership] **in** [year] **is** paid". Adding "[year]" as the second entity variable, is a convenient way to deal with the time aspect in memberships. The alternative way is to formulate PK02 for example as "[fee payment] **is** done". But then, one needs to introduce a new entity type, with the inherent property types "membership of fee payment" and "year of fee payment". Although this formulation is also fully correct, it is recommended to adhere to the principle of minimality, which is often referred to as Ockham's Razor.[1]

---

[1]https://en.wikipedia.org/wiki/Occam%27s_razor

To accommodate the annual occurrence of transactions TK02, we deduce from the same piece of text (being in addition confirmed by the fourth paragraph, to be discussed later) the presence of a third transaction kind. Let us identify it as TK03, name it "fee payment controlling", and formulate the product kind PK03 as "fee payment controlling **for** [year] **is** done". The executing actor role, AR03, can properly be named "fee payment controller". As it holds for all repeating or periodic activities, actors AR03 are not only the executors TK03 but also their initiators (cf. Chap. 10).

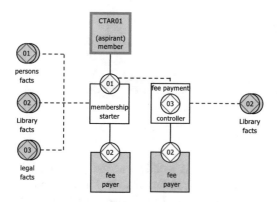

transaction kind	product kind	executor role
TK01 membership starting	PK01 [membership] **is** started	AR01 membership starter
TK02 fee paying	PK02 **the** fee **for** [membership] **in** [year] **is** paid	AR02 fee payer
TK03 fee payment controlling	PK03 fee payment controlling **for** [year] **is** done	AR03 fee payment controller

Fig. 16.1 CSD and TPT of the Library organisation (first part)

Based on the analysis so far, we produce the first part of the CSD and the first part of the TPT in Fig. 16.1. The access links can be deduced from the AM, of which one rule is discussed later. The external facts are contained in the multiple transaction kinds MTK01 through MTK03. In addition, we present the part of the FM that can be deduced from our findings up to now in the OFD in Fig. 16.2. It shows the presence of the core entity type membership (actually the entity class MEMBER-SHIP), as well as the external entity type person and the (by definition external) value type year. The property type 'the member of [membership] is [person]' determines who is the member of a membership. Note that every membership has exactly one associated person as the member but that, conversely, a person may be member in a number of memberships. Although this is not explicitly stated by the case description (and thus has to be validated), it makes perfect sense: by having several memberships simultaneously, one could have more books in loan simultaneously. We assume that the legal age (contained in MTK03) does not change more than once in a year, like the facts that are determined by the Library, and contained in MTK02 (like membership fee and minimal age). The annual fee payment is an aggregation type of MEMBERSHIP and YEAR (cf. Chap. 6).

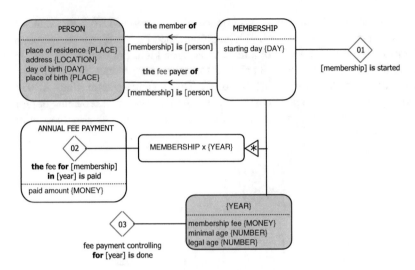

Fig. 16.2 OFD of the Library organisation (first part)

The P-event kind PK01 (which is identical to the product kind PK01 in the TPT) concerns the entity type membership, and the P-event kind PK03 concerns the value type year. The entity type that the P-event kind PK02 concerns is the aggregation of membership and year: every instance of PK02 regards one membership and 1 year.

The attribute types that are listed in Fig. 16.2 can directly be deduced from the part of the case description that we have analysed. Note that the entity type person doesn't have the attributes, surname, first name, and middle initials, for the simple but crucial reason that they are not attributes but names. They just and only serve to refer to particular persons, as discussed in Chap. 5. Names have no ontological relevance, but they may of course very well occur in databases.

Next, the fact type 'paid amount' is an attribute type of the entity type 'fee payment', which is a specialisation of the aggregate entity type 'membership × year'. This specialisation can conveniently be defined graphically, as is done in the OFD.

As an example of an action rule specification, we provide below the one for dealing with requests for memberships. It is assumed that a new instance of membership is created as soon as the first request for it is performed. From then on the membership is referred to by the entity variable [membership].

when membership starting **for** [membership] **is** <u>requested</u>   (TK01/rq)

    with   **the** member **of** [membership] **is some** person

           the payer **of** [membership] **is some** person

           the starting day **of** [membership] **is some** day

assess *rightness:*   **the** performer **of the** request **is the** member **of** [membership]
                    the addressee **of the** request **is a** membership starter
          sincerity: ∗ no specific condition ∗
          truth: **the** starting day **of** [membership] **is the** first day **of some** month;
                    the age **of the** member **of** [membership] **on the** starting day **of**
                        [membership] **is equal to or greater than the** minimal age
                    in the year **of the** starting day **of** [membership];
                    the age **of the** fee payer **of** [membership] **on the** starting day **of**
                        [membership] **is equal to or greater than the** legal age
                    in the year **of the** starting day **of** [membership];

if *performing the action after* **then** *is considered justifiable*
      then   promise membership starting **for** [membership]   [TK01/pm]
             to the performer **of the** request
      else   decline membership starting **for** [membership]   [TK01/dc]
             to the performer **of the** request

The first condition in the rightness division is not a trivial one (cf. Chap. 12). If it is omitted, anyone could perform the request. After execution of the action rule, a particular employee is allocated to the membership as its membership starter.

New members also get a letter of welcome, informing them about the library regulations that they are supposed to know. It is handed over to the new member after payment of the first membership fee, in cash or by bank transfer (in which case one has to provide a debit card). The minimal age for new members is 8 years. Moreover, if a new member is under 18, an adult must be entered as the payer of the fee, and one as the payer of possible fines.

The only ontologically interesting piece of text in this paragraph (marked in red) does not lead to an extension of the essential model because transaction kind TK02 (fee paying) has been identified already. The other parts of the text refer to informational (... *informing them about the library rules* ... and ... *an adult must be entered as the payer* ...) or documental (... *in cash or by bank transfer* ...) matters.

Memberships are automatically extended every calendar year, until they are explicitly ended by the member. The termination of a membership is always per the 1st of January. In addition, the librarian decides every month about ending memberships by the Library. Reasons for ending a membership in this way are e.g. repeatedly late returns of books and/or refusals to pay the fee or the incurred fines. If a membership is ended by the Library, the member may claim the refund of the fee that has been paid for the remaining part of the current year. Refunds are made in cash or by bank transfer.

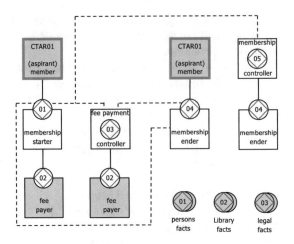

transaction kind	product kind	executor role
TK01 membership starting TK02 fee paying TK03 fee payment controlling TK04 membership ending TK05 membership controlling	PK01 [membership] is started PK02 the fee for [membership] in [year] is paid PK03 fee payment controlling for [year] is done PK04 [membership] is ended PK05 membership controlling for [month] is done	AR01 membership starter AR02 fee payer AR03 fee payment controller AR04 membership ender AR05 membership controller

Fig. 16.3 CSD and TPT of the Library organisation (plus second part)

The red marked text in the first line indicates the presence of a fourth transaction kind, which we will identify as TK04 and name "membership ending". Let us formulate the product kind PK04 as "[membership] is ended" and name the executing actor role (AR04) "membership ender". A possible initiator of transactions TK04 is the member of the membership, thus an actor role within the composite transactor role CTAR01. The other possible ender of memberships is the librarian. According to the second part of text in red, he/she makes such decisions once per month. Clearly, we need another self-activating actor role (like AR03) to model this properly. Let us identify this actor role as AR05, name it "membership controller", name the corresponding transaction kind (TK05) "membership controlling", and formulate the product kind (PK05) as "membership controlling for [month] is done". The analysis up to now leads to the extension of the CM as presented in Fig. 16.3. The access links to the external banks are omitted, in order to keep the diagram readable. In order to specify access rights completely, we will introduce the Bank Access Table later on.

Refunding the membership fee that has been paid for the remaining part of a membership year means ontologically that the payer, that is, the actor AR02, revokes her/his promise in the corresponding transaction TK02, followed by a new transaction TK02 for the remaining amount to be paid, in much the same way as the agreed-upon reduction of the price to pay for the repair in the case Fixit is handled (cf. Chap. 13) (presented in Fig. 16.4). Path 1 (coloured green) represents the successful payment of the fee for the current membership year, and path 2 (coloured tangerine) represents the revoke by the payer of her/his promise to pay. He/she does so in response to the declaration by the librarian that the membership has been ended, thus to the C-event (TK04/da). The revoke may be allowed by the librarian but it may as well be refused, for a valid reason, like a behind on payment.

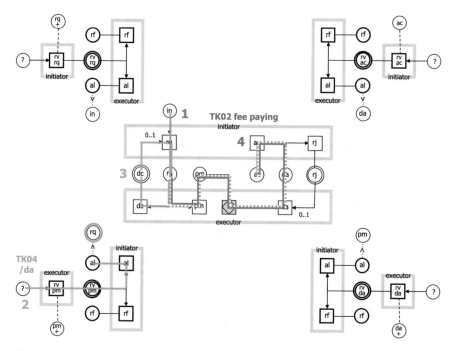

Fig. 16.4 Claiming the refund of the paid membership fee

If it is refused, the main process of the transaction TK02 remains in the state (ac). If it is allowed, this process will be rolled-back to the state (rq), from which the payer can decline the (original) request. In the discussion state (dc), the parties agree on the (reduced) amount that the payer has to pay, after which the librarian performs a renewed request for the agreed upon amount. This is represented by the tangerine-coloured path 3. Finally, the payer pays this amount, represented by path 4 (in blue).

Rolling back the transaction process up to the state (rq), indicated by the dashed green line, logically implies 'undoing' the production act. Undoing the performed fee payment would mean giving back the paid amount to the payer. The second pass of the same transaction process regards paying the reduced amount. The practical solution is to subtract the first amount from the second one and to ask for paying the difference. Because the result of the subtraction is negative, the librarian 'pays' the difference to the payer.

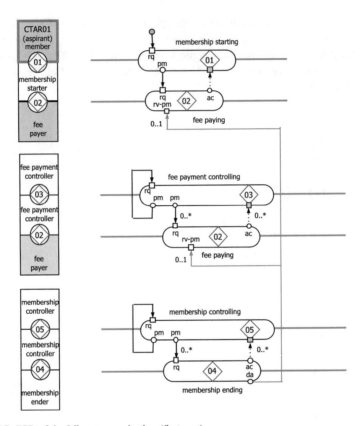

Fig. 16.5 PSD of the Library organisation (first part)

The PM of the case Library, based on the analysis up to now, is represented by the PSDs in Fig. 16.5. It shows how transactions TK02 are enclosed in transactions TK01 and TK03, and how memberships are ended by the librarian (bottom part). In blue, the response link is added that represents the [rv-pm] act by the fee payer in the (last carried out) TK02, in order to get a refund, after the membership has been ended by the librarian (as stated earlier, endings of memberships by members are always per the 1st of January). Although this revoke can be performed in any state of the main process, it is most likely performed from the state (T04/ac), that is, when the membership is ended. As shown, this link must also be drawn to the [rv-pm] act in the shape of TK02 in the upper part of Fig. 16.5, because it can already happen in the first year.

Because the ending of memberships by the members themselves doesn't have enclosed transactions, the (trivial) corresponding PSD is not presented.

Members are entitled to borrow books from the library. Books are put on shelves, sorted by category and title. Normally, there are several copies of the same title. Every book copy is uniquely identified by a bar code. It consists of the ISBN (International Standard Book Number) and a serial number of the book copy. If someone wants to borrow books, he/she has to take the books from the shelves to the out-desk. There, one of the staff members scans the bar codes on the membership card and on the books. These data are automatically entered into LIS, where a loan contract for every borrowed book is created. After this process is finished, the member can take the books along.

This part of the case description regards the borrowing of books, which is a specialisation of the general category of obtaining the usufruct of tangible things,[2] according to the division in Chap. 10 (cf. Table 10.2). Therefore, we start from the general reference model in Fig. 10.19 and its tailored variant in Fig. 10.21.

From the red-coloured parts in this piece of text we deduce indeed the presence of two transaction kinds in the reference model. The first one is about concluding a loan contract. Let us identify it as TK06 and name it "loan completing". Next, let us name the executor role (AR06) "loan completer" and formulate the product kind (PK06) as "[loan] **is** completed". Transactions TK06 enclose a transaction regarding the taking along of borrowed books, as expressed by the third piece of text in red. Let us identify it as TK07 and name it "book taking". Next, let us name the executor role (AR07) "book taker" and formulate the product kind (PK07) as "**the** book **of** [loan] **is** taken".

Note that a loan concerns one book (copy), as also expressed in the second piece of text above in red. As a general rule, and again as an application of Ockham's Razor, it is recommended to have one book per loan, one car per rental, one order entry per order, etc. One may open, however, several loans, rentals, order entries, etc., simultaneously. The advantage is that one or more of the concurrent loans may be completed (after having returned the related book) while the others still go on. So, if a member borrows a number of books at the same time, an equal number of loans are created.

Note also that a formulation of PK07 such as "[book] **is** taken", which one may be inclined to choose as a first attempt, is incorrect. It would imply that every book (copy) can only be taken once in its lifetime. This is obviously not what one wants. The unsuitability of the formulation can easily be discovered by applying the sapience 'verification by instantiation', which we applied before in verifying other fact type formulations (cf. Chap. 12).

Based on the analysis above, we arrive at the extension of the CM of the Library, as expressed in the CSD and the TPT in Fig. 16.6. It contains also the two transaction kinds (and involved actor roles) that can be deduced from the part of the case description above.

There is a maximum number of books that one can have in loan simultaneously, and there is also a maximum loan period. Borrowed books must be returned within this period. When a member returns one or more books, he/she goes to the in-desk and hands the books to a staff member, who then scans the book codes and the membership number, which are automatically entered into LIS. On the screen of the

---

[2]One might disagree with the tangibility of books since it is commonly not the physical representation of the contents that one is interested in, but the contents itself. That is why a digital (electronic) representation (eBook or PDF) is often a good alternative. Nevertheless, we stick to the case description, which is clearly about physical books. An additional argument to do this is that the borrower of a book may have other affordances in mind than reading (cf. Chap. 7).

computer, the staff member sees whether the loan period of a book is exceeded. If it is, the fine to be paid is shown also. Fines have to be paid by the member right away (in cash or by bank transfer).

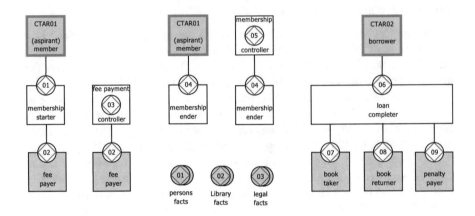

transaction kind	product kind	executor role
TK01 membership starting	PK01 [membership] is started	AR01 membership starter
TK02 fee paying	PK02 the fee for [membership] in [year] is paid	AR02 fee payer
TK03 fee payment controlling	PK03 fee payment controlling for [year] is done	AR03 fee payment controller
TK04 membership ending	PK04 [membership] is ended	AR04 membership ender
TK05 membership controlling	PK05 membership controlling for [month] is done	AR05 membership controller
TK06 loan completing	PK06 [loan] is completed	AR06 loan completer
TK07 book taking	PK07 the book of [loan] is taken	AR07 book taker
TK08 book returning	PK08 the book of [loan] is returned	AR08 book returner
TK09 penalty paying	PK09 the penalty of [loan] is paid	AR09 penalty payer

Fig. 16.6 Final CSD and TPT of the Library organisation

The first and the second red-coloured piece of text in this paragraph indicate the existence of another transaction kind. Let us identify it as TK08 and name it "book returning". Next, let us give the name "book returner" to the executor role (AR08) and formulate the product kind (PK08) as "**the** book **of** [loan] **is** returned". The third piece of text in red gives rise to identifying transaction kind TK09, which we name "penalty paying", with product kind PK09, formulated as "**the** penalty **of** [loan] **is** paid". The executing actor role is AR09, named "penalty payer". Figure 16.6 exhibits the consequent extension of the (final) CSD and TPT, following the reference model in Fig. 10.21.

The figure also contains the (external) multiple transaction kinds MTK01 through MTK03. They are the conceptual stores of facts that are created outside the chosen SoI but needed by the internal actors. MTK01 contains facts about persons, like place of residence and day of birth, and MTK02 contains facts that are created by actors within the Library as a whole, but outside the chosen SoI. Examples are the minimal age of members and the maximum loan period. Their values are typically decided upon (annually) by the librarian. MTK03 contains the current legal age.

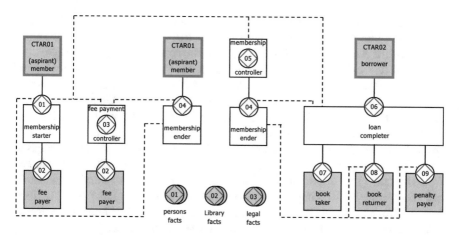

Fig. 16.7 Final CSD plus interstriction structure

Table 16.1 BAT of the Library organisation

Bank Actor	TK01	TK02	TK03	TK04	TK05	TK06	TK07	TK08	TK09	MTK01	MTK02	MTK03
AR01	Ex	In								U	U	U
AR02		Ex									U	
AR03	U	In	In, Ex	U						U	U	
AR04	U			Ex			U	U		U	U	
AR05	U			In	In, Ex					U	U	
AR06	U			U		Ex	In	In	In	U	U	U
AR07							Ex			U		
AR08								Ex		U		
AR09									Ex	U		
CTAR01	In			In						U		
CTAR02						In				U		

Figure 16.6 only shows the interaction structure, thus the set of initiator links between the transactor roles. There are five trees, thus five business processes: TK01 with enclosed TK02, TK03 with enclosed TK02, TK04, TK04 with enclosed TK05, and TK06 with enclosed TK07, TK08, and TK09. There appear to be no impediments between these processes, so there are no process dependencies. There are, however, quite some state dependencies, represented by the interstriction structure, which is exhibited in Fig. 16.7. What is still missing in the figure is the access links from the various actor roles to the external multiple transaction kinds MTK01, MTK02, and MTK03. Adding these access links would make the CSD a mess of dashed lines, however. Fortunately, there is an alternative way to indicate access links. It is the Bank Access Table (BAT), as explained in [1]. Table 16.1 exhibits the BAT for the Library. Next to showing which actor role has reading access to which transaction bank, indicated by a "U" (for Use) at the crossing of the corresponding row and column,

"Ex" indicates the executor actor role and "In" an initiator role of a transaction kind. Full insight into which actor roles use (the instances of) which fact types is gained when also the Bank Contents Table (BCT) and the complete FM are available.

Figure 16.8 exhibits the PSD of the loan completion process (the right part of Fig. 16.6). The main structure of this PSD is what one may expect: the transaction kind TK06 (loan completing) has three enclosed transaction kinds: TK07 (book taking), TK08 (book returning), and the optional TK09 (penalty paying). As discussed in Chap. 10, transactions TK07 and TK08 are initiated from the state requested in the enclosing transaction TK06. The transaction TK06 can be promised when the enclosed TK07 and TK08 are promised. Transactions TK09 are initiated from the state (TK01/pm), which is the usual case. Next, book returning cannot be executed before book taking is finished, represented by the wait link from (TK07/ac) to [TK08/ex] and penalty paying cannot be initiated before book returning is finished, represented by the wait link from (TK08/ac) to [TK09/rq].

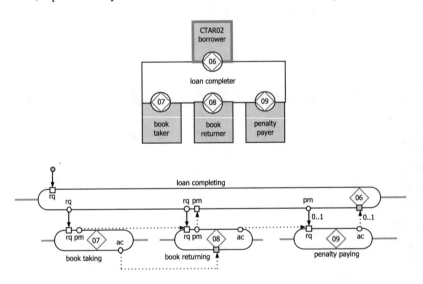

Fig. 16.8 PSD of the Library organisation (second part)

As said, the final and complete OFD is presented in Fig. 16.9. The left part was already discussed earlier (cf. Fig. 16.2), except for the event type PK04 ([membership] **is** ended) and the value class MONTH with the event type PK05 (membership controlling **for** [month] **is** done). The two additions are considered to be self-explaining.

For the right part of Fig. 16.9 we provide the next explanation. The core entity type is 'loan'. The connection with the core entity type in the left part is constituted by the property type '**the** membership **of** [loan] **is** [membership]', of which the domain is the object class LOAN and the range the entity class MEMBERSHIP. There are four event types that concern loans: PK06 ([loan] **is** completed), PK07 (**the** book **of** [loan] **is** taken), PK08 (**the** book **of** [loan] **is** returned), and PK09 (**the** penalty **of** [loan] **is** paid). Note that the latter is optional, as follows from the PSD in Fig. 16.8. Based on these event types, three specialisations of the entity type 'loan' are defined graphically: 'taken loan', 'returned loan', and 'penalty paid loan'. They serve to define precisely two property types and one attribute type.

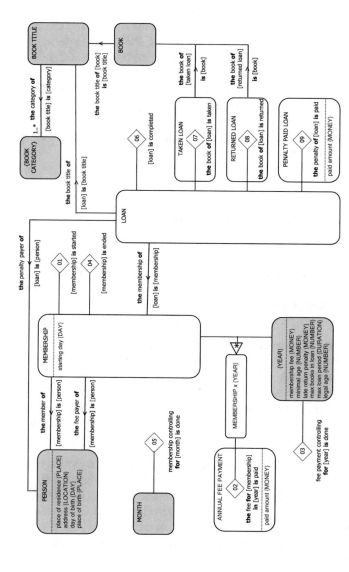

Fig. 16.9 Complete OFD of the Library organisation

The attribute type is 'paid amount', whose range is the value class MONEY. The class may be refined to, for example, EURO (cf. Chap. 6), if needed. The two property types are '**the** book **of** [taken loan] **is** [book]' and '**the** book **of** [returned loan] **is** [book]'. The range of both is the external entity class BOOK. Note that, consequently, the returned book of a loan may be different from the taken book. This can be determined when the book of a loan is returned. Most likely, one of the (declarative) business rules of the Library is that the two books must be the same.

Next, there is an external entity class BOOK TITLE and a value class BOOK CATEGORY. Every book (copy) is a book of some book title. Because one starts a borrowing process by looking for a book of a specific book title, every loan has a particular book title as one of its properties. Which book copy one takes home is actually irrelevant. Finally, to every book title, one or more book categories are assigned, such as novel, thriller, etc., and youth, adult, etc., as an aid in finding the book titles one may want to read. Usually, the book categories are created by the Publisher, but the Library may refine them and add categories.

16.4   Analysis of the Second Phase

Like it holds for the third phase of the case Pizzeria (cf. Chap. 14), the changes in the second phase of the Library compared to the first phase seem to be substantially. Yet, the implications for the essential model that we have produced for the first phase are not dramatic. Let us investigate them by analysing the description of the second phase, again paragraph by paragraph.

After about ten flourishing years, the librarian decides to improve the services of the library substantially by two major changes. The first is that one doesn't need to visit the library in order to become member. It can now be done from home via a web extension of LIS. It implies, however, that payments can only be made by periodic direct debits. Instead of a membership card, members can identify themselves in LIS by means of a membership number and a password. Every member has a personal section in LIS, called MyLIS.

Using a web application to become member, instead of presenting oneself at the desk in the library, is only a change in the way that the steps in transactions TK01 are performed. So, it is only about the lower two levels in Fig. 8.5, thus about implementation. Automating transaction steps doesn't affect the responsibilities of the involved actors (cf. Chap. 11). Therefore, as an example, the popping up of a message on the screen, saying that you have successfully become member of the library, is the declare act in a TK01. The only difference with the way of doing this in the first phase is that the aspirant member and the addressed desk officer communicate via the web application. Note that the decision that you are member is not made by the web application but the desk officer! The fact that you commonly don't know her/him doesn't matter.

A similar reasoning holds for the new way of paying (*by periodic direct debits*), and for using a password instead of a card for identifying oneself.

The creation of a personal section MyLis for members is primarily also a change at the documental (or datalogical) level of communication. It may, however, in addition be a change at the informational (or infological) level, namely if members get access to information they didn't have access to before.

The second major change regards the way in which books are issued and returned. There are no more shelves with books in the library building. Instead there is a central repository in the cellar, where book copies are automatically stored and retrieved by a warehouse system.

In the first phase, one had to take the books to borrow from the shelves. Note that we didn't include this action in the essential model. If one wants, it would mean building a sub-tree under transactor AR07 (book taker), in much the same way as the logistic operations in the case GloLog can be extended (cf. Chaps. 10 and 18). The same holds for modelling the way of working in the second phase (*book copies are automatically stored and retrieved*). The colour purple (as the mix of red and blue) is used to clarify that we are at the edge of 'material production in the O-organisation' and 'material production in the D-organisation' of the disk in Fig. 11.11. If only hard copies are considered, we are in the O-organisation, but if electronic copies, like eBooks or PDFs, are at stake, we are in the D-organisation (cf. Chap. 11).

Either from home, or from desk top computers in the library, one can browse through the catalogue and select the books one wants to borrow. Like it was in the first phase, a loan is created for every book copy. After finishing such a borrow session, the borrowed books are automatically retrieved from the central repository and put in a locker. The member has access to this locker by keying the membership number and the password at the locker wall during five workdays. If the books are not taken out within this period, they are put back in the repository. In addition, one can opt for home delivery, but at an extra charge.

The first piece of text in red is about the logistic operations that we have already discussed above. Because we only deal with hard copies, red is used instead of purple. Accommodating the second piece of text in red would mean extending the essential model with at least a delivery and a payment transactor kind.

Returning books is made as easy as picking up. In the hall of the library building is a conveyer belt on which one can put the returned books, one after the other. The handling of the books, as well as the processing of the corresponding loan, are done automatically. If a fine is incurred, the amount is automatically charged to one's bank account (also through direct debit).

The first and second sentences regard the logistics that we have already discussed above. Like it holds for becoming member via the web application, the blue-coloured pieces of text regard only changes in the lower two levels in Fig. 8.5.

As an extra service, but at an additional charge, one can opt to have the books collected at one's home address.

This implies an extension of the essential model. There is an additional transactor kind needed for transporting the books, and one for paying for this new service.

16.5   Discussion and Conclusions

There are two clusters of business processes in the case Library, one about starting and ending memberships, and one about borrowing books. The product category of the first is creating and changing (cf. Table 10.2) and the product category of the second is obtaining usufruct. So, the reference model of libraries is a combination of the one for clubs or associations in general, like the case Volley (cf. Chap. 12) and the one for renting resources, like the case Rent-A-Car (cf. Chap. 15).

Applying Ockham's Razor leads to conceiving only two core entity types: membership and loan, as well as tailored subtypes, as shown in the OFD in Fig. 16.9. It is the perfect starting point for designing a database as part of the Library Information Systems (LIS), both in the first and in the second phase.

There are two issues that deserve special attention. One is the refund of membership fees in case of the ending of a membership by the librarian. As elucidated in Sect. 16.3, and more specifically in Fig. 16.4, refunding can elegantly be accommodated if one conceives it (quite properly) as revoking the initial promise to pay the last annual fee by the member. This illustrates once more the power of ontological thinking in addressing practical problems.

The other subject is the particular way in which the transactions TK07 (book taking), TK08 (book returning) are enclosed in a transaction TK06, as shown in Fig. 16.8. It is a specialisation of the general case of seizing and releasing a (scarce) resource, as discussed in Chap. 10. Requiring that both the seizing and the releasing of a resource (in the case Library a book) are promised before the usufruct case (in the case Library a loan) can be promised, emphasises that actions like checking-in and checking-out are not non-committal. In this way, no-shows are discouraged effectively. Both the step TK07/pm and the step TK08/pm are 'heavy' commitments. If necessary, they also offer sufficient ground for legal follow-ups.

Reference

1. Dietz, J. L. G. (2019). *DEMO-4 specification language*. Enterprise Engineering Institute.

Chapter 17
Exercise: Case PoliGyn

Abstract The case PoliGyn is an exercise in producing the essential model of an enterprise that offers creation of (tangible and intangible) things: producing diagnoses, and performing clinical and sonographic examinations. The CM, PM, and FM are (partially) presented and discussed. Three, basically general, topics are elaborated, because they have a typical role in PoliGyn. The first topic has to do with the identification and formulation of product kinds. The second one is the order in which enclosed transactions are carried out, and the third one is the delegation of tasks.

17.1   Introduction

The case PoliGyn is an exercise in producing the essential model of an enterprise that offers, in terms of the categories that are distinguished in Chap. 10, the creation of (tangible and intangible) things.

Section 17.2 contains the narrative description of the operational activities in a Policlinic Gynaecology. It is the basis for applying the OER method and producing the essential model (cf. Chap. 12). The analysis of the narrative description is discussed in Sect. 17.3, along with presenting parts of the CM and PM in diagrams and tables. In Sect. 17.4, an exemplifying case is presented and analysed, which leads to developing, partially, the FM of the policlinic. Section 17.5 contains the discussion and conclusions of the exercise.

17.2   Narrative Description

The examination and treatment of patients in the Policlinic (or Outpatient Clinic) Gynaecology, PoliGyn for short, always takes place through referral by a family doctor. Therefore, the description of the processes in PoliGyn starts at the moment that a patient visits her family Doctor. PoliGyn is a department of a hospital. One of the other departments of the Hospital is the Sonographic Lab.

© Springer Nature Switzerland AG 2020

J. L. G. Dietz, J. B. F. Mulder, *Enterprise Ontology*, The Enterprise Engineering Series, https://doi.org/10.1007/978-3-030-38854-6_17

Usually, the family doctor makes an appointment for her/his patient to visit a gynaecologist by calling a desk assistant of PoliGyn. However, the patient can also take the referral letter back home and make an appointment herself. The desk assistant has access to an ICT-system, in which appointments are scheduled. If the patient is pregnant, the desk assistant also makes an appointment with the Sonographic Lab for a sonogram, preceding the appointment with the gynaecologist.

At the settled date and time, the patient checks in at the desk of PoliGyn. There she receives her patient record. The record consists of a folder containing several filled out forms and other kinds of reports. The referral letter from the family doctor is also inserted. If a sonogram is needed, the patient goes first to the Sonographic Lab, with her patient record. The produced sonogram is filed in the patient's folder by the sonographer.

Thereafter, the patient goes to the waiting room of PoliGyn and puts her patient record in a tray that is meant for it. The tray is emptied regularly by an assistant who delivers the correct patient records to the present gynaecologists. Every gynaecologist has access to the automated appointment system and calls the patients into her/his office in the order of appointment.

During the visit, the gynaecologist first diagnoses the patient's problem. He or she does so based on the information provided by the family doctor (in the referral letter), the results of the sonographic examination (if applicable), and one or more clinical examinations, including the anamnesis, that are performed on site.

After the patient's problem is diagnosed, the gynaecologist discusses the possible treatments with the patient, that is, the medical actions that can be taken in order to solve the patient problem. The determination of the treatment, as well as its execution, however, falls outside the scope of the Case PoliGyn.

17.3   Analysis of the Narrative Description

Because it is not possible to question the employees of PoliGyn, we have to apply the second best way of working, as discussed in Chap. 12. It is to study the narrative description and find clues for the presence of original (thus O-organisation) transaction kinds and involved actor roles. We will do this below, paragraph after paragraph. The pieces of text that are taken from the case description are written in italics.

The examination and treatment of patients in the Policlinic (or Outpatient Clinic) Gynaecology, PoliGyn for short, always takes place through referral by a family doctor. Therefore, the description of the processes in PoliGyn starts at the moment that a patient visits her family doctor. PoliGyn is a department of a hospital. One of the other departments of the hospital is the Sonographic Lab.

Although this piece of text does contain indications of essential transaction kinds, we consider it primarily as introductory. PoliGyn will be our focus organisation, with the Sonographic Lab in its environment.

Usually, the family doctor makes an appointment for her/his patient to visit a gynaecologist by calling a desk assistant of PoliGyn. However, the patient can also

*take the referral letter back home and make an appointment herself. The desk
assistant has access to an ICT-system, in which appointments are scheduled. If the
patient is pregnant, the desk assistant also* makes an appointment with the Sonographic Lab for a sonogram, *preceding the appointment with the gynaecologist.*

The first piece of text in red (*makes an appointment for her/his patient to visit a
gynaecologist*) raises an interesting and crucial issue: what does making an appointment mean? Is it the product of a transaction or not? And consequently, are appointments entities or not? In current practice, many information analysts or architects
would be inclined to answer the last two questions in the positive. However, pure
ontological thinking leads us to a different conclusion, namely that making an
appointment is something in the order phase of a transaction. More precisely, it is
the request in a transaction concerning a product that the initiator wants the executor to
bring about, followed by the promise to do it. The notion of appointment refers
specifically to a future point in time at which the product must be brought about.

But what then is the product the red-coloured sentence is about? This is disclosed
in the fifth paragraph of the description: the patient problem being diagnosed. It was
hinted at already in the first paragraph. Thus, we have found the first transaction
kind. Let us identify it as TK01 and name it 'patient problem diagnosing' and let us
consequently name the executor role (AR01) 'patient problem diagnoser'. The
initiator role is taken by some actor role, which we name 'patient', within the
environmental composite transactor role CTAR01.

Considering the patient to be the initiator of a transaction TK01 is a second
important point. Even if the appointment seems to be made by the family doctor
(after all, he/she calls the policlinic), the doctor has nothing more than a delegated
authority. We will come back to it later. As for the product kind (PK01), let us
formulate it simply as '[patient problem] **is** diagnosed'. So, 'patient problem' is a
core entity type in the production world of PoliGyn. Its instances are the distinct
cases of medical care in the policlinic. Every patient problem regards one patient, but
there may be several patient problems associated with the same patient.

It is easier now to understand the ontological meaning of the second piece of text
in red (*makes an appointment with the Sonographic Lab for a sonogram*). This is also
a request, but in another transaction kind, which is about making sonograms. Let us
identify it as TK02 and name it 'sonographic examining' and let us consequently
name the executor role (AR02) 'sonographic examiner'. The product kind (PK02)
can be conveniently formulated as '[sonographic examination] **is** completed'. Normally, there is one sonographic examination per patient problem (or none, because it
is only needed if the patient is pregnant). The concrete outcome is one or more
sonograms.

The third interesting and non-trivial issue concerns the initiator role of transactions TK02. One may be inclined to consider the desk assistant to fill this role.
However, on second thought this cannot be the case. As we will see, the desk
assistant has only delegated authority. The only feasible option is that the
gynaecologists have instructed the desk assistant to always also make an appointment for a sonogram when the patient is pregnant. So the initiators of transactions
TK02 are actors AR01, and every product PK02 is somehow a part of a product
PK01. Figure 17.1 shows the CSD and the TPT of the organisation of PoliGyn.

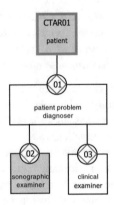

transaction kind	product kind	executor role
TK01 patient problem diagnosing TK02 sonographic examining TK03 clinical examining	PK01 [patient problem] **is** diagnosed PK02 [sonographic examination] **is** completed PK03 [clinical examination] **is** performed	AR01 patient problem diagnoser AR02 sonographic examiner AR03 clinical examiner

Fig. 17.1 CSD and TPT of the PoliGyn organisation

At the settled date and time, the patient checks in at the desk of PoliGyn. There she receives her patient record. The record consists of a folder containing several filled out forms and other kinds of reports. The referral letter from the family doctor is also inserted. If a sonogram is needed, the patient goes first to the Sonographic Lab, with her patient record. The produced sonogram is filed in the patient's folder by the sonographer.

This paragraph offers no new information regarding the essential model. One only reads things about its realisation and implementation. We will elaborate on them later.

Thereafter, the patient goes to the waiting room of PoliGyn and puts her patient record in a tray that is meant for it. The tray is emptied regularly by an assistant who delivers the correct patient records to the present gynaecologists. Every gynaecologist has access to the automated appointment system and calls the patients into her/his office in the order of appointment.

This paragraph is also only about realisation and implementation.

During the visit, the gynaecologist first diagnoses the patient's problem. He or she does so based on the information provided by the family doctor (in the referral letter), the results of the sonographic examination (if applicable), and one or more clinical examinations, including the anamnesis, that are performed on site.

From the red-coloured piece of text, we deduce the presence of a transaction kind TK03, which we name 'clinical examining'. The executing actor role (AR03) is named 'clinical examiner' and the product kind (PK03) is formulated as '[clinical examination] is performed'. The CSD and TPT in Fig. 17.1 already contain this transaction kind. The initiator is clearly AR01. Thus, transactions TK03 are enclosed in a transaction TK01. Note that the role AR03 is filled by the gynaecologist.

The CSD in Figs. 17.1 and 17.2 only shows the interaction structure in the CM. The interstriction structure is omitted for the sake of convenience. There is obviously no (inter-process) impediment structure, since there is only one business process.

After the patient's problem is diagnosed, the gynaecologist discusses the possible treatments with the patient, that is, the medical actions that can be taken in order to solve the patient problem. The determination of the treatment, as well as its execution, however, falls outside the scope of the Case PoliGyn.

This piece of text doesn't lead to changes in the CM because the treatment of the patient problem falls outside the chosen SoI.

Hereafter, we will elaborate only on issues that are mainly about realisation and implementation. One of these issues is the order in which the enclosed transactions TK02 and TK03 are carried out. According to the narrative description, the TK02 (completing the sonographic examination) must be carried out (if at all) before any of the transactions TK03 (clinical examinations) are carried out. However, for actors AR01 (patient problem diagnoser), the order is irrelevant. He/she waits until all results are available and then decides on the diagnosis. Therefore, the described order (first TK02) must be understood as dictated by the existence of a separate Sonographic Lab. If the gynaecologist would dispose of her/his own sonographic instrument (which is quite common nowadays), it is unlikely that some order would be imposed.

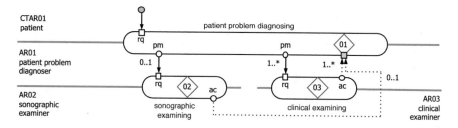

Fig. 17.2 PSD of the PoliGyn organisation

The ontological unimportance of the order of transactions TK02 and TK03 is clearly represented in the PSD of the PoliGyn organisation in Fig. 17.2. Transactions of both kinds can be carried out in parallel. As follows from the narrative description, the cardinality range of transactions TK02 is 0...1 (in other words, TK02 is optional) and the cardinality range of transactions TK03 is 1...* (thus there may be an arbitrary number of transactions TK03, but at least one).

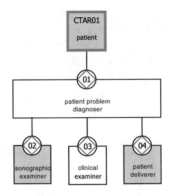

transaction kind	product kind	executor role
TK01 patient problem diagnosing TK02 sonographic examining TK03 clinical examining TK04 patient delivering	PK01 [patient problem] is diagnosed PK02 [sonographic examination] is completed PK03 [clinical examination] is performed PK04 **the** patient **of** [patient problem] **is** delivered	AR01 patient problem diagnoser AR02 sonographic examiner AR03 clinical examiner AR04 patient deliverer

Fig. 17.3 Extended CSD and TPT of the PoliGyn organisation

The other issue we had in mind when making the statement above about realisation and implementation is that the patient must apparently be present herself at the location of the policlinic for carrying out transactions TK02 and TK03. More accurately, her body must be available for examination. The essential model (cf. Figs. 17.1 and 17.2) abstracts from such physical issues. Ontologically speaking, actors can be at any location when entering into and complying with commitments, in transactions of all kinds. The only prerequisite is that it is possible for them to communicate. As a matter of fact, nowadays quite some diagnostic and therapeutic actions are taken with the patient at distance.

In order to be explicit about the requirement that the body of the patient is present on site, another transaction kind must be added, whose product is the delivery of the patient's body (excuse the weird phrasing) to the location of the policlinic and the Sonographic Lab. Adding the transactor kind to the CSD and TPT leads to the extensions as exhibited in Fig. 17.3.

In Chap. 12, the Authorisation Delegation Table (ADT) was introduced for the purpose of showing precisely the delegation of authority between the functionaries in an organisation. In Table 17.1, the ADT of PoliGyn is presented.

Table 17.1 ADT of the case PoliGyn

T/P	TK01/rq	TK01/pm	TK02/rq	TK02/pm
Patient	A			
Family doctor	D			
Desk assistant		D	D	D
Gynaecologist		A	A	
Sonographer				A

There are four tasks where delegation takes place. The first one is performing the request in transactions TK01. Contrary to about 50 years (and longer) ago, there is a common understanding nowadays that the patient is a 'client of age' in health care. Consequently, she is the authorised initiator of transactions TK01. So, if she lets the family doctor make an appointment with the policlinic, she apparently delegates her authority to perform this task. It is marked in the table by an "A" in the row Patient and a "D" in the row Family Doctor, both in the column TK01/rq.

The second delegated task is the promise in transactions TK01. According to the narrative description, this promise is performed by the desk assistant. But when one puts the DEMO glasses on firmly, it becomes clear that it cannot be the case that the desk assistant has the (primarily assigned) authority to perform the promise, because the patient doesn't seek to have her medical problem diagnosed by a desk assistant but by a gynaecologist. The desk assistant is only an intermediary, a convenient way for the policlinic (and for hospitals in general) to organise the making of appointments. Ontologically speaking, it is the gynaecologist who performs acts [TK01/pm], but he/she has delegated this authority to the desk assistant, whom he/she also has given her/his availability for visits. This is marked in the table by an "A" in the row Gynaecologist and a "D" in the row Desk Assistant, both in the column TK01/pm.

The third delegated task is performing the request in transactions TK02, so in making appointments with the Sonographic Lab. One may easily be set on the wrong track by the narrative description. For similar reasons as those provided above, the desk assistant cannot have the primary authority to perform acts [TK02/rq]. Next, despite what we said about the patient being a 'client of age', she also cannot be the authorised performer, although she accepts that making a sonogram is needed (if she is pregnant). Clearly, it is the authority of the gynaecologist to perform acts [TK02/rq], but he/she has delegated this authority to the desk assistant, presumably as one of the instructions that belong to the delegation of the authority to perform the [TK01/pm]. The situation is marked in the table by an "A" in the row Gynaecologist and a "D" in the row Desk Assistant, both in the column TK02/rq.

The fourth delegated task is the promise in transactions TK02. Like it holds for the promise in transactions TK01, it is performed by the desk assistant, however, by virtue of a delegation of authority. In this case, the delegation comes from the sonographer. For similar reasons of convenience, as discussed earlier, he/she has instructed the desk assistant on how to make appointments, which implies that he/she has delegated the authority to perform acts [TK02/pm] to the desk assistant. It is marked in the table by an "A" in the row Sonographer and a "D" in the row Desk Assistant, both in the column TK02/pm.

17.4 Analysis of a Patient Case

In order to validate and deeply understand an essential model, it is often helpful to consider a representative instance of the business process, as presented in Figs. 17.1 and 17.2. We will do so in this section based on thought-up conversations. They start in the consulting room of a family doctor, who calls the Policlinic Gynaecology. During the call, a new instance of patient problem is created. Let us call it 'patient problem 7789'. After every conversation, its normal form (cf. Chap. 12) is presented.

Family Doctor: "I want to make an appointment with doctor Ross for Mrs. Lam. She is pregnant"
Desk Assistant: "I will have a look at the schedule"

CTAR01/Family Doctor: request: AR01/desk assistant: patient problem 7789 is diagnosed; the requested production time is asap

The answer by the desk assistant counts as having reached social correspondence (cf. Fig. 8.5), by which the request is successfully performed. Both the family doctor and the desk assistant have delegated authority to do what they do, as discussed in the previous section.

patient problem diagnosing for patient problem 7789 is requested   (TK01/rq)

Because the patient (Mrs. Lam) is pregnant, the desk assistant also makes an appointment with the Sonographic Lab, following the instructions of the gynaecologist. So there is also a request for a transaction TK02; however, performed implicitly. It implies that a new instance of graphical examination is created. Let us call it 'graphical examination 1913'.

AR01/Desk Assistant: request: AR02/Desk Assistant: sonographic examination 1913 is completed; the requested production time is just before the requested production time of the associated transaction TK01

completing sonographic examination 1913 is requested   (TK02/rq)

Desk Assistant: "On August 4 at 10 o'clock the patient can visit Sonography and at 11 o'clock doctor Ross. Is that okay?"
Family Doctor: "Yes that's fine"

There are two transaction steps performed in this conversation, one in the transaction TK01 and one in the transaction TK02. Their normal forms are presented hereafter. The answer by the family doctor counts as having reached social correspondence (cf. Fig. 8.5), by which the request is successfully performed. Both the family doctor and the desk assistant have delegated authority to do what they do, as discussed in the previous section.

AR01/Desk Assistant: promise: CTAR01/Family Doctor: patient problem 7789 is diagnosed; the promised production time is August 4 at 11 o'clock

patient problem diagnosing for patient problem 7789 is promised   (TK01/pm)

AR02/Desk Assistant: promise: AR01/Desk Assistant: sonographic examination 1913 is completed; the promised production time is August 4 at 10 o'clock *completing sonographic examination 1913 is promised*   (TK02/pm)

The following conversations takes place in the hospital where the patient addresses an assistant at the desk of the policlinic, on August 4, well before 10 o'clock.

Assistant: "Here is your patient record. Take it with you to the Sonographic Lab. Thereafter put it in the tray over there and take a seat in the waiting room"
Patient: "Ok, thanks. I am glad I could come so soon because I am a little worried"

During this conversation, no essential process steps are performed. With reference to the CSD in Fig. 17.2, one may interpret the patient's turning up as the declaration in the transaction TK04.
The following conversation takes place after the sonogram has been made.

Sonographer: "Mrs. Lam, here is your folder, including the results of the sonographic examination"
Patient: "Thanks"

AR02/Sonographer: declare: AR01/gynaecologist: sonographic examination 1913 is completed; the declared production time is August 4 at 10:15 h.

completing sonographic examination 1913 is declared   (TK02/da)

Although he/she is speaking to her, the sonographer is not addressing the patient in this transaction step but the gynaecologist, because he/she is the authorised initiator. The patient is nothing more than a courier who brings the document containing the message (TK02/da) to the gynaecologist. Therefore, the answer "Thanks" can only be interpreted, if one likes to, as expressing the willingness by the patient to transport the folder. Note that the acceptance of the TK02 by the gynaecologist is performed tacitly.
The following conversation takes place in the consulting room of the gynaecologist after all needed clinical examinations are finished.

Patient: "I think I feel much better than during the previous pregnancy"
Gynaecologist: "The baby is okay but you suffer from irregular blood loss. It is not a serious problem, however. I suggest that you come back in a month"

AR01/gynaecologist: declare: CTAR01/patient: patient problem 7789 is diagnosed; the declared production time is August 4 at 11:15 h.

patient problem diagnosing for patient problem 7789 is declared   (TK01/da)

The utterance by the patient has no relevant meaning for the business process. It must be considered as a personal or social expression of her feelings. The utterance by the gynaecologist is first of all the declare act in the transaction TK01: he/she has made a definite decision on the diagnosis of the patient problem. In addition, he/she suggests the patient to come back for another consult. It is up to the patient whether to follow up the advice or not. The acceptance in the transaction TK01 by the patient is performed tacitly, which is quite usual since she doesn't have the medical knowledge to argue about it.

For the correct understanding of the business process in PoliGyn it may be helpful to provide and analyse the FM, in addition to the presented CM and PM. To this end, the OFD of PoliGyn is shown in Fig. 17.4.

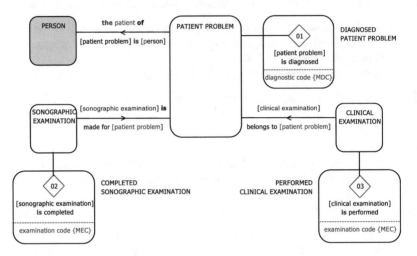

Fig. 17.4 OFD of the PoliGyn organisation

There are three core entity types: 'patient problem', 'sonographic examination', and 'clinical examination'. Instances of these types are created by the PoliGyn organisation (in the broad sense, thus including the Sonographic Lab). There is one external entity type ('person'), and there are two external value types: 'medical diagnostic code' and 'medical examination code', both of the sort categorial (cf. Chap. 21). Note that we adopt the habit in medicine to speak of codes, whereas these codes are actually the names of categories or kinds (cf. Chap. 5). Moreover, in the OFD two abbreviations are used for the sake of convenience: MDC for 'medical diagnostic code', and MEC for 'medical examination code'.

Each of the core entity types has its own (production) event kind: PK01 ([patient] problem **is** diagnosed), PK02 ([sonographic examination] **is** completed), and PK03 ([clinical examination] **is** performed). They represent the coming into existence of unique instances of the respective types. So, once more, a patient problem is specific for the patient and the diagnosis made. During the same patient's visit, one or more other (also unique) patient problems may be identified and diagnosed. Similarly, the instances of the entity type 'sonographic examination' are unique. They are made for a specific patient problem. Next, the instances of the entity type 'clinical examination' are also unique, and related to a specific patient problem. Conversely, however, several clinical examinations may be performed in support of the diagnosis of one patient problem.

Lastly, the extensions of the graphically defined subtypes 'diagnosed patient problem', 'completed sonographic examination', and 'clinical examination' are the proper domains of the mentioned attribute types (cf. Chap. 12).

17.5 Discussion and Conclusions

In Sect. 17.1, the business process in PoliGyn is classified as belonging to the category of creating (tangible and intangible) things. The diagnosis of the patient problem is a typical example of an intangible thing. Taking a cervical smear (as one of the clinical examinations) is a typical example of a tangible thing. Although the chosen category is perfectly applicable to the case PoliGyn, the reader could also have thought of the category of obtaining usufruct, because the 'usage' of the doctor and the sonographer looks quite like the usage of scarce resources. On further consideration, however, these 'usages' appear to be different. The doctor and the sonographer are not seized and released, as, for example, the cars in the case Rent-A-Car (cf. Chap. 15) are. Instead, the doctor and the sonographer are requested to bring about something (a diagnosis, an examination). In order to do this, the patient has to appear at an agreed-upon time and place (to check-in as it is called in the narrative description). To emphasise this prerequisite, we have presented the CSD in Fig. 17.3, where there is an explicit transaction kind that represents satisfying the condition of physical presence.

The case PoliGyn is not very suitable for applying Ockham's Razor in order to minimise the number of core entity types, as we did, for example, in the cases Rent-A-Car and Library (cf. Chaps. 15 and 16). Even the optional sonographic examination is not a good candidate to be linked one-to-one to a patient problem, so that one could speak of the sonographic examination of a patient problem. In medicine, actions are basically contingent on the situation at hand. As an example, the sonographer may decide on the spot to make extra sonograms, in addition to the one that is the norm.

Three things have received special attention in the analysis in Sect. 17.3. One is the identification and formulation of the product that the patient is seeking for. At first sight, it looks like it is to see the gynaecologist. On closer look, it appears that determining or diagnosing the patient problem is more accurate.

The second special thing is the order in which the enclosed transactions TK02 and TK03 are carried out. Although the current implementation requires a specific order, from a purely ontological point of view there is no preference. The (optional) transaction TK02 and the (deemed necessary) transactions TK03 must all be completed before the enclosing TK01 (diagnosing the patient problem) can be completed.

The third quite specific issue in the case PoliGyn is the delegations of authority. Like it holds for the case Pizzeria (cf. Chap. 14), most of them are needed for logical or logistic reasons, namely the delegation of the tasks [TK01/pm], [TK02/rq], and [TK02/pm]. The delegation of performing [TK01/rq] by the patient to the family doctor is a rather fascinating one. It is the result of the becoming 'grown-up' of the patient in health care in the past decades (at least in the Western world). He or she is not only the object of medical care.

Chapter 18
Exercise: Case GloLog

Abstract The case GloLog is an exercise in producing the essential model of an enterprise that offers the transporting and storing of tangible things: goods, containers, ships. The CM, PM, and FM of the GloLog organisation are presented and discussed. Emphasis is put on four topics. The first is the unavoidable need to conceive notions that are not present in the narrative description, but that are nevertheless ontologically crucial: the container content and the ship content. The second is the necessary existence of four distinct, only 'loosely coupled', business processes. The necessity stems from the incompatibility of the case cycles in these processes: sale, purchase, container content, and ship content. The third topic is the distribution of responsibilities: the ontologically necessary ones, as represented in particular by the CM, cannot easily be traced back to the narrative description of the case. The fourth topic is the current implementation of the essential model. Without the help of the essential model, it is almost impossible to clarify the role of the many parties involved and the many document kinds used (respectively to point at their redundancy).

18.1 Introduction

The case GloLog is an exercise in producing the essential model of an enterprise that offers, in terms of the categories that are distinguished in Chap. 10, the transporting and storing of tangible things. It is a slightly adapted version of a case that is studied and analysed in [1].

Section 18.2 contains the narrative description of the operational activities in a conglomerate of enterprises, collectively called GloLog. It is the basis for applying the OER method and producing the essential model (cf. Chap. 12). The analysis of the narrative description is discussed in Sect. 18.3, along with presenting parts of the CM in diagrams and tables. In Sect. 18.4, the essential model is extended with the corresponding PM and FM. In Sect. 18.5, the differences are discussed between the implementation that one would expect, based on the essential model, and the actual implementation. In Sect. 18.6, the current operational problems are addressed. Section 18.7 contains the conclusions of the exercise.

J. L. G. Dietz, J. B. F. Mulder, *Enterprise Ontology*, The Enterprise Engineering Series, https://doi.org/10.1007/978-3-030-38854-6_18

18.2   Narrative Description

General

The case Global Logistics, or GloLog for short, involves logistic operations between countries in the Far-East and The Netherlands. It is coordinated by a firm called Import Export Services (IES for short). One of the tasks of IES is to import consumer electronics products from the Far East for European dealerships (sales companies as well as business groups). The products are transported in containers by ship. IES coordinates the process from sale to delivery of goods to the client, while using the services of a selection of other enterprises. To smoothly operate the transportation of the goods, not only the physical container movements must be executed smoothly, fast, and accurately, but also the information exchanges around it.

Figure 18.1 illustrates the enterprises that are involved, including IES, and how they are related in the physical as well as the information logistics processes. The goods move from the supplier via a shipping company (the ship), a stevedore (the container transshipment in the port of Rotterdam), and a land transportation company (transport from the port of Rotterdam) to IES, which takes responsibility for temporary storage and eventual delivery to the client. The ship broker and the shipping agent play a coordinating role, whilst Customs plays an authoritative role. The last three organisations also have employees in the harbour area, accommodated in the terminal office. Between the different organisations, information is exchanged through telephone, telex, fax, and courier, in order to make sure goods reach their destination as fast as possible.

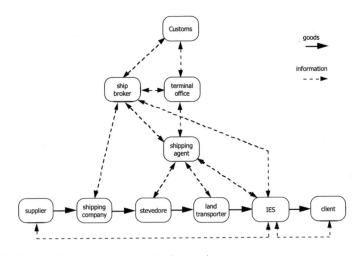

Fig. 18.1 Relationships between the involved enterprises

In the 3 years prior to the time to which this case description applies, the volume of trade has doubled to 4000 containers per year (which is about 800,000 m^3). But the pressure of competition on IES is also large. Therefore, the company is looking at steps that increase the quality of the company's logistics services and decrease costs. It is expected that a decrease in the distribution time will lead to a decrease in costs, in particular because less storage costs will be incurred. In addition, it is expected that redesign of the current business processes will lead to lower processing costs, particularly in terms of time spent per container.

The Global Business Processes
The chain of logistic actions can be described in short as follows. IES processes orders of its clients and places a combined order at a supplier in the Far East. The supplier composes the corresponding shipment, packs it into one or more containers, and brings them to a shipping company, where the containers are loaded on a ship. When the ship is fully loaded, it sails to the harbour of Rotterdam where it is unloaded by the stevedore. Then the containers are picked up by trucks from a land transporter and brought to IES, where the goods are unloaded from the containers. The trucks take the empty containers back to the stevedore. Finally, the client orders are delivered by the IES delivery service. It takes quite some care to ensure this process runs smoothly. We are faced with the following activities and responsibilities:

- IES initiates the shipments and verifies (and corrects if necessary) the shipping documents sent by the supplier, passes these on to the shipping agent, receives the goods and eventually delivers these to the clients. IES plans the container transportation and informs the shipping agent when and where which containers must be picked up.
- The ship broker transfers information to Customs, IES, and the shipping agent, regarding the shipments and the expected arrival times of a ship as well as the time of unloading containers from the ship.
- The stevedore unloads the containers and makes agreements with the shipping company about where and when this is done. The stevedore stores containers on its own grounds until they are picked up by trucks from the land transporter.
- The shipping agent takes care of the handling of the containers by Customs. After the release of the containers, the shipping agent organises the container transportation, in conformity with the planning of IES, from the stevedore's grounds to IES. To this end, the shipping agent makes agreements with the land transporter about which container must be picked up where and at what time, and supplies the land transporter with the documents for picking up the containers from the stevedore.
- The terminal office accommodates the offices of Customs, the ship brokers and shipping agents in the harbour area.

The Business Processes in Detail

Clients of IES place client orders with IES. Based on these orders, IES periodically places a supply order with a supplier. The supplier prepares a shipment for every supply order, which can take up one or more containers. Depending on the harbour from which the order is shipped, the supplier draws up a Waybill (from Singapore) or a Bill of Lading (from Tokyo). A Waybill is a transport document registered under a name, which means that the receiver who is stated on the document must prove her/his identity to be able to receive the shipment. A Bill of Lading (BoL) is "to bearer"; it is the official proof of ownership of the shipment. Both transport documents state which containers they concern, the content of these containers, who is the supplier and who is the receiver, the identification of the transportation overseas, and the parties that must be informed of the arrival of the containers in the harbour . The transport documents (Waybills or BoLs) are sent, together with the remaining documents (invoices and packing lists), to IES per courier. This takes approximately 2 days; the transportation overseas takes roughly 3 weeks. IES administers every Waybill or BoL, verifies whether it corresponds with placed supply orders, makes copies and sends the documents to the shipping agent.

Between 2 and 7 days before arrival of a ship, the ship broker receives the manifest with information regarding the precise cargo on the ship from the shipping company. Every article on board has an article description and a unique article number in this document. A manifest is around 2000 pages on average. On the basis of this manifest, the ship broker draws up a general declaration (GD) which is sent to Customs. The GD is a list of the Waybill- or BoL-numbers of the shipments on board. The ship broker also draws up pre-arrival notices (PaN), which are sent to the receivers mentioned in the manifest.

The shipping agent receives the shipment documents from IES (and other organisations which have shipments on the ship), checks whether these are complete and archives them under the name of the concerned ship. Close to the arrival time of the ship in the harbour, the shipping agent draws up the documents that the truck drivers need in order to receive a container from the stevedore and to drive to IES. It concerns the following documents:

- For every container, the shipping agent produces a CMR (Contrat de Transport International de Marchandises par Route), a European cargo document that must be carried by a truck driver during land transportation.
- For a shipment with a BoL, the BoL is traded by a courier at the ship broker for a delivery order. The ship broker makes a delivery order for every container mentioned in the BoL, upon presentation of which the container can be picked up at the stevedore's premises. For shipments with a Waybill, the presentation of a copy of the Waybill and a proof of identity as the transporter, suffices for the handover of the shipment.
- For every container, a Customs document must be drawn up on which the data about the goods are stated, as specified in the Waybill or BoL, as well as the GD number and the article numbers.

The correct receipt of these documents is not always simple. Next to the article description, the PaN usually (but not always) also contains the article number and the GD number. Sometimes, the shipping agent does not receive a PaN at all because the company is not mentioned in the manifest as one of the parties involved. The article numbers and the GD number are generally also mentioned on the delivery orders. However, for shipments with a Waybill, no delivery orders are made. In such a case, the shipping agent has telephone contact with the ship broker to complete the information necessary for the preparation of the Customs documents.

Using the GD, Customs checks the correctness of the specified data on the Customs documents supplied by the shipping agent, and inspects, if thought opportune, the content of the containers. If the data do not exactly correspond, the shipping agent must provide an explanation. If everything is in order, Customs sends a release statement together with stamped Customs documents to the shipping agent, who then informs IES which containers have been released.

IES determines when the land transport of the released containers can best take place, keeping in mind the urgency of the different shipments and the available unloading capacity at their own grounds, and passes the resulting schedule on to the shipping agent. Based on the planning of IES, the shipping agent gives transportation instructions to the land transporter. These instructions are confirmed by fax; a copy is faxed to the terminal office. The truck driver presents the confirmation fax to the shipping agent's terminal office and receives—provided that the fax corresponds with the copy at the terminal office—the necessary Customs documents, CMR, and Waybill or delivery order. Upon presentation of the CMR and Waybill or delivery order, the stevedore loads the container onto the delivery truck, whereafter the driver drives to IES. IES receives the container and the accompanying documents, unloads the container contents, checks the shipments for completeness and possible damages, stores the goods, and eventually delivers the client orders at the dealerships with IES' own delivery service.

The Current Task Execution
In this section, the previously mentioned tasks of IES and the shipping agent will be elaborated at the task level of individual employees. At the location of IES, there are three employees (referred to as A, B, and C) involved in the receipt of and the administrative settlement of shipments.

Employee A processes the documents that are sent, via a courier, by the supplier in the Far East. The number of sets (BoL or Waybill with packing list, invoice, and other documents) in a courier consignment varies from 1 to 12. The sets are sorted and copied, after which the documents that are necessary for the shipping agent are sent, together with an accompanying letter, in a folder by postal mail to the head office of the shipping agent in Rotterdam (documents that are ready before 16 o'clock are delivered around 11 o'clock on the following working day). The information on the BoLs or Waybills is inserted into the IES database system. For every consignment, a hard copy file (called "on-the-way-archive") is kept with the order form from the supplier, copies of the transportation documents, and the corresponding print-out from the database system.

In agreement with the inventory department of IES, employee B makes the container planning based on the expected arrival times of the ships, PaNs, and the release by the shipping agent. This planning is communicated to the shipping agent by telephone, and confirmed by fax. The planned pick-up times for the containers are filed and a note is made on the planning board. In addition, employee B daily picks up all the files of the containers which are expected that day from the 'on-the-way-archive'. Using the database system, an arrival announcement (AA) is written and passed on to employee C.

Every time a container is delivered by the land transporter, employee C finds the AA concerned, inspects the shipment and sends the AA together with the documents delivered by the truck driver back to employee B. In the case of damage or loss, he/she includes an incident report.

Employee B compares these documents to those in the 'on-the-way-archive' (and reports possible irregularities to employee A), makes copies of the Customs documents and archives these in the file. Those documents that eventually need to be delivered to the client are sent to the order department of IES, together with a copy of the order form. The dispatched container is then erased from the planning board.

At the shipping agent's office in Rotterdam two employees are involved, referred to as D and E. Employee D executes the tasks necessary for the clearance of a container to IES. Employee E executes the tasks concerned with the organisation of the transport from the harbour in Rotterdam to the location of IES.

Employee D checks the documents (BoL or Waybill, packing lists, and invoices) which come in from IES on a daily basis, inputs the data into their own computer system, and archives the documents in the file of the concerned ship. For every container, the computer prints out a CMR. Next, employee D processes the PaNs coming in from the ship broker. Sometimes, the PaN contains all the data needed for making the Customs document for the shipment in question, in which case this is done directly.

Approximately two days before arrival of a ship, employee D makes an inquiry with the ship broker about the availability of the delivery orders. As soon as these are ready to be picked up, the BoLs are taken to the ship broker and traded for the delivery orders. Dropping off the BoLs and picking up the delivery orders is carried out by a courier of the shipping agent who drives to the office of the ship broker by motorbike twice a day.

Based on the delivery orders, employee D prepares the Customs documents if these are not complete yet. If necessary, a phone call is made to the ship broker for the article number and the GD number for the orders without a Waybill (thus those without a delivery order). The Customs documents with the corresponding delivery orders and CMRs are then brought to Customs at the terminal office by motorbike. After release of a container, Customs gives the documents to the employees of the shipping agent at the terminal office where they are later picked up by one of the land transporter drivers. Customs informs the shipping agent's head office per telex that the container is released. A few times a day, employee D checks whether releases have been sent in through telex; if this is the case, an informing fax is sent to IES.

Employee E processes the container planning and transmits it to the shipping agent. He/she searches for the concerned documents and makes agreements per telephone with the land transporter about which truck will pick up which container. For every container employee E makes an agreement in the form of a transportation order. This order is faxed to the land transporter and to their employees at the terminal.

A truck driver working for the land transporter drives into the terminal grounds around the agreed-upon time, walks into the terminal office, picks up the documents from the shipping agent's employees (which he/she only receives if the fax corresponds with the one that is faxed to the terminal office by employee E), drives to the stevedore's grounds and, upon showing the Waybill or delivery order, receives the container and finally delivers it together with the documents at IES.

Current Problems and Failures

IES strives to have all containers at their establishment within 5 workdays after arrival of the ship. The average time it takes in practice is about 5 days; around a third of all containers is delivered later (see Fig. 18.2). As can be deduced from the process descriptions, the distribution time in Fig. 18.2 coheres with a large number of factors. To gain insight into the time span of the different steps in the process, a test was done with a random sample of 200 containers and a number of time intervals were defined, as shown in Figs. 18.3, 18.4, 18.5, 18.6, and 18.7. In all these figures, the horizontal axis shows the number of workdays and the vertical axis shows the number of containers.

IES insists that the transport documents sent by suppliers be at IES seven workdays before the arrival of a ship. Figure 18.3 illustrates that this norm is not met by one-fifth of the containers in the random sample. From one shipment (two containers), the documents even arrived at IES 1 day after the arrival of the ship!

Figure 18.4 exhibits the distribution of the number of workdays that pass between the moment that a ship arrives in Rotterdam and the moment that the containers are released by the shipping agent. The random sample also shows that Customs sometimes approves a shipment before the ship has arrived. It holds for approximately 60% of the containers. Noteworthy are the containers that are approved 13 and 19 workdays, respectively, after arrival. The two shipments in question were heavily delayed as a result of communication problems between the ship broker and the shipping agent.

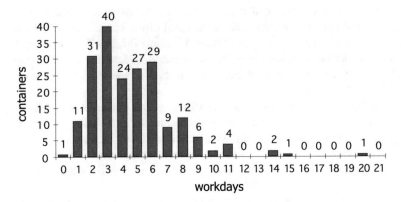

Fig. 18.2 Time between arrival of a ship and delivery of the containers

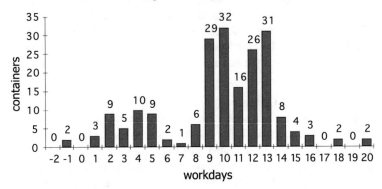

Fig. 18.3 Time between receipt of the documents by IES and arrival of the ship

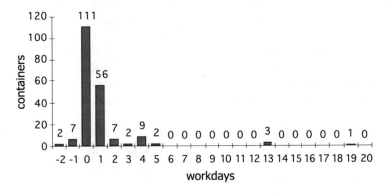

Fig. 18.4 Time between arrival of the ship and release by shipping agent

To determine to what extent the time of release by the shipping agent depends on the moment of release by Customs, date stamps on Customs documents were used to determine the time between the arrival of the ship and the release by Customs. This is illustrated in Fig. 18.5. Comparison of Figs. 18.4 and 18.5 has brought us to study the time difference between release by Customs and release by the shipping agent more closely. This difference is illustrated in Fig. 18.6. The figure indicates that the release of a quarter of the containers is passed on by the shipping agent to IES on the same day as when they are approved by Customs. In less than 10% of the cases more than 1 day passes.

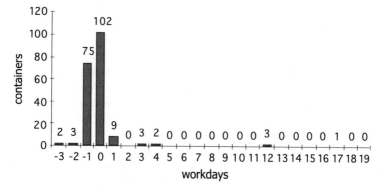

Fig. 18.5 Time between arrival of ship and release by Customs

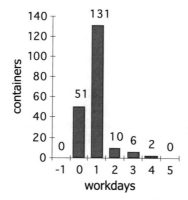

Fig. 18.6 Time between release by Customs and release by shipping agent

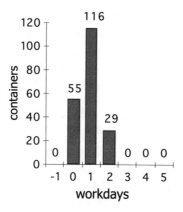

Fig. 18.7 Time between printing of the Customs document and release by Customs

Figure 18.7 illustrates the difference between the day that the Customs documents are printed and the day that Customs approves the shipment. Thus, the graph gives an indication of the speed with which Customs works. One should note, however, that the printed date on the Customs document does not always correspond with the day that it is sent. It often occurs that the Customs document cannot be fully filled in on the day of printing because the GD number or the article number must still be requested at the ship broker. The document can then only be presented at Customs later; thus Fig. 18.7 suggests a longer processing time than it is in reality.

As is indicated in Sect. 18.2, IES thinks that they can decrease costs by decreasing the distribution time of the containers. The relationship between distribution time and costs is most clear when one looks at the demurrage costs: when containers stay on the terminal for more than 3 workdays, IES is charged about 100 euros per container per day. The second factor of importance is the interest burden: as the shipment concerns rather valuable goods (the average container cargo is worth around half a million euro), a day's delay at an interest rate of 6% per year comes down to about 80 euros per container per day. However, the cutting of this cost would not benefit IES, but the supplier. As a third factor, the labour costs can be considered. It seems obvious that improvements in efficiency in the business processes lead to a cut in work time and thus a decrease in labour costs. However, as is it is difficult to prove that 25% less work also leads to a 25% decrease in labour costs (it remains questionable whether the labour force could be decreased by one person), this factor weighs less heavily than the other two.

Next to these three factors, which IES believes to be able to cut costs on, the following costs are also worth mentioning: the transportation per ship from the Far East to Rotterdam (about 5000 euros per container); the transport per truck from Rotterdam to IES (about 400 euros per container); the sending of documents per courier from the Far East to IES (about 150 euros per shipment).

18.3   Analysis of the Narrative Description

Because it is not possible to involve the employees in the various enterprises within GloLog, we have to apply the second best way of working, as discussed in Chap. 12. It is to study the narrative description and find clues for the presence of original (thus O-organisation) transaction kinds and actor roles. We will do this below, paragraph after paragraph. The pieces of text that are taken from the case description are written in italics. Only the text in Sect. 18.2.3 is taken into account; the preceding subsections are merely a summary of it, and Sect. 18.2.4 is merely about the realisation and implementation of the processes that are described in Sect. 18.2.3.

Clients of IES place client orders with IES. Based on these orders, IES periodically places a supply order with a supplier. The supplier prepares a shipment for every supply order, which can take up one or more containers. Depending on the harbour from which the order is shipped, the supplier draws up a *Waybill (from Singapore) or a Bill of Lading (from Tokyo). A Waybill is a transport document registered under a name, which means that the receiver who is stated on the document must prove her/his identity to be able to receive the shipment. A Bill of Lading (BoL) is "to bearer"; it is the official proof of ownership of the shipment. Both transport documents state which containers they concern, the content of these containers, who is the supplier and who is the receiver, the identification of the transportation overseas and the parties that must be informed of the arrival of the containers in the harbour. The transport documents (Waybills or BoLs) are sent, together with the remaining documents (invoices and packing lists), to IES per courier. This takes approximately 2 days; the transportation overseas takes roughly 3 weeks. IES administers every Waybill or BoL, verifies whether it corresponds with placed supply orders, makes copies and sends the documents to the shipping agent.*

From the first piece of text in red (*Clients of IES place client orders with IES*), we deduce the existence of an original transaction kind regarding the processing of client orders. Let us identify it as TK01 and name it "sale completing", as we did for the case Pizzeria (cf. Chap. 14). We use the word "sale" instead of "client order" to emphasise that the transaction concerns a complete sale of IES, not only the order phase. We name the executing actor role AR01 accordingly "sale completer" and formulate the corresponding product kind PK01 as "[sale] **is** completed". The initiating actor role is, as usual (cf. Chaps. 8 and 10), an unknown role within a composite transactor role, which we will identify as CTAR01 and simply name "client".

The next red-coloured piece of text (*IES periodically places a supply order with a supplier*) hints to the existence of two additional transaction kinds. The first concerns the processing of purchases. We use the word "purchase" instead of "supply order" to emphasise that the transaction concerns a complete purchase by IES, not only the order phase (cf. Chap. 5). We identify it as TK02 and name it "purchase completing". Consequently, we name the executing actor role AR02 "purchase completer" and formulate the corresponding product kind PK02 as "[purchase] **is** completed". The third original transaction kind represents the periodic initiation of transactions TK02. Let us identify it as TK11 and name it "purchase controlling". Accordingly, the self-initiating executor role AR11 is named "purchase controller". The product kind PK11 is properly formulated by "purchase controlling **for** [period] **is** done". The length of the period doesn't matter. It can be daily, or weekly, etc. It can even have non-fixed periods, since the production time of the next one is set during the execution of the current transaction TK11 (cf. Chap. 8).

The third piece of text in red (*prepares a shipment for every supply order*) certainly hints also at an original transaction kind; but the question is how to conceive it and consequently how to formulate its product kind. By applying the sapience 'Devising proper concepts' (cf. Chap. 12), we conclude that we don't need an entity type shipment, because there is a one-to-one relationship between purchases and shipments. Let us therefore identify the transaction kind as TK03 and name it "purchase loading". It concerns the loading of the goods of a purchase in one or more containers, as indicated by the fourth red-coloured piece of text (*can take up one or more containers*). Accordingly, the executing actor role AR03 is named "purchase loader" and the product kind PK03 is formulated as "[purchase] **is** loaded". The initiators of transactions TK03 are clearly actors AR02, as a loaded purchase is a sub-product of a completed purchase.

The last interesting piece of text, occurring twice, is "*the transportation overseas*". It gives rise to conceiving an original transaction kind regarding the transport of containers by ship. We identify it as TK14 and name it "sea transport completing". Accordingly, we name the executing actor role AR14 "sea transport completer", and formulate the product kind PK14 as "[sea transport] is completed". It implies the movement of a number of containers, by ship, from a harbour in the Far East to the harbour of Rotterdam.

But who is the initiator of transactions TK14? In other words, who orders a ship to sail? The narrative description of the case doesn't give a clue (also the parts that we have skipped don't). So, we have to rely on what is most likely (and, of course, validate the decision!), which is that the initiator is a self-activating actor role who periodically checks whether a ship can be sent off. Let us identify it as AR12 and name it "sea transport controller". Consequently, we name the related transaction kind TK12 "sea transport controlling" and we formulate the product kind PK12 as "sea transport controlling **for** [period] **is** done". The length of the period is determined by the shipping company, and it need not be fixed, as discussed above.

Between 2 and 7 days before arrival of a ship, the ship broker receives the manifest with information regarding the precise cargo on the ship from the shipping company. Every article on board has an article description and a unique article number in this document. A manifest is around 2000 pages on average. On the basis of this manifest, the ship broker draws up a general declaration (GD) which is sent to Customs. The GD is a list of the Waybill- or BoL-numbers of the shipments on board. The ship broker also draws up pre-arrival notices (PaN), which are sent to the receivers mentioned in the manifest.

This text is only about informational and documental matters. There are no indications of essential transactor roles.

The shipping agent receives the shipment documents from IES (and other organisations which have shipments on the ship), checks whether these are complete and archives them under the name of the concerned ship. Close to the arrival time of the ship in the harbour, the shipping agent draws up the documents that the truck drivers need in order to receive a container from the stevedore and to drive to IES. It concerns the following documents:

- *For every container, the shipping agent produces a CMR (Contrat de Transport International de Marchandises par Route), a European cargo document that must be carried by a truck driver during land transportation.*
- *For a shipment with a BoL, the BoL is traded by a courier at the ship broker for a delivery order. The ship broker makes a delivery order for every container mentioned in the BoL, upon presentation of which the container can be picked*

up at the stevedore's premises. For shipments with a Waybill, the presentation of a copy of the Waybill and a proof of identity as the transporter, suffices for the handover of the shipment.

- *For every container, a Customs document must be drawn up on which the data about the goods are stated, as specified in the Waybill or BoL, as well as the GD number and the article numbers.*

This text is mainly about informational and documental matters. There are, however, indications of the existence of transaction kinds concerning the transport of containers over land. They are marked in red. For a full understanding of the land transport process, we need more information, however. By taking into account already some information from the last paragraph, we can conclude that there must be a transactor role tree that is similar to the one we have found for the sea transport process. So, we identify a transaction kind TK15 and name it "land transport completing". Accordingly, we identify its executing actor role AR15 and name it "land transport completer" and we formulate the product kind PK15 as "[land transport] **is** completed". Where a sea transport is about the movement of all containers on a ship, a land transport is about the movement of one container on a truck.

Similarly, we need a self-activating actor role as the initiator of transactions TK15. Let us identify it as AR13 and name it "land transport controller". Consequently, we name the related transaction kind TK13 "land transport controlling" and we formulate the product kind PK13 as "land transport controlling **for** [period] **is** done". The length of the period is determined by IES (as will be discussed later).

Using the GD, Customs checks the correctness of the specified data on the Customs documents supplied by the shipping agent, and inspects, if thought opportune, the content of the containers. If the data do not exactly correspond, the shipping agent must provide an explanation. If everything is in order, Customs sends a release statement together with stamped Customs documents to the shipping agent, who then informs IES which containers have been released.

From the red-coloured pieces of text, we deduce the presence of two original transaction kinds: one regarding the (physical) inspection by Customs of containers, and one regarding the release of containers, also by Customs. We skip the first one (and provide later the justification of the skipping), identify the second one as TK07, and name it "purchase releasing". Accordingly, we name the executing actor role AR07 "purchase releaser" and formulate the product kind PK07 as "[purchase] **is** released". The reason for "purchase releasing" instead of "container content releasing" is that the initiator of transactions TK07 is obviously actor role AR02 (purchase completer), as it is in the interest of AR02 to get the goods of a purchase released by Customs. The releasing of the individual containers of a purchase could be modelled by a transactor role 'container content releaser', enclosed by TAR07 (cf. Fig. 18.8). Consequently, as long as the contents of one of the containers, containing goods of a purchase, cannot be released, the whole purchase cannot be released.

IES determines when the land transport of the released containers can best take place, keeping in mind the urgency of the different shipments and the available unloading capacity at their own grounds, and passes the resulting schedule on to the shipping agent. Based on the planning of the IES, the shipping agent gives transportation instructions to the land transporter. These instructions are confirmed by fax; a copy is faxed to the terminal office. The truck driver presents the confirmation fax to the shipping agent's terminal office and receives—provided that the fax corresponds with the copy at the terminal office—the necessary Customs documents, CMR, and Waybill or delivery order. Upon presentation of the CMR and Waybill or delivery order, the stevedore loads the container onto the delivery truck, whereafter the driver drives to IES. IES receives the container and the accompanying documents, unloads the container contents, checks the shipments for completeness and possible damages, stores the goods, and eventually delivers the client orders at the dealerships with IES' own delivery service.

The text above is full of hints at original transaction kinds. The first one can be found in "*IES determines when the land transport of the released containers can best take place*". Later in the text, the outcome of the determination is called planning or schedule. The question then is whether making a planning or a schedule is an original transaction. In Chap. 17, a similar problem is discussed, namely making appointments in a policlinic. There, the conclusion is that making appointments (for doing things later) only concerns the order phase of a transaction. The same reasoning holds for making plannings or schedules. It is generating requests for bringing about products at some future point in time. Like scheduling classes for a school, making a transportation planning is not something trivial at all, but the point is that the result is not a change of the state of the production world (cf. Chap. 8). Concluding, the red-coloured piece of text above regards the initiation of transactions in which containers are transported. Let us identify the transaction kind as TK08 and name it "container content transporting" and let us formulate the product kind PK08 as "[container content] **is** transported". The executing actor role AR08 is named "container content transporter". The initiating actor role is clearly AR15 (land transport completer).

The second piece of text in red, "*Based on the planning of the IES, the shipping agent gives transportation instructions to the land transporter*", doesn't add something essentially new, it only tells us that requesting actors AR08 to carry out transactions TK08 is delegated by IES to the shipping agent. We will elaborate on this later.

From the third piece of text in red (*the stevedore loads the container onto the delivery truck*), we deduce the presence of transaction kind TK16 'container content loading', of which the executor role AR16 is named 'container content loader'. The product kind PK16 is accordingly formulated as "[container content] is loaded". The next red-coloured piece of text (*the driver drives to IES*) confirms the existence of transactions TK08, which we have identified already.

From the third piece of text in red (*unloads the container contents, checks the shipments for completeness and possible damages, stores the goods*) we deduce that there is a new transaction kind, which we identify as TK09 and name "container content unloading" by which is meant the emptying of a container. The other actions are considered to be enclosed in a transaction TK09. Accordingly, the executing actor role AR09 is named "container content unloader" and the product kind PK09 is formulated as "[container content] is unloaded". Like it holds for transactions TK16 and TK08, transactions TK09 are initiated by actors AR15 (land transport completer).

The last piece of text in red (*delivers the client orders at the dealerships*) hints at the existence of a transaction kind that concerns the transport of goods of a sale to the client. Let us identify it as TK10 and name it "sale transporting". Accordingly, the executing actor role AR10 is named "sale transporter", and the product kind PK10 is formulated as "[sale] **is** transported". The right initiator role for trans-actions TK10 is AR01 (sale completer), as a transported sale is a sub-product of a completed sale.

The results of the analysis above are represented in the CSD in Fig. 18.8. The tree with double-lined boxes at the top of Fig. 18.8 only serves to clarify that there are four different business processes in the Glolog enterprise. The white-coloured transactor roles constitute the responsibility range (cf. Chap. 10) of the enterprise IES. The other transactor roles are environmental or external (cf. Chap. 10).

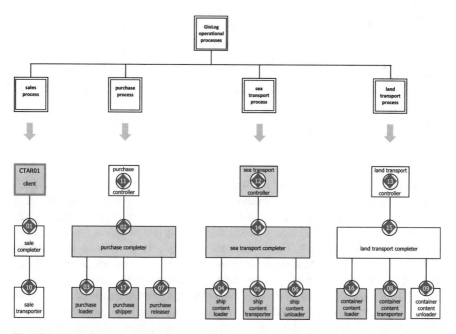

Fig. 18.8 CSD of the interaction structure of the GloLog organisation

The top of the sales process is an actor role within the composite actor role CTAR01. The top of the other three processes are self-activating actor roles: AR11 (purchase controller), AR12 (sea transport controller), and AR13 (land transport controller). As explained in Chap. 10, the reason for having these four processes is the presence of four distinct core entity or case kinds that the GloLog organisation deals with: sales, purchases, ship contents, and container contents.

In Table 18.1, the TPT of the GloLog organisation is shown, corresponding with the CSD in Fig. 18.8. It is revealed from the analysis of the narrative description as presented above. Each of the core case kinds (sale, purchase, container content, ship content) has its own process cycle. Therefore, they cannot be combined in one process. The cycle of the sales process has the highest frequency. The purchase process has a lower frequency, because a purchase encompasses a number of sales. The frequency of the land transport process is on average a bit higher than the one of the purchase process, because the goods of a purchase comprise one or more container contents. The frequency of the sea transport process is by far the lowest one since the charge of a ship comprises in general a huge number of container contents.

Table 18.1 TPT of the GloLog organisation

transaction kind	product kind	executor role
TK01 sale completing	PK01 [sale] is completed	AR01 sale completer
TK02 purchase completing	PK02 [purchase] is completed	AR02 purchase completer
TK03 purchase loading	PK03 [purchase] is loaded	AR03 purchase loader
TK04 ship content loading	PK04 [ship content] is loaded	AR04 ship content loader
TK05 ship content transporting	PK05 [ship content] is transported	AR05 ship content transporter
TK06 ship content unloading	PK06 [ship content] is unloaded	AR06 ship content unloader
TK07 purchase releasing	PK07 [purchase] is released	AR07 purchase releaser
TK08 container content transporting	PK08 [container content] is transported	AR08 container content transporter
TK09 container content unloading	PK09 [container content] is unloaded	AR09 container content unloader
TK10 sale transporting	PK10 [sale] is transported	AR10 sale transporter
TK11 purchase controlling	PK11 purchase controlling for [period] is done	AR11 purchase controller
TK12 sea transport controlling	PK12 sea transport controlling for [period] is done	AR12 sea transport controller
TK13 land transport controlling	PK13 land transport controlling for [period] is done	AR13 land transport controller
TK14 sea transport completing	PK14 [sea transport] is completed	AR14 sea transport completer
TK15 land transport completing	PK15 [land transport] is completed	AR15 land transport completer
TK16 container content loading	PK16 [container content] is loaded	AR16 container content loader
TK17 purchase shipper	PK17 [purchase] is shipped	AR17 purchase shipper

At first sight, the presence of transaction kind TK17 (and the actor role AR17) may seem redundant. It is very appropriate, however, to include it. This becomes evident if one asks the question: "When can an actor AR02 confidently decide that a purchase is completed?" The only reasonable answer is that he/she can do so after the purchase is loaded (PK03), is shipped (PK17), and is released by Customs (PK07). By being shipped is meant delivered at the location of IES. The (true) fact that AR17 is dependent on the progress of other processes (the sea transport process and the land transport process) does not affect the need for the existence of TK17, in order to make the purchase process tree self-contained. This is an important property of transactor role trees (cf. Chap. 10). There are no interactions between these trees, only interstrictions and interimpediments. Lastly, a purchase (PK03) being loaded includes that the containers are brought to the premises of the shipping company.

A tree of processes in the category 'transporting and storing' can generally be extended by conceiving sub-products of the current 'leaf' products. As an example, one can sensibly conceive three sub-product kinds, and the corresponding transaction kinds, of a transaction PK14 ([sea transport] **is** completed): PK04 ([ship content] is loaded), PK05 ([ship content] is transported), and PK06 ([ship content] is unloaded). The addition of these 'leaves' is already contained in the CSD in Fig. 18.8. Note that there is a one-to-one correspondence between sea transports and ship contents, as shown in the OFD in Fig. 18.16.

The processes shown in Fig. 18.8 constitute the SoI of the case GloLog. As said, the white-coloured transactor roles constitute the responsibility range (cf. Chap. 10) of the enterprise IES. So, if one would like to focus on IES, the sea transport process seems to be irrelevant. Seems, though, because there are other relationships with this process. One of kind of these relationships is included in the interstriction structure, as expressed in Fig. 18.9. Note that all external transaction kinds/banks are omitted, for the sake of simplicity. Including them would make the CSD unnecessarily complicated for the purpose of the exercise.

The interstriction structure of an SoI shows the mutual *state dependencies* of the distinct business processes. The access link from AR11 to TK01 expresses that actors AR11 need to know the sales that must be settled, thus from which purchases must be composed. Upon every self-activation, the actor AR11 'sees' the requested and promised transactions TK01 and decides to initiate a transaction TK02 or not. The access link from AR12 to TK03 expresses that actors AR12 need to know the purchases that are loaded in containers and thus from which a ship content must be composed. Upon every self-activation, AR12 'sees' the completed, that is, accepted, transactions TK03 and decides whether to initiate a transaction TK14 or not. The access link from AR13 to TK14 expresses that actors AR13 need to know which containers are waiting in the harbour, ready for land transport. Upon every self-activation, the actor AR13 'sees' the completed transactions TK14 and decides to initiate none, one or more transactions TK15.

The CSD in Fig. 18.10 exhibits the interprocess interimpediment structure in the GloLog enterprise. It shows the mutual *process dependencies* of the distinct business processes in a global way. The details are expressed in the PM, to be discussed in Sect. 18.4. The wait link from TK02 to AR10 expresses that carrying through transactions TK10 has to wait for a specific progress in the transaction TK02 that comprises the specific sale to be transported. The transactions TK10 can already be requested and promised for some time, but they are impeded to proceed until the corresponding transaction TK02 is finished.

We have seen that actors AR12 base the decision to start transactions T14 on the contents of transaction bank TK03, that is, the purchases of which the goods are loaded or are scheduled to be loaded. The wait link from TK03 to AR14 expresses that carrying out transactions TK14 is impeded until the corresponding transactions TK03 are finished. The wait link from TK07 to AR15 represents the condition that purchases must be released before the land transport can be carried out. Note that the transactions TK15 can already have been requested (and promised) because AR13 knows that the finishing of the TK07 is coming. Lastly, the wait link from TK15 to

AR17 expresses that a purchase can be declared shipped as soon as the land transport of the container contents that consists of the goods of the purchase is completed. The cardinality range $1\ldots*$ expresses that the purchase may comprise more than one container content.

In Fig. 18.11, the three organisational structures, as shown in Figs. 18.8, 18.9, and 18.10, are combined, so that one gets a comprehensive overview of the construction of the GloLog enterprise, that is, of the existing transactor roles and of the coordination structures between them.

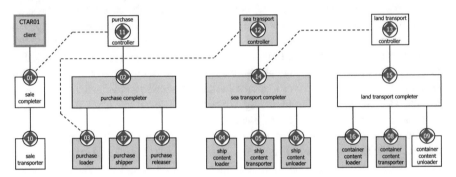

Fig. 18.9 CSD of the GloLog organisation plus interstriction structure

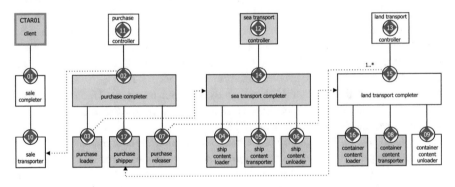

Fig. 18.10 CSD of the GloLog organisation plus interimpediment structure

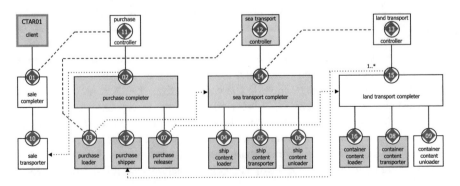

Fig. 18.11 The combined coordination structures in the GloLog organisation

18.4   Extending the Essential Model

In this section, the PM of the GloLog organisation is presented, based on the CM and the narrative description. Since there are four business processes, following from the analysis in Sect.18.3, there are four PSDs. The first one is exhibited in Fig. 18.12. It is the PSD of the sales process, together with the corresponding part of the CSD in the 'click' mode (cf. Chap. 10). The enclosing of a TK10 in a TK01 is in the standard way: from being promised of the TK01, the TK10 is requested, and the TK10 must be accepted before the TK01 can be finished. The explanation of the interprocess wait link from (TK02/ac) to [TK10/ex] is as follows.

Fig. 18.12 PSD of the sales process

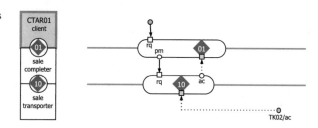

As soon as a TK01 is promised, and the sale thus can become part of a purchase, the corresponding delivery of the goods is requested from the delivery service of IES, so that the people there know that, in the future, goods have to be transported. However, there is a logistic constraint, which is that the goods of the sale must be present on the location of IES. This condition is perfectly represented by the being completed of the purchase in which the sale is contained. The wait link in Fig. 18.12 is a more precise representation of the wait link from TK02 to AR10 in Fig. 18.10.

The PSD of the purchase process is shown in Fig. 18.13, accompanied by the corresponding part of the CSD in the 'click' mode (cf. Chap. 10). The process model is basically standard. Only the enclosing of transactions TK03, TK17, and TK07 needs explanation. The PSD shows that the transactions TK03, TK17, and TK07 within a transaction TK02 are initiated simultaneously, namely as soon as the state (TK02/pm) is reached. However, the order of carrying out TK03 and TK17 is strictly sequential, as indicated by the wait link from (TK03/ac) to [TK17/ex]. The reason is the obvious logistic constraint that a purchase must be completely loaded in containers and that these are brought to the shipping company before it can be shipped.

One might expect a similar wait link from (TK17/ac) to [TK07/ex], but there is no ontological imperative to do so. Like the making of echograms in the case PoliGyn (cf. Chap. 17) does not necessarily precede the (other) examinations, the releasing of a container content by Customs does not necessarily have a precedence condition, except perhaps that the corresponding TK03 (purchase loading) is finished. As mentioned in Sect. 18.2.5, " … Customs sometimes approve a shipment before the ship has arrived. It holds for approximately 60% of the containers". Consequently, there are hardly any logistic constraints for Customs to release shipments.

The other interprocess constraint is that the goods of the purchase must have been delivered (TK15/ac) before the purchase can be completed [TK02/ex]. Having reached the state (TK15/ac) means that the containers containing the goods of the purchase where TK02 is about, are present at the location of IES. It is a logical logistic prerequisite for finishing the transaction TK02. Because the goods of a purchase may be stored in several containers, the cardinality of the wait link is 1...*. It means that all containers in which there are goods of the purchase where the TK02 is about, are emptied. The wait link is a more precise representation of the wait link from TK15 to AR02 in Fig. 18.10.

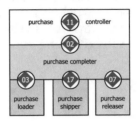

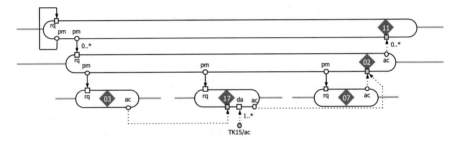

Fig. 18.13 PSD of the purchase process

Despite these logistic constraints, the purchase process is ontologically optimal, that is, the duration of a transaction TK02 is the shortest possible, because of the parallel initiation of the enclosed transactions TK03, TK17, and TK07. The practical meaning of it is that the order phase of the TK17 can already be carried through before the TK03 is finished. In other words, actors AR17 can be fully prepared and ready to start the execution of the TK17. A similar reasoning holds for transaction TK07. The enclosing of transaction kind TK02 in TK11 is the standard way of modelling periodic activities.

Figure 18.14 exhibits the PSD of the sea transport process, together with the corresponding part of the CSD in the 'click' mode (cf. Chap. 10). The process model is basically standard. Only the enclosing of transactions TK04, TK05, and TK06 needs explanation. The PSD shows that the transactions TK04, TK05, and TK06 within a transaction TK14 are initiated simultaneously, namely as soon as the state (TK14/pm) is reached. However, the order of their executions is strictly sequential, as indicated by the wait link from (TK04/ac) to [TK05/ex] and the one from (TK05/ac) to [TK06/ex]. The reason is the obvious logistic constraint that a ship must be completely loaded, that is, contain the corresponding ship content (TK04/ac) before it can sail to its destination (TK05), and it must have arrived at the destination (TK05/ac) before its content can be unloaded (TK06).

The interprocess wait link from (TK03/ac) to [TK04/rq] expresses that containers cannot be put on the ship if they have not been loaded. The wait link is a more precise representation of the wait link from TK03 to AR14 in Fig. 18.10.

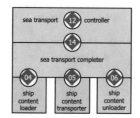

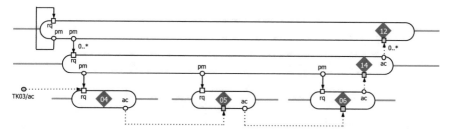

Fig. 18.14 PSD of the sea transport process

Despite these logistic constraints, the process is ontologically optimal, that is, the duration of a transaction TK14 is the shortest possible, because of the parallel initiation of the enclosed transactions TK04, TK05, and TK06. The practical meaning of it is that the order phase of the TK05 and the TK06 can already be carried through before the TK04 is finished. In other words, the actors AR05 and AR06 can be fully prepared and ready to start the execution of the TK05 and TK06, respectively. The enclosing of transaction kind TK02 in TK11 is the standard way of modelling periodic activities.

The PSD of the land transport process, together with the corresponding part of the CSD in the 'click' mode (cf. Chap. 10), is shown in Fig. 18.15. Like the ones for the purchase process and the sea transport process, the model is basically standard, except the enclosing of transactions TK16, TK08, and TK09 in a transaction TK15. The PSD shows that these transactions are initiated simultaneously, namely as soon as the state (TK15/pm) is reached. However, the execution order of the TK16, TK08, and TK09 is, for purely logistic reasons, sequential, as indicated by the wait link from (TK16/ac) to [TK08/ex] and the one from (TK08/ac) to [TK09/ex].

The interprocess wait link from (TK07/ac) to [TK16/rq] expresses that a purchase must be released (by Customs) before its containers can be loaded. The wait link is a more precise representation of the wait link from TK07 to AR15 in Fig. 18.10.

Also the land transport process is ontologically optimal, that is, the duration of a transaction TK15 is the shortest possible, because of the parallel initiation of the enclosed transactions TK16, TK08, and TK09, despite the fact that they are carried out sequentially. The practical meaning of it is that the order phase of the TK08 and the TK09 can already be carried through before the TK16 is finished. In other words, the actors AR08 and AR09 can be fully prepared and ready to start the execution of the TK08 and TK09, respectively.

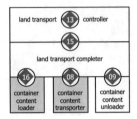

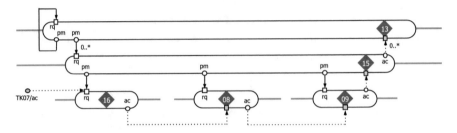

Fig. 18.15 PSD of the land transport process

The second model to be presented in this section is the FM of the GloLog organisation, as far as it can be deduced from the CM and the narrative description (by lack of the AM). The OFD is given in Fig. 18.16. Note that it represents the global FM: it only contains the property types that can be deduced from the narrative description.

The core entity types (represented by white-coloured roundangles) can directly be taken from the TPT in Table 18.1: sale, purchase, container content, ship content, sea transport, and land transport. Their product kinds correspond with the ones in the TPT (cf. Table 8.1). The entity types (actually classes) that are represented by grey-coloured roundangles are external to the modelled processes.

The concepts 'sale' and 'purchase' are straightforward, they have uniquely identifiable instances, which means that although the contents of two sales or two purchases may be exactly the same, they are two distinguishable things. With respect to containers and ships, however, we need to conceive new concepts in order to distinguish the different contents they may have in the course of time (presupposing that containers and ships are reused!). So, it would be incorrect to formulate, for example, PK16 as "[container] is loaded", although the people involved most likely will say that they have loaded a container. However, what they actually mean to say is that they have loaded a container with its current content. Thus, we need the concept of container content (in addition to the concept of container). Therefore, PK16 has been formulated as "[container content] is loaded", PK08 as "[container content] is transported", and PK09 as "[container content] is unloaded". In a similar way, one needs to conceive the notion of ship content (next to the notion of ship). Likewise, the product kinds PK04, PK05, and PK06 are respectively formulated as "[ship content] is loaded", "[ship content] is transported", and "[ship content] is unloaded".

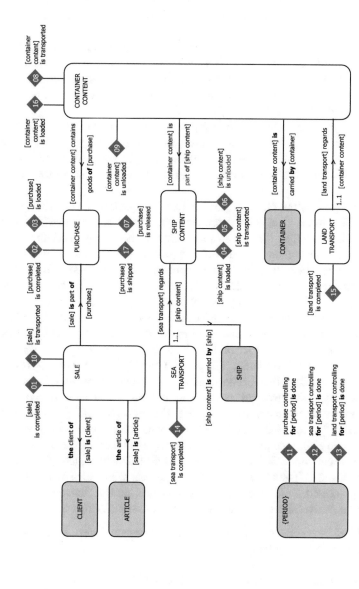

Fig. 18.16 OFD of the GloLog organisation

The other two entity types that need further explanation are sea transport and land transport. By a sea transport is understood moving a specific set of containers over sea that together contain the ship content to be transported (which is the sum of the separate container contents). Consequently, there is a one-to-one correspondence between sea transports and ship contents. This is indicated in the OFD by the 1...1 cardinality range at the domain side of the property type '[sea transport] regards [ship content]'.

By a land transport is understood moving a specific container, containing the container content to be transported over land. Consequently, there is a one-to-one correspondence between land transports and container contents. This is indicated in the OFD by the 1...1 cardinality range at the domain side of the property type '[land transport] regards [container content]'.

In addition to the discussed core entity types, the external entity types 'client', 'article', 'container', and 'ship' are needed, as well as the (external) value type 'period'. We assume that all (production) event types are sufficiently discussed above, so that we can confine ourselves to explaining the remaining property types in the OFD.

The property type '**the** client **of** [sale] **is** [client]' specifies the dealership of IES that is the client in the sale, and the property type '**the** article **of** [sale] **is** [article]' specifies the article which the sale is about. One of the obvious attribute types of 'sale' therefore is the number of items ordered (of the related article). Note that every sale concerns one article. It is the result of applying Ockham's Razor, fully comparable to its application in the case Library (cf. Chap. 16). The property type '[sale] **is** part **of** [purchase]' serves to specify the set of sales in a purchase.

The property type '[container content] contains goods **of** [purchase]' specifies the purchase of which goods are contained in the container content, and the property type '[container content] **is** part **of** [ship content]' serves to specify the set of container contents in a ship content. The property type '[container content] is carried **by** [container]' specifies the specific container carrying the goods of a container content. As said, containers are assumed to be reused and thus to carry many different contents in their lifetime. Likewise, the property type '[ship content] is carried **by** [ship]' specifies the specific ship carrying the goods of a ship content.

There are two additional property types that may be interesting for the operational activities in the enterprise GloLog. One concerns the ship with which a particular sea transport is executed. The other concerns the container with which a particular land transport is executed. Both property types can be derived from existing types. Here are the formal Derived Fact Specifications in DEMOSL (cf. Chap. 21):

the ship **of** [sea transport] **is** [ship] ≡ [sea transport] regards [ship content] **and** [ship content] **is** contained **in** [ship]

the container **of** [land transport] **is** [container] ≡ [land transport] regards [container content] **and** [container content] **is** contained **in** [container]

18.5 The Implementation of GloLog

When comparing the essential model of GloLog, as far as we have revealed it in the preceding sections, with the narrative description in Sect. 18.2, two things catch the eye. One is the quite remarkable difference between the concepts on which the narrative description is based and the ones on which the essential model is built. Probably most notable are the concepts 'container content' and 'ship content'. We consider this matter to be sufficiently dealt with in Sects. 18.3 and 18.4. The other notable issue is the almost ungraspable way in which the essential model is implemented. This holds in particular for the allocation of authorisations to the various stakeholders (including the possible delegations) and for the many documents that serve to facilitate the communication between the stakeholders. We will try to clarify them subsequently.

Table 18.2 Global (left) and detailed (right) ADT of the GloLog organisation

T/P	01	02	03	04	05	06	07	08	09	10	11	12	13	14	15	16	17
customs							A										
ship broker																	
terminal office																	
shipping agent		A	A														
supplier				A	A							A		A			
shipping company						A									A	A	
stevedore																	
land transporter								A									
IES	A								A	A	A		A				A

T/P	TK07/rq	TK07/ac	TK16/rq
supplier	A	A	
shipping agent	D	D	D
IES			A

While reading the narrative description in Sect. 18.2, one gets a picture about who is responsible for what, that appears to be quite misleading, namely, rather different from what the essential model tells us. In order to investigate the issue, we present the global ADT (cf. Chap. 21) of the GloLog organisation in Table 18.2 (left side). On the horizontal axis, the distinct actor roles (AR01–AR17) are listed, and on the vertical axis are the stakeholders (as shown in Fig. 18.1, except the client because the actor roles filled by this stakeholder are outside the SoI). Note that the stakeholders are complete enterprises (companies) instead of functionaries, like in the example ADT in Chap. 21. This explains already the fact that several actor roles are filled by the same enterprise.

An "A" at the crossing of a column (actor role) and a row (enterprise) means that subjects in the enterprise are the primary authorised fillers of the actor role. These allocations can quite straightforwardly be deduced from the narrative description, while having the CM in mind. What strikes one probably most, is that the rows 'ship broker', 'terminal office', and 'shipping agent' do not contain an "A". Regarding the terminal office, this is not surprising because the terminal office is not a distinct enterprise but a housing facility for employees of several enterprises. Most allocations are straightforwardly deducible from the narrative description, but some need further illumination.

The "A" at the crossing of column AR16 and row 'stevedore', means that the stevedore is considered to be the authorised filler of actor role AR16. However, this allocation is questionable since there are two opposing statements in the narrative description. In Sect. 18.2.3, we find the sentence: "Upon presentation of the CMR and Waybill or delivery order, the stevedore loads the container onto the delivery truck, whereafter the driver drives to IES". This sentence could be considered in conflict with the sentence "To this end, the shipping agent makes agreements with the land transporter about which container must be picked up where and at what time, and supplies the land transporter with the documents for picking up the containers from the stevedore", in Sect. 18.2.2. The question thus is whether 'picking up' a container implies loading the container on the truck or not. The narrative description provides no conclusive answer. Therefore, the question can only be answered by validating the two statements in practice. So, either the "A" at the crossing of column AR16 and row 'stevedore' is correct or the "A" should be moved to the crossing with row 'land transporter'.

Regarding the ship broker and the shipping agent, they clearly fill mainly informational or documental actor roles (informing others, handling documents, etc.). Only the shipping agent appears to have also delegated authorisations, two by the supplier and one by IES. They are represented in the detailed ADT in Table 18.2 (right).

The first delegation of authority by the supplier concerns ordering Customs to release (the containers of) purchases, so performing acts [TK07/rq]. It can be deduced from the pieces of text "The shipping agent takes care of the handling of the containers by Customs", and "Using the GD, Customs checks the correctness of the specified data on the Customs documents supplied by the shipping agent, and inspects, if thought opportune, the content of the containers. If the data do not exactly correspond, the shipping agent must provide an explanation. If everything is in order, Customs sends a release statement together with stamped Customs documents to the shipping agent, who then informs IES which containers have been released", in Sect. 18.2.3. The question, however, is whether the shipping agent and the supplier (and Customs as the executor of transactions TK07 for that matter) are aware of it.

The second delegation of authority by the supplier concerns the acceptance of purchase releases by Customs, that is, the performing of acts [TK07/ac]. It can be deduced from the sentence "If everything is in order, Customs sends a release statement together with stamped Customs documents to the shipping agent, who then informs IES which containers have been released", in Sect. 18.2.3. Clearly, the primary authorised party is the supplier, because AR02 is rightly the initiator of transactions TK07. For practical reasons, however, the accept act in these transactions is delegated to the shipping agent.

The delegation of authority by IES concerns requesting the land transporter to pick up containers at the premises of the stevedore, that is, the performing of acts [TK16/rq]. It can be deduced from the sentence "Based on the planning of IES, the shipping agent gives transportation instructions to the land transporter", in Sect. 18.2.3. As discussed earlier, a planning is not an ontological product but a set of requests to complete land transports, each having a specific production time.

The other implementation issue that makes it hard to comprehend fully the operations in the GloLog organisation is the many documents that serve to facilitate the communication between the stakeholders. Let us, therefore, investigate the main document kinds that are mentioned in the narrative description in Sect. 18.2 and try to indicate their role in the identified transaction kinds.

Client Order Form
A document of this kind is produced for every sale. The submitting (by the client) and receiving (by IES) of a filled out client order form is considered to count as performing the act [TK01/rq] in transactions TK01 (sale completing). Such a request is presumably followed by a tacitly performed promise.

Supply Order Form
A document of this kind is produced for every purchase. The submitting (by IES) and receiving (by the supplier) of a filled out supply order form counts as performing the act [TK02/rq] in transactions TK02 (purchase completing), presumably followed by a tacitly performed promise.

Shipment Form
A document of this kind is produced for every shipment, which corresponds one-to-one with a purchase. It is created by the supplier, and it contains information about the purchased goods and the containers in which they are stored. There are two sub-kinds of the shipment form: Waybill and Bill of Lading. On a Waybill, the customer is mentioned (in our case: IES) as the owner of the goods. On a Bill of Lading, no owner of the shipment is mentioned, which means that the bearer of the document is considered to be the owner. Produced by the supplier, shipment forms are used specifically by actors AR07 (Customs) and actors AR15 (land transporters).

Manifest

A document of this kind is produced by the shipping company for every ship content. In a manifest, all goods in all shipments on board are listed, including their article number (as used by the supplier), as well as the numbers of the Waybills or the Bills of Lading of all shipments.

General Declaration (GD)

A document of this kind is produced for every ship content by the ship broker, on the basis of the copy of the manifest that it has got. Basically, a general declaration is a list of the numbers of the Waybills or Bills of Lading of the included shipments. The GD is specifically used by Customs.

Pre-arrival Notices (PaN)

A document of this kind is produced for every ship content by the ship broker, presumably also on the basis of the copy of the manifest that it has got. A copy is sent to the parties that have already also got a copy of the manifest. It is unclear what need the PaN serves.

Customs Document

A document of this kind is produced for every container content by the shipping agent, on the basis of the applicable shipment forms and general declaration. Presumably, the document is sent to Customs. One may consider the sending (by the shipping agent) and the receiving (by Customs) of the Customs document of a container content as the request of a customer (in this case: IES) to release the container contents in a purchase, thus as performing the act [TK07/rq]. Note that a TK07 concerns all container contents in a purchase.

Delivery Order

A document of this kind is produced by the ship broker for every container content in a shipment with a Bill of Lading. The truck driver needs it to get the corresponding container from the stevedore. For shipments with a Waybill, presenting a copy of it suffices, provided the truck driver can identify herself/himself. One may consider presenting the delivery order or Waybill by the truck driver to the stevedore as requesting to load the container on the truck, thus to perform the act [TK16/rq].

CMR

A document of this kind is produced for every container content by the shipping agent, presumably on the basis of the manifest. The CMR is an obligatory European land transport document.

In the discussion of the kinds of documents above we have indicated whether the handing over of a document appears to (or seems to) count as performing a coordination act (or C-act). In such cases, a part of the document would represent (C- and P-) facts that are made known to the settler of the related C-event though the with-clause of the when-clause of the action rule that applies to settling the C-event. Unfortunately, we cannot be more precise about it, because the Action Model (AM) of the GloLog organisation is lacking.

All other parts of the discussed documents concern either facts that are taken into account in the assess parts of the action rules in the AM (cf. Chap. 21), or facts that are not used at all, and thus redundant. Again, we cannot be more precise, because the AM is lacking.

The interstriction structure (cf. Fig. 18.9) comprises three access links. The link from AR11 to TK01 appears to be implemented by sharing the client order forms between the sale completer and the purchase controller. The implementation of the access link from AR12 to TK03 is unclear. The narrative description only tells us that loaded containers are brought to the location of the shipping company. Note that there must be in addition some kind of overall agreement between IES and the shipping companies that the latter take care of the sea transport of these containers. The link from AR13 to TK14 is implemented by providing AR13 with the manifest of a ship content and possibly also the pre-arrival notices. There are actually many more access links, namely to external (multiple) transaction kinds. However, these are omitted for the sake of simplicity.

18.6   Solving the Current Problems and Failures

In Sect. 18.2.5, the current operational problems and failures are presented. Also without the help of the essential model of the GloLog organisation, it is not very difficult to suggest sensible and effective changes in the organisation in order to drive out the current malfunctions. Common sense immediately tells us that it must be able to reduce the number of involved parties and the number of document kinds. But when it comes to selecting the parties to be excluded and the document kinds to be removed, and to fully justify the proposed changes as well, one needs a firm grip to hold. And there is no firmer grip than the essential model, for the simple reason that it abstracts from the things that one wants to change.

Thus, any implementation of the GloLog organisation that is derived systematically from the essential model, will do the job, and will in addition sharply clarify who is responsible for what (and which competences are needed to bear the responsibility), as well as why the actors need the information they have access to. Moreover, the business processes are already optimised at the ontological level, as illustrated by the PSDs in Sect. 18.4. Of course, there are always practical issues one has to handle. For example, there may be huge resistance against abandoning the pre-arrival notices or the CMR, as well as against skipping the involvement of the ship broker and the shipping agent. Be that as it may, the improvement target that was mentioned in Sect. 18.2.5, namely that the receipt of the corresponding documents should at least be 7 days before the arrival of a container in the harbour of Rotterdam, can be met easily by the following measures:

- Make the contents of the transaction banks (including the external ones that we have left out for the sake of simplicity) accessible to all actors in the SoI as determined in the preceding sections.
- Only communicate by means of the existing documents (like the Waybill, the Bill of Lading and the CMR) if it is legally obligatory.

- Automate all communication as far as possible. Then the ship broker and the shipping agent will automatically disappear from the picture. As for the shipping agent, the assigned delegations (cf. Sect. 18.5) can be taken back without problems.

In addition, the problems that are represented by Figs. 18.4, 18.5, 18.6, and 18.7 are all of a purely informational nature. Therefore, they will be solved by taking the measures suggested above.

18.7   Conclusions

The case of the GloLog enterprise, from which we started the analysis and the discussion of possible improvements, is certainly outdated. Nowadays, global logistics operations are automated to a very large extent, both in terms of the physical handling of containers, and in terms of the communication between the involved parties and the storage of data. The point is, however, whether the particular implementation of the processes that one has chosen and installed, can be justified as the best one that could have been chosen. This is quite another story.

Founding the GloLog exercise on the 'outdated' implementation has made it anyhow easy to reveal the essential model of the GloLog organisation, while following the OER method (cf. Chap. 12). One of the outcomes that may be startling for many readers is the presence of four 'loosely coupled' distinct business processes, because of their incompatible case cycles. Although the most common way of understanding the logistic process is the one that is shown in Fig. 18.1, this is a fallacious representation. The 'decouplings', as presented in the CSD (cf. Fig. 18.8), must anyway exist in any implementation, but they may be hidden.

The narrative description in Sect. 18.2 hardly clarifies authorisation and delegation, which means that in the current 'outdated' practice, it must be quite unclear to many involved parties who is responsible for what (if they would give the issue a thought). Although one may wish otherwise, this indefiniteness is not 'automatically' removed by a new state-of-the-art implementation.

In order to keep the analysis and the discussion of the case GloLog within limits, they have been less extensive than those in the other exercises (cf. Chaps. 13–17). Also the absence of payments between the involved enterprises may have surprised (business-oriented) readers. Yet, we believe that the analysis of the case GloLog and its results convincingly clarify that DEMO can very well be applied to what one commonly calls 'real life' situations. For certain, the chapter demonstrates that ontological thinking can provide unexpected and deep insights.

Reference

1. den Hengst-Bruggeling, M. (1999). *Interorganizational coordination in container transport.* Doctoral thesis in Faculty of TPM. Delft: Delft University of Technology.

Chapter 19
Real-Life Applications of DEMO

Abstract A number of real-life applications of the DEMO methodology are presented, varying in size and impact, and in the industrial area that they concern. The selected applications are: (1) The VISI Standard in Civil Engineering, (2) Getting firm grip on software development, (3) Agile Law Making, (4) Enterprise Transformation, (5) Designing Data Warehouses, (6) Enterprise Ontology based Process Simulation, (7) Designing Digital Document Archives, and (8) Air France KLM Cargo—post merger decision making. All applications are reported in the STARR framework.

19.1 Introduction

In the following sections, seven appealing real-life applications of DEMO are presented and discussed. They are selected from a much larger collection of interesting practical studies. The ones that could not be included in this chapter are published on a freely accessible website (being announced on www.ee-institute.org). The following DEMO-applications are discussed in this chapter (their respective authors appearing in brackets):

Section 19.2   The VISI Standard in Civil Engineering
                (Hans Mulder, Niek Pluijmert)
Section 19.3   Getting firm grip on software development (Joost Vermolen)
Section 19.4   Agile Law Making (Mariette Lokin)
Section 19.5   Enterprise Transformation (Eduard Babkin)
Section 19.6   Designing Data Warehouses (Peter Kuipers, Henri Oostindie, Peter Kurstjens)
Section 19.7   Enterprise Ontology based Process Simulation (Sergio Guerreiro)
Section 19.8   Designing Digital Document Archives (Rob Stapper, Peter Hoving)
Section 19.9   Air France KLM Cargo—post merger decision making (Martin Op 't Land)

All applications are reported in the STARR framework (Situation, Task, Approach, Results, Reflection):

© Springer Nature Switzerland AG 2020   409
J. L. G. Dietz, J. B. F. Mulder, *Enterprise Ontology*, The Enterprise Engineering
Series, https://doi.org/10.1007/978-3-030-38854-6_19

The *Situation* in which the case is positioned. It includes, but is not limited to, the context of the case organisation (e.g. market, competition), the characteristics of the case organisation (facts and figures), its challenges and opportunities, important stakeholders, the reason why the project was initiated, a history of earlier attempts, etc.

The *Task* that has been conducted. It includes, but is not limited to, the goals and objectives of the project, its budget and timelines, special requirements, the roles of the various stakeholders, etc.

The *Approach* taken to conduct the task. It includes, but is not limited to, the method used, the various steps in this method, the paradigm or underlying philosophy of the approach/method, the products and deliverables, the way in which the project was planned and managed, the risk management approach and the tools used, etc.

The *Results* of the project. It includes, but is not limited to, the actual benefits for the case organisation and the stakeholders, a cost/benefit analysis, the extent to which the case organisation was actually transformed, etc.

A *Reflection* on the case. It includes, but is not limited to, a discussion about the faced challenges, the way in which the existing methods, frameworks, etc., aided in dealing with these challenges, omissions and limitations found, thoughts on how to 'fix' such omissions and limitations, etc.

Right after the section heading, the name and email address of the contributor (s) is/are mentioned, so that one can directly make contact if one desires to do so. Note that always the DEMO-4 terminology is used (cf. Chap. 12), also if earlier versions of DEMO are actually   applied. All references to publications are put together at the end of the chapter.

19.2   The VISI Standard in Civil Engineering

Hans Mulder (hans.mulder@viagroep.nl) and Niek Pluijmert (pluijmert@inqa.nl)

> *DEMO is a miracle of simplicity*
> (Henk Schaap, project manager VISI)

Situation

VISI is the name of an initiative in the practice of civil engineering in The Netherlands, taken in 1996 in order to improve the communication between the parties in large civil engineering projects (building highways, bridges, tunnels, airports, seaports, dikes, etc.). There have been two unsuccessful predecessors with the same goal. The first one, in the 1970s, tried to set standards for the forms (order forms, invoice forms, forms of various progress reports, etc.) that were exchanged between the parties in a project. Because a solid ground for evaluating form designs was lacking, every party considered their design the best. Therefore, the initiative became a failure. The second attempt, performed in the 1980s, tried to develop and set an EDI standard for data exchange. In hindsight, one can say that both initiatives failed because the abstraction level was too low. In the so-called VISI core team who took the third initiative, in 1996, the key players in civil engineering projects were represented, including Rijkswaterstaat (RWS), a Dutch governmental agency, the main customer in such projects.

Task

The task that the core team had set itself in 1996 was to develop a standard for the communication between the parties in civil engineering projects so that the set-up time of these projects would be shortened considerably, and that failures during the execution, due to miscommunication, would be minimised. It was also recognised that supporting software should be developed so that the effort for all parties to adopt the standard would be as little as possible. Because the two earlier failures had a severe negative impact on the mutual trust of the parties and their willingness to go on a new expedition, utmost attention had to be given to create broad support and to keep everyone on board during what would certainly be a long and difficult journey. But the core team had no clue yet how to go about it.

Approach

In the fall of 1997, several members of the core team attended an introductory course in DEMO at Delft University of Technology. In a short meeting afterwards with the authors of this book, the first step was set towards a long-term collaboration and to the adaptation of DEMO as the methodology for developing the VISI standard. Based on previous experiences, we were able to convince the core team that it is possible to have one general collaboration model for all civil engineering projects, something that was not believed to be possible because of the large variety of building works.

The concepts that convinced them are the ones introduced in Chap. 8: the actor role (notably it being the unit of authority, responsibility, and competence) and the transaction kind (as a standard pattern for coordinating work).

The next important issue was to devise the path towards the adoption of the rather revolutionary new way of thinking about conducting civil engineering projects. To this end, a careful plan was made to introduce the new concepts in the civil engineering world, and explanatory visualisations were made by professional illustrators. One of them is shown in Fig. 19.1.[1] It was used to clarify the 'role-playing' when executing a DEMO model. The different cap kinds represent the different actor roles that the subjects have been assigned.

---

[1]Taken from https://www.bimloket.nl/VISI

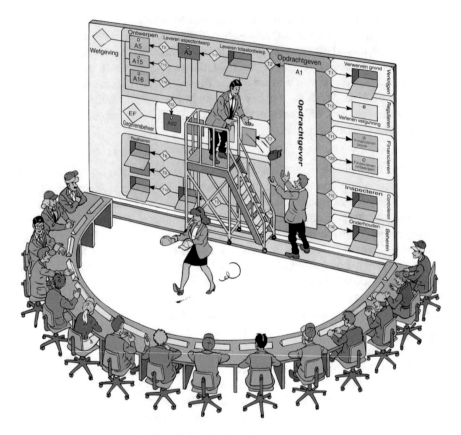

Fig. 19.1 Example of a clarifying VISI illustration

Results

The main result of the efforts of the core team is that VISI is used in practice as an open standard (for over 15 years now), not only in large civil engineering projects, but increasingly also in house-building projects, and even beyond the area of civil and constructional engineering. This is not surprising, since the core of VISI, the transaction pattern is a general pattern of human cooperation, independent of the kind of products that the cooperation is about. A key advantage that users recognise and appreciate is that the usage of VISI, supported by one of the software packages, provides one with a complete and well-structured archive of the actual course of a project. VISI-archives are treasures of data, amenable to various analyses, for example through process mining, with the aim to improve the conducting of future projects. Since 2012, VISI is also the base of an international standard (ISO 29481-2).

Several software companies have developed VISI supporting software packages. One of the interesting outcomes of the analysis (through process mining) of the VISI-archives produced by these software packages is that not all of them followed strictly the transaction pattern. In other words, the developers neglected part of the requirements. Obviously, these failures are corrected.

Initially, only the standard transaction pattern (cf. Fig. 8.8) was adopted by the core team, and consequently included in the requirements to the software developers. Fortunately, in the course of time, it has become clear to the managing institute of the VISI standard that the complete transaction pattern, that is, including the revocation patterns (cf. Fig. 8.10) should be adopted and forcibly implemented in the supporting software packages. In VISI 3.0, this will have been accomplished.

The application of VISI has proven to result in the completion of large projects within time and budget. Recent illustrating examples are the building of the main railway stations in Rotterdam and Delft (www.architectuur.nl 2-2015). Some key publications concerning VISI are: [1–3].

Reflection

VISI offers a communication standard that provides insight into the organisation of construction projects, in particular into the various actor roles (responsibilities) and the project structure. The benefits of VISI include considerable reductions of operational costs, lead time, and failure costs. The standard provides clarity, certainty, and steering aid. Management and employees always have access to up-to-date reports such as time sheets and weekly reports.

The practical usefulness of the DEMO transaction pattern is beyond doubt. However, the simplifications that were initially made to it by the VISI core team, have led to some frustration in practice: 'obvious' and 'natural' courses of action in human cooperation appeared not to be possible. As Albert Einstein or William of Ockham (the right source is unclear) said: everything should be made as simple as possible, but not simpler. Fortunately, the problems will be solved in a future version of VISI.

Another cause of resistance and misunderstanding with respect to VISI is the initial overemphasis on the layout of the messages by which the coordination acts in the transaction pattern are performed. It has led to the widespread misunderstanding that VISI is foremost a document exchange and management system. Certainly, it can also be used as such, but it has a much larger potential: it is a theoretically well-founded and practically highly useful means of organising human cooperation and decision making in large and complex projects. Supported by a proper software package, the resulting VISI-archive offers full transparency of the actual course of a project, also in case the project managers would have liked less. . .

19.3   Getting Firm Grip on Software Development

Joost Vermolen (joost.Vermolen@formetis.nl)

Situation

In 2012, ForMetis was asked to support one of the largest energy players in the Netherlands: Endinet. Endinet operates in the energy market for the supply of gas and electricity to citizens and enterprises. A transition is underway where the energy grid operator and energy supplier are split up into different legal entities due to EU regulations.

There is a need for a central shared information repository system, called Central Connections Register, which captures all customer information and contracts for gas and electricity. The grid operator and the energy supplier, as well as some subcontractors, must have access to the system.

Task

The existing system, which was supplied by ForMetis in an earlier stage to support the process of connecting clients to the energy network (gas and electricity) should evolve into a new system that supports this need. The situation seemed to be a good starting point to introduce the Enterprise Engineering approach (cf. Chap. 2). At the time, ForMetis was working on the implementation of the DEMO engine [4] to generate application software directly from the DEMO models (cf. Chap. 12) of an enterprise. The task ahead seemed to be ideal for introducing and testing the engine.

The task was to rebuild the existing system but keep its data intact and redesign it to meet the new regulations and to support the workforce of the organisation with a workflow that could be fully audited by the supervisor and that would guide the employees through the new way of working. It would be a challenging task because the timeline was strict; little room was left for making mistakes.

Approach

When the project was initiated, several key players of the organisation were trained to elicit the functional specifications for the overall system that met their future needs. This was quite a time-consuming task with room for ambiguity due to a lack of supervision that oversees the problems that may arise. There was also no objective method to measure the quality of the specifications. Next, project management was based on the Waterfall Model where specifications are frozen after they have reached their final stage. This made the timeline even more challenging.

When the implementation phase began, we found that turning a "functional description into a functioning construction" was hard to accomplish. This is where the project needed some pragmatism. The way to solve these misfits was to gradually turn project management into a more agile approach with close links between the implementors and the staff that provided the functional specification. This approach helped enormously to speed up the implementation phase; however, there was a problem that budgets based on supplier offers regarding the earlier functional specifications, were no longer realistic regarding the amount of hours spent.

Results

Relying on the DEMO methodology during the implementation of our part of the system has helped us to get a good overall view of the functionalities that should be supported and the possible pitfalls that we had to overcome. The outcome is that we were the only partners that delivered the functioning system on time despite the short timeframe. During this stage there were serious doubts by the project manager whether our approach was the right choice, but when all parts were put together he had to admit that it really worked. The main publications are [5] and [6].

After the project was completely delivered, we got complimented for both the flexibility of the system and the rigidness of the guidance for the employees to use the system. The department manager told us they could just pick new staff and they would be up and running after half-day's training.

The DEMO Engine holds track of every step in every transaction, which makes auditing easy. Endinet appeared to be the first grid operator that fully complied with the reporting requirements of the governing bodies.

In addition, we conducted a process mining project and found that there were some stages in the overall process that needed attention. Among others, we found that the 'Chinese Wall' between executer and controller had been breached, and that parts of the process were not logical, even contra-productive. Fixing the flaws led to several efficiency gains.

Reflection

The lack of a method to safeguard the quality of functional specifications mentioned earlier, can be tackled by DEMO. In later research and practical experience we have found that generating a DEMO model based on these specifications can help to find omissions and ambiguous situations.

Creating an efficient and elegant user-interface that supports the transaction pattern (cf. Chap. 8) is a challenge and will remain so if we reflect on the past and current implementation. With the help of UX-UI experts and suggestions from clients, we are still seeking for a generic solution that we can use in forthcoming projects.

On numerous occasions we got "squashed" between user's wishes and the need for a consistent software construction. Users often wanted pragmatic shortcuts that led to conflicts between the Coordination World and the Production World. Keeping those worlds clearly separated, or wisely connected by the DEMO Action Model (cf. Chap. 12), helps to overcome these misfits.

Introducing Enterprise Engineering, in particular the DEMO methodology works only if you fully understand the benefits, and if you are able to communicate the benefits with the manager(s) who are responsible for keeping the project on time and within budget.

We see it as a reward for our work, that for the ongoing integration of the total system, Endinet has asked Formetis to take care of it, because we could do it in such an elegant and flexible way.

19.4   Agile Law Making

Mariette Lokin (m.h.a.f.lokin@vu.nl)

Situation

A large part of Dutch legislation is implemented in ICT systems. Due to the massiveness that large government agencies have to deal with, the use of ICT to perform their statutory tasks—further referred to as *digital execution*—has become indispensable. In order to implement the continuous flow of new legislation quickly and efficiently in their ICT systems, various methods of systems development are used, under the heading *knowledge-based working*. The essence of this approach is that knowledge from legislation (rules, data, process steps) is no longer hard coded and thus 'locked up' in the system, but shaped into knowledge models, forming the basis for modular ICT services. In doing so, government agencies aim to increase the agility of the ICT systems and thus of the implementation of legislation.

In recent decades, a great deal of research has been carried out to find ways of supporting knowledge-based working, for example by displaying knowledge in a formalised way, supporting the conversion to automatically executable specifications. However, a method for clarifying the meaning of the legislation is still lacking.

Task

The goal of the performed PhD research [7] was to develop an approach for agile law making, not only aiming at legislation as a product, but also as a process. This led to the following central research question: *To what extent and in what way can digital execution of legislation by national government agencies be taken into account in the legislative process?*

Agile legislation has two dimensions: (1) a product that is clear in terms of structure and meaning, to allow the knowledge required for digital execution to be easily distilled from it; (2) a process that integrates the design of digital execution.

These dimensions have been elaborated in an approach for clarifying the meaning of legislation, consisting of three elements: a *language model*, a *legislative vocabulary*, and the application of *linked data*. Furthermore, possible supporting tools and adjustments in the co-operation between actors in the legislative process, necessary for successful application of the approach, have been described. This case report focuses on the language model, which is partly based on DEMO.

Approach

Legislation is structured in chapters, paragraphs, articles, article parts, etc. (referred to as *formal structure*) and in content elements, such as types and structure of legal norms (referred to as *material structure*). With regard to the content elements, it contains many ambiguities and implicit relations, impeding the conversion to digital execution. The question is whether it is possible to clarify this meaning in the process of drafting legislation, and in the text of the legislation itself (not only in explanatory memoranda).

In order to answer this question, an analysis of the formal and the material structure of legislation has been made, based on the Dutch design requirements for law drafters, and on literature. As the material structure is essential for the design of ICT-driven decision making, it has been further elaborated on the basis of the fundamental legal relations theory of Hohfeld [8] and (its application in) approaches for requirements engineering. As these focus on the legal relations in legislation, another method was needed to distinguish elements related to process and data in legislation. In this, DEMO was found to be very suitable, as legislation bears all the elements of *performa*, *informa*, and *forma* (cf. Chap. 11). Based on the analysis, a language model has been created through which the wording of legal concepts in legislation can be provided with a coloured label (marked as *annotation*) that unambiguously expresses these concepts. The shades of the colours used for the labels match the colours of performa (red), informa (green), and forma (blue).

Results

The language model has been applied to several types of legal provisions in (amongst others) Dutch tax legislation, Aliens Act and Civil and Penal Code. The annotations proved to ameliorate the insight into the meaning of the legislation, both for purposes of digital execution and for manual execution (drafting of instructions, manuals etc.).

In the PhD research, the model has been applied using a regular word processor (Word), which sets limits to its application. It requires multiple acts by the law drafter and is therefore time consuming. However, software applications and techniques are available that may serve as a basis for efficient and effective use of the model. The thesis shows how they can be (further) developed into a special *law editor*, enabling optimal use of the language model.

Reflection

Application of the language model—and through this, the principles of DEMO—in the legislative process, can help to improve the translation of legislation into specifications for ICT systems and work processes. The challenge for successfully implementing the model lies mainly in the changes it requires in the law-drafting process. The worlds of law drafters and system designers are still 'physically' and 'mentally' separated: there is no structural and direct co-operation between these two parties.

Also in the administrative and political arena, the influence of technology on the design and execution of legislation—to be regarded as an independent technological rationality in the process—is not always valued. It is necessary to bridge this gap between 'language' and 'technology', by establishing a different way of working among the various actors in the legislative process. The research report [7] also contains an approach for this, based on agile design methods in ICT.

The need for change is acknowledged by the Dutch Council of State (the highest advisory board on legislation of the government), which in a recent advice on digitisation of government (citing the PhD research) emphasised its importance for safeguarding a legitimate and just government performance.

19.5   Enterprise Transformation

Eduard Babkin (eababkin@hse.ru)

Situation and Task

This contribution concerns a small private company providing various car repairing services to individual car owners in a large industrial city in Russia. The position of the company is stable enough to think about change. The company management would like to have a reliable method of supporting the related decision making. It was proposed to evaluate several transformation alternatives using generic principles of agile enterprise transformation [9–11] and DEMO (cf. Chap. 12). The transformation towards an agile enterprise should include the design and evaluation of several transformation scenarios that will strengthen its position in the market, open new business opportunities, and improve the economic figures.

Approach

Given the objectives above, a combined approach was proposed in order to transform the present structure of the enterprise, namely a combination of DEMO and the theory of transaction costs [12], to have a single and quantitative approach. For estimating the transaction costs, an extension to DEMO was developed: the Transaction Cost Table. On the basis of this table, the CSD (cf. Chap. 12) was extended to indicate the costs for each actor role and each transaction kind. At the border of the organisation, the total costs of the transformation are specified as well. The result is the extended CSD of the current (AS-IS) enterprise (Fig. 19.2).

Using a brainstorming technique, a set of eight semi-structured proposals for restructuring the company was produced. Further evaluation of the proposals was performed by the owners of the company. They selected four proposals for detailed modelling and analysis:

- Removing car washing from the services of the enterprise
- Becoming a car insurance agent
- Opening a spare parts store
- Starting to sell occasions

For each of the four selected proposals, a corresponding CM (cf. Chap. 12) was designed, as the TO-BE model. For a correct estimation of the incurred costs, a business analyst studied statistical data on the market segments of repair, insurance, car sales, and sales of car parts. For each proposal, a Transaction Cost Table was produced as well as the corresponding extended CSD. The resulting tables and diagrams were presented to the company's stakeholders. During the meeting, the forecasts of some types of costs were slightly adjusted, and the final versions of the models were taken as the basis for the selection of the best transformation variant. The final decision was to implement transformations needed for becoming (also) a car insurance agent. This option was recognised as the simplest one, and with the lowest implementation costs. The estimated increase in revenues was 8%.

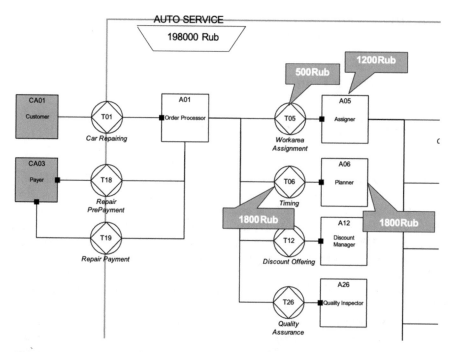

Fig. 19.2   Fragment of the extended CSD of the AS-IS enterprise model

Reflection

The budget of the project included the salary of one business-analyst, who used a set of general-purpose software tools. For drawing the DEMO diagrams, MS Visio was used. Costs calculations were produced in MS Excel. The project lasted 7 months with an average occupancy of the business-analyst of about 12 h per week. In 2017, the company successfully implemented the selected transformation option.

The concepts of DEMO and the abstraction levels were appreciated and fully accepted by the company stakeholders. The results of the cost estimation using the proposed approach were recognised as accurate and appropriate. The constructional changes took place in accordance with the proposed TO-BE DEMO model. The actual costs of restructuring are very close to the predicted values. From the modelling point of view, extensions to DEMO were proposed and a method for estimating costs of changes was developed.

Two typical situations were observed that occurred during the transformation. The first is that after a transformation involving many transaction kinds and actor roles, usually a new transaction kind was suggested: maintaining the enterprise activity in accordance with the DEMO model. It means that the company understood that after the transformation, it is necessary to spend effort and time on assuring that the enterprise's construction actually fits the TO-BE model. The second situation is that when transferring an internal transaction kind to the border (which means outsourcing the transaction kind to external actors), or even or removing it completely, new risks arise, and as a consequence, new transaction costs, such as the risks of litigation, the risk of loss of partners, etc.

19.6   Designing Data Warehouses

Peter Kuipers (peter.kuipers@live.nl), Henri Oostindie (henri.oostindie@nippur.nl), and Peter Kurstjens (peter.kurstjens@qosqo.nl)

Situation

The case concerns a pharmaceutical wholesale company for public pharmacies. It is going through a major transition due to the acquisition of another pharmaceutical wholesale company for hospital pharmacies and almost 100 new public pharmacies. From a small wholesale company with a low-experienced ICT organisation and a tailor-made ERP system to support sales, logistics, and procurement, it suddenly became a midsize wholesale company that needed to comply with new, severer regulations.

A stress test of the existing ERP system showed it would not be able to process the increased amount of sales order lines, almost twice the current volume, as a consequence of the acquisition. A project was started to completely change the supporting ICT application infrastructure. This infrastructure should be built around a standard ERP system with an ESB to integrate the different applications and a data hub to support the applications with the standardised and quality-insured data. Furthermore, a data warehouse needed to be developed to provide the organisation with accurate management information and also enable integration with the data hub for master data management.

Knowledge about the business processes and the way the custom-built ERP system was set up existed mainly in the heads of a few business experts. No documentation was available. The business culture was informal, no-nonsense, and pragmatic. Most project members were external. The technical management of applications, databases, and infrastructure was outsourced to third parties. Governance and project steering came from the board of the company.

Task

The task to be executed is the delivery of a data warehouse, data hub, and the support of the data migration and data cleansing of the overall program. It is assigned to the data team, a small project team within the overall program, which is also responsible for managing the master data. The business analysis has not been completed when development started. There is no overall functional design for the master data. Management does not take ownership and the deadlines are based on external factors, instead of on what would be realistic for the project and the organisation. Moreover, the budget was fixed by the board.

Approach

Enterprise Engineering is chosen as the paradigm to tackle the task, and DEMO was selected as the methodology (cf. Chap. 12). The first step is to create a CM of the whole organisation and to identify all master data objects. Since the business analysis is done parallel to the development, reverse engineering on the existing applications will be applied to gather information for filling in the FM (cf. Chap. 12). The FM is built with Sparx Enterprise Architect and the source systems are reverse engineered utilising automation tool Quipu,[2] supplied by QOSQO.[3] The required ETL code will be generated with Quipu also, making sure that overnight changes in the whole OTAP environment will be captured and information will directly be available for analysis. The data hub supports both the master data management and migration environment.

Results

With the start of the essence of the organisation with DEMO and the needed result for the data warehouse and concepts for the data hub, we had a solid foundation to create the needed structure with Sparx and the needed management information with Quipu, as well as the foundation and environment to be able to do effective master data management. Because of the lack of validation of the CM, the governance for the different concepts, their definitions and business rules, the parallel development, testing, and implementation, we were on the one hand flexible, but on the other constantly shooting at a moving target.

What we did achieve, however, was:

- Providing insight into the structure and the definitions of business information.
- Showing the lack of governance, whereas management and ownership of the business data are crucial.
- Providing insight into how master data objects are created, changed, and ended and who is responsible for which data. However, without actual ownership, the insight is not enough to make effective changes.
- Providing insight into data owners: what data am I responsible for, who can have access to the data, and to whom will the data be distributed to?
- A successful data migration, successful synchronisation of article and stock data between two ERP systems running in parallel, as well as providing information from the data warehouse solution to support process enhancement and bug fixing in the newly live ERP system.

Reflection

As is the case in many projects, the governance and approval steps are vital for good understanding and acceptance of the organisation. The force of moving on because of deadlines is also here a big pitfall. Without a validated CM, the use of the corresponding FM as the basis of the business warehouse is not a solid one. We should have insisted on validating the CM with the business before moving on.

As already mentioned, the major frustrating circumstances were that management did not take ownership, and that the deadlines were based on external factors instead of on what would be realistic for the project and the organisation.

---

[2]https://quipu.nl/

[3]http://www.datawarehousemanagement.org

19.7   Enterprise Ontology Based Process Simulation

Sérgio Guerreiro (sergio.guerreiro@tecnico.ulisboa.pt)

Situation

The case at stake is an agri-food industrial company focusing on the transformation of fresh fruits to preparations that are sold to other companies. Its clients are industries of milk-based products, ice creams, cakes, and beverages products.

To guarantee the product quality, fruit producers are subject to a ratification process before starting to supply fruit. Fruit passes through three stages: (1) raw material, (2) ingredients after raw material preparation, and (3) finished product after ingredients transformation.

Before the end consumer is reached, a complex value chain is executed including the actor roles of client, fruit producer, raw material receptionist, ingredient preparer (e.g. weighing and cleaning), ingredient transformer (e.g. mixing components, adding water, sugar or other products accordingly with the recipe), finished product transporter and storage company (when the agri-food company is not able to locally store all the production). The production starts when a client order is received (produce to order policy). Then, five stages are performed: receiving, supplying, ingredients preparation, ingredients transformation, and dispatch. Besides selling to other companies, a small part of finished products is directly sold to the end consumer.

Task

The project has been conducted to identify the following two objectives: (1) being able to simulate business transactions redesign that maximise value for the company, and (2) supporting management with an approach that is able to estimate the non-observable steps of operational business transactions.

The project involved students that were developing their master thesis on a one semester basis, and the main coordinator of the project.

Approach

Methodologically, a non-documented landscape was presented to the students. The operation of the company was demonstrated in the facilities along with the organisational structure, goals, and ICT main components. Moreover, face-to-face and electronic meetings were established to elicit the detailed requirements of the business processes. From here, the Universe of Discourse (UoD) was documented for future reference. No matter the effort done to clarify the UoD, we observed that an essential description able to avoid misunderstandings was lacking.

To address this limitation, it was decided that an ontological model of the UoD using DEMO will be designed. During the initial meeting to design the core business transactions, many design options were possible. This results from the nature of the previously enunciated problem, for instance, with regard to the client/supplier perspectives that led to an inconsistent information ownership. The DEMO models were presented in a workshop session where the advantages and pitfalls of each model were discussed. This discussion was facilitated by the essential description offered by DEMO. And, a final DEMO model was then reached as the result of group discussion.

Afterwards, the parameters for the simulation tool were estimated in an iterative process by the research team. At this stage, the company's knowledge about their past experiences was of key importance to estimate the main simulation parameters. To obtain this knowledge, non-structured questions were posed to the company, for instance, during the last year, how many trucks had problems while transporting the finish product to storage?

For the simulation tool, the following software solutions were used:

- http://www.graphviz.org/ for visualization
- APPLtoolkit—Approximate pomdp planning (appl) toolkit for processing of Partially Observable Markov Decision Processes, as available at https://github.com/petercaiyoyo/appl
- GNU Octave for results processing
- Matlab, from MathWorks, for processing the Markov Decision Processes

Results

The main results that were delivered to the organisation are: (1) the DEMO CM, consisting of a CSD and aTPT (cf. Chap. 12), of the main business transactions, relevant for stakeholders' awareness and discussion; and (2) two simulation tools to evaluate the delivered business transactions' value. The main publications for these results are: [13] and [14].

Reflection

The benefits obtained are manifold. The solution proposed for the company empowered the managers with pertinent information about the gaps of business transactions steps that occur during operation due to the occurrence of workarounds. In these circumstances, managers are able to decide about the future steps of the business transactions using a decision map that encompasses all the possible future combinations regarding the value delivered for the company. These results are possible due to the deep detail that is offered by the DEMO models, which constitutes a consistent set of business transactions prescribed for this specific organisation.

The attempted intersection between Enterprise Ontology and Operational Research shows that a discrete model of the core operation of the organisation allows for the application of already known approaches for estimation of future behaviour. It has been identified that stochastic approaches could offer a partial solution for the problem at hand, which could be further improved if combined with other solutions, for example, human decision.

The simulation tools still demand a large estimation effort that requires specialised human intervention. For future development, machine learning techniques that are able to estimate the configuration of business transaction behaviour might be considered. Data sets from operation of the business transactions performed by the organisation will be required to train, for example, a neural network. The overall proposed benefit is to minimise the error associated with the human estimation process.

19.8   Designing Digital Document Archives

Rob Stapper (r.stapper@belastingdienst.nl) and Peter Hoving
(pl.hoving@belastingdienst.nl)

Situation

The business processes in the Dutch Tax Office require information from documents
that reside in external document sources. These are physical documents and the
amount is huge. In order to make them more easily accessible to the business
processes, it was decided to create a local digital document archive containing copies
of relevant documents in PDF. Considering the amount of documents and the fact that
a large part of the source documents will never be accessed, it was also decided not to
scan all the documents in one big blow but to build the archive over time on an ad hoc
base. Each time when a document is needed that isn't available in the local digital
archive, a request is sent to the document source for a digitalised copy. The external
document source is willing to deliver the copies under the following conditions:

- A digitalised copy of a document is in principle only requested once.
- On delivery of the digitalised document, the source doesn't have to refer to the
  original request, so that the source can decide to send digitalised documents on
  their own initiative, to anticipate possible future requests.

Staff members in the business processes can subscribe to newly received
digitalised documents that comply with provided specifications. Once a new
digitalised document is received, all the subscribers, whose specifications the document complies with, will receive a message. This way they will be informed about
newly received relevant documents all the time. The requester of a digitalised
document from the source is automatically subscribed to documents with the same
specifications.

Task

The development team is a small team within an overall program. It is responsible
for the design and construction of the software for the interaction with the external
document source. There is a vague idea of the interaction with the external document
source, but the interaction messages with the external document source are
completely defined. There is no view on how to handle exceptional situations.
Business management is represented by a business analyst without any knowledge
of DEMO, but with thorough knowledge of the business requirements and the ability
to decide quickly on design issues.

Approach

Enterprise Engineering is chosen as the paradigm and DEMO as the methodology.
The analysis is done from a product-driven approach. Starting with an inventory of
the products to be delivered from within the scope, we worked our way back to the
products to be obtained from outside the scope, meanwhile recognising intermediate
products, each product eventually resulting in a transaction kind. This way, the
structure of the CM is determined by the products and their cohesion instead of some
process description.

For instance, one of the delivery products we found can be described as a 'copy of a at most one time at the external document source requested digital document copy'. Analysing this back resulted in the need for a 'digital document copy from the document source', a 'digital document copy database', a 'digital document copy request database', and a less obvious product: 'digital document copy recording', a service on behalf of the external document source.

One other delivery product we found can be described as a 'subscription to digital document copy receptions'. Analysing this one back made us realise that one product can result into the delivery of multiple other products over time. Therefore, we modelled it as a transaction kind that allows for it.

Results

Before starting the ICT implementation of the business processes, its complete essential model was produced: the CM, PM, FM, and AM (cf. Chap. 12), and accepted by the business owner. During the ICT implementation no extra essential business information was needed. This demonstrates the completeness of the DEMO methodology. Non-functionals like data sizes and the number of occurrences were added at the start of the ICT implementation.

The essential model was represented in Word, Power Point, and Excel. This way we would be more flexible. Since the project wasn't too big, manually keeping the model consistent would be doable. We also made a Function Point Analysis based on the essential model. It turned out to be quite straightforward.

The ICT-implementation was done in an agile way. The project was fully steered by the essential model. Every transaction kind led to a story that was to be built. Every transaction kind was tested and accepted individually by the business. There was no need for the business to wait for the complete project to be finished before testing the system functionally. How agile can it get? The project results are published in [15] as an example of a 'good place' project environment.

Reflection

Asking the business her acceptance of the essential model as a starting point for the ICT-implementation was a bit of a leap of faith for them. An essential model is a Business model, not an ICT-specific model. The essential model was used as starting point for the ICT development project, not as deliverable. A proper essential model provides all the essential domain knowledge for a domain-model-driven and agile ICT development. Not only can it be used for specifying the ICT products, it can also be used for steering the ICT development project.

The essential model looks like an interesting base for a Function Point Analysis (FPA) on the ICT system. Doing an essential model driven FPA could prevent counting over-complexity of the ICT-implementation as user functionality. This needs further investigation.

Manually maintaining a consistent Enterprise Ontology requires a lot of effort when the scope becomes bigger. Proper tooling is strongly recommended when the scope gets bigger.

19.9   Air France KLM Cargo: Post Merger Decision Making

Martin Op 't Land (martin.optland@capgemini.com)

Situation

In 2005, Air France Cargo and KLM Cargo merged into AFKL Cargo, which is now the no. 1 European carrier of international air freight, serving more than 400 destinations, with local presence in 100 countries. After the merger, the following activities were integrated into a single organisation: Sales, Customer Service (CSO), Revenue Management (RM), Marketing, and Network Development. The operational services (OPS) remained in the original organisations. Since then several attempts were made to move towards a joint ICT systems portfolio (ICT integration).

After some initial studies, the ICT integration was defined as the transition from the legacy environments of Air France (AF) and KLM (KL) to a new ICT environment, to be achieved in three steps: (1) the already integrated commercial organisation, (2) the OPS, (3) the remaining legacy systems.

Air freight is a dynamic business area. The booking of freight for a specific flight usually takes place shortly before departure: the last ones may come in a few hours before. Bookings are evaluated in a revenue management process for profitability. This industry characteristic leads to a highly dynamic process during the final days before flight departure, involving continuous communication and trade-offs between CSO, RM, and OPS. One of the key considerations in moving towards a new common revenue management system as a first step was the potential impact of that new revenue management system on the operational process in the last 24 h.

Task

To ensure well-founded decision making regarding the ICT integration, its basis should be neutral with respect to the merging parties, and enable comparison of the AS IS and TO BE situations. The way of thinking and modelling of DEMO (cf. Chap. 12) was selected, notably, for its implementation neutrality. This resulted in the following assignment: "Within 6 weeks, create neutral and sustainable DEMO-models of the Cargo business, for the current processes in AF and KL. Show in these models: (1) the essential business transaction kinds between commercial and operational domains, with a focus on the last 24 hours before departure; (2) the mapping of the actor roles and transaction kinds on the current AF and KL organisations; (3) the ICT systems that support these transactions; (4) the critical design and migration issues within the preferred scenario and their proposed solution."

Approach

To answer the practical questions about organisation and ICT implementations, actor roles and transaction kinds can be systematically mapped to organisational units and ICT applications [16], in order to find the situations where (1) an actor role is implemented in different organisational units, (2) an actor role is supported by different ICT systems, and (3) actor roles have demanding Quality of Business requirements.

To achieve sufficient buy-in of the resulting analysis on operational integrity, political and organisational sensitive issues should be open to discussion based on observed facts. To this end we developed a four-step approach: (1) creation and validation of the CM; (2) creation of "implementation mappings" of the AS IS situation for the organisation and the ICT systems; (3) identification of critical transaction kinds and its design and migration issues based upon multiple AS IS implementations of the organisation and the ICT systems, and a demanding Quality of Business; (4) evaluation and interpretation of the results in preparation for decision making.

A key role in drafting the CM and creating implementation mappings was played by business event traces. During international workshops, shop floor employees (from both AF and KL) systematically answered for each DEMO coordination step (e.g. "request", "promise") who in the organisation is addressing who, what ICT system is used in that step, and what Quality of Business is needed and what is delivered. This built a solid foundation for validating the DEMO models, the organisational accountabilities and responsibilities and the actual use of the ICT application landscapes.

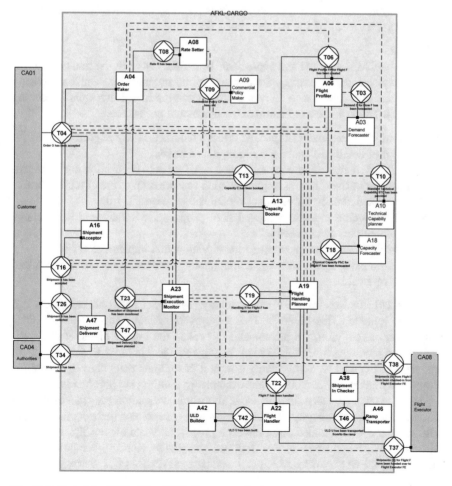

Fig. 19.3 Part of the CSD of the AFKL Cargo organisation

Results

Within the set time frame of 6 weeks and about 65 man-days, AFKL Cargo was able to reach consensus on (1) the DEMO CM as the first neutral and correct model of the essence of its business, and (2) the (very) different implementations of the CM in AF and KL, both in terms of organisation and ICT. Although AF and KL had not cooperated before the merger, the DEMO model appeared to be valid for both airlines. Figure 19.3 exhibits a part of the original CM, consisting of 49 transactor roles and 203 access links. It shows clearly the vital nature of transaction kind T13 (capacity booking), having no less than five initiating actor roles (A04, A06, A16, A19, A23). Note that the diagram in Fig. 19.3 is made in DEMO-2; it may therefore not directly be comprehensible to the reader.

Next, the six critical transactions kinds for the 24 h before departure were determined. By making for the corresponding actor roles actor sheets per organisation (AF or KL) and migration step (AS IS to several TO BE's), management was able to get a clear insight into the impact of the proposed scenario for implementing new ICT systems, and to detect opportunities for simplification of the cases where actor roles were filled by more departments than expected.

Reflection

The DEMO-CM is adopted and appreciated by AFKL Cargo as the first neutral and shared language for discussing the essence of the organisation, and for devising change scenarios. It was also delivered fast, yielding a high Return On Modelling Effort [16]. The key success factors of the conducted project are:

- The intrinsic preciseness of the CM offers a natural and shared stop criterion for the level of detail and enables unambiguous metrics.
- The CM is a neutral model without an AF or KL bias, allowing objective comparison of the different implementation scenarios up to the executive level.
- There existed already a well-educated DEMO-staff on KL-side.
- Directly listening to the operational floor people gave a solid and indisputable underpinning of the conclusions.
- The use of business event traces in identifying actual implementations.
- Early visualising of the results, facilitating communication on management and executive level.

Since DEMO is a 'rational' methodology, emotional and political issues can easily be ignored. This could be overcome by combining DEMO with 'softer' approaches. In addition, we recommend to explain the impact of the clarity, neutrality, and preciseness of DEMO to all key stakeholders in order to enable them to choose whether they want this clarity now and, if so, to let them actively determine the required boundary conditions, for example, in building support and buy-in.

The CM can serve as a 'language' for the whole integration program of AF and KL, including future mergers and alliances, possibly supplemented with the PM and FM, to ensure well-founded discussions on process and data ownership. The CM is also expected to contribute to well-founded business service and component identification in the SOA-world, which is a vital part of AF-KL's ICT strategy.

References

1. Mulder, J. B. F. (2006). Rapid enterprise design. In *Faculteit Elektrotechniek, Wiskunde en Informatica* (p. 160). Delft: Delft University of Technology.
2. Pluijmert, N. J. (2017). VISI revisited. *Lecture Notes in Business Information Processing, 284*, 89–98.
3. Terlouw, L., & Mulder, J. B. F. (2015). *Process mining met VISI*. The Netherlands: CROW Magazine.
4. van Kervel, S. J. H., Dietz, J. L. G., Hintzen, J., van Meeuwen, T., & Zijlstra, B. (2012). *Enterprise ontology driven software engineering*. In ICSOFT 2012. SciTePress.
5. Dudok, E., Guerreiro, S., Babkin, E., Pergl, R., & van Kervel, S. J. H. (2015). *Enterprise operational analysis using demo and the enterprise operating system*. Cham: Springer.
6. Hintzen, J., van Kervel, S. J. H., van Meeuwen, T., Vermolen, J., & Zijlstra, B. (2014). *A professional case management system in production, modeled and implemented using DEMO*. In 8th TEE Workshop: Transformation & Engineering of Enterprises; CBI conference. Geneva.
7. Lokin, M. H. A. F. (2018). Wendbaar wetgeven – de wetgever als systeembeheerder. In *Faculteit der Rechtsgeleerdheid* (p. 390). Amsterdam: Vrije Universiteit Amsterdam.
8. Hohfeld, W. N., & Cook, W. W. (1919). *Fundamental legal conceptions as applied in judicial reasoning, and other legal essays* (114 p.). New Haven, CT: Yale University Press
9. Op' t Land, M. (2006). *Applying architecture and ontology to the splitting and allying of enterprises: Problem definition and research approach*. Berlin: Springer.
10. Op 't Land, M., Proper, E., Waage, J., Cloo, C., & Steghuis, C. (2009). *Enterprise architecture—Creating value by informed governance* (Enterprise Engineering). Berlin: Springer Nature.
11. Tsourveloudis, N., & Valavanis, K. (2002). On the measurement of enterprise agility. *Journal of Intelligent and Robotic Systems, 33*(3), 329–342.
12. Commons, J. R. (1990). *Institutional economics: Its place in political economy*. New Brunswick, NJ: Transaction.
13. Guerreiro, S. (2019). (Re) designing business processes using Markov theory and constrained state, transition and actor role spaces. *International Journal of Knowledge-Based Organizations, 9*(2), 43–61.
14. Guerreiro, S. (2017). *Designing a decision-making process for partially observable environments using Markov theory*. Cham: Springer.
15. Stockbroekx, S. (2019). *The intelligent digital transformation*. Antwerp: Antwerp Management School.
16. Op 't Land, M. (2008). *Applying architecture and ontology to the splitting and allying of enterprises*. Delft: Delft University of Technology.

Chapter 20
DEMO Enhanced Method Engineering

Abstract In this chapter, a number of contributions are presented wherein DEMO is used in combination with an existing and well-accepted approach or activity in the broad field of enterprise engineering, all resulting in improving the quality of the other approach or activity. The selected contributions are: (1) DEMO enhanced Agile Software Development, (2) DEMO enhanced Lean Six Sigma (3) DEMO enhanced BPMN, (4) DEMO enhanced software testing, and (5) DEMO enhanced mining.

20.1 Introduction

Under the heading "DEMO Enhanced Method Engineering" we present in this chapter a number of applications of DEMO of which the common denominator is that they try to improve the effectiveness of some other approach in the broad field of enterprise engineering.

In Sect. 20.2, titled "DEMO Enhanced Agile Software Development", Marné de Vries (University of Pretoria, South-Africa) discusses how the DEMO CM (cf. Chap. 12) can help to keep overview in situations that are basically addressed by applying the story-card method, which is quite popular in agile methodologies. Without such an overview, one easily loses sight of what one is doing.

In Sect. 20.3, titled "DEMO Enhanced Lean Six Sigma", Roland Ettema (Open University, The Netherlands) discusses the improvement of analyses with Lean Six Sigma by combining it with DEMO, notably in finding the real causes of quality problems that appear from correlations-based analysis.

BPMN is a popular business modelling technique, but it suffers from a lack of formality. In Sect. 20.4, titled "DEMO Enhanced BPMN", Steven van Kervel (Formetis, The Netherlands) and Hans Mulder (VIAgroep, The Netherlands) discuss the current drawbacks of BPMN and explain how BPMN can profit from the combination with DEMO.

In Sect. 20.5, titled "DEMO Enhanced Software Testing", René Ceelen (Test Monitor, The Netherlands) explains convincingly the benefits of using the complete transaction pattern (cf. Chap. 8) to set up acceptance performance testing of appli-

© Springer Nature Switzerland AG 2020   431
J. L. G. Dietz, J. B. F. Mulder, *Enterprise Ontology*, The Enterprise Engineering
Series, https://doi.org/10.1007/978-3-030-38854-6_20

cation software. The study thereby demonstrates once more the practical value of the pattern: considering all steps, also the 'exceptional' ones, thus the decline and reject and the revocations.

Process mining is a popular analysis technique, but its application suffers from a lack of semantics of the 'mined' acts or events. In Sect. 20.6, titled "DEMO Enhanced Mining", Linda Terlouw (ICRIS, The Netherlands) shows how DEMO, in particular the complete transaction pattern (cf. Chap. 8), can help in solving this problem. She also appeals for further research of the subject in order to improve insight into organisational problems, notably logistics problems.

The Coordination Structure Diagrams (cf. Chap. 12) that are shown in Figs. 20.1 and 20.4, differ from the ones that are presented in Chap. 10. The reason is that they are expressed in DEMOSL-2, as presented in [1].

20.2   DEMO Enhanced Agile Software Development

Marné de Vries (marne.devries@up.ac.za)

20.2.1   Introduction

Enterprises of today need to ensure that they expand their information system landscape in a dynamic, but coherent and integrated way. Modern software development methodologies have already moved away from the autocratic, plan-driven approaches of the past towards light-weight and agile methodologies that are iterative and incremental. Since agile software development methods were originally intended for small teams, several challenges emerged when agile practices were applied at scale [2].

Enterprise size is one of many scaling factors that need to be considered when adopting an agile methodology at an enterprise. Agile methods and practices may have to be tailored for contexts where scaling factors apply, especially regarding the elicitation and management of requirements [2]. Since additional requirements elicitation practices should be incorporated when scaling factors apply, we believe that the DEMO CM (cf. Chap. 12) could be used to represent a blue print of enterprise operation, a foundation for eliciting requirements and developing supporting information systems. The purpose is not to demonstrate how the CM solves all challenges associated with different kinds of scaling factors. Rather, we acknowledge that the CM will only become useful within agile development contexts if one or more scaling factors apply, since more advanced requirements elicitation and management is needed when scaling factors apply. The CM has the potential to address three main criteria regarding requirements elicitation and management requirements when scaling factors apply: (1) representing the big picture,

(2) creating a shared understanding of the big picture, and (3) providing sufficient structure to ensure traceability of requirements [3].

Yet, agile development stakeholders have different roles and therefore require methods and practices that encourage collaboration, which are easy to understand, and relate to a concrete world [4], rather than the abstract concepts encapsulated in the CM. Hence, we prompted the need to develop an additional method, called the story-card method, to facilitate cognitive understanding of the abstract concepts of the CM [3].

20.2.2   The Story-Card Experiment

The story-card method starts with the story-paradigm of agile methodologies, extracting parts of the enterprise implementation story, linking the story parts to transaction kinds that are included in a CSD (cf. Chap. 12). We demonstrate the story-card method based on the following narrative for an existing enterprise implementation: "Every year, in consultation with the CEO, the enterprise designer selects members for an enterprise governance committee, capturing the selected members on our enterprise design application (EDA). The selected members should also indicate their willingness to become members of the committee. Later, the enterprise designer refers back to the information about selected members to request from every selected member to participate at a workshop. The purpose of the workshop (a periodic event) is that the entire committee evaluates enterprise governance concepts. When committee members arrive at the workshop, the enterprise designer first ensures that all members state their participation by signing an attendance register before the workshop can start. The workshop assistant also captures the attendance data on EDA. The selected committee members often become involved in other projects and then need to resign from the committee. In that case, the enterprise designer consults/communicates with the CEO to replace the committee member, i.e. re-selecting a member."

Based on the narrative, Fig. 20.1 provides a graphical representation of a CSD that consists of four original transaction kinds and four actor roles. Partially explaining the constructs, the actor role 'annual member selector' initiates transactions 'annual member selection'. The same actor role is also the executor of this transaction kind. Furthermore, it initiates transactions 'committee membership starting'. Often, created C- or P-facts (cf. Chap. 8) need to be shared with other actor roles (interstriction). Thus, additional access links are used to indicate access to transaction banks. For instance, the actor role 'governance concepts evaluator' needs to have access to the facts that are contained in the bank 'committee membership starting', since the governance concepts evaluator has to involve members that have already committed themselves to becoming members of the committee.

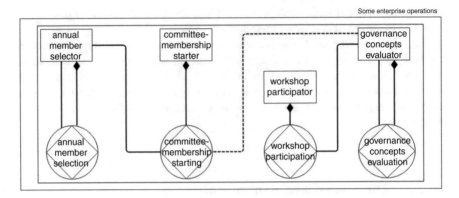

Fig. 20.1 Elementary CSD modelled for the scope "some enterprise operations"

In [3] we presented the story-card method, based on the same narrative. We also evaluated the story-card method, where 21 participants applied the method. The story-card method specifies 5 inputs and 10 method steps. The inputs are: (1) flat working space, such as table or white board, (2) A1 paper, (3) sticky notes of two different colours (red and yellow), (4) a black pen, (5) a colleague's inputs. The method steps:

- Step 1: Inquire from a colleague to explain a short process (about 10–15 activities) that he or she is involved in. Ensure that the process incorporates the use of information technology (e.g. the process followed from requesting vacation leave up to receiving notification about the approval of the request). Explain to your colleague that he or she needs to write the tasks (verb + noun) on yellow sticky notes and position the notes in sequence of occurrence, left to right on a flat working space (e.g. desk or white board).
- Step 2: Take a picture (photo) of the process. (Note that this step was only inserted to ensure that participants that were involved to evaluate the method provided evidence about the initial process.)
- Step 3: Discuss with your colleague all actor roles and write down composite actor roles on yellow sticky notes, adding a smiley face, keeping actor roles aside.
- Step 4: Explain the red-green-blue triangle of production acts (cf. Fig. 11.4), also explaining the universal transaction pattern for actor-collaboration regarding production acts (cf. Chap. 8).
- Step 5: Have a discussion with your colleague as to identify original production acts from his/her process (as mapped out with sticky notes in Step 4).
- Step 6: Classify (in collaboration with your colleague) remaining acts as coordination acts versus production acts.
- Step 7: Remove the original production act notes from the flat surface and phrase appropriate transaction kind descriptions (using adjective + noun) on red sticky notes that are positioned as diamonds on your A1 paper. Collapse initial production act notes underneath re-phrased transaction kind notes.
- Step 8: The remaining activities on your working space should be coordination acts or informational/documental production acts. Remove each of the remaining notes on your working surface and collapse them underneath the appropriate re-phrased transaction kind (red diamond notes) on your A1 paper.

- Step 9: Position the yellow actor role notes on the A1 paper, drawing in (with a black pen) the initiator roles (+ initiator links) and the executing roles (+ executor links) to the transaction kinds, completing the CSD.
- Step 10: Validate your composite CSD with your colleague.

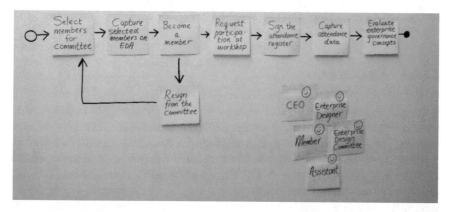

Fig. 20.2 Example of a process to demonstrate method steps 1–3. © Marné de Vries, reprinted with permission

Based on our narrative and an application of the story-card method, Fig. 20.2 presents the result for performing Steps 1–3, whereas Fig. 20.3 resulted from performing Steps 4–10.

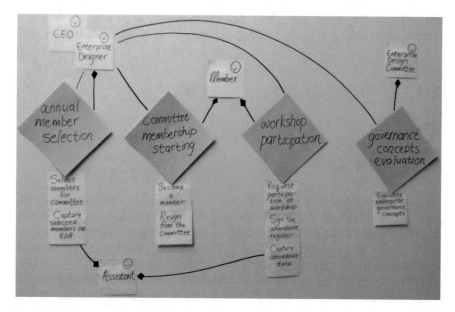

Fig. 20.3 Example of a process to demonstrate method steps 4–10. © Marné de Vries, reprinted with permission

The composite actor roles in Fig. 20.3 would require additional work, transforming them into a network of elementary actor roles. Thus, the yellow sticky notes at the bottom of the diamond-shaped transaction kinds need to be removed from the diagram, whereas the composite actor roles positioned above the diamond-shaped transaction kinds need to be replaced with elementary actor roles. An example of an elementary CSD is presented in Fig. 20.1.

20.2.3   Conclusions

Software development projects at scale involve multiple stakeholders that need to have a common understanding of the enterprise operational context, sharing a common big picture as part of requirements elicitation. DEMO's CSD is useful for representing the enterprise operational context, that is, removing unnecessary clutter of technology implementation detail. Theory indicates that the abstract CM/CSD concepts are concise and used in a consistent way. Yet, agile methodologies require models that encourage collaboration, are easy to understand, and relate to a concrete world, rather than an abstract world. Software development stakeholders need to relate the abstract concepts of the CM/CSD back to a concrete world. The story-card method facilitates collaboration and translation of a concrete world into more abstract (and concise) concepts [3]. The story-card method also improves the possibility of adopting the CM/CSD at an enterprise as a means to represent a common understanding of the enterprise operational context. Participants that were involved in the evaluation of the story-card method represented various different industries and roles [3]. Therefore, we believe that the story-card method would be useful within various different contexts, including contexts where scaling factors apply.

20.3   DEMO Enhanced Lean Six Sigma

Roland Ettema (roland.Ettema@gmail.com)

20.3.1   Introduction

Merck is a worldwide pharmaceutical company with a research lab and plant for the production of birth control pills in the Netherlands. The company struggled for quite some time with an order reliability problem. Three attempts were made already to tackle the problem, by applying Lean Six Sigma[1] (LSS), when the author was called in to assist in the fourth attempt. As the starting point, order reliability was defined (in a CTQ-Tree) as delivering the correct amount of birth control pills on the agreed delivery date. In LSS, a defect order is an order for which the actual amount of pills

---

[1]https://www.leansixsigmainstitute.org

delivered and/or the actual delivery date fall outside a specified deviation, which is 10% for the promised amount, and 30 days for the promised date at Merck.

In the stable market situation of the past, Merck achieved an order reliability above 95%, corresponding with 3.2 sigma. In the current turbulent market, it stays below 72%, corresponding with 2.1 sigma. The sigma value expresses how tightly the values of a quality variable are clustered around the mean. It means that the spread of the quality variable values in the stable market situation was more tightly clustered around the mean than in the unstable situation. Or, in terms of LSS, the company was more in control in the past than presently. In other words, while the general cause of low order reliability was known, it remained unclear why Merck had difficulties in adapting to the market turbulence.

20.3.2   The Case Study

We interviewed the lean six sigma project members from the previous initiatives to learn from the choices that were made in the past. They reported difficulties in identifying appropriate cause-and-effect relationships, and referred to the difficulty of identifying a 'stable' set of process variables, which means that they could not identify a limited set of the most significant and influential process variables.

To cope with this problem, in the fourth initiative we introduced a classification scheme containing ten 'reason codes' representing kinds of reasons why a defect happens. With the help of the scheme, we observed the order fulfilment for 3 months. We noted down each defect order, we recorded the reason and classified it using the scheme. After the observation period and the analysis of the observations, we determined the process variables that had the most influence on the quality variables. This information was presented as a table consisting tuples of variables, where each tuple represents the association between a quality variable (qv) and a process variable (pv), shown in Table 20.1.

To reveal the interactions and mechanisms that facilitate the detected associations (e.g. <qv1, pv1.1>), we sought support in modelling the organisation of Merck with DEMO (cf. Chap. 12). We identified the transaction kinds and actor roles in the part of the organisation dealing with order fulfilment.

Table 20.1 Associations in Merck's order fulfilment organisation

qv	Pv	Occurrence	DEMO	Value range
qv1	**Correct amount**		**[T11]**	**± >10% promised amount**
pv1.1	rc1_planning_error	30 % of rc1	[A04]	−45% < qv1 > 0%
pv1.2	rc7_artwork_change	45 % of rc7	[A05]	0% < qv1 > 30%
qv2	**On time**		**[T11]**	**± >30 days promised date**
pv2.1	rc1_release_delay	42% of rc1	[A06]	−5 days < qv2 > +15days
pv2.2	rc1_production_delay	21% of rc1	[A03]	−5 days < qv2 > +25 days
pv2.3	rc7_ship_doc_delay	25% of rc7	[A08]	0 days < qv2 > + 15 days
pv2.4	rc7_approval delay	20% of rc7	[A08]	0 days < qv2 > + 7 days

We produced the CSD and the TRT. In Fig. 20.4, the CSD is shown augmented with a mapping of the results in Table 20.1 to the corresponding DEMO elements. This is shown in red in the CSD and explained in Table 20.2. The rationale behind the mapping is to identify the transaction kinds and actor roles that control the values of the quality variables and process variables in run-time.

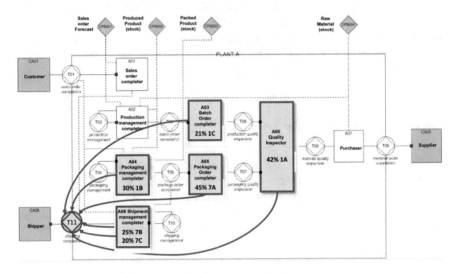

Fig. 20.4   Augmented CSD of the order fulfilment organisation

Table 20.2   Augmentation details of the order fulfilment organisation

RC	Causes	Occ. (%)
1A	Release delay (PI capacity or artwork related)	42
1B	Planning error, packaging material shortage, bulk shortage, order rework	30
1C	Production delays, technical problems	21
7A	Artwork changes (folding carton, leaflets) not on time, artwork approvals delayed, or artwork discussions on release. Optimisation of the artwork change/ COP planning processes	45
7B	Import/Export documents on time (L/C; Import Licence; HUB Invoices) Request at earliest point, strict error checking and follow-up	25
7C	Waiting for approval of the customer for shipment	20

The presented augmented CSD is the result of a mapping activity wherein we mapped variables on actor roles using objective criteria. Otherwise, the mapping would be arbitrary, unguided, and not reproducible. We agreed on three mapping rules. The first states: "Every variable is managed; one actor role is responsible for its values". The second states: "A variable is a subject within a transaction: the initiator and executor are only successful when they agree on the variable's value". The third rule states: "A variable is only mapped once". This constrained mapping leads to an augmented CSD (cf. Fig. 20.4) and a corresponding mapping table (cf. Table 20.2). The augmented CSD shows—in our view—all the entities and activities that are involved in the associations between the quality variables and the process variables. The occurrence rate column in Table 20.2 indicates the portion of a particular process variable that is mentioned in the observations as a cause.

By augmenting the CSD, we created an artefact that combined two kinds of evidence: statistics and organisational modelling with DEMO, thereby finding causal inference support. We learned that several self-activating actor roles are not driven directly by other transactions, but use the available information to determine something, such as an optimal delivery deadline. If we take a closer look at the interstriction structure (cf. Chap. 10) to understand the operation of the organisation, we see how actors rely heavily on information in the transaction banks.

To understand the operation of the causal mechanism that prevents Merck to adapt to the turbulence of the market we asked ourselves: 'are the self-initiating actors informed about the values of the process variables?' This question was raised when an employee expressed doubts about the availability of such information and suggested that informed decision making might be at risk. By using feedback from employees, we could expose multiple limitations in the interstriction structure for the self-activating actors in Merck that prevents the self-activating actors to adapt to changed market circumstances.

20.3.3 Conclusions

We have explained the flexibility of interpreting associations and background information from employees in DEMO aspect models. By applying enterprise engineering in this LSS initiative, we concluded that actor role A01 'Order Completer' has no access to relevant information, which causes issues for order reliability, since A01 is restricted to the information available in the available information system. More specifically, information concerning stock values, planning, and information concerning production delays are not accessible by A01. It is vital that this information is available, to ensure that the delivery date and volume in T01 are feasible.

The focus in regular lean six sigma projects on correlations is useful to isolate and to demarcate the phenomenon to be diagnosed. However, correlations are not sufficient to support a causal description for the phenomenon to be explained. What is needed after the identification of the associational model is an understanding and identification of the organisational entities that should be changed to remedy a problematic phenomenon.

In this case study, a DEMO model was used precisely for this purpose. Furthermore, background information from employees was included in this Enterprise Engineering approach to reveal the mechanism behind the experienced quality problem. From a methodological perspective, the explanations in the diagnosis were subject to statistical, epistemic, and ontological evaluation. All three evaluations were present in this case, respectively from using LSS, from DEMO, and from the coherence between the types of evidence obtained (the association and interaction models). The main reference of the presented case study is [5].[2]

20.4   DEMO Enhanced BPMN

Steven van Kervel (steefk22@telenet.be) and Hans Mulder (hans.mulder@viagroep.nl)

20.4.1   Introduction

Business Process Modelling Notation (BPMN) is an industry standard for workflow procedures, supported by the Object Management Group (OMG).[3] Workflow is a very important technology for achieving business goals in terms of efficiency and effectiveness of their production, while complying with boundary requirements for governance, risk, and compliance [6].

Practice shows, however, that the development of workflow procedures for non-trivial business processes is extremely complex and error-prone. Typically, only the so-called 'happy flow' is modelled. Most of the non-happy process execution must be done ad hoc and 'outside' the business procedure, which is of course an 'unhappy' situation. Most novices in workflow development are tempted and convinced by the easy way a trivial workflow procedure can be developed and executed using today's BPMN suites. The GUIs are of a high quality and the applied BPMN concepts fit intuitively very well to the 'ideas' or 'understandings' of the modellers. Illustrative examples are "This looks like somebody swimming next to others in a swimming pool, so let's call it a swim lane" and "Here somebody is doing something, let's call it an activity". This is the way things become manifest to the naive

---

[2]https://repository.uantwerpen.be/docman/irua/83230a/141806.pdf

[3]http://www.omg.org

observer. However, as extensively discussed in [7], this is deeply flawed because it is not how things in the real world are.

20.4.2   Critical Evaluations of BPMN

Business process languages, in general, and BPMN in particular, have serious drawbacks: the absence of formal semantics, a limited potential for verification, and a message-oriented approach, and the inability to model multi-party collaborations [7].

The lack of formal semantics in BPMN is caused by the heterogeneity of its constructs and the absence of an unambiguous definition of the notation. In contrast to the comprehensively documented syntactic rules, the semantic meaning of the constructs is dispersed throughout the specification document in plain text. BPMN has been critically evaluated within several theoretical frameworks.

The first one is Workflow Patterns [7]. The results of the evaluation indicate that the resource perspective is only supported in a limited way; the data perspective is not fully covered as opposed to the control flow perspective, which is fully supported.

The second evaluation is made by applying the Representation Theory, using the BWW-ontology as a framework. The following findings are reported [7]:

- Concerning ontological completeness, it can be concluded that BPMN lacks representations of state, history, and system structure.
- Regarding construct excess (i.e. BPMN constructs not representing any BWW construct), a number of BPMN constructs have no real-world meaning. An example is Text Annotation.
- Concerning construct overload (i.e. a BPMN construct maps to more than one BWW construct), lanes and pools map to multiple BWW constructs.
- Regarding construct redundancy (i.e. one BWW construct maps to more than one BPMN construct), a transformation can be represented by an activity, a task, a collapsed sub-process, an expanded sub-process, and a transaction. Next, a BWW event can be modelled in BPMN as a start event, an intermediate event, an end event, a message event, a timer event, an error event, a cancel event, a compensation event, and a terminate event.

In comparison with other BPM techniques, which are also evaluated within the BWW framework, BPMN appears to be ontological complete, but it lacks clarity of the constructs. Therefore, the use of BPMN can easily lead to complete, but unclear and potentially ambiguous representations of real-world domains.

A third evaluation framework is the Semiotic Quality Framework, which is based on seven general quality aspects. It identifies five criteria to assess the quality of conceptual modelling languages. Applying the framework to BPMN suggests that BPMN can easily be learned for simple use, and is easy to understand [7]:

- Domain Appropriateness (how suitable is a language for use within different domains): BPMN is suited to model the functional perspective. However, it is not suited to model organisational structures and resources, functional breakdowns, data and information models, strategy, and business rules.
- Participant Language Knowledge Appropriateness (participants know the language and are able to use it): graphical elements of BPMN are clear and easy to learn.
- Knowledge Externalisability Appropriateness (participants' ability to express their relevant knowledge using the modelling language): BPMN is appropriate to model business processes, although it will be very difficult to incorporate knowledge that goes beyond business processes.
- Comprehensibility Appropriateness (audience should be able to understand as much as possible of the language): this category can be divided into understanding the language concepts and understanding the notation. Regarding the latter, readers can easily recognise the basic types of elements as these types are limited in number, intuitive, and very distinguishable from each other. Regarding the language concepts, it is suggested that these are descriptive, accurate, easy to understand, and well defined.
- Technical Actor Interpretation Appropriateness (language suitable for automatic reasoning): it is said that business process diagrams in BPMN are 'with a few exceptions easily translatable to BPEL (Business Process Execution Language)'.[4]

Given the fact that BPMN has some significant drawbacks mainly due to ambiguous and unclear descriptions of their constructs, we present hereafter a first study into alleviating these drawbacks by combining BPMN with DEMO. The study consists of applying BPMN to the case Pizzeria (cf. Chap. 14) and discussing the outcome with the modelling results of the case in DEMO.

20.4.3 The Case Study

In Fig. 20.5, the business process of the Pizzeria (first phase) is modelled in BPMN. While doing this, several issues occurred, mainly due to the ambiguous semantics of the BPMN constructs. For example, how should one model the payment request by Mia to the customer? Two options exist: one can model it as an intermediate message event or as an activity. The same ambiguity pops up when modelling the 'Process Pizza' sub-process: which activities should be part of this sub-process and why?

---

[4]https://www.oasis-open.org/committees/tc_home.php?wg_abbrev=wsbpel

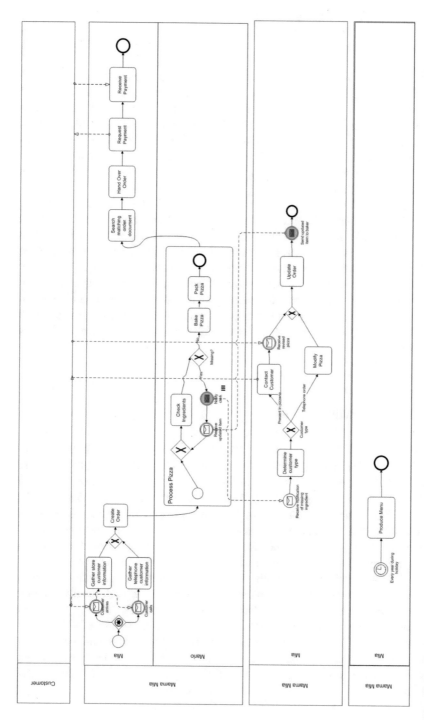

Fig. 20.5 BPMN model of the Case Pizzeria

More generally, which activities should be part of the business process model is to a large extent a subjective opinion of the modeller in BPMN. Aside from revision by end users or other stakeholders, there is no foundation to verify that the model is complete.

Next, there are multiple options to model contacting the customer when some ingredients are missing. Because Mia is the intermediary who has to transfer the customer's preference to Mario, this interaction should be modelled within Mia's lane. Instead of the option we chose in Fig. 20.5, one could also use signalling intermediate events. Again, no preference could be identified from the case description. Finally, the lack of support for the data perspective prohibits a clear overview of the process. For example, the only option that is available to state that an order consists of one or more pizzas is using a text annotation.

An extensive discussion of the way in which a DEMO enhanced version of BPMN could be applied in order to alleviate the identified drawbacks of BPMN is provided in [7]. In includes discussions of the benefits and drawbacks with two distinct groups of potential users: software developers, and business people. Most drawbacks were indicated by the software developers who need more rigour and details in order to use BPMN models as input for producing supporting software. In contrast, the business people pointed out that the use of the core set is sufficient and convenient for modelling concise models, easy to understand by 'the business'. This is also illustrated by the fact that they actually only used a subset of BPMN constructs.

20.4.4 Conclusions

Obviously, BPMN models lack the distinctions as made by the PSI theory (cf. Chap. 8), the OMEGA theory (cf. Chap. 10) and the ALPHA theory (cf. Chap. 11). Therefore, it does not make sense to compare the process model in Fig. 20.5 with the one in Fig. 14.4. BPMN models are not ontological models, that is, abstracted from implementation. They are also not essential, that is, in addition abstracted from realisation. Finally, and as said above, the process model in Fig. 20.5 concerns the 'happy flow'. No attention is paid to the 'unhappy' acts of declining a request, and rejecting a declaration, let alone the four revocation options.

The DEMO methodology, with its underlying theories, provides a formal foundation to BPMN models. Applying DEMO results in high-quality models. It is possible to derive BPMN models from DEMO models, thereby preventing the occurrence of potential anomalies. Moreover, revising existing BPMN models with the help of DEMO can be used to verify completeness and consistency of the modelled business processes, resulting in BPMN models with fewer anomalies. Further research is needed to produce practical guidelines for BPMN modellers.

20.5 DEMO Enhanced Software Testing

René Ceelen (rceelen@testmonitor.com) and Hans Mulder (hans.mulder@viagroep.nl)

20.5.1 Introduction

Software acceptance testing is commonly performed as a kind of black-box testing: a developed software system is compared to the initial requirements and the current needs of its end users or, in the case of a contracted program, to the specifications in the contract. The outcome of an acceptance test is usually the basis for customers on which to determine whether they accept or reject the software product. Thus, acceptance testing is categorically different from other types of testing, where the intent is basically to reveal errors [8].

Software acceptance testing addresses major functional and performance requirements, man–machine interactions, specified system constraints, as well as the external interfaces of the system. The major guide for software acceptance testing is the system requirements document and the primary focus is on usability and reliability.[5] There is currently no industry-wide standard for software acceptance testing. Therefore, in practice, most testing methods are based on best practices. Examples of widely used methods are ISQTB,[6] UTAUT,[7] and TMAP.[8] These methods do not adopt the Enterprise Engineering perspective, and thus do not use ontological models as the starting point for acceptance testing.

20.5.2 The Experiment

By means of a practical case, we investigated the possible advantages or disadvantages of applying enterprise ontological models in software acceptance testing. We applied two types of minimised software acceptance tests (cf. Fig. 20.6): the traditional way (T-way), which is a practical combination of TMAP and ISTQB, and the Enterprise Ontology way (EO-way), both on the same case. The case is about a client who bought a new automated information system to handle its most important business processes. After several workshops with the supplier and employees of the client company to categorise the parameters of the information

---

[5]IEEE: Std 829-Standard for Software Test Documentation. (1983).

[6]ISTQB: http://www.isqtb.org 06 (2010).

[7]IEEE: IEEE Standard 610.12-1990, IEEE Standard Glossary of Software, Engineering Terminology. (1990).

[8]IEEE: Std 1012-Standard for Software Verification and Validation Plans. (1986).

system, a software acceptance test had to be arranged. In this phase, the experiment started.

To compare both ways of testing, two different working approaches were accomplished. The T-way started with analysing the business processes to be handled and dividing them into smaller activities. These activities constitute the basis for the test scenarios. After the test scenarios were completed, the detailed test steps were built, after which the acceptance test could be executed. The EO-way started with building the implementation independent Construction Model (CM) and Process Model (PM) of the business processes to be handled (cf. Chap. 12). Every identified transaction kind in the CM got a complete transaction pattern in the PM: both the 'success flow' and the 'not success flow', containing all 'exceptions' (cf. Chap. 8).

This was the first difference between the two ways of software acceptance testing. The second difference was the way of working in analysing the system documentation. In the T-way, the documentation was read to check and upgrade the detailed test activities. In the EO-way, we built in addition the Fact Model (FM) to ensure the right entity types and fact types were included in the detailed test activities. All test activities were linked to one or more acceptance criteria, based on ISO9126[9] and customer needs (cf. Table 20.3).

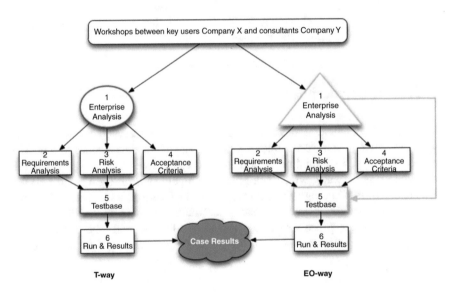

Fig. 20.6 Way of working "traditional way" and "enterprise ontology way"

---

[9]https://www.iso.org/standard/22749.html

Table 20.3 Elements of ISO9126 software quality

Criterion	Description
Stability	The application did not cancel itself or crashed during the testing period as a result of a regular user action and the information is consistent through the system.
Understandability	Buttons, texts, and signals in the application are easy to understand and recognizable for internal and external users.
Financial	The level of certainty that financial data is processed correctly and completely and conforms to the system documentation.
Operational	The level of certainty that operational data is processed correctly and completely and conforms to the system documentation.
Traceability	Every change made is traceable by the user and an undo option is available most of the time.

The complete database of test results of all testers was analysed and presented in a final judgement session. The results of both methods were based on the same acceptance criteria, as shown in Table 20.3. Figure 20.7 shows the findings of the two groups of testers.

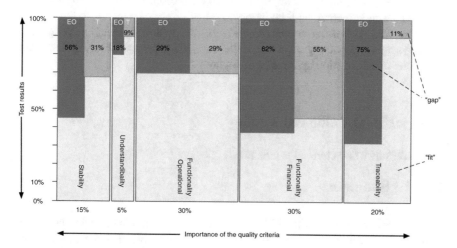

Fig. 20.7 Results based on acceptance criteria T-way and EO-way

The most striking difference is in the criterion Traceability: 75% of all instructions were indicated by the testers in the EO-way as 'non acceptable' versus 11% by the testers in the T-way. The difference can be explained as follows. In the EO-way, one looks for the presence of all steps in the complete transaction pattern (cf. Chap. 8), thus, for example, including the revocation patterns. What the testers found is that many of them were not, or not properly, addressed in the software. This is not surprising because such options are commonly forgotten in the functional requirements specifications, for the simple reason that 'this never happens' in our company.

The results on the other criteria differ as must as on Traceability, but we may safely conclude that the EO-way outperforms the T-way in finding lacking functionalities, errors, and weaknesses. In addition, we observed that the communication between the participants in the EO-way of working was more focused on the software acceptance testing process and on the primary requirements of the company. Our (educated) guess is that this is caused by the completeness and clarity of the DEMO models.

20.5.3   Conclusions

As we have demonstrated above, basing software acceptance testing on DEMO models, thus on implementation independent ontological models of the business process to be supported or handled, has the advantage that one finds much more defects than without doing this. The explanation is simple and clear: the DEMO models, in particular the PM, are based on the theoretically complete transaction pattern, and thus lead to testing the presence of all of them in the software. The most widely used test techniques in practice nowadays, as discussed in Sect. 20.5.1, do not have such a rigid theoretical foundation.

Therefore, when using normative guidance for the development and acceptance of IT systems and both "groups" have the same guidance, we observed the acceptance rate of information systems to be higher.

20.6   DEMO Enhanced Mining

Linda Terlouw (linda.terlouw@icris.nl)

20.6.1   Situation

Many organisations face difficulties getting the right material to the right place at the right moment for carrying out preventive and corrective maintenance to their machines. Preventive maintenance deals with inspecting the current state of a machine, detecting potential problems, and cleaning/replacing items before defects occur. It is scheduled after a certain fixed period or after a certain amount of usage (e.g. working hours of a factory machine or vehicle mileage). Corrective maintenance deals with fixing a machine after a defect has occurred. The demand for items is now less predictable, but quick delivery is as important. Items may be stored at different locations, with different transportation times: the project location (for instance, a construction area or an offshore location), the mechanics workplace (for instance, a garage or a hangar), a local warehouse, a central warehouse, or a warehouse of the supplier.

Organisations must find a balance between inventory costs and service level to the mechanics needing the items. Too little inventory may lead to unnecessary downtime of machines and mechanics waiting instead of working; too much inventory leads to high storage costs, less money available for other business activities, and higher risk of items becoming obsolete, damaged, or stolen.

20.6.2   Task

The task we were faced with was to find the bottlenecks in logistics processes that lead to unnecessary downtime of machines. The task included determining which items should be kept in inventory, and in what amount, to provide an optimal service level to mechanics for preventive and corrective maintenance.

20.6.3   Approach

We extracted data from ERP systems (Infor, SAP, and tailor-made systems), combined these data with data from other enterprise information systems and converted them to a structure suitable for process mining [9]. We mined processes using the inductive mining algorithm [10] to get a first insight into the process. This enabled us to discover: the most frequent activities and process paths, the dependencies between different activities/events, and the time between activities/events.

This type of process mining, however, does not take into account the semantics of the acts/events. Therefore, we combined process mining with DEMO (cf. Chap. 12), notably the PSI theory (cf. Chap. 8), to get a better understanding of the semantics of the business process. We annotated acts/events as either coordination or production acts/events following the complete transaction pattern. This way we could easily detect which business transactions were executed as they should be and which transactions failed somehow.

To find an optimal inventory level, we introduced ideas from Lean Six Sigma on this topic. We used a continuous review model (inventory can be ordered at any moment). We determined for each item type when new items should be ordered and how many, by calculating the inventory reorder point and the optimum order quantity. The inventory reorder point is the level of inventory at which the inventory should be replenished to make sure a certain service level can be guaranteed. Commonly, a higher variation in demand leads to a higher inventory level. In our cases we assumed we cannot influence the demand or the variation (though this might be possible by analysing the maintenance process).

20.6.4   Result

We made custom DEMO enhanced process mining visualisations (cf. Fig. 20.8) for presenting logistics processes. It enabled us to show the process to domain experts in a way that reflects their way of thinking in coarse-grained business transactions instead of fine-grained acts/events registered in IT systems.

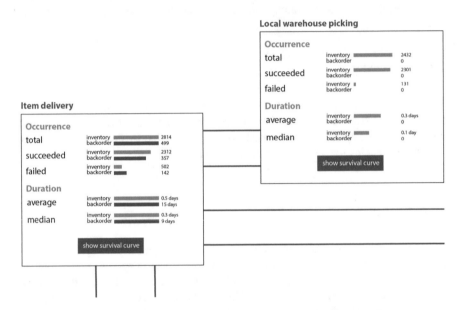

Fig. 20.8 Success rate and duration of business transactions in local warehouse picking

The visualisations show the following metrics per business transaction kind: the total number of successfully executed basic transaction patterns, total number of failed transactions (due to decline, reject, or revocation), the average duration of the transaction (when item is delivered from inventory or backorder), the median duration of the transaction (when item is delivered from inventory or backorder), and the survival curve (how many cases are still 'in the transaction' after a certain period).

Because DEMO processes have a tree structure, we can compare the metrics of an individual business transaction to those of the complete process (which is the root transaction kind). The bars of the metrics in the different transaction kinds are therefore made relative to the values of the metrics of the root transaction kind. We can now easily see which transactions take up most time and which fail frequently. We can show this visualisation for all types of items, but of course we can also slice it for a specific type. When we do this we can view an additional visualisation that shows inventory-related information as depicted in Fig. 20.9. In this figure, we see the monthly number of item requests from mechanics for a certain item type.

The inventory reorder points for service levels of 80, 95, and 99% are calculated automatically. The results can be compared with the actual inventory level to save costs and improve maintenance processes.

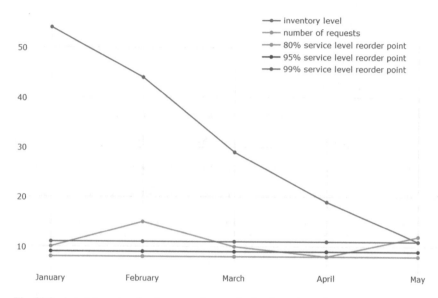

Fig. 20.9 Actual inventory level compared to service level reorder points

20.6.5   Reflection

We have presented above a way to combine fully automated process discovery with manually adding annotations for taking into account the semantics of acts/events in DEMO. We did not only focus on analysing the logistics process itself, but also on determining the optimal inventory level to guarantee a certain service level. We see several ways of further improving our approach.

First, we would like to make a distinction between the different reasons why a business transaction may 'fail' (currently we only distinguish between succeeded and failed). Is it because of a decline, a reject, or a revocation? This can give a better understanding to an organisation of why things go wrong and what to do about it.

A second improvement is to find a way of dealing with declined, rejected and revoked transactions in determining the optimal inventory reorder point. At the moment we exclude them from the calculation, but this is not in all cases the best way to deal with them.

A third improvement is to automatically mine relationships between business transactions, and to see where transactions do not proceed as planned.

References

1. Dietz, J. L. G. (2006). *Enterprise ontology: Theory and methodology* (xiii, 243 p.). Berlin: Springer.
2. Dikert, K., Paasivaara, M., & Lassenius, C. (2016). Challenges and success factors for large-scale agile transformations: A systematic literature review. *Journal of Systems and Software, 119*, 87–108.
3. De Vries, M. (2018). *DEMO and the story-card method: Requirements elicitation for agile software development at scale*. In 11th IFIP WG 8.1 working conference on the Practice of Enterprise Modelling.
4. Patton, J., & Economy, P. (2014). *User story mapping: Discover the whole story, build the right product*. Sebastopol: O'Reilly Media.
5. Ettema, R. W. (2016). *Using triangulation in Lean Six Sigma to explain quality problems*. The Netherlands, Belgium: Radboud University Nijmegen, University of Antwerp.
6. Dudok, E., Guerreiro, S., Babkin, E., Pergl, R., & van Kervel, S. J. H. (2015). *Enterprise operational analysis using DEMO and the enterprise operating system*. Cham: Springer International.
7. Van Nuffel, D., Mulder, H., & Van Kervel, S. (2009). *Enhancing the formal foundations of BPMN by enterprise ontology*. Berlin: Springer.
8. Hsia, P., & Kung, D. (1997). Software requirements and acceptance testing. *Annals of Software Engineering, 3*, 291–317.
9. van der Aalst, W. P. M. (2011). *Process mining—Discovery, conformance and enhancement of business processes*. Berlin: Springer.
10. Leemans, S. J. J., Fahland, D., & van der Aalst, W. M. P. (2014). *Discovering block-structured process models from event logs containing infrequent behaviour*. Cham: Springer.

Glossary[1]

Abstract object Through reasoning by analogy with *concrete objects*, abstract objects are the bare individuals that constitute the core of *abstract things*, and thus are taken as their identity (Chap. 5).

Abstract thing Through reasoning by analogy with *concrete things*, abstract things are *abstract objects* with features. In contrast to concrete things, abstract things only exist in the mind. Examples of abstract things are numbers and booleans, but also lines and circles (Chap. 5).

Access link A link between an *actor role* and a *transaction kind*, indicating that fillers of the actor role have (reading) access to the *facts* in the *transaction bank* of the transaction kind. Consequently, an access link represents the existence of one or more *sharing transaction kinds* between the *O-organisation* and the *I-organisation* of an *enterprise* (Chap. 10).

Act The atomic unit of action in *systems*. Two kinds of acts are distinguished: *coordination acts* and *production acts*. Acts are performed by *actors* (Chap. 8).

Actagenic conversation A business *conversation* in which the participants strive to reach consensus about a *product* that one of them is going to bring about at the other's request (Chap. 8).

Action rule A guideline for *actors* to settle *agenda*. An action rule consists of three consecutive parts: the *event part*, the *assess part*, and the *response part*. Action rules are the imperative equivalent of *existence laws* and *occurrence laws* (Chaps. 8 and 12). [See also Work instruction]

Actor A subject in her/his filling of an *actor role*. An actor is referred to by a tuple <actor role, subject>, commonly noted down as <actor role>/<subject> (Chap. 8).

---

[1] Hereafter, the definitions of the key terms in Enterprise Ontology, as used in this book, are summarised in alphabetical order. At the end of every entry the chapter is indicated between '("and")' where the term is defined.

© Springer Nature Switzerland AG 2020

J. L. G. Dietz, J. B. F. Mulder, *Enterprise Ontology*, The Enterprise Engineering Series, https://doi.org/10.1007/978-3-030-38854-6

Actor role The term 'actor role' has two interpretations. The constructional interpretation is that it represents the *authority* to perform the *coordination acts* and the *production act* within the *responsibility area* of the *executor*, in *transactions* of the *transaction kind* to which the actor role is linked by an *executor link*. The operational interpretation is that it represents the guidelines, ranging from culture (norms and values) to specific *action rules* and *work instructions*, that *actors* filling the actor role apply when they carry out transactions (Chap. 10).

Addressee [property of *coordination act*] the *actor* to whom the *coordination act* is addressed (Chap. 8).

Agenda Plural of *agendum*. At every *point in time*, every *actor* disposes of her/his agenda (Chap. 8).

Agendum A coordination *event* to which the *addressee* of the corresponding *coordination act* has to respond (Chap. 8).

Aggregate A complex of *concrete things* that is not able to act, that is, to bring about changes in some *world* (Chap. 6). [See also System]

Aspect model Partial *ontological model* of an *organisational layer*. An aspect model takes a specific view on the organisational layer and is therefore in itself not a complete ontological model (Chap. 12).

Assess part The part of an *action rule* containing the propositions regarding the *state* of the *coordination world* and the *production world* to be evaluated (Chap. 12).

Attribute Instance of an *attribute type* (Chap. 6).

Attribute type A binary *type*. The *extension* of an attribute type is a mapping from a *concrete* or *abstract class*, called the domain of the attribute type, to an abstract object class, called its range. Cardinality ranges indicate the exact nature of the mapping: $0\ldots1$, $0\ldots*$, $1\ldots1$, $1\ldots*$, or $*\ldots*$ (Chap. 6).

Authorisation One of the two ways in which *authority* can be assigned to *subjects*. The other way is *delegation*. Through authorisation, a subject gets the authority to fill a complete *actor role* (Chap. 8).

Authority The right to perform one or more specific *coordination acts* (and possibly also the *production act*) in *transactions* of some *transaction kind*. Authority can be assigned to a *subject* through *authorisation* or *delegation* (Chap. 8). [See also Responsibility and competence]

Business Term to refer to the *function* perspective on an *enterprise*, in particular the function as perceived by its customers (Chap. 7). [See also Organisation]

Business conversation A conversation that takes place in an institutional setting, and of which the participants aim at achieving a common goal. Four kinds of business conversations are distinguished: *actagenic* conversations, *factagenic* conversations, *reversiogenic* conversations, and *cogitatiogenic* conversations (Chap. 8).

Business process A sequence of *process steps*, which are steps in *transactions* of the *transaction kinds* that are contained in a *business process kind* in the *O-organisation* of an *enterprise* (Chap. 10).

Business process kind A set of *O-transactor roles* (possibly only one) and the *interaction structure* between them, together constituting a tree structure. Every transactor role in the tree is enclosed in a transactor role on the next higher level (except the 'highest' one), and encloses one or more transactor roles on the next lower level (except the 'lowest' ones) (Chap. 10).

Causal link Link between a *coordination act* and its resulting *coordination fact*, indicating that the fact is the immediate result of performing the act (Chap. 8).

Claim to rightness One of the three *validity claims* in a *coordination act*. The claim to rightness regards the *authority* of the *performer* to perform the act (Chap. 8).

Claim to sincerity One of the three *validity claims* in a *coordination act*. The claim to sincerity concerns the sincerity of the *performer* in performing the act (Chap. 8).

Claim to truth One of the three *validity claims* in a *coordination act*. The claim to truth concerns the (potential) existence of the concerned *product* (Chap. 8).

Cogitatiogenic conversation A business *conversation* in which the participants strive to reach consensus about an idea or plan for future action (Chap. 8).

Cognitive correspondence The mutual understanding of actors concerning a *coordination act* at the *informa level* of *communication*. Cognitive correspondence is reached if the *addressee* thinks he/she has understood the semantic content of the communicated *coordination fact* correctly. Success or failure is conveyed by a confirmation or a disconfirmation (Chap. 8).

Commitment The being bound by the *performer* of a *coordination act* to its *intention*. A commitment implies that the performer has the moral obligation to let her/his future actions be in agreement with the intention (Chap. 8).

Communication The sharing of thoughts between *subjects*. It is brought about by exchanging *information* (Chap. 4).

Competence The collective capabilities of a *subject* that makes him/her eligible to be assigned one or more *actor roles* (Chap. 8). [See also Authority and responsibility]

Complex A collection of related *abstract things* or *concrete things*. Two kinds of complexes are distinguished: *systems* and *aggregates* (Chap. 6).

Composite transactor role A collection of *transactor roles*, connected by *initiator links*, and possibly also by *access links* and *wait links* (Chap. 10).

Conceptual complex The conceptualisation of a *concrete complex* as the result of applying a *conceptual schema*, to which the concrete complex conforms. It consists of a number of *conceptual facts* (Chap. 6).

Conceptual fact The thought that emerges in the mind when a *type* is applied to a *thing*. If the thing is a single concrete thing, the fact is an *entity* or a *value*. If the thing is a pair of things, the fact is a *property* or an *attribute*. Formally, a conceptual fact is a (unary or binary) predication of a *conceptual object* (Chap. 5).

Conceptual model A conceptual *complex* that is taken as a model of a *concrete complex*. The model constitutes the understanding of the concrete complex within the applied *conceptual schema* (Chap. 6).

Conceptual object The representation in the mind of a *concrete object* (Chap. 5).

Conceptual schema A coherent collection of related *types*. A conceptual schema works as a mental lens through which one perceives concrete complexes and subsequently creates corresponding *conceptual complexes* in the mind. If the concrete complex is a *world*, the conceptual schema determines the *state* space and the *transition* space of the world (Chap. 6). [See also Type]

Concrete complex A concrete complex is either a (concrete) *system* or a (concrete) *aggregate* (Chap. 6).

Concrete fact A state of affairs in the *world* of a *concrete system*. Although facts only exist in our mind [see *conceptual fact*], people appear to be so used to assuming the existence of a reality, independently of the minds of individual subjects, that we will adopt this philosophical stance and assume the existence of 'objective' concrete facts. A basic prerequisite to this assumption is that the involved people apply the same *conceptual schema* (Chap. 5).

Concrete object The bare individual that constitutes the core of a *concrete thing* and therefore is taken as the identity of the thing (Chap. 5). [See also Abstract object]

Concrete thing A concrete *object* with features. Concrete things are the constituting elements of a *world*. A distinction is made between tangible concrete things, like roses and cars, and intangible concrete things, like purchases and rentals (Chap. 5). [See also Abstract thing]

Construction There are two fundamentally different perspectives on every system: the construction perspective and the *function* perspective. In the construction perspective one considers the composition, the environment, and the structure of the system, without any interest in the function(s) it may offer (Chap. 7).

Coordination act An *act* in a *business conversation*. It has four components or properties: *performer, intention, addressee,* and *product*. The result of a successfully performed coordination act is the immediate creation of the corresponding *coordination fact* (Chap. 8). [See also Process step]

Coordination event The coming into existence of a *coordination fact* (Chap. 8).

Coordination fact *State* element in a *coordination world*. It has four components: *performer, intention, addressee,* and *product*. A coordination fact is the immediate result of a performed *coordination act*. (Chap. 8). [See also Process step]

Coordination world One of the two *worlds* in which the elements in a *system* cause *transitions* (Chap. 8). [See also Production world]

Creation time [*Attribute* of *fact*] The *point in time* at which a *fact* is created. It is less than or equal to the *event time* at which it comes into existence (Chap. 8).

D-actor (role) [Shorthand for *actor (role)* in the *D-organisation* of an *enterprise*]

D-organisation (D from documental) The *organisational layer* of the *organisation* of an *enterprise* in which *documental* production takes place. The ontological model of a D-organisation comprises a number of *D-transactor roles* and the *coordination structures* between them. The D-organisation supports the *I-organisation* by providing *documental services* (Chap. 11).

D-transaction (kind) [Shorthand for *transaction (kind)* in the *D-organisation* of an *enterprise*]

D-transactor (role) [Shorthand for *transactor (role)* in the *D-organisation* of an *enterprise*]

Data set A structured collection of signs. Examples of data sets are customer data, article data, and sales data (Chap. 11).

Declared type A type in a *conceptual schema* that is declared to be contained in the conceptual schema (Chap. 6). [See also Derived type]

Delegation An authorisation may include the right of the authorised person to delegate a part of the assigned *authority* to other subjects. Commonly, delegation concerns a limited number of *process steps* of some *transaction kind* (Chap. 8).

Dependent production fact A production *fact* that comes into existence dependent on, and together with, an *independent production fact* (Chap. 8).

Derived type A type in a *conceptual schema* that is defined on the basis of other (*declared* or derived) types (Chap. 6). [See also Declared type]

Discussion state Transaction *state* in which the *initiator* and the *executor* have to 'sit together' and discuss the cause of having ended up in this state, as well as how to proceed. The standard *transaction pattern* has two discussion states: 'declined' and 'rejected'. The four *revocation patterns* have the discussion state 'revoked' (Chap. 8).

Document An unstructured collection of signs. Examples of documents are reports, books, and letters (Chap. 11).

Documental production In every enterprise, three sorts of *production* can be distinguished: *original*, *informational*, and *documental*. Documental production comprises saving, transforming, and providing *documents* or *data sets*, as well as storing, retrieving, copying, transmitting, and destroying *files* (Chap. 11).

Enterprise The general term to refer to any kind of collaborative activity by human beings. An enterprise commonly is, but need not necessarily be, an economic and/or legal body. Examples of enterprises are: companies, governmental agencies, health care institutions, sports clubs, and building projects. Every enterprise has a *business* and an *organisation* (Chap. 8).

Entity A *typed concrete thing*. Examples of tangible entities are roses and cars; examples of intangible entities are purchases and rentals (Chap. 5).

Essential model The essential model of a *Scope of Interest* is defined as the *ontological model* of its *O-organisation* (Chap. 11).

Event The coming into existence of a *fact*. Events occur instantly, meaning that their duration falls within one *time unit* (Chap. 6).

Event part The part of an *action rule* containing the *agendum* to be settled when executing the action rule (Chap. 12).

Event time [Attribute of *event*] The *point in time* at which an event occurs, and thus a *fact* comes into existence (Chap. 8).

Execution phase The transaction phase in which the *executor* performs the *production act*. It starts when the *transaction state* 'promised' is reached and it ends when the production act is performed (Chap. 8).

Executor One of the two roles that *actors* have in a *transaction*; the other role is *initiator*. The executor in a transaction is *authorised* and *responsible* for performing the *coordination acts* in the executor's *responsibility area* of the *complete transaction pattern* (Chap. 8).

Executor link A link between an *actor role* and a *transaction kind*, indicating that *actors* in the actor role are authorised *executor* in *transactions* of the transaction kind (Chap. 8).

Existence law A (first order) logical formula determining the lawfulness of *states* in a *world* (Chap. 6). [See also Occurrence law]

Extension The extension of a *type* is the set of *objects* that are the identities of the things conforming to the type (Chap. 5). [See also Intension]

Fact *State* element in a *world* (Chap. 6); the result of an *act* (Chap. 8).

Factagenic conversation A business *conversation* in which the participants strive to reach consensus about the *production fact* that one of them has brought about on the other's request (Chap. 8).

File A physical embodiment of a *document* or *data set*. Examples of files are collections of ink marks on paper and optical marks on disk or tape. A document or data set may be inscribed in many files called its copies (Chap. 11).

Focus organisation The part of a *Scope of Interest* where the focus is on (Chap. 10).

Forma Term to refer to the general *competence* of a *subject* to perform *coordination acts* at the *forma level* of communication, as well as *documental production* acts (Chaps. 8 and 11). [See also Informa and performa]

Forma condition The collective prerequisites for reaching *notational correspondence* in performing a *coordination act* (Chap. 8).

Forma level The level of *communication* in performing a *coordination act* at which the *performer* and the *addressee* strive for *notational correspondence* (Chap. 8).

Function There are two fundamentally different perspectives on every system: the *construction* perspective and the function perspective. In the function perspective on an *enterprise* one considers the functions of the enterprise as perceived by its various stakeholders (Chap. 7). [See also Business and service]

I-actor (role) [Shorthand for *actor (role)* in the *I-organisation* of an *enterprise*]

I-organisation (I from informational) the *organisational layer* of the *organisation* of an *enterprise* in which *informational* production takes place. The ontological model of an I-organisation comprises a number of *I-transactor roles* and the *coordination structures* between them. The I-organisation supports the *O-organisation* by providing *informational services* (Chap. 11).

I-transaction (kind) [Shorthand for *transaction (kind)* in the *I-organisation* of an *enterprise*]

I-transactor (role) [Shorthand for transa*ctor (role)* in the *I-organisation* of an *enterprise*]

Independent production fact The core of the *product* that is brought about in a *transaction*. It comes into existence as the direct effect of the accept act by the *initiator*. It is represented by a unary fact (like 'sale 1618 is delivered') or a binary fact (like 'the fee for membership 387 in year 2019 is paid') (Chap. 8). [See also Dependent production fact]

Informa Term to refer to the general *competence* of a *subject* to perform *coordination acts* at the *informa level* of communication, as well as *informational production acts* (Chaps. 8 and 11). [See also Forma and performa]

Informa condition The collective prerequisites for reaching *cognitive correspondence* in performing a *coordination act* (Chap. 8).

Informa level The level of *communication* in performing a *coordination act* at which the *performer* and the *addressee* strive for *cognitive correspondence* (Chap. 8).

Information The expression by a *subject* of thought(s) in a form that is perceivable to other subjects, and that consequently can be communicated (Chap. 4).

Informational production In every enterprise, three sorts of *production* can be distinguished: *original*, informational, and *documental*. Informational production comprises remembering, recalling, and computing *facts* (Chap. 11).

Initiator One of the two roles that *actors* can have in a *transaction*; the other role is *executor*. The initiator in a transaction is *authorised* and *responsible* for performing the *coordination acts* in the initiator's *responsibility area* of the *complete transaction pattern* (Chap. 8).

Initiator link A link between an *actor role* and a *transaction kind*, indicating that *actors* in the actor role are authorised *initiator* in *transactions* of the transaction kind (Chap. 8).

Intension The intension of a *class* is the *type* to which the things that have the *objects* in the class as their identities, conform (Chap. 5). [See also Extension]

Intention [Attribute of *coordination act*] the social disposition of the *performer* of a *coordination act* towards the *addressee*, with respect to a *product*. Examples of intentions are 'request', 'promise', 'decline', 'declare', 'accept', 'reject' (Chap. 8). [See also Commitment].

Interaction structure One of the three coordination structures in an *organisation*. It consists of the *initiator links* between *transactor roles* (Chap. 10).

Interimpediment structure One of the three coordination structures in an *organisation*. It consists of *wait links* between *transactor roles* (Chap. 10).

Interstriction structure One of the three coordination structures in an *organisation*. It consists of *access links* between *transactor roles* (Chap. 10).

Medium level The level of communication in performing a *coordination act* at which the *performer* transmits the file to the *addressee* that carries the *document* or *data set* (possibly containing only one sentence) that must be made perceivable to the addressee (Chap. 8).

Model Any subject using a *complex* A that is neither directly nor indirectly interacting with a complex B, to obtain knowledge about the complex B, is using A as a model of B (Chap. 6). [See also Conceptual model]

Multiple transaction kind A collection of *transaction kinds*. Multiple transaction kinds may be useful if one does not (need to) know exactly the constituent transaction kinds (e.g. because they are outside the *Scope of Interest*) (Chap. 10).

Notational correspondence The degree of mutual understanding of a *coordination act* at the *forma level* of *communication*. Notational correspondence is reached if the *addressee* thinks he/she has understood the form of the message correctly. An example of a form is a sentence in English. Success or failure is conveyed by a confirmation or a disconfirmation (Chap. 8).

O-actor (role) [Shorthand for *actor (role)* in the *O-organisation* of an *enterprise*]

O-organisation (O from original) The *organisational layer* of the *organisation* of an *enterprise* in which *original* production takes place. The ontological model of an O-organisation comprises a number of *O-transactor roles* and the *coordination structures* between them (Chap. 11).

O-transaction (kind) [Shorthand for *transaction (kind)* in the *O-organisation* of an *enterprise*]

O-transactor (role) [Shorthand for *transactor (role)* in the *O-organisation* of an *enterprise*]

Object The bare individual that constitutes the core of a *thing* and therefore is taken as the identity of the thing. An object is *abstract* or *concrete* (Chap. 5).

Occurrence law A (first order) logical formula determining the lawfulness of *transitions* in a *world* (Chap. 6). [See also Existence law]

Ontological model A conceptual *model* of the *construction* and the *operation* of a *system* that is fully abstracted from its implementation (Chap. 9).

Operating principle [property of *system*] The mechanism that makes a system 'tick'. The operating principle of *organisations* is the ability and readiness of the *actors* in the organisation to enter into and comply with *commitments* regarding the bringing about of *products* (Chap. 8).

Operation The operating mode of the *construction* of a *system*. It means that the elements in the system are performing *acts* (Chap. 9).

Operative time [attribute of *product*] The time period[2] during which the product of a *transaction* is operative or valid (Chap. 8).

Order phase The transaction phase in which the *initiator* and the *executor* strive to reach consensus about the *product* that the executor is going to bring about. It starts by performing the 'request' act and ends in the state 'promised'. Ending up in the state 'declined' means that the transaction is in a deadlock (Chap. 8).

Organisation Term to refer to the *construction* perspective on an *enterprise* (Chap. 7). [See also Business]

Organisational layer The organisation of an *enterprise* consists of three organisational layers: the *O-organisation*, the *I-organisation*, and the *D-organisation*. The D-organisation supports the I-organisation by *documental services*. The I-organisation supports the O-organisation by *informational services* (Chap. 11).

Original production In every enterprise, three sorts of *production* can be distinguished: original, *informational*, and *documental*. Original production comprises

---

[2]As discussed in the DELTA theory (Chap. 9), every point in time is actually a time period, but possibly very small. This holds always for the attribute event time. The operative time, however, may be so large (minutes, hours, days) that one preferably speaks of a time period.

manufacturing, transporting, observing, deciding, and judging. They all result in the creation of (new, original) *facts* (Chap. 11).

Performa Term to refer to the general *competence* of a subject to perform *coordination acts* at the *performa level* of communication, as well as *original production acts* (Chaps. 8 and 11). [See also Forma and informa]

Performa condition The collective prerequisites for reaching *social correspondence* in performing a *coordination act* (Chap. 8).

Performa level The level of communication in performing a *coordination act* at which the *performer* and the *addressee* strive for *social correspondence* (Chap. 8).

Performer [Property of *coordination act*] the performing *actor* of a *coordination act* (Chap. 8).

Point in time A particular value on a *time scale*, expressed in one of the corresponding *time units*. Examples: week 36 [week], today [day], tomorrow at 11:25 h [minute] (Chaps. 6, 8, 9 and 12).

Process A sequence of *events* in a *world,* commonly including the sequence of the causing *acts* in the corresponding (discrete event) *system* (Chaps. 8 and 9).

Process step The atomic building block of a *transaction process*. It consists of a *coordination act* and its resulting *coordination fact*. Every process step is of a specific *process step kind* (Chap. 8).

Process step kind [attribute of *process step*] A process step kind is defined by two *properties*: a *transaction kind* and an *intention*. If 'TK01' denotes a particular transaction kind and 'rq' denotes the intention 'request', then 'TK01/rq' denotes a process step kind (Chap. 8).

Product [property of *coordination act*] The product of a coordination act consists of an *independent production fact* together with the associated *dependent production facts* (Chap. 8).

Product kind [attribute of *product*] *Products* of the same product kind are brought about in *transactions* of the same *transaction kind*. Examples of product kinds are: '[membership] is started', '[rental] is completed', 'the fee for [membership] in [year] is paid'. The variables in the formulation of a product kind are placeholders for *entities* (Chap. 8).

Production act The act in a *transaction* by which the *executor* brings about the *product* of the transaction (Chap. 8). [see also Transaction pattern]

Production fact *State* element in a *production world*. A production fact is the result of performing a *production act*. More precisely: the result of a production act is a state of affairs in the production world that gives rise to a number of *conceptual facts* representing the state of affairs (Chap. 8). [See also Product]

Production world One of the two *worlds* in which the elements in a *system* cause *transitions* (Chaps. 8 and 9).

Property Instance of a *property type* (Chap. 6).

Property type A binary *fact type*. The extension of a property type is a mapping from a *concrete class*, called the domain of the property type, to a concrete class, called the range of the property type. Cardinality ranges indicate the exact nature of the mapping: 0...1, 0...*, 1...1, 1...*, or *...* (Chap. 6).

Providing transaction kind The general *D-transaction kind* in which *documents* or *data sets* containing facts regarding the *production world* of an *enterprise*'s *O-organisation* are provided by D-actors to I-actors; the *initiator* role is taken by an *I-actor* in her/his *documental* or 'blue' shape, and the *executor role* by a *D-actor* (Chap. 11). [See also Saving transaction kind]

Remembering transaction kind The general *I-transaction kind* in which *facts* regarding the *production world* of an *enterprise*'s *O-organisation* are made known by O-actors to I-actors in order to remember them; the *initiator* role is taken by an *O-actor* in her/his *informational* or 'green' shape, and the *executor role* by an *I-actor* (Chap. 11). [See also Sharing transaction kind]

Response link A link between a *coordination fact* and a *coordination act*, indicating that the *coordination act* is performed in response to the *coordination event* through which the coordination fact has come into existence (Chap. 8).

Response part The part of an *action rule* containing the *act(s)* to be performed in response to settling the *agendum* in the *event part* (Chap. 12).

Responsibility Disposition of a *subject* to be committed to the *coordination acts* he/she has performed, as well as the *agenda* he/she has to respond to. *Authority* and responsibility are like the two sides of a coin (Chap. 8). [See also Authority and competence]

Responsibility area The set of *process steps* in the (complete) *transaction pattern* for the performing of which either the *initiator* or the *executor* is responsible. Consequently, a distinction is made between the responsibility area of the initiator and the responsibility area of the executor (Chap. 8).

Responsibility range The set of *process steps* in the (complete) *transaction pattern* for the performing of which the fillers of an *actor role* are responsible, both as *executor* in *transactions* of the corresponding *transaction kind*, and as *initiator* in transactions of enclosed transaction kinds (Chap. 10).

Result phase The *transaction* phase in which the *initiator* and the *executor* strive to reach consensus about the *product* that the executor has brought about. It starts by performing the 'declare' act and ends in the state 'accepted' (Chap. 8).

Reversiogenic conversation A business *conversation* in which the participants strive to agree on reverting (turning back) the current *state* in an *actagenic* and/or a *factagenic* conversation, in which they (also) participate (Chap. 8).

Revocation Every step in the *basic transaction pattern* (so 'request', 'promise', 'declare' or 'accept') can be revoked, at any time and from any state in the main *transaction process*. The effect of a successful revocation is that the state of the main process is 'rolled-back' to the previous basic state (accepted → declared, declared → promised, promised → requested, requested → initial state) (Chap. 8). [See also Reversiogenic conversation]

Revocation pattern A pattern of *process steps* through which one can revoke one of the steps in the *basic transaction pattern* (Chap. 8). [See also Revocation]

Saving transaction kind The general *D-transaction kind* in which *documents* or *data sets* containing facts regarding the *production world* of an *enterprise*'s *O-organisation* are given by I-actors to D-actors in order to save them; the *initiator* role is taken by an *I-actor* in her/his *documental* or 'blue' shape, and the *executor role* by a *D-actor* (Chap. 11). [See also Providing transaction kind]

Scope of Interest (SoI) The delineation of the (part of the) *enterprise* or the collection of enterprises that one wants to study (Chap. 10).

Self-activating actor role An actor *role* is called self-activating if its fillers are *initiator* as well as *executor* of the same *transaction* (Chap. 10).

Sentence The syntactic form in which thoughts, especially *facts*, are expressed (Chaps. 5 and 8).

Service The functional appearance of a *product* to its consumers (Chap. 8).

Sharing transaction kind The general *I-transaction kind* in which *facts* regarding the *production world* of an *enterprise*'s *O-organisation* are made known by I-actor to O-actors; the *initiator* role is taken by an *O-actor* in her/his *informational* or 'green' shape, and the *executor role* by an *I-actor* (Chap. 11). [See also Remembering transaction kind]

Social correspondence The degree of mutual understanding of a *coordination act* at the *performa level* of *communication*. Social correspondence is reached if the *addressee* thinks he/she has understood the *intention* of the message correctly. Success or failure is conveyed by a confirmation or a disconfirmation (Chap. 8).

State At any *point in time*, a *world* is in some state, defined as the set of *facts* that have come into existence up to (and including) the point in time (Chaps. 6, 8 and 9).

Subject A human being in her/his quality of social individual, in particular her/his ability to enter into and comply with *commitments* (Chap. 8).

Subsystem A thing x is a subsystem of a *system* y if and only if x is a system, and if $C(x) \subseteq C(y)$; $E(x) \subseteq (C(y) \setminus (C(x)) \cup E(y)$; $S(x) \subseteq S(y)$ (Chap. 9).

System A complex of *concrete things* that is able to act, that is, to bring about changes in the corresponding *world*. Formally, a (homogeneous) system can be defined as a triple (C, E, S), where C is a set of concrete things of the same category, called the composition of the system; E is a set of concrete things of the same category as the elements in C, called the environment of the system; S is a set of influencing bonds among the elements in C and between them and the elements in E, called the structure of the system (Chap. 9). [See also Aggregate]

Thing An object together with its features. Only through the features can a thing be known or recognised. The features may change in the course of time; the object always remains the same. A distinction is made between *abstract things* and *concrete things* (Chap. 5)

Time scale A division of a (discrete and linear) time dimension in consecutive pieces of equal length (duration), called *time units* (Chaps. 9 and 12).

Time unit The unit for indicating or measuring amounts of *time* on a *time scale*. The length of a time unit depends on the needed precision. Examples: day, hour, minute, second (Chaps. 9 and 12). [See also Point in time]

Transaction The building block of *business processes*. The result of a successfully carried out transaction is the coming into existence of a *product*. Every transaction is of a specific *transaction kind* (Chap. 8).

Transaction bank The conceptual store associated with a *transaction kind*, in which all *coordination facts* and all *production facts* are stored in all of its carried out *transactions* (Chap. 10).

Transaction kind [*attribute* of *transaction*] There are two interpretations of the term *transaction kind*: the constructional interpretation and the operational interpretation. In the constructional interpretation, it represents the *complete transaction pattern*. Examples of transaction kinds: membership_starting, rental_completing. Transactions of the same transaction kind concern *products* of the same *product kind*. In the operational interpretation, the transaction kind is conceived as a *transaction bank* (Chaps. 8 and 10).

Transaction pattern A structured collection of *process steps*, alternately taken by actors in two roles: one fills the *initiator* role and the other the *executor* role in the transaction. The *basic transaction pattern* consists of the process steps 'request', 'promise', 'declare', and 'accept' (Note: in between the promise and the declare act, the *production act* is performed; it precedes immediately and unconditionally the declare act, but it is not considered a process step itself). The *standard transaction pattern* contains in addition the process steps 'decline' and 'reject'. The *complete transaction pattern* consists of the standard transaction pattern and the four *revocation patterns* (Chap. 8).

Transaction phase A transaction *process* consists of three consecutive phases: the *order phase*, the *execution phase*, and the *result phase*. They may partly or wholly be 'repeated' as the effect of *revocations* (Chap. 8).

Transaction process A sequence of *process steps* within the *complete transaction* pattern. Process steps of the same kind may occur multiple times, as the effect of *revocations* (Chap. 8).

Transaction state The state of a *transaction (process)* is defined as the most recently performed *process step* (Chap. 8).

Transactor role Since every *actor role* is connected by an *executor link* with exactly one *transaction* kind (and vice versa), the combination of the two constitutes a transactor role (Chap. 8).

Transition A change of *state* of a *world* (Chaps. 6 and 9).

Type A prescription of form (both concrete and abstract). Type works like a template that can be applied to *things* or pairs of things. If and when the form of a thing (or a pair of things) conforms to an applied type, a *fact* starts to exist. The fact is an instance of the type. A distinction is made between *conceptual facts* and *concrete facts* (Chap. 5).

Validity claim In performing a *coordination act*, three validity claims are raised by the *performer* and validated by the *addressee*: the *claim to rightness*, the *claim to sincerity*, and the *claim to truth*. The response to a *coordination event* will depend on the degree to which the three *validity claims* are accepted by the addressee (Chap. 8). [See also Action rule]

Value (1) A *typed* abstract *thing*. Values are commonly ordered in *value scales*. Examples of values are days, meters, and boolean values (Chaps. 6 and 12).

Value (2) The intensity of the experience that is evoked in a *subject*'s mind by the recognition of an affordance. This notion of value is commonly expressed in economic or monetary terms (Chap. 7).

Value scale An ordered class of *values* (according to definition 1). A value scale has a dimension (like time, length, mass, temperature, or money) and a scale unit (like minute, meter, gram, degree Celsius, or euro) (Chaps. 6 and 12).

Wait link A link between a *coordination fact* to a *coordination act*, indicating that performing the *coordination act* must wait until the *coordination fact* does exist, that is, the corresponding event has occurred (Chaps. 10 and 12).

Work instruction Guideline for performing a *production act* (Chap. 12). [See also Action rule]

World With every system, a world is associated in which the effects of the *acts* by (the elements in) the system take place. More specifically, the effect of an act is the creation of a *fact* in the system's world (Chaps. 6, 8, and 9).

Printed in the United States
by Baker & Taylor Publisher Services